Troubleshooting
NetWare for the 386

Michael Day and Ken Neff

Troubleshooting NetWare for the 386

Featuring expert tips and techniques for maintaining a healthy, productive NetWare 3.11 LAN

M&T BOOKS

 M&T Books
A Division of M&T Publishing, Inc.
501 Galveston Drive
Redwood City, CA 94063

Limits of Liability and Disclaimer of Warranty
The Author and Publisher of this book have used their best efforts in preparing the book and the programs contained in it. These efforts include the development, research, and testing of the theories and programs to determine their effectiveness.

The Author and Publisher make no warranty of any kind, expressed or implied, with regard to these programs or the documentation contained in this book. The Author and Publisher shall not be liable in any event for incidental or consequential damages in connection with, or arising out of, the furnishing, performance, or use of these programs.

Library of Congress Cataloging-in-Publication Data

Day, Michael, 1961-
    Troubleshooting NetWare 386/ by Michael Day and Ken Neff.
    p. cm.
    Includes index.
    ISBN 1-55851-223-3: $34.95
    1. Operating systems (Computers) 2. NetWare (Computer file)
I. Neff, Ken, 1957-   II. Title
QA76.76.063D4 1991
005.7'1369--dc20   91-20763
                                                              CIP

Project Editor: Tova F. Fliegel   **Cover Design:** Lauren Smith Design
Editor: Barbara Hume   **Layout:** Ellen Silvia
Art Director: Nancy Cutler

94 93 92 91   4 3 2 1

i

Contents

WHY THIS BOOK IS FOR YOU 1

INTRODUCTION: THE SCIENCE AND ART OF
TROUBLESHOOTING 3
Basic Troubleshooting Techniques 3
   Identifying the Nature of the Problem 4
      Analyze the Symptoms 5
      Form a Hypothesis 7
   Isolating the Cause of the Problem 7
      Test Your Hypothesis 8
      Reach a Conclusion 9
   Resolving the Problem 9
Interpreting Network Error Messages 9
   Where Error Messages Come From 10
      Messages at the File Server Console 10
      Messages at Workstations 11
   What Error Messages Say 11
   When Error Messages Occur 12
      Errors at Initialization 12
      Errors at Run Time 13
      Errors During a Consistency Check 13
   Error Message Severity Levels 13
      Status Messages 14
      Warning Messages 14
      Fatal Messages 14
   Sources for Error Message Documentation 14

Keeping Network Logbooks 15

Building a Troubleshooting Foundation for the Future 15

PART ONE: OVERVIEW OF NETWARE V3.X

CHAPTER 1: THE NETWARE V3.X OPERATING SYSTEM ...21

The Client-Server Model 22

    NetWare: The Specialized Server Operating System 23

    Basic Operating System Functions 24

Four Main Components of the NetWare v3.x Operating System 25

The NetWare Loader 28

The NetWare Kernel 30

    NetWare Memory Manager 31

        Flat Memory Model 31

        Dynamic Memory Allocation 32

        No Virtual Memory 32

        No Memory Protection 33

        NetWare v3.x Memory Types 33

        Kernel Memory 34

        Permanent Memory 35

        Alloc Memory 35

        File Cache Memory 36

        Memory Tuning 37

    The NetWare Scheduler 38

    The IPX Protocol Stack 39

        Structure of an IPX Packet 40

        ECBs and ESRs 43

        The IPX Internal Network 44

    NetWare Core Protocols (NCPs) 44

    Router 47

    NetWare's Cache System 49

        Problems with Caching Data 49

How NetWare Caches Data 51

The File System 51

File and Record Locking 53

Transaction Tracking System 55

Device Driver Interface 56

The NLM Environment 57

CLIB 58

Streams 59

Sequenced Packet Exchange 60

Communications Services 60

Queue Services 60

Application Services 61

The Bindery 62

Login Processing and Security 62

Accounting Services 63

Diagnostic Services 64

Message Services 65

Print Services 65

Architecture Summary 65

CHAPTER 2:EVOLUTION OF NETWARE V3.X **67**

Features New with NetWare v3.1 67

Transport Layer Interface (TLI) 68

Print Server Software 69

Resource Tracking 71

Remote Management Facility (RMF) 72

Features New with NetWare v3.11 73

Enhancements of v3.1 Features 74

New Product Packaging 75

Benefits of NetWare v3.x Evolution 75

CHAPTER 3:PROTOCOL AND WORKSTATION SUPPORT....77

Communication Through Protocol Stacks 77

NetWare's Protocol Engine..79

    Open Data-Link Interface 80

    NetWare Streams 81

Multiple Name Spaces 81

Media-Level Protocols 83

    Media Access Protocols 83

        CSMA/CD..83

        Token Passing 83

    Networking Hardware 84

        Ethernet 84

        Token Ring 84

        Arcnet 85

NetWare's Transport and Service Protocols 85

    Internetwork Packet Exchange 85

    Sequenced Packet Exchange 86

    NetWare Core Protocol 86

    NetBIOS Emulation 86

Other Protocols Supported by NetWare...86

    OS/2 Environment Protocols 87

        Named Pipes 87

    Macintosh Environment Protocols 88

        LocalTalk 89

        AppleTalk and AppleShare 90

    AppleTalk Filing Protocol 90

    UNIX Environment Protocols 90

        TCP/IP Transport Stack 90

        Network Filing System (NFS) 91

    IBM's SNA Environment Protocols 91

    OSI Standard Protocols 92

Workstation Environments 92

The DOS Workstation 93

    Getting a LAN Connection 93

    DOS and the NetWare Shell 94

The Windows Workstation 96

The ODI Workstation 96

The OS/2 Workstation 97

    Key Differences between OS/2 and DOS Workstations 97

    Interaction with the OS/2 Kernel 97

    The OS/2 Workstation-to-LAN Connection 98

The Macintosh Workstation 98

    Establishing a LAN Connection 99

    Some Specific Macintosh Challenges 99

Other Workstation Environments 100

PART TWO:NETWARE V3.11 INSTALLATION

CHAPTER 4:TOPOLOGIES AND CABLING STRATEGIES..103

Network Topologies 103

    The Linear Bus Topology 103

    The Ring Topology 104

    The Star Topology 105

Cabling Types 106

    Coaxial 106

    Twisted Pair 106

    Fiber Optic 107

General Cabling Concepts 108

    Cable Installation Rules 108

    Network and Node Addresses 111

    Common Addressing Mistakes 113

Arcnet Cabling Concepts 114

    Components Associated with Arcnet 116

    Rules for Low-Impedance Arcnet Networks 117

Troubleshooting Tips for Arcnet Cabling 118
Ethernet Cabling Concepts 120
   Thin Ethernet Cabling 121
      Components Associated with Thin-Cable Ethernet 121
      Rules for Thin-Cable Ethernet Networks 122
   Thick Ethernet Cabling 123
      Components Associated with Thick-Cable Ethernet 123
      Rules for Thick-Cable Ethernet Networks 124
   Troubleshooting Tips for Ethernet Cabling 125
Token-Ring Cabling Concepts 127
   Components Associated with Token-Ring Networks 128
   Rules for Token-Ring Networks 129
   Troubleshooting Tips for Token-Ring Cabling 129

CHAPTER 5:NETWARE V3.11 SERVER INSTALLATION....131
Server Installation Overview 131
   Decision Checklist 132
   Server Installation Steps 133
Choosing to Boot NetWare from a DOS Partition 133
   Creating a DOS Partition 135
   Preparing the Server and Booting It with DOS 135
   Loading NetWare and Deleting Existing Partitions 136
   Creating a New DOS Partition 141
   Formatting the DOS Partition 142
   A Note About FDISK vs. INSTALL 143
   Using INSTALL to Perform a Low-level Format 144
Installing NetWare v3.11 on the Server 144
   Running SERVER.EXE 144
      Server Name 145
      Internal IPX Number 146
   Loading NetWare Disk Drivers 147

Running the INSTALL NLM 148

Deciding on the Number of Drives 149

Setting Up NetWare Partitions 149

Setting the Hot Fix Information 152

Mirroring and Duplexing Partitions 153

Creating NetWare Volumes 157

Adding Volume Segments 161

Finishing the Volume Creation Process 162

Variations for Servers with More Than One Disk 162

Copying the System and Public Files 162

CHAPTER 6: LOADING SERVER LAN DRIVERS **165**

Open Data-Link Interface Drivers 165

Media and Frame Types 167

802.3 Frames 167

Ethernet II Frames 167

802.2 Frames 168

Ethernet SNAP Frames 168

Loading LAN Drivers 171

LAN Driver Options 172

INT=number 172

DMA=number 173

PORT=number 174

MEM=number 175

FRAME=frame type 175

(HL3) NAME=board name 175

NODE=number 176

RETRIES=number 177

SLOT=number 177

TBC=number 178

TBZ=number 178

Binding Transport Protocol Stacks to LAN Drivers 178

Checking Driver Parameters with the CONFIG Command................... 179

CHAPTER 7: LOADING NLMS AND EDITING SERVER BOOT
FILES 183
Loading NLMs on the Server 183
    Common NLMs 184
    Loading the Monitor NLM 184
    Dependent NLMs vs. Automatic NLM Loading 186
Creating the Server Boot Files 187
    Creating the STARTUP.NCF File 189
    Creating the AUTOEXEC.NCF File 190
Editing the Server Boot Files 191
    Sample STARTUP.NCF File 191
    Sample AUTOEXEC.NCF File 193
Using Alternate .NCF Files 196

CHAPTER 8: TROUBLESHOOTING THE SERVER
INSTALLATION 197
Installation Trouble Spots 198
Installation Problems and Their Solutions 198
    Warning Regarding Memory Conflicts 200

CHAPTER 9: INSTALLING NETWARE WORKSTATIONS 211
Installing a DOS Workstation 211
    Installing a LAN Adapter in a DOS Workstation 212
    Installing the DOS Workstation Software 213
    Using SHELL.CFG to Optimize the Workstation Software 215
    Logging In from a DOS Machine 218
    Troubleshooting the DOS Workstation Installation 219
DOS Workstation Memory Management 221
    Types of Memory in a DOS Workstation 222
    Using Novell's Expanded/Extended Memory Shells 222
    Troubleshooting Expanded and Extended NetWare Shell Problems 224
    Troubleshooting DOS Environment Problems 225

Using Microsoft Windows on the Network 226
   Installing Windows on the Network..226
      Checking for Proper NetWare Shell Versions 227
      Copying the Windows Program Files to the Network 228
      Setting Up Windows User Files 228
      Setting Windows Parameters in SHELL.CFG 229
   Logging In from a Windows Workstation 230
   Troubleshooting Windows Workstations 231
Installing a DOS ODI Workstation 234
   Creating an ODI Boot Diskette 234
   Logging In from a DOS ODI Workstation..237
   Troubleshooting DOS ODI Workstations 238
Installing Diskless Workstations 240
   Loading the Remote Program Load NLM at the Server 241
   Creating One Boot Image File for All Workstations 242
   Creating Multiple Boot Image Files 243
   Remote Boot Considerations for ODI Workstations....................................247
   Logging In from a Diskless Workstation 247
   Troubleshooting Problems Specific to Diskless Workstations 248
Installing an OS/2 Workstation 248
   Steps for Installing the Requester on the Workstation 249
   Modifying the CONFIG.SYS File 249
   Installing the NetWare OS/2 Utilities on the Server 252
   Logging In from an OS/2 Workstation 253
   Troubleshooting the OS/2 Workstation..254
Installing the Macintosh Network Software 255
   Logging In from a Macintosh Workstation..256
   Troubleshooting Macintosh Workstations 257

CHAPTER 10: INSTALLING AN EXTERNAL ROUTER..........261
Uses for External Routers 261
Planning the Router Installation 262

Dedicated Protected Mode 262

Nondedicated Protected Mode 263

Checking Hardware Compatibility..264

Recording Information About the Router 264

Installing an External Router 264

Starting an External Router 267

Starting a Dedicated Router 267

Starting a Nondedicated Router 267

Switching Between Console and DOS Mode 268

Maintaining the Router 268

The ROUTER.CFG File 269

Router Console Commands 269

The CONFIG Command 270

The DOWN Command 270

The TRACK ON and TRACK OFF Commands 270

The VAP Command 271

Troubleshooting Your Router 272

CHAPTER 11: UPGRADING TO NETWARE V3.11....................275

Upgrading from NetWare v2.x 276

Benefits of Using UPGRADE.EXE 277

Shortcomings of UPGRADE.EXE..278

Upgrading Execute-Only Files 278

Upgrading User Passwords 280

Handling NetWare v2.x-Specific Files 280

Dealing with Copy Protection 280

Mapping Between Old and New Directory Security 281

Duplication of Users or Groups 281

Two Methods for Running UPGRADE.EXE 282

The Transfer Method 282

The Archive Method 283

UPGRADE.EXE Features You Should Not Ignore 285

Potential Upgrade Problems 286
    Combining Multiple v2.x Servers 288
    Upgrade Safeguards 289
Troubleshooting the Upgrade Process 290

PART THREE: DIRECTORIES, APPLICATIONS, AND USERS

CHAPTER 12: INCORPORATING A SECURITY SCHEME.....295
NetWare v3.11 Security Concepts 295
    Login and Password Restrictions 295
        Password Restrictions 296
        Station, Time, and Other Account Restrictions 297
    NetWare Rights Security 298
        Trustee Rights Assignments 299
        The Inherited Rights Mask 299
        Effective Rights 300
    Attribute Security 301
        Directory Attributes 302
        File Attributes 303
        Other File Attributes 305
    The NetWare Bindery 305
Setting Up NetWare Security 306
    Using SYSCON to Set Up NetWare Security 306
        Setting Up User Security 306
        Setting Up Group Security 309
    Using FILER to Set Up NetWare Security 310
    Using SETPASS to Change User Passwords 312
    Using ALLOW to Modify Inherited Rights Masks 312
    Using FLAGDIR to Set Directory Attributes 314
    Using FLAG to Set File Attributes 315
    Using GRANT to Establish Trustee Rights 317
    Using REVOKE to Withdraw Trustee Rights..................318

Using REMOVE to Delete Trustees 319

Utilities for Finding Security Problems 320

Using RIGHTS to Display User Rights 320

Displaying User and Group Trustees with TLIST 321

Displaying Security Information with WHOAMI 321

Repairing the Bindery with BINDFIX and BINDREST 322

Checking for Holes with SECURITY 323

Other Methods of Locating Security Holes 324

Protecting the Network from Viruses 325

Tight Security—The First Line of Defense 325

Use Only Diskless Workstations 326

Limit Workstations with Floppy Drives 326

Have Only One Supervisor 327

Use Workgroup Managers and Operators 328

Disallow Access Control Rights 328

Restrict Rights in Shared Directories 328

Control Modem Use 329

Use Anti-Virus Software 329

Keep Adequate Backup Copies 330

Making a Secure System More Usable 331

CHAPTER 13: SETTING UP DIRECTORIES **333**

NetWare Directory Structure Concepts 333

Directories NetWare Creates Automatically 335

Directories You Should Create on the Server 336

DOS Directories 337

Application Directories 339

Data Directories 340

Home Directories 341

Creating Directories on the Server 342

Using DOS Commands to Create Directories 342

Using FILER to Create Directories 343

Using SYSCON to Create Home Directories 344
Directory Management Utilities..346
Limiting Directory Space with DSPACE...346
The "User Restrictions" Option 346
The "Directory Restrictions" Option 348
Checking Directory Space with CHKDIR 350
Renaming Subdirectories with RENDIR 350
Listing Directory Information with LISTDIR 351
Listing File Information with NDIR 351

CHAPTER 14: INSTALLING APPLICATIONS..............................**357**
Using Separate Directories and Groups to Simplify Access to Applications 357
Installing the Applications 358
Tips for Installing NetWare-Aware Applications 358
Test New Applications Rigorously 359
Bring Up New Applications One at a Time 360
Printing from Applications Designed for Network Printing 360
Tips for Installing Applications that Aren't NetWare-Aware...........................361
Troubleshooting General Application Problems..362
Troubleshooting Applications that Aren't Sufficiently Network-Aware 369
Common Single-User Application Problems 370
Configuration Files 370
Requirement to Install on a Particular Drive 372
Hard-Coded Directory Paths 373
Controlling Multiple-User Access to Files 373
Hard-Coded Temporary Files 374
Printing from Applications Not Designed for Network Printing 374

CHAPTER 15: SETTING UP USERS AND GROUPS.............**375**
NetWare User and Group Concepts 375
User Accounts 375
User Login Scripts..376

Using Groups to Simplify Administration 377
Distributing Network Management 377
    User Account Managers 378
       What User Account Managers Can Do 378
       What User Account Managers Can't Do 379
    Workgroup Managers 379
       What Workgroup Managers Can Do 379
       What Workgroup Managers Can't Do 379
Utilities for Creating Users and Groups 380
    Using the SYSCON Utility to Create Users 381
    Using the MAKEUSER Utility to Create Users 383
    Using the USERDEF Utility to Create Users 386
       Using the Default Template 386
       Creating a Custom Template 387
Creating User Groups 389
    Creating Groups in SYSCON 389
    Assigning Trustee Rights to the Groups 390
    Adding Users to a Group 391
Assigning User Account Managers and Workgroup Managers 391
    Creating User Account Managers 391
    Creating Workgroup Managers 392
Listing User Information with USERLIST 392

CHAPTER 16: CREATING LOGIN SCRIPTS 395
How NetWare Login Scripts Work 395
    The Default Login Script 395
    The System Login Script 396
    User Login Scripts 396
Setting Up Login Scripts 396
    Login Script Commands and Variables 398
    How to Use the Login Script Commands 403

ATTACH 403

BREAK ON or BREAK OFF 404

COMSPEC 404

DISPLAY or FDISPLAY 405

DOS BREAK 406

DOS SET 406

DOS VERIFY 407

DRIVE 407

EXIT 408

EXTERNAL PROGRAM EXECUTION (#) 408

FIRE PHASERS 409

GOTO 409

IF...THEN 410

INCLUDE 412

MACHINE NAME 413

MAP 414

MAP Command Variations 414

The Shell Descriptor Area and Login Script Identifiers 415

PASSWORD_EXPIRES 416

PAUSE 416

PCCOMPATIBLE 417

REMARK 417

SHIFT 418

WRITE 420

Using Identifier Variables with WRITE 420

Using Super-Characters and Compound Strings 421

Sample Login Scripts 422

Sample System Login Script 423

Sample User Login Script 424

Troubleshooting Tips and Suggestions for Login Scripts 424

CHAPTER 17: SETTING UP MENU INTERFACES....................**427**

Examining NetWare's MENU Utility...427

    NetWare's MAIN Menu..428

    Looking at the MAIN.MNU File 428

        How Menu and Submenu Titles Are Defined.....................429

        How a Window's Position Is Defined 429

        How Menu Colors Are Defined..430

        How the Menu's Options Are Defined 431

    Summary of Menu Script File Rules...................................431

Creating A Custom Menu Script...432

    Accessing Network Applications in MENU 434

    Accessing NetWare Menu Utilities in MENU 435

    Running Command-Line Utilities through MENU 436

    Using Special Characters in Menu Files 438

Accessing the Menu from the Login Script 439

MENU and Terminate-and-Stay-Resident Programs....................440

Using the COLORPAL Utility 440

    Changing Menu Colors for a Single Workstation 441

    Changing Menu Colors for the Entire LAN 441

    How COLORPAL Affects Monochrome Monitors 441

Troubleshooting Custom Menus 442

Other Menu Alternatives...442

    Saber Menu 442

    LANShell 443

CHAPTER 18: RESOURCE ACCOUNTING.................................**445**

Resource Accounting Concepts 445

    Uses for Resource Accounting 446

    Services You Can Charge For 447

        Block Reads 447

        Block Writes 447

        Connect Time 448

Disk Storage 448

Service Requests 449

Accounting Servers 449

The Accounting Audit File 449

NetWare's Accounting Utilities 450

Determining Appropriate Charge Rates 450

Example of Charge Rate Calculation for Connect Time 453

When to Remove Accounting 453

Setting Up Resource Accounting 454

Activating Resource Accounting 454

Setting Charge Rates 455

Assigning User Account Balances 457

Uninstalling Accounting 458

Using NetWare's Accounting Utilities 459

The ATOTAL Utility 459

Monthly Audit File Maintenance 461

Troubleshooting Resource Accounting Problems....................462

PART FOUR: NETWARE PRINTING

CHAPTER 19: SETTING UP NETWARE PRINTING 467

NetWare Printing Concepts...467

The Trouble with Network Printing 468

The Network Printing Model 469

NetWare Printing Utilities 471

Network Printing Problems Solved 472

Advantages of Network Printing 473

How NetWare Print Queues Work 473

Queue-Printer Relationships 475

More About Print Jobs 476

Print Queue Operators 477

Print Queue Users 477

How NetWare Print Servers Work 478

Interaction with Print Queues 479

Print Server Operators 480

Print Server Users 480

Ways to Set Up NetWare Printing 480

Print Server NLM (PSERVER.NLM) 481

External Print Server (PSERVER.EXE) 482

Workstation-Based Printing (RPRINTER.EXE) 484

Devising a Network Printing Plan 486

Setting Up Printing..487

Installing Printer Hardware 487

Setting Up Printing with a Print Server 488

Creating Print Queues 488

Creating the Print Server Account 489

Defining the Printers Supported by the Print Server 490

Assigning Queues to Each Printer 493

Enabling the Print Server on Additional File Servers 494

Starting the Print Server 495

Starting PSERVER.NLM 495

Starting PSERVER.EXE...496

Starting the Remote Printer Software...497

Changing the Print Server Configuration 499

Changing Printers and Queue Assignments.............................499

Stopping and Restarting the Print Server 500

Making a Remote Printer Private 501

Troubleshooting Printing 502

CHAPTER 20: USING THE NETWARE

PRINTING UTILITIES...515

Overview of NetWare's Printing Utilities 515

Establishing Printer Definitions with PRINTDEF 516

Starting PRINTDEF 519

Defining a Print Device 519

Importing Predefined Print Definitions 520

Copying Existing Print Definitions 520

Creating Your Own Printer Definitions 521

Defining Device Functions 522

Defining Print Modes 525

Defining Print Forms 527

Saving the PRINTDEF Database 529

Creating Print Job Configurations with PRINTCON 529

Starting PRINTCON 530

Creating a New Print Job Configuration 531

The "Edit Print Job Configuration" Window 531

PRINTCON's Options 532

Settings Used Only with CAPTURE 534

Precautions for the CAPTURE Options 535

Specifying the Queue, Printer, and Modes 535

Saving the New Configuration 536

Designating the Default Configuration 537

Copying Your Configurations for Other Users 537

Specifying PRINTCON Configurations in NetWare Utilities 538

Using the CAPTURE Command 538

CAPTURE's Options 539

Specifying Where Data Will Be Printed 540

Determining When Data Will Be Printed 540

Determining How Data Will Be Printed 542

Capturing Data to a Network File 544

Viewing the Current CAPTURE Status 545

Using CAPTURE with Network Applications 545

Using the ENDCAP Command 547

Using the NPRINT Command 547

NPRINT's Options 548

Using the PSC Command 549

PSC's Options 549

   The STAT Option 550

   Options for Stopping and Starting the Printer......................551

   The MOUNT FORM Option 552

   Other PSC Options 552

PART FIVE: MANAGEMENT AND TROUBLESHOOTING

CHAPTER 21: MEMORY MANAGEMENT AND PERFORMANCE TUNING 559

NetWare Memory Types 559

Volume Memory Requirements 561

Special Memory Requirements 562

   LSL Packet Receive Buffers 562

   Indexed Files 562

   Btrieve 563

   NLM Applications 563

   TCP/IP Support 563

   NetWare for Macintosh, NetWare NFS, and NetWare OSI 563

Memory Use While Mounting Volumes 564

Memory Use During File Service 565

Memory Use by NLMs 565

   Using MONITOR to View NLM Memory Usage 565

   MONITOR's "Resource Utilization" Option 568

   Other MONITOR Options 571

MONITOR's Server Memory Statistics 571

   What to Do When Cache Buffers Are Low 572

   The "SET Maximum Alloc Short Term Memory" Command 573

   The "SET Reserved Buffers Below 16 Meg" Command 574

NetWare's Consistency Checks 574

   What to Do When the Server Fails a Consistency Check 575

Tools for Detecting NLM Errors 576
SET Commands for NLM Developers 576

CHAPTER 22: FILE SYSTEM MANAGEMENT 579

NetWare File System Data Structures 579

    NetWare Volumes 580

    Disk Blocks 580

    The File Allocation Table 581

    The Volume Directory Table 582

    Redundant Copies of the FAT and Directory Table 582

    Troubleshooting FAT and Directory Table Problems............583

Directory Caching 584

    Directory Hashing 584

    Viewing Directory Cache Buffers in MONITOR 585

File Caching 586

    Cache Buffer and Disk Block Size......................................587

    How Caching Works for Disk Read Requests 588

    How Caching Works for Disk Write Requests 589

    Viewing File Cache Statistics in MONITOR 590

    How Many Cache Buffers Do You Need 591

NetWare's SALVAGE and PURGE Utilities 592

SET Commands for Tuning the NetWare File System 594

    "File Caching" Category 594

    Minimum File Cache Buffers 594

    Minimum File Cache Buffer Report Threshold 595

    Dirty Disk Cache Delay Time..596

    Maximum Concurrent Disk Cache Writes 597

    "Directory Caching" Category 598

    Directory Cache Buffer NonReferenced Delay 598

    Maximum and Minimum Directory Cache Buffers 600

    Dirty Directory Cache Delay Time 600

    Maximum Concurrent Directory Cache Writes 601

Directory Cache Allocation Wait Time 601

"File System" Category 602

Immediate Purge Of Deleted Files 602

Minimum File Delete Wait Time 602

File Delete Wait Time 603

Maximum Percent of Volume Used by Directory 603

Extended File Attributes 604

NCP File Commit 605

Maximum Subdirectory Tree Depth 606

Turbo FAT Re-use Wait Time 606

"Locks" Category 608

Maximum File Locks 608

Maximum Record Locks 609

Troubleshooting Application Error Messages 610

CHAPTER 23: SYSTEM FAULT TOLERANCE 613

Hot Fix 613

Read-After-Write Verification 615

Write Redirection 617

Read Redirection 617

Random Media Errors vs. Bad Media 617

Checking Hot Fix Redirection in MONITOR 618

Disk Mirroring and Duplexing 619

Unmirroring Disks 619

Remirroring Disks 620

Transaction Tracking 620

Flagging a File Transactional 621

Disabling and Enabling TTS 623

The Transaction Backout Procedure 624

The TTS$LOG.ERR File 625

Explicit and Implicit Transactions 627

Using SETTTS 627

Workstation Deadlocks 628

TTS-Related SET Commands 629

    Maximum Transactions 629

    Auto TTS Backout Flag 630

    TTS Abort Dump Flag 631

    TTS Unwritten Cache Wait Time 631

    TS Backout File Truncation Wait Time 632

Troubleshooting Fault Tolerance Problems 632

CHAPTER 24: DISK/VOLUME MANAGEMENT 635

Disk Management Concepts 636

    Disk Interfaces and Controllers 637

    Disk Drivers 638

    NetWare's Device Numbering Scheme 639

    Partitions 641

Volume Management Concepts 643

    Volume Names 643

    Volume Size 643

    Volume Segments 644

    Volume Block Size 645

    Useful NetWare Commands and Utilities 645

    The INSTALL Utility 646

        INSTALL's "Disk Options" 646

        INSTALL's "Volume Options" 652

    The LOAD Command 654

    The UNLOAD Command 655

    MOUNT, VOLUMES, and DISMOUNT 656

    MONITOR's Disk-Related Information 657

        Disk I/O Statistics 657

        The "Disk Information" Option 659

    SET Commands for Disk and Volume Management 666

"Memory" Category 666

"File System" Category 666

"Disk" Category 667

"Miscellaneous" Category 667

The VREPAIR Utility 668

When to Run VREPAIR 669

Running VREPAIR 670

The CHKVOL Utility 675

The VOLINFO Utility 675

Other Disk and Volume Analysis Tools 676

Troubleshooting Network Disk Problems 677

General Disk Troubleshooting Procedure 678

Problems When Loading Disk Drivers 681

Problems When Mounting a Volume 683

Other Disk-Related Problems 685

CHAPTER 25: LAN DRIVER/COMMUNICATION

MANAGEMENT 687

LAN Communication Concepts 687

Packets, Headers, and Frame Types 689

The LSL and Multiple Link Interface Drivers 691

Transport Protocols and NetWare Streams 692

Ethernet Frame Types 693

Other Frame Types 698

Useful Console Commands and Utilities 698

The LOAD Command 698

Hardware Configuration Parameters 699

Board Identification Parameters 700

Load-Time Configurable Parameters 701

The UNLOAD Command 702

The BIND Command 703

Binding IPX 703

Binding Other Novell-Supplied Protocols 705
Binding Third-Party Protocols 705
The UNBIND Command 706
Changing a Network Number 706
The PROTOCOL Command 707
The PROTOCOL REGISTER Command 708
The CONFIG Command 708
The DISPLAY NETWORKS Command 709
The COMCHECK Utility.. 710
MONITOR's "LAN Information" Option 712
Generic LAN Driver Statistics 714
Custom LAN Driver Statistics 719
Ethernet Boards 719
Token-Ring Boards 721
Arcnet Boards 724
Other Communication-Related SET Commands 726
Troubleshooting LAN Communication Problems 726
General LAN Communication Problems 728
Problems When Loading LAN Drivers.. 732
Problems When Binding Protocols 735
Internetwork Routing Errrors 737

CHAPTER 26: UPS AND POWER PROTECTION......................**739**
The Importance of Power Protection 739
Disturbances to Commercial Power 740
Types of Power Protection 741
Types of UPS Systems Available 742
Off-Line UPS 742
On-Line UPS 743
Intelligent Power Systems 744
Implementing Power Protection on Your Network 744
What Network Components to Protect... 745

UPS Power Rating 745
NetWare's UPS Monitoring Feature 747
    UPS-Monitoring Hardware 747
      Setting UPS Jumpers 748
    Loading UPS.NLM 748
Relevant Console Commands 750
    The UPS STATUS Console Command 751
    The UPS TIME Console Command 752
Troubleshooting the UPS System 753
    UPS Initialization Messages 754
    Server Shutdown Messages 755
    UPS Messages Sent to Workstations 755
    Low Battery Messages 756

CHAPTER 27: BACKUP AND RESTORE MANAGEMENT.....759
Backup Program Features 759
    NetWare File System Compatibility 760
    Backing Up Open Files 760
    Backup Rate 761
    Error Handling 761
    Backup Media Support 762
      Magnetic Tape 762
      Optical Disks 763
      Removable Hard Disks 763
    "Convenience" Features 764
      Unattended Backup 764
      Image and File-by-File Backups 764
      Miscellaneous Features 765
Implementing an Effective Backup Plan 765
    Recommended Backup Schedule 765
    Rotating Backup Media 766
    Storing Backup Media Off-Site 767

Backup Security 767

Structuring Directories to Facilitate Backup 768

Backup Programs Available for NetWare v3.x 768

The SBACKUP Program 769

SBACKUP Software 769

SBACKUP.NLM 770

SIDR.NLM 770

TSA.NLM 771

TSA-311.NLM 771

Backup Device Drivers 771

Other Required Modules 772

Gearing Up for SBACKUP 773

Editing the DIBI2$DV.DAT File 774

Setting Server Parameters 774

Loading the Backup Device Driver 775

Loading the TSA and SBACKUP Modules 776

Backing Up Data 778

Selecting the Target Server 778

Selecting the Working Directory 779

Setting the Backup Options 780

Running the Backup Session 783

Viewing the Backup and Error Logs 784

Restoring Data 785

Selecting the Target Server for a Restore 785

Selecting the Working Directory for a Restore 785

Setting the Restore Options 786

Running the Restore Session 788

Unloading the SBACKUP Modules 788

Troubleshooting Backup and Restore Problems 788

CHAPTER 28: REMOTE MANAGEMENT 795

Styles of Network Management 795
   Centralized Network Management 796
   Distributed Network Management 796
Knowing Your Network 797
Tools for Managing Your Network 798
   Management Products Available from Novell 798
   Management Products from Other Sources 799
   NetWare's Support for Enterprise Management Systems 799
The FCONSOLE Utility 800
NetWare's Remote Management Facility 801
   Remote Management Software 801
      Direct Connection Configuration 802
      Asynchronous Connection Configuration 803
      Redundant Connection Configuration 805
   Management and Troubleshooting Uses for RMF 806
   Security Precautions for RMF 807
   Setting Up a File Server for RMF 808
   Running a Remote Console Session 809
      Starting RCONSOLE at a Network Workstation 810
      Starting ACONSOLE at a Network Workstation 810
      Starting ACONSOLE at a Standalone PC 812
   Remote Console's "Available Options" Menu 813
      Scanning Directories with RMF 814
      Transferring Files to the Remote Server 814
      Copying New NetWare System Files to the Remote Server 816
   Specific Administrative Tasks 817
      Updating a LAN Driver with RMF 818
      Updating a Disk Driver with RMF 819
      Rebooting a Server Remotely 820

APPENDIX A: COMMON HARDWARE CONFIGURATIONS..823

APPENDIX B: LAN, DISK, AND BACKUP DRIVERS..............827

APPENDIX C: NETWARE NAME SERVICE 835

APPENDIX D: SOURCES OF ADDITIONAL HELP...................851

INDEX 857

Preface

Novell's mid-1989 release of NetWare v3.0 introduced a new generation of network operating systems. A complete rewrite of the company's popular 80286-based NetWare product, NetWare 386 (as it was called back then) was the first 32-bit network operating system specifically designed to take advantage of the advanced features of Intel's 80386 and 80486 microprocessors. The technical superiority of NetWare 386 received industry-wide praise. LAN administrators, installers, designers, and consultants welcomed its drastically simplified installation, its improved memory usage scheme, its dynamic self-configuration capabilities, and its innovative loadable module technology. NetWare 386 also rose above previous design limitations, providing support for up to 250 users, 4GB of memory, and 32TB (terabytes) of disk storage.

Today, two revisions and one official name change later, NetWare v3.11 is the most sophisticated network computing platform Novell has to offer. It is ideally designed for use in "enterprise" networks where many different types of computing systems must coexist, communicate, and share both data and applications. The connectivity features available with NetWare v3.11 bring together IBM PCs and PS/2s running DOS, Windows, or OS/2; Macintosh computers running in their native environment; Unix machines using TCP/IP and Sun's Network File System; and the emerging OSI-compliant systems. With management links to IBM's NetView and other vendors' Simple Network Management Protocol products, NetWare LANs are no longer solitary islands in a vast sea of minicomputer and mainframe systems; they're becoming an integral part of the overall corporate information structure.

What does all this technobabble have to do with troubleshooting? Put simply, it emphasizes that in NetWare v3.x you're dealing with an extremely complex product. Even a small LAN with fewer than twenty users can contain dozens of hardware components running numerous software packages from a multitude of different vendors. The more complex the product is, the more complex the process of isolating and correcting problems becomes.

There was a time, in the early days of PC networking, when relatively little prior knowledge and expertise was required to manage the network. Often the people who knew the most about DOS were automatically elected to be the network supervisors—and somehow they got by, notwithstanding the frustrations of trial-and-error networking.

Needless to say, the new generation of sophisticated, multivendor networks ushered in by NetWare v3.x calls for a new breed of supervisor. Now more than ever before, the job requires a solid understanding of network hardware and software, a thorough grasp of classic troubleshooting methods, and a certain amount of skill, experience, and intuition.

This book provides advanced technical information, installation guidelines, and management/troubleshooting techniques that both beginners and veterans can draw upon to hone their network skills. It is meant to be used along with your Novell manuals and other network reference books. Of course, no book can substitute for actual hands-on experience, nor can the written word endow you with any kind of knack for knowing what's wrong. Expertise in troubleshooting comes only through doing. But by reading and applying what you learn in this book, you'll be able to make the most of your experience, building up your personal arsenal and quickly raising your level of troubleshooting expertise.

How This Book Is Organized

As we considered various approaches to troubleshooting NetWare v3.x, it became clear that the old adage "An ounce of prevention is worth a pound of cure" applies as much to networks as to human health. Most problems can be avoided if you (1) understand the relevant technology, and (2) properly install and set up the network in the first place. The overall organization of this book reflects this emphasis on prevention. That's why we have dedicated a large part of the book to concepts, installation, and setup procedures.

- The Introduction is a primer on network troubleshooting in general. It gives a model for analyzing and resolving faults, and it contains guidelines for interpreting error messages and other symptoms.

- Part One presents an overview of the NetWare v3.x computing environment. If you're new to NetWare or if you want to gain a foundational understanding of the technology, read this part first. Many of the discussions later in the book assume you've read and understood the concepts presented in the overview.

- Part Two deals with installing NetWare v3.x. Its coverage includes the cabling, server, workstations, and external routers. Installers will be particularly interested in this section.

- Part Three gives advice on setting up directories, applications, and users, including chapters on NetWare security and resource accounting. System supervisors will find this section of particular interest.

- Part Four is dedicated to one of the most trouble-prone aspects of networks: printing. This section goes through the selection and configuration of the various print server options available with NetWare. It also includes a troubleshooting section and a discussion of the printing utilities.

- Part Five contains specific management and troubleshooting information, grouped under general categories such as memory, disks, and LAN drivers. Each chapter contains more in-depth conceptual information about its respective topic, then presents specific setup and management procedures and lists of common problems and solutions. Technicians and support personnel can refer to the troubleshooting sections of these chapters to build up their library of solutions.

Several appendices contain supplemental material that may be of interest.

- Appendix A lists common configurations used by various hardware components most often found in DOS-based servers and workstations.

- Appendix B lists the LAN, disk, and backup device drivers included with NetWare, matching each with its respective hardware.

- Appendix C introduces the NetWare Name Service, Novell's add-on product for managing access to multiple servers and resources by grouping them into administrative domains.

- Appendix D lists third-party products and other resources that are useful in managing and troubleshooting NetWare v3.x networks.

While this organization follows the overall chronological flow of a new installation, you don't have to read the entire book from front to back. We expect that many readers will be familiar with at least some aspects of Novell networking, and will turn to this book only for clarification and guidance concerning a particular topic. To accommodate this random-access approach, we've tried to modularize each chapter as much as possible, defining relevant terms and explaining necessary concepts in an appropriate context.

Entire volumes could be (and in some instances have been) written on any given aspect of networking with NetWare v3.x. Indeed, reams of technical bulletins and huge technical support databases contain only a small percentage of the possible errors and problems that you might encounter in a given combination of network hardware and software. Thus, any single reference that purports to cover the issues surrounding network management and troubleshooting must necessarily be limited in its scope.

To provide the most useful information for the widest possible audience, we've tried to focus on those troubleshooting and maintenance concerns common to the most typical NetWare v3.x networks. About 90 percent of network problems occur over and over again in almost all installations. The remaining 10 percent occur very infrequently, and mainly in atypical configurations. This book covers the bulk of the 90 percent, leaving treatment of the rarest problems to more appropriate resources (such as authorized dealers, tech support lines, and electronic bulletin board forums).

While this book includes an overview of the NetWare v3.x operating system and how it interacts with various desktop computers, space does not permit ground-up discussions of the DOS, OS/2, Macintosh, and Unix operating systems. We assume the reader is familiar with the basic operation of these platforms. Helpful references are listed in Appendix D.

Throughout this book, names of keys on the keyboard are enclosed in pointed brackets, as in <Enter> and <F1>. The names of programs and files are given in all capital letters, as in INSTALL and AUTOEXEC.NCF. We have tried to keep command formats as easy-to-read as possible. Commands that you are to type at the keyboard are shown in **boldface** type or enclosed in quotation marks. For variables in *italics*, substitute the appropriate information; for example, in place of the variable *servername* in a command, you would type the name of your file server. Variable information in error messages is shown in italics as well. Optional parts of a command are enclosed in square brackets ([...]). Unless noted otherwise, don't include the brackets when you type the command.

Statistics show that a certain amount of downtime is inevitable, even in the most carefully planned and expertly managed network. Our aim is to help you minimize that downtime, thus saving your organization what would otherwise be lost due to disrupted productivity. We hope you find this compilation useful as you rise to the challenges of working with NetWare v3.*x*.

Michael Day
Ken Neff
October 1991

Why This Book Is For You

Installing, managing, and troubleshooting complex systems like NetWare v.3*x* networks is a challenge even for the most knowledgeable computer technician. Handling the job effectively requires a versatile arsenal of tools, techniques, and training, along with a solid understanding of the underlying technology.

Troubleshooting NetWare for the 386 is a valuable addition to any network troubleshooter's toolbox. It contains a wealth of detailed information about how the NetWare v3.*x* operating system works, what features it offers, and how to install and set up a network. Throughout the book, you'll find tips for avoiding common pitfalls and techniques for solving those problems that so often pop up to plague network administrators.

Newcomers to NetWare v3.*x* and seasoned veterans alike will benefit from this book's technical overview and conceptual discussions. This material is intended to provide the insights necessary to understand and work more confidently with the myriad of components in a high-end NetWare network. The setup, management, and troubleshooting information in this book is also designed to appeal to a wide range of audiences:

- If you're a NetWare designer, consultant, or installer, you'll find practical advice on how to properly configure and install NetWare v3.*x* servers, workstations, and routers. You can also use the book as a research tool in planning a customized network.

- If you're a NetWare supervisor or MIS staff member, you'll find useful suggestions for setting up network security, directories, applications, and users. You'll also find the management sections of the book helpful in dealing with the day-to-day maintenance of the network.

- If you're a NetWare service technician or support provider, you can use the troubleshooting sections to enhance your knowledge base and raise your level of expertise in isolating and fixing network problems.

As a single-source reference for network troubleshooting methods, technical concepts, setup procedures, management practices, performance tuning tips, and fault resolution techniques, *Troubleshooting NetWare for the 386* is an indispensable tool for anyone charged with keeping a high-end NetWare network running.

Introduction: The Science and Art of Troubleshooting

Troubleshooting—the process of detecting, isolating, and repairing faults in a given system—is often described as a combination of science and art. As a science, troubleshooting requires that you understand the operation of the system and the relationship between symptoms and underlying causes. As an art, it demands a certain amount of intuition, skill, and experience.

Since this book is a troubleshooting guide for Novell's high-end NetWare v3.*x* network operating system, its main purpose is to help you gain the requisite scientific foundation. However, so as not to neglect the artistic side, this introductory chapter deals with the actual "craft" of troubleshooting. We'll present a simple, three-step procedure that many expert troubleshooters use in diagnosing and resolving network problems. We'll also discuss how to analyze and interpret error messages, and we'll emphasize the importance of keeping configuration and error logs.

One of the best ways to learn any art or craft is to observe and emulate the methods used by those who are good at it. With this foundation to build on, you can more effectively develop your own skill and intuition as you gain experience of your own. This chapter allows you to figuratively "peek over the shoulder" of a pro troubleshooter, thus gaining valuable insights into the fine art of troubleshooting a NetWare network.

Basic Troubleshooting Techniques

A NetWare network is a classic example of a dynamic system—one in which a number of discrete components work together to form a functional whole. Each component has one or more specific relationships to other components in the system, and each component has one or more expected behaviors. A network is dynamic because its components can change, both in terms of their existence within the system and in terms of their expected behavior.

The main challenge in troubleshooting a dynamic system lies in isolating which of the various components is at fault. Seasoned troubleshooters and network technicians follow a very precise procedure to diagnose the source of a problem. By emulating this procedure, you can often eliminate some of the more obvious problems yourself. If you end up calling for help, you can provide more accurate information for the technician to go on.

The rules that troubleshooting pros follow are actually quite simple and are based on nothing more than common sense. They are:

- Identify the exact nature of the problem.
- Isolate the cause of the problem.
- Resolve the problem.

While there are numerous variations and alternative methods, this three-step "identify-isolate-resolve" process forms the basis of successfully troubleshooting problems in most networks. The following sections discuss each step in greater detail.

Identifying the Nature of the Problem

Most network problems are heralded by something catastrophic: An application hangs, communication between servers and workstations ceases, or the server itself crashes. Sometimes an error message appears on the file server or workstation monitor; other times you receive no message at all. Since many error messages are vague and hard to decipher, they're often of little help even when they do appear.

When a problem occurs, there is often intense pressure from both users and management to get the network back up *immediately*. A common mistake made under this type of pressure is to start fiddling with this component or that without thoroughly examining the symptoms first. The danger with this approach is that, in many cases, the most obvious symptoms may have little to do with the actual problem and can lead you off on a costly tangent. So don't just reboot the server as a knee-jerk reaction. Like a master detective, you've got to gather your clues before you can solve the case.

Figure I-1 illustrates a cyclical process you can use when diagnosing network problems. The four steps in the cycle are to be repeated continuously until you have ultimately identified the problem.

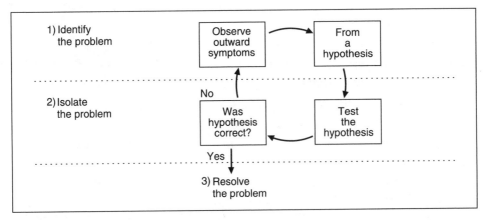

Figure I-1: A four-step, cyclical process for properly diagnosing network problems.

Analyze the Symptoms

The first step in identifying a problem is to analyze the outward symptoms. If you do get an error message, write it down exactly as it appears on the screen. (A good place to do this is in a network error log, which we will explain further later in this chapter). The wording of error messages and whether they appear at the server or at a workstation are important clues to where they came from (more on that later, too).

The file server or a workstation may simply hang, or cease operation with no clue as to why. In this case, look for other signs: Does the machine still have power? Is the monitor dead? Will the computer accept any keyboard input at all? Is the disk access light still flashing?

Also look at the context in which the problem occurred. Try to ascertain what kind of activity was occurring on the network at the time. What NetWare Loadable

Modules (NLMs) were loaded in the server? How many users were logged in? What applications were they running?

Make a note of which workstations are still operational, if any. If the problem is limited to a single workstation or a group of workstations connected to the same piece of hardware, suspect that piece of hardware first. If the problem affects all workstations running a certain application, that application may be the culprit. If none of the workstations can access the file server, something may be wrong with the LAN communications channel in the file server (NetWare OS, LAN drivers, network boards, cabling, routers, and so on).

Consider also whether anything has changed since the network last functioned properly. For example, if you've just finished running INSTALL or UPGRADE and you can't get the server to boot up, there's a pretty good chance that something went wrong during the installation or upgrade. If the file server ran fine until you added that new network interface board or disk drive, chances are the new component is causing the problem. Even something as minor as deleting a line in a CONFIG.SYS or other configuration file can cause big problems on a network. Keep a detailed record of every hardware and software change in your network configuration logbook (described later in this chapter).

If the problem occurs while you're trying to boot the file server, note how far the boot-up process is able to proceed. Did the server die immediately after reset, or did everything proceed normally until the time came to initialize network interface boards or mount volumes?

Finally, if the server is no longer functioning, reboot it and see if the problems happens again. Problems that reoccur in exactly the same way over and over are easier to identify than problems that occur intermittently. If the problem occurs while a certain application is running, try to reproduce the problem with another application or with no applications running. This helps determine whether the problem is related to a specific application.

Once you've noted everything you can about the problem, you're ready to make an educated guess about what's causing the observed symptoms.

Form a Hypothesis

Of all the aspects of troubleshooting, this is the area where experience and expertise are the most helpful. To form a valid hypothesis that's consistent with the symptoms, you must be familiar with the types of network problems that can cause the observed deviation from normal. You also need a good understanding of the protocols and applications running on the network.

Naturally, inexperienced troubleshooters will have a harder time figuring out which components to suspect first. Hopefully, reading this and other NetWare reference books will help steer you in the right direction until you gain more troubleshooting experience.

Even experienced troubleshooters will want to use some of the various tools available for diagnosing network problems. One of the most useful, though initially hard to learn, is the network analyzer. These devices connect to the network and analyze the packets being sent over the wire. They can display a variety of information about transmit speeds, packet types, and protocol errors. Many analyzers come with prepackaged tests you can run. Some of the newest product releases incorporate on-line troubleshooting guides that give you tips on the likely causes of certain symptoms.

Another useful tool is the benchmark test. Knowing what the normal operation of the network "looks" like can help you more easily recognize unusual situations. Naturally, you must run these tests before a problem occurs in order to get an accurate picture of "normal" network operation. Novell and many third-party vendors provide benchmarking programs you can use to gather this baseline data. One such test, called PERFORM2, is available on NetWire (Novell's technical forum on CompuServe). Check with your authorized reseller or NetWare users' group for others.

Isolating the Cause of the Problem

After following the above suggestions for identifying the possible source of the problem, you're ready to perform various tests involving the likely cause. As you do so, you should be able to conclude whether or not your hypothesis is correct.

Test Your Hypothesis

There are several methods you can use to test your hypothesis. One technique often used by experts is "swapping," or replacing the suspected faulty component with a similar component that you know works. This method is most effective when you are familiar with the expected behavior of each component and already have a good idea of what could be causing the problem.

It's vital that you swap only one component at a time. If you replace a length of cable, the network interface board, and the file server's power supply all at once and the problem is resolved, you won't know for sure which piece was the source of the problem.

If you suspect a hardware problem, remove the questionable component and replace it with an identical component to see if anything changes. If you just added a new piece of hardware, swap that piece first. One advantage of a network is that you usually have similar network hardware components available in other machines on the LAN. Many network managers keep a small inventory of spare parts on hand just for swapping purposes so they don't have to pilfer them from functional machines.

The same principle applies to software problems. If you just added a new piece of software or loaded a new application on the server and now other network applications won't work, remove the new software and see if normal network operation is restored. Whenever you change a software configuration file or batch file, keep a backup copy of the old one in case the new one is causing the problems.

Another method you can use when you aren't as familiar with some of the system components is the simple process of elimination. In this method, you use the knowledge you have about the other components to make a judgement concerning a specific component about which you may know very little. Start out by assuming that every component could be the source of the problem. Then examine each component one by one and observe whether or not the rest of the system behaves as expected. If so, you can remove that component from the list of possible candidates; if not, the component in question remains a candidate for causing the fault.

Reach a Conclusion

Following each experiment, you must decide whether your hypothesis is correct. If you executed the other steps correctly, this step is usually the most straightforward. Naturally, if the problem remains the same, you know your hypothesis was incorrect. If the problem goes away, you know you have found the source of the problem. A more challenging case is when the problem remains but the outward manifestations differ after you change one of the components. As you gain experience, you will come to know what your conclusion should be for each possible outcome of the experiment. In the event that the test results are unfamiliar, you must expand or revise your view of the problem so that you can better associate the symptoms with the observed test results.

As you saw in Figure I-1, the troubleshooting process is cyclical. If the results of one test are inconclusive, you must look more closely at the symptoms and form another hypothesis. Most of the time, you need to change the problem environment before reexamining the symptoms. For example, you might want to remove a node from the network and then observe the symptoms again.

Resolving the Problem

Once you've isolated the faulty component (or components), you must somehow compensate for the fault. The three main options here are to repair, replace, or work around problematic components. For malfunctioning hardware, your only choices are to repair or replace the component. For software components, you can often employ some type of work-around to fix the problem. For example, if you find that a certain version of the NetWare workstation shell is causing problems, you can either upgrade the shell to the latest version or configure the shell differently via options in the NetWare SHELL.CFG file. The troubleshooting sections of this book give numerous suggestions for resolving various problems you're likely to run into.

Interpreting Network Error Messages

Few things are more frustrating than receiving an error message and not being able to determine what the message means or where it came from, let alone how to eliminate the problem that caused the message. One reason error messages are so cryptic is that they're written into the code by engineers who speak an entirely different language than most other people.

Following are some hints for interpreting system and error messages in the NetWare LAN environment. Classifying an error message according its source, its subject, and time of occurrence can be very helpful in solving the problem that generated the error.

Where Error Messages Come From

Most network supervisors don't realize how many different pieces of software are combined to form a NetWare network. The open architecture of NetWare v3.11 leaves room for a myriad of third-party add-ons to the core NetWare operating system. Many error messages that appear on workstations and file servers may not be generated by NetWare at all, but rather by a third-party LAN driver, disk driver or NLM, by network application software, or by a workstation operating system (DOS, OS/2, Unix, or the Macintosh OS).

Determining the source of the error message can be extremely useful in identifying the problem and eliminating it. The primary key to determining where an error message originates is to observe whether the message is displayed on the file server console or on the workstation.

Messages at the File Server Console

Error messages that appear on the file server console could be generated by any of these software pieces:

- The file server cold boot loader
- The core NetWare operating system
- Operating system drivers (LAN drivers, disk drivers, backup drivers, or others) that have been loaded on the server
- Other server-based applications (NLMs) running at the server

Since drivers and NLMs may be written by third-party vendors, these often generate error messages that don't appear in Novell documentation. One way to tell where an error message originated from is to look at how general or specific the wording of the message is.

LAN drivers, disk drivers, and NLMs usually generate specific error messages that use the actual name of the component involved. For example, disk drivers often generate disk-specific error messages such as "Unable to reset the PS/2 MFM disk controller." LAN drivers generate LAN hardware-specific errors such as "Error Resetting 3C505 Etherlink Adapter."

Error messages generated by the operating system are typically more general and don't mention disks or boards by name: for example, "Problem with drive 01: Error reading disk redirection data" or "Warning! LAN A DEAD." The cold boot loader generates messages relating to the file server's attempt to boot from a hard disk drive, such as "Checksum error in load file."

Messages at Workstations

Error messages displayed on a workstation could be generated by the NetWare shell, the workstation operating system, or a specific application. However, a few error messages generated by the file server operating system appear at workstations instead of at the file server console. Since third-party vendors can supply shell LAN drivers as well as operating system drivers, the error messages these drivers generate may not appear in Novell documentation. But, like file server errors, general references or specific products named in the message can often help pinpoint the error's source.

For example, a workstation LAN driver will generate a specific LAN error message, such as "Error initializing IBM Token-Ring board." Errors that use network terminology, such as "Network Error on Server JUNGLE: Error writing to network" are usually generated by the NetWare shell. Workstation operating systems (DOS, OS/2, and the like) produce general file or memory errors, while applications often display messages referring to application-specific details.

What Error Messages Say

The subject of an error message can be helpful in determining the source of the message and the solution to the problem. Generally, file server console error messages can be classified into one of the following groups:

- The internal operation of the NetWare operating system

- The LAN communication channel
- The disk drives and disk channels
- NetWare disk mirroring and duplexing
- The Transaction Tracking System (TTS)
- The Hot Fix feature
- UPS monitoring
- Printing

The most common error messages occur in the disk drive and system fault-tolerance areas, such as "Mirroring turned off on volume VOL1 (drive 02 failed)" or "Invalid mirror definition table. Run INSTALL."

When Error Messages Occur

Generally, NetWare error messages can occur during three distinct stages of network operation. Initialization errors are those that occur when you're booting up the file server. Run time errors are those that occur after the network has been running for a period of time. A third type of error, the consistency check error, can occur either during bootup or during normal operation, whenever the OS checks its data for internal consistency.

Errors at Initialization

Initialization errors occur after the file server is reset or turned on, while the operating system software is being loaded. They don't occur after the server has been running for a period of time. Initialization errors are usually fatal errors that halt the system. (Fatal errors are often called "abend" errors because they cause an *ab*normal *end*ing to whatever was running.)

Bootup errors could be caused by improperly configured hardware and software, or by a hardware failure. Examples of these errors include "Invalid Redirection Index Table" and "Time out error configuring disk Coprocessor" at the file server, and "A File Server could not be found" at the workstation.

Errors at Run Time

Run-time errors occur after the OS has been properly loaded and initialized and has been running normally for a time. These error messages are typically caused by hardware failure or power disruptions, though a few are caused by erroneous conditions occurring on the network. Examples of run-time errors are: "Abend: NMI Interrupt," "ERROR! Address collision with SLASHER," and "Problem with drive 01: Mirror drive was shut down."

Errors During a Consistency Check

NetWare's multitasking kernel checks the data stored in memory at various points to ensure that it's consistent with the operation being performed. Most of these consistency checks are performed just before or after critical operations, such as writing data blocks from cache memory to disk. If any of the checks fail, it means that critical data has been corrupted and that continued operation will worsen the situation. Therefore, almost all consistency check errors are fatal and abend the file server.

Examples of consistency check messages are "Dirty cache block has no dirty bits set," "Fatal File System Error: zero First or Current Cluster" and "Stack overflow detected by kernel." Usually the text message generated by a consistency check error is cryptic and difficult to understand unless you know the internal architecture of the NetWare operating system.

Most consistency check errors are caused by memory data corruption. Memory corruption means that data in portions of the system memory are erroneously changed. This condition is commonly attributed to poor power line conditioning on the file server or to hardware memory failure. The latter is particularly true if Non-Maskable Interrupt (NMI) errors frequently occur on the system, since these errors are generated mainly by improperly functioning hardware. Poorly designed applications can also trigger an NMI error.

Error Message Severity Levels

Not every message you receive from NetWare halts the operation of the network and abends the file server. In addition to these types of messages, which are classified as "fatal," some are considered status messages, while others are considered warning messages.

Status Messages

Status messages simply inform you of current operating system conditions or the successful completion of a process. Most of these messages aren't considered errors and typically don't require you to take any specific action, but they can help you in managing the network. Examples of status messages are "Address change detected for JUNGLE," "UPS has been enabled" and "Re-mirroring successfully completed."

Warning Messages

Warning messages indicate that, although processing can continue despite the condition mentioned in the message, you should resolve the potential problem condition as soon as possible. If you ignore warning messages, the problems can reoccur and can quickly become serious. Examples of warning messages are "Hot Fix turned off on drive 02 (volume 03)," "FAT Entry 015A out of bounds in REPORT.OCT," and "Batteries are low. Server will go down in one minute."

Fatal Messages

Abend or fatal error messages are always serious and always halt the system. In errors affecting the file server, the server halts and the error message displays on the console. No further processing takes place until the system is rebooted. Abend errors are usually generated when the software discovers that data being processed is erroneous to the point that automatic recovery is not possible. If the file server continues processing, the result could lead to additional data corruption. Therefore, the system halts operations to prevent further damage.

The majority of abend errors are caused by hardware problems involving memory or disk drives. Examples of fatal error messages are "Abend: Attempt to configure nonexistent drive," "General Protection Interrupt," and "Invalid op code interrupt."

Sources for Error Message Documentation

Many available documents contain specific information on error messages. The NetWare v3.11 *System Messages* manual describes most NetWare-specific error messages for both file servers and DOS workstations, although many of the file server messages actually apply only to NetWare v3.0 and v3.1.

Novell's Electronic Bulletin Board Service, NetWire, and the technical bulletins Novell sends to dealers and distributors are other good sources for advice on NetWare problems and solutions. Many v3.11 error messages not found in the *System Messages* manual are documented on NetWire and in the technical bulletins.

Third-party vendors who supply drivers or NLMs for NetWare v3.x may also supply error message documentation with their software. For application-specific error messages, check the manuals that came with the application. Appendix A of the *IBM Disk Operating System Reference* manual contains DOS-specific error messages.

Keeping Network Logbooks

You should keep a network *configuration* logbook describing the exact settings and parameters of each hardware and software component on your network. The Novell installation manuals contain worksheets you can use to get your logbook started by collecting information about the current configuration of your workstations, servers, and routers. Every subsequent hardware and software change, no matter how minor, should be recorded in the logbook. This configuration logbook will come in handy when you have to call out for support. The first questions support technicians ask is how the file server, workstations, and NetWare operating system are configured.

We recommend that you also keep a network *error* logbook, either as part of the configuration logbook or separately. The same types of problems tend to reoccur frequently on local area networks. Keep a detailed record that describes every network problem and its solution, no matter who does the repairs: you or a professional service technician. This logbook will be an invaluable resource for future troubleshooting. When future errors occur, you can check through the logbook to see if that error happened before and if so, what the solution was.

Building a Troubleshooting Foundation for the Future

In this introduction, we've emphasized that truly effective troubleshooting is possible only when the troubleshooter understands what's going on beneath the surface of the network. We've encouraged you to obtain what we'll call a "deep" knowledge of NetWare; that is, a knowledge of the underlying workings of the operating system, its data structures, communications services, and so on. A troubleshooter with a deep knowledge of NetWare will always be more effective than one with a superficial knowledge.

Another reason for striving to obtain this deep knowledge is that NetWare is constantly being revised. In the past, new revisions of NetWare have come out as often as twice in the same year. There's a good chance that future versions of NetWare v3.x will appear very different on the surface than the present version, even though the basic operation of the OS remains fundamentally the same. A deep knowledge of NetWare will help you take these changes in stride.

Here are four final suggestions for improving your effectiveness as a network troubleshooter. First, maintain a fundamental curiosity. As you deal with NetWare, constantly ask yourself "How does that work?"—then stay curious until you find out the answer. Our experience is that learning driven by curiosity stays with you far more easily than knowledge obtained by other methods.

Second, set aside some time for learning more about NetWare. Many networking professionals fall into the trap of becoming too busy sawing to sharpen the saw. It is a paradox that we often work so long and so hard at effectively maintaining the network that we lose touch with the technology and actually become less effective in the long run. Another trap is to gain just enough expertise to build up a "comfort zone" from which you never venture out. It takes discipline (and often a great deal of convincing upper management) to make time for taking classes or reading books that will help you branch out into new areas where you may not have much experience.

Third, study more than just NetWare. Now that NetWare v3.11 is equipped to interoperate with DOS, Windows, OS/2, Unix, TCP/IP, NetView, SNMP products, and a variety of other hardware and software components, you can't afford to be ignorant of the larger world of computer networks. An understanding of how things like Ethernet, TCP/IP, and NetBIOS really work will give you valuable insights into how they fit in—and what kinds of problems they can cause—with NetWare.

Fourth, broaden your troubleshooting arsenal. This book focuses on the tools that come with the basic NetWare v3.11 operating system software. However, Novell itself and a host of third-party vendors offer numerous other products that are extremely useful in troubleshooting networks. These include network analyzers, cable scanners, protocol decoders, PC diagnostics programs, and even "programmer" tools such as debuggers and disassemblers. The so-called "physical layer" tools (analyzers and scanners) allow you to see inside the wire to investigate what is happening at the packet level. Sometimes this is the only way to discover a network fault, particularly when you're dealing with physical network problems that often manifest themselves as software problems. Although programming expertise is not a prerequisite for being a good troubleshooter, debuggers and disassemblers allow you to look inside a computer while it is executing code. This is sometimes the only way to find out what's really going on at the code level. Besides, experimenting with debuggers and their ilk is a great way to learn more and satisfy that basic curiosity we mentioned earlier.

By following the methods and suggestions we have presented in this introduction, you can build up troubleshooting skills that will serve you far into the future. Your abilities will also become more "portable," meaning you will be able to use the same techniques when troubleshooting systems other than NetWare v3.11. Not only will you become a better, more versatile troubleshooter, you will become more of an asset whatever your current assignment is in the networking industry.

Part One:

Overview of NetWare v3.x

At the heart of every Novell network lies the NetWare operating system. The more you know about the inner workings and functions of this sophisticated operating system, the better prepared you will be to troubleshoot when something goes wrong.

This overview section serves as an introduction to basic NetWare concepts and features. Those who are new to networks in general, and to NetWare v3.11 in particular, should read the entire overview. A solid understanding of what goes on inside the operating system provides the foundation upon which we'll build in the rest of the book.

- **Chapter 1: The NetWare v3.x Operating System** introduces the main components of the NetWare operating system and explains how they provide various network services. Many discussions later in the book assume that you have read this chapter and understand at least the basic workings of NetWare.

- **Chapter 2: Evolution of NetWare v3.x** details the changes made to the operating system and the features added since the release of NetWare 386 v3.0. If you've just upgraded to NetWare v3.11 (or are contemplating such an upgrade), read this chapter to get a quick overview of what's new.

- **Chapter 3: Protocol and Workstation Support** outlines the basics of the NetWare v3.x protocol engine, which enables the operating system to oversee communication between a variety of network protocols. It also explains how NetWare can support DOS, Windows, OS/2, Macintosh, and Unix workstations on the same network.

CHAPTER 1

The NetWare v3.*x* Operating System

When troubleshooting a NetWare v3.*x* network, your success hinges largely on how clearly you understand the role of the NetWare operating system and how it provides various services to network users. This is especially true when you're faced with uncommon network problems outside the realm of your everyday experience with LANs.

The purpose of Part One in this book is to explain in a general way the architecture of the NetWare v3.*x* operating system. By reading this first chapter, you'll come to understand how NetWare is different from operating systems like DOS and OS/2 and why this difference is important to you as a network trouble-shooter. You'll also see why topics such as network file systems, protocols, routers, and server memory protection are important troubleshooting concerns.

Much of the discussion in this chapter and in Chapter 3 is theoretical. (Chapter 2 details the differences between NetWare v3.11 and previous releases of NetWare 386. This information is directed to those who are familiar with NetWare but new to v3.11.) If you're comfortable with your present theoretical foundation in the NetWare v3.*x* architecture and communication protocols, or if you simply want to dive into the hands-on installation and troubleshooting information, you can skip directly to Part Two (Chapter 4). Later, if you find you need some clarification on these architectural principles, you can always refer to these overview chapters.

The Client-Server Model

One of the primary characteristics of a NetWare LAN is its use of the client-server networking model. In the client-server model, the *server* is an object that provides resources to one or more *client* objects. These resources are well-defined and known to both the server and its clients. To obtain a resource from the server, a client makes a request to the server using a series of messages. The server provides the resource through a series of responses to the client's messages. These messages and responses must be understood by both the server and the client.

The first important requirement of the client-server model, then, is that both the client and the server must be "intelligent" objects. By "intelligent," we mean simply that both the server and client must be able to perform enough of their own processing to form a valid message and to make a valid reply to a message.

The intelligence of the client is in contrast to the "dumb" terminals connected to centralized host systems such as mainframes and minicomputers. In such host-based systems, the dumb terminal doesn't perform its own processing. Rather, it serves as an input/output station for the host computer, which performs all the processing.

On a NetWare LAN, the clients are personal computers. Because they contain their own CPU and processing capabilities, they're intelligent according to our definition. As a specially- configured personal computer, the server is also intelligent. To access network resources, clients execute programs which request the use of network files, printers, or communication devices from the server.

The second important requirement of the client-server model is that both the client and the server must know and understand a common set of messages and responses. The client must know which resources are provided by the server and which resources are not provided. This well-defined system of resources, messages, and responses is known as a "protocol."

One interesting aspect of the client-server model overlooked by many LAN users is that both the client and the server pieces may reside on the same computer. With NetWare, however, the client and the server reside on different computers.

NetWare: The Specialized Server Operating System

The NetWare v3.*x* operating system is designed specifically to be a server. According to our definitions, that means NetWare provides a well-defined set of resources to its clients, and does so using a protocol, or well-defined set of messages and responses. The primary resources provided by NetWare include the following:

- File service
- Network routing
- Device sharing (printers and communications devices)
- Message delivery

To focus on its role as a server OS, NetWare v3.*x* eschews many design features considered necessary for general-purpose operating systems. As a specialized operating system, NetWare is like the pitcher on a baseball team who concentrates on one critical role—that of eliminating opposing batters. Other players on the team are less specific in their efforts: they must field and hit. Some team members fulfill the role of "general purpose" or "utility" players, having the ability to play several positions. At the professional level, however, baseball pitchers typically focus on pitching to the detriment of their hitting abilities.

Similarly, NetWare v3.*x* focuses on providing network services to network clients. NetWare isn't a general-purpose "utility" operating system. For example, it offers extremely limited graphics and user-interface capabilities; those it does offer exist to provide a workable administrative console and little else.

On the other hand, DOS, OS/2, and the Macintosh OS are general-purpose operating systems. They're designed to focus mainly on the user of the computer, rather than on the network. Accordingly, each has an extensive set of user-interface mechanisms, but no built-in support for the client-server model. They assume all resources required by their applications are local resources unless the user instructs them otherwise.

NetWare, on the other hand, provides specific, previously-defined resources to network clients, which themselves run general-purpose operating systems. By design, NetWare assumes that it's providing resources to remote clients over some type of network hardware. It assumes that all user interface and graphics support is provided by the client operating system. It further assumes that applications focusing on the user of the computer are executing on the clients, and therefore limits its role to providing network resources to those applications.

Later in this chapter, you'll see what NetWare's special focus means in terms of its technical design features. For now, the important thing to remember is that NetWare isn't designed to do the same things that DOS, OS/2, and the Macintosh OS are designed to do.

Basic Operating System Functions

All operating systems, including NetWare, DOS, OS/2, and the Macintosh OS, provide a group of fundamental routines. These include the ability to schedule and execute programs, the ability to store and retrieve data (this ability is typically called a "file system"), and the ability to allocate and manage RAM. In addition, an operating system should always provide a way for programs to communicate with computer hardware. Like most operating systems, NetWare provides this last service through a device driver interface.

Some operating systems, such as OS/2, have the ability to execute more than one program at a time. When an operating system has the ability to do this, we refer to it as a "multitasking" operating system. A multitasking operating system should further provide a mechanism for communication among concurrently executing programs. The ability of a multitasking operating system to allow communication among the programs or processes currently executing is called an "Inter-Process Communication," or IPC mechanism.

NetWare possesses these traditional operating system functions, but implements them in a non-traditional fashion. As a result, the design of NetWare tends to confuse people. For example, most traditional operating systems don't mix their memory management routines with their file system, but NetWare does. Most traditional operating systems don't include networking protocols as one of their core components, but NetWare does. Most traditional operating systems use their file system for IPC, but NetWare uses its networking protocols for IPC.

We could list other peculiarities of NetWare's design, but the point we want to emphasize is that while NetWare has most elements of a traditional operating system—it manages memory, schedules processes, runs device drivers, and so on— it is specifically designed to do network server tasks as efficiently as possible. Since NetWare continually services requests for access to files, its dominant architectural feature is its file system (in the sense that most of its executing instructions belong to the file system). In fact, NetWare could be described as a "file system with a scheduler and a protocol stack."

But don't forget the baseball player analogy. Just like a pitcher who performs a single task (attempt to eliminate opposing batters) over and over, NetWare has a focused role to play. All of the obvious characteristics of NetWare v3.x—its file system, memory management techniques, NetWare Loadable Module (NLM) architecture, and others—are part of NetWare for a good reason. Each component contributes directly to NetWare's ability to perform as a network operating system within the client-server model.

As you read more about NetWare v3.x's architecture, you'll come to understand how these components work and why they're critical to a high-performance, highly optimized operating system like NetWare.

Four Main Components of the NetWare v3.x Operating System

It's useful to think of the NetWare v3.x operating system as consisting of four basic components: the NetWare loader, the kernel, the NetWare Loadable Module (NLM) environment, and the application services.

- The NetWare loader initializes the server's hardware in preparation for execution of the NetWare kernel. After the kernel executes, the loader allows NLMs access to the NetWare kernel.

- The kernel is the fundamental code of an operating system. All code executing on a computer resolves eventually into execution of some kernel code. The kernel, therefore, is the most critical and, if all goes well, the most efficient part of the operating system. NetWare's kernel includes routines that provide its file system, scheduler, memory management, and network ing services.

- The NetWare NLM environment encompasses both the loader and the kernel, and provides scheduling, memory management, and all the necessary resources for NLMs. Software developers can write NLMs that extend the NetWare kernel by providing additional resources, and the NetWare loader makes these resources "visible" to the NetWare kernel.

- NetWare's application services provide basic networking functions that are available to NLMs running on the same machine and also to remote clients running on the same network.

Each component of NetWare—the loader, the kernel, the NLM environment, and the application services—operates at a higher level (further removed from the hardware) than the component preceding it, and each component leverages the services of the preceding components to do its job. For example, the NetWare bindery is built using (among other things) the NetWare file system. Figure 1-1 shows how these four basic NetWare components stack up.

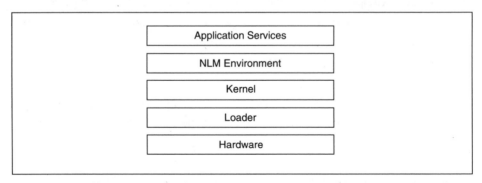

Figure 1-1: The four main parts of the NetWare v3.11 OS architecture—the loader, the kernel, the NLM environment, and the application services—use each others' services to perform their tasks.

While Figure 1-1 helps describe the concepts behind NetWare, it isn't entirely correct; it implies a hierarchical relationship among NetWare v3.x components that doesn't really exist. Moreover, it draws distinctions where actually there may be no distinction to be drawn. Figure 1-2 shows another conceptual description of the NetWare v3.x architecture.

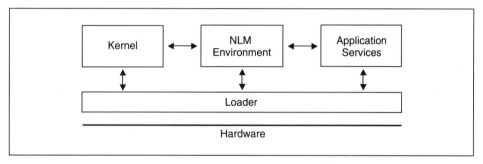

Figure 1-2: The components of the NetWare v3.11 OS behave primarily as peers, rather than in a hierarchical fashion.

While Figure 1-2 shows a more realistic depiction of the NetWare v3.x OS architecture, Figure 1-1 is more useful for our purpose here, because it presents a clear order for our discussion of the various elements of the NetWare operating system.

The remainder of this chapter, then, proceeds as in Figure 1-1, beginning with the NetWare v3.11 loader and ending with the application services offered by NetWare v3.11. Where appropriate, we'll divide these main components still further into sub-elements, thus providing the correct level of detail for the topic at hand.

Figure 1-3 shows a detailed, component-by-component breakdown of the NetWare v3.11 architecture.

NetWare v3.11 loader
- 386 protected-mode program loader
- Dynamic run-time linker

NetWare v3.11 kernel
- System executive
- Memory manager
- Scheduler
- IPX protocol stack
- NetWare Core Protocols (NCPs)
- Router
- Cache system
- File system
- File and record locking
- Transaction tracking
- Device driver interface

NLM environment
- CLIB (C Library)
- Streams
- SPX (Sequenced Packet Exchange)
- Communications services
- Queue services

Application services
- The bindery
- Login processing and security
- Accounting services
- Diagnostic services
- Message services
- Printing services

Figure 1-3: Each main component of the NetWare v3.x architecture consists of numerous other elements.

The NetWare Loader

The NetWare v3.x loader has two simple but critical functions. First, the loader executes from DOS, saves the DOS context, switches the server's processor from real mode to protected mode, and loads the NetWare kernel. Once the kernel is loaded, NetWare is up and running.

The second critical function of the loader is to act as a run-time linker, loading and linking additional modules to the NetWare kernel. Such modules are called NetWare Loadable Modules, or NLMs.

The function of a linker is to make addresses of executable routines available to the operating system. Thus, when it loads an NLM, the NetWare loader makes the addresses of NLM routines available to the operating system and, in certain cases, to other NLMs. We refer to the NetWare loader as a dynamic load-time linker for two reasons:

- It does its linking when the NLM is loaded.
- It allows you to unload NLMs after they have been linked.

Load-time linking allows you to configure the NetWare operating system by loading device drivers and NLMs from the console, rather than by using a special linker such as the one contained in Novell's NETGEN program. (NETGEN, as you may know, is the NetWare v2.1*x* installation program. NETGEN permanently links all device drivers to the NetWare v2.1*x* operating system during the installation procedure.)

NLMs are flexible; they can be distinct programs, disk or LAN drivers, protocol stacks, or libraries of code. When loaded, NLMs are linked by the loader, becoming in essence an extension of the kernel. The key is that the NetWare loader allows you to load and unload NLMs dynamically as you need them.

When you read about the NLM environment later in this section, you'll see how the loader provides NLMs with access to the core services of the NetWare kernel. This material will be critical to your ability to understand the role of NLMs and how they're different from traditional application programs.

In Part Two of this book, you'll read about NetWare v3.11 installation and how you must use the NetWare loader to run the core NetWare NLMs. The loader also allows you to retain DOS in the server's memory after the kernel executes. This retention of DOS allows you to load NLMs from DOS drives (including "DOS" network drives) while file service is occurring.

The NetWare Kernel

The NetWare v3.x kernel is the code that performs the core processing of the operating system. Everything you can possibly coax NetWare into doing eventually results in the execution of some kernel code.

For example, when your workstation requests data from a NetWare file, it forms a series of messages and sends those messages to the server. The server receives those messages from the network and investigates them. The code that investigates network messages is part of the NetWare kernel, so already your workstation's request has caused some kernel code to be executed. When NetWare reads the file, it uses kernel code to do so. Forming the response to your workstation's messages is also accomplished by the server using kernel code.

The kernel allocates and reclaims server memory, provides NLMs with access to server resources such as drives, ports, and the network (using device drivers), and runs the NetWare v3.x file system. Most kernel code is executed over and over—literally thousands of times—for each line of higher-level code. Thus all kernel code must be fast and reliable.

Here is a more detailed list of the components within the NetWare v3.x kernel:

- Memory manager
- Scheduler
- IPX protocol stack
- NetWare Core Protocols (NCPs)
- Router
- Cache system
- File system
- File and record locking
- Transaction tracking
- Device driver interface

Glancing at this list, you'll see some elements you wouldn't expect to find in the kernel of a traditional operating system. For example, NetWare includes a *router* as part of its kernel. (The *router* is a specialized routine that keeps track of internetwork addresses and uses its knowledge of the network layout to act as a "traffic cop" to network packets seeking their destination node.)

Because it's a specialized network operating system, NetWare also places its native IPX protocol stack and its file system within its kernel. Further, it uses its native protocol stack as a type of IPC mechanism. Components such as the protocol stack, router, and file system are just as much part of the NetWare kernel as its device driver interface and memory manager.

The sections below explain each component of the NetWare kernel in more detail.

NetWare Memory Manager

The NetWare v3.x memory manager is characterized by the following design attributes:

- Flat memory model
- Dynamic allocation of memory
- No virtual memory
- No memory protection

The two most significant characteristics of the NetWare v3.x memory manager are its use of the flat memory model and its dynamic allocation and reclamation of memory. Both characteristics contribute to the relative efficiency and flexibility with which NetWare manages its memory resources.

Flat Memory Model

A *flat* memory model allows an operating system (such as NetWare v3.x) to address all available memory using a continuous range of memory addresses. Previous versions of NetWare (v2.x and earlier) use a *segmented* memory model, which forces the operating system to addresses memory using a series of segments. (Segments are 64KB in this case.) The use of segmented memory reduces the flexibility with which an operating system can manage its memory. Moreover, segmented memory makes it difficult for an operating system to maintain data structures larger than a single segment or data structures which cross segment boundaries.

The use of a segmented memory model allowed previous versions of NetWare to address up to 16MB of memory using the Intel 80286 processor, which otherwise (without segmentation) could address only 64KB of memory. However, with the advent of the 32-bit 80386 processor, NetWare v3.x is able to address up to 4 gigabytes (GB) of memory without resorting to segmentation.

Dynamic Memory Allocation

Dynamic allocation and reclamation of memory means that an operating system (such as NetWare v3.x) responds to externally-imposed requirements by altering its memory configuration (within certain bounds such as total installed memory). For example, as the number of its active clients increases, a NetWare v3.x server can allocate more memory toward the storage and processing of requests for service made by such clients.

Conversely, as the number of its active clients falls, a NetWare v3.x server can reclaim a portion of its memory that was previously allocated for service requests. When so reclaimed, the memory is then available for some other purpose, such as caching of data, or is simply held by NetWare in reserve for some unknown future requirement.

The key benefit of NetWare v3.x's dynamic memory allocation and reclamation is that NetWare can optimize its memory heap "on the fly," so to speak, in response to actual network conditions. Consequently (with a couple of exceptions that we'll cover shortly), NetWare's memory configuration is neither a network management nor a network troubleshooting concern. This condition is in stark contrast to earlier versions of NetWare (versions 2.1x and earlier), which encouraged meticulous tuning of NetWare's static memory parameters at installation time.

No Virtual Memory

One element of memory management that NetWare *doesn't* have is virtual memory. *Virtual memory* refers to the ability of an operating system (such as Unix or OS/2) to address more memory than is physically installed on the machine, using a medium such as a disk drive as a secondary memory device. Virtual memory in NetWare would be self-defeating, because NetWare uses all memory not required by the kernel or NLMs for file system caching. If NetWare did have virtual memory, it would use the extra address space to virtualize its file cache to a disk-based swap file. The result would be the ironic situation of having to cache file system data to a disk-based swap file. This process would not only defeat the advantages of file system caching, but would add significant overhead to NetWare's execution.

No Memory Protection

A second element of memory management that NetWare doesn't have is memory protection, or the ability of an operating system to control access to memory addresses depending on the "privilege level" of the task requesting access to a given memory address. The primary purpose of memory protection is to protect the kernel and its data structures from corruption by a less critical program, such as an application.

While NetWare v3.*x* could gain some benefit from memory protection, its need for such protection is less critical than that of general-purpose operating systems. This is because the vast majority of application-based processing on a NetWare LAN is performed by clients. Applications that do run on the server as NLMs typically require free access to the most privileged NetWare data structures anyway, which is just what memory protection attempts to prevent.

NetWare v3.x Memory Types

NetWare v3.*x*'s memory management facility has grown more capable and sophisticated with each incremental release of the product, beginning with v3.0 and continuing with v3.11. However, the basic NetWare v3.*x* memory architecture remains unchanged.

While the concepts behind NetWare's memory usage may be difficult for the novice network supervisor to grasp, knowing about the different types of NetWare memory is important for the following reasons:

- NetWare error messages often refer to memory pools.
- Many of the SET commands for tuning the server involve memory parameters.
- It will help you know when to add more memory to the server.
- It's a must for troubleshooting memory management problems.

Upon initialization, NetWare v3.*x* maintains four classes, or pools, of memory:

- *Kernel memory*, which contains the NetWare kernel and which remains static while NetWare is running

- *Permanent memory*, which NetWare uses to maintain its fundamental data structures, such as communications buffers, volume tables, and others

- *Alloc memory*, which NLMs use

- *Cache memory*, which NetWare uses to cache its file systems

Of these four classes of memory, kernel memory is static, while the other three types of memory are dynamic to some degree or another. Permanent memory is the least dynamic of the three, while cache memory is the most dynamic.

Kernel Memory

When you execute SERVER.EXE from DOS, the NetWare Loader initializes an area of server memory above the 1MB address and loads the kernel into that memory. From the time the kernel executes until the time you shut down the server, the kernel memory remains static. In other words, kernel memory remains dedicated to the NetWare v3.*x* kernel; it isn't available for any other use as long as the kernel is running.

However, despite the fact that the server's processor now runs in protected mode and under the control of the NetWare kernel, memory below the 1MB address continues to contain DOS. The reason DOS remains in memory is that you may need to use the server's floppy drives to load more NLMs or other software stored on the server's DOS partition or on DOS floppy diskettes. NetWare uses DOS to let you do this.

If you don't need DOS any more, you can unload DOS from memory by using the REMOVE DOS console command. Once you remove DOS from the first megabyte of server memory, that memory becomes available to NetWare as cache memory.

Permanent Memory

Permanent memory is dedicated to core NetWare data structures such as communications buffers and directory information. Communications buffers are special areas of memory used by NetWare to send and receive data to and from the network. Permanent memory is semi-dynamic; that is, part of it is static in that it has a base configuration that never changes as long as NetWare is running. The rest of permanent memory is dynamic.

For example, when NetWare initializes permanent memory, it sets up a series of communications buffers; as more users connect to the server, NetWare may increase the number of its communications buffers. The original buffer configuration represents a base-level data structure, contained in permanent memory.

As the number of buffers grows, NetWare allocates "semi-permanent" memory and dedicates it to the large buffer structure. Semi-permanent memory is dynamic in that NetWare can allocate it for core data structures that need to be expanded; but, once allocated, semi-permanent memory remains dedicated to the data structure for which it was allocated and can't be returned to NetWare's pool of available memory.

Alloc Memory

Alloc memory is memory allocated by NetWare for short-term purposes and for use by NLMs. NetWare must be able to create and destroy data structures in order to fulfill short-term processing requirements that occur repeatedly: for example, each time a user connects to a server and later disconnects from it, or when an application locks a file and later releases the file lock.

Moreover, NLMs frequently request memory from the NetWare memory manager. Unlike NetWare's core data structures, which remain in place for the duration of NetWare's execution, these data structures tend to be short-lived. However, the need for them arises continually.

NetWare v3.*x* maintains its alloc memory as a set of available memory addresses in a chain, or linked list, and cycles through that list to fulfill such requests. Using a linked list of memory addresses allows NetWare to initialize its alloc memory only once, but retain the ability to use the same chunk of memory repeatedly to fulfill allocation requests. The linked list structure prevents memory fragmentation and memory leakage, two problems associated with short-term recurring memory operations.

Every time an NLM requires memory, NetWare delivers that memory to the NLM from the alloc memory pool. When the NLM is finished with the memory, it returns the memory to NetWare's alloc pool. NetWare can then "recycle" that memory by placing it back on the linked list of available alloc memory.

However, as the memory requirements of NLMs increase, NetWare's alloc pool may become depleted. When this happens, NetWare appropriates more alloc memory from its cache memory, possibly reducing server performance. Moreover, once NetWare has "stolen" from its cache in order to increase the size of its alloc pool, that memory remains in the alloc pool and doesn't return to cache. Normally, this isn't a problem because a server's NLM configuration remains fairly stable.

For example, you don't generally load and unload NLMs the way you might load and unload programs on your workstation. Rather, you settle on a set of NLMs that provide the services your network requires, and you leave them loaded and running indefinitely.

To prevent severe cache depletion, NetWare can limit the size of its alloc pool. The default maximum size of the alloc pool is 2MB, but you can set the maximum size as low as 50KB or as high as 16MB. In Chapter 21, you'll read how to track NetWare's use of its alloc memory, and you'll learn what you can do to tune it more closely to your specific installation.

File Cache Memory

All memory not being used as kernel, permanent, semi-permanent, or alloc memory is available for file caching. Typically, file cache memory on a NetWare v3.*x* server consists of around 70% of total memory, making file cache memory far and away the dominant memory type.

NetWare's file cache memory is simple in concept but sophisticated in its implementation. The idea is simple: By maintaining file data in fast cache buffers, NetWare can increase its file service performance dramatically. However, file caching is made a complex proposition by many factors, including data integrity, file and record locking, concurrency and synchronization, and latency. NetWare's file cache architecture addresses each one of these factors during its normal operation, which means that you probably won't have to tinker with NetWare's caching parameters much if at all.

File cache memory is the most dynamic of NetWare v3.x's memory types. For one thing, NetWare is continually recycling individual cache buffers, which act as a temporary storage area for file data. Furthermore, NetWare draws on file cache memory to expand its semi- permanent and alloc memory pools. Again, once NetWare has allocated memory from its file cache into either semi-permanent or alloc memory, that memory never reverts back to file cache.

NetWare further categorizes its file cache memory as either *non-moveable cache memory* or *moveable cache memory*. Non-moveable cache memory is similar to alloc memory in that it's appropriate for short-term requirements that arise repeatedly. Non-moveable cache memory buffers are maintained in a linked list, from which they're allocated to cache file data; upon release, they're recycled back onto the linked list. The significant aspect of non-moveable cache memory is that NetWare can return it to use as file cache buffers after it's freed by an NLM.

Moveable cache memory is just like non-moveable cache memory, except that NetWare can move it to different physical memory addresses in order to maintain an efficient memory heap. (A memory "heap" is the total memory available for use by the operating system.)

Memory moving is a common method used by operating systems (such as the Macintosh OS, OS/2, and NetWare v3.x) to eliminate memory fragmentation and to make memory management in general more efficient. NetWare maintains moveable cache buffers in a linked list, from which NetWare allocates them to cache file data. Like non-moveable cache buffers, they're recycled by NetWare upon release.

The overhead NetWare requires to maintain moveable memory makes sense only for data structures that are relatively long-lived. That's why NetWare fulfills short-term file caching requirements out of its non-moveable cache, but fulfills all other file caching requirements out of its moveable cache.

Memory Tuning

The optimum memory configuration for a NetWare v3.x server is a moving target that changes according to external events. For example, the number of active nodes, the number of open files, the average size of open files, the applications being run by workstations, the applications being run on the server, the type of transport protocol in use, and more, all affect the optimum server memory configuration.

Much of NetWare's memory management architecture is dedicated to the notion of dynamic memory tuning. If you use the MONITOR utility to watch the memory configuration of a NetWare v3.x server, you'll notice that it continually moves toward an equilibrium point that represents optimum use of server memory.

However, that equilibrium point changes every time something happens on the network. For example, if you approach a server and begin loading NLMs, one after the other, you'll see file cache memory go down while alloc memory goes up. That's what dynamic tuning is all about. In Chapter 21, you'll read how to tune and troubleshoot those few aspects of memory management NetWare doesn't tune by itself.

The NetWare Scheduler

As a multitasking operating system, NetWare v3.x can run multiple tasks concurrently. A plain-vanilla NetWare v3.11 server, for example, has several processes running at all times. In addition to file service processes, the polling process, the cache update process, and more, NetWare v3.11 runs its own router, accepts input from its console, maintains printer queues, and so on. Each of these processes represents a distinct executing object within the server. Furthermore, NLMs themselves can consist of multiple processes.

The NetWare Scheduler is the group of kernel procedures that controls the execution of all other processes. The primary job of the scheduler is to ensure that only one process has control of the server's CPU at a given instance. In simple terms, each active process cycles through a queue maintained by the scheduler. When a process reaches the head of the queue, it gains control of the server's CPU and resumes execution. When the executing process relinquishes control of the server's CPU, it halts execution and goes back into the scheduler's queue. Then a different process gains control of the server's CPU, and so on.

In general, NetWare's scheduler is non-preemptive. That is, it doesn't preempt the executing process by forcing it to halt its execution and to place itself back on the scheduler's queue. Rather, the scheduler allows the executing process to retain control over the server's CPU until the process itself relinquishes control of the CPU. The alternative, a preemptive scheduler, forces an executing process to relinquish control of the host's CPU after a predefined number of execution cycles.

A non-preemptive scheduler is the most efficient type in an environment that makes heavy use of shared memory, as NetWare does. (NetWare's file cache memory is a good example of shared memory.) The potential problem with a non-preemptive scheduler is that a rogue process can fail to relinquish control of the CPU in a timely manner, thus locking other active processes out of the execution cycle. For this reason, NLMs should be written so that they execute functions quickly, and tested to ensure that they don't block other processes out of execution for inordinate periods of time.

NetWare allows some processes to have a higher execution priority than other processes, which means simply that high-priority processes can cut in front of lower-priority processes in the scheduler's queue. NetWare's scheduler has become more sophisticated with the release of NetWare v3.10 and v3.11. As a result, you have finer control over the workings of the scheduler.

The IPX Protocol Stack

Understanding Novell's native communications protocol—the Internetwork Packet eXchange (IPX) protocol—is critical to understanding how NetWare works. The IPX "protocol stack" refers to that code within the kernel responsible for forming, sending, receiving, and processing units of transmission called "packets."

IPX doesn't define the physical-layer network (in other words, the "cards and cable" you'll read about in Chapter 4) over which it sends data. Instead, it uses a well-defined interface to communicate with various network transport protocols.

When IPX "sends" or "receives" a packet, it doesn't do so directly to a network interface board, but instead sends and receives packets to and from a piece of software called a LAN driver. It's the LAN driver's job to communicate directly with the networking hardware, accounting for all things peculiar to a specific type of networking adapter or topology. Because these peculiarities are abstracted by driver software, IPX doesn't have to make any distinctions among types of networking hardware, as shown in Figure 1-4.

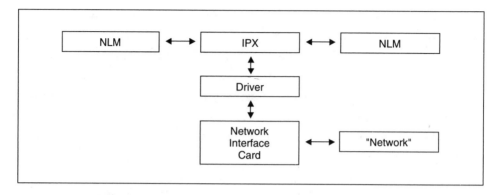

Figure 1-4: IPX doesn't communicate directly with networking hardware, but instead with a LAN driver, which allows IPX to generalize differences among different types of networking hardware.

Structure of an IPX Packet

IPX itself is a simple, but robust and fast, communications protocol. Figure 1-5 shows the basic structure of an IPX packet.

```
Offset    Content                        Size
- - - - - - - - - - - - - - - - - - - - - - - - - - - - - - - -

0         Checksum                       2 Bytes
2         Length                         2 Bytes
4         Transport Control              1 Byte
5         Packet Type                    1 Byte

6         Destination Network            4 Bytes
10        Destination Node               6 Bytes
16        Destination Socket             2 Bytes

18        Source Network                 4 Bytes
22        Source Node                    6 Bytes
28        Source Socket                  2 Bytes

30        Data Portion                   0 - 546 Bytes
```

Figure 1-5: An IPX packet is a structure consisting of numerous data fields.

In Figure 1-5, as in most computer literature, "offset" refers to the location of a data structure element relative to the beginning of that structure. Offsets are usually numbered in bytes, though not always.

The first 30 bytes of an IPX packet (offsets 0-29) are what is known as the *IPX Header*; the remainder of the packet, if there is a remainder, contains the packet's data. (An IPX packet doesn't have to contain any data, but it must always have a 30-byte header.) IPX packets can be of varying length, up to 576 bytes (including the header). The actual length of a given IPX packet is contained in the header's Length field (offset 2).

Each packet header also contains the source and destination *network* addresses, the source and destination *node* addresses, and the source and destination *sockets*.

- A *network address* is the 4-byte LAN address, and typically refers to a network segment. For example, a server with two Ethernet cards attached to it identifies the networks attached to each card, respectively, using a distinct LAN address for each one.

- A *node address* specifies a single station attached to the LAN. A LAN may have many nodes attached to it.

- An IPX *socket* plays two roles. A particular IPX packet's source or destination socket may signify what type of information is in that IPX packet's data field. For example, a packet with a source or destination socket of 453h is commonly understood by NetWare to contain internetwork routing information. Novell has defined several such "well-known" sockets, including 451h (file service packet),456h (diagnostic packet), and others. Think of a socket as a defining variable that affects how IPX behaves when it processes a specific packet.

An engineer friend of ours offers this analogy for understanding IPX network, node, and socket addresses: Think of an apartment building in your town. To send a letter to a specific apartment, you must know what street the building is on, the address of the building, and the apartment number. The IPX network number is like the street address; the node number is like the building address; the socket number is like the apartment number.

Just as there may be several apartments located in a single apartment building, there may be several IPX sockets active within a single computer. To send an IPX packet to a program, you must know the network number, the node number, and the socket number, as shown in Figure 1-6.

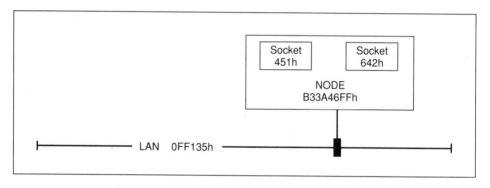

Figure 1-6: An IPX packet's destination network address, node address, and socket address work together to identify a specific destination for that packet. Individual nodes can have multiple sockets open simultaneously.

Applications can also use sockets for their own purposes. For example, two applications wishing to communicate with each other over the network can negotiate sockets with which to do so. If two applications agree to communicate over socket 5000h, for example, they can safely ignore packets addressed to other sockets. Each can also safely assume that a packet destined for socket 5000h is a communication from the other application.

NetWare uses sockets to filter and route packets internally. For example, a NetWare router listens for packets with a destination socket of 453h and processes them differently from packets with a destination socket of 451h.

ECBs and ESRs

IPX is closely linked to the following design elements of NetWare:

- Event Control Blocks (ECBs)
- Event Service Routines (ESRs)

The next few paragraphs discuss ECBs and ESRs and how NetWare uses these structures to provide resources to network clients.

Remember from the apartment analogy that a single LAN may have multiple nodes attached to it, and a single node can have multiple sockets. Sockets are represented within the node as elements of a RAM-based data structure called an Event Control Block (ECB). An ECB controls the formation, reception, and processing of IPX data. It's common for IPX-based workstations to have several ECBs active at a given time, and each ECB can potentially define a different socket. This is especially true of multitasking nodes, including NetWare v3.x servers.

ECBs are said to be "listening" or "sending." A listening ECB is waiting to receive an IPX packet; if the listening ECB has defined a destination socket, it's listening specifically for packets with a matching destination socket. A sending ECB submits itself to IPX, which uses the ECB to form an IPX packet.

Another point about IPX that's critical to how NetWare v3.x works is the notion of an Event Service Routine (ESR). An ESR, like a socket, is an element of an IPX Event Control Block. When a listening ECB receives a valid packet, it triggers its ESR. The ESR itself is a function pointer (the address to where a particular routine resides in memory). IPX triggers the ESR by executing the function at the address pointed to by the ESR.

For example, suppose an application creates a listening ECB with a socket of 700h. Furthermore, the ECB has an ESR that causes the string "Time to take a break" to be displayed on your workstation. As soon as IPX receives a packet with the destination address of the workstation, it copies the packet and submits the copy to the ECB. Since the ECB is listening specifically for packets with a destination socket of 700h, it will discard packets that have different destination sockets. However, if the ECB receives a packet with a destination socket of 700h, it places the packet's data in its receive buffer and triggers the ESR, causing the string "Time to take a break" to be displayed on the workstation's screen.

The use of ESRs is optional; many NetWare-aware applications don't use them. However, NetWare itself makes heavy use of ESRs, as you'll soon discover.

The IPX Internal Network

The ability of NetWare v3.x to load and unload NLMs "on the fly" means that the OS can't anticipate how many concurrently running processes will need to communicate with each other, and it can't afford to make any assumptions in this regard. Moreover, the number of such processes, and the degree to which they need to communicate among themselves, may change rapidly.

The result is that every NetWare v3.x server must have an internal IPX "network" before it can run. Logically, the server's *internal* IPX network is equivalent to the IPX networks associated with the server's LAN adapters. An NLM is to the server's internal IPX network what a node is to the server's LANs. Through the internal IPX network, NLMs can send and receive IPX packets among themselves, define and trigger ESRs, and, in short, use IPX just as any other network application can.

A NetWare v3.x server, then, is really a self-contained network running at ultra-high speeds. When two NLMs running on the same server wish to communicate, they do so just as two physically separated nodes would do over a network. This form of inter-process communication within the server works exactly as it does between server and workstation.

The use of an internal IPX network for IPC is a precursor of what is becoming known in the industry as a "message passing architecture." As such, NetWare v3.x's internal IPX network is only one form of IPC provided by NetWare. Other forms include semaphores and shared memory. NLMs can even define their own methods of IPC if they need to.

NetWare Core Protocols (NCPs)

NetWare Core Protocols (NCPs) are a proprietary set of well-defined messages that control server execution. The current method for passing NCPs to the server is through a specially-flagged IPX packet, although there's no technical barrier to transmitting NCPs using other datagram protocols such as the User Data Protocol (UDP) used in TCP/IP- based networks.

Historically, Novell has maintained tight control over the definition of NetWare NCPs because they're the *key* to NetWare. A client node may have a perfectly good IPX/SPX stack and an active physical connection to a server; yet, without knowledge of NCPs, that client won't be able to coax any services out of the server. Figure 1-7 shows how NCPs work.

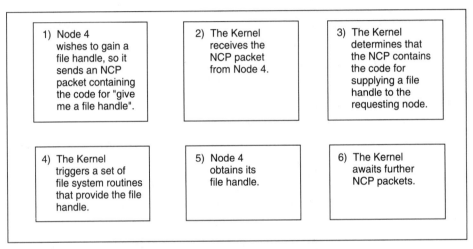

Figure 1-7: NetWare uses NCPs to provide services to its clients.

What's happening in Figure 1-7 is really pretty simple. Both the server and the client have within their memory space a table of valid NCPs. The server's NCP table reflects the OS services exported by that kernel; the client's NCP table reflects the types of services required by that client. Since each specific NCP, when invoked, triggers a series of kernel routines, both the client and server must know exactly what each NCP means, when to invoke it, and what to expect after invoking it.

For example, if the client needs to obtain a file handle from the server, it searches its table of NCPs until it locates the NCP that causes the server to provide a file handle. The client then packages the code number for that NCP into a specially-flagged IPX packet and sends that packet to the server. The server, upon receiving the packet, immediately notices that it's an NCP packet and unwraps it to obtain the NCP code number.

Upon obtaining the NCP code number sent by the client, the server searches its NCP table until it finds the NCP corresponding to the code number sent by the client. As soon as the server matches the packet's code with its corresponding NCP, it triggers a predefined set of kernel routines. The result is that the client now has a file handle provided for it by the server.

In actual execution, NCPs are different and more complicated than represented here. (The server's data structure isn't necessarily a table, for example.) In addition, NCPs are usually invoked in groups, rather than singly. However, the idea is the same.

It's important to note that the client node requesting NCP services can be another kernel process or NLM running on the server that processes the NCP request. In fact, that's the key to message passing; it's more efficient than the traditional method of having client nodes make system calls.

NCPs really are the key into NetWare. Novell keeps tight wraps on them for a couple of reasons. First, as the capabilities of the NetWare v3.x OS increase or change, the NCPs must change correspondingly. In fact, NCPs undergo continual change, a fact which simply reflects the successful evolution of the NetWare OS. Second, as you can see, it's critical that both the client and the server be in complete agreement as to what each NCP means. If even one bit of one NCP is out of synch between a server and a client, NetWare won't work correctly.

IPX, NLMs, NCPs, and the server's internal network all are tightly integrated with each other, making a NetWare server the logical equivalent of the physical network it serves to integrate. Understanding the internal roles of these kernel components is the key to understanding how NetWare can deal efficiently with network clients. NCPs, which are tightly integrated with IPX, are a network extension of the server's internal message passing architecture. The result is that NetWare is equally efficient at servicing the requests of network clients *and* at executing the system calls of its own linked NLMs.

Applications designed to run on NetWare can, in effect, create their own "core" protocols through the use of Event Service Routines (ESRs), as described earlier. ESRs work much the same way as NCPs do for NetWare v3.x servers. One difference is that NCPs are well-defined and "hard coded" into the NetWare kernel and client software, while ESRs are more dynamic.

Router

Each NetWare server provides a routing service to the network. At the very least, this routing service allows a single-server network to provide communications across multiple LAN segments, as shown in Figure 1-8.

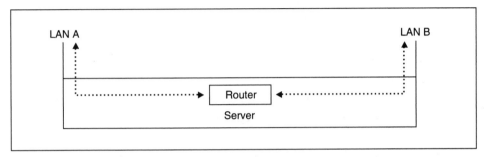

Figure 1-8: Routing can be as simple as providing single-server communications among different LAN segments.

However, NetWare's inherent routing services are most useful in a multiserver environment, where there are many LAN segments and possibly several different paths between two given nodes, as shown in Figure 1-9.

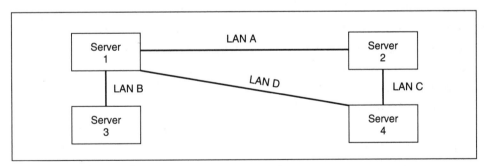

Figure 1-9: NetWare's routing services are most useful in a situation where there are many LAN segments and many servers.

The portion of the NetWare v3.*x* kernel that performs routing between networks is referred to simply as the *router*. The router is a series of routines that maintain a "picture" of the internetwork from a specific server's point of view. The routing information contained within each server includes:

- All the networks, or LAN segments, known to the server;
- For each known network, the number of intermediate networks between the server and that particular network; o Each server known to the server in question;
- For each server known to the server in question, how many intermediate networks are between the two servers.

This "picture of the internetwork" is called a *routing table*, and each server's table is different.

At regular intervals (the default interval is one minute), NetWare servers broadcast their routing table to every other server on each local LAN. To do this, they use a special type of IPX protocol called the Routing Information Protocol (RIP). A NetWare server is continuously receiving updated routing tables from other servers.

Each individual server continually uses RIP information from other servers to check against its own internally maintained routing table. If a server detects inconsistencies between RIP information and its own routing table, it will generate alerts declaring some type of routing problem. You can watch RIP information as it comes over the wire by using the NetWare TRACK ON console command (described in Chapter 10).

The advantage of NetWare's internal router is that changes in the configuration of an internetwork are dynamically reflected network-side in server routing tables. For example, if you add a server or a LAN to your internetwork, NetWare will automatically perform updates of internet-wide routing tables. Likewise, if you remove a server or a LAN, NetWare will remove that server or LAN from internet-wide routing tables. This allows for maintenance-free internetwork routing provided that you follow the rules for assigning network addresses.

For especially large or complex internetworks, you can use special software that comes with NetWare v3.*x* to create standalone, or external, routers. External routers are different from NetWare's internal router because the external router does nothing except route IPX packets, while NetWare's internal router is simply one among many components of the NetWare server. External routers can help to lessen the routing load of a NetWare server, freeing its resources to provide other services, such as file or print services.

NetWare's Cache System

When we discussed NetWare's memory manager earlier in this chapter, we introduced the different types of memory (kernel, permanent, alloc, and cache) NetWare maintains. Cache memory, you may recall, was the largest single type of memory in a NetWare v3.*x* server. Now you'll learn what NetWare does with all its cache memory.

The basic purpose of NetWare's cache system is to speed access to data stored within the NetWare file system. The premise is simple: since RAM access is faster than disk access, use cache memory to store data in RAM, and then clients can gain access to the data faster than if the data were stored only on disk.

Problems with Caching Data

There are several problems inherent with caching, each of which NetWare v3.*x* solves in an interesting way.

The first problem is that available disk storage is usually hundreds of times larger than NetWare's cache memory, which means that only a portion of the NetWare file system can be cached. To complicate this problem, NetWare can't be certain how much cache memory it will have when it boots.

So how does NetWare know which portions of the file system to cache? Well, NetWare *assumes* that certain data, such as volume directories, will always be requested, so it caches those data structures automatically when it mounts a volume. Directory caching allows NetWare to quickly locate a file's place within a NetWare volume.

Upon booting and mounting its volumes, NetWare proceeds to cache data as soon as it's requested by a client. However, depending on the size of the server's file cache memory, this can only continue for a short time (specifically, until NetWare fills all its cache memory with data from its file system).

To handle the problem of all available cache memory being filled up, NetWare keeps track of how often clients request access to certain files (and portions of files). When its cache space is full, it flushes the least recently used file (or portion of a file) from cache memory. NetWare then uses the newly-available space within its cache memory to speed access to the next non-cached piece of data requested by a client by loading that data in the just-flushed cache buffer. Whenever NetWare flushes data from its cache memory, it does so by first writing the data to its correct place on the appropriate NetWare volume, and then by overwriting its newly freed cache memory.

Depending on how often or in what way clients request data to a specific file, NetWare may cache the entire file, part of the file, or none of the file. This leads to another problem. How does a client know, when it writes data to a cached file, that the data has actually been stored on disk?

For some applications this is an important factor, because cache memory is volatile; its contents disappear as soon as the NetWare server goes down or power is disrupted. Disk memory, however, is more permanent. If a file resides in cache and not on disk, that file will be vaporized if the server goes down due to a power failure or some other aberrant event.

This is, in fact, a shortcoming of cache memory, and many systems do little or nothing to address it. This happens because most cache systems are implemented separately from the file system, a situation which allows for a growing disparity between what cache believes the state of the file system to be and what the file system believes about itself.

The only way an application can be certain its data has been flushed from cache and onto disk is by using NetWare's Transaction Tracking System (TTS). (TTS, it turns out, is a excellent solution; you'll read more about it shortly.) However, NetWare addresses the problem of maintaining synchronization between its cache and file systems by integrating cache and file system to the point that they're really the same thing.

How NetWare Caches Data

Whenever NetWare caches data, it does so by reserving a physical disk block (a unit of storage within the NetWare v3.11 file system), transferring that block's data to cache memory and creating a logical link between the physical disk block and the cache buffer that holds data from that block. This link between a cache buffer and a physical disk block allows NetWare to manipulate disk blocks and also reflects the effects of such manipulation on cache buffers that are linked to the disk blocks, thus maintaining synchronization between its disk-based file system and its RAM-based cache memory.

While the NetWare v3.11 memory manager initializes and maintains cache memory, cache manipulation is performed by the NetWare file system, which ensures that cache and disk storage are fully synchronized. This synchronization, though complex, removes most of the concerns for data integrity raised by large-scale data caching. In addition, it allows NetWare's cache to use all of the data synchronization services, including file and record locking, that are integral to the NetWare v3.x file system. (We'll discuss these synchronization services a little later in this chapter.)

The File System

NetWare's file system is a set of routines and data structures that read, write, move, organize, delete, and generally maintain data on NetWare v3.x volumes. As part of the NetWare kernel, the file system inherits some important attributes, such as the ability to move data in 32-bit chunks.

Like the NetWare v3.x operating system as a whole, the file system is focused on providing services to clients in a networked environment: specifically, on providing file service. The most important data structures of the NetWare file system include volumes, partitions, disk blocks, cache buffers, hash tables, directories, and files.

A volume is the primary structure of the NetWare file system. All NetWare servers must have at least one volume (the SYS volume) mounted at all times. However, a server can optionally have up to 64 volumes mounted at once. Each volume can span up to 32 storage segments, and each of a volume's segments can reside on a different physical drive.

When you span a NetWare volume over more than one physical drive, the file system automatically performs "striped" reads and writes. This means that it reads or writes data from each of the volume's multiple drives concurrently. Striped reads and writes can speed file system operations significantly, depending on the server's configuration.

Files stored on a NetWare v3.x server consist of a file descriptor and a chain of disk blocks. A file's descriptor is part of the volume directory, which is cached automatically as described in the caching section above. Disk blocks are units of storage that the NetWare file system uses to store data. NetWare tracks the status of each disk block and maintains information about it that is useful for file caching and directory maintenance.

When you create a NetWare v3.x volume, you can select a size for that volume's disk blocks. The available sizes are 4KB, 8KB, 16KB, 32 KB, or 64KB. Large block sizes speed the transfer of large files, but waste storage space for volumes containing many smaller files. (The default block size is 4KB.)

NetWare v3.11 allows you to alter the size of its cache buffers so they match the size of the file system's disk blocks. As you would expect, the valid sizes for NetWare v3.x cache buffers are 4KB, 8KB, or 16KB. This is yet another example of how closely NetWare's cache memory and file system are integrated.

The NetWare v3.x file system allows for some big-time data structures. For instance, a single NetWare file can be up to 4GB in size. A single NetWare v3.x server can maintain up to 1,000,000 concurrently opened files, up to 1,000,000 file or record locks, or some combination of each, provided the total number of file handles and locks is equal to or less than 1,000,000.

In addition to these mainframe-class file system limits, the NetWare file system supports sparse files, or files with large areas of no data (holes) in them. Sparse files are commonly used by database management systems to speed record access.

Much of the logic of the NetWare v3.x file system is designed to allow as many clients as possible to gain access to as much data as possible as quickly as possible. Consequently, the file system also contains considerable logic to handle data contention—cases in which several clients attempt to manipulate common data at the same time.

Most of this logic involves mechanisms to prevent data contention from occurring in the first place. However, because some data contention is inevitable, the file system contains sufficient logic to reduce the negative effects that data contention has on file service performance, and also to ensure the integrity of data in the face of contention.

File and Record Locking

File and record locking are two mechanisms used by the NetWare file system to resolve data contention. As such, the ability to provide clients with record and file locks is a critical element of NetWare's ability to function in a client-server environment.

When the NetWare file system locks a file, the client that initiated the locking procedure by opening the file "owns the lock," so to speak. Other clients that attempt to open the file while the first client holds the lock can do so, but with Read access only. In other words, the first client to open a file can read and write to the file, while clients who open the same file subsequently can only read the file. When the first client closes the file, the NetWare file system releases the file lock, and the next client attempting to open the file receives its own file lock.

The NetWare file system can lock entire files or portions of files. The former type of lock is called a *file lock*, while the latter type of lock is called a *record lock*. Both types of locks—file locks and record locks—allow subsequent clients to open the file for reading, but not for writing. That way, multiple clients can open a file for reading, but only a single client can open the file (or a portion of a file, as in a record lock) for reading and writing.

It may seem odd that a client would want to lock only a portion of a file rather than an entire file. Database applications are a good example of the need for record locking. Many databases are implemented as large files, and database records are stored in individual portions of those files. To read or write a single record, the database application will request a lock on only the portion of the file containing the desired record.

Figure 1-10 shows a simple 12KB file consisting of three 4KB blocks. Block 1 begins with offset zero and ends with offset three; block 2 begins with offset four and ends with offset seven; block 3 begins with offset eight and ends with offset eleven.

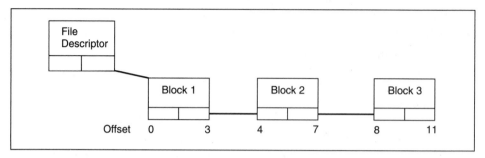

Figure 1-10: This is a simple 12KB file consisting of three 4KB blocks.

Obtaining a file lock on the file shown in Figure 1-10 would result in the situation represented in Figure 1-11, with the entire file locked.

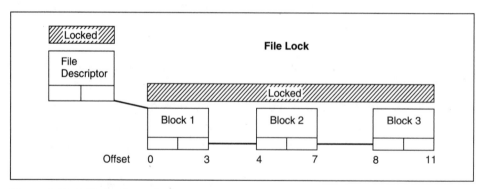

Figure 1-11: A file lock results in the entire file being locked.

A record lock, on the other hand, would result in a situation like that represented in Figure 1-12. When requesting a record lock, the client defines the beginning and ending offsets of the record within the target file.

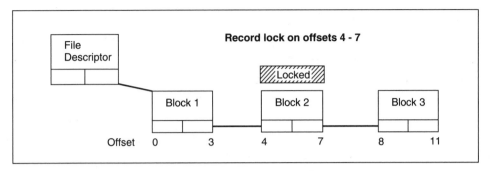

Figure 1-12: With record locking, only a portion of the file is locked at a time.

Transaction Tracking System

.Novell's Transaction Tracking System (TTS) provides the ability of NetWare's file system to associate one or more file updates into a single logical unit called a transaction. Further, the NetWare file system ensures that every update within a transaction is successfully written to disk, or none of the updates are written to disk.

A good example of how transaction tracking works is an imaginary order entry system— perhaps like the one your business uses. When a customer calls your service representative and orders $100 worth of your product, a good order entry system will place a shipping order to your warehouse for $100 worth of product and bill the customer's account for $100. Both the shipping order and the billing are part of the same transaction.

If the order entry system were to create a shipping order without also billing the customer, your company would be in the position of shipping product without billing for it. Naturally, you want the order entry system to ensure that the billing and shipping orders are both generated (and for the same amount) without error. If there is an error, you want the order entry system to erase the entire transaction and start over from the beginning.

TTS ensures that groups of logically-related items are processed together, and that NetWare treats them as a single operation that either succeeds or fails. Many types of database applications can benefit from transaction tracking, including inventory systems, accounting systems, and so on. In short, transaction tracking is applicable to any data application that organizes data into records and fields. A database record is, after all, nothing more than a logical grouping of distinct data items. And when a database program writes a record to a database, it's performing a transaction. Thus, TTS provides benefits to a wide range of possible applications.

Two things are notable about the Netware v3.x Transaction Tracking System. The first is that TTS is integrated tightly with the NetWare file system. Transaction tracking code is present in even the lowest-level file input and output routines and is a vital part of NetWare's record and file locking system.

The second important aspect of TTS is that it's designed to work in a network environment. This is important because many things can go wrong in a networked environment, and most problems are completely unpredictable. Internally, NetWare v3.x manages transactions using a combination of station numbers and station tasks in addition to file handles. This treatment reflects the distributed nature of networks. It also allows individual transactions to span multiple files and multiple server volumes.

Applications can take advantage of transaction tracking by using NetWare's programming interface. Designing an application for TTS is actually easier than coding one without it, because NetWare's TTS function calls perform all the necessary file and record locking automatically. Applications not designed to use TTS may be able to benefit from *implicit* transactions, or transactions that are generated by NetWare itself whenever an application requests a file or record lock on a properly flagged file.

NetWare doesn't use transaction tracking on every file; you must explicitly declare a file as being *transactional* via the NetWare FLAG command. Some files, such as the bindery files, are transactional by default. You can turn TTS on or off using NetWare's DISABLE TTS and ENABLE TTS console commands.

Device Driver Interface

All the services provided by the NetWare v3.x kernel are of little use if they can't be exported to some object other than the kernel itself. For example, the NetWare file system is useless unless it can communicate with a physical storage device. Likewise, NetWare's routing services make no sense unless the kernel has some way to communicate with other network nodes. That's where NetWare's device driver interface comes into play.

A *device driver* is a piece of software that translates requests from the kernel into a sequence of instructions for some physical device, such as a network adapter card or a drive controller. In NetWare v3.x, device drivers are special NLMs, and, as such, can be loaded and unloaded dynamically just like other NLMs.

The two most obvious types of device drivers you'll use with NetWare v3.x are LAN drivers and disk drivers. LAN drivers always have the file extension .LAN, while disk drivers always have the extension .DSK.

NetWare's device driver interface is a well-defined (and well-documented) set of requests the kernel is allowed to make to the various types of devices. When an engineer creates a device driver, he or she translates the set of valid requests for that particular type of device into a series of device-specific instructions. NetWare's device driver interface thus places a software layer in between the kernel and the various physical devices one may use with a NetWare server. This makes it possible for the same NetWare kernel to support many different devices. To support a different device, you just load a different device driver.

Like the NetWare v3.x kernel, device drivers can move data in 32-bit chunks and can address up to 4GB of memory. Netware v3.x's 32-bit wide device driver interface allows the fastest possible pathway between the kernel and its devices, provided the driver is designed and coded correctly. Device drivers are critical to both the performance and the reliability of a NetWare server. An inefficient device driver can totally negate the efficiency of NetWare's kernel code, and an error-prone device driver can totally negate NetWare's internal integrity checks.

The NLM Environment

The NetWare v3.x NLM environment is a group of services that NetWare provides to other NLMs. Some of the components that make up the NLM environment are special, lower-level NLMs that use private variables and kernel hooks not available to third-party developers. Other components of the NLM environment are technically part of the kernel, but are built upon one or more of the kernel services discussed above. Regardless of how they're implemented, each component of the NLM environment helps to integrate the raw services provided by the NetWare kernel into a coherent and complete environment for running server-based applications.

The NLM environment, as outlined earlier, consists of the following components:

- CLIB (C Library)
- Streams
- SPX (Sequenced Packet Exchange)
- Communications services
- Queue services

We'll explain each of these components briefly.

CLIB

The NetWare v3.*x* C Library (or CLIB—pronounced "see libe" with a long i) is the main programming interface to the NetWare operating system, providing access to the hundreds of low-level routines exported by the kernel. The CLIB is actually an NLM, albeit one with a rather intimate knowledge of the NetWare kernel. CLIB knows all about the innermost data structures and routines that are the "private parts" of NetWare.

CLIB builds a comprehensive collection of function calls out of NetWare's private code and data, and it exports those function calls to every active process running on the server. Other NLMs that wish to gain access to the operating system do so by using the functions made public by CLIB. Not only does this protect the kernel's private code and data, but it also protects developers from being affected by changes within the kernel. As long as developers write their NLMs using CLIB function calls, their NLMs will continue to run as intended on subsequent versions of the operating system.

Figure 1-13 illustrates how CLIB relates to other NetWare components.

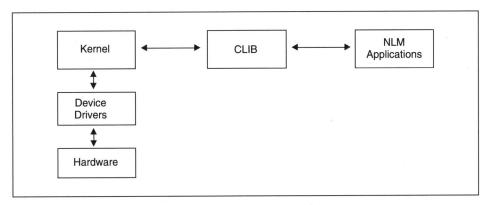

Figure 1-13: CLIB constructs a comprehensive set of function calls using the kernel's private code and data, and exports those function calls to all active processes.

CLIB provides application developers with a spartan but complete set of programming tools. In addition to the services provided by the NetWare kernel, especially IPX and its associated communications services, CLIB provides access to other higher-level NetWare data structures such as the bindery and queues. CLIB also provides an ANSI C library set, plus some additional screen handling and utility functions. Like NetWare itself, the CLIB programming environment is specialized; it focuses on providing functions useful to the type of "back end" processing typically performed by servers.

Streams

STREAMS is a special environment for moving data among the server's memory structures and devices. STREAMS allows different devices or processes to exchange data without having to worry about the exact format of that data. Applications can gain access to NetWare communications services, such as SPX, using STREAMS.

Like CLIB, STREAMS is a special NLM that knows all about the private code and data structures of the NetWare kernel. Not only does STREAMS simplify the movement of data within NetWare, it also makes it less error-prone because it establishes a standard data exchange protocol that is the same regardless of the underlying protocol.

Sequenced Packet Exchange

Sequenced Packet Exchange, or SPX, provides NetWare servers and clients with a connection-oriented communications protocol that perform rigorous error checking. SPX uses IPX to send and receive packets, but adds to the standard IPX method by establishing and maintaining "sessions" between two nodes and by sequencing packets exchanged by two nodes sharing a session.

IPX makes no effort to ensure that packets arrive at their destination in the same order in which they were sent by the originating node. In fact, on an internetwork, it isn't uncommon for IPX packets sent from the same host to take different routes to their destination, therefore arriving out of sequence. Not only does SPX arrange packets in the proper order, but it resends packets that are missing or out of sequence.

The overhead required to sequence packets and to maintain sessions between nodes causes SPX to be less efficient than its underlying datagram service (IPX). However, the extra reliability is sometimes required by certain applications. SPX (as well as IPX) is available to NLMs via the CLIB. Clients gain access to SPX via their shell software.

Communications Services

Communications services are an integration of IPX, SPX, and the associated data structures and routines necessary for an application to make effective use of these two protocols. For example, NetWare's communications services allow applications to construct and make use of Event Control Blocks (discussed earlier), establish and dismantle SPX sessions, and initialize Event Service Routines (also discussed earlier). While it's possible to do all of these things without an integrated library such as NetWare's communications services, the existence of such a library greatly simplifies the task.

Queue Services

NetWare provides applications with the ability to create and maintain queues—special data structures that organize items of information. Moreover, NetWare allows applications to associate queues with active processes.

The most obvious example of the association of a queue and an active process is the NetWare print server. A print server is an active process that formats print jobs and submits them to a particular printer. A print server obtains jobs for printing from a print queue. Applications can define their own queues and "job servers" using NetWare's queue services.

For example, an application may wish to maintain a list of files for sorting and submit that list to a process that sorts the data within those files. In the terminology of queue services, the list of files is a queue and the process that sorts the files is a queue server. NetWare uses queue services internally for many of its functions.

Application Services

As you've proceeded through this overview, you've gained a piece-by-piece description of how NetWare v3.*x* is put together. The discussion has proceeded from the most fundamental portions of NetWare (the NetWare loader and kernel) and worked its way "upward" to NLM and application services.

Admittedly, this classification of NetWare's components is somewhat arbitrary. However, the basic structure of the discussion has been to describe the low-level parts of NetWare first, then to proceed up a level. For example, the components of the NLM environment are generally constructed out of kernel components. What we refer to as NetWare's "application services," generally speaking, build upon the NLM environment. The next level up from application services consists of the NetWare administrative and user utilities, which you'll read about in Parts Two through Five of this book.

NetWare's application services include the following:

- The bindery
- Login processing and security
- Accounting services
- Diagnostic services
- Message services
- Print services

The Bindery

The bindery is a flat-file database maintained by NetWare that defines server objects such as users, groups, queues, job servers, and so on. The bindery itself is hidden from users for several reasons, including network security and reliability concerns.

An API allows applications to create, define, manipulate, and delete bindery objects. For example, the NetWare command-line utility MAKEUSER uses the bindery API to create user objects.

Some temporary or dynamic data structures rely heavily on information located in a server's bindery. For example, whenever a user logs in to a NetWare server, the server maintains information about that user's connections in a dynamic connection table. The server connects that user's connection information to the definition of that user, which is stored in the bindery. Applications can then obtain information about that user's active connections through the bindery API.

Likewise, the NetWare file system maintains for each file and directory a list of that file or directory's *trustees* (users who have access rights to the file or directory). To do this, the file system must obtain user object identification numbers from the bindery. When a NetWare server boots, one of the first things it does is open the bindery. If it can't do so, the server won't be able to run. Moreover, applications that wish to take advantage of NetWare's services must be able to obtain information from the bindery. For example, an application that wishes to use NetWare's print services must first obtain information about network printers and queues from the bindery.

One interesting thing about the bindery is that it is by default a transactional file. That is, NetWare uses TTS to handle any read or write operation NetWare performs on the bindery. This preserves the integrity of the bindery as a database of critical information.

Login Processing and Security

To log in to a NetWare server, you must do so with a *username* that corresponds to a user object defined in that server's bindery. One property of every user object in a server's bindery is a *password*. NetWare won't allow you to log in to a server unless the username and password you enter are both defined within the same user object.

Once you successfully log in to a NetWare server, you carry your user object definition around with you everywhere you go. Other bindery objects, such as printer queues, have as part of their definition a list of users who are authorized to gain access to that object. When you attempt to change the definition of a printer queue, for example, NetWare checks your user object definition against the list of authorized users for the printer queue. If your user object definition doesn't match the printer queue's definition of authorized users, NetWare won't allow you to alter that printer queue's bindery information.

Groups are also bindery objects, and for security purposes NetWare treats them in much the same way as it treats users. When you add a user to a group, that user's object definition inherits the security attributes defined in the group's bindery object. NetWare also allows individual users to obtain security equivalences. For example, if you define a user as having the security equivalence of a supervisor, that user inherits the security attributes of the bindery supervisor object. (Every NetWare server has within its bindery a default supervisor object, which has all rights and privileges for that server.)

Not all security information is maintained within the bindery. For example, all the security information for files and directories is maintained by the NetWare file system. Each file or directory has list of object IDs and a rights bit map (sequence of bits) that, together, contain the cumulative user object IDs of all users who have rights to gain access to that file. When you attempt to read a file, NetWare tries to resolve your user object ID with the file's read access bit map. If NetWare is unable to do so, it won't permit you to read that file.

As you've probably surmised, NetWare's security services are closely linked with its bindery and with its file system. In fact, the only way applications can read or alter the security attributes of bindery objects is through NetWare's bindery API. Likewise, the only way applications can read or alter the ownership and trustee information of files is through NetWare's file system API.

Accounting Services

Using accounting services, NetWare 3.x servers can maintain a record of server resources and processing consumed by a user. For example, accounting services can track the amount of disk storage a user is consuming, the amount of connect time a user is consuming, successful logins and logouts by a user, requests for NetWare services made by the user, and disk blocks read or written by the user. Using the accounting services API, applications can define accounts- specific resources and can submit charges for that account to the user.

Accounting has two purposes. First, accounting creates an *audit record* for each of the server resources mentioned above. The accounting audit log then becomes a useful tool for network managers. Second, supervisors can establish *account limits* and charge users for their consumption of server resources. This can be useful for commercially-oriented applications such as on-line databases. Or companies can use accounting reports for internal billing purposes—for example, when the Production Department is consuming disk storage on the Marketing Department's server, and so on.

Using the menu utility SYSCON, you can establish account limits for user objects defined in the bindery. When a user exceeds his or her account limit for one or more of the server resources tracked by the NetWare accounting system, the server will log the user out (after several warnings). Account charges and balances are maintained by NetWare as attributes of specific user objects. The accounting system doesn't maintain user accounts in any form of currency, but simply as units; you can define the currency value of single units, such as dollars or pennies.

If you want to use the accounting system only as an auditing tool, you can provide users with an unlimited account balance. This approach causes NetWare to accumulate charges for users, but makes it impossible for the server to log off users because users can never exceed their account limits.

Diagnostic Services

Diagnostic services are a network management tool available to DOS and OS/2 clients. To gain access to NetWare's diagnostic services, an application must use the NetWare diagnostics API. Applications can request information about a node's client software, including its machine type, operating system version, shell statistics, IPX statistics, SPX statistics, connection information, network address, and more. Applications can also obtain information about NetWare servers and bridges, including some routing table information. NetWare's diagnostic services also provide some simple tests that applications can use to diagnose driver and network faults.

Some NetWare utilities make use of diagnostic services, but this is an area of NetWare that remains largely unexploited by third-party application developers.

Message Services

Using message services, applications can send and receive short (126 or fewer bytes) text-based messages, either by broadcasting them as a datagram or by piping messages as a connection-oriented pipe between two or more nodes. The most obvious example of NetWare's message services is the SEND command-line utility. Using SEND, users can pass messages to other logged-on users. When a user receives such a message, it's displayed at the bottom of his or her monitor screen (or in a dialog box for Windows nodes).

Print Services

The NetWare v3.*x* print services are a collection of APIs that allow users to redirect their nodes' printer ports to a NetWare printing queue and configure and submit printing jobs to a queue. NetWare provides a fairly comprehensive set of command-line utilities to support printing, and these utilities all use NetWare's printing services. NetWare's printing utilities include CAPTURE, PRINTCON, NPRINT, and others.

NetWare's print services use the lower-level queue management services, discussed earlier, in combination with some databases that NetWare creates solely in support of its printing features. Many of today's major applications, such as WordPerfect, make use of NetWare's print services in order to provide their users with a simpler interface to network printing. This is particularly important in light of the fact that many users (and administrators) find network printing an intimidating feature.

Architecture Summary

This overview of the NetWare v3.*x* architecture has highlighted just the most prominent services made available by NetWare. Many of NetWare's features make use of the elements you've just read about to construct more complex services.

As a specialized server operating system, NetWare has a focused and relatively simple kernel that emphasizes network and file-oriented processing. NetWare's kernel architecture includes dynamic memory management, non-preemptive process scheduling, IPX network communications, routing, file services, and a device driver interface. These are the most basic tools NetWare uses to support complex and large internetworks.

The NetWare kernel itself maintains a self-contained IPX network that it uses to provide interprocess communications, but which NetWare servers can also use to communicate with network nodes. NetWare Core Protocols are a set of well-defined messages that NLMs and network clients can use to control the execution of NetWare servers. In addition, applications can use IPX Event Service Routines to define their own set of messages to control their execution.

NLMs are dynamically linked code modules that can be programming libraries, device drivers, or server-based applications. CLIB is an NLM that provides a programming interface to other NLMs, including much of the console software you'll use to configure and manage your NetWare server.

The NLM environment includes SPX, a connection-oriented communications protocol built upon IPX; Streams, an interface that NetWare v3.11 servers use to move data internally and around the network; communications services, which provide NLMs and client applications with the ability to establish, maintain, and shut down network connections; and queue services, which allow NLMs and client applications to maintain linked list data structures within the server itself.

NetWare's application services, which are used mostly by clients, include the bindery, a database of server objects such as users, groups, and printer queues that is maintained by the server; login processing and security, which client applications can use to gain access to NetWare servers and their resources and which provide network security; accounting services, which both serve as a network management tool and have commercial applications; diagnostic services; message services; and printing services.

Server-based applications make use of both the NLM environment and NetWare's application services, while client-based applications generally make use of NetWare's application services. All NetWare utilities, both command-line and menu-based, use the items discussed in this overview to provide a fairly comprehensive interface to the NetWare operating system.

As you read further in this book, you'll be able to place the installation, maintenance, and troubleshooting information in the context of the NetWare v3.x architecture as it has been presented to you. We hope this information will assist you in your job of managing the network.

CHAPTER 2

Evolution of NetWare v3.*x*

Although NetWare v3.*x* is in a reasonably early stage of its life cycle, it has already seen three fairly substantial releases. The first release, of course, was the introduction of NetWare 386 v3.0. The second release was NetWare 386 v3.1. The current release, as of this writing, is NetWare v3.11 (notice that "386" has been dropped from the official product name).

Both versions 3.1 and 3.11 are evolutionary, rather than maintenance, releases. Taken together, they represent a significant increase in the capabilities of NetWare 386 over what its initial release offered. While the architecture of NetWare v3.11 is essentially unchanged from the first release (v3.0), the internal workings of the operating system have been refined, reworked, and generally made more sophisticated with each subsequent release.

Features New with NetWare v3.1

NetWare v3.1 includes several new features. Foremost among these are:

- The introduction of a multiprotocol Transport Layer Interface (TLI)

- PSERVER, the NetWare print server product

- Resource tracking, which allows the operating system to manage server resources being used by NLMs

- NetWare's Remote Management Facility (RMF), which allows most console administration and management tasks to be performed from a network workstation.

In addition to the obvious features listed above, NetWare v3.1 includes a more complete integration of name space support within the file system, further integration of BTRIEVE, CLIB, and STREAMS into the workings of NetWare, network management alerts, and more. Name space support allows the NetWare file system to provide file access to non-DOS clients (such as the Macintosh) using their native file system.

Overall, NetWare v3.1 represents a more mature operating system that provides several important new features. Now let's look at the major new features in more detail.

Transport Layer Interface (TLI)

TLI was originally introduced by AT&T as part of its Unix operating system. The problem that existed in Unix was that it supported two major transport services—TCP/IP and Xerox Network Systems (XNS). Moreover, some Unix implementations supported a TCP/IP programming interface called *Berkeley Sockets,* while others did not. In addition, the Open Systems Interconnect (OSI) networking model loomed on the horizon as a potential third option for Unix network programming.

TLI addressed these problems by introducing a single transport-independent programming interface to the network. Because TLI was designed to generalize differences between different (and incompatible) transport layers, it allowed programmers to write a single program that would work over a network, regardless of the underlying protocol.

The NetWare v3.1 implementation of TLI, while faithful to the AT&T implementation as introduced in Unix, is not completely compliant. In addition, it works with only one transport suite—NetWare's IPX/SPX. However, the inclusion of TLI into the NetWare OS is one of the most significant aspects of NetWare v3.1, because it laid the foundation for the more spectacular multiple transport support introduced in version 3.11.

Print Server Software

NetWare's print server (PSERVER) software allows you to configure NetWare print servers and queues independently of the NetWare server. For example, you can use a DOS machine anywhere on the network as a print server capable of supporting multiple queues and multiple printers. PSERVER represents a significant advance over NetWare's previous printing system, which forced you to attach printers directly to a server, as shown in Figure 2-1.

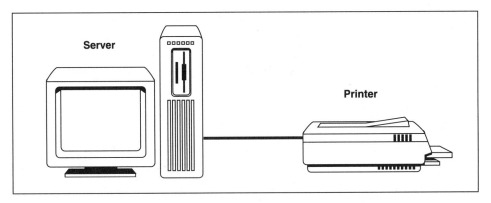

Figure 2-1: Previous versions of NetWare required that a network printer be attached directly to a server.

Using PSERVER, you can place printers closer to the users of that printer rather than close to the server, as shown in Figure 2-2.

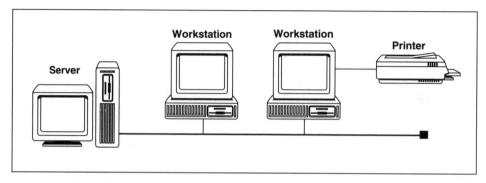

Figure 2-2: PSERVER allows you to attach printers to a workstation in the vicinity of people who are using the printer.

The printer setup shown in Figure 2-2 is significant mostly because it allows users to maintain the printer queue without having to run to the server closet. Moreover, users can make a quick check on the status of the print server by glancing at its console.

But PSERVER is more than a convenient method of setting up and using network printers. It also represents an opening up of NetWare's network printing model. PSERVER is built on top of NetWare's queue services (described in Chapter 1). Specifically, PSERVER is a special type of *queue server*, and print queues are special types of queues.

PSERVER advertises itself as a print server using NetWare's Service Advertising Protocol, or SAP. NetWare queue servers are logically similar to regular servers (servers that run the NetWare OS), except that they don't participate in any NetWare routing; rather, queue servers register their existence with regular servers, which perform the necessary routing that allows users to gain access to queue servers.

It's true that NetWare's queue services and SAP existed prior to NetWare v3.1. However, PSERVER is significant because it uses queues and SAP to provide one of the most critical functions of NetWare: printing. PSERVER shows how it's possible to use NetWare's architecture to distribute specific services over the network, rather than concentrating them at a single machine.

NetWare v3.1 provides two versions of PSERVER: an NLM version, which runs at the server; and an EXE version, which runs on any DOS workstation. After all this discussion of distributing services over the network and removing them from the main server, it may seem odd to run PSERVER as an NLM. However, the architecture of PSERVER is the same, regardless of whether it's running on a NetWare server or on a NetWare workstation. The important thing is that PSERVER users have the option of establishing printing services wherever they want.

Chapters 19 and 20 discuss NetWare printing in more detail.

Resource Tracking

Resource tracking allows the NetWare kernel to manage resources it allocates to NLMs. When an NLM stops executing without releasing system resources (an all-too-common programming bug), the OS can now reclaim those resources, cycling them back into the pool of available server resources. By making NLMs more reliable, resource tracking also makes the NetWare operating system itself more reliable.

Thanks to the inclusion of resource tracking in v3.1, you can use the MONITOR utility to view an NLM's use of server resources. This is a handy troubleshooting tool for network administrators. For example, the version of MONITOR shipped with v3.1 allows an administrator to approach the console, select the MONITOR "System Module Information" menu item, and view resources being used by that module. Resources displayed by MONITOR v3.1 include alloc memory, device locks, event registration (using ECBs, described in Chapter 1), non-moveable memory, processes, and screens. For each type of resource, MONITOR v3.1 displays detailed information about that resource, such as the number of bytes it constitutes and the number of outstanding events.

The addition of resource tracking in NetWare v3.1 involved major work within the kernel's memory allocation routines and other areas. The irony is that many users still don't know that resource tracking is available in the OS. If anything, resource tracking made its own existence harder to detect because it prevented errors and crashes, which are the types of things users usually notice and remember. In other words, by making the OS more reliable, resource tracking masked its own existence from the average user.

The interesting thing about the way resource tracking was implemented in NetWare v3.1 is that it allows some fascinating possibilities for device-kernel-NLM interaction that otherwise would be unattainable. Like the inclusion of TLI, resource tracking in v3.1 laid the foundation for more spectacular features and services in the future.

Chapter 21 explains more about how to use NetWare's new resource tracking feature in troubleshooting network problems.

Remote Management Facility (RMF)

The NetWare v3.1 Remote Management Facility is a terrific feature that, all by itself, makes life much easier for network managers. RMF allows any user with console privileges to "run" the server console from a remote workstation, thereby changing the way NetWare v3.1 servers are configured and maintained.

The new components in release 3.1 that make all of this possible are REMOTE.NLM, RSPX.NLM, and RCONSOLE.EXE. REMOTE.NLM and RSPX.NLM are loaded by the server, typically at server boot time, and provide the server with all the logic and network intelligence required to establish a remote screen session. RCONSOLE.EXE is the DOS component of RMF that allows a standard DOS workstation to establish a remote screen session with the server.

When the v3.1 server loads REMOTE and RSPX, it is then able to use SAP to advertise itself as a "remote" server (for lack of a better term). When a network manager runs RCONSOLE from his or her workstation, the workstation presents the manager with a menu of all available "remote" servers.

Upon selecting a server and providing the correct password, the manager can run all the console programs and use all the console commands just as if he or she were sitting at the actual server console. This includes the ability to load and unload NLMs, drivers, and protocol stacks, as well as the ability to use console programs such as MONITOR or INSTALL interactively. Note that a single manager, sitting at his or her workstation, can perform maintenance or troubleshooting on multiple servers or on all available "remote" servers. For the first time, NetWare allowed an administrator to perform 90% of his or her network-wide server tasks from a single node.

The first time most adminstrators had occasion to use the NetWare v3.1 RMF was when upgrading the server from NetWare v3.0 to v3.1. If you're a network adminstrator, service technician, or manager, you probably know that RMF usage expanded quickly from this first instance. Some of the imaginative uses RMF was put to in short order included:

- Viewing server routing information using the TRACK ON and TRACK OFF, DISPLAY SERVERS, DISPLAY NETWORKS, and RESET ROUTER commands

- Viewing resource tracking information using MONITOR

- Remotely installing new NLMs or utilities from a floppy disk to the server

Significantly, the value of RMF increases every time Novell or a third-party developer releases another NLM, because it allows loading and configuration of that NLM from a remote station.

While the average NetWare user doesn't use (and probably doesn't know about) RMF, it's safe to say that Novell would incite a riot by network managers and administrators if it announced RMF was going to be discontinued in a future version of NetWare. That's how invaluable this utility has become to those who do most of the work involved in networking.

Chapter 28 discusses the use of NetWare's Remote Management Facility in more detail.

Features New with NetWare v3.11

NetWare v3.11, the current version of NetWare "386," goes a long way toward fulfilling the promise of NetWare's 32-bit, specialized architecture. NetWare v3.11 has a special attraction for large-site, multiprotocol networking customers because many internetworking features necessary for true enterprise-wide communications are present in version 3.11. These include:

- Kernel-level support for three major transport protocols: IPX/SPX, TCP/IP, and AppleTalk

- Enhanced network management abilities, including many options for users of IBM's Systems NetWork Architecture (SNA)

- File service to DOS, OS/2 HPFS, Macintosh, Network File System (NFS), and OSI clients

- A new, more robust, backup architecture (SBACKUP.NLM)

- Better STREAMS and TLI modules

- A more complete NLM environment via an improved CLIB

These new NetWare v3.11 features are more than cursory. For example, AppleTalk support in v3.11 includes a full-scale AppleTalk Phase II stack, including routing services.

NetWare's new TCP/IP support includes the ability to encapsulate, or *tunnel*, IPX packets within IP packets. This means that NetWare IPX clients on opposite ends of a TCP/IP internetwork can communicate as if they were connected directly over an IPX network. To do this, NetWare v3.11 must be able to route IP packets, which it does.

NetWare v3.11's SNA capabilties include a full-featured communications server enabled for IBM's NetView network managment facility.

Enhancements of v3.1 Features

Many of the features introduced in NetWare v3.1, such as TLI and network management, are more meaningful in the context of v3.11. For example, TLI now supports both IPX and TCP/IP, and many NetWare device drivers have the ability to convey information about their state to the server console. The RMF now works over wide-area links and can create server boot floppies, allowing a network administrator to reboot a server remotely.

Some features present in pre-v3.11 releases of NetWare have been reworked to support these new abilities. For example:

- Many hardware dependencies have been isolated to the NetWare loader, allowing NetWare to run without modification (except to the loader) on non-standard hardware such as the NetFrame and certain Japanese DOS computers.

- NetWare's new backup facility, SBACKUP, allows the server to back up data regardless of its native format. For example, SBACKUP can archive data residing on Macintosh clients, provided the appropriate client software resides on such machines.

- The NetWare utilities have been reworked to support all the file system name spaces supported by the server.

New Product Packaging

NetWare v3.11 is marketed and packaged differently from its predecessors. For example, it's available in three different versions, supporting 20, 100, and 250 users. Each version, regardless of the numbers of users supported, has the same set of features.

Further, some advanced options are bundled separately from the standard NetWare package. While AppleTalk and TCP/IP transports are included in the standard NetWare package, the file service and client modules for these protocol stacks are packaged separately. Likewise, the communications server is sold as a different product. An OSI client package that makes use of NetWare v3.11's underlying IP support is also a separate package.

Benefits of NetWare v3.x Evolution

The interesting thing about all the new features that are part of the v3.11 release is that NetWare accomplishes them using the same basic (albeit more mature) architecture introduced with release 3.0. Most of the new features are implemented as NLMs, demonstrating the inherent flexibility that the NLM environment affords the basic operating system.

Another practical consequence of NetWare v3.*x* development is that many of the new features shore up some of NetWare's weak areas that have become evident throughout its use. For example, the ability to tunnel IPX packets through a TCP/IP internetwork does much to improve NetWare's viability as a wide-area networking platform. Likewise, the ability of many NetWare device drivers to take advantage of network management features within the OS makes it easier to manage large internetworks. And the continued evolution of CLIB and TLI makes it easier to write software that is able to use NetWare's communications abilities.

CHAPTER 3

Protocol and Workstation Support

The NetWare v3.11 operating system features a sophisticated protocol engine capable of supporting a variety of network communication protocols. It is this protocol engine that allows NetWare to provide services to DOS, OS/2, Macintosh, and Unix clients, as well as participate in larger enterprise networks.

This chapter covers the basic concepts of network communication through protocol stacks and introduces the protocol stacks NetWare v3.11 is equipped to handle. This information will provide a foundation for understanding and troubleshooting protocol-related problems.

Communication Through Protocol Stacks

A *communication protocol* is a set of rules that define precisely how communication takes place over a network. Typically, these rules govern how to establish and maintain a channel for communication, and how to package information so it can be sent across that channel.

Most protocols are implemented in several layers, giving rise to the term "protocol stack." When information is exchanged between two computers on a network, they both must use the same protocol stack. To package data from an application and transmit it over the network, the sender follows the rules starting at the top of the stack and works down to the bottom layer. The receiver uses the same rules, only in reverse order, to unpack and access the data.

Various models have been developed to standardize the functions available at various protocol levels. One that is widely accepted is the seven-layer OSI Reference Model developed by the International Standards Organization. Communication through a layered protocol stack is shown in Figure 3-1.

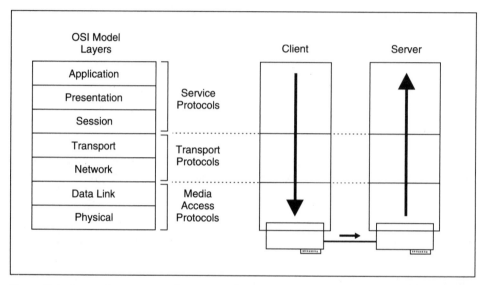

Figure 3-1: Computers communicate over the network through layered protocol stacks.

Since NetWare was originally developed at about the same time the OSI model was being solidified, there is a close but inexact correlation between NetWare communication functions and the OSI layers. For the purposes of our discussion, we'll group communication functions into three simpler classifications:

- *Media protocols.* The lower layers of the stack specify how data is trans formed into electronic signals so it can be transmitted by the network interface card onto the physical cabling media.

- *Transport protocols.* The middle layers specify how to establish a network communication connection, or session, and encapsulate data into specially-designed "packets" for transport over the network. They define a form of peer-to-peer communication between two systems.

- *Service protocols.* The rules at the upper layers of the stack determine how applications deal with data from the network and how they can access network services. Protocols at this level also define how a client (usually a workstation) makes requests from the server.

NetWare's Protocol Engine

NetWare has always supported a large number of network interface cards and cabling topologies at the media level. Up until recently, however, the protocols you could use at higher levels were limited to those offered by Novell. Meanwhile, a number of other network protocols have been developed by various organizations over the years.

To facilitate interoperability between NetWare and other network systems, Novell has incorporated a number of technologies into the NetWare v3.11 multiple protocol support engine (as shown in Figure 3-2).

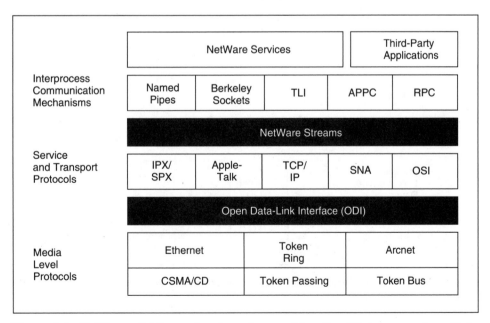

Figure 3-2: NetWare v3.11's protocol engine enables the OS to support multiple communication protocols.

Open Data-Link Interface

Traditionally, the pathway between a network interface card and a network communication protocol has been a one-lane street. LAN drivers could recognize and transmit only one type of packet using a single protocol stack. If you wanted to connect a workstation to another network system besides NetWare, you had to install a second network card and driver, then reboot the workstation whenever you wanted to change to the second protocol.

With NetWare v3.*x*, this one-lane communication pathway has been expanded into a multi-lane highway capable of handling traffic over a number of different protocol stacks. The key component that makes multiple protocol support possible is the Open Data-link Interface (ODI), developed by Novell with the initial help of Apple Computer. ODI provides a standard interface for allowing transport protocols to share a single network card without conflict. Figure 3-3 gives a closer look at how ODI works.

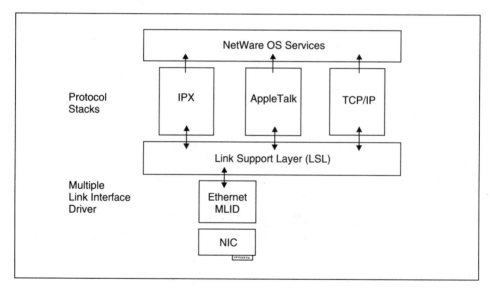

Figure 3-3: The Open Data-Link Interface a network interface card communicate over more than one protocol stack.

By using LAN drivers written to ODI specifications, a network board can handle more than one protocol at a time. In effect, you have a "logical" network card through which different protocol packets can be sent on the same card over a single network cabling system. The workstation can use a different protocol stack without being rebooted. In this way, you can use a single network card to connect to both NetWare and non-NetWare networks (such as TCP/IP or AppleTalk).

NetWare Streams

In the previous chapter, we introduced NetWare Streams as a standard data exchange protocol. NetWare Streams is a key technology for establishing transport protocol-independent communication between varying network protocols. Originally developed by AT&T, the Streams interface forms a two-way data transfer path that can be manipulated through simple operations such as open, read, write, and close. It can also be multiplexed so that a single upper stream can provide access to multiple lower streams, each leading to a different protocol stack with a different API. This allows network requests (for example, Btrieve or SQL requests) to travel over a variety of transports (IPX/SPX, TCP/IP, or OSI) using a variety of interprocess communication mechanisms (APPC, NetBIOS, or Named Pipes). Novell implements Streams as a set of NetWare loadable modules.

Multiple Name Spaces

Another important element that enables NetWare to support multiple protocols is the multiple name space capability of the NetWare file system. Remember that, among other things, a file system defines how files are recorded onto a mass storage device: how long file and directory names can be, what characters are legal to use in these names, and what additional information can be stored besides just the names.

To accommodate multiple users and provide fast file I/O, Novell built its own proprietary file system for use on the file server. The original NetWare file system was patterned after the hierarchical system used by Unix, with some ideas incorporated from the CP/M and DOS file systems as well. Even though the NetWare file system was not the same as that used by DOS, DOS workstations could read and write files on the server by making the appropriate NCP requests.

As the need arose to store other types of files (such as OS/2 and Macintosh files) on the server, Novell enhanced the file system to accommodate *multiple name spaces*. Multiple name spaces allow more than just the DOS naming convention to be used to identify the same file or directory. With name spaces, NetWare assigns each file and directory a DOS-compatible name by default. Files created on other types of workstations can use their own naming conventions. For example, a file created on a Macintosh workstation retains its full Macintosh file name and attributes when stored on a NetWare file server. If the file is accessed by a DOS workstation, it sees the DOS-compatible file name.

By loading the appropriate name space NLM, NetWare v3.11's "universal" file system can support name spaces for files created on the following types of computers:

- DOS/Windows workstations using DOS's File Allocation Table system
- OS/2 machines using the High Performance File System (HPFS)
- Macintosh computers using AppleTalk Filing Protocol (AFP)

Through optional Novell products, NetWare servers can store files created on the following:

- Unix workstations using the Network File System (requires NetWare NFS)
- OSI clients using the File Transfer, Access and Management (FTAM) file naming conventions (requires NetWare FTAM)

Now that we've discussed how NetWare supports multiple protocols, let's take a closer look at what those various protocols are.

Media-Level Protocols

Novell pioneered the concept of LAN media independence. By encouraging network hardware vendors to write specialized *drivers* (programs that enable a network card to send and receive packets over the network cable) for NetWare, Novell has been able to support a wide assortment of network interface cards and cabling. Here is a brief rundown of the media-level protocols supported by NetWare.

Media Access Protocols

Media access protocols define exactly how network interface cards transfer data to and from the network cable. Two types of media access protocols are most commonly used in LANs: CSMA/CD and token passing.

CSMA/CD

Carrier Sense Multiple Access with Collision Detection is the most commonly used media access control scheme. With CSMA/CD (sometimes referred to as "carrier contention"), a station that needs to send a packet first checks the cable. If no other packets are currently being transmitted on the cable, the station sends its packet immediately. If it senses other packets on the cable, the station waits a predetermined amount of time and tries again. Since all stations are contending for use of the cable, it is possible for two stations to attempt to send packets at the same time, resulting in a collision. When this happens, neither packet survives to reach its intended destination. CSMA/CD provides various means for stations to detect collisions and retransmit the packets when the cable is not busy.

CSMA/CD was developed by Xerox, DEC, and Intel as part of the original Ethernet specifications. It has since been standardized by IEEE committee 802.3 and is now included as an OSI standard.

Token Passing

With token passing, a specialized type of packet called a *token* is passed around the ring in physical order from one station to the next. A station that needs to transmit data must wait for the token. If no one else is sending data with the token, the station grabs the token, marks it as "busy," and resends it along with a data packet. The "busy" token and its accompanying data continue around the ring until they reach the station the data is intended for. That station copies the data and passes the still "busy" token along. When the token arrives back at the original sender, the station removes the "busy" identifier from the token and relinquishes control of it. If the station needs to send more data, it must wait for the token to come around again. Because it guarantees that only one station is transmitting at any given time, the token passing media access method eliminates the possibility of collisions.

This token passing scheme, originally devised by IBM for its Token Ring Network system, has been standardized by IEEE committee 802.5 and is now also included in the OSI standards.

Networking Hardware

In most cases there is a one-to-one relationship between a particular type of network hardware and a media access protocol. The three main hardware/protocol combinations used in most LANs are Ethernet, Token Ring, and Arcnet.

Ethernet

In Ethernet networks, stations are typically connected using a linear bus topology. Ethernet cable types include thick coaxial, thin coaxial (RG-58), and twisted pair. The Ethernet protocol uses the CSMA/CD media access method and provides a transmission speed of 10 megabits per second (10Mbps).

A number of slightly different packet specifications (or *frame types*) have emerged from various groups involved in the development of Ethernet. NetWare can support the following Ethernet frame types: Ethernet II, Ethernet 802.3, Ethernet 802.3 with 802.2, and Ethernet 802.3 with 802.2 and the SNAP extension. (These frame types will be explained later.)

Token Ring

IBM devised the Token Ring network wiring system. In Token Ring networks, stations are connected in a ring topology using either shielded or unshielded twisted pair cable. Token Ring uses the token passing media access method. The original Token Ring specification provides a transmission speed of 4Mbps; newer versions offer 16Mbps.

As with Ethernet, several frame types have been developed for Token Ring. NetWare supports both IBM Token Ring and Token Ring SNAP frame types.

Arcnet

Arcnet networks typically use RG-62 coaxial cable or twisted pair cable laid out in either a star or bus topology. They employ a variation of the token passing media access method called *token bus*. However, the specific method used with Arcnet is not an IEEE standard. In Arcnet's token passing implementation, each station is assigned a unique address. The token is passed around in logical ring order. In other words, it moves from one address to the next in sequential order, independent of the physical ordering of stations on the cable. The original Arcnet specification provides a transmission speed of 2.5Mbps; newer versions offer faster speeds.

NetWare's Transport and Service Protocols

In Chapter 1, we discussed how the IPX protocol stack is built in to the OS itself. Figure 3-4 shows the other transport and service protocols developed by Novell for use in a native NetWare environment consisting of only DOS, Windows, and OS/2 workstations.

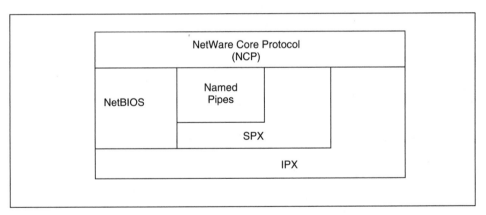

Figure 3-4: The native NetWare protocol stack used by DOS, Windows, and OS/2 clients.

Internetwork Packet Exchange

Novell patterned its Internetwork Packet Exchange (IPX) protocol after the Xerox Network Service protocol. IPX is a connectionless transport mechanism optimized for use on LANs. It makes a "best effort" to deliver all packets to their destination, but does not guarantee delivery. IPX does not have to establish an actual connection between the sender and receiver, nor does it provide any packet sequencing mechanism. This allows IPX to transport packets quickly, with a minimal amount of overhead.

Sequenced Packet Exchange

As we mentioned in the previous chapter, Novell's Sequenced Packet Exchange (SPX) is a connection- oriented interface that provides guaranteed delivery and packet sequencing. Used by applications requiring reliable data transfer, SPX establishes a virtual circuit, or session, between two connections and provides for acknowledgement when packets are received.

NetWare Core Protocol

The previous chapter introduced Novell's NetWare Core Protocol (NCP), which defines procedures that the OS follows to accept and respond to workstation requests. NCP service protocols exist for every service a workstation might request from a file server. Common requests handled by the NCP include creating and destroying a service connection, manipulating directories and files, opening sema-phores, altering drive mappings and security, and printing.

NetBIOS Emulation

NetBIOS is a high-level, peer-to-peer communications protocol developed by IBM and used by numerous application vendors. Like SPX, NetBIOS establishes a session between two stations that want to exchange data. Since many developers consider it a standard application interface, a significant number of NetBIOS-based applications have been written. To support these applications, Novell provides a NetBIOS emulator in the NetWare protocol stack.

Other Protocols Supported by NetWare

Here is a quick rundown of some of the other protocols currently supported by NetWare v3.11. As indicated below, these protocol stacks are either built into the operating system itself or available as add-on NetWare loadable modules.

OS/2 Environment Protocols

The NetWare v3.11 operating system also provides additional protocol support for OS/2 clients. Workstations running OS/2 communicate on the network through the NetWare Requester for OS/2 software. This software is loaded at the workstation. The OS/2 Requester uses IPX/SPX as its transport protocol and NCP as its service protocol, as shown in Figure 3-5.

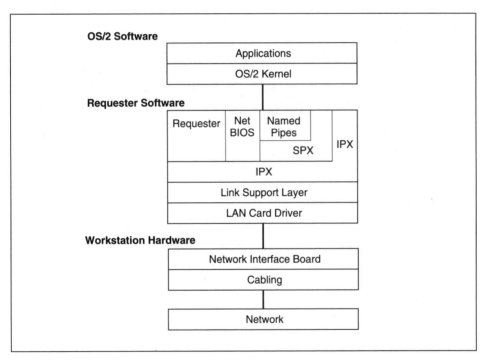

Figure 3-5: This diagram illustrates the architecture of the NetWare Requester.

Named Pipes

Note that the NetWare Requester also provides support for the *named pipes* interprocess communication mechanism that is often used by OS/2 applications. On an OS/2 workstation, you often have more than one application, or *process*, running at the same time. A number of sophisticated distributed applications (such as Lotus Notes and Microsoft's SQL Server) rely on being able to pass data from a process running in one machine to a process running in another. To facilitate this type of communication across the network, Microsoft developed an interprocess communication mechanism called Named Pipes. The NetWare Requester for OS/2 supports Named Pipes on OS/2 workstations as well as on DOS workstations (through a TSR program supplied with the Requester).

Novell provides a supplemental set of OS/2-specific utilities as well. These utilities, which are installed in a separate directory on the file server, replace SYSCON, FILER, and other DOS-specific NetWare utilities.

Unlike NetWare v2.2, NetWare v3.11 supports the long file names that are possible with OS/2's High Performance File System (HPFS). Available since OS/2 v1.2, HPFS lets OS/2 users store files under names that exceed the eight-character length limitation imposed by DOS. When OS/2 users store such files on a NetWare v3.11 file server with the OS/2 name space loaded, NetWare automatically assigns them a DOS-compatible name in addition to the long name.

Macintosh Environment Protocols

NetWare v3.11 supports Macintosh clients through the multiple name space feature and an optional set of NetWare loadable modules. Together, these NLMs form NetWare for Macintosh v3.0, a separate Novell product. NetWare for Macintosh allows Macintosh files to be stored on a NetWare server and accessed by both Macintoshes and non-Apple systems. Figure 3-6 shows the important protocols used in the Macintosh environment.

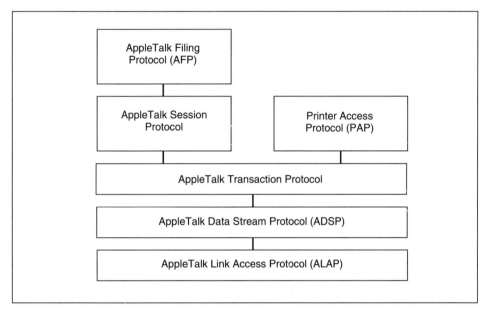

Figure 3-6: These are some of the protocols used in the Macintosh environment.

Through a set of NLMs included with the optional NetWare for Macintosh product, NetWare v3.11 provides support for the entire AppleTalk protocol suite. The suite includes AppleTalk Filing Protocol (AFP), AppleTalk Data Stream Protocol (ADSP), Printer Access Protocol (PAP), and others. This support allows Macintosh computers to access files and services on NetWare servers through their native AppleTalk interface.

LocalTalk

Every Macintosh computer comes with the hardware needed to interface to LocalTalk, a wiring scheme frequently used to connect Macs in a small network. NetWare for Macintosh v3.0 supports LocalTalk through ODI-compatible drivers. However, LocalTalk communication is slow (230 kilobits per second) and therefore not very useful in larger networks.

AppleTalk and AppleShare

AppleTalk is actually a suite of network protocols built in to every Macintosh computer. These protocols provide the rules necessary for Macintoshes to communicate over a network. AppleTalk client software ships with every Macintosh. Networked Macintosh computers generally run software called AppleShare, a more advanced protocol that uses AppleTalk as its default network transport protocol. It is traditionally run on LocalTalk wiring, but more and more Macs are being connected to Ethernet, Token Ring, and Arcnet cabling systems via an add-on network interface card. NetWare for Macintosh v3.0 supports both AppleTalk Phase I and Phase II routing methods. You can purchase the AppleTalk protocol stack separately.

AppleTalk Filing Protocol

Macintosh computers use a proprietary filing system called the AppleTalk Filing Protocol (AFP). This system allows file names to be up to 32 characters long and handles both the data fork and resource fork inherent to all files created on a Macintosh. The data fork contains the actual data, while the resource fork holds icons and other graphical information related to the file. NetWare for Macintosh v3.0 supports AFP 2.0.

UNIX Environment Protocols

NetWare v3.11 file servers can participate in the standard Unix computing environment through built- in support for the TCP/IP transport protocols and the optional NetWare NFS product. NetWare NFS includes a Unix name space utility.

TCP/IP Transport Stack

NetWare v3.11 includes Novell's own implementation of the Transmission Control Protocol/Internet Protocol originally developed by the U.S. Department of Defense. Designed mainly for wide-area networks that run over leased phone lines, TCP/IP is an established standard used by many universities and government agencies to link dissimilar computer systems across large networks. Most Unix systems use TCP/IP for their network transport. By supporting TCP/IP, NetWare servers can participate in this standard computing environment.

Through its TCP/IP transport stack, NetWare has the ability to route TCP/IP packets as well as IPX/SPX packets between any connected Ethernet, Token Ring, or Arcnet cabling systems. In addition, you can attach a NetWare v3.11 file server to an existing TCP/IP wide area network and "tunnel" IPX packets across the WAN. Tunneling simply means encapsulating the IPX/SPX packet within a TCP/IP datagram and sending it via TCP/IP links.

NetWare's TCP/IP stack provides two other important capabilities:

*   An SNMP agent that can supply information to a Simple Network Man agement Protocol-based TCP/IP console application. The NetWare v3.11 server can then receive SNMP alerts and remote configuration information.

*   Support for commonly-used Unix APIs such as AT&T Streams/TLI and Berkeley Sockets v4.3. Thus developers can write NLMs using familiar TCP/IP interfaces.

Network Filing System (NFS)

NFS is a distributed file system that allows a server to share its resources with another computer on a network. Developed by Sun Microsystems, NFS is widely used to access files on Unix-based systems. An optional Novell product called NetWare NFS lets Unix clients see the NetWare file system as an extension of their native file system and access NetWare volumes using the standard Unix mount command. NetWare NFS also allows Unix clients access to NetWare's printing services to submit documents to NetWare print queues.

IBM's SNA Environment Protocols

IBM developed its System Application Architecture (SAA) in the 1970s as a standard way to define communications between terminals and mainframes. It is the grand scheme IBM has instituted company-wide to tie all of its products together. The network part of SAA is called System Network Architecture, or SNA. SNA defines a seven-layer protocol that corresponds closely (but not exactly) to the OSI protocol stack. Novell and other companies support these SNA protocols in order to communicate with IBM mainframe and minicomputer hosts.

NetWare v3.11 includes an SNA transport stack that can be used to communicate network management information to IBM hosts. These "alerts," as they are called, help NetWare fit into enterprise-wide SNA management systems (such as IBM's host-based NetView).

An optional product called NetWare for SAA provides LAN-to-host connectivity. This product enables NetWare clients to establish full communication sessions with IBM hosts.

OSI Standard Protocols

Another optional Novell product, NetWare FTAM, implements major protocols from all seven layers of the OSI reference model. These protocols include:

- FTAM
- ACSE
- Presentation
- ASN.1
- Session
- Transport Class 4
- CLNP

By supporting these OSI protocols, NetWare v3.11 fulfills the basic requirements of the U.S. GOSIP 1.0 specification. Once the NetWare FTAM modules are loaded on the server, FTAM clients can transfer files between NetWare and any other OSI-compliant system.

Workstation Environments

One of the greatest benefits of NetWare v3.11 is its ability to support a variety of different workstation environments, even within a small LAN. While network installers and supervisors may be familiar with the concepts involved in networking a DOS workstation, they may have had little or no experience with the challenges of networking and troubleshooting LAN workstations based on Macintosh, OS/2, or Windows, or workstations that address multiple protocols via Novell's ODI (Open Data-Link Interface).

The following sections describe the manner in which each of these workstation environments intercommunicates within a NetWare v3.11 LAN.

The DOS Workstation

In the NetWare environment, the file server manages access to shared applications and stored files, while the majority of the actual application processing takes place at the workstation. Most NetWare workstations today are Intel-based personal computers operated by some version of DOS.

As you turn on a DOS workstation, the workstation establishes a DOS "environment" by loading device drivers and other environmental variables from the CONFIG.SYS file. The workstation then loads COMMAND.COM and looks for an AUTOEXEC.BAT file, which contains instructions for other workstation parameters such as PROMPT or PATH commands or terminate-and-stay-resident (TSR) applications.

The AUTOEXEC.BAT file also loads IPX.COM, which contains the network files, and NETx.COM, which is the NetWare shell. As we discussed in the previous section, IPX serves as a sort of "syntax" for communicating from the workstation to the NetWare LAN. When you generate a NetWare shell through WSGEN, you are establishing a set of specifications for sending communications through the network interface card to the LAN. WSGEN then links IPX to these specifications, thereby creating a hardware-specific "LAN driver" which can format data for transmission onto the LAN cable.

Getting a LAN Connection

When the IPX driver loads itself from within the AUTOEXEC.BAT routine, it establishes a channel for communication between the network interface board and its attached cable and the network server. Next, the NetWare shell (the generic portion of the network connection) is loaded and proceeds to operate on top of IPX.

The NetWare shell uses IPX to locate and establish a connection with the network server, or, in the case of a multi-server internet, with the closest server. In fact, with NetWare v3.11 you can set up a command in SHELL.CFG or NET.CFG to designate a specific server. As the shell connects to the server, the AUTOEXEC file then moves to the SYS:LOGIN directory and presents the user with the logical network login drive.

The user is now able to initiate a LOGIN request to a specific LAN server. If the user is requesting access to a different server than the one he or she is physically connected to, NetWare will route the request to the appropriate server on the internet, thereby giving the user a logical connection. As the designated server responds to the user's request, it answers through the best route available at the time of connection. The NetWare shell then drops the connection to the original server and establishes a connection to the server the user has named. NetWare v3.11 allows users to specify a "preferred server" within the SHELL.CFG or NET.CFG file to reduce the logistics of locating and connecting to a server other than the closest server at hand.

Once the connection is in place, the LOGIN command checks to ensure that the username you've entered is recognized by the server's bindery. If so, the server will invite you to enter your password— and you're now on your way.

DOS and the NetWare Shell

Once a connection is established, NetWare uses that connection to communicate with DOS. When an application wants DOS to perform a specific task, it issues an Int 21h command to get DOS's attention, then it gives DOS the necessary information to accomplish the task. DOS looks up the function in its function table, executes the request, then returns the necessary information or procedure to the application.

In the NetWare environment, however, the NetWare shell becomes a redirector that "takes over" all Int 21h calls. As applications make requests to Int 21h, the shell determines whether the call should be handled by the server or at the workstation.

If the request requires the server, the shell translates the DOS request into a NetWare Core Protocol (NCP) request packet and sends the request to the appropriate server. The server processes the request and then responds. The transaction is entirely transparent to the application (and to the user). The application proceeds to operate just as if it were dealing entirely with DOS. The entire process is illustrated in Figure 3-7.

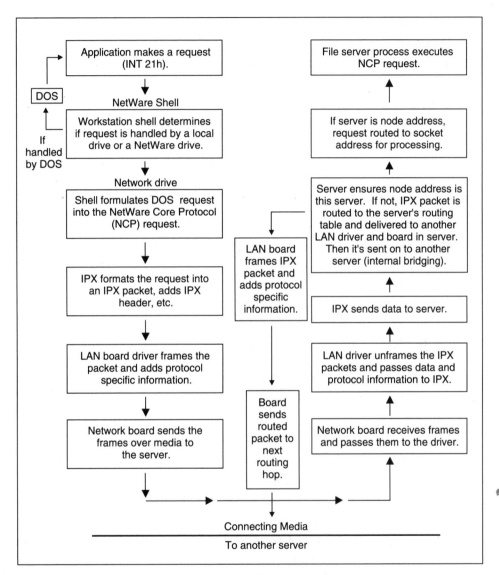

Figure 3-7: This figure shows what happens when an application makes a request on a DOS workstation.

The Windows Workstation

Microsoft Windows is actually a graphical user interface (GUI) designed to run on top of MS-DOS on a standard Intel-based personal computer. However, Windows typically takes over many of the standard operating system tasks from MS-DOS. For this reason, the Windows interface is often referred to as an operating environment. In the past, Windows has been somewhat oblivious to the network environment.

For the first time, however, Windows 3.0 provides rudimentary network capabilities. Microsoft includes a NetWare device driver set within Windows 3.0. In addition, NetWare support for Windows requires several Novell-supplied files which are included in NetWare v3.11.

To establish Windows workstations in the NetWare environment, you must first establish the NetWare server(s) with INSTALL and then set up the NetWare DOS workstations as usual. Microsoft provides a utility called EXPAND.EXE to uncompress all Windows files and copy those files from the Windows diskettes into a shared server directory. The Windows SETUP program features a /N parameter (/N for "network") that installs only user-specific files at the individual workstation, leaving the bulk of the Windows program files on the server.

The ODI Workstation

In the Multiple Protocol Support section of this chapter, we discussed the concept of the Open Data- link Interface (ODI). In basic terms, ODI allows you to create a "logical network interface board" which accepts multiple communication formats (protocols) over one physical network board and wire.

At the workstation level, ODI allows you a certain flexibility in terms of communication. For example, you can allow your DOS workstations to communicate with other systems or internetwork resources through IPX/SPX, AppleTalk, and TCP/IP protocols (so long as you have versions of these protocols which support the ODI specification) without adding extra network boards to the workstation. Furthermore, you can elect to speak to any of these varied resources without having to stop and reboot your machine.

After the initial LAN is in place, you can convert a standard PC into an ODI workstation through a separate installation process, using the DOS ODI workstation software available from Novell.

The OS/2 Workstation

NetWare v3.11 includes the NetWare Requester for OS/2 v1.3, which enables OS/2 v1.3 workstations and application servers to operate on a NetWare LAN.

Key Differences between OS/2 and DOS Workstations

The NetWare DOS shell is able to steal DOS interrupts and essentially act as a DOS front end, As a result, NetWare can filter workstation and application commands before DOS even sees them. But because OS/2 is a multitasking operating system, its basic design premise is to protect the workstation hardware from misguided processes and to protect concurrent processes from interfering with each other. Therefore, the NetWare requester for OS/2 must communicate with the OS/2 workstation in a very different fashion than the way in which the standard NetWare shell communicates with DOS.

Whereas the NetWare shell acts as a *front* end to the DOS workstation environment, grabbing interrupts without the permission or knowledge of DOS, the OS/2 Requester includes a device driver which is allowed the privilege of residing at the *back* end of OS/2 to pick up and act upon the interrupts OS/2 doesn't know how to handle. In fact, it's the requesting nature of the transaction that leads to the name NetWare Requester for OS/2.

Interaction with the OS/2 Kernel

The OS/2 requester system is actually facilitated by two types of files: device drivers and daemons. The device drivers run in the privileged "Ring O" of the OS/2 kernel, which means, basically, that the device driver registers itself with the OS/2 operating system as the authorized agent to perform a certain function or to handle a particular interrupt line.

There are actually two types of OS/2 device drivers: base drivers, which are the pre-installed, standard drivers that make it possible for the system to run; and installable drivers, such as the NetWare Requester for OS/2 drivers, which enable network communication. The installable drivers must be included in the CONFIG.SYS file.

The daemon files, in contrast, are executable programs that run at Ring 3 and that are tightly coupled with the device driver roles. As the LAN administrator, you will often see a pair of both types of files- -device drivers and daemons—in CONFIG.SYS

97

for the purpose of performing a single action. The device driver deals with the low-level part of the system operation, while the daemon file handles higher-level functions such as the screen image and keyboard I/O.

The OS/2 Workstation-to-LAN Connection

As with any LAN workstation, the software connection from the OS/2 workstation to the network begins with a LAN card driver—a device driver specifically designed to carry communications between the workstation operating system and the network interface card.

The next layer of the interface is the Link Support Layer (LSL), which acts as a buffer between the device driver and the protocol stack. In the current NetWare Requester for OS/2, the protocol stack is IPX/SPX; however, the LSL can conceivably support multiple concurrent protocol stacks. From the LSL, the data emerges through the IPX/SPX protocol stack.

In addition to IPX/SPX support, the NetWare Requester includes support for two more protocols: Named Pipes and the NetBIOS emulator. Named Pipes is a protocol designed to facilitate interprocess communications on OS/2 nodes. The NetBIOS emulator is a functional equivalent to the NetBIOS protocol for DOS—it provides another form of guaranteed delivery (in addition to SPX). Either of these protocols may be accessed by OS/2 applications through direct programming calls.

The final piece of the puzzle is the NetWare Requester itself. This is the component which sits on top of IPX and allows IPX to send packets back and forth to the file server when network services are required.

The Macintosh Workstation

NetWare for Macintosh v3.0 is not included with the basic NetWare v3.11 operating system, but it is available from Novell as a separate product. The NetWare for Macintosh v3.0 software operates as a set of NetWare loadable modules, or NLMs. Prior to NetWare v3.11, network administrators had to install NetWare for Macintosh as a series of Value-Added Processes (VAPs) on a NetWare v2.15 server or external router. This was accomplished from a DOS workstation through a separate installation process, after the initial NetWare LAN was in place. In NetWare v3.11, however, you can choose to have NetWare for Macintosh automatically established during INSTALL.

Establishing a LAN Connection

The first requirement for a Macintosh LAN workstation is, of course, an Apple Macintosh PC. The second requirement is a Macintosh-specific network interface card.

Every Macintosh has a built-in network interface card that uses a Macintosh-specific, physical-level protocol called LocalTalk. Most PC networking vendors, including Novell, are able to support the LocalTalk protocol.

However, because LocalTalk is a relatively slow protocol (230Kbps), most LAN administrators choose to network Macintosh workstations via separately installed Macintosh Ethernet, Arcnet, or Token-Ring cards.

From the physical layer, the Macintosh workstation communicates with network environments through the AppleTalk (or AppleTalk Phase 2) suite of networking protocols. This creates an interesting challenge for NetWare, which uses IPX/SPX as its standard network protocol stack.

Novell addresses the Macintosh workstation through its support of the AppleTalk protocols running as NLMs at the server. When the AppleTalk modules are loaded, they intercept AppleTalk messages, translate them into an equivalent IPX message, and carry the translated message to the NetWare file server. Responses from the NetWare file server follow the same path in reverse.

Some Specific Macintosh Challenges

Because of the differences between NetWare and AppleTalk, there is no one-to-one correspondence between IPX/SPX and AppleTalk functions. A function which corresponds to a single instruction in AppleTalk may equate to a series of several instructions in IPX. Likewise, a single IPX instruction may translate to several AppleTalk instructions after it passes through NetWare for Macintosh. As a result, the network error messages a Macintosh workstation displays may not accurately portray the actual problem on the LAN.

Another challenge comes when you attempt to back up or copy Macintosh files from a DOS workstation on the LAN. It's important to remember that Macintosh files are comprised of two parts: a resource fork and a data fork. If you attempt to use DOS's XCOPY to copy Macintosh files, you'll receive only the data forks—the formatting information in the resource forks will stay behind.

The NetWare v3.11 version of NCOPY has a switch you can set to copy both forks of Macintosh files. However, unless you remember to explicitly set this switch, NCOPY, too, will copy only the data forks of the files.

Furthermore, you'll need to ensure that any NetWare archiving products you buy have the ability to back up both DOS and Macintosh files.

Other Workstation Environments

As mentioned previously, NetWare v3.11 also supports Unix, FTAM, and SNA clients through optional Novell products. Each of these environments is complex in its own right; to explain each one to those who are unfamiliar with them would require more space than we can afford. To keep the information in this book manageable and focused, we will concentrate on DOS, Windows, ODI, OS/2, and Macintosh clients. See Appendix D for suggested references on these other types of clients NetWare v3.11 supports.

Part Two

NetWare V3.11 Installation

The chapters in Part Two are dedicated to the installation process and troubleshooting common problems encountered during this process. Nothing is more important than making sure you have a successful and solid installation. This section of the book will give you information pertaining to your cabling, file server, workstation, and router installations.

- **Chapter 4: Topologies and Cabling Strategies** discusses network topologies and how they relate to cabling schemes. It explains the concepts, specifications, and limitations for installing Arcnet, Ethernet, and Token-Ring networks.

- **Chapter 5: NetWare v3.11 Server Installation** walks you through the preliminary steps of installing the file server on a new network, up to the point where you are ready to load LAN drivers.

- **Chapter 6: Loading Server LAN Drivers** takes you through the process of loading and configuring LAN drivers for the network boards in your file server.

- **Chapter 7: Editing the Server Boot Files** explains how to boot the newly installed server and edit the commands in the AUTOEXEC.NCF and STARTUP.NCF files.

- **Chapter 8: Troubleshooting the Server Installation** details common problems encountered when installing the server and gives tips for solving them or avoiding them altogether.

- **Chapter 9: Installing Workstations** covers the basic steps of configuring and installing a network interface card, as well as a step-by-step process for creating the workstation's networking software.

- **Chapter 10: Installing an External Router** covers the basic steps for successfully configuring and installing a NetWare router.

- **Chapter 11: Upgrading to NetWare v3.11** explains the procedures involved in upgrading an existing NetWare v2.x, v3.0, or v3.1 file server to NetWare v3.11.

CHAPTER 4

Topologies and Cabling Strategies

Before installing your LAN, you need to understand the types of cabling and topologies that you can choose from. When selecting a topology (and an appropriate network protocol to support that topology), you must weigh the advantages and disadvantages of each. One of the best features of NetWare is that it supports virtually any topology/protocol choice.

Network Topologies

The term "topology" refers to the physical layout of your workstations, servers, gateways, hubs, and cabling. You should be familiar with three basic topologies: bus, star, and token.

The Linear Bus Topology

The *linear bus* topology is probably the most common of physical network layouts. The bus topology is associated with the Ethernet protocol described in the Overview. As shown in Figure 4-1, the cabling in a bus topology consists of a single or central cable to which the workstations and servers are connected. This topology can use coaxial and twisted-pair cabling.

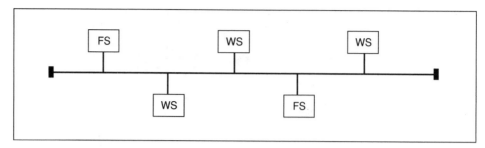

Figure 4-1: The bus network topology uses one central cable.

The bus topology has advantages and disadvantages. One advantage of the bus topology is that the bus cabling scheme makes it easy to connect a new workstation on the bus without disrupting other workstations or servers. Networks based on bus topologies can be relatively cheap and easy to install. The major disadvantage of the bus topology is that a break (open) or short anywhere along the length of the cable can halt data transmissions for the entire network.

The Ring Topology

The *ring* network topology (associated with the IBM Token-Ring network protocol) is much like the bus in that each workstation and file server is attached to a central cable. As shown in Figure 4-2, the workstations and the file server are connected together to form a ring. The workstations and file servers take turns passing information from one to another until the information reaches its final destination.

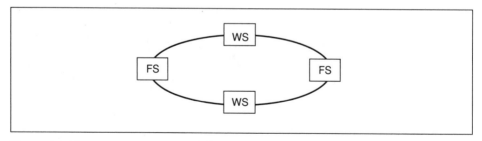

Figure 4-2: The ring network topology connects all nodes in a circle.

Like the bus topology, the ring topology has its advantages and disadvantages. The major disadvantage of the Token-Ring topology is that each node on the ring must handle the data being transferred. If by chance one node on the ring fails to handle the transfer of data, that failure could interrupt the network's operation. The advantage of a Token-Ring topology is that only one node on the ring can transmit at any given time, thereby eliminating the transmission collisions that frequently occur with a bus topology.

The Star Topology

In a *star* topology, the workstations are directly wired to the file server or to a central wiring hub. Traditionally, the star topology was associated with the Arcnet protocol; however, Ethernet networks which comply with the current 10Base-T standard may be configured in a physical hierarchical star topology. As shown in Figure 4-3, the classic star topology gives each workstation a dedicated line between itself and the server.

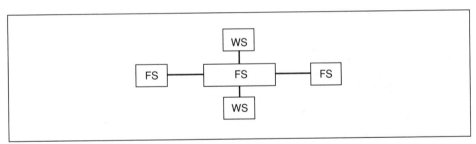

Figure 4-3: The star network topology connects each workstation to the central server.

This classic star topology resembles a multiuser, or time-sharing, system. Because there is a dedicated line between the file server and workstation, this topology can decrease the amount of cable bandwidth being used, and can therefore increase the overall performance of the LAN. The star topology is also inherently fault-tolerant; a break in the cabling will affect the network's ability to communicate with a particular workstation, but has no affect on network communications to the rest of the LAN. The major disadvantage of the star topology is that it requires more cabling than either the bus or the ring.

Very few networks today use the classic star topology where the server is the central point of attachment. Rather, in the physical layout of Arcnet and Ethernet 10Base-T networks, the server and the workstations are attached to a central hub or wiring concentrator. Other hubs can be attached to the first hub, forming a string of stars.

Cabling Types

Your cabling choice will depend somewhat on the type of protocol/topology and LAN adapters you choose. The basic cabling choices available today include *coaxial, twisted-pair,* and *fiber optic.*

Coaxial

Coaxial cable is probably the most common cable choice for microcomputer networks. Coaxial cable itself is more expensive than unshielded twisted pair (hubs can be expensive, even if cables are not), but it is more resistant to electromagnetic interference and noise. Figure 4-4 shows a typical coaxial cable.

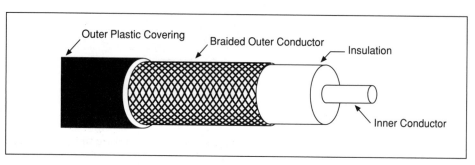

Figure 4-4: In standard coaxial cable, several layers of insulation surround a central copper wire.

Twisted Pair

Twisted-pair cabling comes in two varieties. *Shielded twisted-pair cabling* is designed to be less susceptible to noise interference than coax or unshielded twisted pair. Shielded twisted-pair cabling is most appropriate for Ethernet or Token-Ring networks.

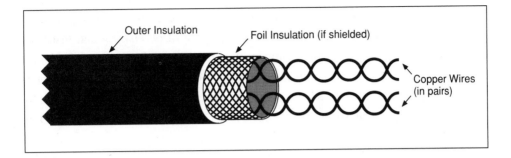

Figure 4-5: In twisted-pair cabling, the conductors are wound around each other and enclosed in an insulative sheath.

Unshielded twisted-pair (*UTP*) cable, similar to telephone cable, is widely used in today's network installations. The advantage of this type of cabling is that it is relatively inexpensive, easy to install, and easy to maintain. The main drawback is that you need extra equipment (hubs and transceivers) to use unshielded twisted pair.

Fiber Optic

Fiber optic cabling is an evolving type of physical network media. The major benefit offered by fiber optic cabling is that it provides a path for high-speed transmission (100Mbps or more) and it is not susceptible to noise.

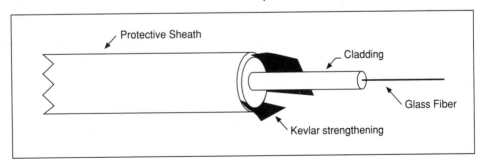

Figure 4-6: In fiber optic cable, a hair-thin glass or plastic core is surrounded by a protective outer covering.

In the past, the major disadvantage of fiber optic cabling was its higher cost, particularly for installation. Now, however, the cost of purchasing and installing fiber optic cable and equipment is comparable to the price of shielded and unshielded twisted-pair cabling. The remaining price difference is in the cost of LAN adapters for fiber optic networks, which are still more expensive than standard adapters for copper media, particularly in the area of Fiber Distributed Data Interface (FDDI) 100Mbps network implementations.

Today, many vendors provide fiber optic network products based on glass fiber optic cabling. One of these vendors, Codenoll Technology Corporation, has also introduced a series of products based on Plastic Optical Fiber (POF). Current POF technology allows network workstations and other devices to be located as far as 50 meters from the POF concentrator. POF technology can transmit data at a rate of 10Mbps. Fiber optic networks which require FDDI 100Mbps bandwidths, or which require cable runs of more than 50 meters, still require glass fiber today.

General Cabling Concepts

Before you install your cable, we recommend that you consult the Novell installation supplement for the particular LAN adapter. These supplements explain the limitations and rules for the various types of LAN adapters and cabling supported by NetWare.

Third-party board manufacturers usually supply their own documentation, along with a NetWare- compatible LAN driver. This documentation often contains special instructions for configuring and installing the board and its cabling on a Novell network. Use these instructions in addition to the Novell installation manuals and supplements.

Cable Installation Rules

When installing your cabling, you can eliminate many potential problems by following a few basic rules.

1. Always follow the cabling requirements.

   Take the time to research the cabling specifications of your network. All too often, people don't understand the specifications or they cut corners on them.

Remember to stay within the lengths specified, terminate correctly, obey the rules of hub installations, and ground the cable correctly.

2. Always test connections or cables before installation.

This area of the cabling installation is the most overlooked, probably because most of us assume that any cable we purchase or make will work the first time it's installed. Several simple ways to test your cabling would be to test the connection at each workstation, and to test each segment of cable with an easy-to-use cable testing tool.

3. Establish a user-friendly cabling system.

A user-friendly cabling installation allows the user to do normal day-to-day work without accidently damaging the cabling system. To enhance the user-friendly characteristics of the system, make sure that the connectors on your cables are installed correctly, leave enough slack in the cable for a little movement, and keep the cables out of areas where users may walk on them or run their chairs over them.

4. Establish a fault-resistant cabling scheme.

Before installing the cabling, you may want to review your cabling scheme to prevent total failure of the network if a cabling problems should happen. You may want to ask yourself what would happen if one hub or segment of the network were to fail. If all the workstations are connected to one segment of the cabling and a failure occurs on that cable, it can affect everyone. With distributed cabling scheme, on the other hand, you can avoid a total network failure if one cable fails.

In Figure 4-7, the first illustration shows a network that would experience total failure if the cable failed. In the second illustration, the workstations are divided into two different cabling segments and bridged together by a file server. If one segment failed, only the workstations on the faulty cable segment would be affected.

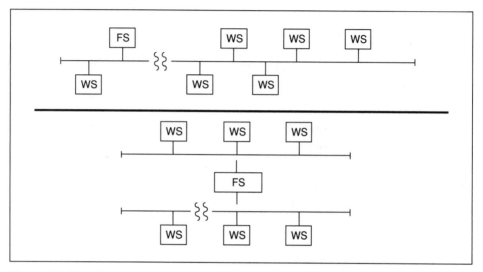

Figure 4-7: The right cabling scheme can prevent the failure of the entire network.

6. Follow local laws for cable installations.

    Before even purchasing your cable, check your local laws to verify the codes for installing cables. Some ordinances may require that you use a specific type of coated cable. There may also be some guidelines for installing cables around vents and lights.

7. Know about useful troubleshooting tools.

    The Microtest Cable Scanner and similar products are useful for troubleshooting cables. We recommend that you purchase a cable tester; it can save you hours of downtime while you're trying to find a cabling problem.

Network and Node Addresses

Before installing any components on the network, you should understand the concept of network and node addresses and how they relate to the network. Together, these two addresses directly affect the way network and internetwork workstations and servers communicate with each other.

The purpose behind network and node addressing is to allow the data intended for a specific workstation to use the network address to locate the network on which the workstation resides, and then to locate the correct workstation on that network.

A *node address* is the address of the LAN adapter in the workstation or file server. This address must be unique; that is, it must be different from any other node address on the *immediate* network (but not the internetwork). The type of LAN adapter (Arcnet, Ethernet, or Token-Ring) you select will determine how these addresses are established. If you're using Arcnet, you must choose a unique node address (hexadecimal address) for the network and move jumpers or switches on the adapter accordingly. If you're using Ethernet or Token-Ring, the node addresses are already uniquely assigned and hard-coded onto the card.

A *network address* is an eight-digit hexadecimal number that uniquely identifies a network. You can arbitrarily designate this address, which may include symbols anywhere within the hexadecimal ranges of 1 to FFFFFFFE (such as AAAAAAA1, or BADBEEF).

On a single-server network, you don't need to be concerned about address conflicts, since there is only one server on the network to assign an address for. Figure 4-8 shows a single network configured with one network address.

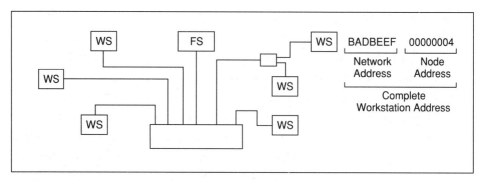

Figure 4-8: This single network is configured with one network address.

In a multiple-server network, the file servers on that network must have the same network address; however, each server (and each LAN adapter) within the network carries a unique node number. Figure 4-9 illustrates what a multiple server network configuration might look like.

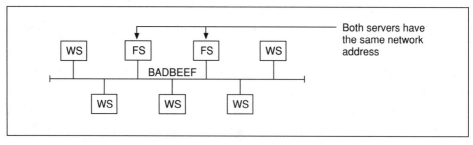

Figure 4-9: This multiserver network requires the same network address on all its file servers, but a unique node number on each.

A multiple-server internetwork consists of two or more networks (cabling systems) connected together via an internal or external router to form an internetwork. In this case, the file server or external router that brings the networks together must have a network address and a node number which identifies it with each of the networks the router supports. Each of the networks brought together in an internetwork must have a unique network address.

For example, in Figure 4-10 you can see how the file server (internal router) ANIMAL brings together two networks with different network addresses.

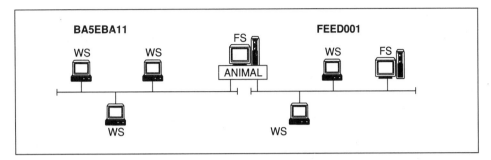

Figure 4-10: Two networks with different network addresses are brought together in one file server.

You bring together two networks by installing two LAN cards in the server and specifying a different network address on each card. Note the node addresses on both sides of the network. LAN adapters, in the case of Arcnet, can have the same node addresses as long as they exist on different networks. With Ethernet or Token-Ring, however, the node addresses are hard-coded on the cards.

Addressing configurations for external routers are the same as for a file server. The network addresses of the LAN adapters within the router must match the addresses of the LANs being brought together.

If you have nondedicated file servers or nondedicated routers on the internetwork, the DOS process within the nondedicated server or router must have a unique network and node address as well.

In NetWare v3.*x*, each server also has an *internal IPX number*, an eight-digit hexadecimal address used to identify the file server itself. The internal IPX number must also be unique across the internet. When the server advertises its file services, it provides the internal IPX address (which are always assigned a node address of 1).

Common Addressing Mistakes

A common mistake on an Arcnet LAN is duplicating the node address when you move a workstation from one network to another. The best way to avoid this error is to buy an Arcnet troubleshooting software product that lists the nodes currently being used on the LAN. If you have a single-server network, you can simply log every workstation into the server and do a USERLIST /A to display the workstations' node addresses.

In a multiserver network environment, the network administrator may forget that each server's network address must be the same. If the servers aren't communicating with each other, or if you're receiving "Router Configuration Errors" at the file server's console, it's possible that incorrect server addressing is your problem. To correct this problem, reconfigure the file server or external router that has incorrect network address to prevent it from conflicting with the rest of the network.

In a multiserver internetwork environment, you can run into problems if a network address conflicts with other network addresses. You can spot this problem if the servers on the internet won't communicate with each other or if you start receiving "Router Configuration Errors" at the file server console. To correct this problem, make sure your cabling is connected to the correct LAN adapters on the file server or external router. You may also want to verify that the network addresses on the file servers and external routers are correctly defined.

Arcnet Cabling Concepts

This section offers a brief review of Arcnet cabling concepts. Remember to consult your manufacturer's supplement about the limitations of the media you have chosen.

Arcnet uses a token bus topology which runs at 2.5Mbps. You can use Arcnet with coaxial, twisted- pair, or fiber optic cabling.

There are two types of Arcnet network boards: low-impedance and high-impedance. The low- impedance Arcnet layout is a star topology that has it own set of rules, as illustrated in Figure 4-11.

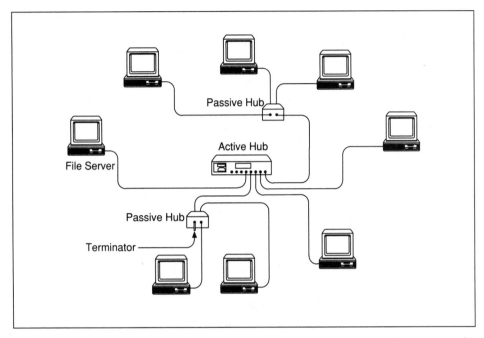

Figure 4-11: This illustration shows the basic layout of a low-impedance Arcnet network.

A high-impedance Arcnet network is based on the bus topology. A maximum of eight high-impedance Arcnet station can be connected together in a series. The basic layout is shown in Figure 4-12.

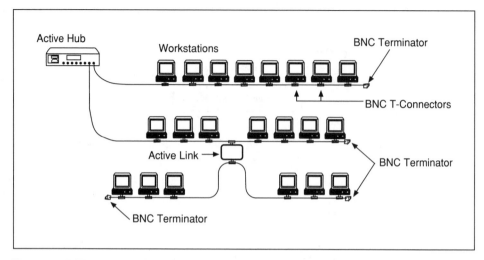

Figure 4-12: This illustration shows the basic layout for high-impedance Arcnet network.

Components Associated with Arcnet

If you will be dealing with Arcnet cabling, you need to become familiar with some of the components found in Arcnet networks. For the sake of explaining Arcnet cabling concepts and troubleshooting, we'll concentrate on a low-impedance, coaxial configuration. If you're using another type of cabling for Arcnet, the rules concerning length and the cable-dependent components (such as BNC connectors) may differ from the ones presented here. Consult your manufacturer or reseller for information specific to the type of cards, cabling, and hubs you are using.

Figure 4-13 shows the components commonly used in low-impedance Arcnet networks.

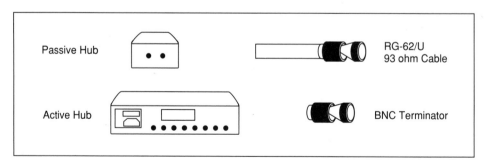

Figure 4-13: This diagram illustrates the components of a low-impedance Arcnet network.

- **Active Hubs.** The active hub relays network signals and amplifies the strength of those signals. BNC (Bayonet-Neill-Concelman) ports are located on the back of the hub (twisted-pair and fiber optic hubs will have different types of ports) to bring together the cabling from other active hubs, passive hubs, and workstations. Unused ports on the active hub do not require termination.

- **BNC Terminators**. 93-ohm BNC terminators prevent reflections of the network signals. You attach them to the unused ports on passive hubs.

- **Cabling**. If you're using coaxial, use RG-62/U 93-ohm coaxial cable. At the end of each cable is a BNC connector that can link into a workstation, hub, or terminator.

- **Passive Hubs**. A passive hub relays the network signals. It contains four BNC ports to which workstations, an active hub, and terminators can be connected. Note that any unused port on the passive hub must be terminated with a 93-ohm terminator. Also, remember that you can't connect a passive hub to a passive hub; the ports on the passive hub can only connect to active hubs, workstation and terminators.

Rules for Low-Impedance Arcnet Networks

1. A single Arcnet network can have only 255 different node addresses (for workstations and fileservers, starting from the server LAN adapter out). Node addresses 0 and 256 (FFh) are not available.

2. Each Arcnet adapter on the network (from the server LAN adapter out) must have a unique node address.

3. You can connect active hubs only to other active hubs, passive hubs, file servers, and workstations.

4. Don't create loops from one port of the active hub to the other, either through an other active hub or passive hub to the original hub.

5. Don't connect one passive hub to another passive hub.

6. Don't connect an active hub to a passive hub and then to another active hub.

7. Don't create loops from one port on the passive hub to the other.

8. Be sure to terminate any unused port on a passive hub with a 93-ohm terminator.

9. Consult your installation supplement for cable length limitations.

For a small company, a network administrator may want to use Arcnet because it is generally inexpensive compared to Ethernet and Token-Ring. That doesn't mean that Ethernet or Token-Ring won't work on such a small a network, or that Arcnet won't work on a large network. It simply means that you should consider the disadvantages and advantages of each.

Once you've installed an Arcnet network, you may need to consult the following section for some specific Arcnet troubleshooting help.

Troubleshooting Tips for Arcnet Cabling

Before going through these basic troubleshooting tips, verify that your workstation will at least load IPX.COM. (We'll explain this file in Chapter 9.) In *most* cases (there's always an exception), if IPX.COM won't load successfully, you must focus your troubleshooting efforts on making sure that your workstation can communicate with the LAN adapter. We'll discuss how to troubleshoot this problem in detail in Chapter 25.

The following common troubleshooting tips are for those cases in which you loaded IPX.COM successfully, but you can't find a server on the network.

Problem: One or a few workstation(s) can't log in to the network.

Solutions:

Verify that the cable to the workstation(s) is connected. Sometimes cables look like they're connected to the workstation, but the connector on one end may be loose. Verify that the connector hasn't become loose by gently but firmly pulling on the cable while the connector is still attached to the network adapter or hub.

Check the cabling and the passive and active hubs directly associated with the workstation(s) for continuity and termination. A common problem experienced with Arcnet is an active hub losing its power. Use an ohm-meter or cable tester to verify that the cable has continuity.

You can use the COMCHECK utility supplied with NetWare to check the continuity between workstations on the network. This utility is explained in Chapter 25.

Verify that you don't have any interrupts or I/O conflicts. For this purpose, you can use software tools like Symantec's Norton Utilities or Central Point Software's PC Tools.

Problem: You start experiencing a lot of network errors or a periodic hanging.

Solution:

Do a USERLIST/A to make sure that each node address on the network is unique. Make sure that no station has the node address of 0 or FFh. Brightwork's ARCmonitor offers a good utility you can use for finding the current Arcnet node addresses on the network.

Ethernet Cabling Concepts

Ethernet networks are generally associated with coaxial cabling. There are two types of Ethernet coaxial cabling: thick or thin.

Most Ethernet adapters will work with both thick or thin cable. Your choice between thick or thin cabling will determine the length of Ethernet cabling your network will be able to support. We recommend that you consult the installation supplement for your specific adapter for information concerning allowable Ethernet cabling lengths.

Before we move into the concepts behind thin and thick Ethernet, it's important to note how 10Base-T (twisted-pair Ethernet) works. To use 10Base-T, you'll need a transceiver that will transmit and receive signals on the twisted-pair cabling. Some current Ethernet adapters have this twisted-pair transceiver built into the card. If your Ethernet adapter doesn't have a built-in twisted-pair transceiver, you must attach an external transceiver to a thick Ethernet cable port (DIX).

In a large network, the twisted-pair cabling scheme is often advantageous, for several reasons. First, thin Ethernet cabling segments may not be able to carry the signal correctly over long distances. Second, with thick and thin cable you have a greater possibility of a cabling failure because there are more connectors. Third, when many workstations exist on the same cabling segment and the segment fails, the workstations will lose their connections. Finally, managing thin and thick Ethernet networks can be a real headache for the network administrator.

Using twisted-pair can help eliminate the increased possibility of total cable failure; at the same time it lets you expand the lengths of your Ethernet network. It's easier to install, since the twisted-pair cables can be installed with the phone cabling. It's also much easier to manage, especially when you probably have enough to do during a day without worrying about the need to keep the cable functioning. The only drawback is that it will probably cost more for twisted-pair, but you must carefully weigh that extra expense against the costs that would be incurred from the potential increase in downtime if another cabling scheme were used.

The following sections discuss the primary characteristics of thin and thick Ethernet cabling schemes.

Thin Ethernet Cabling

The standard thin Ethernet cable is a 0.2-inch diameter 50-ohm coaxial cable (RG-58A/U). Thin Ethernet uses the transceiver that's internal to the Ethernet adapter.

Components Associated with Thin-Cable Ethernet

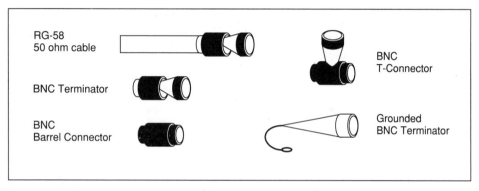

RG-58
50 ohm cable

BNC Terminator

BNC
Barrel Connector

BNC
T-Connector

Grounded
BNC Terminator

Figure 4-14: Shown here are the components used on a thin-cable Ethernet network.

- **BNC Connectors.** A BNC connector jack connects the network adapter to the trunk segment of the thin Ethernet cable. You can either purchase thin Ethernet cable in pre-cut pieces, with standard BNC connectors attached to each end, or purchase the cable in bulk and attach BNC connector plugs to the ends of the cable yourself. The BNC connectors allow you to connect the cable to T-connectors, barrel connectors, or other BNC hardware components.

- **BNC Barrel Connectors.** A barrel connector joins two pieces of thin BNC Ethernet cable.

- **BNC T-Connectors**. A BNC T-Connector joins two pieces of thin Ethernet and leaves a connection in the cable for a LAN adapter to attach to.

- **BNC Terminator.** You can use a BNC 50-ohm terminator to "terminate" a thin Ethernet cable. You must place a BNC terminator at one end of the cable segment and place a "grounded" BNC terminator (a terminator which

121

includes a grounding wire) on the opposite end. The purpose of the terminator is to stop signal reflections on the wire.

- **Grounded BNC Terminator**. This BNC 50-ohm terminator a grounding wire, which you must use to terminate one end of the Ethernet trunk.

Rules for Thin-Cable Ethernet Networks

1. In a thin-cable Ethernet network, the BNC T-Connectors must be directly hooked up to the Ethernet card. You can't add cable between the BNC T-Connector and the Ethernet adapter.

2. You must install a BNC 50-ohm terminator at the end of each trunk segment.

3. One of the two terminators on the trunk segment must be grounded.

4. As you install a thin Ethernet network, try to keep cabling splices to a minimum. Use unspliced cable lengths between network stations wherever possible. The fewer splices you make in the cable, the more reliable and easier to troubleshoot your network will be.

If you're sure your network trunk cable will never exceed 3,035 feet (925 meters), thin Ethernet may be your preferable cabling choice. Thin Ethernet is less expensive and easier to install than thick Ethernet cable. Figure 4-15 shows the basic layout of a thin Ethernet network.

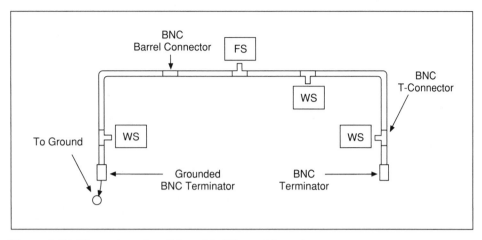

Figure 4-15: Shown here is a thin-cable Ethernet layout.

Thick Ethernet Cabling

Standard thick Ethernet employs a 0.4-inch diameter 50-ohm coaxial cable. It uses an external transceiver to help transmit and receive network signals.

Components Associated with Thick-Cable Ethernet

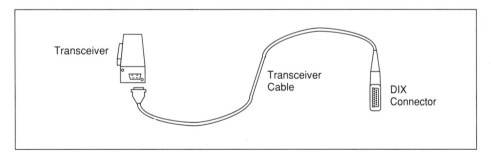

Figure 4-16: Shown here are the components used on a thick-cable Ethernet network.

- **DIX (Digital Intel Xerox) Connector.** Thick Ethernet cable requires either a DIX male connector plug or DIX female connector socket. The DIX connector plug connects the cable to a network adapter board. The DIX connector socket may be attached to an external transceiver.

- **N-Series Male Connectors.** These connectors are installed at both ends of the thick cable. In most circumstances, you'll buy thick cable in large quantities and put on these connectors after the cable has been cut into lengths.

- **N-Series Terminators.** An N-Series 50-ohm terminator is used to "terminate" the cable. Each end of the trunk cable segment must have a terminator. One of the two terminators must contain a grounding wire and must be grounded to earth.

- **N-Series Barrel Connectors.** These connectors are used to connect two pieces of thick Ethernet cable.

- **Transceiver.** Transceivers transmit and receive network signals on a thick Ethernet network. You need a transceiver only if you're using thick Ethernet.

- **Transceiver Cable.** This cable server to connect the station to external transceivers on thick Ethernet. At each end of the transceiver cable exists a DIX connector with male and female ends. The male DIX connector attaches to the Ethernet adapter and the female DIX connector attaches to the transceiver.

Rules for Thick-Cable Ethernet Networks

1. A terminator must be located at each end of the trunk segment.

2. One of the two terminators on the trunk segment must be grounded.

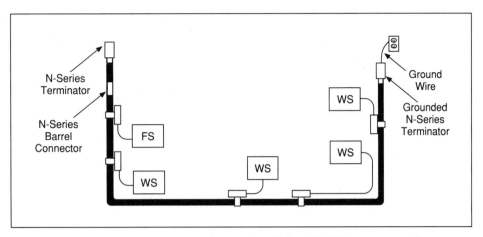

Figure 4-17: Shown here is the basic layout of a thick-cable Ethernet network.

Troubleshooting Tips for Ethernet Cabling

Before you go through the following troubleshooting tips, verify that your workstation will at least load IPX.COM. (We'll explain this file in Chapter 9.) In *most* cases (remember there is always an exception), if IPX.COM won't load successfully, you must focus your troubleshooting efforts on making sure that you workstation can communicate with the LAN adapter. We'll discuss how to trouble-shoot this problem in detail in Chapter 25.

The following common troubleshooting tips are for those cases in which you loaded IPX.COM successfully, but you can't find a server on the network.

Problem: Your workstation can't find a server.

Solutions:

Make sure that your cable is properly connected to the Ethernet adapter. Sometimes the cable simply isn't properly attached to the LAN adapter or transceiver. This the first place to check when you can't communicate with the network.

Use the COMCHECK utility provided with NetWare to check the cable continuity between two workstation on the network. We'll explain this utility in Chapter 15.

If you just installed an Ethernet adapter, you may want to verify that it's configured to support your thick or thin Ethernet cabling choice. You can configure most Ethernet adapters—for example, the Novell NE2000—by adjusting a jumper(s) on the card. If you have a Micro Channel or EISA Ethernet adapter, you can run a configuration utility to set the adapter for "Thick (DIX)" or "Thin."

Make sure your Ethernet card is correctly seated in the workstation's expansion slot. You can do this by turning off the power to the workstation, taking off workstation cover, and firmly pressing the card down into the expansion slot.

Verify that you that you don't have any interrupt or I/O conflicts with the LAN adapter. A common problem is a conflict between the Ethernet adapter and a port with a modem or mouse installed on it.

Some Ethernet cards have a jumper that will adjust the timing between the microcomputer and the Ethernet adapter. For more information about a possible conflict, you may want to consult the supplement manual that came with your adapter or contact the Ethernet adapter manufacturer.

Verify that you're using the Ethernet standard (Ethernet II or IEEE 802.3) on the workstation software that is currently compatible with your file server configuration. Failing to confirm this compatibility is a common mistake in multiple-protocol environments. For more information on the Ethernet standards, you may want to refer to Chapter 25 to learn how to adjust your Ethernet standard.

Problem: Multiple workstations can't log in to a file server, even though you know that your file server is working.

Solutions:

If you've just done a new installation, you may want to test each of your cables for continuity. Each piece of the network cable should be properly tested to avoid a break or "open" in the bus. If the cable has an "open" in the bus, the workstations won't be able to communicate with the network.

To test the cable for continuity, you can use an ohm-meter or a cable testing tool, such the Microtest Cable Scanner.

Check for incorrect termination or no termination. Make sure that you terminate the ends of the cable segments. If the ends of the cable aren't properly terminated, none of the workstations will be able to communicate with the LAN.

Use the COMCHECK utility provided with NetWare to check the continuity between two workstations on the network. We'll explain this utility in Chapter 25.

Token-Ring Cabling Concepts

In this section, we explain basic Token-Ring concepts. Consult your Token-Ring adapter supplement for specific information concerning cable lengths and other Token-Ring requirements.

Components Associated with Token-Ring Networks

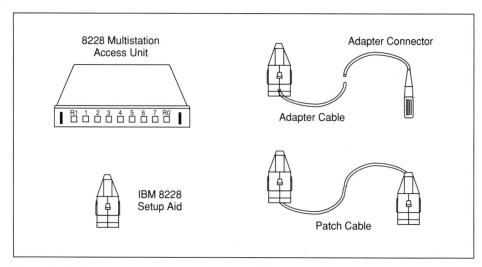

Figure 4-18: Shown here are the components used on a Token-Ring network.

- *Adapter Cables.* An adapter cable consists of Type 6 cable that has an IBM Cabling System Connector on one end and a connector that interfaces with the Token-Ring adapter on the other.

- *Multistation Access Unit (MAU).* A MAU is made up of 8-16 ports that are used to connect workstations to the network. Along with those ports are "Ring In" and "Ring Out"(RI and RO) ports that connect other MAUs to form a ring.

- *Patch Cables.* A patch cable consists of Type 6 cable that has IBM Cabling System Connectors on each end. You can use patch cables to link together MAUs and workstations. You can also connect them to each other.

- *Setup Aid.* You can use a Setup Aid to test a MAU before installing it. This is a helpful tool for avoiding possible installation problems.

Note: Currently, other types of cabling (besides IBM Type 6) can be used with a Token-Ring network. You may want to consult IBM or a reseller for more information about the available types of cabling. For this explanation, we'll concentrate on Type 6 cabling.

Rules for Token-Ring Networks

1. If more than one MAU exists on the network, they must be connected together with patch cables to form a ring. Use the Ring In and Ring Out (RI/RO) ports to connect the MAUs together. Connect the Ring Out of one MAU to the Ring In of another MAU until the whole forms a ring.

2. If only one MAU exists on the network, the Ring In and Ring Out ports need not be connected with patch cables.

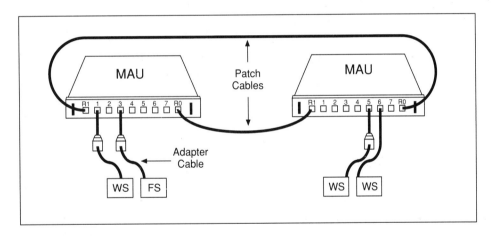

Figure 4-19: Shown here is the basic layout of a Token-Ring Network.

Troubleshooting Tips for Token-Ring Cabling

Problem: A workstation can't find a file server.

Solutions:

Check to make sure that your cables are plugged correctly into the MAU port and the Token-Ring adapter. To make sure your cable is connected properly to the MAU, you should hear the connector "click" when you plug it into the

Most Token-Ring adapters come with a diagnostic utility to make sure the Token-Ring adapter is working correctly.

Problem: No workstations on the ring are working.

Solution:

Be sure you've correctly connected the Ring In on one MAU to the Ring Out on another MAU.

CHAPTER 5

NetWare v3.11 Server Installation

Server installation time is your best opportunity to prevent problems down the road. In other words, if you plan your installation well, you'll have less occasion for troubleshooting the server, because a good installation will allow you to avoid potential problems. Our philosophy is that it pays to take time up front, during the installation, to make certain that everything you do is correct and well planned. This chapter introduces the NetWare v3.11 server installation procedure and gets you started on your way to a successful server implementation.

Server Installation Overview

As is the case with most software, installing NetWare v3.11 on a server involves numerous options. Some of these installation options are more important to get right the first time than others. For example, while it's a simple thing to change a server's LAN configuration (network addresses, NICs, and so forth), it's impossible to change a volume's block size once you've created that volume. In addition, many of NetWare v3.11's dynamic parameters are subject to the server's hardware configuration (for example, the amount of RAM installed in the server).

Other installation options, while easily changed, have the potential to cause problems if you haven't thought things through ahead of time. For example, conflicts among network addresses or server names will cause problems with NetWare routers. The server must be able to support sufficient I/O, memory, and interrupt options for the number and combination of adapter cards you'll be using on the server. Finally, you should plan your server installation under the assumption that your network will grow, which can mean the server will have to support more users than you currently have, more drives or volumes, and more networks.

Decision Checklist

Compared to earlier versions of NetWare, version 3.11 is easy to install—so much so that it almost encourages a shoot-from-the-hip attitude on the part of the installer. That's all right if you really know what you're doing. For the rest of us, however, it's a good idea to make a checklist of configuration options and decisions you'll have to make during the course of installation. Here's a general decision checklist you can use.

1) Do you want to boot the server from a DOS partition?
2) What will be the server's name?
3) What will be the server's internal IPX number?
4) How many drives will the server have?
5) Do any of the drives need non-NetWare partitions?
6) Will any drives be mirrored or duplexed?
7) How many volumes will the server have?
8) Will any volumes span multiple drives?
9) What will be the block size for each volume?
10) What name spaces will you use on which volumes?
11) How many LAN segments will the server have, and what will be their addresses?
12) What protocol stacks and frame types will you require for use with the server's LANs?

This decision checklist is not meant to replace a file server hardware worksheet you may decide to maintain. The NetWare v3.11 *Installation* manual provides a useful template for such a worksheet, and we encourage you to make full use of it, both for installation and maintenance purposes. Rather, this is a minimal list of decisions that you'll need to make during the course of the installation.

Server Installation Steps

The basic steps for installing NetWare v3.11 are:

1. Set up the server to boot both DOS and NetWare (including the creation of a DOS partition if desired).
2. Run SERVER.EXE to load NetWare and assign a server name and internal IPX number.
3. Load NetWare v3.11 disk drivers.
4. Load the INSTALL utility and create NetWare partitions on all drives.
5. Mirror drives together, if desired for fault tolerance.
6. Create NetWare volumes on the drives.
7. Copy NetWare's system and public files to the SYS volume.
8. Load NetWare v3.11 LAN drivers.
9. Edit the STARTUP.NCF and AUTOEXEC.NCF files.

Your answers to the items outlined in the decision checklist above will determine the exact steps you take when performing the tasks outlined in these installation steps. NetWare v3.11 offers countless variations of the same basic installation procedure, and these variations depend on your specific server hardware, your NetWare site, and how you will use your NetWare v3.11 server.

Because of the large number of installation options NetWare offers you, we'll try to explain what each step entails, and at the same time offer insight into why NetWare requires each step and what is happening under the surface. That way, if your specific installation requires some steps we don't cover in the next few chapters, you'll still have a solid understanding of the installation procedure as a whole.

Choosing to Boot NetWare from a DOS Partition

The first installation decision you'll have to make is whether to boot NetWare from a floppy diskette or from a DOS partition on the server. Booting from a DOS partition from is recommended for a number of reasons. First, as we explained in Chapter 1, the NetWare Loader is contained in a DOS executable file named

SERVER.EXE. This means that your server will always boot NetWare from DOS. NetWare v3.11 allows you to retain a DOS partition on your server's C: (boot) drive. Using a DOS partition drive speeds booting significantly, because the only alternative is to boot from a floppy diskette in the A: drive.

Another less generally-applicable reason for maintaining a DOS partition on a server is that it allows you to occasionally use the server machine as a DOS workstation. Many NLM developers use this approach because they can compile and link NLMs under DOS, and then run them on the same machine after executing SERVER.EXE. You may have your own reasons for using a server machine as both a DOS and a NetWare platform.

Note that if all of your server's hard drives are connected to a Novell Disk Coprocessor Board (DCB), you won't be able to boot from a DOS partition, because DOS is incapable of addressing DCB-based drives. At least one disk must be connected to a non-DCB internal hard disk controller.

The tradeoff with maintaining a DOS partition on your server is that the disk space used for DOS is unavailable for use by NetWare. For example, if your server has a 300MB drive and you use 30MB for a DOS partition, NetWare then has only 270MB to work with. However, you can choose the size of your DOS partition (Novell recommends a minimum size of 3MB), so this is a minor problem. Whether you maintain a DOS partition or not has absolutely no effect on the server's use of memory, since it must load DOS regardless. And either way, you can remove DOS from the server's memory after booting the server using the REMOVE DOS console command.

Another slight drawback of maintaining a DOS partition on your server is that it makes the installation process slightly more cumbersome. The instructions that follow assume that you have decided to boot NetWare from a DOS partition. We'll try to guide you smoothly through this potentially confusing procedure.

Creating a DOS Partition

The process for creating a DOS partition on a NetWare drive consists of four main steps:

- Prepare the server machine for basic operation and boot it with DOS.

- Load NetWare and use the INSTALL NLM to zap any partitions that may exist on the drive.

- Use the DOS FDISK.COM program to create a small DOS partition and to make that partition active.

- Format the DOS partition as a "system" partition (containing the hidden DOS system files and COMMAND.COM).

Once you've completed these steps, you run the NetWare INSTALL utility again to create a NetWare partition out of the remaining space on the C: drive.

The following sections contain step-by-step instructions for completing these initial NetWare v3.11 installation procedures.

Preparing the Server and Booting It with DOS

1. When the server machine boots from DOS, it must be able to recognize the hard drive(s) you've installed in it. So before you begin, verify that you've provided the server machine with correct information about its DOS configuration. For an Industry Standard Architecture (ISA) machine, this means running SETUP; for an Extended ISA (EISA) machine, it means running the EISA configuration utility; for a PS/2 Micro Channel machine, it means running the machine's Reference diskette.

2. Once you've made sure the server and its hard disks are installed and configured correctly, boot the machine using DOS v3.*x* or higher.

3. If you have any data you wish to preserve on the C: drive, back it up now. Once you zap existing partitions on the server machine, the data stored in those partitions is gone forever.

Loading NetWare and Deleting Existing Partitions

1. Insert the SYSTEM-1 diskette you received with your NetWare v3.11 software package in drive A: and type

    ```
    A:\SERVER <Enter>
    ```

    at the DOS prompt.

2. As NetWare loads, it prompts you for a server name and an internal IPX network number. What you enter for these parameters at this point is of no lasting consequence. However, you must obey the rules when entering this information. Specifically, the server name can contain any alphanumeric characters, plus hyphens, or underscores. The IPX network number can be any hexadecimal number from one to eight digits long. (Hexadecimal digits include the numbers 1-9 and the letters A-F.) Type an appropriate name and number, pressing <Enter> after each one.

3. Once you've entered the server name and network number, the server displays other information such as a speed rating and NetWare version. When you see the colon (:) prompt, NetWare v3.11 is running on the server. However, you can't gain access to the server's disk drive(s) until you load the disk driver.

    If your server is an ISA or EISA machine, load the disk driver by inserting the SYSTEM-2 diskette in the A: floppy and typing

    ```
    LOAD A:ISADISK <Enter>
    ```

    at the console command line.

    If your server is a PS/2 machine, the driver to load depends on the type of drive(s) you have installed. If you have a PS/2 with an ESDI controller, substitute PS2ESDI for ISADISK in the command line example above; for a PS/2 MFM controller, substitue PS2MFM; for a PS/2 SCSI controller, substitute PS2SCSI. (Some machines, such as the Compaq SYSTEMPRO with an Intelligent Drive

Array, require a vendor-supplied disk driver other than ISADISK.DSK. If you have such a machine, you should have received the appropriate driver with your machine.)

4. When you load a disk driver, NetWare prompts you for memory address, I/O address, and interrupt settings. To assist you in setting these values, NetWare provides you with a default settings which, if you accept them, will not conflict with any other drivers currently loaded. If your disk controller is set at its factory default setting, the defaults should work. If it isn't, enter the settings that match those on the disk controller hardware.

Once you've successfully loaded the appropriate disk driver, NetWare v3.11 can talk to its hard drive. Now you need to load the INSTALL NLM and zap any existing partitions on the C: drive.

5. To load INSTALL, insert the NetWare SYSTEM-2 diskette in drive A: and type

```
LOAD A:INSTALL <Enter>
```

from the console command line. When INSTALL loads, you will see the screen shown in Figure 5-1.

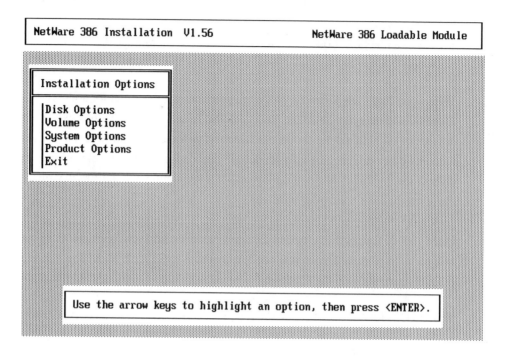

Figure 5-1: When you start INSTALL, the first screen you see contains the "Installation Options" menu.

6. To zap pre-existing partitions on the server's C: drive, select "Disk Options,"
    the first item on the "Installation Options" menu. INSTALL displays another
    menu called "Available Disk Options," as shown in Figure 5-2.

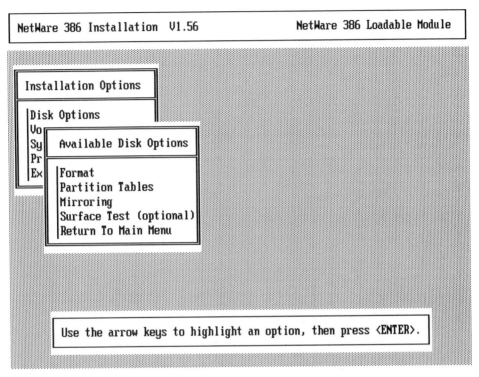

Figure 5-2: The next screen in INSTALL contains the "Available Disk Options" menu.

Note that the first item on the "Available Disk Options" menu is "Format."
Formatting a disk is strictly optional. Most disks come from the manufacturer
with a low-level format already performed, so you should rarely have to
format a disk using INSTALL. The primary exception to this rule is older
disks, which may benefit from a fresh low-level format because they've suffered
a decrease in viable sectors due to aging of the media.

7. Select "Partition Options," the second item on the "Available Disk Options"
   menu. Choosing this option causes INSTALL to display a partition table similar
   to the one in Figure 5-3 that shows the existing partitions on the drive, if any, and
   free disk space, if any. Additionally, INSTALL displays a "Partition Options"
   menu, which has four items: "Change Hot Fix," which allows you to alter the

number of blocks set aside by NetWare for recovery from media errors; "Create NetWare Partition," which does just what it says; "Delete Partition," which will delete anyexisting partition, regardless of its type (Unix, DOS, NetWare, and so forth); and "Return To Previous Menu," which takes you back to the "Available Disk Options" menu.

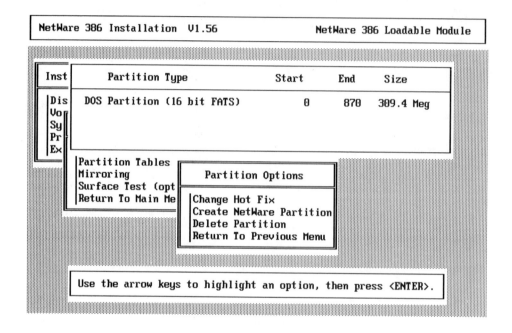

Figure 5-3: When you select "Partition Options," INSTALL displays the current partition table and the "Partition Options" menu.

8. Highlight each partition displayed in the partition table at the top of the console screen and select "Delete Partition." When you're finished deleting partitions, the partition table should contain just one item—"free space."

9. That's it for now—press <Esc> until you return to the "Installation Options" menu and select "Exit" to exit INSTALL. Then, at the colon prompt, type the DOWN command to halt the server.

Creating a New DOS Partition

Now you need to reboot DOS and run the FDISK program to create a bootable DOS partition.

1. Insert your DOS boot diskette in drive A: and reboot the server with DOS.

2. To start FDISK, be certain that a floppy diskette containing FDISK.COM is in the current drive, and type

    ```
    FDISK <Enter>
    ```

    from the DOS prompt. FDISK presents you with four options, as shown in Figure 5-4.

    FDISK Options

    Current Fixed Disk Drive: 1

    Choose one of the following:

    >   1. Create DOS partition
    >   2. Change Active Partition
    >   3. Delete DOS partition
    >   4. Display Partition Information

    Enter choice: [1]

    Press ESC to return to DOS

Figure 5-4: DOS's FDISK program includes four options for working with partitions.

To be sure you deleted the pre-existing partitions correctly, you can select option 4, "Display Partition Information," to confirm that there are no existing partitions on the drive.

3. Select option 1, "Create DOS Partition" (the exact wording of the options might differ from DOS version to DOS version).

4. FDISK prompts you further to select from three sub-options. Select the first, "Create Primary DOS Partition."

5. At this point, you need to decide the size of your DOS partition. FDISK assumes that you want to use the entire drive as a "primary" DOS partition, and takes the liberty of entering this optionas a default. Override the default by answering "No" to the "Use entire space as DOS partition" prompt (again, the wording may vary, depending on your version of FDISK). Enter the size of the DOS partition you've decided on (we recommend a minimum of 3MB). FDISK will create the partition for you.

6. Now that a primary DOS partition is present on the server's C: drive, you must set that partition as the "active" partition by choosing option 2 on the FDISK menu, "Change Active Partition." If you fail to do this last step, the machine probably won't recognize the partition when you try to reboot it. The DOS partition must be "active" in order for the machine to boot from it.

7. Exit FDISK by pressing <Esc>. FDISK will reboot your machine automatically whenever you have altered the machine's partition information.

Note that to reboot the machine using DOS, you'll need to have a floppy book diskette in the machine's A: drive. Once the machine reboots with DOS, you're ready to format the DOS partition.

Formatting the DOS Partition

1. Be certain that the A: drive contains a disk with the DOS utility FORMAT.COM. From the DOS prompt, type

```
FORMAT C: /S <Enter>
```

The /S (system) option causes FORMAT to format the C: drive's active DOS partition and also place the hidden DOS system files and COMMAND.COM on the partition. During the format, FORMAT will tell you what percentage of the partition it has formatted, and will continually update this statistic.

The format should progress at a regular pace; if it doesn't, you may have problems with your drive, in which case you'll need to perform a low-level format using INSTALL (as explained under "Using INSTALL to Perform a Low-level Format" below).

2. When the format is complete, FORMAT will copy the hidden DOS system files and COMMAND.COM to the new DOS partition. (If you don't have a floppy with the DOS system on it in the A: drive, FORMAT will prompt you to insert a DOS system disk.)

3. After a successful format, you can copy all the DOS utilities and files to the partition, making it an honest-to-goodness DOS boot partition.

4. You might also want to copy the entire NetWare SYSTEM-1 disk to the DOS partition: this will make it easier and faster to perform the remaining installation steps.

A Note About FDISK vs. INSTALL

You may have noticed that one of the FDISK options allows you to delete existing DOS partitions. Why, then, did we have you go through the hassle of running NetWare and loading INSTALL just to delete partitions, when FDISK can do it for you? The answer is that while FDISK might work, INSTALL will always work.

The reasons for this situation are rather arcane. Suffice it to say that the information NetWare gives you about a drive may not always coincide with the information FDISK gives you about a drive. FDISK makes assumptions about drive configurations that aren't necessarily true for hardware configurations you may be using with NetWare. Additionally, FDISK isn't smart enough to know about non-DOS partitions (such as NetWare or Unix partitions.) You'll probably save time by doing it the right way (running NetWare and loading INSTALL rather than simply running FDISK), thus ensuring that you'll only have to do it once.

Note also that after deleting any existing partitions using INSTALL, you must create the DOS partition first and then create the NetWare partitions. If you do it in the opposite order, the machine probably won't be able to boot from the DOS partition, because virtually every BIOS expects a bootable DOS partition to start within the first 32MB of the disk.

Using INSTALL to Perform a Low-level Format

As we mentioned above, performing a low-level format on a NetWare drive is strictly optional. You may need to perform this low-level format, however, if you're having problems formatting the DOS partition. The DOS FORMAT utility, when formatting a DOS partition, occasionally detects bad sectors on the partition it's formatting. When this happens, FORMAT will "lock out" the sector, preventing DOS from using it. FORMAT's status message tells you that this is happening. So far, so good. However, because FORMAT is only working with a portion of the total drive (you've reserved the majority of drive space for NetWare), finding bad sectors in the DOS partition is a clue that there may be more bad sectors on the drive. In this case, you'd be wise to perform a full format using INSTALL and to start over from scratch with FDISK and then FORMAT.

Installing NetWare v3.11 on the Server

Now that you've got a good, solid DOS partition from which to boot the server machine, you're ready to do the NetWare installation proper, which includes running SERVER.EXE and progressing from there.

Running SERVER.EXE

At this point, you've already run SERVER.EXE once, so you know how to load it. You also know how to enter a server name and an internal IPX network number. This time through, however, you *must* settle on a server name and network number that you want to use when the server is running in its actual production environment. You must get these parameters correct this time through, because INSTALL keeps track of everything you do from the time you load SERVER.EXE and uses the information to create the server's STARTUP.NCF and AUTOEXEC.NCF boot files.

Here are some guidelines for choosing an appropriate name and internal IPX number for your NetWare v3.11 server.

Server Name

The server name can be up to 47 characters long, provided it doesn't contain any periods or spaces. If you're installing a server on an existing network with other NetWare servers, you need to be certain that the server name is unique. The NetWare internal router will only keep information on one instance of a server name; if there are duplicate server names on an internetwork, the router won't be able to direct NetWare traffic correctly. Most conspiciously, NetWare's login and messaging utilities won't function as expected. Moreover, there is no good reason to use duplicate server names.

One way you can check for any existing servers with the name you want to use for the new server is to use the NetWare SLIST utility. SLIST is a client utility, so from a DOS or OS/2 IPX workstation, type

```
SLIST ServerName <Enter>
```

If there's already a network server with the name you've chosen, SLIST will display the name of that server, along with its network and node addresses, and tell you whether or not you're attached to the server. If there is no server on-line with that name, SLIST will display a message "*ServerName* not found." Remember, however, that this only means that there are no servers on-line with that name. Or there could be another server with that name on-line, but the primary server you're attached just doesn't know that yet. Or there could be another server with that name not currently on the internetwork.

Here's another tip: Try to give each server you install a name that is informative. For example, if you're installing a server for the engineering department, call the server "ENGINEERING." Not only does this type of naming convention tell users what's stored on the server, but it also gives you an indication of the physical location of the server, which is important when you're called on to maintain or troubleshoot the server. Giving servers informative names also makes it easier for users to navigate multi-server networks.

Internal IPX Number

The server's internal IPX number, like any other IPX network address, must also be unique. The address can be from one to eight hexadecimal digits (numbers 1-9 and letters A-F). Giving a server an internal IPX network address that is the same as another address on the network will definitely cause routing problems.

Once again, you can use the SLIST utility to determine existing network numbers. However, because SLIST was written to display server names, it's not quite as easy to use it to obtain internetwork IPX addresses. Here's how to do it. From the DOS command line, type:

```
SLIST <Enter>
```

Executing SLIST without specifying a server name causes the workstation to display all servers currently on the network. The workstation will display every server listed in your primary server's routing table. But you don't care about server names: you're looking for IPX addresses. SLIST displays those, too; it just doesn't sort them for you like it does for server names.

If you're installing a server on a large internetwork (one that has many NetWare servers), a handy trick is to redirect the output of SLIST to a text file. Then you can open the resulting text file with a text editor and do a search for the IPX address you're planning to use for the new server's internal network number. DOS allows you to redirect the output of its console to a text file using the ">" operator, like this:

```
SLIST > TextFile <Enter>
```

One final note about the server's internal IPX network number and the SLIST utility. On an internetwork, each server must have a unique internal IPX number. The SLIST utility, while it displays all external network numbers, only displays internal network numbers for NetWare v3.x servers.

Another way to discover existing network numbers is to go to the console of a NetWare server already running on the internetwork and issue the DISPLAY NETWORKS command.

The IPX network numbers for a server's LANs need not be unique, but must be consistent with existing IPX network segments, if any. For example, Figure 5-5 shows two NetWare servers that share a common network segment.

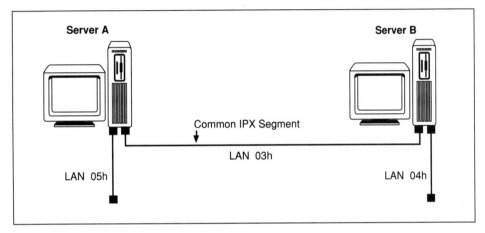

Figure 5-5: Two NetWare servers that share a common IPX network must communicate with that network using the same address.

Note that the servers in Figure 5-5 each have three IPX addresses:

- A unique internal IPX address
- A common shared-segment IPX address
- An additional non-shared IPX network

Since a server's internal IPX network is logically the same as the physical network or networks the server is attached to, you must consider all network numbers when assigning a unique internal IPX address to a server.

Loading NetWare Disk Drivers

After you enter the server's name and internal IPX number, you're ready to load the appropriate disk driver. If you've created a DOS boot partition as described previously in this chapter, this is probably at least the second time you've loaded the disk driver. So you should already know how to do it. If necessary, refer to the steps under "Loading NetWare and Deleting Existing Partitions" above.

Running the INSTALL NLM

INSTALL.NLM is the focal point for the rest of the server installation process. The critical tasks you use INSTALL for include:

- Creating NetWare partitions

- Implementing fault tolerance (in the form of Hot Fix, mirroring, and duplexing)

- Creating NetWare volumes

- Installing the NetWare "System" and "Public" files

- Creating and editing the server boot files

If you've created a DOS partition on your server's drive, as outlined above, you already know a little bit about INSTALL, because you used it to delete existing partitions from the server's C: drive. However, there are a few more things you need to know about INSTALL before you use it to bring up a production server.

As shown in Figure 5-1, INSTALL's main menu contains five options. As we will explain in the rest of this chapter, the "Disk Options" allow you to format and partition disks, mirror or duplex disks, and perform an optional surface test of a disk. Under "System Options," you create and edit server boot files (to be covered in Chapter 7). "Product Options" is a feature you may use later to install optional or third-party NetWare products. The "Exit" option takes you out of the INSTALL utility.

Before you do any serious work with INSTALL, you need to make some decisions regarding how you're going to set up the server's disks and what level of fault tolerance the disk volumes will have. (Each volume can have a different level of fault tolerance.)

Deciding on the Number of Drives

The question of how many drives the server will have is an important one to answer, for several reasons. Assuming that you've set up a small DOS partition on the server's C: drive, you still have a lot of flexibility regarding how you use the remainder of the server's disk drive resources. For instance, NetWare allows you to hook up external disk drives housed in a separate subsystem to a disk channel controller in the server.

In planning your disk space usage, it's helpful to know the basic decisions involved in setting up a disk to run NetWare. The first step to take is to create "raw" NetWare partitions on all of the server's remaining drive's or drive space. After creating NetWare partitions on all the server's (non-DOS) drives or drive space, you need to decide whether or not you want to mirror or duplex the server's drives. The next decision you must make is how many volumes to create. Further, you must decide the physical configuration of each volume, including the size of its Hot Fix table, its block size, and its physical configuration (that is, how many segments spanning how many physical drives will comprise the volume).

Each of these decisions is based at least in part on how many drives you have. This is obviously true with regard to mirroring and duplexing. However, these decisions can also affect the performance characteristics of NetWare volumes and the memory requirements of the server machine, as you will see shortly.

Setting Up NetWare Partitions

In the last section, we referred to NetWare partitions as "raw" partitions. It's useful to think of NetWare partitions as being homogeneous raw material, which you can mix and match to form volumes. In other words, a NetWare v3.11 volume can consist of several partitions. Moreover, a volume can consist of several partitions each of which resides on a different drive. However, a single drive can contain at most one NetWare partition.

Note that you can create a NetWare volume out of a portion of a partition. For example, if you have a 600MB NetWare partition, you can use that partition to create two separate volumes, perhaps each containing 300MB of space. When you segment a partition in this manner, you are using "segments." Remember, a NetWare partition

149

is the raw material of which volumes are made; a partition "segment" is the part of a partition that is actually conscripted by a volume.

Here is how to create a NetWare partition on your server's disks.

1. If you haven't already done so, load INSTALL. (The instructions for loading INSTALL are listed earlier, in the section on creating a DOS partition.)

2. From the INSTALL "Installation Options" menu, select "Disk Options." The "Disk Options" menu will appear.

3. If you have more than one hard drive installed on the server machine, the "Disk Options" menu will display a list of available drives contianing NetWare partitions. Select the appropriate drive. Then select the "Partition Tables" option. INSTALL will then display a table of existing partitions. The server console screen should look much like the one shown earlier in Figure 5-3.

   Here's where you need to pay close attention. If you're working with a C: drive on which you've already created a DOS boot partition, INSTALL's partition table will display that partition. The DOS boot partition should be fairly small, and there should be a significant amount of free space listed in the partition table.

   However, if you're working with another drive (not the boot drive), what you see depends on the type of drive you're working with, and what previous uses, if any, that drive has served. Since you want to create a NetWare partition on the drive, you should delete all existing partitions. (Once again, be careful: don't delete the DOS boot partition you've already created. Here's a hint: when you select the "Partition Tables" option from INSTALL, INSTALL will access the drive to read the partition table. Watching the drive lights will tell you which drive you selected!)

   If you need to delete partitions, use the "Delete Partition" item on the "Partition Options" menu. Once you've wiped the drive clean of existing partitions (with the exception of the DOS boot partition on the C: drive), you're ready to create a new NetWare partition on the drive.

4. To create a NetWare v3.11 partition, select "Create NetWare Partition" from the "Partition Options" menu. INSTALL will display a "Partition Information" window similar to the one shown in Figure 5-6.

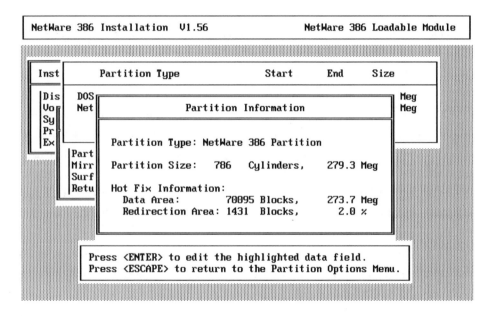

Figure 5-6: When you create a NetWare partition, INSTALL displays a "Partition Information" window.

The "Partition Information" window shows the type of partition you're creating (a NetWare 386 partition), the size of the partition in cylinders and megabytes, and Hot Fix information for that partition. You can edit the size of the partition and the Hot Fix information.

You should probably use all of the drive's cylinders for the NetWare partition. However, if you want, you can decrease the number of cylinders for the NetWare partition by editing that field in the window.

Setting the Hot Fix Information

The Hot Fix information shows how many blocks of the NetWare partition will be available for data and how many blocks will be held in reserve for redirection if any NetWare blocks go bad during the life of the drive. It's normal for a small number of blocks to go bad over time due to the aging of the drive's media. When these blocks fail, NetWare locks them out dynamically and redirects their data to one of the "hot fix" blocks held in reserve.

The default, which INSTALL automatically fills in for you, is to hold 2% of the drive's space in reserve for Hot Fix redirection. For most drives, 2% should be sufficient. However, if you're working with an older drive, or if you have some reason to be wary of the efficacy of the drive's media, you can increase the size of the redirection area by editing this field in the "Partition Information" window.

Note that the larger you make the Hot Fix redirection area for a partition, the smaller that partition's data area will be. However, once you create a volume using a specific partition, you can increase that partition's Hot Fix redirection area, but only by destroying volumes that are using that partition. This fact should give you reason to pause—at least long enough to make an intelligent decision regarding the size of the Hot Fix redirection area.

When you are finished creating the NetWare partition, the console screen should display the final partition information as in Figure 5-7. Press <Esc> to return to the "Available Disk Options" menu.

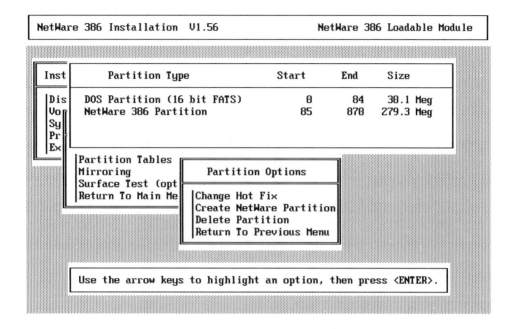

Figure 5-7: INSTALL displays final partition information in the partition table portion of the screen.

Mirroring and Duplexing Partitions

Mirroring and duplexing are two enormously effective ways you can reduce your chances of losing data and minimize server downtime. What NetWare v3.11 does when you mirror or duplex partitions is simple: it treats both partitions as the same logical partition, maintaining the same data on both.

For example, when you write data to a mirrored partition, NetWare writes data to both partitions. When one partition fails, NetWare automatically switches to the other partition. There is no downtime and no loss of data. Later, you can replace the drive containing the mirrored partition. By remirroring the partition to the new drive (the one you just used to replace the bad drive), you can restore the server to its pre-failure state. The best part is that file service for the mirrored partition continues to be operational while you're doing this.

Technically, you don't write data to partitions; you write data to volumes. But volumes are created within the NetWare partitions. So in reality, when you write data to a volume built from mirrored partitions, NetWare maintains synchronization between the mirrored partitions, which includes updating the volume data that resides on those partitions.

Here's another technical clarification: You should certainly down the server and power down the server machine before you replace a physical drive. But the remirroring process occurs in the background, so you can bring the server back up and remirror the partition while users are logged in to the server.

This leads to another important point about mirroring. NetWare v3.11 volumes can span multiple partitions (and, by inference, multiple drives). So when an unmirrored partition goes down, it takes part of a multi-partition volume down, but not the whole volume. It will take part of the volume FAT table down, rendering the volume useless. Because NetWare requires access to the entire volume, you should always mirror multi-partition volumes.

The reasoning behind this recommendation is simple. If one partition of a multi-partition volume fails, the entire volume fails. And the more partitions a volume is comprised of, the greater the chances are that that volume will fail. Mirroring can balance these probabilities and even increase them in your favor.

Mirroring has become a generic term that entails both mirroring and duplexing. In reality the two are different, and duplexing is preferrable. Mirroring means that NetWare maintains data synchronization between two partitions connected to the same drive controller. Duplexing, on the other hand, means that NetWare maintains data synchronization between two partitions connected to different controllers. So mirroring protects you against drive failure, but not controller failure, while duplexing protects you against both types of faults.

Note that duplexing isn't an INSTALL function per se, but happens automatically when you mirror two partitions that are connected to different controllers. So the process for mirroring and duplexing is the same. You can ensure that you're in reality duplexing drives by always "mirroring" partitions residing on different physical devices. (That's why INSTALL provides you with that information.)

Here are the steps to mirror or duplex a partition in INSTALL.

1. Select "Mirroring" from the INSTALL "Available Disk Options" menu. IN-STALL will display the "Partition Mirroring Status" window. This window displays all available NetWare partitions nd their mirroring status.

   Each partition has a logical partition number. Partition numbers are logical, while device numbers are physical. For example, the boot drive can have multiple logical partitions. NetWare v3.11 treats partitions as logical devices. "Not Mirrored" means that the partition isn't mirrored.

2. Select the partition you want to mirror from within the "Partition Mirroring Status" window and press <Enter>.

3. INSTALL will display a further window called "Mirrored NetWare Partitions." This window displays each partition and its synchronization status. Note also the Partition (logical) device number and the Device (physical) device number for each partition. Unmirrored partitions that have no data problems are always "in sync."

   With the partition you wish to mirror highlighted in the "Mirrored NetWare Partitions" window, press <Insert>.

4. INSTALL will display a list of partitions available for mirroring to the selected partition in the "Available Partitions" window. Highlight the partition you wish to mirror to the first partition and press <Enter>.

To be available for mirroring to the selected partition, a partition must be of greater or equal size to the partition you wish to mirror. An available partition doesn't need to reside on the same type or size of drive (or indeed on the same controller, which is how duplexing is possible). If you mirror a partition to a larger partition, the resulting mirrored partition is only as large as the smaller of its two component partitions. For this reason, it's a good idea to mirror partitions that are approximately the same size.

Note that you can mirror up to 15 partitions to the same partition. Each time you mirror a partition, you decrease your chances of data loss due to physical device failure by a factor of the device's reliability. For example, imagine you've got three drives, each with one partition:

Device	Partition	Failure Rate
Device 0	Logical partition 1	3%
Device 1	Logical partition 2	3%
Device 3	Logical partition 3	3%

As you can see, each device (and hence partition) has a 3% chance of failure. If you use partition 1 unmirrored, your chance of losing data due to physical device failure is 1 multiplied by the failure rate, or

$$1 \times .03 = .03$$

Let's say that you mirror partition 2 to partition 1. Now you've got reduncancy, and your chance of losing data due to physical device failure is:

$$1 \times .03 \times .03 = .0009$$

Let's say further that you mirror both partition 2 and partition 3 to partition one. Now you've got double redundancy. Your chance of losing data due to physical device failure is now

$$1 \times .03 \times .03 \times .03 = .00003$$

This example shows how redundancy can increase the reliability of your server. Mirroring is a highly effective fault-tolerance mechanism that's incredibly inexpensive when placed in the context of its effectiveness.

Here are a couple of final tips about mirrored NetWare v3.11 partitions. First, you can unmirror and remirror partitions without disturbing file service. This means that you're not stuck with your mirroring or duplexing structure after you set it up for the first time.

Second, you can increase or decrease the Hot Fix area (and conversely, decrease or increase the data area) of a partition after you've created the partition. However, doing so destroys NetWare volume information that may reside on that partition.

Creating NetWare Volumes

Now that you've created partitions, defined the Hot Fix area of each partition, and possibly mirrored partitions, you're ready to create volumes. Volumes (actually logical organizations of data) are the primary component of NetWare's file service. In Chapter 1, we discussed how NetWare caches volume File Allocation Tables and disk blocks in order to speed file service. The caching occurs regardless of how you define your volumes, but there are a couple of things you need to do when creating volumes to ensure that NetWare gains the greatest performance benefit of caching. We'll describe these precautions shortly.

Given the partitions you've created, you should have a very good idea regarding how you'll set up your volumes. Here are some important facts you should know before we discuss the volume creation procedure.

- By default, the first volume you create is the SYS volume. The SYS volume has five default directories: SYSTEM, PUBLIC, MAIL, LOGIN, and DELETED.SAV. Later on, when you're finished creating volumes, IN-STALL will copy the NetWare OS files into the SYS:SYSTEM directory, the NetWare utilities into the SYS:PUBLIC directory, and the login utilities into the SYS:LOGIN directory. DELETED.SAV is reserved for deleted files that aren't purged upon deletion.

- Volumes can have different block sizes. Once you select a block size for a volume, you can't change the block size without destroying the volume. This means that you should decide on block sizes before you create the volumes. Block sizes have implications for caching, which we'll discuss shortly.

- You can increase the size of a volume by adding additional partitions. However, you can never decrease the size of a volume without destroying the volume.

- A file server can have up to 64 volumes. A single volume can be up to 16 terabytes (TB) in size. However, because NetWare caches the File Allocation Table for each volume, the real limit on a server's storage capacity is its RAM, rather than its volume capacity. In other words, the server will run out of cache memory before you bump up against the limit of 32TB combined volume space.

Here are the steps to create a volume in INSTALL.

1. Select "Volume Options" from the INSTALL "Installation Options" menu. INSTALL will display a window showing all current volumes, if any.

2. Press <Ins> and INSTALL will display a "Volume Information" window. Because you're creating a volume, you can edit the fields within this window. A sample screen is shown in Figure 5-8.

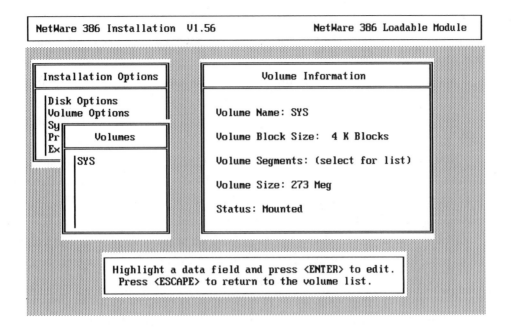

```
┌────────────────────────────────────────────────────────────────────┐
│ NetWare 386 Installation   V1.56            NetWare 386 Loadable Module │
└────────────────────────────────────────────────────────────────────┘

  ┌─────────────────────────┐   ┌──────────────────────────────────────┐
  │ Installation Options    │   │          Volume Information           │
  ├─────────────────────────┤   ├──────────────────────────────────────┤
  │ Disk Options            │   │                                      │
  │ Volume Options          │   │   Volume Name: SYS                   │
  │ Sy┌───────────────────┐ │   │                                      │
  │ Pr│     Volumes       │ │   │   Volume Block Size:   4 K Blocks    │
  │ Ex├───────────────────┤ │   │                                      │
  │   │ SYS               │ │   │   Volume Segments: (select for list) │
  │   │                   │ │   │                                      │
  │   │                   │ │   │   Volume Size: 273 Meg               │
  │   │                   │ │   │                                      │
  │   │                   │ │   │   Status: Mounted                    │
  └───┴───────────────────┴─┘   └──────────────────────────────────────┘

            ┌──────────────────────────────────────────────┐
            │ Highlight a data field and press <ENTER> to edit. │
            │ Press <ESCAPE> to return to the volume list.    │
            └──────────────────────────────────────────────┘
```

Figure 5-8: When you create a new volume, INSTALL displays a "Volume Information" window.

Volume Name. If this is the first volume, INSTALL will have already filled in the "Volume Name" field with "SYS." You can edit any volume name except the default name of SYS for the first volume. We suggest you use short names such as VOL1 or DATA for subsequent volumes.

Block Size. The default block size is 4KB. Other available block sizes are 8KB, 16KB, 32KB, and 64KB. The block size of a volume can affect its performance. Larger block sizes generally offer greater performance. However, if the block size is more than twice the size of the average data file, the perfomance effects are minimal.

For servers with more than a gigabyte of storage, another factor in selecting a block size is the amount of RAM the server has. Each block requires 23 bytes of cache; if a volume has name space support, each block requires the default 23 bytes of cache, plus 9 bytes for each name space it supports. While this calculation will overestimate RAM requirements for servers with more than a gigabyte of storage, it is better to be prepared, rather than surprised.

According to our calculation method, a 1GB volume with 4KB blocks and no name space support will therefore require 6,029,312 bytes (around 6MB) of RAM just for file, directory, and FAT caching, and for other volume overhead. Remember, each block requires 23 bytes; there are 262,144 4KB blocks on a 1GB volume.

Now, if you create the same 1GB volume using 8KB blocks, you'll have half as many blocks to cache. (There are 131,072 8KB blocks on a 1GB volume.) Cache requirements for a 1GB volume with 8KB blocks are around 3MB. The same principal applies for 16KB, 32KB, and 64KB block sizes.

Finally, the larger the block size, the less efficient the volume will be in using all its space to store files. On average, half of a block will be wasted at the end of each file on a given volume. For example, each file occupies at least one block. A 1KB file occupies at least one block. If you're working with a volume that has 4KB blocks, a 1KB file consumes 4KB of volume space. For a volume with 8KB blocks, that same 1KB file consumes 8KB (one block) of volume storage.

It's best to keep the volume block size small for overall faster file I/O. However, if your server machine is short on RAM, or if most of your files are large, you can use a larger block size.

Now let's discuss the implications a volume's block size has for the cache. NetWare allows you to configure the size of its cache buffers by using a special command-line switch when you start SERVER.EXE. The basic rule is that cache buffers larger than a volume's block size decrease server performance. (In fact, NetWare won't mount a volume that has a smaller block size than its cache buffers.) Cache buffers that match a volume's block size provide the greatest performance benefits. Finally, cache buffers smaller than a volume's block size have no negative effect on performance.

It seems obvious that you should always set NetWare's cache buffer size to be equal to the volume block size. However, what do you do when you have several volumes of different block sizes? The answer is that you set NetWare's cache buffer size equal to the block size of the volume with the smallest blocks. For example, imagine the following volume configuration:

SYS: 8KB blocks
DATA: 16KB blocks
ARCHIVE: 32KB blocks

If you boot a server with the above volume configuration, you'll realize the greatest caching benefits with 8KB cache buffers. To set NetWare v3.11's cache buffers to 8KB (8,192 bytes), start SERVER.EXE by typing at the DOS prompt:

```
SERVER -C8192 <Enter>
```

When NetWare boots, it will display a message stating that the cache buffer size is 8192 bytes (8KB). If you omit the "-C" option when executing SERVER.EXE, NetWare v3.11 will initialize using its default cache bufffer size of 4KB. If you try to initialize NetWare v3.11 with a cache buffer size larger than the block size of a particular volume, NetWare will refuse to mount that volume.

Once you decide what a volume's block size will be, edit the "Volume Block Size" field in the "Volume Information" window.

Adding Volume Segments

So far you've named the volume, set the volume's block size, and learned about the relationship between volume blocks and cache buffers. You still need to define the size of the volume by adding partition space to it. (Remember, partitions are the "raw materials" of which volumes are constructed.) A NetWare v3.11 volume can consist of up to 32 segments. Typically, each segment will consist of a one-partition disk (the entire disk has one NetWare partition on it), although you can create multiple volume segments on a single partition.

To add a segment to a volume, highlight the "Volume Segments" field of the "Volume Information" window and press <Enter>. If the server has only one hard disk, NetWare v3.11 assumes you want to use the entire NetWare partition for the first volume (SYS). It calculates the number of blocks available on the partition and

161

fills that number in as the default. If you want to create other volumes in that single NetWare partition, decrease the segment size to your preference and press <Esc.>

Note that when you create a volume, the "Volume Segments" field determines the number of blocks the volume should have. For an existing volume, the "Volume Segments" field is strictly for adding segments to the existing volume.

Finishing the Volume Creation Process

INSTALL will ask you if you want it to create the volume as you have defined it: answering "Yes" to the prompt causes NetWare to create the volume. INSTALL will then return you to the "Volume Information" window.

To mount the new volume, highlight it within the window and press <Enter>. Once again, INSTALL will display the "Volume Information" window (the one you just used to edit the block and segment size and to create the volume). This time, move the cursor to the "Status" field and press <Enter>. NetWare will display a two-item menu, with the items "Mount Volume" and "Dismount Volume." Select "Mount Volume" and press <Enter>.

Variations for Servers with More Than One Disk

If the server has more than one hard disk, INSTALL will behave a little differently when creating volumes from the way we've just described it. Rather than displaying the "Volume Information Window" immediately after you select "Insert New Volume," INSTALL displays a window showing partitions available for additional volume segments. To add a segment, highlight a partition from the available list and press <Enter>. Continue adding segments until you've defined the volume as you wish (up to 32 segments). Note that you can add segments to the volume later without destroying data or bringing the server down.

After you select segments for a volume, the remainder of the volume creation procedure is the same as for a single-disk server as described above.

Copying the System and Public Files

At this point, your server possibly has a DOS boot partition with the DOS system files on it. It certainly has a SYS volume, and may have additional NetWare volumes. The one remaining task in INSTALL is to copy the NetWare system and public files to the appropriate directories on the SYS volume.

1. From the INSTALL "Installation Options" menu, select "System Options."

2. Select "Copy System and Public Files." INSTALL will prompt you to place the SYSTEM-2 diskette in the A: drive. INSTALL will then begin downloading files from the floppy diskette to the SYS:SYSTEM and SYS:PUBLIC directories.

3. When INSTALL has finished downloading files from the SYSTEM-2 diskette, it will prompt you to insert the next diskette, and so on, until it has downloaded all the files it needs.

The SYSTEM-1 diskette contains the files necessary to get NetWare v3.11 running and to provide it with the ability to address its volumes (disk drivers). We recommended earlier that if your server has a DOS boot partition, you should copy the entire SYSTEM-1 diskette to that partition. The SYSTEM-1 diskette contains an important NLM called VREPAIR. VREPAIR is important because it can repair damaged NetWare v3.11 volumes. Since NetWare loads its NLMs from the SYS volume, why should you copy VREPAIR to the DOS boot partition? If the server's SYS volume is damaged, it won't have access to its NLMs, so it won't be able to load them. If VREPAIR is on the SYS volume, NetWare won't be able to load the very NLM that can repair its SYS volume. That's why VREPAIR is on the DOS boot volume. (You'll read more about VREPAIR in Chapter 24.)

If you wish, you can do a quick check to be certain VREPAIR is on the DOS boot partition by going to the server console and typing:

```
LOAD C:\VREPAIR <Enter>
```

When VREPAIR loads, select the "Exit" option, and NetWare v3.11 will unload it for you. If VREPAIR doesn't load, you may want to recopy the SYSTEM-1 diskette to the DOS boot partition and restart NetWare. It's nice to know you have VREPAIR handy in case you need it.

CHAPTER 6

Loading Server LAN Drivers

Once you get your NetWare v3.11 server running with its disks properly set up, it is time to load the LAN drivers you'll need to support network communication. As NetWare v3.x has evolved to support different transport protocols, its LAN drivers have necessarily become more sophisticated. At the very minimum, you must assign to a LAN driver a network address and hardware parameters (interrupt, I/O port, memory addresses, and DMA) that don't conflict with other devices when you load it. However, depending on your server's configuration and site, you may need to assign and define quite a bit more when loading a LAN driver.

This chapter explains how to properly load and configure LAN drivers on your server. Before we get into the actual instructions, however, we need to explain a little bit about NetWare's Open Data-Link Interface specification and what frame types are.

Open Data-Link Interface Drivers

NetWare v3.11 server LAN drivers conform to the NetWare Open Data-link Interface (ODI) specification. The ODI driver specification separates the different modules of a LAN driver into protocol stacks, hardware-specific modules (HSMs), and media-specific modules (MSMs).

- Protocol stacks correspond to transport protocols such as IPX/SPX, AppleTalk, and TCP/IP.

- HSMs correspond to specific network interface boards, such as the NE2000, Token-Ring Adapter/A, and 3C505.

- MSMs correspond to specific media types, such as Ethernet, Arcnet, and Token-Ring.

In addition, a Link Support Layer (LSL) provides a multiplexing interface between transport stacks, HSMs, and MSMs, allowing a single board to service multiple protocol stacks concurrently. Figure 6-1 is a block diagram of how ODI drivers work on a v3.11 server.

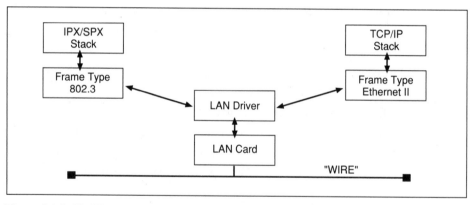

Figure 6-1: In NetWare's server-based ODI model, the server can support multiple transport protocols (in this case, IPX/SPX over Ethernet 802.3 and TCP/IP over Ethernet II).

Each component of the ODI specification communicates with the components above and below it, using a well-defined interface. In Figure 6-1, the HSM is communicating with the LAN adapter below it and the Link Support Layer (LSL) above it. The LSL is multiplexing two different MSMs—Ethernet using the 802.3 frame type, and Ethernet using the Ethernet II frame type. Each MSM is communicating with a different transport stack: Ethernet 802.3 is communicating with IPX/SPX, and Ethernet II is communicating with TCP/IP. The LSL is multiplexing the two media and protocol stacks to the HSM.

Media and Frame Types

You may be wondering what the difference is between media types and frame types. The distinction between these two entities is important primarily for NetWare v3.11 servers using a media type of Ethernet. Basically, a particular frame type is a variation of a media type. Each frame type represents a slightly different method of encapsulating data for its media. Most NetWare v3.11 Ethernet MSMs support four different frame types:

- 802.3 (the default frame type)

- Ethernet II

- 802.2

- Ethernet SNAP

802.3 Frames

802.3 is the default frame type for NetWare ODI drivers. You should use 802.3 only if you're running IPX/SPX and no other protocol stack. 802.3 frames encode the packet length within the third field of the packet (see Chapter 1 for a discussion of the fields in an IPX packet). Other Ethernet frame types use the third field to specify the higher-level transport protocol that is encapsulated within the Ethernet packet. The data length encoded in 802.3 Ethernet frames is useful to NetWare, but not required.

If you're running transport protocols other than IPX/SPX on the same Ethernet network, 802.3 frames don't supply the Link Support Layer with any information regarding the specific transport packet encapsulated within the Ethernet packet. This defeats the LSL's protocol multiplexing mechanism.

Ethernet II Frames

Ethernet II frames are exactly the same as 802.3 frames, except that they use the third field of the packet to store a value indicating which type of transport packet is encapsulated within the Ethernet packet. When you use Ethernet II frames, for example, the LSL can discover whether there is a TCP/IP packet, an IPX/SPX packet, or some other type of packet encapsulated within the Ethernet packet. Ethernet II frames are required to support TCP/IP on a NetWare v3.11 server.

802.2 Frames

802.2 frames are the same as 802.3 frames, except they have Logical Link Control (LLC) information encoded within them immediately following the 802.3 length field. LLC information provides drivers with the ability to maintain logical connections, or sessions, much the same way the NetWare's SPX does. 802.2 frames also have space for other information about transport packets encapsulated within the Ethernet packet.

If you're installing NetWare v3.11 on an internetwork where 802.2 frames are active, you must configure NetWare to also use 802.2 frames. If you don't, NetWare v3.11 can possibly "break" internetwork nodes by broadcasting non-802.2 Ethernet frames. ("Breaking" a node renders it incapable of functioning on a network.)

Ethernet SNAP Frames

SNAP stands for "Sub-Network Address Protocol" and represents yet another frame type that contains higher-level transport protocol information. SNAP was originally developed to allow encapsulation of IP datagrams and Address Resolution Protocols (ARP) packets within either the 802.2 or 802.3 Ethernet frames. However, SNAP is now also used by non-Ethernet media drivers such as Token-Ring, and for transports other than TCP/IP, such as AppleTalk Phase II.

Like 802.2 frames, SNAP frames are encapsulated within 802.3 or Ethernet II frames. The first three SNAP data fields are exactly the same as the first three fields of 802.2 frames, ensuring that SNAP and 802.2 are compatible. The remainder of SNAP information includes protocol information and an "ethertype" field, like the type field in Ethernet II frames. You can use SNAP frames on a NetWare v3.11 server to support TCP/IP over either Ethernet media or Token-Ring media.

Figure 6-2 summarizes the four different frame types we have discussed here.

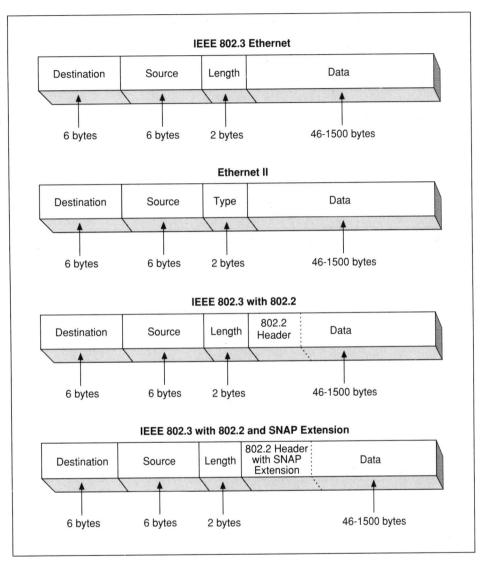

Figure 6-2: NetWare v3.11 supports four types of Ethernet frames.

Server-based ODI and the sophistication it brings to NetWare v3.11 means you have many options when loading LAN drivers:

- You can bind multiple packet types to a single LAN adapter.

- You can bind multiple transports to a single LAN adapter.

- You can use multiple LAN adapters, each supporting a single transport.

- You can use a single LAN adapter that supports multiple transports.

- You can use any combination of LAN adapters, frame types, and transports supported by the server's hardware and the LAN adapters installed on that server.

Figure 6-3 shows a NetWare v3.11 server's MONITOR screen displaying four supported frame types bound to a single NE2000 Ethernet board.

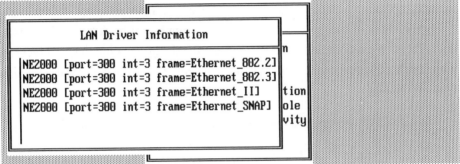

```
NetWare v3.11 (20 user) - 2/20/91          NetWare 386 Loadable Module
```

```
                    Information For Server KAITLIN

    File Server Up Time:    0 Days 21 Hours 14 Minutes  0 Seconds
    Utilization:            2          Packet Receive Buffers:    10
    Original Cache Buffers: 2,657      Directory Cache Buffers:   29
    Total Cache Buffers:    2,144      Service Processes:          1
    Dirty Cache Buffers:        0      Connections In Use:         1
    Current Disk Requests:      0      Open Files:                 8
```

```
              LAN Driver Information

 NE2000 [port=300 int=3 frame=Ethernet_802.2]
 NE2000 [port=300 int=3 frame=Ethernet_802.3]
 NE2000 [port=300 int=3 frame=Ethernet_II]
 NE2000 [port=300 int=3 frame=Ethernet_SNAP]
```

Figure 6-3: ODI allows a single NE2000 board to support four different Ethernet frame types.

Note that the I/O port and interrupt are the same for each "logical" board, because it is the same physical board. But the frame type is different for each instance of the driver. The Ethernet II frame is bound to TCP/IP, while the other frames are bound to IPX.

We'll explain more about ODI, LAN drivers, and frame types—and how to troubleshoot related problems—in Chapter 25. For now, follow the instructions below to load the LAN drivers you need on your NetWare v3.11 server.

Loading LAN Drivers

In Chapter 1, we explained the NetWare v3.11 Loader and how it links NLMs to the kernel at load time. ("Load time" simply means the time you load the NLM from the server console.) We also explained that LAN and DISK drivers are special types of NLMs. Therefore, the method of loading LAN drivers is basically the same

171

as for loading NLMs: You load LAN drivers (and all other NLMs) using the NetWare LOAD command, typed from the server console. However, loading LAN drivers is a bit more complicated because of things such as transports, media types, frame types, interrupt, I/O port, and memory options.

Before we explain the syntax for loading LAN drivers, we should warn you that there is no single set of command-line options that covers every LAN driver. Different LAN adapters support different hardware options, and different drivers support different configuration options. Further, different bus types in the server machine, such as ISA, EISA, and Micro Channel, affect both the hardware and software options available for a particular driver and LAN adapter.

Some types of machines support a greater number of installed LAN adapters than others. We recommend that you rely on the documentation that you received with your hardware (both server hardware and network interface hardware) for these types of details.

To load LAN drivers, use this syntax, typed from the server console:

```
LOAD [path] DriverName [parameters] <Enter>
```

Loading a driver initiates communication between the driver and the LAN adapter. Binding a transport protocol stack to the driver name or board name (note that you can assign a board a logical name) initiates communication between the NetWare v3.11 kernel and the board via the transport protocol stack.

LAN Driver Options

We've already discussed some of the more important optional parameters by explaining transport protocols and frame types. Here is a detailed explanation of some of the more common options. (Remember, the options available to you depend on your specific LAN adapter, driver software, and server machine.)

INT=number

All Intel-based computers allow devices, such as LAN or disk drivers, to notify the CPU they are in need of service by generating an interrupt. For example, if a LAN adapter receives data from the network, its driver generates an interrupt. As soon as possible, the machine's CPU will turn its attention to the LAN adapter's driver and processes the driver's data.

Interrupts do more than notify the machine's CPU that a device is in need of service. Each device on a machine is assigned a distinct interrupt number. Not only does this allow the machine's CPU to identify the device in need of service, but it ensures that only one device present on the system bus can be serviced by the CPU at a given time.

The critical thing here is that each device (disk controller, LAN adapter, and so on) must be configured to use a different interrupt. In addition, drivers for specific LAN adapters support a finite set of available interrupts. You should consult the documentation you received with the LAN adapter and driver for a list of supported interrupt values.

If you try to load a NetWare v3.11 network driver using an unsupported interrupt or an interrupt already in use by another device, NetWare will refuse to load the driver. If you load a network driver without specifying the interrupt, NetWare will prompt you to select an interrupt and will display a set of available (supported and not already in use) interrupts for that LAN adapter and driver.

DMA=number

DMA refers to Direct Memory Access. Intel-based computers have DMA controllers that device drivers can use to transfer data from DMA-enabled devices, such as LAN or disk adapters, directly to system memory.

When a LAN adapter receives a packet from the network media, it "unwraps" the packet, removing the header (which contains addressing information) and the trailer (which usually contains error correction information). The remaining information should be a higher-level transport protocol packet, such as an IPX packet. This is the data that needs to be copied into a receive buffer in the machine's system memory.

DMA-enabled devices allow the machine's DMA controller to copy data to buffers in the machine's system memory. While the data is being copied, the machine's CPU can perform other tasks. Non- DMA devices, on the other hand, must rely on the machine's CPU to transfer data from a LAN or disk adapter to system memory.

All things being equal, a DMA-enabled device will always provide better performance than a non-DMA device, because of the reduced load on the machine's CPU. Note that DMA is appropriate for disk adapters as well as LAN adapters. In either case, the principle is the same, and the advantages of DMA are equally desirable.

The DMA parameter is the DMA controller number (located on the server) that the LAN driver will use to transfer the "unwrapped" packet to system memory. You must specify the DMA controller number when you load the driver. For a list of supported DMA controllers, consult the documentation for the LAN adapter and driver in question.

Note that you should only have to specify a DMA controller for ISA-based LAN adapters. Both EISA and Micro Channel adapters allow you to use configuration software to set DMA controllers. You must configure these adapters before you begin the NetWare v3.11 installation process as part of the hardware setup. If you have EISA- or Micro Channel-based server hardware, consult the documentation you received with the server machine.

One exception here involves using an ISA-based LAN adapters in an EISA-based server machine. In this case, you must configure the LAN adapters using the jumpers on the board. Also use the EISA configuration to inform the server machine of the board's DMA configuration.

PORT=number

The PORT parameter specifies an I/O address that a server's processor uses to send or receive data from a peripheral. When you assign a port number to a LAN adapter, you're specifying the I/O address the server's processor will use to communicate with the adapter's driver. The PORT parameter applies only to ISA-based LAN adapters and drivers; both EISA and Micro Channel machines establish port addresses during the setup process.

The port addresses supported by a specific LAN adapter are defined by that adapter's driver. If you omit the port parameter when loading a LAN driver, NetWare v3.11 will prompt you to enter a port address and will display a list of valid, unused port addresses.

MEM=number

The MEM parameter specifies a range of memory that will be shared by the device driver and the NetWare operating system. "Shared memory" is memory that both the driver and the OS can read from and write to. NetWare uses shared memory as an efficient method of transferring data from a driver to the OS.

Drivers that require this parameter will have a small set of supported memory addresses, so you should consult the documentation that you received with the LAN adapter and driver to discover what these addresses are. For drivers to which the MEM parameter applies, it is not optional; if you load the driver without specifying an address, the driver will prompt you for an address and will display for you a list of addresses that are both supported and not currently in use by another driver.

FRAME=frame type

We discussed frame types earlier in this chapter. In addition to the Ethernet frame types discussed, IBM Token-Ring and PC Network drivers support 802.2, 802.5, and SNAP frames. (802.5 is the ANSI standard for token-passing media.) Consult the documentation for the LAN adapter and driver in question.

NAME=board name

Because you can use multiple LAN adapters of the same type in a server, NetWare v3.11 allows you to identify each board with a name of up to 17 characters. This is useful, for example, if you have two NE2-32 boards installed in your server and you want to bind a different transport protocol to each board, as follows:

```
LOAD NE2-32 SLOT=1 NAME=ipxspx FRAME=Ethernet_II <Enter>

LOAD NE2-32 SLOT=2 NAME=tcpip FRAME=Ethernet_II <Enter>

BIND IPX TO ipxspx <Enter>

BIND IP to tcpip <Enter>
```

The first command above loads the NE2-32 driver, links it to the NE2-32 EISA Ethernet board installed in slot 1 of the server, names the board "ipxspx," and forces it to broadcast Ethernet II frames.

175

The second command loads the same NE2-32 driver re-entrantly, links it to a second NE2-32 EISA Ethernet board installed in slot 2 of the server, names the board "tcpip," and forces it to broadcast Ethernet II frames.

The remaining two commands bind IPX to the board named "ipxspx" and IP to the board named "tcpip," respectively.

When NetWare loads a driver "re-entrantly," it means that the driver has been loaded at least once, and NetWare is getting a request to load the driver once more. Rather than load the entire driver again, NetWare initializes additional data structures and buffers for a second device, but uses the previously- loaded driver code to service the device for which you are loading the driver again. Re-entrant loading of device drivers results in more efficient use of server memory.

Once you name a LAN adapter, you can use the board name on the console command line instead of the name of the LAN driver. Because the LAN driver is used re-entrantly (the same driver can be loaded more than once), whenever you have more than one adapter of the same type installed in a server, it isn't enough to refer to the adapter by the name of its driver. If you do, NetWare will have to prompt you to select a specific adapter and will display a list of loaded drivers of the same type by their slot numbers, interrupt settings, or some other distinguishing factor, depending on the type of adapter in question. It's much easier to name each adapter of the same type when you're using more than one LAN adapter in the server.

You can also specify more than one name for the same LAN adapter whenever you're using more than one frame type with that adapter. To assign a second frame type to a board, you must load the adapter's LAN driver re-entrantly. When you do so, you can simply specify a unique name for the driver.

NODE=number

NODE overrides the 12-digit hexadecimal number assigned to NE-1000 and NE-2000 Novell Ethernet boards. Every Ethernet board has a unique hexadecimal address burned into its firmware. When the board broadcasts on the network, it uses this address as its node number. Node numbers are designed to be unique. Every manufacturer of Ethernet boards is assigned a range of node numbers to burn into its boards to ensure there are no conflicting Ethernet addresses on a given network. If you choose to override the node address of an NE-1000 or NE-2000, verify that the node address you specify is indeed unique, or you'll cause routing problems on the network.

RETRIES=number

RETRIES is an optional parameter that specifies how many times a driver will attempt to resend a network packet after failing to send the packet the first time. A certain number of failures to send a packet is normal for Ethernet and Arcnet adapters because the possibility exists for packet collisions. (Token-Ring networks should never have packet collisions because of the way they are designed.) Both Ethernet and Arcnet were designed to recover gracefully from collisions by trying again to send the packet. The RETRIES parameter allows you to define how many retries can occur before the packet transmission is deemed a failure by NetWare v3.11.

The default for most LAN adapters and drivers is to retry a packet transmission five times. Under normal conditions, five retries should be sufficient to transmit a packet successfully. However, under high-load conditions or on high-traffic LAN segments, it may be necessary to increase RETRIES to a higher number. Most drivers will allow you to set RETRIES as high as 255.

NetWare v3.11 will not report a transmission error until the driver has already exceeded its RETRIES parameter. Therefore, if you receive transmission errors, you should assume that the server has exceeded its retry count for the driver in question and raise the driver's retry count. The only way to do this is to unload the driver and load it again with a higher number for the RETRIES parameter.

SLOT=number

SLOT applies to EISA- or Micro Channel-based servers, but not to ISA-based servers. SLOT simply informs the driver where to look for the LAN adapter you wish to link to the driver. For example, to load a NE2-32 driver and link it to a NE2-32 adapter located in slot 3 of the EISA-based server, use "SLOT=3" as a parameter when you load the driver. If you specify an incorrect SLOT value, NetWare v3.11 can't initialize the LAN adapter, so it won't load the driver.

177

TBC=number

TBC applies only to the TOKEN driver, which supports both ISA and Micro Channel-based Token-Ring adapters. TBC stands for "Transmit Buffer Count" and specifies the number of transmission buffers the TOKEN driver should maintain. The range of buffers is zero to two, with the default setting being two.

TBZ=number

This parameter applies only to the TOKEN driver. TBZ specifies the size of each transmission buffer you create using the TBC parameter. The valid range is 96 to 65,535 bytes, with the default size being zero. When you set TBZ to zero, the buffer size becomes the maximum packet size allowed by either the LAN adapter or the operating system, whichever is lower.

Binding Transport Protocol Stacks to LAN Drivers

Once you load a network interface driver successfully and link it to a LAN adapter, you still have to BIND a protocol stack to the driver. Until you do, the driver won't transmit or receive any network packets. Because NetWare v3.11 LAN drivers are all written to the ODI specification, you can bind multiple transport protocol stacks to the same driver via the ODI link-support layer. The basic syntax for the BIND command is:

```
BIND Protocol TO LANDriver | BoardName [Driver Param-
eter...] [Protocol Parameter] <Enter>
```

The BIND command links a transport protocol stack, such as IPX/SPX, to the link-support layer of the LAN driver. Note that you can use either the LAN driver name or the board name, as discussed above.

One important point about the BIND command concerns its optional driver parameters. These are the same driver parameters you use when loading the LAN driver. However, when used with the BIND command, their purpose is not to configure the driver, but rather to identify a specific LAN adapter when more than one board of the same type is active at the server. In other words, you're only specifying driver parameters in order to single out a specific board to which you wish to bind the transport protocol stack in question. You can't configure drivers using the BIND command.

Protocol parameters vary according to the protocol stack you're binding. The only protocol parameter supported by IPX is a hexadecimal network number. For example:

```
BIND IPX TO NE2000 [INT=3] NET=00HBABEE <Enter>
```

Alternatively, if you named a LAN adapter when you loaded its driver, you could specify a name rather than a driver parameter such as the adapter's interrupt in the example above:

```
BIND IPX TO ipxspx NET=00HBABEE <Enter>
```

NetWare v3.11's TCP/IP stack supports the following NET parameters:

Parameter	Meaning
ADDR	IP network address
MASK	IP subnetwork mask (optional)
BCAST	Broadcast address (optional)
GATE	Gateway address (optional)
DEFROUTE	Establishes node as an IP gateway via RIP (optional)
ARP	Use Address Resolution Protocol (optional)
COST	Number of hops for IP routing purposes (optional)
POISON	IP routing parameter (optional)

For more information on NetWare's TCP/IP BIND parameters, see the Novell NetWare v3.11 *TCP/IP Transport Supervisor's Guide*.

Checking Driver Parameters with the CONFIG Command

The greatest potential for problems in the area of LAN drivers is specifying LOAD or BIND parameters that are incorrect or that conflict with other defined parameters at the server. Of all parameters, the source of the most problems is the "NET=*number*" parameter.

NetWare v3.11 provides a handy way for you to check the server's active LOAD and BIND parameters quickly, using the CONFIG console command. At the server console, simply type

```
CONFIG <Enter>
```

Here is an admittedly contrived example of the CONFIG console command's output:

```
File server name: KAITLIN
IPX internal network number: 000BABEE
NetWare NE2000 v3.11 (910131)
Hardware setting: I/O Port 300h to 31Fh, Interrupt 3h
Node address: 00001B330479
Frame type: Ethernet_802.3
No board name defined
LAN protocol: IPX network 0000BABE

NetWare NE2000 v3.11 (910131)
Hardware setting: I/O Port 300h to 31Fh, Interrupt 3h
Node address: 00001B330479
Frame type: Ethernet_II
Board name: Ethernet_II
LAN protocol: ARP
LAN protocol: IP address: 1.1.1.1 net mask: FF.0.0.0

NetWare NE2000 v3.11 (910131)
Hardware setting: I/O Port 300h to 31Fh, Interrupt 3h
Node address: 00001B330479
Frame type: Ethernet_802.2
No board name defined
No LAN protocols are bound to this LAN board
:
```

Note that you're asking for trouble if you use the 802.3 Ethernet frame type with a multiprotocol network. We included that parameter in this example just to show the different types of information you can obtain by using the CONFIG command.

The first item of information CONFIG gives is the server's name and its internal IPX network number. Then, for each logical network board, CONFIG shows the name and version of its driver, the hardware settings the driver was loaded with, the node address of the LAN adapter the driver is linked to, the frame type transmitted by the adapter and driver, the board name (if any), and the transport protocol stack bound to the adapter and driver.

CHAPTER 7

Loading NLMs and Editing Server Boot Files

The final phase of the NetWare server installation is to load the other NLMs you will need, and then edit the two server boot files (STARTUP.NCF and AUTOEXEC.NCF) automatically created in the process. With the proper commands in these boot files, your server can re-establish the desired configuration every time it is booted up. This chapter explains the NLMs commonly used on a NetWare v3.11 server and gives a general discussion of how to load NLMs. It then looks at how to create and edit the STARTUP.NCF and AUTOEXEC.NCF boot files for your server.

Loading NLMs on the Server

Although each NetWare v3.11 site is different, some NLMs that ship with NetWare are used by all or most NetWare v3.11 servers. For example, every NetWare v3.11 server runs INSTALL at least once. Another common NLM is MONITOR, which allows you to track NetWare's use of server resources. This section covers the loading of NLMs you are likely to run on your server most, if not all, of the time.

Common NLMs

Your server is likely to require most or all of the following NLMs during its day-to-day operation:

NLM Name	Function
MONITOR.NLM	Displays NetWare's use of server and OS resources
STREAMS.NLM	Provides NetWare STREAMS environment
CLIB.NLM	Provides NetWare v3.11 C interface
REMOTE.NLM	Provides the NetWare v3.11 Remote Console
RSPX.NLM	Provides a transport service for REMOTE.NLM
UPS.NLM	Provides UPS monitoring for the server
MAC.NAM OS/2.NAM NFS.NAM	Provide name spaces for Macintosh, OS/2 HPFS, and NFS file systems
NMAGENT.NLM	Collects and monitors server data for use by IBM's NetView network management program

At this point, you should load all the NLMs you know the server will require. Before you load these NLMs, consult the NetWare v3.11 *System Administration* manual for information about NLM parameters.

Loading the Monitor NLM

Let's start out by loading MONITOR. From the server console, enter this command:

```
LOAD MONITOR <Enter>
```

NetWare v3.11 will load MONITOR. The server console screen should appear similar to Figure 7-1.

```
 NetWare v3.11 (20 user) - 2/20/91              NetWare 386 Loadable Module

                        Information For Server KAITLIN

    File Server Up Time:    0 Days  0 Hours 23 Minutes  4 Seconds
    Utilization:                0 │ Packet Receive Buffers:    10
    Original Cache Buffers: 2,657 │ Directory Cache Buffers:   25
    Total Cache Buffers:    2,231 │ Service Processes:          1
    Dirty Cache Buffers:        0 │ Connections In Use:         1
    Current Disk Requests:      0 │ Open Files:                 8

                       ┌─────────────────────────┐
                       │     Available Options    │
                       ├─────────────────────────┤
                       │Connection Information    │
                       │Disk Information          │
                       │LAN Information           │
                       │System Module Information │
                       │Lock File Server Console  │
                       │File Open / Lock Activity │
                       │Resource Utilization      │
                       │Exit                      │
                       └─────────────────────────┘
```

Figure 7-1: When you load NetWare v3.11's MONITOR NLM, the console displays this initial screen.

The first thing you may have noticed about the command to load MONITOR is that you didn't have to specify a path on the console command line (such as "LOAD A:MONITOR"). The reason is simple. When you copied the NetWare system and public files to your server, INSTALL placed MONITOR.NLM in the server's SYS:SYSTEM directory, which is the default directory for NLMs. When you load an NLM without specifying a path, NetWare v3.11 assumes the NLM is in the SYS:SYSTEM directory, and searches for it in that directory.

You may wish to explore some of MONITOR's options and screens just to get a feel for how it works and what it does. The "Connection Information" option displays a list of users that currently have an active service connection with the server (meaning they are either logged in or attached). For each connection, you can see what files they have open, what file/record locks are in use, how many requests they have made to the server, and so on. You can find out who has a particular file open or locked by using the "File Open/Lock Activity" option. "Lock File Server Console" lets you password- protect the server's keyboard to prevent unauthorized users from entering console commands.

For more information about the "System Module Information" and "Resource Utilization" options, see Chapter 21. Further information about the "Disk Information" option is given in Chapter 24. The "LAN Information" option is covered in Chapter 25.

Dependent NLMs vs. Automatic NLM Loading

Many NetWare v3.11 NLMs depend on other NLMs being active and loaded. If you try to load an NLM for which a dependent NLM is not active, NetWare v3.11 may refuse to load it. For example, if you attempt to load BCONSOLE.NLM (Btrieve Console) without first loading BTRIEVE.NLM (upon which BCONSOLE is dependent), you'll see the following error messages:

```
:load bconsole
Loading module
BCONSOLE.NLM BCONSOLE
Loader cannot find public symbol: GetBCommStats
Load file referenced undefined public variable.
Module BCONSOLE.NLM NOT loaded
:
```

These messages indicate that BCONSOLE didn't load because it couldn't find a public variable called GetBCommStats in NetWare's memory space. GetBCommStats is a variable that BTRIEVE.NLM exports whenever it is active; BCONSOLE couldn't find the variable GetBCommStats because BTRIEVE was not active. The result is that BCONSOLE didn't load.

Another example of a dependent NLM is RSPX.NLM, which is dependent on REMOTE.NLM. If you try to load RSPX without first loading REMOTE, RSPX will not load. (Try it if you wish.)

BCONSOLE and RSPX are two examples of NLMs that don't load if other NLMs upon which they are dependent are not already loaded. However, this type of behavior is not universal. Many NLMs, if they discover that an NLM upon which they are dependent isn't active, will load the NLMs upon which they depend automatically. The best example of this behavior is CLIB.NLM, which is dependent upon STREAMS.NLM. If you attempt to load CLIB without first loading STREAMS, CLIB will load STREAMS for you. Some LAN drivers that are aware of NetView will auto-load NMAGENT.NLM, the NetWare v3.11 NetView agent.

Whenever you try unsuccessfully to load an NLM, chances are that you must first load another NLM, then load the NLM in question. Another possibility is that the NLM you're trying to load isn't in the SYS:SYSTEM directory and the NetWare v3.11 loader can't find it. A tip as to which possibility is behind the failure to load an NLM is the message you receive from the server console. If the console displays the message "Unable to find *NLM name*," you know that the NLM isn't in the SYS:SYSTEM directory. (Or, if you specified a path for the NLM, it isn't in the directory named by the path).

Otherwise, if the console displays a message similar to "Loader cannot find public symbol: *symbol name*," it found the NLM you wish to load, but discovered that another NLM must be loaded first.

Creating the Server Boot Files

When you install a NetWare v3.11 server and load NLMs for the first time, INSTALL keeps track of all the console commands you type and uses them to create the server boot files. Although you can edit the server boot files later, it's easier to load all the NLMs the server will use during the installation session, which causes INSTALL to create the boot files for you.

NetWare 3.11 maintains two boot files: STARTUP.NCF, which is located on the DOS boot partition; and AUTOEXEC.NCF, which is located on the SYS volume.

The purpose of STARTUP.NCF is simply to load the appropropriate disk drivers and name spaces. As soon as NetWare v3.11 loads its disk driver(s) and name space(s) from the STARTUP.NCF file, it automatically mounts the SYS volume, providing it with access to the AUTOEXEC.NCF file. NetWare then loads the AUTOEXEC.NCF file and proceeds with its initialization, using the commands contained in AUTOEXEC.NCF.

If you've loaded the NLMs you anticipate using during normal server operation, you're ready to create the server boot files. To do so, the INSTALL NLM must be loaded on the file server. Press <Alt><Esc> at the server console to cycle through the active console screens. If INSTALL is loaded, you should come across its screen. If it isn't loaded, load INSTALL by typing LOAD INSTALL <Enter> at the console. Figure 7-2 shows the INSTALL "Installation Options" menu.

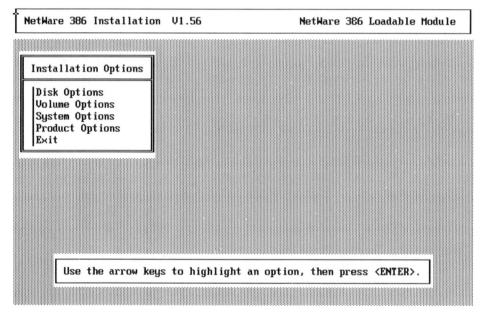

Figure 7-2: You can access the server boot files by selecting "System Options" from INSTALL's "Installation Options" menu.

Now, to create the server boot files, select "System Options" and press <Enter>. The "Available System Options" menu will appear.

```
    Available System Options
  ┌─────────────────────────────┐
  │Copy System and Public Files │
  │Create AUTOEXEC.NCF File     │
  │Create STARTUP.NCF File      │
  │Edit AUTOEXEC.NCF File        │
  │Edit STARTUP.NCF File         │
  │Return To Main Menu          │
  └─────────────────────────────┘
```

Creating the STARTUP.NCF File

To create the STARTUP.NCF file, select the "Create STARTUP.NCF" option and press <Enter>. INSTALL will then prompt you for a path where it should store the STARTUP.NCF file, as shown:

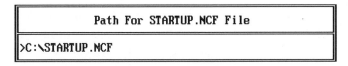

This path should point to the server's DOS boot partition (or floppy, if you're booting the server from a floppy).

When you enter (or accept) the path to the server's DOS boot partition, INSTALL will create the STARTUP.NCF file using information it infers from the current server configuration. Your server console screen should appear similar to Figure 7-3. Remember that your console display will probably be different, depending on the commands you used to start your server.

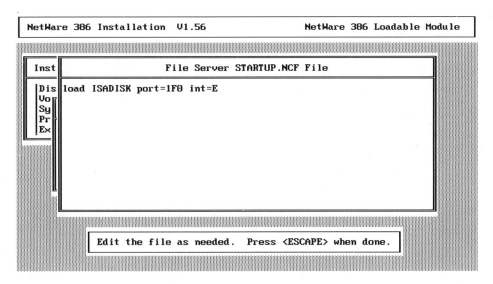

Figure 7-3: This is an example of a minimal STARTUP.NCF file created by INSTALL.

As indicated at the bottom of the screen, you can edit the STARTUP.NCF file as needed. For example, if you forgot to load name space modules (MAC.NAM, OS/2.NAM, or NFS.NAM), insert the commands for doing so here. When you've finished editing, press <Esc>, and INSTALL will save the STARTUP.NCF file to the server's DOS boot partition.

Remember that the purpose of STARTUP.NCF is to load the disk driver(s) and the name space(s) necessary to provide NetWare v3.11 with access to its SYS volume, and that's all. (The SYS volume mounts automatically, so you don't need to include a MOUNT command for it.)

Creating the AUTOEXEC.NCF File

Now you need to create an AUTOEXEC.NCF file. This file should include all the additional commands you will want the server to initialize with during normal operation. INSTALL starts the file for you based on information it derives from the current server configuration.

To create the AUTOEXEC.NCF file, select "Create AUTOEXEC.NCF" from the INSTALL "Available Systems Options" menu.

When you select the "Create AUTOEXEC.NCF", INSTALL displays its ready-made file for you; you don't need to provide it with a path name. That's because INSTALL assumes you want the file stored in the SYS:SYSTEM directory.

Your server console should now look much like the one shown in Figure 7-4. The specific commands you see in the AUTOEXEC.NCF file will depend on the console commands you type during your initial INSTALL session.

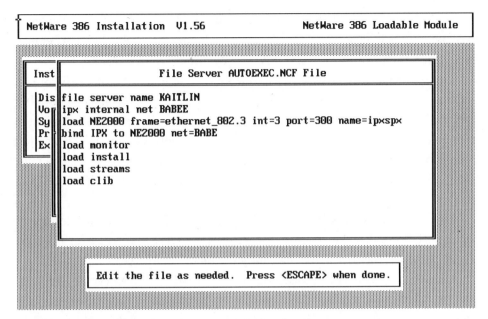

```
NetWare 386 Installation  V1.56              NetWare 386 Loadable Module

┌──────────────────────────────────────────────────────────┐
│ Inst │          File Server AUTOEXEC.NCF File             │
│ Dis│ file server name KAITLIN                             │
│ Vol│ ipx internal net BABEE                               │
│ Sy│ load NE2000 frame=ethernet_802.3 int=3 port=300 name=ipxspx │
│ Pr│ bind IPX to NE2000 net=BABE                           │
│ Ex│ load monitor                                          │
│   │ load install                                          │
│   │ load streams                                          │
│   │ load clib                                             │
└──────────────────────────────────────────────────────────┘

        Edit the file as needed.  Press <ESCAPE> when done.
```

Figure 7-4: INSTALL creates an AUTOEXEC.NCF using the console commands you enter during the installation process.

To save the newly created AUTOEXEC.NCF file, press <Esc> and answer the prompt "Save AUTOEXEC.NCF File?" by selecting "Yes" and pressing <Enter>.

Editing the Server Boot Files

After you create the server boot files using INSTALL, you can edit them at any time to add, change, or remove commands or parameters.

Sample STARTUP.NCF File

Let's look at a sample STARTUP.NCF file. (We added the line numbers for reference purposes.)

```
1    set cache buffer size=8192
2    load ISADISK.DSK port=1F0 int=E
3    load MAC.NAM
4    load OS2.NAM
```

Remember, the STARTUP.NCF file, located on the server's DOS boot volume, executes only as long as it takes for the server to mount the SYS volume. After that, execution resumes from the AUTOEXEC.NCF file.

Line 1 sets the cache buffer size for the server to 8KB (8,192 bytes). This is an optional command that we discussed in Chapter 5. If you don't specify a cache buffer size, NetWare v3.11 will initialize its cache buffers to 4KB, which is sufficient in most cases. The server's cache buffer size must be only as large as the smallest volume block size the server will encounter. As explained in Chapter 5, you must specify the server's cache buffer size either when you execute SERVER.EXE from the DOS command line or in the STARTUP.NCF file.

Line 2 loads the server's disk driver using an I/O port and an interrupt as parameters. Note that the specific disk driver or drivers you will load from the STARTUP.NCF file depend on the configuration of your server.

Lines 3 and 4 load name space modules for the Macintosh and OS/2 HPFS file systems. The server requires these modules to be loaded in order to support the alternate name spaces. In addition to these two name space modules, NetWare v3.11 also supports the Network File System (NFS) using the module NFS.NAM, which you can purchase as a separate product.

A short aside: In order to support alternative name spaces, you must explicitly add the name space support to each volume you want to store non-DOS files on. For example, if you want a volume to support Macintosh files, you must add Macintosh name space support to that volume using the following command:

```
ADD name space MACINTOSH to volume VolumeName <Enter>
```

The ADD command is strictly a one-time deal for each volume and name space pair. However, you must load the name space module every time the server boots, which is why the "LOAD NameSpace" command is in the STARTUP.NCF, while the "ADD NameSpace" command isn't.

Note that adding name space support to a volume approximately doubles the memory required to cache that volume for each name space you add. This is true regardless of whether or not you actually store any non-DOS files on the volume.

Sample AUTOEXEC.NCF File

Now let's look at a sample AUTOEXEC.NCF file:

```
1    echo on
2    # Name server and initialize internal network
3    file server name KAITLIN
4    ipx internal net BABEE

5    # Load NLMs
6    load install
7    load monitor
8    load streams
9    load clib
10   load remote coolbop
11   load rspx

12   # Load LAN driver with frame type and board name
13   load ne2000 frame=ethernet_802.3 int=3 port=300 name=ipxspx

14   # Bind ipx to board "ipxspx" with network number "babe"
15   bind ipx ipxspx net=babe

16   # If you have volumes other than SYS, mount them here
17   # using the MOUNT <volume name> command

18   # Secure console by removing DOS, preventing date and time
19   # changes, and disabling the NetWare debugger
20   secure console

21   # start router tracking screen
22   track on
```

Before diving into an analysis of the sample AUTOEXEC.NCF, let us first point out the meaning of the pound (#) signs scattered at the beginning of some lines in the file. When it encounters a "#" character at the beginning of a line in an AUTOEXEC.NCF file, NetWare v3.11 ignores that line and proceeds to the next one. In other words, you can use the "#" character to add comments to an

AUTOEXEC.NCF file.

Line 1 uses the "echo on" statement to cause NetWare to echo its startup commands as it executes them. With echo on, not only do you see the results of each command, such as "Volume VolumeName Mounted," but the commands themselves are also echoed on the console in the same form in which they're entered in the boot file.

The sole purpose of the "echo on" statement is for debugging of the server boot files. For example, if a statement in one of the boot files failes to execute properly (a module or driver didn't load, a volume didn't mount, or some similar problem), you can see the exact command echoed to the console in the same form it takes in the AUTOEXEC.NCF file. To turn echoing off, simply omit the statement from the AUTOEXEC.NCF file, or change it to "echo off."

Note that you can also use the echo on/off statement in the STARTUP.NCF file. You might, for example, wish to have STARTUP.NCF commands echoed, but not AUTOEXEC.NCF commands. In this case, you could place "echo on" in the STARTUP.NCF file, and "echo off" in the AUTOEXEC.NCF file. Or you could restrict echoing to a series of commands in a single file by bracketing those commands with "echo on" and then "echo off."

Line 2, as you may have inferred already, is a comment. Line three names the server, while line 4 assigns the server's internal IPX network, which must be a unique hexadecimal number of one to eight digits. (See the section on naming IPX networks in Chapter 5.)

Lines 6 through 10 load the server NLMs. You should load NLMs from the AUTOEXEC.NCF file only if you anticipate that those NLMs will decome part of the server's normal configuration. Remember that you can load and unload NLMs any time the server is up and running, so it's a good policy to leave infrequently used NLMs unloaded until you need them. (This leaves more memory available for cache buffers.)

Note lines 10 and 11. These lines load the Remote Console (with a password "coolbop") and its transport service. The Remote Console allows you to gain access to the server's console from a network workstation, just as if you were at the console itself. The Remote Console is covered in detail in Chapter 28.

Lines 13 and 15 load a LAN driver, link it to a LAN adapter, and bind the IPX/ SPX protocol stack to the driver and adapter. Your server's AUTOEXEC.NCF may have more drivers, boards, frame types, and protocols to load, but the syntax is the same as in this example.

Note the comment lines 16 and 17, which, in this example, are placeholders for the MOUNT commands you would use for a multivolume server. Remember that the SYS volume mounts automatically. Because a single NetWare v3.11 volume can be several gigabytes in size, you'll rarely wish to have multiple volumes simply for the sake of storage space. However, there are other reasons. For example, you may wish to have different name space configurations on different volumes. Or you may wish to have different block sizes on different volumes, and so on.

Line 21 issues the SECURE CONSOLE command. SECURE CONSOLE doesn't lock the console (which you can do using a separate command from within MONITOR), but closes three security holes left available to someone who has physical access to the console. First, SECURE CONSOLE removes DOS from the server's memory. This is to prevent an individual from inserting a floppy diskette into one of the server's floppy drives and loading an NLM via the floppy diskette. It's fairly simple for a programmer to write an NLM that can change passwords, trustee rights, create users and assign security levels to users, delete users, "dump" the bindery to disk, and so on. However, with DOS removed from memory, it's impossible for an individual to load an NLM that isn't already in the NetWare v3.11 file system.

The second thing SECURE CONSOLE does is to disable the console TIME command. The TIME command allows you to change the server's date and time. By changing the server's date and time, an individual can bypass access restrictions you can set from within the SYSCON utility. For example, you can limit a user's network access to certain days or certian hours. If a user can only log in to the network during normal working hours, for example, that user could approach the console in the middle of the night, change the server's time to a normal working hour using the TIME command, and log in to the server. SECURE CONSOLE closes this security hole.

Finally, SECURE CONSOLE disables the NetWare v3.11 internal debugger. An individual who has sufficient knowledge can do just about anything he or she pleases using the NetWare debugger, so SECURE CONSOLE simply makes the debugger inactive.

Line 23 starts the NetWare v3.11 router tracking screen, which displays all routing activity within the server. We like to have this screen active, because it gives us a good indication of what's happening in the larger arena of the network. The TRACK ON and TRACK OFF console commands are covered in Chapter 10.

Using Alternate .NCF Files

SERVER.EXE supports three command-line parameters that allow you to use an alternate STARTUP.NCF file, or no *.NCF files at all. The syntax is:

```
SERVER -S [Path]FileName (to boot with a different
              STARTUP.NCF file)

SERVER -NA  (to boot without using the AUTOEXEC.NCF file)

SERVER -NS  (to boot using no *.NCF files whatsoever)
```

There is no command-line support for booting SERVER.EXE using an alternative AUTOEXEC.NCF parameter. That's because both the name and path of the AUTOEXEC.NCF file are fixed. (Just as the name, but not the path, of the DOS AUTOEXEC.BAT file is fixed.) The server's AUTOEXEC.NCF file is always stored in the SYS:SYSTEM directory.

You can, however, boot using an alternative AUTOEXEC.NCF by renaming the server's AUTOEXEC.NCF file to AUTOEXEC.BAK (or something similar), creating a new AUTOEXEC.NCF file using a text editor, and copying the new file to the server's SYS:SYSTEM directory.

CHAPTER 8

Troubleshooting the Server Installation

Those of you with experience in installing NetWare v2.x servers will quickly realize that NetWare v3.11 features a much more intuitive and flexible installation procedure than NetWare v2.x. However, you shouldn't infer from the relative elegance of NetWare v3.11's installation process that you're dealing with a simple operating system. NetWare v3.11 is a complex entity, made even more so by the creation of networking links to other servers and workstations.

Installing a NetWare v3.11 server is a rigorous task. Unless you understand fully what you're doing in each step of the installation process, you'll probably experience some errors and setbacks. The saving grace of NetWare v3.11's installation procedure—and what makes it superior to NetWare v2.x installation—is that you can always backtrack from a mistake gracefully, figure out what went wrong, and try again.

Because of the many factors influencing the installation of a NetWare v3.11 server, it's impossible for us to discuss every potential installation problem. Consequently, we recommend that you read thoroughly the overview of the NetWare v3.x operating system in Chapter 1. By doing so, you'll be better equipped to troubleshoot unforseen errors you encounter during the installation process. If you're upgrading from NetWare v2.x to NetWare v3.11, we also recommend you read Chapter 11, "Upgrading to NetWare v3.11," before attempting the upgrade.

Installation Trouble Spots

As you read in the previous chapters, server installation consists of four main steps:

- Creating NetWare v3.11 partitions and volumes using the INSTALL NLM

- Loading and configuring device drivers and NLMs

- Installing the SYS:SYSTEM and SYS:PUBLIC files

- Creating and editing the server boot files (STARTUP.NCF and AUTOEXEC.NCF)

During the first two steps above, you must make several explicit decisions, including the size, number, and block size of NetWare v3.11 volumes, network addresses, and network frame types. You also must load and configure system NLMs correctly.

Of all the tasks involved in installing a NetWare v3.11, those entailed in the first two steps above offer the greatest opportunity for errors. If you evaluate the first two steps above, you'll notice that their common denominator is they involve the low-level work of getting the NetWare v3.11 operating system to function correctly with the server machine and network hardware. And virtually all of the complexity of networking concerns the successful interaction of the network operating system with the server and networking hardware.

Installation Problems and Their Solutions

What follows is a discussion of what our experience proves are the most likely problems you'll encounter during server installation.

Problem: NetWare v3.11 recognizes only the first 16MB of memory.

Solution: Because of the design of most server machines, including Industry-Standard Architecture (ISA), Extended ISA (EISA), and Micro Channel designs, NetWare v3.11 by default recognizes only the first 16MB of server memory. This isn't a fault of NetWare, but is a result of the PC ROM BIOS program which is a part of all standard Intel-based personal computers.

In order to recognize and address memory above 16MB, you must instruct NetWare v3.11 explicitly as to the beginning address and limit of server memory above 16MB. To do this, you can use the REGISTER MEMORY console command. (Note: for EISA server machines, you don't use the REGISTER MEMORY command, but instead use a special SET parameter, which we will discuss shortly.)

The syntax for REGISTER MEMORY is as follows, from the server console:

```
REGISTER MEMORY Start Length <Enter>
```

where *Start* is the hexadecimal address of the seventeenth megabyte of memory, and Length is the amount in hexadecimal of the total server memory above 16MB. For example, register an additional 4MB of memory above 16MB (for 20MB of total server memory), the console command line is as follows:

```
REGISTER MEMORY 1000000 400000 <Enter>
```

The table below shows some common command-line parameters for registering memory above 16MB.

Total Memory	Start (hex)	Length (hex)
20MB	1000000	400000
24MB	1000000	800000
28MB	1000000	C00000

To register memory above 16MB for an EISA machine, use the console SET command as follows:

```
SET Auto Register Memory Above 16 Megabytes: on <Enter>
```

You should place either the REGISTER MEMORY or the "SET Auto Register Memory Above 16 Megabytes" commands in the server's AUTOEXEC.NCF file immediately after the lines defining the server's name and its internal IPX number.

Warning Regarding Memory Conflicts

Most 16-bit (ISA) disk or LAN adapters can't perform I/O using memory addresses greater than 16MB. If you successfully register memory greater than 16MB and also load device drivers for such adapters, NetWare v3.11 will experience memory addressing conflicts when attempting device I/O to these devices. Such conflicts will likely cause the server to go down and can result in corrupted data.

The only solution is to ensure that your ISA adapters are capable of addressing memory above 16MB. To do this, you should check with the adapter's vendor.

The preferred solution is to run NetWare v3.11 on an EISA machine. EISA adapters are, by design, capable of addressing memory above 16MB.

Problem: NetWare v3.11 runs out of memory when trying to mount a volume.

Solution: NetWare v3.11 requires more memory to mount a volume than it does to run with the volume mounted. This is due to the extensive consistency checking NetWare performs on volume data structures as part of the mounting process. You'll probably receive one of the following error messages when this occurs:

```
Attempt to allocate memory to read volume definition
     tables failed
Attempt to allocate memory to hold NetWare partition
     information failed
```

The best solution is to install additional memory in the server. However, if you have added name space support to the volume in question, you can use VREPAIR.NLM to remove one or more supported name spaces. This has the effect of reducing the amount of server memory required to mount the volume. It is, however, a destructive solution: It destroys extended attributes for files stored on the volume.

Problem: NetWare v3.11 runs out of memory when loading NLMs or when an NLM attempts to allocate memory.

Solution: The bottom line here is that the NetWare v3.11 server is out of memory. You read in Chapter 1 about NetWare v3.11's dynamic memory management. You may recall how NetWare v3.11 allocates memory for NLMs on an "as-needed" basis. Consequently, you're never guaranteed when you attempt to load an NLM that NetWare will be able to allocate sufficient memory for the NLM to run. Moreover, after the NLM is loaded and running, the possibility still exists that the NLM will fail in a request for NetWare to allocate more memory.

When NetWare v3.11 fails to allocate memory to load an NLM, or when a run-time NLM request for memory fails, you'll a message similar to "unable to allocate short term memory," or "unable to allocate *MemoryType*," where "memory type" is the particular memory pool from which the NLM requested memory. Another common vein of out-of-memory error messages is "Out of memory *Error*," where "error" is usually a specific type of memory, the request for which failed.

The first thing you should do is check MONITOR's main screen to see the state of the different memory pools in the NetWare v3.11 server. (For details on how to do this, read Chapter 21. Chapter 21 tells you what the MONITOR memory statistics mean and how to explore them further.)

If the problem occurs when you're attempting to load an NLM, the next thing to do is unload at least one other NLM and then try again to load the NLM in question. Unloading an NLM can free additional alloc memory, which NetWare v3.11 can use to fulfill requests to load an NLM.

One short-term fix you can apply to the server's memory management methods is to reduce the minimum number of cache buffers. By doing so, you allow NetWare v3.11 to free file cache buffer memory for use by NLMs. You can reduce the minimum number of cache buffers by using the NetWare v3.11 console SET command:

```
SET minimum file cache buffers: Number
```

where *Number* is the lowest number of file cache buffers the server will allow. The lowest valid number you can use with this SET parameter is 20, meaning that the NetWare v3.11 server will allow file cache buffers to be depleted for use by NLMs until the number of cache buffers reaches 20. As soon as the number of cache buffers reaches 20, NetWare v3.11 will refuse requests by NLMs (and the operating system itself) for further memory allocations.

Note that you can still free alloc memory after NetWare reaches its minimum level of cache buffers by unloading NLMs.

You read in Chapter 5 how to calculate NetWare v3.11 server memory requirements. You may recall from that chapter that volume block size and name space support affect the server's memory requirements. You can decrease memory requirements by using VREPAIR to remove volume name space support (see Chapter 24). You can also reduce server memory requirements by destroying a NetWare volume and re-creating it with a larger volume block size. Both of these steps, however, are destructive: They cause you to lose data. When you remove name space support, you lose extended attributes for files on the volume; when you destroy and re-create a volume, you lose all the data on the volume.

The best solution, as with all cases of insufficient memory on a NetWare v3.11 server, is to install more memory.

Problem: NetWare v3.11 can't load an NLM.

Solution: There are two cases (aside from insufficient memory, which is a different situation) in which NetWare v3.11 won't even attempt to load an NLM. The first case is when NetWare can't find the NLM in one of its volumes or a DOS partition. The second case is when NetWare can't find a loader symbol required by the NLM. Loader symbols represent library functions imported by the NLM, without which the NLM can't execute.

NetWare searches for NLMs in directories stored in the global variable "SEARCHPATH." By default, the search path includes SYS:SYSTEM. So when you attempt to load an NLM, NetWare v3.11 searches for that NLM in its SYS:SYSTEM directory.

You can add paths to the NetWare v3.11 search path using the SEARCH console command. The syntax for SEARCH is as follows, from the server console:

```
SEARCH [add [Number] Path]
SEARCH [del [Number]]
```

The first parameter, "add," causes SEARCH to add the second parameter, "path," to NetWare v3.11's search path. For example,

```
SEARCH add 2 SYS:PUBLIC\NLM <Enter>
```

causes Netware to search for NLMs first in the SYS:SYSTEM directory (the first element in the search path) and second in the SYS:PUBLIC\NLM directory.

To display the NetWare v3.11 server's current NLM search path, execute SEARCH with no parameters:

```
SEARCH <Enter>
```

NetWare will display on the server console information like this:

```
Search 1:[Server Path] SYS:SYSTEM Search 2: [DOS Path] C:
```

To remove a path from the server's NLM search path, execute SEARCH using the DEL parameter and the number of the path you wish to remove. For example:

```
SEARCH DEL 3 <Enter>
```

causes NetWare v3.11 to remove the third NLM search path.

Note that you can't execute SEARCH if you've previously executed the SECURE CONSOLE command at the NetWare v3.11 server console. SECURE

CONSOLE disables SEARCH, removes DOS from the server's memory, and prevents you from changing the server's date or time. SECURE CONSOLE doesn't delete the server's search path, but it does prevent you from altering the search path. Furthermore, SECURE CONSOLE makes it impossible to load NLMs from a DOS path, regardless of whether or not a DOS path is currently defined in the server's search path.

A second reason NetWare will refuse to load an NLM is if the NetWare v3.11 Loader is unable to export library functions the NLM in question wishes to import. Library functions are routines exported by Library NLMs (such as CLIB). For example, when you load CLIB, it exports all its functions, making those functions available to be called by other NLMs.

If you fail to load CLIB and subsequently attempt to load an NLM that requires functions exported by CLIB, NetWare may not be able to load the NLM in question. Note that this is true not only for NLMs that import CLIB functions, but for any NLM that imports functions. (We don't know of an NLM that doesn't import functions, although this is theoretically possible.)

Whenever NetWare v3.11 refuses to load an NLM because the loader can't find a symbol exported by the NLM in question, you will see a console error similar to this one:

```
Loader cannot find public symbol: Symbol
```

where Symbol is the name of the function required by the NLM in question.

The solution to this problem is to consult the documentation of the NLM you're attempting to load. You should search specifically for a table of NLMs that the NLM in question relies on for functions to import. When you discover the NLM or NLMs upon which the NLM you're attempting to load is reliant, load those NLM(s) first, and then attempt to load the NLM in question.

Problem: NetWare v3.11 can't load an NLM from its DOS volume or from a DOS floppy diskette.

Solution: Assuming you've set up the NetWare v3.11 server's search path correctly, as described previously, the problem here is that DOS is disabled on the server.

You can disable DOS by using either the REMOVE DOS console command or the SECURE CONSOLE console command. Both of these commands remove DOS from the NetWare v3.11 server's memory. As soon as DOS no longer resides in the server's memory, NetWare v3.11 no longer has access to its DOS partition or its floppy diskette drives.

The solution is to reboot the server and load the desired NLM from the DOS partition or floppy diskette. If you've placed either the REMOVE DOS or SECURE CONSOLE command in the NetWare v3.11 server's AUTOEXEC.NCF file, you'll have to execute SERVER.EXE from the DOS prompt using the -NA parameter as follows:

```
SERVER -NA <Enter>
```

The -NA parameter causes SERVER.EXE to execute without running its AUTOEXEC.NCF file.

Problem: NetWare v3.11 is unable to mount volume SYS.

Solution: Virtually every failure on the part of a NetWare v3.11 server to mount its SYS volume indicates some type of corruption of at least one operating system or file system data structure.

When NetWare v3.11 initializes its internal data structures, it performs exhaustive "consistency checks." A consistency check in this context means NetWare tests the format and contents of all its internal data structures against a set of pre-defined criteria. If a data structure fails a consistency check, NetWare v3.11 will fail to initialize.

Most of the internal consistency checks performed by NetWare v3.11 occur during the course of mounting volumes. Volumes contain directory tables, a File

Allocation Table (FAT), file chains, and more. Further, NetWare constructs file cache buffers, directory buffers, caches the FAT, and more, all in the course of mounting a volume.

Mounting the SYS volume is the most critical operation NetWare v3.11 performs during initialization, because the SYS volume contains the bindery files, transaction tracking data, and other important operating system information, without which NetWare v3.11 can't operate. If any of the critical data structures stored on the SYS volume are corrupt, NetWare won't mount the SYS volume.

The first thing you should do when NetWare is unable to mount the SYS volume is load and run VREPAIR.NLM. VREPAIR will identify corrupt volume data structures and attempt to repair them. We've found VREPAIR to have a very high success rate in repairing damaged NetWare v3.11 file systems.

You should always store a copy of VREPAIR on the server's DOS partition or on a floppy diskette. If you store VREPAIR on the server's SYS volume, then you'll be unable to load and run VREPAIR if the SYS volume becomes unmountable.

Problem: NetWare v3.11 won't bind a protocol stack to a network board.

Solution: The most common cause of failure to bind a protocol stack to a network interface board is an error in one of the BIND parameters. The syntax for bind is as follows, from the server console:

```
BIND Protocol [TO] LANDriver | BoardName [Driver Parameter...]
[Protocol Parameter ...] <Enter>
```

The first two conditions you must meet when using the BIND command are: first, Protocol must represent a valid protocol stack, such as IPX/SPX; and second, you must specify a valid LAN driver or board name (if you've named the board) to which NetWare v3.11 should bind the valid protocol stack.

If you're specifying a protocol stack other than IPX/SPX, you must have loaded that protocol stack using the LOAD command. For example, to load TCP/IP, you must issue a **LOAD tcpip** command; to load AppleTalk, you must issue a **LOAD**

appletlk command.

The board name or driver name to which you're binding the protocol stack must also be loaded. For example, if you're binding IPX/SPX to an NE2000 board, you must first have loaded the NE2000 LAN driver.

Finally, you must specify correct protocol and driver parameters for the protocol and driver you wish to unite with the BIND command. These parameters vary according to the protocol stack and driver in question, so you should check the protocol and driver documentation carefully. Typical driver parameters include interrupt numbers, memory addresses, and I/O addresses. Typical protocol stack parameters include network addresses, domain or zone names, and so on.

Since command-line parameters for the typical BIND command are fairly complex, we recommend that you double-check the entire console command line before executing a BIND command.

Note that a successful binding of a protocol stack to a board doesn't entail correct BIND parameters for your network and server. Rather, it entails valid BIND parameters. That is to say, you may have specified valid network numbers according to the network number syntax, but just because a network number is valid according to network syntax doesn't mean it is consistent with network numbers on your internet. If you specify a network number that is inconsistent with the configuration of your internet, the NetWare server will report routing configuration errors.

Problem: Router configuration errors are being displayed on the NetWare v3.11 console.

Solution: You bound IPX/SPX to a network interface board driver using a network address that conflicts with information stored in network routing tables maintained by other servers on the network. The NetWare v3.11 server is now receiving routing tables from other network servers, noticing the network address conflict, and generating the console error message.

Whenever you bind a protocol stack to a driver and board that are physically attached to a previously existing LAN segment, you must specify a network address that is consistent with the address other servers on that LAN segment are using to send and receive data over that LAN segment.

You should remove the protocol stack from the network interface board immediately, using the UNBIND console command. The syntax for UNBIND is the same as for BIND, except you don't specify any protocol parameters. The UNBIND command removes the protocol stack from the driver and causes the NetWare v3.11 server to cease broadcasting over that driver and board.

The next thing you need to do is find out why you specified a conflicting network address when you originally bound the protocol stack to the driver. Perhaps you made a typographical error in the BIND command line. If the NetWare v3.11 server has multiple network adaptor boards, perhaps you bound IPX/SPX to the wrong driver and board. Perhaps you have incorrect documentation of network addresses. Regardless of the source of the error, you should ensure that you have correct address information before attempting once more to bind the protocol stack to the driver and board.

Problem: Users can't log in to the server even though they use correct passwords.

Solution: NetWare v3.11 assumes all passwords sent to it over the network are in encrypted format by default. Older versions of NetWare workstation utilities (such as LOGIN and ATTACH) don't encrypt passwords before sending them to the server over the network.

If workstations are using older versions of the NetWare utilities, you should upgrade all workstations on the network to v3.11 utilities. Doing this will cause workstations to emit encrypted passwords, thereby solving the problem.

Another option is to configure the NetWare v3.11 server to accept unencrypted passwords. You can do this with the console SET command:

```
SET allow unencrypted passwords=on <Enter>
```

If your NetWare v3.11 server supports Macintosh workstations, you may want to allow unencrypted passwords. However, if you've purchased NetWare for Macintosh v3.0, you can configure Macintosh workstations to emit NetWare v3.11-supported encrypted passwords. To do this, refer to the NetWare for Macintosh v3.0 documentation.

Problem: Macintosh users can't "see" the NetWare v3.11 server from within the Chooser.

Solution: Make sure that you've loaded AFP.NLM at the NetWare v3.11 server. Even though you may have loaded and configured AppleTalk support correctly, Macintosh clients won't be aware of the NetWare v3.11 server until you initialize Appletalk Filing Protocol (AFP) support on the server by loading AFP.NLM.

If AFP.NLM is loaded and Macintosh clients are still not aware of the NetWare v3.11 server, you should ensure that you loaded APPLETLK.NLM correctly and used correct network and zone addresses when you bound APPLETLK to the network driver and board. It's likely that you loaded and bound APPLETLK using valid zone and network addresses that are inconsistent with existing AppleTalk networks. Consult the NetWare for Macintosh v3.0 documentation for details.

Problem: Macintosh users can't mount a NetWare v3.11 volume.

Solution: Even if you've correctly loaded, configured, and bound APPLETLK.NLM and you've loaded AFP.NLM, Macintosh clients will be unable to mount NetWare v3.11 volumes unless you've explicitly added support for the Macintosh name space to those volumes.

To add Macintosh name space support to a volume, use the ADD console command from the server console:

```
LOAD mac <Enter> ADD name space macintosh to volume
VolumeName <Enter>
```

The first command, LOAD, causes the NetWare v3.11 server to load the MAC.NAM module, which is necessary in order for the server to process Macintosh file requests. The second command, ADD, installs Macintosh support on the volume named by the *VolumeName* parameter.

CHAPTER 9

Installing NetWare Workstations

Installing a workstation correctly is just as vital as installing the server correctly. Every network workstation installation includes both hardware components (network interface card or LAN adapter) and software components (client operating system, NetWare client software, and so on). This chapter reviews some simple, basic steps for installing and maintaining a successful network environment for each of the workstation types supported by NetWare v3.11.

Installing a DOS Workstation

For many years, the PC networking industry revolved mainly around computers running IBM's PC-DOS and Microsoft's MS-DOS operating systems. As a result, many people still think of NetWare as a product strictly for networking DOS-based PCs. What these people don't realize is that the first release of NetWare was actually designed for computers running CP/M (an early predecessor to MS-DOS). It was the runaway success of the IBM PC, XT, and AT machines in the mid-80s that convinced Novell to switch its main emphasis to DOS.

Today, DOS-based workstations remain one of the primary client platforms supported by NetWare, forming by far the largest installed base of NetWare workstations. Novell is continually upgrading its software offerings for DOS clients in the form of enhanced shells and timely support for new releases of DOS.

This section explains how to install a LAN adapter and the necessary NetWare workstation software in a machine running PC-DOS or MS-DOS.

Installing a LAN Adapter in a DOS Workstation

The exact procedure for installing a LAN adapter will vary, depending on the type of board (Ethernet, Token-Ring, Arcnet), the type of machine (PC/AT, notebook-type PC, or Macintosh), and the bus type (standard AT, Microchannel, or EISA). It is a good idea to read through the manufacturer's supplement manual for information concerning the limitations and configuration of your particular adapter.

Before installing the LAN adapter into your computer, make sure that your adapter is configured to avoid possible interrupt and I/O conflict with the computer. Refer to the supplement manual for the possible configurations. The specific configuration the adapter board uses must correspond with the correct driver in the NetWare software shell in order to allow the network adapter to "talk" to the LAN. If your adapter has the capability of using different types of media (twisted-pair or coaxial), make sure that that is appropriately configured on your LAN card.

If you're installing LAN adapters based on the Extended Industry Standard Architecture (EISA) or IBM's Micro Channel Architecture (MCA) technologies, you must run a software configuration program on the machine in which you are installing the adapter.

With most types of microcomputers (the exception being notebook computers with no expansion slot), the LAN adapter is placed in an expansion slot inside the computer. Here are the steps to follow in physically installing the adapter in your computer.

1. Check and record the settings on the adapter before the installation.

2. Turn off the power to the computer.

3. Properly ground yourself while working with hardware equipment.

4. Remove the cover of your machine to gain access to the bus expansion slots.

5. Remove the metal bracket covering the hole in the back of the computer.

6. Gently push the LAN adapter into the expansion slot, taking care that
    connectors protruding from the mounting bracket clear the opening.

7. Make sure the adapter is carefully fastened down (usually with a screw).

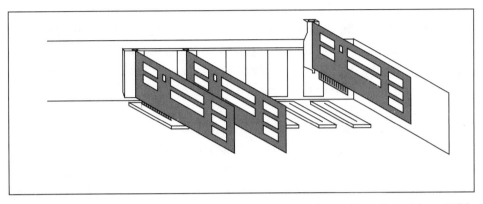

**Figure 9-1: A LAN adapter is installed just like any other add-on board in a DOS
workstation.**

Installing the DOS Workstation Software

The DOS workstation network software installation consists of generating a file
called IPX.COM (unique to the LAN adapter and configuration you're using) and
other associated files to boot up the machine on the network. We'll cover each step
you need to successfully get your workstation communicating with the network.

Before attempting to install the workstation software, you should have installed
the LAN adapter in the workstation, as explained.

1. Boot a workstation containing a high-capacity drive with DOS version 3.0
    or above.

2. Find the working copy of the diskette labeled WSGEN and insert it into the
    floppy diskette drive.

3. At the DOS prompt, type "WSGEN <Enter>."

4. After reading the introductory screen, press <Enter>.

5. Highlight the LAN driver that corresponds with the LAN adapter you installed in the workstation and press <Enter>.

   If the LAN adapter you want isn't on this list, press <Ins>. Then insert a diskette with a name like LAN_DRV_*xxx* (this diskette should have come with the LAN adapter) in the floppy disk drive and press <Enter>. Now highlight the LAN adapter you need from the expanded list and press <Enter>.

6. After selecting the correct LAN driver, highlight the configuration option that matches the settings on the LAN adapter and press <Enter>.

   If the configuration you need isn't listed, choose another non-conflicting one and set the LAN adapter to match. Some LAN drivers allow you to use Novell's JUMPERS utility to configure the generated workstation software (IPX.COM) to a custom configuration. (For instructions on running JUMPERS, refer to the NetWare v3.11 *Installation* manual.)

7. After choosing and configuring the LAN driver, you will be asked if you want to generate the workstation software or terminate the generation. Answer "Yes" to generate the IPX.COM file for the selected configuration. The resulting IPX.COM file will be stored on the WSGEN diskette (if you are running WSGEN from diskette) or in the WSGEN directory (if you are running WSGEN on the network).

8. Copy the newly-generated IPX.COM file to your workstation boot disk.

9. Copy the NET3.COM (for DOS 3.*x*) or NET4.COM (for DOS 4.*x*) from the WSGEN diskette or directory to the workstation boot disk. (Novell also has a NET5.COM for DOS 5.*x*; this file ships with Microsoft's DOS 5.0 and will also be included in the NetWare v3.11 Update Kit.)

10. If you're running applications that require the NetBIOS emulator, copy the following files from WSGEN to the workstation boot disk:

    NETBIOS.EXE
    INT2F.EXE

11. Create an AUTOEXEC.BAT file to load the appropriate networking software for the workstation. You can do this by using the DOS COPY CON command or a text editor. For example, a typical AUTOEXEC.BAT file might contain these commands:

    IPX
    NET4
    F:
    LOGIN

If you're using the NetBIOS emulator, your AUTOEXEC.BAT might look like this:

    IPX
    NET4
    NETBIOS
    INT2F
    F:
    LOGIN

Using SHELL.CFG to Optimize the Workstation Software

In its default state, the NetWare shell is equipped to handle most network functions. However, some applications (notably those involving multitasking, database access, electronic mail, or peer-to-peer NetBIOS functions) require some adjustments to the shell's defaults. Old applications written for previous versions of NetWare might also require some shell modifications to work with NetWare v3.11.

To optimize the workstation's network parameters for these types of applications, you can place various commands in a file called SHELL.CFG. This file is nothing more than a simple text file containing various parameter settings. You can also use SHELL.CFG to modify parameters that affect printing, network communications, and other options pertaining to the local workstation and its interaction with the network.

Note: SHELL.CFG is the shell configuration file associated with traditional DOS workstations. For workstations that use the DOS ODI software, the configuration file is named NET.CFG. Either file name will work. How ever, Novell is slowly phasing out its non- ODI workstation software; if you are planning to upgrade your DOS workstations to ODI drivers, name the configuration files NET.CFG now so you don't have to rename them when you upgrade. Place the SHELL.CFG commands at the beginning of the NET.CFG file, with no spaces or tabs preceding the commands.

Before you create a SHELL.CFG file, review the options given in Appendix B of the NetWare v3.11 *Installation* manual. You only need to include those options that change the defaults listed in the manual. Here are some of the most useful options for DOS workstations:

CONFIG OPTION=*n*

This option temporarily changes the configuration used by the workstation's IPX.COM file when you reboot the machine. It is most useful when you are tracking down a possible hardware conflict and need to see if a different configuration option will solve the problem. The variable *n* refers to one of the configurations listed in WSGEN for the workstation's LAN driver. To change the IPX.COM file permanently, run WSGEN.

LOCAL PRINTERS=0

This setting is recommended for all workstations that do not have a printer attached locally. It prevents the workstation from hanging if a user types the

<Shift>-<PrintScrn> keystroke combination.

LONG MACHINE TYPE=*XXXXXX*

This option tells the shell what type of machine it is running on (the default long machine type is "IBM_PC"). The long machine type is read by the shell when the %MACHINE variable is accessed in the login script. If you have a different brand of workstation (such as a Compaq or Epson) that came with its own version of DOS, replace the variable *XXXXXX* with a string of up to six characters identifying the brand ("COMPAQ" or "EPSON", for instance). Then use that character string in the DOS subdirectory name containing your machine's version of DOS on the server. For example, if you have a Compaq workstation running Compaq DOS v3.31, create a directory named COMPAQ/MSDOS/V3.31 on the server for the DOS system files. Then include the line "LONG MACHINE TYPE=COMPAQ" in the SHELL.CFG file so your machine can access DOS from that directory.

SHORT MACHINE TYPE=*XXXX*

This option is similar to the long machine type, except it is used when the workstation must access a different NetWare overlay file. This string (up to four characters) is read by the shell when the %SMACHINE variable is accessed in the login script. By default, the short machine type of "IBM" allows the workstation to use the IBM$RUN.OVL file when running the NetWare menu utilities. The only time you need to change the short machine type is if your workstation's monitor does not display NetWare's default menu colors correctly (this occurs on certain machines in which a color monitor is connected to a monochrome adapter). Changing the short machine type to "CMPQ" lets such machines access the CMPQ$RUN.OVL file, which contains a black-and-white color palette for NetWare menus.

PREFERRED SERVER=*XXXXXX*

On a network that has more than one file server, the shell initially attaches to whichever server responds to it first. This may or may not be the server you ultimately want to log in to, but poses no problem unless there are no free connections on that nearest server. Including this option in the SHELL.CFG file allows the shell to poll up to five servers for an available connection. Once it has a connection, the shell proceeds to connect to the server specified as the preferred server.

Check the setup documentation for your network applications to see if they require other options in the SHELL.CFG file. Once you have decided which options you need to include, create the SHELL.CFG file using the DOS COPY CON command or a text editor. For each option, follow the correct syntax as defined in the NetWare manual.

In order to take effect when the network software (shell) is loaded, the SHELL.CFG file must be stored in the same directory as the IPX.COM and NET*x*.COM (or XMSNET*x*.COM or EMSNET*x*.COM) files.

Logging In from a DOS Machine

After you've created your DOS workstation's boot disk, reboot your machine to initialize the NetWare shell. Since the AUTOEXEC.BAT has the LOGIN command in it, you will be prompted to enter your login name. If this is your first time logging in, use the username SUPERVISOR so you will have all rights to the server for setting up other user accounts.

If you have a multiple file server network, you must specify both the file server's name and your username (unless you have included the "PREFERRED SERVER=" option in the SHELL.CFG file). Separate the two names with a backslash (\). For example, to specify server JUNGLE and username SUPERVISOR when prompted to enter the username, type:

```
JUNGLE\SUPERVISOR <Enter>
```

If your username has a password assigned to it, you'll be prompted to enter the password. (If you're logging in as SUPERVISOR for the first time, you won't have a password.) NetWare doesn't display the password on the screen as you enter it, so type carefully. When you have finished typing the password, press <Enter>.

Troubleshooting the DOS Workstation Installation

For troubleshooting purposes, you must be able to differentiate between a problem specific to the computer and a problem related to networking components (LAN adapter, NetWare shell, or cabling). If the computer is functioning correctly, you should be able to boot the workstation with DOS without loading the NetWare shell. If the workstation can't boot DOS, you can assume that the problem lies with the computer itself, unless the LAN adapter hangs the machine. If the machine boots DOS but has problems trying to get on the network, you can assume that you're having a problem with one of networking components of the workstation.

Here are some basic problems and solutions associated with a DOS workstation.

Problem: The workstation software won't load, hangs, or gives an error message when you execute IPX.COM.

Solutions: This problem basically means that IPX can't initialize the LAN adapter. Do the following:

Make sure that your IPX.COM configuration matches the LAN adapter installed in the workstation. You can check your IPX.COM configuration by typing "IPX I <Enter>" at the DOS prompt.

Verify that your LAN adapter configuration doesn't conflict with other interrupts or I/O settings.

Verify that your LAN adapter is seated completely in the workstation bus expansion slot.

Sometimes the IPX.COM file can become corrupted. In this case, use the WSGEN utility to create a new IPX.COM.

Move your LAN adapter to another bus expansion slot. Make sure you don't have a 16-bit adapter in an 8-bit slot.

Try another LAN adapter card.

Problem: When executing NET*x*.COM, a workstation can't find a file server.

Solutions: This problem means that your workstation can't establish communication with a file server on the network. Follow these steps:

Make sure your cable is properly connected to the LAN adapter. A poor connection here is so common that it's the first logical thing to check when you can't communicate with the network.

Verify that you don't have any interrupt or I/O conflicts with the LAN adapter. It's common to find that the LAN adapter conflicts with a port with a modem or mouse installed on it.

Use the COMCHECK utility provided with NetWare to check the cable continuity between two workstations on the network (see Chapter 25).

If you've installed a LAN adapter with different cable ports, verify that it's configured for the type of cabling you're using. For instance, you can configure most Ethernet adapters for thick or thin cabling types by adjusting a jumper(s) on the card. If you have a Micro Channel or EISA adapter machine, configure the adapter by using a configuration utility provided with the computer.

If you're running Ethernet, verify that you're using the Ethernet standard (Ethernet II or IEEE 802.3) that is currently compatible with your file server configuration. Failure to do so is common in multiple-protocol environments. (For more information on Ethernet standards and frame types, see Chapter 25.)

Problem: The workstation can successfully log in to the network, but periodically the workstation will hang.

Solutions: This problem originates either from the computer or from the network components in the workstation (the LAN adapter or the NetWare shell). Follow these procedures:

Make sure you're using the latest available version of the NetWare shell. Sometimes the file server has been upgraded but the workstation shell hasn't.

Verify that the LAN adapter doesn't have an interrupt or I/O address conflict with the workstation.

Try another LAN adapter to see if that eliminates the hanging problem.

If several workstation hang at the same time, check the cable segment or other connection hardware that the workstations have in common (such as a wiring concentrator or hub).

If none of these solutions solves your problem, look for something wrong with the computer itself.

DOS Workstation Memory Management

Managing limited memory can be one the most challenging aspects of maintaining a DOS workstation. The DOS machine's limitation of 640KB of RAM can be a serious challenge when it comes to integrating DOS workstations into the LAN.

To troubleshoot workstation memory, you must first understand the different types of memory and then be able to recognize the common memory problems likely to arise. This section reviews basic workstation memory concepts and then provides some memory troubleshooting tips.

Types of Memory in a DOS Workstation

DOS workstation memory can be divided into three different categories: conventional, expanded, and extended.

- *Conventional memory* consists of the first 640KB of available memory, which is used by DOS's CONFIG.SYS and COMMAND.COM, by TSRs, and by applications. The next 384KB is reserved memory for addressing video cards, hardware drivers, and other devices. The NetWare shell also takes up some of this memory, but the exact amount NetWare requires depends on the type of shell you are using.

- *Expanded memory* is memory above the 1MB range. You can access expanded memory by swapping the memory above 1MB a "page" at a time through a memory window in the 384KB of reserved memory. This requires a memory manager compatible with the LIM/EMM (Lotus/Intel/Microsoft/ Expanded Memory Manager) specification to do the swapping.

- *Extended memory* is also memory above the 1MB range, but it is set up differently in the PC's BIOS. To access extended memory for DOS-based applications, you must use an memory manager (such Microsoft's HIMEM.SYS) to address the first 64KB area above the 1MB range. The memory manager must be compatible with the XMS (eXtended Memory Specification) standard.

Using Novell's Expanded/Extended Memory Shells

NetWare v3.11 comes with two other kinds of workstation shells besides NET*x*.COM. These shells allow you to store the NetWare workstation shell in expanded or extended memory, thus reducing the amount of conventional memory NetWare requires. This solution is especially helpful if you discover that you don't have enough conventional memory to run the applications you need.

The expanded memory NetWare shell (EMSNET*x*.EXE) moves most of the shell out of conventional memory and puts it into expanded memory. This shell loads approximately 33KB of its code into expanded memory, leaving only about 7KB in conventional memory.

To use EMSNET, your workstation must have access to an expanded memory manager. The expanded NetWare shell is written to the LIM/EMS v4.0 memory manager specification. The expanded memory manager (EMM.SYS) is generally included with the expanded memory boards.

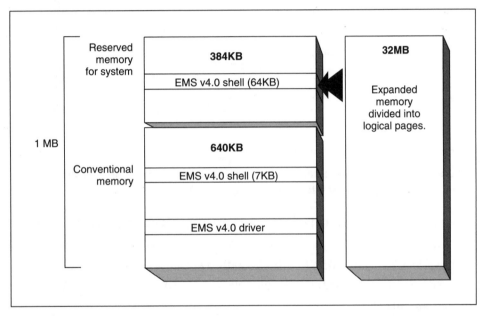

Figure 9-2: NetWare's expanded memory shell takes about 7KB of conventional memory and loads the rest into expanded memory.

NetWare's extended memory shell (XMSNETx.EXE) moves most of the shell out of conventional memory and puts it into addressable memory above the 1MB range. Approximately 34BKB is placed in extended memory, and about 6KB is left in conventional memory.

To use the extended memory NetWare shell, make sure an extended memory manager is loaded. The shell is written to support XMS v2.0 or compatible memory managers. An example of an extended memory shell is Microsoft's HIMEM.SYS.

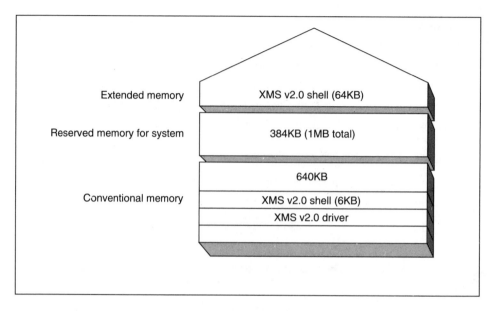

Figure 9-3: The NetWare extended memory shell takes about 6KB of conventional memory and loads the rest into extended memory.

Troubleshooting Expanded and Extended NetWare Shell Problems

This section discusses two of the most common errors specific to the EMSNET*x*.EXE and XMSNET*x*.EXE shells. (For information about other errors that pertain to the expanded and extended NetWare shells, refer to the NetWare v3.11 *Installation* manual.)

> **Problem:** When you load EMSNET*x*.EXE or XMSNET*x*.EXE, you receive the following error message:

```
No Expanded Memory Manager present. Cannot continue initialization.
```

or

```
No Extended Memory Manager present. Cannot continue initialization.
```

Solution: Make sure you load the appropriate memory manager for either expanded or extended memory, respectively. The memory manager should be compatible with the LIM/EMS v4.0 specification for expanded memory, or with the XMS v2.0 specification for extended memory.

Problem: When you load EMSNET*x*.EXE, you receive the following error message:

```
Expanded Memory Manager is not v4.0 or better. Cannot continue
initialization.
```

Solution: Make sure your Expanded Memory Manager (EMM) driver is compatible with LIM/EMS v4.0 or above.

Troubleshooting DOS Environment Problems

One of the most common memory problems that occurs in a DOS workstation is the lack of DOS environment memory. This problem is due to the large number of environmental settings (such as drive path statements and mappings, and other variables) that exist when the workstation logs into a network. A DOS environment shortage is indicated by the following messages when you log into the file server:

```
Could not add "USER=JOHN" to the local environment variables.
```

    or

```
Could not execute external program "capture", not enough memory.
```

    or

```
There is no room to expand the PATH environment variable with
the mapping: "S16:=JUNGLE/SYS:PUBLIC/UTILS"
```

If you receive any of these messages, you should increase your DOS environment space. To do that, use a text editor to create or modify the CONFIG.SYS file with the following parameter:

```
SHELL=C:COMMAND.COM /P /E:512
```

The "C:" represents the disk location where the file COMMAND.COM can be found. The "/P" switch tells DOS to run the AUTOEXEC.BAT file upon bootup. The "/E" parameter defines the environmental space you want use. In this example, the environment is set at 512 bytes.

Using Microsoft Windows on the Network

Microsoft Windows 3.0 is not really a separate desktop operating system; it is a graphical user interface that runs on top of DOS. As such, Windows is installed more like an application than like a workstation operating system such as DOS or the Macintosh OS. Therefore, you don't need to worry about Windows from the standpoint of creating the workstation shell and the communications link between the workstation and the network server. Rather, your primary concern in providing access to Windows is in setting up the Windows program files on the server in a proper fashion, and in making sure your applications can run within Windows, and, if desired, multitask.

Installing Windows on the Network

The issues involved in installing Windows 3.0 on a Novell network are many and complex. The following discussion summarizes the main points to consider. (For a more complete discussion of the subject, refer to Novell's "NetWare and Microsoft Windows Integration" Application Note published in January 1991. Appendix D provides ordering information.)

The recommended way to set up Windows on a network, according to the Microsoft documentation, is to install the bulk of the Windows program files on the server, thus leaving a minimal number of files to be installed at the individual workstations. Although this method saves local disk space (a full copy of Windows eats up about 800KB per user) and is easier to upgrade, it can reduce performance on the network due to increased traffic when running Windows.

If your workstations all have local hard disks with plenty of free space, it might be preferable to install a full copy of Windows locally at each workstation. This reduces the amount of Windows-related traffic on the network, increases the operating speed of Windows, and allows standalone Windows operation should the network go down. However, it is harder to maintain because each workstation has its own set of .INI files that you have to change one at a time if a change becomes necessary.

The installation guidelines given below refer mainly to the first method of installing Windows. To install Windows fully at each workstation, refer to the Microsoft documentation.

Checking for Proper NetWare Shell Versions

Before you install Windows on the file server, it's especially important to ensure that all workstations on the network are running the correct version of the NetWare shells. This includes IPX.COM, along with one of the three shell files: NETx.COM, EMSNETx.EXE, or XMSNETx.EXE. If you have a choice between EMSNETx.EXE and XMSNETx.EXE, choose the XMSNET file, since Windows uses extended, not expanded, memory in its Standard and 386 Enhanced modes.

The NetWare shell files must be at least v3.01a or higher to work properly with Windows 3.0. The shell files shipped with the first release of NetWare v3.11 will work, but they have since been updated to v3.03 for IPX and v3.20 for the shell. If you want the latest shell versions, they are available from the NetWire portion of CompuServe.

The other Novell-provided files you'll need for working with Windows are also available on CompuServe. These include IPX.OBJ, TBMI.COM, TASKID.COM, and VPICDA.386; the updated NetWare utilities (including MAP, LOGIN, GRANT, RIGHTS, TLIST, and BINDFIX), which work with the newest NetWare DOS shells); and NETWARE.PIF (which allows you to specify certain run- time options for NetWare utilities in Windows).

A number of other Microsoft-supplied files for working with NetWare are included on the Windows 3.0 installation diskettes. These are NETWARE.DRV, NETWARE.HLP, NETWARE.INI, NWPOPUP.EXE, VNETWARE.386, and VIPX.386.

Copying the Windows Program Files to the Network

Next, create a directory named WINDOWS for the shared Windows files beneath the APPS directory in SYS:PUBLIC. Map drive F: to this directory and copy the EXPAND.EXE program into it from the first Windows installation diskette.

From within this new directory, create a batch file to expand the Windows files and install them on the server, using the batch file instructions in the Windows documentation:

```
a:
for %%i in(*.*) do f:\windows\expand %%i F:\windows\%%i
f:
```

With this batch file, you can begin the Windows installation by inserting each of the Windows diskettes into drive A: as the program instructs.

Setting Up Windows User Files

At this point, configure each of the workstations that will access the shared Windows directory. The first step is to run the Windows SETUP program (with the /N parameter) for each workstation. The /N parameter lets the program know that this is network workstation. The SETUP program will ask you where the personal Windows files should be stored. You may choose to store these files in the user's personal directory on the file server or on the workstation's local hard disk.

The SETUP program is equipped to automatically make the required changes to each workstations AUTOEXEC.BAT and CONFIG.SYS files. But note one significant installation factor: Windows makes use of temporary "swap" files. Unless you tell it otherwise, Windows will assume that it should store the swap files in the same directory as the Windows startup files—the shared directory on the server. This creates several problems: not only do the users need Modify or Write privileges in the Windows directory in order for Windows to operate, but shuttling the temp files back and forth across the network cable creates extra traffic, and therefore slows LAN performance.

A better alternative is to use the TEMP environment variable in CONFIG.SYS to direct the temp files either to a personal directory, or, better still, to a directory on the workstation's own hard drive, like this:

```
SET TEMP=C:\TEMP
```

In Windows' 386 Enhanced mode, however, you can specify a permanent location for the swap file on a local DOS drive. (Refer to the Microsoft *Windows User's Guide* for specific instructions on how to do this.)

Since Microsoft Windows runs on DOS, you need the same type of configuration as you do for DOS when running Windows. Remember to use the proper version of the IPX and NET*x* shell files. You may want to use the XMSNET*x*.COM or EMSNET*x*.COM shells to free up some additional conventional memory space.

Setting Windows Parameters in SHELL.CFG

To run Windows on a DOS workstation, you should make some adjustments in the workstation's SHELL.CFG (or NET.CFG) file. (Refer to Appendix B of the NetWare v3.11 *Installation* manual for details on these and other SHELL.CFG file settings.)

The first three settings are essential for Windows to run smoothly:

```
SHOW DOTS=ON
FILE HANDLES=60
ENVIRONMENT PAD=14
```

The SHOW DOTS parameter allows you to move up the NetWare directory structure in Windows by selecting the ".." option in Windows' directory lists.

The number of FILE HANDLES must be increased from the default of 40 because of the number of files held open is usually greater with Windows (Windows itself opens 14 files). Be sure to also change the CONFIG.SYS files parameter to FILES=60 to match the shell setting.

The ENVIRONMENT PAD increase gives you room to add search drives to a Windows "virtual machine" (a separate DOS session running under Windows). This is especially important when you are running DOS applications in Windows' 386 Enhanced mode, since Windows freezes the current DOS environment when it starts and doesn't allow you to modify it while Windows is running.

If you will be multitasking applications in Windows, include this parameter in the SHELL.CFG file:

```
MAX TASK=Number
```

The MAX TASK parameter specifies the maximum number of tasks that can be active at the same time. Since Windows can have several tasks open at the same time, you'll probably need to increase the number of tasks. The default number of concurrent tasks is 31, but you can enter any number between 20 and 128.

Logging In from a Windows Workstation

Network users should first log in to the network server and then invoke Windows. You must make sure, of course, that both the user's personal directory and the shared Windows directory are part of the user's path. The path to the personal directory must *precede* the path to the main Windows directory in the path statement. The Windows SETUP program can help you make this specification a permanent part of the user's AUTOEXEC.BAT. Alternatively, you can place corresponding NetWare search drive mappings (in correct order) in the user's login script (see Chapter 16).

Instruct your users *not* to log in or out of NetWare servers using the Windows Control Panel "Network" option. This option does not work properly with NetWare. (If you need the ability to attach to other NetWare servers from inside Windows, get the NetWare Tools for Windows software recently released by Novell in their NetWare Windows Workstation package.)

By default, Windows and DOS applications running under Windows keep track of NetWare drive mappings independently. So if you map a drive while in one application and then switch to another one, the new drive mapping will not be recognized by the second application. If you want Windows to make NetWare drive mappings effective throughout all applications, add the following line to the [NetWare] section of the SYSTEM.INI file:

```
NetwareShareHandles=true
```

If you run Windows in 386 Enhanced mode, you can make all new drive mappings stay in effect when you exit Windows by adding the following line to the [NetWare] section of SYSTEM.INI:

```
RestoreDrive=false
```

You'll have to exit Windows and restart it for these settings to take effect.

If users will be working in Windows most of the time (and with the Windows File Manager in particular), they may want to use the MAP ROOT version of the NetWare MAP command to set up their network drive mappings. MAP ROOT prevents the File Manager from scanning every network drive starting at the volume level and proceeding down through directory levels they may not even have access rights to. It is much faster and easier for users if they get a list of the directory each network drive is actually mapped to when they click on a network drive icon in Windows.

One last tip for using Windows on the network. It is possible for the same network file to be accessed at the same time from two different DOS applications running on the same workstation. For example, if a user opens two instances of a database program in separate DOS windows, the user can access the same data file at the same time. This can result in corrupted or lost data. At present, there is no way to avoid this danger except to make users aware of the problem and caution them against it.

Troubleshooting Windows Workstations

Here are some tips for troubleshooting common problems when installing and using Windows on the network.

Problem: The Windows SETUP program hangs or displays errors when loading.

Solutions: The Windows SETUP program is designed to automatically sense what type of hardware it is being run on and make settings accordingly. Certain hardware configurations can cause SETUP to hang when it attempts to read the system information. One case in particular is with LAN adapters that use I/O address 2E0h (the default setting for some Arcnet boards). SETUP expects this address to indicate an 8514 video adapter. To disable SETUP's automatic hardware detection, add the /I parameter to the command (SETUP /I). A better solution, however, is to change the I/O address of the LAN adapter to somewhere in the 300h range.

If you get the "Update network shell" error in SETUP, the workstation does not have a recent enough version of the NetWare shell files. Make sure that IPX and the shell are v3.01a or higher.

If you get the error "Cannot create WIN.COM," you are trying to run SETUP /N with Windows files that have not been uncompressed. Run the Windows EXPAND.EXE program as described above to uncompress the Windows program files, then try SETUP /N again.

Another common problem occurs when using SETUP to scan network disks for applications. By default, NetWare v3.11 limits the number of outstanding directory searches to 51. On a large network disk, SETUP may have to scan many more directories than that before it is finished, and you will get the error "You exceeded your outstanding NCP directory search limit." You can increase this limit via the "SET maximum outstanding NCP searches=n" console command. The valid range is from 10 to 1,000 searches.

Problem: Windows hangs when loading.

Solutions: First check to see if Windows will load in any of its three modes: Real mode (WIN /R), Standard mode (WIN /S), and 386 Enhanced mode (WIN /3). If Windows won't load in 386 Enhanced mode but will run in the other two modes, check for problems in the [386Enh] section of the SYSTEM.INI file. If Windows will only run in Real mode, you probably have problems with your XMS memory manager (consult the memory manager's documentation for possible solutions). If Windows won't load in any mode, something is wrong in your Windows configuration or setup.

Make sure the workstation has enough memory to run in the desired mode. Real mode runs in 640KB; Standard mode requires 1MB; 386 Enhanced mode requires a 386 or better CPU and at least 2MB of memory.

Avoid using IRQ 2 or IRQ 9 for a LAN adapter. These interrupts are more complex to service than others, and they can cause problems when running Windows in 386 Enhanced mode. The best solution is to run WSGEN to change the shell's configuration setting to another non-conflicting interrupt. If you must use IRQ 2 for the LAN adapter, use the Novell-supplied VPICDA.386 driver in place of Microsoft's VPICD.386 driver. You change the driver in the [386Enh] section of the SYSTEM.INI file. (Note that some 16-bit VGA adapters use IRQ 2, which can also cause problems when trying to run with Windows. Refer to the manufacturer's documentation for alternate settings.)

On certain PCs, if you have a serial mouse connected to COM1 (which uses IRQ 4) and your LAN adapter is set to IRQ 3, you may not be able to access the network. This problem occurs mainly with Ethernet adapters. Run WSGEN to change the LAN driver setting to another non-conflicting interrupt.

Check for LAN adapters that use memory addresses in the D000-DFFF range (the IBM Token-Ring adapter with 16KB shared RAM is one). Windows uses this address range for its default EMS page frame. Either set the LAN adapter to use another base memory address, or include the following statement in the SYSTEM.INI file to exclude the memory segment used by the LAN adapter (the example range shown is that used by the IBM Token-Ring adapter):

```
EMMExclude=D000-D7FF
```

If you are using the XMSNET*x* or EMSNET*x* shell and Windows hangs when loading, either switch to the NET*x* shell or upgrade to Windows 3.0a (which corrects a memory allocation bug in Windows 3.0).

Problem: When printing to a network printer from within Windows, you experience bad page breaks, font problems, or incomplete print jobs.

Solution: First, disable Windows' print spooler by changing the spooler statement to No in the [windows] section of the WIN.INI file. (You'll have to exit Windows and restart it for this to take effect.) Then run NetWare's PRINTCON utility (as described in Chapter 20) and make sure all of the print job configurations used with Windows have the following settings:

Suppress Form Feed: Yes
Autoendcap: No
Enable Timeout: No

If users use CAPTURE to redirect local output to network printers, make sure they include the "NFF NT NA TI=0" options in the CAPTURE command.

Installing a DOS ODI Workstation

As we mentioned in Chapter 3, the Open Data-link Interface (ODI) expands the workstation's capability to use multiple protocols on the same card and network cabling. In the next few pages, we'll discuss how to install, use, and troubleshoot workstations using ODI.

Before installing the ODI drivers, make sure that you have a working copy of the WSGEN diskette, that the LAN adapter is configured and installed (including having the cables attached), and that you have at least 80KB available for workstation software while leaving at least 512KB for applications.

Creating an ODI Boot Diskette

These steps represent a sample installation of ODI boot files.

1. Create a bootable DOS diskette. You can do this by using the DOS FORMAT command with a /S parameter.

2. Copy the correct shell file from the WSGEN diskette to the newly created boot disk. Your choice of shell files will depend on what type of memory space you want your users to use and on the DOS version you're using. (The "*x*" in these file names is a variable representing the DOS version. A "3" here signifies DOS 3.*x*, a "4" signifies DOS 4.*x*, and a "5" signifies DOS 5.*x*.)

    *   **NET*x*.COM** will be loaded into the workstation's conventional memory (640KB).

    *   **EMSNET*x*.EXE** will be loaded into the workstation's expanded memory (LIM 4.0 EMS compatible). This file moves about 33KB of the shell to the expanded memory on a workstation. About 7KB will still remain in conventional memory. Use this shell to relieve potential "RAM cram" in your conventional memory (640KB).

    *   **XMSNET*x*.EXE** will be loaded into the workstation's extended memory (XMS 2.0 compatible). This file moves about 34KB of the shell to extended memory, which is addressed above the 1MB memory range. About 6KB will still remain in conventional memory (640KB). Use this file to release needed conventional memory.

3. Copy the following required workstation files from the DOSODI directory on the WSGEN diskette:

    *   **LSL.COM**—the Link Support Layer

    *   **RPLODI.COM**—Copy this file only if the boot diskette is used for remote booting.

    *   The **LAN driver** associated with the LAN adapter you have installed. For example, you might use a file by the name of NE2000.COM if you're installing ODI files for a workstation with a NE2000 Ethernet adapter.

- **IPXODI.COM**—the ODI protocol stack ODI file. This file will be dependent upon the protocol you need.

- **NETBIOS.EXE** and **INT2F.COM**—if your applications require a NETBIOS emulator.

- **ROUTE.COM**—if you have a Token-Ring network with IBM routers.

- **LANSUP.COM**—if you're using IBM PC-Net or Token-Ring.

- Other optional files determined by configuration and usage of your workstation. You can also copy them from the DOSODI directory on the WSGEN diskette.

4. Create a CONFIG.SYS file by using the DOS COPY CON command or a text editor. This file will contain parameters specific to the workstation environment settings. We recommend that you set the files (FILES=*number*) equal to 35 and the buffers (BUFFERS=*number*) equal to at least 20.

   If you're using a memory-resident memory manager, such as Microsoft's HIMEM.SYS, you must install a parameter in this file pertaining to the memory manager you're using. Consult your DOS manual for more information pertaining to the CONFIG.SYS file.

5. Create an AUTOEXEC.BAT file that will execute the ODI file you copied to the diskette. The files must be loaded in the following order:

   Link support layer
   LAN drivers
   Protocol stacks
   Shell file

For example, if you're creating an AUTOEXEC.BAT for a workstation with an NE2000 Ethernet card on an IPX network and with a conventional DOS shell, the AUTOEXEC.BAT would look something like this:

```
LSL
NE2000
IPXODI
NET3
```

6. (Optional) You may want to create a NET.CFG file to be used when loading the ODI workstation boot files. Use the NET.CFG to specify certain configuration parameters pertaining to the workstation interaction with the LAN adapter and network. The default configurations don't require you to create this file, but you should know about it in case something pertains to your setup. For example, you can configure your ODI drivers for a different interrupt, port address, frame type, and protocols. We recommend that you read the *NetWare ODI Shell for DOS* manual for more information about implementing the NET.CFG file.

For example, to change the interrupts, I/O addresses (IRQ=2 and PORT=320), and frame type (Ethernet II) of an Ethernet card, create a NET.CFG that looks something like this:

```
LINK DRIVER NE2000
    INT=2
    PORT=320
    Frame=ETHERNET_II
```

Logging In from a DOS ODI Workstation

After you've created your DOS workstation's boot disk, you can reboot your machine to initialize the NetWare shell. Since the AUTOEXEC.BAT has the LOGIN parameter in it, you'll be prompted to enter your login name. If this is your first time logging in, use the username SUPERVISOR (which has all rights to the file server). If you have a multiple-server network, you must specify your file server's name and your username. For example, to specify server JUNGLE and username SUPERVISOR when you're prompted to enter the username, type:

```
JUNGLE/SUPERVISOR <Enter>
```

If your user name has a password, you'll be prompted to enter it. If you're logging in as SUPERVISOR for the first time, you won't have a password.

Troubleshooting DOS ODI Workstations

For troubleshooting purposes, you must be able to differentiate between a problem specific to the computer and a problem related to the networking components (LAN adapter, NetWare shell, or cabling). If the computer is functioning correctly, you should be able to boot the workstation to DOS without loading the NetWare shell. If the workstation can't boot to DOS, you can assume that the problem lies with the computer itself, unless the LAN adapter hangs the machine.

If the machine boots to DOS but has trouble trying to get on the network, you can assume that you have a problem with one of the networking components of the workstation.

If you start getting error messages when loading the network shell, you may want refer to the *NetWare ODI Shell for DOS* manual.

Here are some basic problems and solutions associated with a DOS ODI workstation.

Problem: The workstation can't load ODI LAN adapter drivers (such as NE2000.COM), or it receives the "Fatal: *LAN Adapter* NIC command port failed to respond" error.

Solutions: Basically, this error message means that the LAN driver can't initialize the LAN adapter. Perform the following checks:

Make sure you've correctly installed and configured the LAN adapter.

Make sure your LAN adapter and the LAN driver configuration settings are correct. You can use the NET.CFG file to specify the LAN driver configuration (interrupts, I/O addresses, and so forth). Refer to the *NetWare ODI Shell for DOS* manual for information about creating and configuring the NET.CFG file.

Make sure the LAN adapter is correctly seated in the workstation bus expansion slot.

Verify that you don't have a hardware conflict (interrupts, I/O addressing and so forth)between the LAN adapter and the computer.

Move your LAN adapter to another bus expansion slot.

There's always a possibility that the LAN adapter is bad. Try another LAN adapter.

Problem: A workstation can't find a file server when executing NET*x*.COM or XMSNET*x*.COM or EMSNET*x*.COM.

Solutions: This problem usually means that your workstation can't establish communication with a file server on the network. Follow these steps:

Make sure that your cable is properly connected to the LAN adapter. This problem is so common that it's the first thing to check when you can't communicate with the network.

Verify that you don't have any interrupt or I/O conflicts with the LAN adapter. It isn't uncommon for the LAN adapter to conflict with a port which has a modem or mouse installed on it.

Use the COMCHECK utility provided with NetWare to check the cable continuity between two workstations on the network. We explain this utility in Chapter 25.

If you've installed a LAN adapter with different cable ports, verify that it's properly configured for the type of cabling you're using. For instance, you can configure most Ethernet adapters for thick or thin cabling types by adjusting a jumper(s) on the card. If you have a Micro Channel or EISA machine, configure the LAN adapter by using the configuration utility provided with the computer.

If you're running Ethernet, verify that you're using the Ethernet standard (Ethernet II or IEEE 802.3) that's currently compatible with your file server configuration. You can configure the Ethernet type in the NET.CFG file. (For more information on Ethernet frame types and how to configure workstations, routers, and servers for them, refer to Chapter 25.)

Problem: The workstation can successfully log in to the network, but periodically the workstation will hang.

Solutions: This problem can arise from either the computer or the network components in the workstation (LAN adapter or the NetWare shell). Here's a list of items you should check for problems originating with the network components of the workstation:

Make sure you're using the latest available version of the NetWare shell. Sometimes the file server has been upgraded but the workstation shell hasn't.

Verify that the LAN adapter doesn't have an interrupt or I/O address conflict with the workstation.

Try another LAN adapter to see if that eliminates the hanging problem.

If none of these solutions works, you need to start looking for a problem with the computer itself.

Installing Diskless Workstations

If you don't want your workstation to boot from a floppy or if you have a diskless workstation, use the following procedures to boot up to the network. The boot files that the workstation needs will be located at the file server. A combination of these files make up a "boot image file."

The whole concept behind the diskless or remote boot workstation is to allow the ROMs on the LAN adapter to find a file server and use the server's image file to boot itself to the network.

If you're using a diskless workstation, make sure that a boot PROM is installed and configured on the LAN adapter. For further information, use the supplemental documentation that comes with the LAN adapter. (In some cases, the adapter comes built into the diskless workstation.)

Loading the Remote Program Load NLM at the Server

According to the kind of LAN adapters your diskless workstations have, you need to load the appropriate "remote program load" NLM at the server. The available RPL NLMs are:

ETHERRPL	For Ethernet workstations
TOKENRPL	For Token-Ring workstations
PCN2RPL	For IBM PC Network II workstations

For example, to set up the server for remote booting of Ethernet workstations, first load ETHERRPL by typing this command at the server console:

```
LOAD ETHERRPL <Enter>
```

Next, bind the ETHERRPL protocol to the Ethernet LAN driver in the file server by typing:

```
BIND ETHERRPL LANDriver [DriverParameters] <Enter>
```

Replace *LANDriver* with the name of the driver you are using. If you have loaded the driver more than once, repeat this step.

Replace *DriverParameters* with any parameters required for the driver. By default, the ETHERRPL protocol stack accepts ETHERNET_802.2 frames. If the boot ROM on your Ethernet adapters uses a different frame type, bind that frame type to the ETHERRPL protocol stack.

Note: To have the remote program automatically load the NLM when you boot the server, add the two commands shown above to the server's AUTOEXEC.NCF file.

Creating One Boot Image File for All Workstations

If you have several diskless workstations that boot identically (same LAN driver, DOS version, and AUTOEXEC.BAT), you need to make only one boot image file.

To create the remote boot image file on the server, follow these steps. (*You must use a workstation that has a floppy drive to complete this procedure.*)

1. Boot a currently networked workstation up to DOS.

2. Create another bootable diskette.

3. Copy the appropriate IPX.COM for the LAN adapter in the diskless workstation and the correct NET*x*.COM to the bootable diskette you've prepared.

4. Create an AUTOEXEC.BAT file by using the DOS COPY CON command or a text editor. Your AUTOEXEC.BAT may look like this:

   ```
   IPX
   NET3
   F:
   LOGIN
   ```

5. Copy the AUTOEXEC.BAT file to the SYS:LOGIN directory or to any other default directories specified by the login script. (For information on creating and using the login script, see Chapter 16.)

6. From the machine on which you created this boot disk, log in as SUPERVISOR on the file server to which the diskless workstation will be booting. For installation procedures, the workstation *must* have a floppy drive in which to insert the boot disk you just created.

7. Insert the boot disk that you just created for the diskless workstation.

8. With the NetWare MAP command, map drive F: to SYS:SYSTEM and drive G: to SYS:LOGIN.

9. Change to drive G: and type

    ```
    F:DOSGEN <Enter>
    ```

The DOSGEN utility will use the information from the boot diskette in the A drive to create a file called NET$DOS.SYS. This file will be copied to the SYS:LOGIN directory.

10. The final step is to flag NET$DOS.SYS Sharable Read-Only with the NetWare FLAG command. The command will look like this:

    ```
    FLAG NET$DOS.SYS S RO <Enter>
    ```

Creating Multiple Boot Image Files

In order for different configurations of diskless workstations to boot on the same network, you must follow these procedures to ensure that each diskless workstation will attach itself to the file server. For example, workstation configurations may vary according to their particular LAN adapters. Therefore, you must create different boot files for each workstation to reflect that workstation's specific environment.

1. Gather the information on the different types of workstation configurations for which you need to create boot image files. This information includes the type and configuration of the LAN adapter.
    Several workstations may have the same type of configuration, or perhaps only one needs a different boot configuration.

2. Boot a machine to DOS (this machine *must* have a floppy drive).

3. Using DOS 3.*x* or higher, create a bootable floppy. You'll use this bootable floppy to create the remote boot file on the server. If you find yourself needing to install multiple image boot files, you may want to use this diskette each time you create the image file, modifying it appropriately according to the configuration you need.

4. Copy the appropriate IPX.COM and NET*x*.COM files to the newly created diskette. (If you need information on creating an IPX.COM file, refer to "Installing the DOS Workstation Software" above.)

   Make sure the IPX.COM matches the configuration of the LAN adapter in your workstation.

5. Create a unique batch file for each workstation or workstation group you have. As a network administrator, you have a great deal of flexibility here. For example, you may name them OPTION1.BAT for one configuration, OPTION2.BAT for the next, and so on. These batch files should have at least the following lines (NET3 for DOS 3.*x* and NET4 for DOS 4.*x*):

   ```
   IPX
   NETx
   F:
   LOGIN
   ```

6. Copy the newly created batch file (OPTIONx.BAT) to the file server's SYS:SYSTEM directory and to any other default directory defined in the login script. Copying the file to the server's SYS:SYSTEM directory and to the workstation's default directories will ensure that the workstations boot up to the correct server.

7. You must create an AUTOEXEC.BAT file on the diskette to execute one of the

batch files (OPTIONx.BAT) you created in step 6. For example, the AUTOEXEC.BAT file should contain a statement similar to this one:

```
OPTION1.BAT
```

8. With the diskette you created in the workstation, use the MAP utility to map drive F: to SYS:SYSTEM and drive G: to SYS:LOGIN.

9. Change to the G: drive and run the DOSGEN utility to create the image file on the file server. When you run this utility, specify the name of the new image file. For management purposes, we recommend that each image file you create be associated numerically with the batch file (OPTION1.BAT) you created. To run DOSGEN, type the command with the following syntax:

```
F:DOSGEN A:BOOT1.SYS <Enter>
```

10. Each image boot file you create you should flag Shareable Read-Only by going to the SYS:LOGIN directory and typing

```
FLAG BOOT1.SYS S RO <Enter>
```

11. By using the workstation node address, you can make clear which workstation uses which image file. To do this, create a remote reset boot file (BOOTCONF.SYS) containing the workstation network and node addresses and the image file information associated with it.

There are two ways to determine the address of the LAN adapter. The first is to read the actual physical setting on the adapter (as with an Arcnet adapter). Some diskless workstation manufacturers may include the node address with the documentation or on the back of the diskless workstation.

The second way is to use the server's TRACK ON console command. This method works for Ethernet and Token-Ring adapters, which have the node address hard-coded into the adapter. TRACK ON will display information pertaining to packets going in or out of the file server. To determine the address of a LAN adapter, turn on the diskless workstation and let it try to log in to the server. When it tries to log in, the TRACK ON utility on the server's console will display the workstation's address. For each diskless workstation, you must go through this process of finding its node address. (For more information on using the TRACK ON utility, refer to Chapter 10.)

12. By using the DOS COPY CON command or a text editor, create a remote reset file (BOOTCONF.SYS) in the SYS:LOGIN directory. In this file you'll specify the diskless workstation's network and node address and the image file that it will be using to boot. The syntax should be similar to this:

```
0x[network address],[node address]=[boot image file name]
```

(The first character of the syntax is the number zero.) For example, a workstation located on the BADBEEF network with the node address 00001B014EA5, with the associated image file, may require a line in the BOOTCONF.SYS that looks like this:

```
0xBADBEEF,00001B014EA5=BOOT1.SYS
```

For each diskless workstation you install, you must give the BOOTCONF.SYS the information it needs to boot up with the correct image file.

If you have several servers on one network, you must copy the image files and the associated boot files to the other file servers' SYS:LOGIN directories. This procedure will ensure that whatever file server your workstation tries to attach to will be valid.

Remote Boot Considerations for ODI Workstations

If you want to remotely boot a DOS ODI workstation, you must include the RPLODI.COM file in the workstation's boot image file. RPLODI.COM is located on the WSGEN diskette under the DOSODI subdirectory. You must load RPLODI.COM immediately after LSL.COM and before any ODI LAN drivers. Here is a sample AUTOEXEC.BAT for an ODI workstation boot image file:

```
LSL.COM
RPLODI.COM
NE1000.COM
IPXODI.COM
NET3.COM
```

RPLODI.COM does not affect the amount of memory available for applications running on the workstation.

Logging In from a Diskless Workstation

After you've created the appropriate file discussed above, you can reboot your diskless machine. The workstation should then go to the file server and look for the NetWare shell. Since the boot image file is configured to execute the LOGIN parameter immediately after loading the shell, you'll be prompted to enter your login name. If this is your first time logging in, you should use the user name SUPERVI-SOR (which has all rights to the file server). If you have a multiple-server network, specify your file server's name and your username. For example, to specify server JUNGLE and username SUPERVISOR when prompted to enter the username, type:

```
JUNGLE/SUPERVISOR <Enter>
```

If your user name has a password, you'll be prompted to enter it. If you're logging in as SUPERVISOR for the first time, you won't have a password.

Troubleshooting Problems Specific to Diskless Workstations

Here are some tips for troubleshooting common problems encountered when installing diskless workstations.

Problem: A diskless workstation can't find a network server.

Solutions: Check these possible causes:

Verify that your cabling is properly set up and attached to the workstation.

Make sure that the image file was correctly set up with the correct IPX.COM and other files.

If you have several servers on one network, make sure that the image files are copied to the other file servers on that network.

Verify the configuration of the LAN adapter: for example, make sure you have the right jumper settings for interrupt, port, and boot ROM.

Installing an OS/2 Workstation

Whereas virtually any Intel-based personal computer can serve as a DOS or Windows workstation, the OS/2 workstation has a greater set of requirements. Unlike DOS, which requires just 640KB of RAM, an OS/2 workstation can easily require 2MB or more. For an OS/2 workstation, you should select a computer with at least 6MB to 8MB of RAM, if not more.

The OS/2 operating system itself will require approximately 14MB to 20MB of disk storage. Therefore, a PC with a hard disk is required. Although it is feasible to boot the OS/2 workstation from a floppy disk drive, most OS/2 users choose to boot the system from the local hard drive.

Finally, it's important to remember that you can't create an OS/2 network workstation on a diskless PC. Diskless systems boot from specialized boot ROMs on their internal network interface boards. On current diskless PC offerings, however, the boot ROMs are designed to work only with DOS.

Steps for Installing the Requester on the Workstation

The NetWare Requester for OS/2 routes the request between the workstation and the file servers. The NetWare Requester installation basically consists of three steps: copying the NetWare Requester files to the workstation's local hard drive, modifying the CONFIG.SYS file, and installing the NetWare utilities for OS/2. The NetWare utilities for OS/2 are specifically designed to be used with OS/2 workstations.

Here are the steps for the requester:

1. Make sure you've installed the LAN adapter in the workstation.

2. Make sure you've installed OS/2 on the workstation on which you're putting the requester.

3. Boot your workstation up to OS/2 and insert the REQUESTER diskette into drive A.

4. Choose the OS/2 "Full Screen" option and then change to drive A.

5. Type "INSTALL <Enter>."

6. Follow the prompts to install the Requester files to specific directories on the local hard drive. If a directory isn't listed on the screen, press <Ins> and enter the name of the directory. If you enter the name of a directory that doesn't exist, you'll be prompted to create it. After selecting the location you want for the files, you'll be prompted to answer "Yes" or "No" to continue the installation and copy the files to the local hard disk.

Modifying the CONFIG.SYS File

1. The first step in this process is to copy the CONFIG.PST file into the

CONFIG.SYS. Do this by typing:

```
COPY CONFIG.SYS + CONFIG.PST <Enter>
```

2. If you haven't copied the NetWare Requester .DLL files to the OS2\DLL directory or the hard disk root directory, you need to modify a statement in the CONFIG.SYS file. The statement LIBPATH must have C:*directory* at the end of it. The directory is the place where you installed the OS/2 Requester.

3. Add the drive and specification to your PATH statement in the CONFIG.SYS. For example, your path statement may look like this:

```
L:\OS2
```

4. The next step is to remove the "rem" statement from the statement in your CONFIG.SYS that is associated with the LAN adapter you're using in your workstation. For example, if you were to install a Novell Ethernet NE2000 and remove the "rem" from the statement, it would look like this:

```
DEVICE=C:\Directory\NE2000.SYS
```

Directory signifies the place where you installed the NetWare Requester.

> **Note:** You can use a NET.CFG file to specify the configuration settings (interrupts, I/O addresses, and so forth) for your LAN adapter. You can also use it to specify different protocols you may want to use. Refer to your *NetWare Requester for OS/2* manual.

5. If you're going to use NetWare PCONSOLE and PSC print utilities or Named Pipes (or any programs associated with SPX), you must remove the "rem" from

the following statements in the CONFIG.SYS:

```
REM DEVICE=C:\Directory\SPX.SYS REM
RUN=C:\Directory\SPDAEMON.EXE
```

6. To use Named Pipes, you may choose one of two procedures. The first is to use Named Pipes without defining your workstation as a Named Pipes server. To do this, you must remove the "rem" from the following statements:

```
REM DEVICE=C:\Directory\SPX.SYS REM
RUN=C:\Directory\NPDAEMON.EXE
```

The second choice is to have your workstation act as a Named Pipes server. To do this, remove the "rem" from the following statements and define the *ComputerName*:

```
REM DEVICE=C:\Directory\NMPIPE.SYS REM
DEVICE=C:\Directory\NPDAEMON.EXE ComputerName
```

Directory signifies the place you installed the NetWare Requester and *ComputerName* represents the name you want for the Named Pipes server. But remember: never use duplicate names on an internetwork.

7. The NetWare Requester installation has two parts. First, install the Requester with the NWREQ.SYS file. Second, install the file system with the NWIFS.IFS file. You must modify your CONFIG.SYS by adding the following statement to it:

```
IFS=C:\Directory\NWIFS.IFS
```

This statement must appear in the CONFIG.SYS as follows:

```
DEVICE=C:\Directory\NWREQ.SYS
IFS=C:\Directory\NWIFS.IFS
RUN=C:\Directory\NWDAEMON.EXE
```

8. To use NETBIOS, remove the "rem" from the following statements in the CONFIG.SYS:

```
REM DEVICE=C:\Directory\NETBIOS.EXE REM
RUN=C:\Directory\NBDAEMON.EXE
```

Installing the NetWare OS/2 Utilities on the Server

Follow these steps to install OS/2-specific utilities for NetWare. You should have the utilities on each server that has a workstation logging in to it. To prevent any possible confusion between DOS and your OS/2 utilities, we recommend that you create a separate directory for the utilities.

To make things simpler when logging in to the file server, you may want to copy the LOGIN and SLIST utilities to the hard disk on the OS/2 workstation. With the utilities on the hard disk, you need not be attached to the file server to use the LOGIN utility to log in to a file server.

1. Log in to the server on which you want to install the utilities. Do this by choosing the "Full Screen" option, placing the OS2UTIL-1 diskette in drive A:, changing to drive A:, and then typing

   ```
   LOGIN [ServerName]/SUPERVISOR <Enter>
   ```

   SUPERVISOR is the default user with all rights to the server. (We'll discuss SUPERVISOR more fully in Chapter 15.)

2. Next, create an OS2 subdirectory in the server's SYS:LOGIN and SYS:PUBLIC directories. You'll store the utilities in this subdirectory.

3. Using NetWare's MAP command, map the following drives:

   L: to SYS:LOGIN/OS2

and

P: to SYS:PUBLIC/OS2

4. Place the OS2UTIL-1 diskette into drive A:, change your drive to A:, and then type

```
SERVINST <Enter>
```

5. Follow the prompt that will be given. The utilities will then be copied to the SYS:LOGIN/OS2 and SYS:PUBLIC/OS2 directories.

6. Flag the utilities to protect them from possible deletion by changing your default drive to P: and typing

```
FLAG L: *.* S RO <Enter>
FLAG P: *.* S RO <Enter>
```

7. The last step is to modify the system login script by typing "SYSCON <Enter>" at the P: drive, selecting "Supervisor Options" from the main menu, and then choosing "Edit System Login Script." Add the following command to the system login script:

```
MAP L:=SYS:LOGIN
```

Logging In from an OS/2 Workstation

To log in to a file server, you must make sure that you've completed the LAN adapter installation and installed the Requester for OS/2. Follow these steps to log in to the file server:

1. Reboot and bring up your workstation to OS/2.

2. Choose the OS/2 "Full Screen" option.

3. Go to the L: drive (or wherever you have the NetWare LOGIN utility located).

4. Then type

```
LOGIN ServerName/UserName <Enter>
```

5. If you have a password associated with the username, you'll be prompted to enter it.

Troubleshooting the OS/2 Workstation

Before you start troubleshooting an OS/2 workstation, it's important for you to review the configurations you set during the installation.

Problem: You can't find a file server.

Solutions: This problem usually stems from the LAN adapter being unable to talk with the server. Check these possible causes:

Verify that your cable to the LAN adapter is attached.

Make sure that your LAN adapter is completely seated in the workstation bus expansion slot.

Make sure that you've selected the correct setting for the type of cabling you're using on the network. For example, Ethernet can be set to thick or thin.

Check the CONFIG.SYS to make sure that the correct LAN driver was selected and that the associated LAN driver is located on the workstation hard disk. For example, if you're using a Novell NE2000 Ethernet adapter, make sure that you have the following statement in the CONFIG.SYS:

```
DEVICE=C:\Directory\NE2000.SYS
```

Directory signifies the place where the OS/2 requester is installed. Also make sure that NE2000.SYS is located in that same directory.

Make sure that NET.CFG file settings match the LAN adapter settings. Refer to the *NetWare Requester for OS/2* manual for more information on creating and modifying the NET.CFG file.

Installing the Macintosh Network Software

Installing a Macintosh computer on the network is relatively easy compared to working with DOS or workstation installations. Probably your toughest task is to make sure you have the right version of the Macintosh system software. When we go through each of the installation steps, we'll tell you which version of the Macintosh system software you must have installed.

1. Verify that you have AppleShare software version 2.0 or greater installed in the System Folder. To check this, open the System Folder by clicking on the icon. After the System Folder is open , make sure you see the AppleShare icon. If you don't see the AppleShare icon, you must install it. If you do see the AppleShare icon, click on it and select "Get Info" from the "File" menu to display information about the currently installed AppleShare software.

2. If you're going to print from your Macintosh to a network printer, the Macintosh workstation must be running LaserWriter Version 5.2 or above or ImageWriter Version 2.7 or above. You can check these versions by going to the System Folder and clicking on the icon representing the device you want information about and then selecting "Get Info" from the "File" menu.

3. Verify that the Macintosh System Version is 6.0 or above and the Finder is 6.1 or above. You can check the version by choosing "About the Finder" from the Apple menu.

4. Verify that the Macintosh Chooser Version is 3.3 or above. You can check the version by opening Chooser from the Apple menu. The version will be displayed in the right-hand corner of the Chooser menu.

5. If you're using LocalTalk (Macintosh's physical level network protocol) to communicate on the network, you must verify that you've installed the cable to

the built-in port.

6. If you're using EtherTalk (Macintosh's Ethernet shell for Ethernet adapters), you must install the Ethertalk software in the System Folder. Most Macintosh Ethernet vendors will supply you with a software EtherTalk installer. After you've finished installing the software, go to the Control Panel from the Apple menu, choose "Network," and make sure it's set up for EtherTalk. Refer to the supplement that comes with your Ethernet adapter for more information on the installation of the adapter and software.

Logging In from a Macintosh Workstation

After you've installed the LAN adapter and the networking software (including the Macintosh software configuration for the file server), you should be able to log in to the file server.

1. Boot up your Macintosh client.

2. Open the Macintosh Chooser from the Apple menu, then click on the AppleShare icon in the Chooser dialog box.

3. After you click on the AppleShare icon, the defined AppleTalk zones will appear. When you select the different zones (if you have multiple zones), the file servers within that zone will be displayed. Also notice the place for entering your login name in the Chooser dialog box.

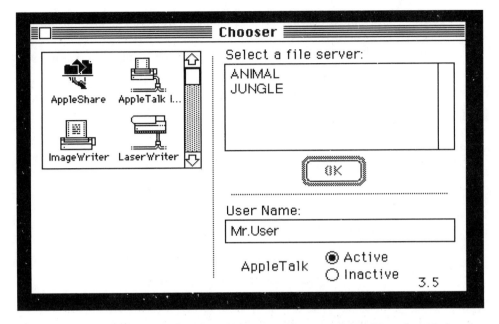

4. To log in to the server, double-click on the server name. You should then be prompted with the option of changing the your username. Also, if a password is associated with that username, you must enter it. The server volumes will be listed to select from; to open a server volume, double- click on it, or click in the check box next to the volume to save the username and password and to select the volumes that will automatically mount every time you start up.

5. The server volume icon should then appear on the desktop (just like your local hard disk).

6. To log out of the server, drag the server volume icon(s) into the Trash.

Troubleshooting Macintosh Workstations

Here are some tips for troubleshooting common problems encountered when installing and using Macintosh workstation on the network.

Problem: The AppleShare icon doesn't appear while you're in Chooser.

Solution: This problem usually results from the Apple Workstation software not being installed on the Macintosh workstation. To correct this, install the AppleShare Workstation software supplied with the Macintosh.

Problem: The Macintosh client can't find a file server.

Solutions:

Verify that your cables are plugged in correctly.

Verify that your cable port on the LAN adapter is set correctly. For example, on Ethernet the cable port may be set to thick or thin.

Verify that you set up the Macintosh for either the built-in network or any other LAN driver you're planning use. For example, you may have installed an Ethernet adapter to use on the network. To select the driver for this adapter you must first go into the Control Panel from the Apple menu, select the Network icon, and then select the appropriate driver.

Make sure you've verified that your NetWare for Macintosh NLMs on the file server are correctly working. (Refer to Novell's NetWare for Macintosh 3.0 manuals for specific troubleshooting information.)

Problem: While you're using the MultiFinder, you run out of memory when trying to open the folder on the network. For example, you might get an error message like this one:

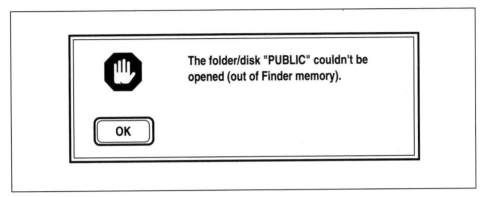

Solution: Increase the "Application Memory Size" value for the Macintosh Finder. To do this, open the System folder and click *once* on the file named "Finder". Using the mouse, pull down the File menu to "Get Info" and in the lower right-hand corner of the window, change the application memory size from 160K to 512K for an 80MB drive, or 800K for a 160 MB drive.

CHAPTER 10

Installing an External Router

An external router is an optional part of your network. It is a networked computer whose purpose is to efficiently manage the routing of packets to different segments of the network. The first section of this chapter discusses how to plan and install an external router on your network. The latter half is devoted to managing and troubleshooting the router.

Uses for External Routers

The most common use for an external router is to connect two different types of cabling systems. For example, you can use an external router to link an Ethernet and a Token-Ring network together, as shown in Figure 10-1.

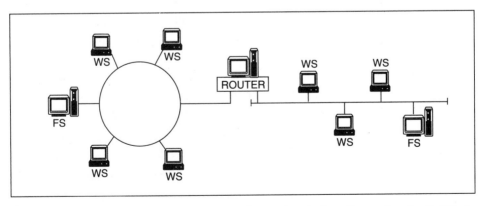

Figure 10-1: An external router connects up to four networks together and routes NetWare packets between dissimilar cabling systems.

Of course, you can accomplish the same thing by installing several network boards in the NetWare v3.11 file server, which includes an internal router. However, establishing an external router is often cheaper than purchasing a new file server every time you need to connect different cabling types. On a busy internetwork, using external routers also offloads much of the routing traffic from the servers.

You can also use a router to divide a large network into several smaller segments. Although this is a viable scenario for growing a network, it's not necessarily an optimum configuration. Installing the router adds another node through which packets must pass to get to their destination. While this configuration slows the overall network throughput, it is a workable solution for alleviating a routing bottleneck or distributing network traffic more evenly across the internet.

Planning the Router Installation

Before attempting to install an external router, you should decide which external router mode you're going to use, make sure that your hardware is NetWare-compatible, and fill out an information sheet that gives information on how the router will interact with the network. Here are some guidelines to use in planning your router installation.

Deciding Which Router Mode to Use

NetWare v3.11 offers three external router modes: dedicated protected mode, nondedicated protected mode, and dedicated real mode. You should base your choice on factors such as performance, hardware compatibility, and risk of router failure. The following sections address the advantages and disadvantages of each option.

Dedicated Protected Mode

A dedicated protected mode router is a computer dedicated to operate only as a router. The principal advantages of a dedicated router are higher performance (when compared with nondedicated mode) and greater reliability. Because a dedicated mode router is committed to performing just one task— routing data to different segments of the network—the router's processor is free to move data more quickly on and off the cable. Furthermore, since no other applications are running on the machine, there is less chance of the machine crashing from an application conflict or user error.

The primary disadvantage of a dedicated mode router is that you have to commit a workstation machine to this task. Because this type of router runs in protected mode, you must use a machine based on the Intel 80286, 80386, or 80486 microprocessors with a minimum of 512KB of memory. No fancy monitor, mouse, or other peripherals are required to run the dedicated router software. If you will be running NetWare v2.x VAPs (such as the Print Server VAP included with NetWare v3.11) on the router, you'll need more RAM (the router can have up to 8MB of RAM if needed).

Nondedicated Protected Mode

A nondedicated protected mode router is a computer which serves as both a router and a user workstation on the LAN. The primary advantage of this mode is the full utilization of your hardware investment, since the nondedicated router can also run applications.

The primary disadvantage of a nondedicated router is decreased performance and lower reliability. Because the machine is used for workstation tasks, the processor may not always be free to respond to a routing request. In addition, the presence of applications and user input may increase the probability of machine failure.

Since the nondedicated router also runs in protected mode, you must use a machine based on the Intel 80286, 80386, or 80486 microprocessors. The router software requires about 300 to 500KB of memory (depending on how many networks it is connecting). In addition, you'll need enough memory for DOS and whatever applications will be run on the workstation. The maximum amount of RAM is 8MB. Because of memory and performance constraints, we recommend that you *not* run VAPs on a nondedicated router.

Dedicated Real Mode

A dedicated real mode router is much like the dedicated protected mode router in that its only task is to route information. The difference is that this real mode router can be run on machines based on the Intel 8086 or 8088 microprocessor. (The real mode router can also be set up on computers based on the 80286, 80386, or 80486 microprocessors.) The disadvantage of a dedicated real mode router is that it can access only 1MB of memory, which is insufficient for handling VAPs.

Checking Hardware Compatibility

In general, the NetWare router software will run on any IBM PC XT, AT, and PS/2 model computer. However, some restrictions apply, especially for IBM-compatible machines. Novell offers a service that certifies whether a certain brand of hardware is compatible with NetWare products. If you have an off-brand PC that you want to install as a router, check first with your NetWare Authorized Reseller to confirm that your hardware is compatible with NetWare. This simple step can help you eliminate hours of frustration when installing your router.

Recording Information About the Router

The NetWare v3.11 *Installation* manual provides a Router Configuration Worksheet that will be helpful during the installation. We recommend that you fill out this worksheet before performing the installation. This worksheet will not only help you during the installation, but will also serve as a permanent record of the router installation for future troubleshooting.

Installing an External Router

Now that you've made your preparations, you're ready to perform the router installation. The first step is to install the hardware itself. After you obtain the computer and set it up to run DOS, you must correctly configure the network interface cards and install them into the future router. Make sure that no conflicts occur with other hardware in the computer. (Consult the card's installation supplement to determine appropriate installation configurations.)

The software installation consists of several easy steps. During this part of the installation, we recommend you use the Novell-provided Router Configuration Worksheet. Your primary goal in running the NetWare ROUTEGEN program is to create a file by the name of ROUTER.EXE. You'll use this file to bring up your router after you've booted DOS on the machine.

1.   Boot your router machine with DOS version 3.0 or higher.

2. If you haven't made a working copy of the NetWare ROUTEGEN diskette, do so now.

3. Insert the working copy of the ROUTEGEN diskette into the floppy diskette drive.

4. At the DOS prompt, type "ROUTEGEN <Enter>." A screen will appear, giving some simpleinstructions on the installation. After you've read the intructions, press <Enter>.

5. ROUTEGEN displays a screen showing the different router modes. Highlight the name of the mode you're installing and press <Enter>.

6. If you've chosen the nondedicated mode, you must enter a unique network address for the nondedicated workstation process running in the router. This address must be different than all other network addresses used on the internet.

7. When prompted, enter the number of communication buffers that your router will need. The default is 150, but you can select any number between 40 to 1,000. Because the communication buffers take a minimal amount of RAM, we suggest that you use at least the default number. Increasing the number of buffers can improve the performance of the router.

8. You must now select the appropriate LAN drivers to match the LAN cards you installed in the router. If you filled out the Novell-provided Router Configuration Worksheet, refer to it for this information. Highlight "Driver" and press <Enter> to see a list of available drivers.

    To select a driver, highlight the one you want and press <Enter>. If the LAN card driver you need isn't on the list, insert the diskette provided by the network interface card manufacturer (labeled LAN_DRV_*XXX*) and press <Ins>, then <Enter>. You can now select the driver from the expanded list which should include the driver for the network interface card you are installing.

9. After selecting the LAN driver, specify the configuration of the adapter by highlighting "Configuration option" and pressing <Enter>. Choose the configuration that matches the settings on the network card, preferably the default option (Option 0) that the network boards are set to at the factory, and press <Enter>.

If none of the configurations matches what you need and the "JUMPERS Configurable" option appears for the driver, select that option. You can then use the NetWare JUMPERS utility to create a customized configuration after you finish the router generation program. (Refer to the NetWare v3.11 *Utilities Reference* manual for detailed information on using JUMPERS.)

10. As prompted, enter a valid network address for the LAN adapter. This address must be different than any other network address being used anywhere on the internet.

11. Repeat steps 8 through 10 for each LAN adapter installed in the router. You can install up tofour LAN adapters in an external router (two if you're using only Token-Ring adapters).

If an asterisk (*) appears next to a selected option, it indicates a conflict with another selected configuration. Go back and reconfigure the driver with a non-conflicting option.

12. When you've completed the configuration and no conflicts exist, record the configuration information on the Router Configuration Worksheet. Then press <F10> to generate the router software (ROUTER.EXE).

Before you start up your router, you need to copy the ROUTER.EXE file from the ROUTGEN diskette (or from the ROUTEGEN directory if you ran the program from the network) to a bootable DOS diskette. Use the DOS version 3.0 or higher FORMAT command with the "/S" parameter to create a bootable disk, then copy ROUTER.EXE onto that diskette.

Starting an External Router

Once you've completed the generation of ROUTER.EXE and copied it to a bootable diskette, you're ready to intialize the router. The process is slightly different for dedicated and nondedicated routers. Follow the instructions in the appropriate section below.

Starting a Dedicated Router

For a dedicated external router, we recommend that you create an AUTOEXEC.BAT file that will initiate the ROUTER.EXE file. You can do this by using a the DOS COPY CON command or a text editor. The file needs only one line:

    ROUTER

If you boot the external router from a hard disk, copy the ROUTER.EXE file to the root directory and use the same AUTOEXEC.BAT file to start up the router.

Starting a Nondedicated Router

The nondedicated router uses the same startup command ("ROUTER") as does the dedicated router. In addition to the ROUTER.EXE file you generated with the ROUTEGEN program, copy the CONSOLE.COM file, from the \LOGIN subdirectory of the NetWare DOSUTIL-1 diskette, to the router boot diskette. You also need a CONFIG.SYS file with the "FILES=" and "BUFFERS=" parameters set to at least 20 each.

With the nondedicated router, you first run the ROUTER command to bring up the router. Then you load NET3, NET4, or NET5 (depending on the version of DOS you're using) so that the machine can operate as workstation on the network. Here's an example of how your AUTOEXEC.BAT might look for bringing up your router:

    ROUTER
    NET3
    F:
    LOGIN

The router will start, then the shell will load and the user will be prompted to enter his or her login name. Once the name and password are entered correctly, the user can work on the network in the same way as on other DOS workstations. As a precaution, though, if the user turns off the workstation, the router will be shut down as well. Train your nondedicated router workstation users to simply log out when they are finished working, leaving the router running.

Switching Between Console and DOS Mode

There are two commands you need to remember when you have to toggle between the router console and the DOS mode: CONSOLE and DOS.

Use the CONSOLE command to switch from the DOS mode to the router console. Enter the command as follows from the DOS prompt:

CONSOLE <Enter>

In response, the current DOS screen will disappear and the router console prompt (:) will appear. You can then proceed to enter the router console commands listed in the next section. If a user application was running before the switch, its operation will be suspended until the user switches back to DOS mode.

To switch from the router console to DOS mode, use the "DOS" command. At the colon prompt (:), type:

DOS <Enter>

The computer will revert to its DOS workstation mode and the user can continue working where he or she left off in DOS.

Maintaining the Router

Once the router is up and running, the routing function begins without any further intervention from you. However, you may find it necessary to reconfigure the router if you are running VAPs on it, or use other console commands to maintain and troubleshoot the router.

The ROUTER.CFG File

The usual way to load VAPs on an external router is to copy the VAP files onto the router's boot diskette. The router software then detects the presence of the VAPs and asks you, during the bootup routine, if you want to load them. You must answer either "Yes" or "No" before the bootup process can continue.

NetWare allows you to create a ROUTER.CFG file to overcome some of the limitations inherent to the normal router initialization procedure. For example, if you want the router to be able to boot up without anyone having to respond to the VAP load prompt, you can create a DOS text file containing this line:

VAP WAIT *n*

For *n*, substitute the number of seconds (between 10 and 360) you want the router to wait before automatically loading the VAPs.

If your VAP files are too large to fit on the boot diskette, you can set another path in which NetWare will look for these files. To specify an alternate location for VAP files, include this line in the ROUTER.CFG file:

VAP DISK *Path*

You can specify any valid driver letter or directory path for the Path variable. If you specify drive A, you can load VAPs from only one diskette. If you have more VAPs to load than will fit on a single diskette, copy them to a hard disk directory and alter the VAP DISK path accordingly.

Router Console Commands

The following router console commands will help you maintain and troubleshoot your router:

CONFIG
DOWN
TRACK ON/TRACK OFF
VAP

A nondedicated router must be in "console" mode (as explained above) before you can enter these commands.

The CONFIG Command

Use this command to identify the current configuration of the router. As shown here, the CONFIG command gives specific information about the address and configuration of router's LAN card:

```
LAN A Configuration Information:
    Network Address: [BADCAB1E] [00001B45EF9A] Hardware Type:
    NetWare Ethernet NE2000 V1.00EC (881004) Hardware Set-
    tings: IRQ = 3, I/O Base = 300h, no DMA or RAM

LAN B Configuration Information:
    Network Address: [ FEED001] [00001BAEF330A] Hardware Type:
    NetWare Ethernet NE2000 V1.00EC (881004) Hardware Set-
    tings: IRQ = 2, I/O Base = 320h, no DMA or RAM
```

The DOWN Command

This command brings down the router correctly. Never just turn off a router to shut it down. The DOWN command gives the router time to notify other routers on the internetwork that it is going down and that its routes to other network segments will no longer be available. The other routers then adjust their routing tables accordingly.

The TRACK ON and TRACK OFF Commands

The TRACK ON command displays information about network packets that are being sent and received in the router. (The TRACK ON command can also be run from a file server to diagnose the routing function of the server.) From a troubleshooting perspective, this display is extremely useful when you're really not sure if a router, server, or workstation is communicating with the network. As shown below, TRACK ON displays vital information about servers, the network, and connection requests.

```
IN [BADCAB1E:00001B056AE7]          ANIMAL   1
     JUNGLE 2
IN [BADCAB1E:00001B056AE7]          FEED001 1 OUT
[BADCAB1E:FFFFFFFFFFFF]             ANIMAL 1
     JUNGLE   2
```

The syntax for interpreting the TRACK ON information is:

Direction [*NetworkAddress:NodeAddress*] *ServerName Hops ServerName Hops ...*

or

Direction [*NetworkAddress:NodeAddress*] *NetworkAddress Hops ...*

When using this command for basic troubleshooting purposes, you should concentrate on the direction (IN and OUT) information. If your router (or server) is receiving and transmitting information, you'll see both "IN" and "OUT" packets in the TRACK ON display. The "IN" designates a packet coming into the server. "OUT" signifies a packet going out. The network and node address of the machine sending or receiving the packet is shown in brackets.

To demonstrate how you might use this information, let's assume that only "OUTs" are being displayed for one of the network addresses with no "IN" showing up at all—and you know you have a workstation trying to communicate. From this information, you can determine that the router is trying to talk (represented by an OUT) with some network segment, but nothing on that segment can find the router (represented by an IN). In this case, look at your cabling to make sure the physical communication channel between the workstation and the router is intact.

If no information at all appears when you type TRACK ON, your router may be down. Use the TRACK OFF command to turn off the display of the TRACK ON command.

The VAP Command

Use this command to display the current VAPs loaded on the router, along with any console commands or usage parameters each VAP recognizes.

Troubleshooting Your Router

Here's a list of possible router problem scenarios and their solutions.

Problem: A workstation can't send information from one side of the router to the other.

Solutions:

Verify that the cables are correctly attached to each network adapter in the router.

If you're using Ethernet cable, make sure you have set the Ethernet card to use thick or thin cable, according the your network cabling type.

Verify that your router isn't down by using the TRACK ON command (as explained previously). If the router is DOWN, nothing will be displayed when you do a TRACK ON.

Verify that the router is "routing" information by using the TRACK ON command at the router console.

Problem: When booting the router, you receive a LAN card initialization error on the router's console similar to this one:

```
Initializing LAN A Error Initialing LAN Driver: NE2000 Hardware
Fails To Respond. The router will be shut down.
```

Solutions:

Make sure the physical configuration of your LAN adapter and the software configuration for that adapter (specified in ROUTEGEN) are the same. Use the CONFIG console command to display the current software configuration of the LAN adapter.

Reseat the LAN adapter in the router's bus expansion slot.

You may need to replace the LAN adapter that didn't initialize with one known to be good.

Problem: The error message "Invalid configuration parameter" appears when you're loading the VAPs on the router.

Solution: This message represents an invalid parameter in the ROUTER.CFG file. To correct the error, make sure you didn't misspell one of lines in the ROUTER.CFG. Make sure that your variables are being correctly used. Also check for unneeded spaces and lines.

Problem: A real mode router runs out of memory when loading VAPs.

Solution: Real mode allows the router to use only 640KB of memory. This is not enough memory to run VAPs. Switch to a protected mode router and install more memory if necessary. Also check for unneeded spaces and lines.

CHAPTER 11

Upgrading to NetWare v3.11

Upgrading a NetWare server to v3.11 is a critical operation that many users face. The only situation where you don't need to perform some type of upgrade operation is if you're building the very first NetWare network at your site. Here is a list of possible upgrade situations.

Upgrade Tasks

Installing a new v3.11 server on an existing LAN
- Install NetWare v3.11 on new server
- Copy v3.11 utilities to existing servers

Convert a v3.x server to v3.11
- Back up the v3.x server
- Copy v3.11 SYSTEM-1 files to server's DOS partition
- Boot server and install v3.11 system and public files
- Copy v3.11 utilities to other existing servers

(contintued)

Convert v2.x server to v3.11
- Back up the v2.x server twice using UPGRADE.EXE
- Perform v3.11 installation from scratch to v2.x server machine
- Install v3.11 workstation software on one workstation machine
- Save v3.11 NET$LOG.DAT file
- Convert and restore the v2.x bindery using UPGRADE.EXE
- Convert and restore the v2.x file system using UPGRADE.EXE
- Boot the server using NetWare v3.11
- Install v3.11 system and public files
- Restore NET$LOG.DAT file
- Re-install execute-only files
- Set user passwords o Edit system and user login scripts
- Copy v3.11 utilities to existing servers
- Back up the v3.11 server

As you can see from this list, upgrading a NetWare server can be a daunting task with some tricky steps. There are some dangerous pitfalls, which we'll cover in this chapter. Note that this chapter isn't intended as a substitute for the "Upgrade" section of the NetWare v3.11 *Installation* manual. Rather, this chapter is a troubleshooting guide, the intent of which is to alert you to potential problems specific to your NetWare installation. Consequently, you should read this chapter before reading the upgrade instructions in the NetWare v3.11 *Installation* manual.

Upgrading from NetWare v2.x

By far the most difficult upgrade to execute is converting a NetWare v2.x server to a NetWare v3.11 server. There are several reasons for the difficulty of a v2.x to v3.11 upgrade, including the following:

- 2.x and v3.11 servers have a different bindery format
- 2.x and v3.11 servers have a different file system
- 2.x and v3.11 servers have a different security model

These differences have an effect not only on the server itself, but also on the utilities by which users gain access to the server. Consequently, you must upgrade workstation and utility software across an entire NetWare internetwork as part of the upgrade process. (NetWare v3.11 workstation software and utilities are backwardly compatible with v3.x and v2.x servers, but the opposite is not true.)

Benefits of Using UPGRADE.EXE

Novell's UPGRADE.EXE program was designed to preserve your present NetWare environment, while allowing you to move up to the more powerful NetWare v3.11 platform. The benefits of using UPGRADE.EXE are:

- It preserves the bindery.
- It preserves the directory structure and rights.
- It preserves the original file ownership.
- It allows you to use the pre-upgrade server machine as the post-upgrade server.
- It automates and formalizes the entire upgrade process.

There is an alternative to performing a formal upgrade using UPGRADE.EXE. You can install NetWare v3.11 on a fresh machine (provided the machine is appropriately configured, with a 386 or better processor, lots of RAM, and ample disk storage), and start from scratch. You can even duplicate the old server's bindery and directory structure and transfer the old server's files over the network using the NCOPY.EXE utility. After transferring the files from the old server to the new server, you can "recycle" the old server machine by converting it to a workstation.

The problem with doing a "manual upgrade" is that you can't duplicate the old server's environment with total fidelity. For example, copying data from the "old" server to the "new" server changes file ownership and creation dates. And duplicating NetWare's security structure from one server to another is an intricate and tricky task. The more heavily used the "old" server is, the more difficult and time-consuming a manual upgrade becomes, with possibly uncertain results.

The formal upgrade process, using UPGRADE.EXE, affords you a structured method of reproducing the old server's bindery and directory structure with a high degree of fidelity to the old server. It allows you to convert server data from the v2.x or v3.x format to the v3.11 format, while preserving ownership and security information.

Another advantage of using UPGRADE.EXE is that it allows you the option of archiving a complete NetWare v2.x server environment to tape, converting the NetWare v2.x server environment to an equivalent v3.11 environment, and restoring the NetWare v3.11 environment from tape to the same machine. In other words, you don't need a second server-class machine upon which to base the new v3.11 server. You can simply use the "old" machine and the "new" platform. (If you wish, you can also use UPGRADE.EXE to transfer the NetWare v2.x environment to a brand-new machine.)

Shortcomings of UPGRADE.EXE

Our opinion is that UPGRADE.EXE is your best method of converting a NetWare v2.x server to a v3.11 server. However, UPGRADE.EXE leaves several gaps in the new platform you should be aware of:

- It can't transfer files flagged Execute-Only.
- It can't decrypt v2.x user passwords.
- You can't use v2.x-specific files (VAPs and applications using outdated APIs) on a v3.11 server.
- Some applications' copy protection interferes with UPGRADE.
- It leaves potential holes in directory security.
- It can duplicate certain bindery group objects.

Here are some ways to work around these shortcomings of the UPGRADE program.

Upgrading Execute-Only Files

One advantage the NetWare file system has long enjoyed over standard DOS file systems is the ability to flag files as "execute-only." By flagging a file Execute-Only, you cause NetWare to deny any type of access to the file by clients, except for the purpose of executing the file. This means clients can't copy or read the file, or write to the file. You can only delete the file. As the supervisor, you can't remove a file's Execute-Only attribute.

Flagging a file as Execute-Only has several advantages, including virus protection and enforcement of software licenses. However, UPGRADE.EXE can't archive or transfer Execute-Only files. In fact, there is no way to transfer an Execute-Only file from NetWare to tape, or from one NetWare server to another.

The only way to make sure that Execute-Only files are on your new NetWare v3.11 server is to manually install them on the new server from their original floppy diskettes. You should do this after using UPGRADE.EXE to successfully upgrade to the new server.

If you don't know which files are flagged Execute-Only, you can use the NetWare FLAG utility to discover them. For example, to produce a list of all .EXE and .COM files and save the list to a file, type these commands at the command line:

```
FLAG *.EXE SUB > exe.txt <Enter>
FLAG *.COM SUB > com.txt <Enter>
```

The first command specifies "*.EXE" for the file name. This causes FLAG to list attributes for all files having the .EXE extension. Likewise, the second command causes the FLAG utility to list attributes for files having the .COM extension. If you execute the above command lines from a NetWare v2.x volume's root directory, the "SUB" option causes NetWare to display attribute information for files in the volume root directory and also in all subdirectories.

The ">" symbol in the command examples above causes DOS to redirect its output to the file specified immediately following the ">." Because FLAG is likely to produce a lengthy listing of files and their attributes, it's helpful to redirect all output to a file, which you can then browse, using a text editor, at your leisure. Redirecting the FLAG output to a file also gives you a permanent record of files and their attributes.

After executing FLAG as shown in the examples above, you should investigate the output files. You'll be looking for something similar to this:

```
FILE.EXE  [- - - X - - - -]
```

All files with an "X" in their list of attributes are ExecuteOnly files. These files are the ones you must re-install manually on the new server.

Upgrading User Passwords

NetWare v2.x stores user passwords as encrypted character strings. While UPGRADE.EXE can read the encrypted passwords, it can't decrypt them. Consequently, UPGRADE.EXE can't set user passwords on the new v3.11 server. After successfully restoring the old server environment to the new v3.11 server, you must therefore restore user passwords manually. The best method for doing this is to assign a new password to each user, and then encourage users to change their passwords in the near future.

If you ask users to change their own passwords, you should check to make sure they have the capability to do so. You can grant users the ability to change their own passwords by going into the SYSCON utility and selecting the "User Options" menu. Once you've selected the "User Options" menu, highlight the name of the user you want to be able to change his or her password, and select "Account Restrictions." SYSCON will present you with a window having, among other things, an option to grant this ability to the highlighted user.

Handling NetWare v2.x-Specific Files

VAPs, of course, don't run on NetWare v3.11. In addition, some network applications use outdated NetWare APIs not supported by NetWare v3.11. You should delete VAPs from the NetWare v2.x server before running UPGRADE.EXE.

You won't be able to identify network applications that use outdated APIs by running them on the v2.x server. If possible, the best thing to do is to test them on a v3.11 server *before* running UPGRADE.EXE. If you experience problems during the test, remove the offending applications from the v2.x server before you run UPGRADE.EXE. We'll discuss implementing a pre-upgrade testing program at the end of this chapter.

Dealing with Copy Protection

Copy protection is a generally nasty method of enforcing software licensing agreements. Some copy protection schemes are hostile to the NetWare file system and can disrupt the functioning of UPGRADE.EXE. If you have applications with copy protection on your v2.x server, you should contact the application vendor for instructions on moving the application to the new v3.11 server.

Mapping Between Old and New Directory Security

The NetWare v3.11 file system has a richer security architecture than its v2.x counterpart. One problem, however, is that there isn't always a direct correspondence between v2.x security settings and v3.11 security settings.

After you run UPGRADE.EXE, you should verify directory trustee assignments and directory effective rights for all users to make certain that there are no security holes on the new v3.11 server. The best strategy for doing this is to isolate a group of directories that contain sensitive data and check them first. If you notice any security holes in these sensitive directories, you should close them up and then check every directory tree on the server for similar security holes. See Chapters 12 through 15 for instructions on defining security for NetWare users and directories.

Duplication of Users or Groups

By default, every NetWare server has a group named EVERYONE and a user named SUPERVISOR. When you restore the NetWare v2.x server environment to the new v3.11 server, UPGRADE.EXE will replace the v3.11 server's default SUPERVISOR and EVERYONE objects with those of the old v2.x server. If you don't want UPGRADE.EXE to do this, you must explicitly tell it not to. (UPGRADE.EXE prompts you at the critical moment for your wishes concerning this matter.)

Duplication of users or groups is especially troubling when you're combining two or more v2.x servers to a single v3.11 server using UPGRADE.EXE. Not only will each v2.x server have its own SUPERVISOR and EVERYONE definitions, but there is potential for other duplicate users and groups.

To solve this problem, UPGRADE.EXE allows you to rename duplicated users and groups on the new v3.11 server.

Two Methods for Running UPGRADE.EXE

There are two different methods you can use to run UPGRADE.EXE to upgrade from NetWare v2.*x* to NetWare v3.11.

The Transfer Method

The transfer method assumes you've got a new machine upon which to place the upgraded NetWare v3.11 server environment. By attaching the new machine to the same network as the v2.*x* server, you allow UPGRADE.EXE to transfer the entire v2.*x* environment over the network directly to the new v3.11 server machine. Figure 11-1 shows how the transfer method works.

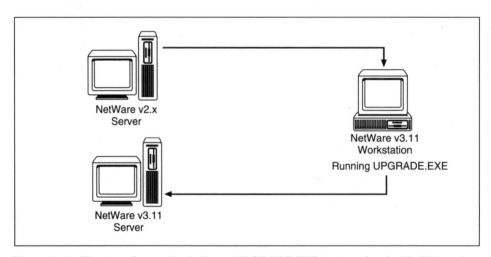

Figure 11-1: The transfer method allows UPGRADE.EXE to transfer the NetWare v2.*x* server environment directly to the new v3.11 server machine.

If your NetWare v2.*x* server has an 80286 processor, you must have a new machine for the NetWare v3.11 server. NetWare v3.11 requires an 80386 or higher processor in order to run.

The advantages of using the transfer method are:

*   It's faster than the archive method.
*   The v2.*x* server remains whole throughout the upgrade process.

The transfer method of running UPGRADE.EXE is faster than the archive method because it allows UPGRADE.EXE to move the server environment over the network directly to the new machine. The archive method, which stores the NetWare v2.*x* environment temporarily to tape, involves more steps and uses a slower media.

The second advantage of the transfer method is that you don't need to destroy the NetWare v2.*x* server environment until after the upgrade is complete. This gives you an extra safety hatch, so to speak, if anything goes wrong during the upgrade process.

The disadvantage of the transfer method is that it requires a second server-class machine. Because NetWare servers typically have large amounts of RAM and large hard-disk storage capacity, a server machine is significantly more expensive than a workstation machine. Frequently users will balk at the expense of a second server-class machine.

The Archive Method

The archive method of running UPGRADE.EXE stores the entire NetWare v2.*x* server environment to tape archive. Once the v2.*x* environment is stored to tape, you destroy the NetWare v2.*x* environment and install NetWare v3.11 on the same server machine. Finally, you run UPGRADE.EXE again, which converts and restores the NetWare v2.*x* environment to the v3.11 server. Figure 11-2 shows how the archive method works.

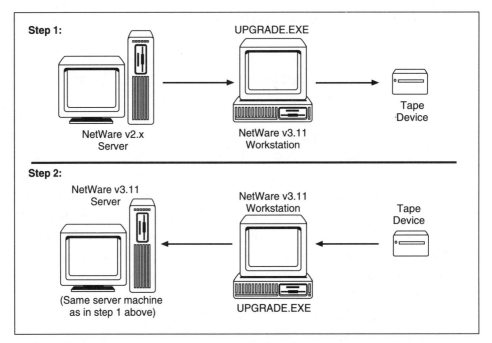

Figure 11-2: The archive method of running UPGRADE stores the entire NetWare v2.x server environment to tape temporarily, and then converts and restores that environment to the same machine, which now has NetWare v3.11 installed on it.

In case your tape archiving device doesn't have the capacity to archive the entire NetWare v2.11 environment to a single tape cartridge, you can instruct UPGRADE.EXE to archive the server's bindery and data separately. You can even split the v2.x server's data among multiple tape cartridges if you need to.

The advantage of the archive method is that it allows you to perform an upgrade to NetWare v3.11 using a single server machine. The disadvantages of the archive method are as follows:

- It's slower than the transfer method.
- It's more complicated than the transfer method.
- It may require splitting NetWare v2.x bindery and data among multiple tape cartridges.

We recommend that you use the transfer method of UPGRADE.EXE to upgrade your server if at all possible. NetWare v3.11 deserves a heavy-duty server machine to run on, and if your NetWare v2.x server machine is old or underconfigured, you should consider buying a new machine for NetWare v3.11. You can always recycle the old v2.x machine as a workstation.

Hardware factors aside, the transfer method is superior to the archive method because it's a simpler procedure. The archive method, with its extra intermediate steps, presents more opportunities for the upgrade process to fail.

UPGRADE.EXE Features You Should Not Ignore

Regardless of whether you use the transfer or archive method to upgrade to NetWare v3.11, there are some important features of UPGRADE.EXE you should take advantage of:

- Selecting the working directory
- Excluding files from the transfer
- Renaming duplicate files and directories

The working directory is the directory where UPGRADE.EXE stores its log files. UPGRADE.EXE creates and maintains a record of the entire upgrade process and stores this record within the directory you designate as the working directory.

A working directory can be located on the v3.11 target server, on another server located on the same network (but not the v2.x server from which you are upgrading), or on a local hard drive attached to the workstation from which you are running UPGRADE.EXE.

We recommend that you locate the working directory on another server (if one is available) or on a local hard drive. If you locate the working directory on the NetWare v3.11 target server, you run the slight risk of losing the UPGRADE.EXE log files in case something goes terribly wrong during the upgrade process. This is an especially troubling prospect, because the sole purpose for which UPGRADE.EXE maintains its log files is to recover from errors occurring during the upgrade process.

Excluding files from the transfer allows you to ensure that v2.*x*-specific applications don't get transferred to the new NetWare v3.11 server. In addition, you can exclude outdated or unneeded data files from the upgrade process, thereby shortening the time to upgrade.

Causing UPGRADE.EXE to rename duplicate files and directories provides an extra measure of insurance against unintended data loss as result of the upgrade process. Every NetWare server has by default a SYS:SYSTEM, SYS:PUBLIC, SYS:MAIL, and SYS:LOGIN directory. Because you must install NetWare v3.11 on the new server before transferring the v2.*x* environment to it, these directories will, by definition, exist on the target server. If you don't instruct UPGRADE.EXE to rename duplicate files and directories, it will overwrite the existing directories on the target server.

If you allow UPGRADE.EXE to rename existing files and directories, it will change the extension of the duplicate files or directories to allow them to co-reside on the server with the duplicates that were there first. After the upgrade process, you can go through the renamed duplicate files and move or delete them according to your requirements.

Renaming duplicate files requires extra hard disk space on the NetWare v3.11 server. For example, if you have 6MB of duplicate files, you'll need 6MB of free and clear space on the v3.11 server in order to store the renamed duplicate files. But the advantage of renaming duplicate files is that you have more discretion over the upgrade process.

Potential Upgrade Problems

While UPGRADE.EXE attempts to hide the complexities of transferring a complete server environment to a new and totally different operating system (NetWare v3.11), you shouldn't remain ignorant of certain technical details. You should pay special attention to these facts:

- NetWare v3.11 requires more hard disk space than v2.x to store an equivalent amount of data

- The NetWare v3.11 SYSTEM and PUBLIC directories occupy more space than their v2.x counterparts.

- NetWare v3.11 uses different device drivers than v2.x.

Because of differences in the NetWare v3.11 and v2.x file systems, your server machine will require greater hard disk capacity than the v2.x server did to store the same amount of data. While the differences in storage capacity requirements are difficult to calculate, you should plan on 5% data expansion or more as result of the upgrade process.

The factors that determine the exact amount of data expansion you will experience as result of the upgrade process include the total number of files you're transferring, the average size of those files, the volume disk block size on the v3.11 target server, and more. As a rule, the smaller the average size of files you are transferring, the greater the total amount of data expansion you'll experience during the upgrade process.

If you're planning on adding new name space support to the NetWare v3.11 server, you should plan on at least an additional 5% expansion of data for each name space module you're planning to use.

By definition, NetWare servers place operating system-related files in the SYS:SYSTEM directory, and utility programs in the SYS:PUBLIC directory. NetWare v3.11 requires more space for both its operating system-related files and its utility programs than NetWare v2.x does. Consequently, you should allow for at least 2MB of additional storage for the SYS:SYSTEM and SYS:PUBLIC directories when upgrading from a v2.x server to a v3.11 server.

Device driver support is an issue you should address when planning your purchase of NetWare v3.11. Some device drivers supported by NetWare v2.x may are not currently supported by NetWare v3.11. Furthermore, if you're purchasing a new server machine along with NetWare v3.11, you should ensure that disk and LAN drivers for that machine are available for NetWare v3.11.

Novell has made an effort to ship drivers for popular LAN adapters and hard disks with the NetWare v3.11 operating system. If you're planning on using Ethernet, Arcnet, or Token-Ring adapters, you should have little problem finding compatible LAN drivers for your NetWare v3.11 server. However, if you're planning to install an FDDI or other less-common LAN, be sure that LAN drivers are available for NetWare v3.11. Furthermore, if you're planning to use a non-standard server machine such as a NetFRAME, make sure that disk and LAN drivers for NetWare v3.11 are available.

If you have doubts about device driver support for your disk or LAN hardware, contact the vendor of each device in question before attempting to upgrade your server from NetWare v2.x to v3.11.

Combining Multiple v2.x Servers

It's possible to combine two or more NetWare v2.x server environments into a single NetWare v3.11 server environment. In fact, with the increased capacity of NetWare v3.11 over v2.x, it makes sense to combine servers in such a manner.

The primary problem you'll encounter when combining NetWare v2.x servers is duplication of bindery objects such as users and groups, as well as file duplication. You already know that the user SUPERVISOR and the group EVERYONE exist on every NetWare server. In addition, you know that the SYS:SYSTEM, SYS:PUBLIC, and SYS:LOGIN directories exist on every server. Furthermore, the NET$LOGIN.DAT file, which contains the server's system login script, exists on every server.

You may have created your own duplicate bindery objects, directories, and files on the servers you wish to combine. For example, you may have defined on each server a LOTUS123 group that includes users of the popular spreadsheet package. Perhaps you've defined duplicate print queues or backup users. Individual users will almost certainly exist on more than one server.

The only way to tackle the problem of duplicate bindery objects, directories, and files when combining servers is careful pre-upgrade planning. During the pre-upgrade planning, you should decide how you'll combine duplicate server entities. Perhaps the best option is to go through the new NetWare v3.11 server after the upgrade and combine duplicate entities by hand, using the SYSCON utility.

If you're using NetWare's resource accounting feature on the NetWare v2.x servers you're combining, use SYSCON to go through each user's account on each v2.x server and record the user's current account balance for that server. You should then calculate a cumulative account balance for the user and record that balance. After the upgrade, go through each user's account on the new v3.11 server and restore that user's account to its pre-upgrade cumulative balance.

Upgrade Safeguards

A successful upgrade is one that results in a close duplication of the old NetWare v2.x server on the new v3.11 server. "Close duplication" means that you don't lose data unintentionally during the course of the upgrade, and that you preserve bindery objects, directories, and files to the greatest degree possible. There are several things you can do to ensure the success of your server upgrade, including:

- Run a NetWare v3.11 test server for several weeks prior to the upgrade.

- Test all your network applications on a NetWare v3.11 server prior to the upgrade.

- Back up the NetWare v2.x server at least twice prior to the upgrade.

- Perform a "test restoration" of the NetWare v2.x server prior to the upgrade.

Running a NetWare v3.11 test server prior to the upgrade assumes you have a new server machine on which you can install the new operating system. If at all possible, we recommend you install and run a test server. During the test period, which should last from two to four weeks, you should determine if:

- The server hardware is stable when running NetWare v3.11.

- The NetWare v3.11 server participates successfully in your internetwork.

- Applications you're planning to run on the NetWare v3.11 server execute successfully.

- The backup hardware you're planning to run with the NetWare v3.11 server does in fact work.

- The UPS hardware and software works with NetWare v3.11.

A period of two to four weeks is long enough to ensure that most problems likely to occur will, in fact, occur. You should ensure that the NetWare v3.11 server remains on-line for two successive weeks. If the server goes down, you should attempt to isolate the problem. Depending on the configuration of your server machine and the applications you're planning to run on it, the testing period can entail some intensive troubleshooting.

Most problems likely to arise during a test period involve incompatible server hardware or ill-behaved server applications. We strongly recommend that you run NetWare v3.11 on Novell-certified hardware only. We further recommend that you do not attempt to run suspect applications on the NetWare v3.11 server.

To test your backup hardware and software with the NetWare v3.11 test server, you should perform at least two successful backups and restorations of server data. To test your UPS hardware and software with the NetWare v3.11 test server, disconnect the UPS hardware from its power supply and observe the behavior of the server, thus confirming that the UPS system performs up to your expectations.

Troubleshooting the Upgrade Process

If you follow the upgrade instructions contained in the NetWare v3.11 *Installation* manual, as well as the safeguards you've just read about, you shouldn't experience any catastrophes resulting from the upgrade. However, that doesn't mean you won't have any problems. Here's a discussion of some problems you may encounter, as well as their solutions.

Problem: UPGRADE.EXE aborts during transfer or restore session.

Solution: UPGRADE.EXE will abort if it loses its connection to the NetWare v3.11 target server, the source device (which is either the old v2.*x* server or a tape device), or some other run-time error. The primary concern you should have is the state of the bindery on the target server. Consequently, you should restore the v3.11 target server's bindery before re-starting UPGRADE.EXE.

To restore the v3.11 server's bindery, log in to the v3.11 target server as SUPERVISOR and run the BINDREST.EXE utility. The command-line syntax, from the workstation command line, is:

```
BINDREST <Enter>
```

After running BINDREST.EXE, delete the bindery map file for the old v2.x server. UPGRADE.EXE creates a bindery map file for the old server, which it uses to monitor the progress of the bindery transfer and conversion. To delete the bindery map file, use the UPGRADE.EXE "List Bindery Map Files" option to select the bindery map file for the old v2.x server. Once you've selected the file, you can delete it by pressing the <Del> key.

Problem: UPGRADE.EXE can't transfer Macintosh files.

Solution: You haven't loaded Macintosh name space support on the NetWare v3.11 target server. Stop the UPGRADE.EXE session. From the console of the v3.11 target server, load the Macintosh name space module:

```
LOAD MAC.NAM <Enter>
```

Once you've loaded the Macintosh name space module, you can restart the UPGRADE.EXE session and continue with the upgrade.

Problem: UPGRADE.EXE will not execute the transfer.

Solution: You can't transfer the server environment if users other than yourself are currently connected to either the v2.x source server or the v3.11 target server. Note that "connected" does not necessarily mean "logged in."

Note also that NetWare v2.*x* VAPs typically log in to the server as special types of users.

UPGRADE.EXE will present you with a list of connections to either the source or the target server. Remove these connections by selecting them and pressing the <Delete> key. Ensure that logins are disabled for both servers by executing the DISABLE LOGIN console command. Continue with the upgrade process.

Problem: The workstation running UPGRADE.EXE hangs with no error notification.

Solution: You may be experiencing driver problems at the workstation. Note that if you're using the archive method of running UPGRADE.EXE, you may be experiencing conflicts between the tape device driver and other TSRs loaded at the workstation. Ensure that only the tape device driver and the NetWare v3.11 workstation shell software is installed at the workstation and re-try running UPGRADE.EXE.

If the problem persists, try changing the interrupt or I/O settings for the tape device driver, the workstation LAN adapter, or both.

Part Three

Directories, Applications, and Users

Once you have the network properly installed, you can use this section of the book to help you establish user accounts and applications so you can put the network to use.

- **Chapter 12: Incorporating a Security Scheme** tells you how to take advantage of the security features in NetWare v3.11 and how to plan and establish a strong security scheme before the users ever enter the LAN.

- **Chapter 13: Setting Up Directories** helps you establish a directory structure to keep the network server in order and to make the network easier to maintain and to use.

- **Chapter 14: Installing Applications** offers hints and troubleshooting advice for getting your applications to run smoothly on the LAN.

- **Chapter 15: Setting Up Users and Groups** shows you how to take advantage of the NetWare group concepts. This chapter also gives several alternatives for establishing network user accounts.

- **Chapter 16: Creating Login Scripts** explains how NetWare login scripts work and helps you set up user login scripts for your network.

- **Chapter 17: Setting Up Menu Interfaces** shows you how to make the network easier to use by establishing customized menu interfaces, using either the NetWare MENU utility or one of the many third-party menu interface tools.

- **Chapter 18: Using NetWare's Resource Accounting** describes how to set up charge rates to charge your network users for their use of server resources.

CHAPTER 12

Incorporating a Security Scheme

Because of the distributed nature of data on a network, security is a major issue for most installations. Many people fear that if their files are not stored locally, under their own control, the information will be wide open to everybody. To protect network data from unauthorized access, NetWare provides three basic types of security: login/password restrictions, rights security, and attribute security. These types of security form three "doors" through which a user must successfully pass before accessing any data stored on the network. If a user lacks the proper keys for any one of these doors, that user is effectively barred from the data. With a little knowledge and planning, you can combine these types of security to establish just the right level of access to network data.

This chapter reviews NetWare security concepts, provides step-by-step examples for setting up security on a NetWare v3.11 server, and discusses some utilities that can be used to maintain the server's security scheme. It also includes a section on preventing computer viruses on the network.

NetWare v3.11 Security Concepts

The security features in NetWare v3.11 restrict who can use the network, determine which directories and files they can use, and determine what the users can do with the files (such as reading or modifying a file). This section looks at the three levels of NetWare security in more detail.

Login and Password Restrictions

Login security determines who can access the server, when they can access the server, and which workstation they can log in from. NetWare enforces these restrictions through assigned usernames, user passwords, and administrator-controlled account restrictions.

In order for users to log in to the server, they must know their individual usernames. This is the network's first line of defense. If someone tries to log in using a username unknown to the server, the server will prevent that person from logging in. In most cases, however, usernames aren't very hard for an intruder to figure out. For example, it's easy to guess that a user named John Smith may have a username of either JOHN or JSMITH.

Because usernames are fairly easy to guess, NetWare includes an optional password feature that can be associated with the username. If the network administrator has specified that users must have a password, each user must enter the correct password before being able to successfully log in. If a user enters an incorrect or misspelled password, NetWare denies that user access to the server.

Password Restrictions

NetWare protects the user password in several ways. First, the LOGIN program refrains from echoing (displaying) the password on the monitor as the user types it in. In addition, the operating system can impose various other restrictions to make passwords as secure as possible. As the network administrator, you can configure each of these features in SYSCON according to the network's specific needs.

The *password length limitation* prevents users from using short passwords that may be easy for someone else to guess. You can adjust the minimum password length anywhere from 2 to 45 characters. To be secure, passwords should be at least five or six characters long.

The *periodic password change* feature forces users to change their passwords after a certain number of days. Typically, users should change their passwords every 30 to 60 days. In organizations such as banks or government agencies where data is highly confidential, passwords should be changed more frequently.

The *unique password* feature prevents users from using the same password over and over. To prevent repeated passwords, the server is equipped to remember the last eight passwords that anyone has used. It also requires that the passwords be in use for a period of at least one day between changes. This prevents a user from changing the password eight different times in a day and then using his or her favorite password again.

The *limited "grace" login* feature lets users continue to log in a specified number of times after their passwords have expired. When the password first expires, the operating system reminds the user to enter a new password. If the user doesn't do so, the system reduces the remaining limited grace number by one. If the user doesn't enter a new password before the grace login number reaches zero, the system will lock out that particular user account.

Station, Time, and Other Account Restrictions

User account restrictions provide added login protection to prevent unauthorized access to the LAN. These features allow you to further restrict how and when users can access the server. They also help prevent successful entry by intruders using common methods of attack. These features are optional and configurable to meet the needs of your network.

NetWare's *station restrictions* let you restrict a user to log in only from certain assigned workstations. By specifying exactly which network and node addresses the user must log in from, you can prevent an intruder from logging in as a user assigned to a different workstation.

The *time restrictions* prevent users from logging in to the file server during specified days and hours. For example, you may want to prevent users from logging in to the file server on weekends or during the daily backup.

Another restriction is how many concurrent connections a single user can have. This prevents users from logging in all over the network and taking up file server connections needlessly. You can also place restrictions on the length of time users accounts will be valid. This feature is useful in academic environments where accounts for a particular class must all expire after the end of the term or semester.

When a user's account expires, NetWare locks the account to prevent possible entry by an intruder. User accounts will also be locked when the maximum number of failed password attempts is exceeded, or when an account's balance is depleted. If the number of password attempts is exceeded, the network will temporarily lock the account for a specified period of time. If the account expires or is depleted, the network locks the account until you reactivate it.

NetWare Rights Security

Once a user has successfully logged in to the network, access to specific directories and files is further controlled by NetWare's rights security. The rights a user has define what that user can do within a network directory and its subdirectories, as well as what he or she can do with particular files in those directories. NetWare v3.11 features eight different rights, each of which is identified by its first initial (or identity initial).

NetWare v3.11 Rights

Identity Initial	Right Name	Function
S	Supervisory	Gives the user all rights in the directory, its files, and its subdirectories. It is usually granted to workgroup managers and user account managers to give them complete control over a portion of the directory structure. The S right cannot be filtered out by an Inherited Rights Mask.
R	Read	Allows the user to open a closed file and read its contents (if it is a data file) or run the program (if it is an executable file).
W	Write	Allows the user to open a closed file and write to it or modify its contents.
C	Create	Allows the user to create files and subdirectories in the directory.
E	Erase	Allows the user to delete files and subdirectories in the directory.
M	Modify	Allows the user to change the attributes of the directory, its files, and its subdirectories; the user can also rename them (but not change the contents of files).
F	File scan	Allows the user to see the directory's files in a directory listing.
A	Access control	Allows the user to change trustee assignments and the Inherited Rights Masks for the directory, its files, and its subdirectories.

Trustee Rights Assignments

In NetWare v3.*x*, you can assign any combination of these eight rights at both the directory and the file level. When you grant NetWare rights to a user, the user becomes a "trustee" of the particular directory or file. Thus, this type of rights assignment is known as *trustee rights*.

While granting rights on a user-by-user basis is appropriate for small networks with few users, the preferred method in large networks is to grant rights to groups. In SYSCON, you can create groups for users who perform similar tasks, who have similar needs for information, or who use the same applications, printers, or print queues. You can then use either SYSCON, FILER, or GRANT to assign appropriate rights to the entire group at once (as explained later in this chapter).

Trustee rights assignments directly affect only the directory in which they are assigned. However, users' rights "flow down" the directory structure to all subdirectories unless they are filtered out at some lower level by means of the Inherited Rights Mask.

The Inherited Rights Mask

As an added precaution, every directory and file created on the NetWare file server has an *Inherited Rights Mask* that can further restrict what rights can be exercised. As its name implies, the Inherited Rights Mask (or IRM) determines what rights can be inherited from a higher directory level.

By default, the IRM contains the full set of NetWare rights (no restrictions). If you want to prevent certain rights from being inherited from a parent directory, you must remove those rights from the child directory's IRM using either FILER or the ALLOW utility (as explained later in this chapter). You must have the Access Control right to modify the IRM.

If you're used to working with NetWare v2.*x* and its Maximum Rights Masks, the concept of the Inherited Rights Mask can be confusing. In many ways, the IRM functions exactly opposite from the Maximum Rights Mask. Whereas the Maximum Rights Mask filters out what trustee rights can be exercised in a directory (thus superseding any trustee rights assignment), the IRM filters out what effective rights can flow down from the parent directory. An explicit trustee assignment in the directory supersedes any restrictions imposed by that directory's IRM.

The IRM affects only the specific directory or file in which it is modified. If you change the IRM for one directory, the default IRM (which allows all rights to be inherited) remains in effect for all subdirectories unless you change them as well. Likewise, if you change the IRM for one file in a directory, the IRMs for the other files remain at the default unless you change them too.

Effective Rights

A user's *effective* rights are those rights the user can actually exercise in a given directory or file. Effective rights are determined by looking at the combination of trustee rights assignments and the IRM. There are three keys to understanding effective rights:

- If a user has been granted rights to a directory or file, either through a user or group trustee assignment or through a security equivalence to another user, the user's effective rights equal the trustee rights, regardless of the IRM at that level.

- In the absence of an explicit trustee assignment, the user's effective rights are inherited from the parent directory, unless some of the rights are filtered out by the directory's IRM.

- The Supervisory right throws off the whole effective rights equation. If a user has been granted the Supervisory right, he or she automatically has all rights in that directory and in all subdirectories. The Supervisory right cannot be restricted by the IRM at some lower level.

Figure 12-1 summarizes how NetWare determines a user's effective rights in a directory and for a specific file.

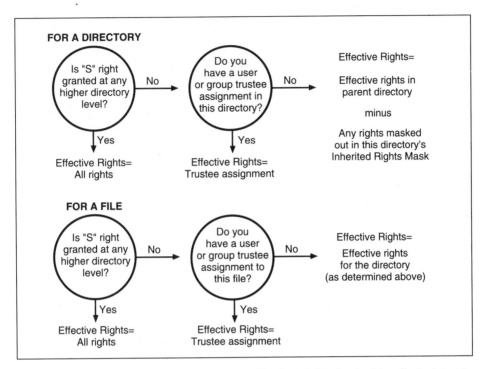

FOR A DIRECTORY

Is "S" right granted at any higher directory level?

No → Do you have a user or group trustee assignment in this directory?

No → Effective Rights=

Effective rights in parent directory

minus

Any rights masked out in this directory's Inherited Rights Mask

Yes ↓

Effective Rights= All rights

Yes ↓

Effective Rights= Trustee assignment

FOR A FILE

Is "S" right granted at any higher directory level?

No → Do you have a user or group trustee assignment to this file?

No → Effective Rights=

Effective rights for the directory (as determined above)

Yes ↓

Effective Rights= All rights

Yes ↓

Effective Rights= Trustee assignment

Figure 12-1: NetWare determines a user's effective rights by looking first at trustee assignments, then at the effective rights allowed to flow down from above by the Inherited Rights Mask.

Here's an analogy to help you remember how the IRM and effective rights relate. Suppose you find out your rich uncle has died and left you $7 million. To your dismay, the IRS intervenes and takes away $3 million for inheritance tax. The portion of the original amount you can actually spend is only $4 million. Think of the $7 million as the seven NetWare rights (excluding the Supervisory right) granted at a higher directory level. The IRM is like the IRS—it always takes away. In this analogy, three of the original seven "rights" were filtered out, leaving the remaining four as your effective rights.

Attribute Security

The third level of NetWare security consists of attributes, which are special properties you can assign to specific files and directories. For example, you can assign particular attributes to a file to prevent users from deleting or modifying the file by mistake.

Attributes override effective rights, preventing tasks that rights would otherwise allow. For example, a user cannot delete a file flagged with the Delete Inhibit attribute, even if that user has the Erase right in the directory. Attributes apply equally to the user SUPERVISOR and users with the Supervisory right. However, these users have the Modify right and can change the attributes if they have to.

The NetWare v3.11 attributes fall into three categories: directory attributes, file attributes, and system attributes. You should become familiar with the various attributes, because they will be helpful to you as you set up and maintain your network security scheme.

Directory Attributes

You can assign attributes to directories to prevent users from renaming or deleting them. You can also designate directories as hidden or system directories. The following directory attributes can be assigned in FILER or with the FLAGDIR utility (as explained later in this chapter). You must have the Modify right in the directory.

Attribute	Identity Initial(s)	Description
Hidden	H	This attribute hides directories from DOS DIR scans. However, the NetWare NDIR command will show the hidden directories to a user who has the File Scan right.
System	Sy	This attribute also hides directories from DOS DIR scans. However, the NetWare NDIR command will show the directory to a user who has the File Scan right.
Purge	P	This attribute causes NetWare to immediately purge all files in the directory when they are deleted. Purged files cannot be retrieved with the SALVAGE utility.

Delete	D	This attribute prevents users from deleting the directory even if Inhibit they have the Erase right. However, a user with the Modify right could remove the Delete Inhibit attribute and then delete the directory.
Rename	R	This attribute prevents users from renaming the directory even if Inhibit they have the Modify right. However, a user with the Modify right could remove the Rename Inhibit attribute and then rename the directory.

File Attributes

You can also assign attributes to individual files to protect them from accidental erasures or modifications. You can also designate files as hidden or system files. The following file attributes can be assigned in FILER or with the FLAG utility (as explained later in this chapter). You must have the Modify right to the directory or file.

Attribute	Identity Initial(s)	Description
Hidden	H	This attribute hides files from DOS DIR scans. Users can locate files with this attribute by using the NetWare NDIR command, but only if the user has the File Scan right.
System	Sy	This attribute is used on system files (the files an operating system needs tooperate). NetWare's system files are stored in the SYS:SYSTEM directory. The System attribute hides the files from DOS DIR scans, but users can seethe files by using the NetWare NDIR command if they have the File Scan right.
Read Only	Ro	If a file is flagged Read Only, users can't write to, change, erase, or rename the file even if they have Write and Erase

rights. (NetWare's FLAG utility automatically assigns the Delete Inhibit and Rename Inhibit attributes along with Read Only.)

Read Write   Rw   This attribute allows users to both read the file and write to it (modify its contents). All files are flagged Read Write by default. Users with the Modify right can change this attribute.

Shareable   S   This attribute allows several users to simultaneously access the file. It is normally used along with the Read Only attribute. By default, all files are Nonshareable when first created or copied to a NetWare server. Application program files should be flagged Shareable Read Only.

Execute Only   X   This attribute prevents files from being copied or backed up. It can be assigned only to files with .COM and .EXE extensions. Use this attribute with caution; once you've assigned it, you can't remove it without deleting the file altogether. Make sure you have a backup copy of the file before assigning this attribute. Also, some applications do not run correctly when flagged Execute Only.

Copy   C   This attribute applies only to Macintosh workstations. It prevents Mac Inhibit users from copying the file even if they have the appropriate rights. However, a Mac user with the Modify right could remove the Copy Inhibit attribute and then copy the file. (DOS machines ignore this attribute.)

Delete Inhibit   D   This attribute also applies only to Macintosh workstations. It prevents Mac users from deleting the file even if they have the Erase right. However, a Mac user with the Modify right could remove the Delete Inhibit attribute and then delete the file. (DOS machines ignore this attribute.)

Other File Attributes

NetWare v3.11 uses other file attributes that are not security-related. Here is a list of these attributes.

Attribute	Identity Initial(s)	Description
Archive	A	This attribute is automatically assigned when a file Needed is created or modified since the last backup. It is the same as the DOS archive bit.
Purge	P	This attribute causes NetWare to immediately purge the file when it is deleted. Purged files cannot be retrieved with the SALVAGE utility.
Transactional	T	This attribute is assigned to files that you want to be protected by NetWare'sTransaction Tracking System (TTS).It should be assigned only to database files that contain transactional data.
Read Audit	Ra	NetWare doesn't currently use this attribute.
Write Audit	Wa	NetWare doesn't currently use this attribute.

Later in this chapter, we'll show you how to use NetWare utilities to display and modify NetWare file and directory attributes.

The NetWare Bindery

NetWare stores the security information for users, groups, directories, and files in a special-purpose database called the bindery. The bindery is made up of three components that assist in controlling access to the network and protecting NetWare's security: objects, properties, and property data sets.

- An *object* can be a user, group, file server, print server, or any other entity (physical or logical) that is named. The OS assigns a unique ID number for each bindery object.

- Each bindery object can have one or more *properties* associated with it. Properties consist of password information, account restrictions, account balances, the groups the user belongs to, and so forth.

- The *property data* sets are values assigned to the bindery object's properties.

In NetWare v3.11, the bindery is made up of three separate files which are located in the SYS:SYSTEM directory. The NET$OBJ.SYS file contains object information; the NET$PROP.SYS file contains property information; and the NET$VAL.SYS contains property values.

Setting Up NetWare Security

NetWare v3.11 provides numerous utilities for setting up your network's security: SYSCON, FILER, SETPASS, ALLOW, FLAG, FLAGDIR, GRANT, REVOKE, and REMOVE. This section briefly explains these utilities and provides examples of how to use them.

Using SYSCON to Set Up NetWare Security

You can use the SYSCON utility to set user account security features, as well as trustee rights and security equivalences for both users and groups. (We discussed these security features earlier in the chapter.) We'll show how to set up the user security features and then move on to security features for groups.

Setting Up User Security

Here's how to set up login and user account security in SYSCON:

1. Make sure you're logged in as SUPERVISOR.

2. At the workstation command line, type **SYSCON <Enter>.**

3. Select the "User Information" option from the "Available Topics" menu. A list of the current server users will appear.

4. To modify the security rights of a current user, highlight the username and press <Enter>. If the user doesn't exist, you'll need to add the username by pressing <Ins>. (For more information about setting up users, see Chapter 15.)

   After you've selected a user, the "User Information" menu will appear.

```
╔════════════════════════════════════╗
║        User Information            ║
╠════════════════════════════════════╣
║ Account Restrictions               ║
║ Change Password                    ║
║ Full Name                          ║
║ Groups Belonged To                 ║
║ Intruder Lockout Status            ║
║ Login Script                       ║
║ Managed Users and Groups           ║
║ Managers                           ║
║ Other Information                  ║
║ Security Equivalences              ║
║ Station Restrictions               ║
║ Time Restrictions                  ║
║ Trustee Directory Assignments      ║
║ Trustee File Assignments           ║
║ Volume Restrictions                ║
╚════════════════════════════════════╝
```

The options pertaining to security are described briefly below. menu gives you the options of setting account restrictions, password, security equivalency, time restrictions, and trustee directory assignments.

Account Restrictions. Select this option to set account restrictions such as password length, forced periodic password changes, and so forth. A window displaying the current account restriction information will appear. Make the necessary adjustments and press the <Esc> key to save and exit.

Change Password. Use this option to set or change the user's password. You'll then be prompted to enter a new password. After you've entered the password, you'll be prompted to enter the same new password again. This procedure verifies that you typed it correctly the first time. Non-SUPERVISOR users must enter the existing password (if any) before they can change the password.

Groups Belonged To. With this option, you can make the user a member of a group. Assigning a user to a group gives the user the same rights as the group has.

Security Equivalence. Use this option to make the user security equivalent to another user. A screen displaying the current security equivalences will appear. Press <Ins> to see a list of other possible equivalences. Select the user or group you want this user to be security equivalent to.

Station Restrictions. Use this option to restrict a user's login capabilities to specific workstations. Within this option, you can specify the network and node addresses from which the user must log in.

Time Restrictions. Use this option to restrict the time period during which a user can log in to the server. A window will appear displaying the current time restrictions. Each asterisk (*) represents a half-hour time period during the week. To restrict a time block, replace the asterisk with a space.

Trustee Directory Assignments. Use this option to assign the user trustee rights to certain directories. A list of the current trustee directory assignments will appear. Press <Ins> to specify the directory in which you're assigning trustee rights. You can either type in the full directory path here, or you can press <Ins> to look at the possible directories. As you select each directory, you'll see the cumulative directory path displayed.

Once the desired path is displayed, press <Esc> to cause the search for the correct path to stop. You can then either press <Enter> to make the user a trustee of that directory, or you can type in a new directory name beyond the displayed path. If you add a new directory, you'll be prompted to verify the creation of that directory.

After you've selected the directory to which you want to assign trustee rights, you'll see the selected path appear in the "Trustee Directory Assignment" list. You'll notice that Read and File Scan rights are the default rights assigned. To assign other trustee rights, select the directory from the "Trustee Directory Assignments" list. A list will appear of the current trustee rights that are already assigned to that directory. Press <Ins> to list other possible trustee rights that can be assigned to the directory. You can select several rights by marking them with the <F5> key; then press <Enter>. If you accidentally grant an inappropriate trustee right, highlight that right and then use <Del> to revoke it.

Trustee File Assignments. Use this option to assign the user trustee rights to specific files. The procedure is similar to the one explained above for assigning rights to directories, only you select files instead of directories.

Setting Up Group Security

Once a user is a member of a group, the trustee rights assigned to the group become valid for the user. Here's how to assign trustee rights to a group in SYSCON:

1. From the "Available Topics" menu in SYSCON, select the "Group Information" option. A list of the current group names will appear.

2. Select the group name for which you want set up security features. A menu titled "Group Information" will appear. To add a new group, press <Ins> and specify the group name. (For more information about creating groups, see Chapter 15.)

3. From the "Group Information" menu, select the "Trustee Directory Assignments" option. A list of the current trustee directory assignments will appear. Press <Ins> to specify the directory to which you're assigning trustee rights. You can either type in the full directory path, or you can press <Ins> to look at the possible directories. As you select each directory, you'll see the cumulative directory path displayed.

   Once the desired path is displayed, press <Esc> to end the search for the path. You can then either press <Enter> to make the user a trustee of that directory, or you can type in new directory beyond the displayed path. If you add a new directory, you'll be prompted to verify the creation of that directory.

   After you've selected the directory to which you'll be assigning trustee rights, you'll see the selected path appear in the "Trustee Directory

Assignment" list. Notice that the default rights assigned are Read and File Scan. To assign other trustee rights, select the directory from the "Trustee Directory Assignments" list. A list will appear of the current trustee rights assigned to that directory. Press <Ins> to list other possible trustee rights that can be assigned to the directory. Select the rights by using the <F5> key to mark them; then press <Enter>. If you accidentally grant an inappropriate trustee right, select the right and press <Del> to revoke it.

Using FILER to Set Up NetWare Security

FILER is a comprehensive utility for viewing and assigning directory trustee assignments. The difference between SYSCON and FILER is that with SYSCON you see security assignments from a user's perspective, and with FILER you see security assignments from a directory and file perspective.

Here's how to use FILER to modify attributes, set Inherited Rights Masks, and assign trustee rights for directories and files:

1. Make sure you are logged in as SUPERVISOR so you have the security rights to make changes within FILER.

2. From the workstation command line, type **FILER <Enter>.**

3. Use the "Select Current Directory" option to specify the directory in which you want to work.

4. Once the desired directory appears at the top of the screen, select the "Current Directory Information" option from the "Available Topics" menu. A "Directory Information" window appears.

```
╔══════════════════════════════════════════════════════╗
║          Directory Information for PUBLIC             ║
╠══════════════════════════════════════════════════════╣
║                                                      ║
║  Owner: SUPERVISOR                                   ║
║                                                      ║
║                                                      ║
║  Creation Date: August 2, 1991                      ║
║                                                      ║
║  Creation Time: 3:45 pm                             ║
║                                                      ║
║  Directory Attributes: (see list)                   ║
║                                                      ║
║  Current Effective Rights: [SRWCEMFA]               ║
║                                                      ║
║  Inherited Rights Mask: [SRWCEMFA]                  ║
║                                                      ║
║                                                      ║
║  Trustees: (see list)                               ║
║                                                      ║
╚══════════════════════════════════════════════════════╝
```

5. To view or set the directory's attributes, highlight "(see list)" to the right of "Directory Attributes:" and press <Enter>. Press <Ins> to add attributes to the "Current Flags" list. You can mark several attributes at once with the <F5> key. Press <Esc> to return to the "Directory Information" window.

6. To set the directory's IRM, highlight the "Inherited Rights Mask" field and press <Enter>. The current rights allowed in the IRM are displayed in the "Inherited Rights" list. To remove rights from the list, highlight them and press <Del>. (Note that you can't remove the Supervisory right). To add rights back in, press <Ins>. Press <Esc> to return to the "Directory Information" window.

7. To make trustee assignments in the directory, highlight "(see list)" to the right of "Trustees:" and press <Enter>. From here on, the procedure for assigning rights works the same as in SYSCON. To add a user or group trustee, press <Ins> and select the trustee from the resulting list. Then highlight the user or group name and press <Enter> to assign or withdraw rights. To remove existing user or group trustees altogether, highlight them and press <Del>.

8. To perform similar tasks in a subdirectory of the current directory, press <Esc> to return to the "Available Topics" menu, then select "Directory Contents" for a list of the directory's subdirectories and files. When you select a subdirectory, a "Subdirectory Options" menu appears. Select the "View/Set Directory Information" option to access a window similar to the one shown above.

Another useful option in the "Subdirectory Options" menu is called "Who has rights here." Select this option to see a list of every user and group that has effective rights in the subdirectory. This list is sometimes better than using the TLIST command because TLIST only shows explicit trustee assignments. FILER also shows those who have rights that are inherited from an explicit assignment at a higher directory level.

9. To view or set file attributes, IRMs, and trustees, select "Directory Contents" from the main menu. Then select a file (or multiple files using the <F5> key) from the resulting list of subdirectories and files. A "File Options" menu will appear. Select "View/Set File Information" to perform the tasks described above for the selected files.

Using SETPASS to Change User Passwords

Changing passwords at the network prompt through the SETPASS utility allows users to synchronize their passwords on all servers on which they use the same login name. The command format for SETPASS is:

```
SETPASS [ServerName][/UserName]
```

If you are attached to more than one server, SETPASS asks if you want to synchronize your password across all of the servers. This saves time and eliminates the problems of maintaining multiple passwords on multiple servers.

Using ALLOW to Modify Inherited Rights Masks

You can use the ALLOW command to change the Inherited Rights Mask of a directory of file. You need the Access Control right to change the IRM, but any user can run ALLOW to see the current IRM. Here is the command format for ALLOW:

```
ALLOW [Path [RightsList]]
```

Replace Path with a drive letter or full path name for a directory. Include a file name (or file pattern using the wildcard ? and * characters) for specific files. Here's a list of options you can use in ALLOW:

Option	Description
ALL	Use this option in place of *RightsList* to allow all eight trustee rights to be inherited (the default IRM setting).
N	Use this option in place of *RightsList* to allow no rights to be inherited. (Note that if the Supervisory right has been granted at a higher level, the "N" option can't prevent that right from being inherited.)

To specify other combinations of rights in the IRM, use the following abbreviations in your *RightsList*, inserting a space between each letter:

R   Read
W   Write
C   Create
E   Erase
M   Modify
F   File Scan
A   Access Control

For example, to allow only Read and File Scan rights to be inherited in the SYS:DATA\SALES directory, use the command like this:

```
ALLOW SYS:DATA\SALES R F <Enter>
```

To view the current IRM for all files and subdirectories of the current directory, type the ALLOW command with no parameters.

Note that the rights you specify in the ALLOW command are not added to the existing IRM, but completely replace the previous IRM setting. Thus, if the IRM already allows Read and File Scan and you want it to also allow Write and Create, you must include all four of these rights (R F W C) in the *RightsList* of the ALLOW command.

Remember that the Supervisory right is a special case; it cannot be filtered out in a directory's IRM.

Using FLAGDIR to Set Directory Attributes

You can use the FLAGDIR utility to display and change directory attributes. You must have Modify rights in the directory to use the FLAGDIR utility. Here is the basic format for the FLAGDIR command:

```
FLAGDIR [Path [Options]]
```

Replace *Path* with either a mapped drive letter or a full directory path. Here's a list of the *Options* you can specify:

Option	Description
HELP	Displays the usage format and available options.
D	This option affects the Delete Inhibit attribute that prevents users from erasing the directory.
R	This option affects the Rename Inhibit attribute that prevents users from renaming the directory.
P	This option affects the Purge attribute that causes files in the directory to be purged immediately upon deletion.
H	This option affects the Hidden attribute that hides directories from DOS DIR scans.
SY	This option affects the System attribute that hides system directories that contain files used by an operating system.
N	The "Normal" option cancels any other attributes that have been set and resets the directory to its default state.

Use the + or - characters to indicate whether you want to add or delete directory attributes. Place the appropriate character *in front of* the options. For example, to add the Hidden directory attribute to a directory in the SYS volume called GAMES, type:

```
FLAGDIR SYS:GAMES +H <Enter>
```

You can modify more than one attribute at a time. For example, to remove both the Hidden and SYstem attributes from the GAMES directory, your command would look like this:

```
FLAGDIR SYS:GAMES -HSY <Enter>
```

You can use FLAGDIR without any options to display the current directory attributes. For example, to find the attributes for the directory GAMES, type:

```
FLAGDIR SYS:GAMES <Enter>
```

Using FLAG to Set File Attributes

You can use the FLAG utility to change file attributes. To use FLAG, you need File Scan and Modify rights. Here is the format for the FLAG command:

```
FLAG [Path/FileName [Options]]
```

Replace *Path/FileName* with the path (if necessary) and name of the files you want to affect. You can use the wildcard characters (? and *) to specify a group of files. Here's a list of options you can use with the FLAG command.

Option	Description
N	Use this "Normal" option to reset files to the default attributes (Nonshareable/Read Write).
ALL	Use this option to assign all attributes (except Execute Only and Copy Inhibit) to thespecified files. The "ALL" option flags all affected files Read Only, not Read Write.
SUB	Add this option at the end of the command to flag files in all subdirectories (you don't need to insert a slash before the option, just a space).

Use the + or - characters to indicate whether you want to add or delete file attributes. Place the appropriate character *in front of* the attribute names, abbreviated as follows:

RO   Read Only
RW   Read Write
S   Shareable
A   Archive Needed
H   Hidden
Sy   System
T   Transactional
P   Purge
CI   Copy Inhibit
DI   Delete Inhibit
RI   Rename Inhibit
X   Execute Only (must be SUPERVISOR to assign)

For example, to delete the Archive Needed attribute from all files with the .DAT extension, your command would look like this:

```
FLAG *.DAT -A <Enter>
```

You can affect more than one attribute at a time. For example, if you want to add both the Shareable and Read Only attributes to all .DAT files in SYS:DATA\SALES, your command would look like this:

```
FLAG SYS:DATA\SALES\*.DAT +SRO <Enter>
```

Use the FLAG utility without any options to find out what the current file attributes are. For example, to find attributes for all the .EXE files in a directory, type:

```
FLAG *.EXE <Enter>
```

Using GRANT to Establish Trustee Rights

The GRANT utility is much like SYSCON and FILER in that you can use it to give users and groups trustee assignments. Use this command format for GRANT:

GRANT *RightsList* [FOR *Path*] TO [USER | GROUP] *Name*

Here's a list of the available trustee assignment options that you can grant to users and groups:

Option	Description
ALL	Use this option in place of *RightsList* to grant the specified user all trustee as signments.
N	Use this option in place of *RightsList* to take away all trustee rights for the specified user or group.
/SUB	Add this option to the end of the command to grant the same rights in all subdirectories of the directory.
/FILES	Add this option to the end of the command to grant the specified rights to the individual files in the directory.

To grant other combinations of rights, use the following abbreviations in your RightsList, inserting a space between each letter:

S   Supervisory
R   Read
W   Write
C   Create
E   Erase
M   Modify
F   File Scan
A   Access Control

For example, to grant user JACOB Read, Write, and File Scan rights to the SYS:DATA\SALES directory, use the command like this:

```
GRANT R W F FOR SYS:DATA\SALES TO USER JACOB <Enter>
```

Note that the rights you specify in the GRANT command are not added to the existing rights for the users or group, but completely replace any previously granted rights. Thus, if a user already has Read and File Scan rights and you want the user to also have Write and Create rights, you must include all four of these rights (R F W C) in the *RightsList* of the GRANT command.

Using REVOKE to Withdraw Trustee Rights

Use the REVOKE utility to take away directory trustee assignments from a user or group. Here is the command format for REVOKE:

```
REVOKE RightsList [FOR Path] FROM [USER | GROUP] Name
```

Here's a list of the available trustee assignment options that you can take away from users and groups:

Option	Description
ALL	Use this in place of *RightsList* to revoke all trustee rights from the specified user or group.
SUB	Add this option to the end of the command to revoke the specified rights in all subdirectories.
/FILES	Add this option to the end of the command to revoke the specified rights for all files in the directory.

To revoke other combinations of rights, use the following abbreviations in your *RightsList*, inserting a space between each letter:

S   Supervisory
R   Read
W   Write
C   Create
E   Erase
M   Modify
F   File Scan
A   Access Control

For example, to take away Read and Write trustee rights from user JACOB in the SYS:DATA\SALES directory, the command would look like this:

```
REVOKE R W SYS:DATA\SALES FROM USER JACOB <Enter>
```

Note that when you use REVOKE, the user or group remains listed as a trustee of the directory, even if you revoke all rights. Revoking all rights from a user or group in a directory prevents them from inheriting any rights from higher directory levels, because it is the trustee rights assignments that determine what rights a user has in a directory.

Using REMOVE to Delete Trustees

Use the REMOVE utility to delete a user or group from the directory's trustee list. Don't confuse this utility with the REVOKE utility, which takes specific trustee rights away from the user or group, but allows the user or group to continue to be listed as a trustee of the directory. When you use REMOVE, the user or group is no longer listed as a trustee of the directory, but they may still have rights in the directory if any are inherited from above.

Here is the command format for REMOVE:

```
REMOVE [USER | GROUP] Name [FROM Path]
```

For example, to remove the user JACOB from the SYS:DATA\SALES directory's trustee list, your command would look like this:

```
REMOVE USER JACOB FROM SYS:DATA\SALES <Enter>
```

Add the "/SUB" option at the end of the command to remove the specified user or group as a trustee in all subdirectories of the directory.

Add the "/FILES" option at the end of the command to remove the specified user or group as a trustee of all files in the directory.

Utilities for Finding Security Problems

To help you maintain security and troubleshoot security problems, NetWare offers the following utilities: RIGHTS, TLIST, WHOAMI, BINDFIX, BINDREST, and SECURITY.

Using RIGHTS to Display User Rights

Use the RIGHTS utility to display the effective rights a user has been granted. Here is the command format:

```
RIGHTS [Path]
```

To execute this utility, type **RIGHTS <Enter>** in the directory where you want to see the effective rights the user has, or add a directory path to view your trustee rights in another directory.

When using this utility, remember to consider file attributes and file trustee rights assignments. For example, a user may have Read and Write rights to a directory, but if the files in that directory are flagged with the Read-Only attribute, you can't write to an existing file unless the attribute is changed to Read-Write.

Displaying User and Group Trustees with TLIST

Use the TLIST utility to view the trustee list of a directory or a file on a server you're attached to. Here is the command format for TLIST:

```
TLIST [Path] [USERS | GROUPS]
```

To display the trustee information for a certain directory, type in the directory path after the TLIST command. For example, to find who has trustee rights to the SYS:SYSTEM directory, use the command like this:

```
TLIST SYS:SYSTEM <Enter>
```

If you execute the TLIST command without any parameters, you'll see both user and group trustees. To see either one or the other, add "USERS" or "GROUPS" at the end of the command. For example, to see only the user trustees of the SYS:SYSTEM directory, execute the TLIST command like this:

```
TLIST SYS:SYSTEM USERS <Enter>
```

To see only the group trustees of SYS:SYSTEM, execute the TLIST command like this:

```
TLIST SYS:SYSTEM GROUPS <Enter>
```

The TLIST utility is helpful to a network administrator who needs to quickly find out who has been assigned rights in different directories on the file server. For example, you may be concerned that a user may have rights to a confidential directory on the server. By using TLIST, you can quickly find out which users have what trustee rights to that confidential directory.

Displaying Security Information with WHOAMI

You can use the WHOAMI utility to find security information about the user who is currently logged in. WHOAMI displays group memberships, security equivalences, effective rights, object supervisor information, workgroup manager

321

information, and general system information. The command format for WHOAMI is:

```
WHOAMI [ServerName] [Options]
```

Here's a list of the options you can include with WHOAMI.

Option	Description
/S	Displays security equivalence information for the specified server.
/G	Displays group membership information for the specified server.
/W	Displays workgroup manager information.
/R	Displays effective rights on the servers to which the user is currently attached.
/SY	Displays general system information.
/O	Displays object supervisor information, including the groups and users being supervised.
/A	Displays all the information in the above WHOAMI options.

Repairing the Bindery with BINDFIX and BINDREST

Use the BINDFIX utility to correct problems with the NetWare bindery. The possible symptoms of a bad bindery are:

- A username can't be deleted

- A user's password can't be changed

- User's rights can't be modified

- An error message referring to the bindery appears on the server

- An "unknown server" error occurs while printing even on the default servers

Before using BINDFIX, make sure that all users are logged out of the file server and that you are logged in as SUPERVISOR. We recommend that after all users have logged out, you disable logins before starting BINDFIX. You can disable the login either from the server console or through the FCONSOLE utility. If you disable logins, it will allow you to verify that the bindery is intact before allowing users to log back in.

To execute BINDFIX, change to the SYS:SYSTEM directory on the file server and type

```
BINDFIX <Enter>
```

When BINDFIX is executed, NetWare closes the bindery files so users can't access them. As a precaution, BINDFIX makes a backup of the bindery files in case you experience problems with the rebuilt bindery. BINDFIX then starts rebuilding the bindery files. As it does so, you'll see the current BINDFIX tasks displayed on the screen.

BINDFIX scans all mounted volumes and removes any nonexisting users from all trustee lists. You'll also be prompted to delete the mail directories and trustee rights of users who don't exist on the file server.

A final bindery check determines if BINDFIX was successful or not. If it was not, you'll need to run the BINDREST utility to restore the previous version of bindery files to the file server. Again, you must be logged in as SUPERVISOR to use this utility. From the SYS:SYSTEM directory, type

```
BINDREST <Enter>
```

When BINDREST is executed, the backup versions of the bindery files that BINDFIX made will be restored to their original state.

Checking for Holes with SECURITY

Use the SECURITY utility to scan the file server for possible security violations. It will look for users without passwords, account restrictions that aren't sufficiently secure, supervisor equivalency rights, root directory privileges, excessive rights in system directories, and accounts without a login script.

To use this utility, you must log in as SUPERVISOR. Because this utility is mainly used by the supervisor and not by regular users, it's stored in the SYS:SYSTEM directory on the file server. The command format for this utility is simply:

```
SECURITY <Enter>
```

To redirect the displayed information to a file for reviewing or printing, use the DOS redirector (>) command. For example, to redirect the information from this utility to a file called SECURE.TXT, type:

```
SECURITY > SECURE.TXT <Enter>
```

We recommend using this utility frequently to find any possible security holes in your file server.

Other Methods of Locating Security Holes

In addition to using NetWare utilities such as SECURITY.EXE to locate security loopholes, you might consider third-party products such as Bindview 3.0c from the LAN Support Group of Houston, Texas.

Bindview is a report generator for NetWare that allows network administrators to create templates for customized reports about various aspects of the network: for example, server performance statistics, workstation statistics, disk space utilization, user accounts, and security equivalences.

In the area of network security, for example, you could generate a report to list every username on the network, tell you what rights each user has, which users are supervisor equivalent, which users are using their last names or their initials for passwords, and which users have chosen passwords such as "secret" or "private" that are easy to guess. By displaying this information in a table, BindView makes it easy to spot weak areas. These weak areas might include too large a number of supervisor equivalents coupled with easy-to-guess passwords, or users who have received indirect rights (through trustee assignments or security equivalences) that are greater than you intended them to have.

This information simplifies the task of locating and eliminating vulnerable security spots. The more users on your network, of course, the more valuable a report-generator product such as Bindview is likely to be.

Protecting the Network from Viruses

Another critical aspect of network security is protecting your network from computer viruses. A lack of knowledge on how viruses work and the lack of proper security are major factors in virus proliferation.

Tight Security—The First Line of Defense

The first line of defense against virus infiltration is to ensure that you're actually using the NetWare security features described in this chapter. For instance, if you keep your executable files in directories that have only Read and File Scan rights, a virus won't be able to copy itself into the directory.

A virus can reach no further into the network than the users themselves are able to go. Therefore, we suggest you keep user security tight by enforcing the following rules:

- Whenever feasible, LAN workstations should be diskless machines with remote boot PROMs.

- Only two workstations should have floppy disk drives: a workstation for SUPERVISOR and a workstation to test and load software.

- There should be only one designated supervisor per server(s)—and no supervisor equivalents.

- Whenever possible, delegate supervisor tasks to workgroup managers and operators.

- Do not grant users Access Control or Supervisory rights in their personal directories.

- No one should be allowed to create or modify executable files in a shared directory—they're strictly for data files.

- Set consistent, company-wide policies for modem control.

- Use virus-scanning software on a regular basis.

- Modify your backup procedure to account for virus infiltration.

Each of these suggestions is explained in more detail next.

Use Only Diskless Workstations

A number of viruses are designed to attach themselves to the workstation's COMMAND.COM file or to the boot sector on the workstation's hard disk or boot diskette. Other viruses attach to DOS's hidden files—IBMBIO.SYS and IBMDOS.SYS. Viruses that attach to these files are very difficult to detect.

If you don't have diskless machines, you can't really control what users put on the network. However, you should take every measure possible to discourage users from bringing in utilities and programs from home. For example, if Ted brings in a utility from home that he claims he can't live without, someone in the next office is likely to see the utility and want a copy as well. Therefore, Ted may grant the other person rights to access his directory, and before long, many users are employing the utility Ted brought from home.

The danger is that the utility may have a virus and end up infecting each of the participant's directories and from there infect executable programs throughout the server. For security purposes, the best alternative may be to purchase diskless workstations or convert existing workstations into diskless workstations.

You can turn a workstation into a diskless workstation by installing remote reset PROMs on the workstation's network interface board. Then disable or disconnect the floppy drives and hard disk drives from the controller and power supply. For AT-based computers, run the SETUP program to tell the CMOS memory that the computer no longer has a floppy or hard disk drive. If you don't tell SETUP of the changes, you will usually get errors. (However, more advanced AT and 386/486-based machines will try to run even if the hardware doesn't match the CMOS information.)

Limit Workstations with Floppy Drives

You should have only two workstations on the network with floppy drives: the system administrator's workstation and another workstation whose sole purpose is to load software onto the network. The second workstation should have two floppy disk drives, but no hard disk (because it could get infected); thus you will have to boot the workstation from a write-protected floppy diskette. To date, no known virus can get onto a write-protected diskette.

Before placing the write-protection tab on that floppy diskette, copy virus-checking software as well as the IPX.COM and NET*x*.COM files onto the diskette. Be sure to check all programs before setting up an AUTOEXEC.BAT file to run them automatically. The boot diskette should contain only the COMMAND.COM, CONFIG.SYS, AUTOEXEC.BAT, IPX.COM, and NET*x*.COM files—that's all you really need to have to log in to a server. You can load everything else from login scripts or at the network prompt.

When you purchase new software, regardless of where you get it (even from a commercial vendor), load the new software in one drive and run the virus-scanning software in the other drive before you copy the program to the network. (Since many software packages come on more than one diskette, you may have to scan multiple diskettes.) Then load the software into a directory where no one has rights except the person installing the program.

It's also worth noting that many software packages come compressed on the diskettes, a form which most virus-scanning software can't adequately scan. If you install compressed files, be sure to scan those files both before and after the installation procedure. Use *only* the workstation with virus- scanning software to install network software packages.

Have Only One Supervisor

Because viruses need to write to or modify files in order to spread, you should use NetWare's full security capabilities to protect the network from unauthorized use. But remember, logging in as SUPERVISOR or adding supervisor-equivalent privileges to your username gives you full reign over the server's entire directory structure. This means you could infect the whole directory structure if your workstation becomes infected with a virus. If your workstation is housing a virus and you log in as SUPERVISOR or equivalent, every executable program on the network can become infected. Even if you don't give yourself full access privileges to a directory, viruses can work from the potential rights you have. So if a file is flagged Read-Only, viruses (through your supervisor-equivalent potential) can flag the file Read-Write, infect the program, then reflag the file back to Read-Only. As a matter of precaution, no one should ever have supervisor- equivalent privileges.

Unless the software package specifically requires it, never install the software as SUPERVISOR. Instead, log in as a person with Modify or Supervisory rights—sufficient rights in the directory to install and flag the files. Supervisors shouldn't log in as SUPERVISOR unless they actually need full supervisory privileges to perform a task.

Use Workgroup Managers and Operators

Depending on which NetWare operating system you're running, you can delegate many directory and user creation functions to workgroup managers. For example, in NetWare v3.11, the supervisor can set up workgroup managers and have those functions performed through those managers. You then don't have to log in as SUPERVISOR to create a user account; the workgroup manager can do it.

The supervisor can also set up FCONSOLE and PCONSOLE operators to eliminate the need to log in as SUPERVISOR for many day-to-day tasks. The person acting as system administrator shouldn't have Write rights to user directories or to the SYS:PUBLIC directory. Those rights should be saved for the person who installs software, or (for user directories) for the supervisor.

Disallow Access Control Rights

For virus protection, users shouldn't be allowed to have even Read and File Scan rights to other users' directories. To see why not, suppose Ted has all rights to his directory and Pam has Read and File Scan rights to Ted's directory. If Ted's workstation and subsequent network directories become infected, Pam can copy infected files or execute an infected program, which will also infect her directories. If you restrict Pam so she never has access to Ted's directories, you won't have the copying problem.

With NetWare v3.11, the simplest way is to *not* grant users Supervisory or Access Control privileges to their personal directories. Then they can't grant other users rights to their directories.

Restrict Rights in Shared Directories

Group-access directories are the hardest places to control viruses, for they are the focal point of information exchange. The essential rule is that you don't grant multiple users rights to a directory where more than one user has Write rights to the files within. The user with Write access may write to a file that others will subsequently read. But if you can read a file, you can also copy it to another directory and consequently infect other directories.

If you must grant multiple users Read/Write access to the same directory, educate your users. Be sure they don't place .COM, .EXE, .OVL, .SYS, or any other kind of executable files, in the shared directory. Group directories should contain data files only.

Control Modem Use

You also need to control the use of modems on the network. One such control mechanism is to have them on one workstation controlled by an administrator who makes sure that no bulletin board numbers are called. Users with dial-in privileges can also cause contamination when they use modem access for executable file transfer from remote workstations.

Some employees use modems to transfer files back and forth so they can work at home instead of at the office. Other employees access the network to run programs in their work directories from their home computers. If the accessed network server does not have proper security and a user's executables are infected at work, that user stands the chance of also infecting the remote workstation. You will need to set up strong company policies on how remote workstations are allowed to access the network.

Use Anti-Virus Software

There are a number of anti-virus packages on the market. Some virus-scanning software packages run on workstations and only run when you scan software with them. Other types of scanning software run as TSRs that continually look over executables for signs of infection. You can also purchase scanning NLMs that continually look for viruses when users execute programs.

Because each company's needs are different and the available programs are different (and continually changing), purchasers must look into this area themselves. Probably the best source is dealers who carry network virus scanning software and who can assess your needs. Another way to learn about available anti-virus software is to ask other users or bulletin board SysOps what they've found useful. User groups are also a good source for this kind of information.

How often you scan depends on how often you install programs or on how much freedom your users to have to install software. If users have floppy drives in their workstations, scan at least once a week (if not continually) for viruses. You'll also want to scan the network occasionally just to ensure that nothing is infected.

In some cases, updates and new software may detect a virus that the old software couldn't recognize. This means you have inadvertently installed infected software on the network. When this happens, you may need to restore entire volumes from your backup tapes in order to flush the infection from the server.

The NetWare NDIR command provides a quick way to check shared network directories for unauthorized programs that might be viruses. At least once a day, change to the directory you are concerned about and type the following NDIR commands:

```
NDIR ALL *.EXE CREATED AFTER Date
NDIR ALL *.COM CREATED AFTER Date
```

Substitute yesterday's date for *Date*. NDIR will scan for any .COM and .EXE files with creation dates more recent than yesterday. To make this check easier, include these two commands in a batch file and have the results of each one redirected to a file (add the ">" symbol, followed by a file name at the end of each command).

Note that this simple scan for new program files may not be sufficient to detect all viruses; a "smart" virus can circumvent this check by resetting the file's creation date.

Keep Adequate Backup Copies

A good time to back up is after scanning for viruses, for you at least know that your present version of anti-virus software hasn't detected a virus. But the version that comes out tomorrow may detect a virus that's already there. So the crucial element isn't how often you back up, but how long you keep the backup tapes.

As a case in point, a certain company backed up every week, but kept only a month's worth of backup tapes. Three months later, they discovered the server was infected by a virus. When they went back through their tapes, they discovered that each tape set was also infected. They had no backup tapes from which to restore their system because they'd recycled their tapes too soon.

The best procedure for handling backup copies is to get on a rotation: back up every week, then every four weeks make a copy as a monthly backup. Make monthly backups for a year, then make a yearly backup as well.

How often you should back up is based on how much data you can afford to lose. If you can afford to lose a day's worth of information, then back up once a day. If you can afford to lose a week's worth of information, then back up once a week.

Making a Secure System More Usable

Some companies may find the secure approach a bit too confining. For example, many will refuse to implement diskless workstations. If you do stay with workstations that have floppy drives, be sure to write-protect all boot diskettes. With protection tabs, you at least have boot diskettes that can't be infected.

By using workstations with disk drives, you open the network to a couple of virus avenues. For example, users with machines at home might download utilities from bulletin boards, a common source of viruses. Or users might bring in software that has been infected by viruses and install that on the network. Companies must set up a policy to keep track of incoming software as well as equipment. It's a good idea to have all incoming software scanned for viruses; otherwise, ban new software from any source but mainstream vendor channels—and scan even that software.

As the whole network industry becomes more knowledgeable about network security, and as you set up proper security, you can better protect your network data from the dangers of virus infiltration.

CHAPTER 13

Setting Up Directories

This chapter introduces the directory structure used on NetWare v3.*x* file servers. It discusses ways to organize your own directory structure for easy management and explains how to create directories and subdirectories on a file server. It then presents some useful NetWare utilities and commands for working with server directories.

NetWare Directory Structure Concepts

The NetWare directory structure lets you store your files on the server in an organized manner. NetWare v3.*x* incorporates its own file system that is a hybrid of flat-file and hierarchical structures. On the server, NetWare stores files in a flat-file structure, which means they are written in simple, chronological order, just as they come in; however, once the files are on the disk, NetWare uses a hashing algorithm to create the organized, hierarchical directory structure you see when you work with directories and files.

NetWare's file-system hierarchy begins with the file-server name itself. The server's disks are divided into volumes (such as SYS), which form the next level in the file system. As a fixed amount of disk space, the volume corresponds to the root directory level on a hard disk. It is the starting place for creating directories and files. Beneath any directory, you can create and store other directories (called "subdirectories") and more files.

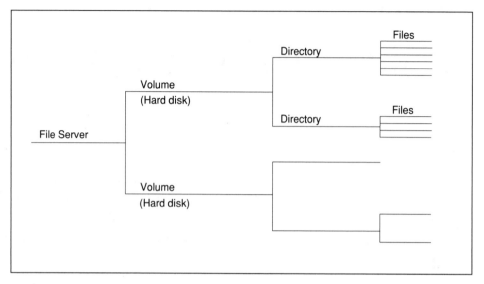

Figure 13-1: NetWare's hierarchical file system allows you to organize applications and data files.

Each directory and file has a name. Together, the server, volume, directory, subdirectory, and file name constitute a full directory path. A typical directory path on a NetWare file server looks like this:

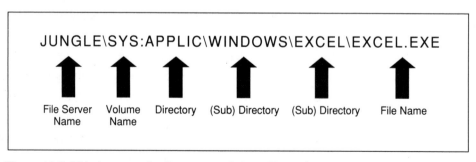

Figure 13-2: This is a sample directory path for a file server.

Note that NetWare allows you to use either a backslash (\) or a forward slash (/) to separate directory levels, while DOS recognizes only the backslash.

To access files within the directory structure, you can use either DOS or NetWare commands to move from one directory to the next. (These commands are explained later in this chapter.)

Directories NetWare Creates Automatically

Every NetWare file server, when installed, contains a volume named SYS. It is the first and primary volume, under which the installation program creates five directories: SYSTEM, PUBLIC, LOGIN, MAIL, and DELETED.SAV.

- The SYSTEM directory contains the NetWare operating system itself, the bindery, and other system files. The utilities within this directory are designed specifically for the network supervisor to use in performing administration tasks.

- The PUBLIC directory contains NetWare utilities that all users can access.

- The LOGIN directory contains NetWare utilities needed for logging in to the server.

- The MAIL directory contains subdirectories associated with each user's ID number on the file server. These directories can be used for NetWare-compatible mail programs. They also contain users' login scripts and print-job configurations.

- The DELETED.SAV directory holds deleted files whose original directories no longer exist. Until the files are purged, you can use the NetWare SALVAGE utility to recover deleted files from this directory.

Directories You Should Create on the Server

Managing directories and files can be a challenging task for most system administrators. But if you take the time to plan and organize the directories from the beginning, you can save yourself many administrative difficulties in the day-to-day maintenance of the network.

It is up to each network administrator to decide what types of directories are needed and how they'll be used. Since the needs of every organization differ, we can't prescribe exactly how you should set up your directory structure. We can, however, give some general guidelines that can be applied in most situations.

The main guideline is to keep the directory structure as simple and logical as possible. The primary function of a directory is to hold a set of files that belong together: all of the program files for an application, or all chapters of a book. The secondary function of a directory is to act as an organizational tier, under which you can group other related directories. For instance, you can create a directory called APPS and then, under that, create separate subdirectories for each network application (more about this later). This type of directory usually contains no files.

When you're planning your directory structure, avoid having too many levels. Besides being more difficult to navigate up and down, long directory paths can cause problems for some applications. For example, some programs provide a fixed-length field in which you must enter the full path and file name of the files you want to work with. If the path is too long to fit in the field, you won't be able to access the file. Keep in mind also that although NetWare allows a directory path to be up to 255 characters long (including delimiters), DOS limits paths to 127 characters.

On a NetWare server, you should not mix executable files and data files in the same directory, because the two types of files require different access rights. Avoid storing any files at the volume (root) level in NetWare. Remember from Chapter 12 that effective rights flow down the directory structure until filtered out by explicit trustee assignments or the Inherited Rights Mask. If you grant rights at the root level, you may inadvertently be giving users rights to directories on the volume that they shouldn't have access to.

Here are a few examples of the types of directories that are generally recommended when you set up a NetWare network.

DOS Directories

For convenience when working in DOS-based applications, you can copy the DOS system files onto the network. This way, users can access and run DOS utilities without having to insert DOS diskettes at their workstations. Since different workstation vendors provide their own versions of MS-DOS (IBM's PC-DOS and Compaq DOS, for example), you must provide a way for users to access the directory containing their specific version of DOS. Since the SYS:PUBLIC directory is used for files that relate to many users, and since all users by default have Read and File Scan rights to the PUBLIC directory, we recommend that you create DOS directories under SYS:PUBLIC.

Because of the capabilities of NetWare's login script variables (see Chapter 16 for a complete discussion of login scripts), we recommend that you set up DOS directories according to the following convention:

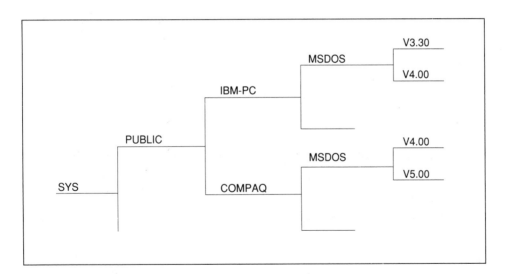

Figure 13-3: This logical directory structure for DOS files works best with login script variables.

For each machine-specific version of DOS used on your network, create a directory with a six-letter name directly under the SYS:PUBLIC directory. This directory name is associated with the "long machine type" specified in the SHELL.CFG file (see Chapter 9 for an explanation of SHELL.CFG options) and corresponds to the %MACHINE variable in the login script. Since the NetWare shell's default long machine type is "IBM_PC," use that directory name for the version of DOS used by the majority of your DOS workstations. If you have workstations that use another vendor's implementation of MS-DOS, such as Compaq DOS, create another directory called COMPAQ under SYS:PUBLIC. (Remember to set the long machine type name to "COMPAQ" in those workstations' SHELL.CFG files.)

Next, under each "long machine type" directory, create a subdirectory that represents the generic operating system type you'll be using. The default for all versions of MS-DOS and PC-DOS is "MSDOS." Therefore, you should name all these subdirectories MSDOS. This directory level corresponds to the %OS variable in the login script.

The final DOS directory levels should specify the DOS version. For example, if you have two Compaq workstations, one using Compaq DOS version 3.31 and the other using Compaq DOS version 4.00, your DOS directory paths will look like this:

SYS:PUBLIC\COMPAQ\MSDOS\V3.31
SYS:PUBLIC\COMPAQ\MSDOS\V4.00

This last directory level corresponds to the %OS_VERSION variable in the login script. This is where you actually copy the DOS system files from the user's original DOS diskettes. (Note that the DOS licensing agreement requires every DOS workstation to have its own copy of DOS, even if the user is running DOS from the network.)

Adhering to this DOS directory-naming convention lets you use the following generic search drive mapping in the system login script:

MAP S2:=SYS:PUBLIC/%MACHINE/%OS/%OS_VERSION

As long as the user's long machine type is correctly set, the shell will map the search drive to the appropriate DOS directory for that workstation.

This naming convention is also used by the default template in the NetWare USERDEF utility (a simple program for creating multiple user accounts at once, described in Chapter 15). If you don't plan to use USERDEF's default template to create users, you can safely eliminate the empty "MSDOS" directory level in the DOS directory path. This directory level is a holdover from the early days of NetWare, before MS-DOS became firmly established as the primary operating system for IBM- compatible PCs.

Application Directories

For management reasons, it's best to create a directory for applications and install all your applications below this directory. Keeping these files in a logical place makes it easier for you to manage upgrades and changes.

Keep in mind the different workstation-platform applications that will be installed on the file server. For example, you may have DOS, Windows, OS/2, and Macintosh applications stored on the server, all from the same software manufacturer. For instance, you might have a version of Microsoft Excel for Macintosh and a version of Microsoft Excel for Windows. To keep the two separated for the sake of manageability, create a separate subdirectory for each workstation platform (named, for example, WIN and MAC) below the main application directory. Under the application platform directory, create a subdirectory for each application and store its program files there. With this convention, your application directory structure may look like Figure 13-4.

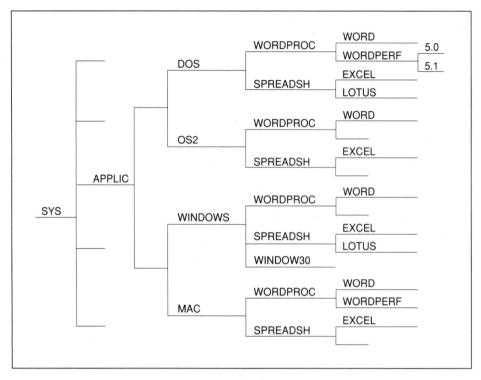

Figure 13-4: Use separate directories to keep DOS, Windows, OS/2, and Macintosh applications logically organized.

Data Directories

You can create a data directory to store data files that are shared on the system. Within a data directory, you can then organize the data files in subdirectories that are specific for certain groups. For example, if you have an accounting and sales database, the directory structure may look like Figure 13-5.

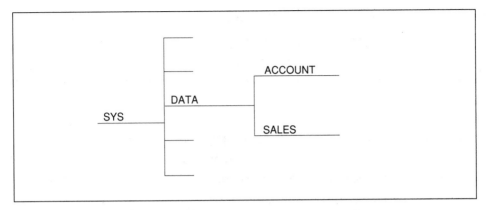

Figure 13-5: Data files must also fit logically into the directory structure.

Home Directories

Home directories are specifically for users' personal files. For login script and management benefits, we recommend that you create a directory level specifically for containing user directories. A common approach is to create a directory called HOME or USERS, under which you can create individual subdirectories for each user. You then give each user rights to that directory.

For ease of use, we recommend that you name each user's home directory with that user's login name. This naming convention will prove helpful when you want to use a login script variable tox map the user's home directory (see Chapter 16.) For example, if a user's login name is JSMITH, the home directory name may look like this:

```
SYS:USERS\JSMITH
```

Home directories serve as a convenient place for applications such as WordPerfect and Lotus 1-2-3 to create their temporary files. Users can also store personal setup and configuration files in their home directories.

Creating Directories on the Server

To create the directory structure on the file server, you can use the DOS MD (Make Directory) command. If you prefer using menus to using the command line, create the structure in NetWare's FILER or SYSCON utility. The following sections briefly describe how to use these different methods of creating directories.

Using DOS Commands to Create Directories

First, let's look at using the DOS **MD** command to create directories. (Of course, you must have Write rights where you're creating a directory, but that's not usually a problem for the network administrator.)

To create a directory using this command, first go to the directory beneath which you want to create a subdirectory. At the network prompt, type **MD** and then the name of the directory. The directory name can contain up to a maximum of eight characters, a period, and a three-character extension (just like a DOS file name). For example, to create a directory called DATA, type:

```
MD DATA <Enter>
```

There are two ways to use the MD command to create subdirectories in the DATA directory. The first way is to type the MD command and then state the path with the new directory name. For example, to create a SALES subdirectory in the DATA directory, from the volume's root, type:

```
MD DATA\SALES <Enter>
```

The second method is to use the DOS CD (Change Directory) command to go from the root directory to the DATA directory. For example, to change to the DATA directory, at the DOS prompt of the volume's root, type:

```
CD DATA <Enter>
```

While you're in the DATA directory, you can use the MD command to create the SALES directory. Simply type:

```
MD SALES <Enter>
```

If you accidentally create a directory, you can remove it by using the DOS RD (Remove Directory) command. Any directory that you remove using this command must be empty; it must contain no files or subdirectories. For example, to delete the SALES directory, type:

```
RD SALES <Enter>
```

or

```
RD F:\DATA\SALES <Enter>
```

Using FILER to Create Directories

The FILER utility provides a simple, menu-driven method for creating directories. To create a directory in FILER, follow these steps.

1. Log in as **SUPERVISOR**.

2. From the workstation command line, type **FILER <Enter>.**

3. To select your current directory, choose the "Select Current Directory" option from the "Available Topics" menu. An entry box will appear, displaying the current directory path.

4. Type the directory path to the location you want. Or, if you want to select a subdirectory below your current directory, press <Ins> to list the current directories available. (The easiest way to avoid having to select the current directory is to go to that directory before executing FILER.)

5. After you've entered the desired current directory path, press <Enter>.

6. Select "Directory Contents" from the "Available Topics" menu. A list of the directory's contents will be displayed.

7. To create a new subdirectory, press <Ins>.

8. As prompted, enter a new subdirectory name and press <Enter>.

If you accidentally create a directory, you can remove it in FILER by following these steps:

1. Select "Directory Contents" from the "Available Topics" menu. A list of the current subdirectories and files will be displayed.

2.   Highlight the name of the directory you want to delete and press <Del>. From here, you'll be given several options for deleting the directory. These options include the ability to delete the files in the subdirectory or to delete the entire directory structure.

Using SYSCON to Create Home Directories

The SYSCON utility is useful for creating user home directories at the same time you're creating user accounts. You can set up this utility to prompt you automatically for the verification of a user's home directory, eliminating the need to create each user's home directory individually and manually. To use this feature, follow these steps:

1. Make sure that you're logged in to the file server as SUPERVISOR to create user accounts and directories.

2. From the workstation command line, type **SYSCON <Enter>**.

3. Select the "Supervisor Options" option from the "Available Topics" menu.

4. Select the "Default Account Balance/Restrictions" option from the "Supervisor Options" menu. A screen will appear with the default account balance and restriction information.

5.   Enter **Yes** in the "Create Home Directory for Users:" field.

6.   To save and exit, press <Esc>.

From now on, whenever you're creating a new user with the SYSCON utility, you'll be prompted to verify the creation of a user's home directory. At the same time, the path of the home directory will be displayed and the user's login name will appear as the last directory name on the path. If this path is incorrect, enter the correct path for the user's directory. When you enter the path to the user's directory, SYSCON will record the directory entered as the default home directory (excluding the user's login name, which is unique).

For example, if you create two users named BARNEY and FRED, you'll be prompted to verify the path of the each user's home directory. If you create BARNEY first, the user default home directory path appears in a window, possibly looking something like this:

```
SYS:BARNEY
```

To place the home directory for BARNEY under a parent directory called USERS, enter the correct directory path in the window. For example, change the directory path to:

```
SYS:USERS\BARNEY
```

The server will then recognize that the SYS:USERS directory is the parent directory for all user home directories, unless otherwise specified. When the user FRED is created, therefore, the home directory path will look like this:

```
SYS:USERS\FRED
```

Directory Management Utilities

Besides FILER and SYSCON, NetWare offers several other utilities for working with directories. These include DSPACE, CHKDIR, RENDIR, LISTDIR, and NDIR.

Limiting Directory Space with DSPACE

DSPACE is NetWare's Disk SPACE management utility that lets you limit the total amount of disk space a user can use in a volume. It also lets you limit the maximum size of a directory and its subdirectories. These limitations help you prevent certain users from hogging too much of the server's disk with unnecessary files.

When you start the DSPACE utility by typing **DSPACE <Enter>** at the workstation command line, the "Available Options" menu appears:

```
┌──────────────────────────────┐
║       Available Options      ║
╠══════════════════════════════╣
║Change File Server            ║
║User Restrictions             ║
║Directory Restrictions        ║
└──────────────────────────────┘
```

The "User Restrictions" Option

To limit the total amount of volume space a user can use, follow these steps:

1. Select "User Restrictions" from the main menu. Your username and a list of the users you manage on the current server are displayed.

```
┌──────────────────────────────┐
║ Users on Server JUNGLE       ║
╠══════════════════════════════╣
║ GUEST                        ║
║ KNEFF                        ║
║ MDAY                         ║
║ SUPERVISOR                   ║
└──────────────────────────────┘
```

2. Highlight the user you want to restrict and press <Enter>. DSPACE displays a list of volumes defined on the current server.

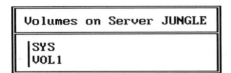

Volumes on Server JUNGLE
SYS
VOL1

3. Highlight the volume you want to set limitations for and press <Enter>. The "User Disk Space Limitation Information" window appears.

```
┌────────────────────────────────────────────────────┐
│      User Disk Space Limitation Information          │
├────────────────────────────────────────────────────┤
│                                                      │
│  User:    GUEST                                      │
│                                                      │
│  Volume: SYS                                         │
│                                                      │
│  Limit Space:      No                                │
│                                                      │
│  Available:             Kilobytes                    │
│                                                      │
│  In Use:          2396 Kilobytes                     │
│                                                      │
└────────────────────────────────────────────────────┘
```

The user and volume you selected are displayed in the window. The other fields are used to limit the amount of space the user can own on that volume, as described below.

Limit Space. This field indicates whether or not the user has a disk-space limitation. The default is "No." Change the option to "Yes" to set the space limit in the "Available" field. (To remove a disk-space restriction, set the "Limit Space" field back to "No.")

Available. This field shows the user's current space restriction, if any. You can change the number of kilobytes shown to make the total volume space available to the user larger or smaller. The "In Use" field shows the amount of space currently owned by the user.

The "Directory Restrictions" Option

This DSPACE option lets you set the maximum possible size for a directory, as well as a minimum size for all directories in the path. There are numerous situations in which you would want to impose a limit on the size of directories. For example, if you are running a DOS application that doesn't function well in a large volume, you can use DSPACE to limit the application directory's size. You can also use DSPACE to put a cap on the size of users' home directories.

Before you use DSPACE, you must determine an appropriate size limit for the directory. The procedure depends on what type of directory you are limiting:

- For an application directory, load all the program files first. Then run CHKDIR (as explained under "Checking Directory Space with CHKDIR" below) to see how many kilobytes of space the files take up. Add about 10 percent as a safety margin, and use the total as the upper limit for the application's directory.

- For home directories, decide how many kilobytes of volume space you want to allow altogether for users' personal work space. Divide this amount by the total number of users to get the amount of space per user. Use the resulting amount as the maximum size for each user's home directory.

Here's how to set the directory restrictions in DSPACE:

1. If necessary, start DSPACE by typing **DSPACE <Enter>**. Then select "Directory Restrictions" from the "Available Options" menu. The current directory name appears in the "Directory for Space Restriction Information" entry box.

```
Directory for Space Restriction Information:
JUNGLE\SYS:PUBLIC
```

2. Enter the directory path for the directory you want to restrict.
   If you don't know the exact directory path, press <Ins> and select the directory path

one level at a time. When the desired directory path appears in the box, press <Esc>.

3.   Press <Enter> to access the "Directory Disk Space Limitation Information"
     window.

```
┌─────────────────────────────────────────────────────────────┐
│    Directory Disk Space Limitation Information                │
├─────────────────────────────────────────────────────────────┤
│                                                               │
│   Path Space Limit:              K Bytes                      │
│                                                               │
│   Limit Space: No                                             │
│                                                               │
│   Directory Space Limit:             K Bytes                  │
│                                                               │
│   Currently Available:       33800 K Bytes                    │
│                                                               │
└─────────────────────────────────────────────────────────────┘
```

   This window displays the current space limitations, if any, for the selected
directory. Set the desired directory limitations as described below:

   Path Space Limit. This field indicates the minimum size for all directories along
the selected path. If a directory above your selected directory has a smaller space
limit, that limit will also be enforced on the current directory.

   Limit Space. This field indicates whether or not the directory has a space
restriction. The default is "No." Change the option to "Yes" to set the space limit in
the "Directory Space Limit" field. (To remove a previous disk space restriction, set
the "Limit Space" field back to "No.")

   Directory Space Limit. This field shows the directory's current space restriction,
if any. The default is 1,024 kilobytes (1 MB). You can change the number of kilobytes
shown to make the total possible size of the directory larger or smaller.

   Currently Available. This field indicates how much space is currently available
in the selected directory. The number includes the path space limit as well as the
amount of space in use by the selected directory's subdirectories and the free space
on the volume.

Checking Directory Space with CHKDIR

The CHKDIR (CHecK DIRectory) utility displays the directory space limitations for the specified directory and its volume. The command format for CHKDIR is:

```
CHKDIR Path
```

Replace *Path* with a mapped drive letter or the full path of the directory you want to check. You don't need to specify a path if you change to the desired directory first. CHKDIR displays information as follows:

```
Directory Space Limitation Information For:
JUNGLE\SYS:USERS\GUEST

Maximum      In Use      Available
992,960 K    898,568 K   94,392 K    Volume Size
             7,184 K     94,392 K    \USERS\GUEST
```

The "Maximum" column displays the maximum storage capacity of the volume (in kilobytes) and the maximum storage capacity of the directory (if the directory has a space restriction). In this example, the directory has no space restrictions.

The "In Use" column displays the number of kilobytes currently in use on the volume and in the specified directory. In this example, SYS:USERS\GUEST uses almost 7,200 kilobytes of disk space.

The "Available" column displays the number of kilobytes available to the user on the volume and in the specified directory.

Renaming Subdirectories with RENDIR

NetWare's RENDIR (REName DIRectory) command is a quick way to rename a directory. The format for this command is:

```
RENDIR OldDirectory TO NewDirectory
```

You must be one level above the directory you want to rename. Substitute the appropriate old and new names for the subdirectory you are renaming. When you rename directories, remember to adjust any references to those directories in login scripts, batch files, or application configuration files.

Listing Directory Information with LISTDIR

NetWare's LISTDIR (LIST DIRectory) command displays various information about directories below the current directory. The format for this command is:

```
LISTDIR [Option]
```

Typing LISTDIR without any options produces a simple listing of subdirectories under the current directory. Here are the other options you can include:

Option	Description
/A	Displays the entire directory structure from the current directory on down, including all subdirectories, Inherited Rights Masks, and creation dates.
/R	Displays only the Inherited Rights Masks of the subdirectories.
/D	Displays only the creation dates and times of the subdirectories.
/S	Displays only the subdirectory structure from the current directory on down.

Listing File Information with NDIR

You can use NDIR to view and sort a directory's files and subdirectories according to name, file size, date created, date last accessed, date last archived, file attributes, or owner. You can also see information about Macintosh and other files (such as OS/2 and Unix files) with long names.

In its simplest form, you issue NDIR commands the same way you issue DIR commands in DOS. For example, the command

```
NDIR *.COM <Enter>
```

provides a list of all files with a .COM extension in the current directory. Here is a sample of the basic NDIR output for the above command typed in the SYS:PUBLIC directory:

```
JUNGLE/SYS:PUBLIC

Files:          Size      Last Updated    Flags        Owner

CONSOLE COM     103       8-25-87 7:57a   [RoS------DR] SUPERVISOR
NBACKUP COM     10,346    12-06-90 5:15p  [RoS------DR] SUPERVISOR
NFOLIO COM      10,410    8-14-90 0:00    [RoS------DR] SUPERVISOR

    20,859 bytes in 3 files
    28,672 bytes in 7 blocks
```

Note that NDIR shows a little more information than DIR does, including the NetWare file attributes and owner.

You may also add one or more options to the basic NDIR command to see additional information. Here is the basic command format:

```
NDIR [Path] /[Format Option] [Flag Option] [Sort Spec]
     [Restriction] [Option]
```

For Path, you can substitute a mapped drive letter or a full directory path, up to and including the filespec (file name or file pattern using the * and ? wildcard characters). Or you can substitute a string of up to 16 filespecs (separate each filespec with a comma). For example, to list all of the .EXE, .COM, and .BAT files in the current directory, type:

```
NDIR *.EXE,*.COM,*.BAT <Enter>
```

Here's a list of the various NDIR options, grouped according to the categories shown in the command format above. The parts of the option names shown in capital letters indicate the abbreviations you can use to invoke these options. Note that you must include a slash (/) before you type any of the options.

The format options affect what type of display format NDIR uses.

Format Option	Description
DATES	Displays, in addition to the date and time of the last update, the NetWare last archived date/time, the last accessed date, and the creation date/time. Also shows which files have the Archive bit set.
RIGHTS	Displays the file attributes, the Inherited Rights Masks, and the user's effective rights to the current directory's files and subdirectories.
MACintosh	Displays only Macintosh files and subdirectories in the current directory. When you list only Macintosh files or subdirectories, they appear with their Macintosh names.
LONG	Displays Macintosh, OS/2, and NFS long file names for the files, depending on which name spaces are loaded on the volume.

The flag options are used to select files with certain attributes. You can precede the attribute abbreviation with "NOT" to see all files *except* those having the specified attribute.

Flag Options	Description
RO, S, A, X,	RO=Read Only, S=Shareable, A=Archive Needed, X=Execute Only
H, SY, T, I,	H=Hidden, SY=System, T=Transactional, I=Indexed,
P, C, D, R	P=Purge, C=Copy Inhibit, D=Delete Inhibit, R=Rename Inhibit

The sort spec options allow you to sort the listing according to various keys. Precede each option name with the keyword "SORT" in the command. To reverse the normal sort order (alphabetical, chronological, ascending), precede the option name with "REV SORT."

Sort Spec Option	Description
OWner	Sorts the list of files by owner.
SIze	Sorts the list of files by size.
UPdate	Sorts the list of files by the last update date and time.
CReate	Sorts the list of files by the creation date and time.
ACcess	Sorts the list of files by the last accessed date and time.
ARchive	Sorts the list of files by the last archived date and time.

UNsorted   Displays the list of files in the order in which they would appear with the DOS DIR command.

The restriction options let you narrow down the NDIR listing according to a number of variables. In place of the "EQ" (equal to) operator, you can substitute "LEss than," "GReater than," "BEFore," or "AFTer." You can also precede the operator with "NOT" to see all files except those that match the restriction option.

Restriction Option	Description
OWner EQ*Username*	Displays only files whose owner matches the specified username.
SIze EQ *Number*	Displays only files whose size matches the speci fied number of bytes.
UPdate EQ *Date*	Displays only files last updated on the specified date.
CReate EQ *Date*	Displays only files created on the specified date.
ACcess EQ *Date*	Displays only files last accessed on the specified date.
ARchive EQ *Date*	Displays only files last archived on the specified date.

Here are the generic options you can add at the end of the NDIR command.

Option	Description
FO	Displays files only, not subdirectories.
DO	Displays subdirectories only, not files.
SUB	Displays the requested information for all subdirectories under the specified path.
C	Displays the information continuously; does not pause the display between each screenful.
HELP	Displays a help screen showing NDIR usage and possible options.

Whenever you want to add any of these NDIR options (except /HELP), you must include some type of directory path in front of the option(s). You can use a period (.) to represent the current directory or a backslash (\) to represent the root of the directory. To request a series of options, simply leave a space between each of the options you want to request. For example, the command

```
NDIR . H /SUB <Enter>
```

would show you all the files flagged Hidden starting at the current directory level on down through all subdirectories and their subdirectories.

The command

```
NDIR \ NOT S SUB
```

would show you all the files not flagged as Shareable starting at the volume (root) level on down through all directories and their subdirectories.

CHAPTER 14

Installing Applications

Installing applications can be one of the trickiest aspects of setting up the network, especially if your applications do not come with network-sepcific instructions. This chapter addresses the issues involved in setting up both network and non-network applications on your server.

Using Separate Directories and Groups to Simplify Access to Applications

Now that a growing number of networks are supporting many types of workstations and several desktop operating environments such as Windows and OS/2, the network will end up housing multiple versions of the same applications to support DOS workstations, OS/2 workstations, and Macintosh computers. If the applications are all stored in the SYS:PUBLIC directory, users can become confused as they try to sort out which version of WordPerfect or Excel they actually need.

In Chapter 13, we talked about creating a separate directory called APPS in which to place subdirectories for each application. This approach differs from the traditional one recommended by the NetWare documentation, in which network administrators create a separate subdirectory in SYS:PUBLIC for each application on the network. Then, below the APPS directory, create a separate subdirectory for each workstation operating system and environment your network supports.

You may want to create some additional subdirectories as well. Perhaps you'll want a subdirectory for DOS utilities, for example, and a directory for supervisor troubleshooting tools that only you, or a group manager or supervisor equivalent, can access. When you install the various applications, you can simply put them in the appropriate subdirectories.

Next, you'll need to map the users' network and search drives to the applications they need to use. The easiest way to do this is to create groups (see Chapter 15) for each application you installed, assign the appropriate rights, and then make each user who needs the application a member of that group. Using IF...THEN statements (see Chapter 16) in your system login script enables you to map the needed application directories to members of that application group. For example, if a new employee needs WordPerfect, all you need to do is verify the license agreement and add the employee to the WordPerfect group. Once you make the new employee part of the group, the server automatically assigns the appropriate rights and mappings.

Setting up the applications directories in this way will take some extra time at the beginning, but it can save you a great deal of frustration as the network and the number of applications grows later on.

Installing the Applications

After you've created the appropriate directories, your next step is to install applications for the network. Many popular applications now come in both standalone and network versions. The two are sometimes included in the same package; other applications require you to purchase the network capabilities as an add-on package.

The basic steps for installing applications include copying the program files for each application into the correct directory you have created, and then setting the appropriate attributes for these files. Be prepared to change the directory structure, access rights, login scripts, user groups, batch files, and search paths, if necessary, to make the applications work. (See Chapter 15 for setting up users and groups, Chapter 16 for login scripts, and Chapter 13 for directory structures.)

The next sections give some tips that you may find helpful when installing applications on the file server.

Tips for Installing NetWare-Aware Applications

If the application includes instructions for installing the program on a network, your course is somewhat easier. Turn to these directions and follow them.

Once the installation is complete, flag the application files as Shareable Read Only (S RO). This flagging step is important because the default file attribute is Read Write, and you don't want network users to be able to overwrite the application's program files.

Note: Some applications require both Read and Write privileges in order to operate because the application has to write temporary files. We'll deal more specifically with these applications in the troubleshooting portion of this chapter. In general, however, we suggest that you deal with these applications by placing the specific files that require Write privileges either in a directory where the user can have Read Write privileges or in the users' home directories. We do not recommend that you grant Write privileges to the public application directories.

You can use either FLAG or FILER to change the file attributes (see Chapter 13). Finally, if the application modifies or creates lines in the AUTOEXEC.BAT or CONFIG.SYS file, you'll need to add these lines to the appropriate files on the workstation's boot diskettes. (See Chapter 9.) For convenience, and to make troubleshooting easier, we recommend that you implement these commands through the "Group" function within SYSCON, which allows you to make the addition for every appropriate user at once.

Test New Applications Rigorously

Before you initiate a new application on the network, you should make sure it works with your particular server hardware, network interface cards, printers, and workstations. Some ways to get this information include attending user groups, reading related articles, calling the product vendors, and checking related topics in Novell's testing reports. For a large network, you may want to set up a product testing environment away from the production file server(s) where you can evaluate new products and ensure that they work properly before you introduce them into the primary LAN.

Bring Up New Applications One at a Time

Bring up applications on the LAN one at a time, starting with the easiest program. Particularly in the case of TSR (memory-resident) applications, if the application has a problem running on the network or if conflicts between applications occur, bringing the applications aboard one at a time will help you identify which application is causing the problem. In the case of TSRs, your problem may simply be an aspect of the order in which the TSR applications are loaded. Try changing the order of TSRs before you assume the application is bad. There are some TSR programs that won't operate correctly unless they're the last one loaded, for example.

Beyond the troubleshooting aspects of the applications, bringing the programs on-line one at a time will help users get acclimated to the network environment. If they have access to all of the applications at once, users may experiment with new applications before they've been properly trained, and may either fail miserably and assume they're unable to use the network versions of the programs or run into problems that demand your immediate help. We recommend that you get the easier applications such as word processing installed and running smoothly first, and then install the more complex applications such as groupware programs and server-based database applications.

Printing from Applications Designed for Network Printing

Many applications are already aware of the network environment. Documentation for these products includes instructions for accessing network print services.

In some cases, establishing print services for the applications can be particularly tricky. If you're having trouble with the print services, as a last resort you can issue a CAPTURE command to redirect the output of either LPT1 or LPT2 to the file server, then set up the application to print to the LPT port you've CAPTUREd.

The one point you'll need to remember here, however, is that NetWare v3.x sends print jobs to print queues rather than to printer numbers. If the application asks you to specify printer numbers, you'll need to set up spooler assignments at the file server console to route these print assignments into the appropriate queues. (If you use CAPTURE, however, make sure that your application isn't also queueing the print jobs—otherwise you'll be queueing the print jobs twice.)

Another point to be aware of is that files that include tables or graphics tend to print very slowly over the network. If you intend to use desktop publishing or any kind of graphics applications on the network (possibly even WordPerfect), you may want to enhance the print speed with a product such as LANSprint, from Digital Products Inc. (based in Watertown, Mass.). LANSprint is a hardware/software print server that uses Direct Memory Access (DMA) to speed up the process of getting graphics files off the network and into the printer.

For more information on NetWare printing, see Chapters 19 and 20.

Tips for Installing Applications that Aren't NetWare-Aware

Many application problems on a network can arise if you install applications that are either single-user applications or are not sufficiently network-aware.

One important point bears mentioning here: It's certainly feasible to access single-user applications from the network file server, and there are troubleshooting helps and third-party tools that can assist you in getting these applications to operate smoothly on the network. The primary third-party product in this category is Net-Aware, from Network Associates (of Santa Barbara, Calif.). This product helps you isolate and correct standalone application problems on a NetWare LAN. (We'll describe this tool in more detail later in this chapter.)

Legally, however, it's imperative that you purchase sufficient licensing rights to support your applications' use by multiple workstations on the LAN. Our advice in this regard is that you either get a network version of the software or buy enough single units of the software to cover the number of users you'll need to support on the LAN.

Certain software utilities such as Brightwork's SiteLock or Connect Computer's Turnstyle can ensure that your network doesn't exceed its software licensing rights. Some third-party menu packages such as Intel/LANSystems' LANShell include the capability to manage software licensing limits as well. We suggest you implement such a program.

If you have a license agreement to use the application on the network, but the application has no instructions for installation on a network, turn to the area of the documentation that tells how to install it on a hard disk. (In the next section, we'll show you how to get around the typical problems that may occur.)

After the installation is finished, be sure to flag the application files as Shareable Read Only (S RO). The default file attribute is Read Write, and you normally don't want network users to be able to overwrite the application files (see the Note above for some exceptions to this rule). You may use either FLAG or FILER to change the file attributes (see Chapter 13).

Finally, if the application modifies or creates lines in the AUTOEXEC.BAT or CONFIG.SYS file, you must add these lines to the appropriate files on the workstation's boot diskettes. Be certain your additions don't conflict with the other programs you're loading through these files.

Troubleshooting General Application Problems

This section lists the most common causes for applications not running, or not running properly, on the network and suggests possible solutions for each one.

Problem: You have insufficient rights to install the application.

> **Solution:** Some applications check for rights at the root directory when they're being installed. In these cases, use the MAP ROOT command to make the application's current directory a root directory. Be sure you're logged in as SUPERVISOR to install these applications.

Problem: The application won't install on NetWare.

> **Solution:** Check to see if the application uses the PC LAN Network Program's LAN Installation Check (B800h Interrupt 2Fh) or the SHARE Installation Check (INT 2F). These checks verify that the application is running on a LAN.
>
> To correct the problem, load either SHARE.COM or INT2F.COM (Rev 2) on the workstation. The INT2F.COM file is located on the WSGEN diskette.

Problem: A user has insufficient rights to run the application.

Solution: If you can run the application when you're logged in as SU-PERVISOR, but not when you're logged in as a user, you need to grant the correct trustee assignments to users.

You may accomplish this in one of the following ways:

- Create a group for the application and grant the group all rights to the application's directory. Then delete one right from the trustee assignment, log in as a member of the group, and attempt to run the application. Do this with one right at a time until you've determined which rights the users need to run the particular application.

- Keep in mind that, in addition to the Write right, users will usually need Create, Erase, Modify, and File Scan rights if they write to files.

- As we mentioned earlier, some applications create temporary files. In many cases, the application tries to create temp files in the same directory as the data files. Users need at least Write, Create, Erase, Modify, and File Scan rights at the directory level for these types of applications (and Read rights as well, if they're in a directory where data files are stored). You may want to map a search drive to the application and have users try running the application from a home directory, to which they have all rights, to determine if the temp files are the source of their problem.

Problem: The application won't run at all.

Solution: If the application won't run, it may be that the users need Write access to the program file. In this case, flag the file Shareable/Read Write (S RW). Normally, if an application is having problems with a file, it will display the name of that file, either in an error message or in a pop-up window on top of the application.

If the application uses a software interrupt that NetWare also employs, the workstation will hang. If you have an interrupt conflict, call your application developer or Novell for assistance.

Your workstation may also hang if you press the <Shift><Print Screen> keys when none of your LPT ports are captured and no local printers are attached to your workstation. To prevent this, include the following line in the SHELL.CFG file on your workstation boot disk:

```
LOCAL PRINTERS=0 <Enter>
```

Problem: A workstation can't find the application.

Solution: If the workstation can't find the application files, you need to map a search drive to the file server directory that contains the application's executable files. Check for missing search drive mappings in the user or system login script.

If you create groups for your applications, as we suggested earlier, you can use the IF...THEN command in the system login script (in SYSCON) to set up search mappings for the entire group at once.

Another possible cause is if the application is installed too deep in the directory structure. We suggest you use the MAP ROOT command to make the current directory a root directory, then run the application. If the application still doesn't run, you may have to reinstall the program after making the MAP ROOT change. Your other alternative, of course, is to install the application in a directory off the volume root; however, for maintenance and security purposes, we recommend you solve the problem through MAP ROOT instead.

Problem: An application requires changes to the local DOS environment.

Solution: Read the application's documentation to determine whether you'll need to make changes to the workstation's local CONFIG.SYS file. Then make any required modifications (such as additional file opens or additional memory for the DOS environment) directly to the CONFIG.SYS file.

Problem: There are conflicts between the SHELL.CFG and CONFIG.SYS parameters.

Solution: Check for any conflicts between the network's SHELL.CFG and the workstation's CONFIG.SYS. If your application needs 50 file opens, for example, use the same value for the CONFIG.SYS option (files=50) and the SHELL.CFG option (file handles=50).

Problem: An application uses an interrupt that conflicts with a network adapter.

Solution: Check to be sure the application isn't attempting to use the same DOS interrupt your workstation and server's network adapters are using. If you filled out the NetWare worksheets when you installed the network, it will be easier to identify the adapter's interrupts.

You may need to contact the vendor to find out what interrupt your application is using. If there's a problem, change the interrupt setting on the network boards to allow the application to run.

Problem: The application can't find NetBIOS.

Solution: Check the application documentation to see if the program requires NetBIOS. If it does, add the NETBIOS.EXE and INT2F.COM files to the boot diskette. Also add the NETBIOS command to the AUTOEXEC.BAT file. NETBIOS.EXE and INT2F.COM come with NetWare on the WSGEN diskette.

Problem: The application can't deal with network drives.

Solution: Check to see if the application uses Absolute DiskRead-INT 25H or Absolute Disk Write- INT 26h. These interrupts are not valid function calls for NetWare, because they transfer control directly to the DOS driver. Therefore, an application that uses these interrupts will have to be run from the local workstation disk.

Problem: The application requires unique workstation names.

Solution: Check to see if the application uses the Get Machine Name function call (5E))h Interrupt 21H). This function checks for the IBM PC Network Program and ensures that all workstations on the LAN have a unique call number. It's easy to correct this problem. Simply assign each user's workstation a unique name in the user login script by using the SET command and typing MACHINE="NAME." The name can be anything you want it to be, but you should enter it in capital letters, as in the following example:

```
SET  MACHINE="DORALEE"
```

Problem: Users are getting "Access Denied" errors or are having trouble reading application files.

Solution: The users may have insufficient trustee rights to the directory in which the application is stored. If a file seems to keep losing its Shareable (S) flag, the application is either resetting the file attributes or re-creating the file. This can happen when an application reads a file into a temporary working file for modification. When the modification is done, the application may actually delete the original file and rename the temporary file to the original filename. This causes the original file attributes to be lost.

To correct this problem, either use the Net-Aware utility to redirect the temporary files to a personal directory or ask the software developer to create a temporary file for you that includes a Shareable flag.

Some applications limit the number of concurrent users through the use of an internal semaphore. For example, if an application has a limit of five users, the semaphore will prevent a sixth user from entering the application. In some cases, the workstation that is denied access may hang. In other cases, the application may appear to hang until the fifth user exits the program, thereby making room for the sixth, at which time the sixth user can enter the application and the program continues to run.

If you're having this problem, your best solution is to buy an extended software license.

Problem: Users get the "File Not Found" error message when they start the application.

Solution: Several application problems can result in "File Not Found." First, check the trustee rights granted to the user, and make sure the users have been granted sufficient rights in the application's directory. (You'd need at least Read and File Scan rights to see if the file is there.)

Next, check the status of the file. You can find out through FCONSOLE or MONITOR whether the file may already be open and in use at another workstation. In some cases, the DOS "file lock" message may be interpreted by the application as "File Not Found."

Next, check the search drive mappings. Map a search drive to the directory that contains the application's executable files. If the mapping solves the problem, add a search drive mapping to the login script.

Finally, the problem may result from the user's not having adequate rights in the root directory to allow the application to find and open the appropriate file. The easiest way to solve this problem is to either change the user's rights to include the entire directory path or use the MAP ROOT command to make the application's current directory a root directory. Make sure that you're logged in as Supervisor while you're installing these kinds of applications.

Problem: The application requires write access to its program files.

Solution: As we mentioned earlier in the chapter, some applications require the ability to write temporary files as they execute. If this is the case, and if there's nowhere the application can write to, it can't run.

This problem is caused either by insufficient file attributes or by insufficient rights. First, you'll need to use FLAG to change the file to Read Write (Rw). If the file you're writing to doesn't exist on the hard disk you're using, the NetWare shell will begin a search for the file and may find it in one of the search drives. If the file is found on a network drive, NetWare checks for appropriate rights. If you don't have sufficient rights in that directory, you can't write to the file.

You have a couple of options here: (1) Include a path along with the filename when you're writing to a file. This will prevent the network shell from initiating a search. (2) Copy the file into a directory where you have Read, Write, Create, Erase, and Modify rights. Many applications require more than just the Write capability because they may delete the original file and actually re-create it when you save your changes.

Problem: The application won't run because the file or record is locked.

Solution: If the application is using file locking functions for DOS 3.x but the workstation didn't boot up with DOS 3.x, the application won't work. In this case, simply ensure that the workstation is booted with DOS 3.1 or above.

You may run into trouble with the file locking function if you're using the application from a search drive and you're attached to multiple servers. In this case, log in directly to the file server you need without attaching to other file servers on the internet.

Finally, check to see if your application is designed to run in the network environment. If it isn't, don't map network search drives to the application's directory. In these cases, have each user map a local drive to the application and execute the application from there.

Problem: The software is designed for single-user use.

Solution: Check your application documentation to see if it gives any specific help for getting the software to run on a LAN. If it doesn't, check the troubleshooting hints we've provided in the section above. When you purchase LAN licensing rights to some applications, they require that you place a "key diskette" in the workstation's floppy drive before the application will run on a LAN. Most applications designed for LAN use avoid requirements like this.

The next section gives more tips for troubleshooting problems with single-user applications on a network.

Troubleshooting Applications that Aren't Sufficiently Network-Aware

In this section, we'll list some of the most common problems associated with non-network-aware applications. Then we'll offer some suggestions for solving these problems. One of the most helpful tools we've discovered for dealing with uncooperative applications is the Net-Aware utility from LANSMITH (mentioned previously in this chapter). Net-Aware contains a TSR module called "Monitor" that allows the network administrator to observe the program files' "opens" and "searches" as an application operates (or attempts to operate) on a LAN. Examining these opens and searches can help you find the source of the application's trouble.

Common Single-User Application Problems

Once you've identified the problem, Net-Aware lets you implement a specific "rule" to correct the problem. We'll describe how the rules work as we walk through the common problems below.

Configuration Files

Most every application has a configuration file that stores information about the user's preferences and about hardware devices. Because different users are likely to have different preferences for the program settings, and because the network is likely to include multiple hardware types, most network administrators prefer to have a private configuration file for each user and workstation. You can store these files either on the local workstation hard disks or on the users' home directories on the LAN.

Using Lotus 1-2-3 v2.2 as an example, we'll walk through the solution to this problem. (Note: Lotus 1-2-3 v2.3 is designed to be installed on a network; if you're using this version, simply follow the NetWare installation instructions at the back of the manual and you'll be fine. But if you've already purchased multiple copies of Lotus v2.2 for the users on your network, as many network administrators have, follow these instructions to make the user-specific configurations work.)

Rather than resort to installing the application separately on each workstation's hard disk, you should install the program just once, in the appropriate file server direcory, and then perform your user-customization work with just the configuration files. In the Lotus example, there are two configuration files: 123.SET, which contains information about the video device and printer being used; and 123.CNF, which contains the users' personal preferences, such as where they want to store worksheet files.

Lotus allows you to define multiple 123.SET files with different names. You can then specify these "alternate" files when loading Lotus by naming them on the command line (for example, LOTUS MONO).

The administrator's trick is to set an environment variable (in other words, a "rule") for each node that indicates which SET file to use, and then to create a batch file to ensure that when the user loads Lotus, the workstation invokes the appropriate file.

For example, let's assume you define an environment variable named 123SET. The batch file that loads Lotus will contain the line *Lotus %123SET%*. From then on, every time the batch file runs it replaces the variable 123SET with a request for the appropriate SET file. Dealing with the 123.CNF file is not quite so easy. Since Lotus is programmed to look for the 123.CNF file in the current subdirectory, the best solution is to put a customized copy of 123.CNF at each user's local directory.

This is a workable solution, as long as users remember to run Lotus from the same subdirectory every time. (One of the ways to help them remember would be to have them invoke the Lotus application through a customized menu—we'll show you how to create one in Chapter 17.) In any case, this alternative is much easier than implementing a standalone installation at every workstation.

As another alternative, you can create several versions of the hardware configuration files (one for VGA, one for CGA, and so forth). Next, you can create a single batch file for each type of configuration: for example, 123VGA or 123MONO. Finally, you can create an entry in AUTOEXEC.BAT to force the user's workstation to select the correct batch file from the server each time the particular application (in this case, Lotus) is invoked.

If you're using Net-Aware, you can solve the problem of multiple user configuration files by defining a Net-Aware file-swapping "rule" that swaps in the user's own specific configuration file whenever the Lotus program attempts to open or search for the 123.SET file.

```
┌─────────────────────────────────────────────────────────────┐
│  ┌───────────────────────────────────────────────────────┐  │
│  │        CHOOSE A USER TO DEFINE A SWAP RULE FOR         │  │
│  ├───────────────────────────────────────────────────────┤  │
│  │ CSNAPP    │ Cheryl Snapp                               │  │
│  │ DSNAPP    │ Doug Snapp                                  │  │
│  │  ┌──────────────────────────────────────────────────┐ │  │
│  │  │   LIST OF FILES WITH SWAP RULES DEFINED FOR JSMITH│ │  │
│  │  ├──────────────────────────────────────────────────┤ │  │
│  │  │                      ■                            │ │  │
│  ├──┴──────────────────────────────────────────────────┴─┤  │
│  │           DEFINE SWAP RULES FOR JSMITH                 │  │
│  ├───────────────────────────────────────────────────────┤  │
│  │ FILE NAME │ 123.SET                                    │  │
│  │ BECOMES   │ \JSMITH\123.SET                            │  │
│  │ MAKE SWAP │ when programs try to OPEN or SEARCH for this file. │
│  └───────────────────────────────────────────────────────┘  │
└─────────────────────────────────────────────────────────────┘
```

In this case, you define the rule just once, then insert a variable (%LOGIN_NAME%). The variable will instruct the utility to apply the rule to each user in order to redirect the Lotus program to the correct directory path for each user's personal application configuration file. The end result is the same as in the previous example, but the process is faster.

Requirement to Install on a Particular Drive

Many applications request that you install the program files in the root directory. In the network environment, not only would doing this create a great deal of confusion (as we discussed earlier), but it would also pose a security risk.

If the installation requires you to place the program files in the hard disk's root directory (analogous to the volume level in NetWare), you must use the NetWare MAP utility in conjunction with NetWare v3.11's ROOT command to map a fake root to the appropriate network directory. For example:

```
MAP ROOT G:=SYS:APPS\WINDOWS\WORDPROC   <Enter>
```

Place this command in the system login script to make it permanent.

If the application requires you to install the program files on a specific drive, such as C: or D:, go ahead and install the program in the correct NetWare directory, then use the MAP and ROOT commands to create a map to that directory from the application's preferred drive letter, as follows:

```
MAP ROOT C:=SYS:APPS\DOS_APPS\DBASE   <Enter>
```

NetWare will display the following message:

```
Drive C: currently maps to a local disk.
Do you want to assign it to a network drive? (Y/N) Y
```

Then place this command in the system login script to make it permanent.

If you're using Net-Aware, implement a file-swapping "rule" to replace the root directory or hard disk directory with the acceptable network directory path. In a few cases, applications may be incompatible with network search paths. In these cases, you must either employ the Net-Aware utility or install the application as a standalone program on the individual workstations' hard drives.

Hard-Coded Directory Paths

In some cases, applications store the user's data in hard-coded subdirectories (such as \DATA). In the network, however, this forces all users to share the same subdirectory. Since there's only one set of user data, only one user can access the application file at a time.

In this case, you must either install the application as a standalone program on the workstation's hard drive, for the users who need it, or use Net-Aware to swap in a separate subdirectory path for each user's data.

Controlling Multiple-User Access to Files

Single-user applications use several different methods of opening and closing data files. Most applications employ some type of locking structure that holds the file open from the time it's read into memory until the time it's saved. If another user attempts to access the data file during this time, he or she will be denied access.

In some cases, such as standalone spreadsheet applications, the application may hold a worksheet file open only when it's actually being written to or read from disk. The rest of the time, other users are free to open the file and access the same worksheet on their workstations. Other applications hold program files open the entire time a user is working in the application and don't close the program files until the user exits the application altogether.

A possible solution to these problems is to make sure users keep their own data files in their own personal directories. Since no other network users have rights to a particular user's home directory, the user can work on his or her private data without the risk of interference.

Hard-Coded Temporary Files

In some cases, you must deal as well with the issue of hard-coded temp files. Most progams make use of temporary files to store data while you're running the program. Unfortunately, some programs store those files in hard-coded subdirectories with fixed file names (like TEMP.DAT).

In a case like this, you must either use the application only as a standalone program, or live with the fact that only one user will be able to access the application at a time, or use Net-Aware to redirect the temporary files to appropriate user-specific directory paths.

Printing from Applications Not Designed for Network Printing

If you're using applications not designed for network printing, you'll need to use NetWare's CAPTURE, ENDCAP, NPRINT, and PCONSOLE utilities to print. You'll find an explanation of these utilities in Chapter 20.

CHAPTER 15

Setting Up Users and Groups

This chapter will give you help in setting up users and groups. It will also tell you how to distribute network management responsibilities by using user account managers and workgroup managers. We'll provide some basic tips you may want to consider during the process of setting up users and groups.

NetWare User and Group Concepts

Everyone who uses the server needs a unique username. Associated with each user are an optional password and restrictions, a login script, and rights. For administration purposes, you can establish groups of users who have common rights and mappings. To help with the administration of users and groups, you can define two types of managers on the server: *user account managers* and *workgroup managers*.

User Accounts

We've already mentioned that each user on the server must have a unique username. We recommend that you come up with a convention for creating usernames and stay with that convention for all users. You can choose from any number of different naming schemes. We'll describe four: given name, surname, given name with surname initial, or initial(s) and surname.

- Given name—This naming convention consists of simply using the person's first name as the username. For example, you may have user names such DANIEL or MARIANNE. This type of naming convention is all right with a small group in which you don't have several users with the same first names.

- Surname—This naming convention consists of using just the last name of the user. For example, you may have a user with the last name NEFF. This naming convention is all right unless you have several users with the same last name.

- Given name with surname initial—This naming convention consists of using the person's given name and the first initial of the surname. For example, you may have a user with the username RYANN or ERICN. The obvious problem would be having more than one user with the same given name and first surname initial.

- Initials and surname—This naming convention consists of using the user's given name initial(s) with the surname. For example, Ryan K. Neff may have the username RNEFF or RKNEFF. This naming convention is the least likely to cause duplicate usernames on a file server.

In Chapter 12, we mentioned the password concepts for user accounts. At this point you may want to review the "User Security" section in Chapter 12.

The important concept to remember about passwords is that the network's security will be only as tight as you set it up to be. By requiring longer passwords and more frequent password changes, you can get a more security-tight server on the password level.

User Login Scripts

User login scripts are much like configurable batch files. By using login scripts effectively, you can make the login procedure, drive mappings, and workstation environment much easier to use. In Chapter 16, we'll discuss in detail how the login scripts work and how to set up your own login scripts.

In Chapter 12, we discussed the concept of rights in detail. You can set up each user to have certain trustee rights to certain directories and files. Another rights privilege you may want to consider is the concept of user equivalencies. For example, you may make an assistant the security "equivalent" of his or her supervisor for the purpose of allowing that person to assist in facilitating certain networking tasks. (For more specific information about rights and equivalencies, see Chapter 12.)

When you create a user, the file server assigns that user a hexadecimal ID number. You can see this ID number in SYSCON by choosing the user's name and selecting the "Other Information" option.

Along with the creation of this ID number is the creation of a mailbox that is stored in the SYS:MAIL directory. For example, if a user has the ID number of 0E54F438, the mailbox would be located in the directory SYS:MAIL\0E54F438. Within this mailbox may be included user login scripts and print job configurations. The user is assigned all rights to this directory except Access control. *Do not* delete the mail directory, even if you aren't using electronic mail. This directory will be used for the login scripts and print job configurations.

Using Groups to Simplify Administration

When you need to give a user rights and establish the network drive mappings, the simplest procedure is to accomplish the task for all appropriate users at once by defining a user group. For example, you may have several users who need access to a certain database. Rather than assigning rights to the database directory for each of these users, one by one, you can define a group, give the group rights to the database directory, and then insert the appropriate usernames into the group. The result is that each of the users gets the rights that are assigned to the group.

Groups are also convenient for mapping network drives. As we'll show you in Chapter 16, if a person is a member of a group, you can set up the group login script to map each user in the group automatically to a certain network drive and/or directory.

To summarize, the concept of groups allows you to avoid unnecessary work in the process of assigning user rights to specific applications and then mapping the users to the correct application drives and directories.

Distributing Network Management

If you have experienced NetWare users on your network, you may want to think about establishing user account managers and workgroup managers. Assigning these two system management responsibilities to your most skilled users can let you share the tasks of creating users, assigning users to groups, or modifying login scripts. You can then devote more of your time to actual troubleshooting.

To help you understand the potential of this kind of distributed network management, we'll explain the duties of *user account managers* and *workgroup managers.*

User Account Managers

You can assign the job of user account manager to any existing user or group member. That user's task will be to manage specified users and groups. If a workgroup manager creates a user, the workgroup manager automatically becomes a user account manager for that user.

What User Account Managers Can Do

Once assigned, a user account manager can:

- Delete managed users and groups

- Assign managed users to a managed group

- Assign a managed user to user account manager

The user account manager can also modify certain options in SYSCON's "User Information" submenu. These options don't require file rights:

- Account Balance

- Account Restrictions

- Change Password

- Full Name Groups Belonged To (only if the groups are managed groups)

- Login Script

- Managed Users and Groups Managers

- Security Equivalences

- Station Restrictions

If assigned sufficient file rights in the directory structure, a user account manager can also assign directory trustee rights and disk space restrictions.

What User Account Managers Can't Do

User account managers can't perform these tasks, which are reserved for SUPERVISOR or equivalent users:

- Create users and groups Assign managed users to a group that the user account manager doesn't manage Modify the login restrictions of their own user accounts (unless they've been granted the rights to manage their own accounts)

Workgroup Managers

Workgroup managers have responsibilities similar to those of the supervisor. They act as assistants to the supervisor by creating and managing users, groups, and print queues.

The workgroup managers' rights do not entirely replace the network supervisor's role. For example, workgroup managers can manage only the users and groups they create or those assigned to them for account management. Workgroup managers don't acquire rights to the directory structure or file system unless those rights are specifically granted to them by the network supervisor (which we don't recommend).

What Workgroup Managers Can Do

Once assigned, a workgroup manager can:

- Create users and manage their accounts

- Create groups and add users they manage to those groups

- Delete users they have created

A workgroup manager must be assigned directory trustee rights in order to assign or modify directory trustee rights or assign or modify disk space restrictions.

What Workgroup Managers Can't Do

Workgroup managers can't perform these tasks:

- Assign any rights the supervisor hasn't assigned them

- Create a user and assign that user supervisor equivalency

379

- Create another workgroup manager

- Manage users or groups they haven't created (unless they've been designated as the user account manager of the users or groups)

- Modify any login restrictions of their own accounts (unless they've been granted management rights of their own accounts)

Utilities for Creating Users and Groups

In NetWare v3.11, you can choose from among three utilities to create users on the file server. These utilities are SYSCON, MAKEUSER, and USERDEF. You can modify existing users or create groups only in the SYSCON utility.

Use SYSCON for creating individual users. We recommend this utility if you have many user specializations (in terms of trustee assignments or login scripts, for example) or you're adding one or two new users to a server. After your initial installation, you'll probably find SYSCON most useful for quickly creating users.

Use the MAKEUSER utility for the initial installation if most of your users have basically the same account configuration. MAKEUSER is the best utility for creating users at a school or college, for example. By creating a user standardization file (.USR) each time a class must be added to or deleted from the system, MAKEUSER will eliminate extra steps you'd have to follow in SYSCON.

Use the USERDEF utility if you have several users with similar account configurations. For example, suppose you have a database system on a file server. Each user has pretty much the same configuration to use the database. You can create a template for granting users the rights to access a particular database. Once you've created the template, every time a new user needs those same rights to the database you can use the USERDEF template to set up the user properly and quickly. Later in this chapter, we'll show you how to create a USERDEF template.

The following sections show you how to use these utilities to create users. For each utility, we give a step-by-step explanation, along with examples. We'll also discuss which utility to use for specific user- and group-creation situations.

Before creating *any* users, take the time to gather information about your network users. Plan out the users' needs before doing the installation. Planning ahead will save you from having to go back to redo or add more information. Worksheets like the ones in the NetWare manuals are quite helpful. Here's a quick list of some questions you might want to ask:

- What account restrictions will be necessary?

- What trustee rights will the user need?

- What applications (for groups) will they need to access?

- What will their usernames be?

- What is each user's full name?

- How much disk space will each user need?

Using the SYSCON Utility to Create Users

To help you understand how to use SYSCON to create a user, let's assume that you want to create a user named MARY. Here's a step-by-step explanation of the process of creating users with SYSCON.

1. Before creating any users, define the default account restrictions for users. These restrictions include login restrictions, disk space restrictions, and a description of the location of all user directories. You won't have to do this every time you want to create a user, but you should define a default for most users you'll be creating.

   Define these restrictions by starting SYSCON and selecting "Supervisor Options" from the main menu. Then select "Default Account Balance/ Restrictions." (For more information about what these account restrictions do, review Chapter 12.)

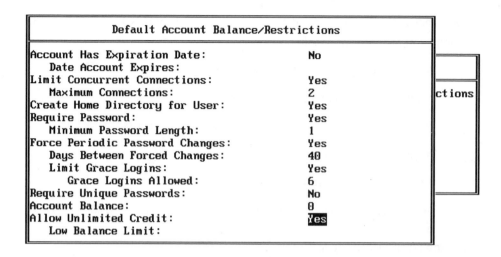

After you've made the appropriate settings, exit by pressing <Esc>.

2.   Choose the "Default Time Restrictions" option to define the default periods during which users can log in.

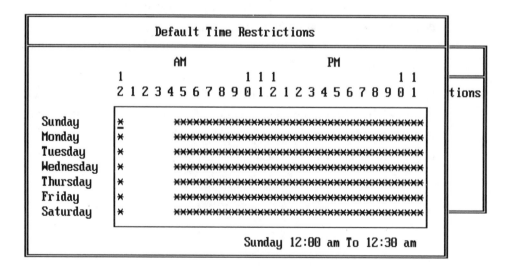

After you've defined the time restrictions, exit by pressing <Esc>. Keep pressing <Esc> until you return to the "Available Topics" menu.

3. Select the "User Information" option from the "Available Topics" menu. A list of the current user names (at least SUPERVISOR and GUEST) will appear in a window titled "User Names."

4. Press <Ins> and type the user name "MARY" in the "New User" entry box. Then press <Enter>.

   The user MARY will now appear in the list of users.

5. Select MARY from the list; a menu titled "User Information" will appear with some options you can use to configure the new user's environment. At this point, you may want to go through most of the items on this menu, creating the environment the user needs. (See Chapter 12 for setting up user security, Chapter 13 for directory creation, Chapter 14 for creation information dealing with applications, and Chapter 16 for information on establishing a login script.)

Using the MAKEUSER Utility to Create Users

Before using MAKEUSER to create users, you need to understand how this utility works. When using MAKEUSER, you first create a .USR file for each user. After creating the .USR file, you'll be able to process the information specified in the .USR files. The MAKEUSER utility includes the options for creating and processing the .USR files.

The .USR file consists of keywords used to create and assign rights for new users. If you have questions about the syntax for using the keywords, you can use the HELP <F1> key. We will briefly discuss how to use these keywords and provide some samples. (For more information about MAKEUSER keywords, refer to the NetWare *v3.11 Utilities Reference* manual.)

Here is a list of the MAKEUSER keywords you will use when you create the .USR file:

MAKEUSER Keywords

#ACCOUNT_EXPIRATION *month day year*
#ACCOUNTING *balance, lowlimit*
#CLEAR or
#RESET
#CONNECTIONS *number*
#CREATE *username* [*;fullname*] [*;password*] [*;group*] [*;directory [rights]*]
#DELETE *username*
#GROUPS *group*
#HOME_DIRECTORY *path*
#LOGIN_SCRIPT *path*
#MAX_DISK_SPACE *number*
#NO_HOME_DIRECTORY
#PASSWORD_LENGTH *length*
#PASSWORD_PERIOD *days*
#PASSWORD_REQUIRED
#PURGE_USER_DIRECTORY
#REM or REM
#RESTRICTED_TIME *day, start, end*
#STATIONS *network, station*
#UNIQUE_PASSWORD

Here is a list of restrictions you must follow when using the MAKEUSER keywords. Each keyword must be on a separate line. For example,
#CREATE MJONES^
#CONNECTIONS 1

- The #CREATE or #DELETE keyword *must* be in every .USR file that you create. Any other keywords are optional.

- The #CREATE keyword must have a caret (^) character to terminate a line at any point.

- If you don't use all variable options after the keyword, enter a caret (^) to terminate the line. For example, to create a user (MJONES) without using the other options (fullname, password, and so forth) enter the line like this:

#CREATE MJONES^

- Use the #CLEAR or #RESET keyword to mark the beginning of a new set of keywords within a .USR file. Any keywords before the #CLEAR or #RESET will not affect the keywords below that command. For example, suppose you want to create three users: Jack, Fred, and Cathy. You want to restrict Jack and Fred to one connection, and you want to make Cathy a member of the MARKETING group. To do this, create a .USR file like this one:

#CONNECTIONS 1
#CREATE JACK
#CREATE FRED
#CLEAR
#CONNECTIONS 2
#CREATE CATHY

- If a keyword is specified more than once, only the last value is used; all previous values will be ignored.

As an example of using MAKEUSER, here are the steps for creating a user named ALAN.

1. From a network drive, type **MAKEUSER <Enter>**.

2. Select the "Create New USR File" option from the "Available Options" menu.

3. MAKEUSER presents a script box, complete with a text editor, for creating generic user definitions. Enter the keywords and values for your user accounts, along with any other parameters specific to the accounts. For our example, you would enter the keyword "#CREATE ALAN" in the script box.

4. After entering the keywords, press <Esc> to exit. Specify what you want the name of the .USR file to be and save the .USR file. Let's name our sample file ALAN.USR.

5. Select the "Process USR File" option from the "Available Options" menu. You'll then be prompted for the .USR file name. Press <Ins> to list the current .USR files that have been created. Highlight and select the USR file you want to process (ALAN.USR in this case). The name of the .USR file will appear in the prompt window.

6. Press <Enter> to begin processing the .USR file.

After the processing is complete, the MAKEUSER utility will display the name of a result file. By using the DOS TYPE command or a text editor, you can view the results of the MAKEUSER processing for the .USR file you selected. The result file will give you information about any errors that happened when processing the .USR file.

Using the USERDEF Utility to Create Users

Use the USERDEF utility for creating multiple users. Along with creating users, you can set up basic login scripts, specify a home directory, establish print job configurations, assign account and disk space restrictions, and set minimal login and password security.

Using USERDEF consists of three steps: choosing between the default template and a definable custom template, doing some preliminary work before using one of these templates, and then actually running USERDEF.

The default template is a basic template that's already set up and ready for use.

Using the Default Template

To use the USERDEF default template, you must complete the following preliminary steps. Then you can use the USERDEF utility.

1. If you're going to use the accounting features, specify the accounting parameters within the SYSCON utility.

2. Using the PRINTDEF utility, copy the print device definitions that match the printers on your network. For example, you may have a user who wants to print some reports in a certain font. You can define the proper escape

codes in PRINTDEF. (For more information about this utility, refer to Chapter 20.)

3. Using the PRINTCON utility, create print job configurations for the user Supervisor. You can copy these configurations for the new user. (For more information about this utility, see Chapter 20.)

Now you can use the USERDEF utility to start creating users and their associated configurations. Here are the steps.

1. At the command line, type **USERDEF <Enter>** to start USERDEF.

2. Choose the "Add Users" option from the "Available Options" menu.

3. Select the "Default" template from the "Templates" list.

4. A list of the current users will appear. To create a new user, press <Ins>. You'll then be prompted to enter the user's full name and then the login name. Repeat this step for every user you want to create with the default template.

5. After you've defined the new usernames, press <Esc>. Follow the USERDEF prompts to complete the creation of the new users you've just defined.

After the new users' definitions have been processed, a "MakeUser Result" screen will appear, indicating any errors USERDEF encountered while creating the new users.

Creating a Custom Template

A custom template is perfect for creating several users who have similar configuration parameters. For example, a group of data entry clerks might have similar login scripts, default directories, group assignments, and account restrictions.

Before creating and using a custom template, complete these preliminary steps.

1. If you're using the accounting options, install these options in SYSCON. (For more information about the Accounting features, see Chapter 18.)

2. In SYSCON, create any user groups that your potential users will be using.

3. Create the parent directory for the users' home directories. For example, create the USERS directory for a user's home directory path of

SYS:USERS\JOHN.

4. Create the users' application directories.

5. Using the PRINTDEF utility, copy the print device definitions that match the printers you'll be using on the network. You may want to use this utility to help make the data entry clerks' printer style. (Chapter 20 covers this utility in more detail.)

6. Using the PRINTCON utility, create print job configurations for user Supervisor. You can then copy these configurations for the new user. (Chapter 20 covers this utility in more detail.)

After you've taken care of the preliminary work, follow these steps to create a custom template and use it to create similar users.

1. Type **USERDEF <Enter>** to start the USERDEF utility.

2. Select "Edit/View Templates" from "Available Options." A list of previously created templates will appear.

3. Press <Ins> to create a new template for the data entry clerks. You'll be prompted to enter an arbitrary name for the custom template you're creating. This name should be different from the names of the other templates you've created. After you've entered a name, press <Enter>.

4. A menu will appear, giving you two choices: "Edit Login Script" and "Edit Parameters." Choose the "Edit Login Script" option to modify the login script for the custom template you created. Choose the "Edit Parameters" option to modify the user's default directory, print configuration, group assignments, account balance, and restrictions. (See Chapter 16 for information about the login script and Chapter 12 for information about the account parameters.)

After making the necessary modifications, press <Esc> to exit and save.

5. Select "Add Users" from the "Available Options" menu. A menu displaying

the currently available templates will appear.

6. Select the custom template you created. A list of the current users will appear.

7. To add a username, press <Ins>. You'll then be prompted to enter the full name and the login name. Repeat this step for each user you want to create with the custom template.

8. After you've defined the new users you want to create, press <Esc>. Follow USERDEF's prompts to continue with the creation of the new users you defined.

After the new users' definitions have been processed, a "MakeUser Result" screen will appear, indicating any errors USERDEF may have encountered while creating the new users.

Creating User Groups

You create user groups by using SYSCON to create the groups, assign trustee rights, and assign users to that group. Before actually creating the group, you need to decide on the trustee right assignments and the users to assign to the group. As discussed earlier in the chapter, creating groups can make assigning trustee rights and mappings easier.

To help you understand how to create groups, we'll use an example of creating a group called COMMON. The COMMON group uses an area for sharing files among other users.

Creating Groups in SYSCON

Here is a step-by-step explanation of how to create this COMMON user group.

1. After logging in as SUPERVISOR, type **SYSCON <Enter>** to start SYSCON.

2. Select the "Group Information" option from the "Available Topics" menu. A list of the current groups will appear.

3. Press <Ins> and enter the new group name COMMON. The new group COMMON will be added to the list of the defined groups.

4. Select "COMMON" from the list of groups. A "Group Information" menu will appear for that specific group.

5. To help you remember the purpose of the group, you have the option of entering a full name that will describe the group in more detail. Select the "Full Name" option from the "Group Information" menu. Type a full name for the group (for example, "User common area for sharing files") and press <Enter>.

Assigning Trustee Rights to the Groups

To assign trustee rights to the group COMMON, follow these steps.

1. If necessary, start SYSCON and choose "Group Information." Select "COMMON" from the list of groups.

2. Select the "Trustee Directory Assignments" option from the "Group Information" menu. This option is for assigning trustees to a group. (Some groups may not have trustee assignments if they're used only for mapping purposes.)

3. Press <Ins> to enter the directory path for the group's trustee assignments. You'll be prompted to enter the directory path where you're assigning directory rights. If you're not sure of the directory path, you can press <Ins> to list the possible volumes, directories, and subdirectories. By selecting the volume, directories, and subdirectories, you'll start building a directory path. When you've entered the directory path, press <Enter>.

4. To assign trustee rights to the directory you selected, highlight the directory and press <Enter>.

5. Press <Ins> to list the available trustee rights. In this example, the group COMMON allows users to share files, so you need to grant them all rights. Using the <F5> key, mark each of the rights you want the group to have in the selected directory. After you've marked the rights, press <Enter> to add the rights.

6. Press <Esc> to return to the "Group Information" menu.

Adding Users to a Group

After you've defined the trustee rights, you can assign the users who need to share files to the COMMON group. Here's how.

1. Select the "Member List" option from the "Group Information" menu. A screen will appear with a list of any users currently assigned to the group.

2. To assign users as members of the group, press <Ins>. A screen will then appear, listing current users who are not assigned as members of the group.

3. Highlight the names of the users you want assigned to the group by using the <F5> key. After you've selected the users, press <Enter>.

The selected users are now members of the group. They will have the same trustee rights to the directories in which you granted rights to the group.

Assigning User Account Managers and Workgroup Managers

At this point, we'll go through the process of using SYSCON to assign users and workgroup managers. To make these assignments, you must be logged in as SUPERVISOR. You can assign user account managers one at a time, or you can assign a group to be a user account manager.

Creating User Account Managers

As an example of how to assign a user account manager, here are the steps for making user MICHELLE a user account manager over PAUL, TED, and HEATHER:

1. At the command line, type **SYSCON <Enter>**.

2. Select the "User Information" option from the SYSCON "Available Topics" menu.

3. Select "MICHELLE" from this list; a "User Information" menu will appear.

4. Select the "Managed Users and Groups" option from the "User Information" menu. A list will appear.

5. Press <Ins> to view a list of "Other Users and Groups." Select PAUL, TED,

and HEATHER from the list by highlighting the username and marking it with the <F5> key. After you've marked all three users, press <Enter>.

Creating Workgroup Managers

As an example of assigning a workgroup manager, here are the steps for making user CHRIS a workgroup manager:

1. At the command line, type **SYSCON <Enter>**.

2. Select "Supervisor Options" from the "Available Topics" menu.

3. Select "Workgroup Managers" from the "Supervisor Options" menu. A list of the current workgroup managers will appear.

4. Press <Ins> to add a new workgroup manager. A list of "Other Users and Groups" will appear. Select "CHRIS" from this list. "CHRIS" will then appear in the list of "Workgroup Managers." Press <Esc> until you return to the "Available Topics" menu.

5. Select the "User Information" option from the "Available Topics" menu. Select "CHRIS" from this list of users.

6. Highlight and select the "Managed Users and Groups." Press <Ins> to list the users and groups not currently being managed by CHRIS.

7. Select the users or groups (or both) that you want the workgroup manager to manage. To select several users or groups at one time, highlight each user or group and press the <F5> key. After you've marked the name(s) you want, press <Enter>; they'll be added to the "Managed Users and Groups" list.

Listing User Information with USERLIST

NetWare provides a utility called USERLIST that you can use to list information about the users currently logged in to a file server. The format for the command is:

```
USERLIST [Server/][UserName] [Option]
```

With no parameters, USERLIST displays all users currently attached to the default server and the date and time they last logged in to that server:

```
User Information for Server JUNGLE
Connection     User Name      Login Time

1              JHANCOCK       8-02-1991 8:03 am
2              *CSMITH        8-02-1991 8:30 am
3              PJONES         8-02-1991 7:59 am
4              GUEST          8-02-1991 9:30 am
```

You can specify a server other than your default server, as long as you are attached to it. Include the server's name in place of *Server*, followed by a slash (/). The slash signifies that you mean a server name, not a username.

To view information about only one user, specify that name in place of *UserName*. You can use wildcard characters (* and ?) to see information about several users at a time (for example, D* for all users whose names begin with "D").

Here are the options you can use with USERLIST. Precede the option name with a slash (/).

Option	Description
/A	Displays users' network and node addresses along with the connection numbers and login times.
/O	Displays the object type (user, print server, and so on) of the entity using each server connection.
/C	Scrolls through the list continuously without pausing after each screenful.

Typing USERLIST /A is a quick way to gather node addresses when you are troubleshooting possible node address conflicts. It also helps identify exactly which workstation generic users such as GUEST and SUPERVISOR are logged in from.

CHAPTER 16

Creating Login Scripts

A login script is made up of commands that set environmental variables, create network drive mappings, and/or control the execution of a program upon logging in. A login script is much like a batch file. This chapter will review the different login scripts, explain how to set them up, and then give you some troubleshooting and network management pointers. The exciting thing about login scripts is that they let you be as creative as you want.

How NetWare Login Scripts Work

In this chapter, we'll discuss three different login scripts: the default login script, the system login script, and user login scripts (sometimes called personal login scripts).

The three kinds of login scripts work in a specific order. When a user logs in to a server, the system login script (if there is one) executes first. The user login script operates next. The default login script executes *only* if no user login script exists. If a user login script does exist, NetWare ignores the default login script.

The Default Login Script

As mentioned above, the default login script is executed if no user login script exists. This simple login script is coded into the LOGIN.EXE file and provides the basic instructions that NetWare uses when you first log in as SUPERVISOR. The default login script looks like this:

```
WRITE "Good %GREETING_TIME, %LOGIN_NAME."
MAP DISPLAY OFF
MAP ERRORS OFF
Remark: Set 1st drive to most appropriate directory.
MAP *1:=SYS:;*1:=SYS:%LOGIN_NAME Remark: Set search drives (S2
machine-OS dependent).
```

```
MAP  S1:=SYS:PUBLIC;  S2:=S1:%MACHINE/%OS/%OS_VERSION
Remark: Now display all the current drive settings.
MAP DISPLAY ON
M A P
```

The important thing to remember about the default login script is that it will always execute unless a user login script exists. Even if you aren't using user login scripts because all necessary drive mappings are taken care of in the system login script, you should create user login scripts that consist of just a space or a remark statement. The file server will still consider that a login script and thus not run the default login script when you don't want it to.

The System Login Script

As network administrator, you create the system login script, which should control the general login parameters for the file server. Within the system login script, you can place commands for mapping network drives, mapping search drives, setting up environment variables, or setting commands that relate to groups of users. Because you create the system login script in SYSCON, other users may view it. You must remember, therefore, never to place non-public information, such as passwords, in the system login script.

User Login Scripts

The user login script controls specific login parameters for a particular user. Only users who have rights to change their own passwords can create and modify their own login scripts.

Like the system login script, the user login script contains commands for mapping network drives, mapping search drives, and setting environmental variables. You can also set it up so that the user is taken directly into a menu system (such as one created with Novell's MENU program) that takes over right after the user login script executes.

Setting Up Login Scripts

You can create and modify login scripts in the NetWare SYSCON utility. To set up a system or user login script, you must first become familiar with the commands you can use. After we've reviewed the commands, we'll discuss the essential parts of the system login script. Last, we'll give some examples of setting up both the system and user login scripts.

We recommend that when you create login scripts, you use comments in the login scripts that will "document" what the various commands are for. This will not only help you maintain the login scripts, but it will be of immense help to someone else who has to come in after you and try to figure out what you've done with your login scripts.

Here's how to access the system login script in SYSCON:

1. Start the SYSCON utility by typing **SYSCON <Enter>** at the command line.

2. Select "Supervisor Options" from the main menu.

3. Choose "System Login Script." A window appears, in which you can insert the login script command and variables.

Here's how to access a user's login script in SYSCON:

1. After starting SYSCON, select the "User Information" option from the "Available Topics" menu.

2. A list of the currently defined users will appear. Highlight the name of the user for whom you want to create or modify a login script.

3. After selecting the user, you'll see a "User Information" menu with several user configuration options. Select the "Login Script" option from this menu.

4. If no login script yet exists for the user, you will be prompted to copy an existing login script from another user. This feature lets you reuse commands from one login script without having to type in duplicate commands for every user. If you don't want to copy an existing login script, press <Esc>. A window will appear for inserting login script command and variables.

Login Script Commands and Variables

The next pages contain two tables: a table of login script commands and a table of login script identifier variables. First, we'll give you a brief description of what these commands and variables are, and then we'll explain how to use each of them in a login script. Keep in mind that you won't need to use every command or variable; they're available, however, if you need them.

You use the login script commands to cause something to happen with every login. The login script identifier variables consist of values that you can use in the login script. The combination of the login script commands and the login script identifier variables helps to make the login script.

Login Script Commands

Command	Description
ATTACH	Use this command to attach to additional servers that exist on the network.
BREAK	Use this command to determine whether or not the login script execution can be interrupted by the <Ctrl><Break> or <Ctrl><C> key sequences.
COMSPEC	Use this command to locate the proper COMMAND.COM (the DOS command processor) the workstation will need when exiting programs.
DISPLAY or FDISPLAY	Use this command to display the specified text file on the workstation's screen during the execution of the login script.
DOS BREAK	Use this command to control the type of commands that can be interrupted by pressing <Crtl><Break>.
DOS SET	Use this command for setting a DOS environment variable to a specified value.

DOS VERIFY	Use this command to ensure that data copied to a local drive is copied correctly.
DRIVE	Use this command to set the default drive that will be in effect when the login script finishes executing.
EXIT	Use this command to exit the login script (thus aborting any further execution of login script commands).
#(External program name)	Use this command to temporarily execute a program that resides outside of the login script.
FIRE PHASERS	Use this command to produce a phaser sound while the login script executes.
GOTO	Use this command to execute a portion of the login script out of the normal top-to-bottom sequence.
IF...THEN	Use this statement to set conditions governing when login commands within the statement will be executed.
INCLUDE	Use this command to run login script commands in separate "subscript" files.
MACHINE NAME	Use this command to set a machine name of up to 15 characters to identify the workstation (not the same as the six-character long machine name)
MAP	Use this command for mapping network drives and search drives for the users.
PAUSE	Use this command to cause the login script to pause until the user presses a key.

PCCOMPATIBLE	Use this command to inform the login program that a work-station is an IBM PC compatible.
REMARK	Use this command to insert descriptive comments in the login script.
SHIFT	Use this command to shift the command line parameters to the next variable.
WRITE	Use this command to write a specific message to the work-station screen during login.

Login Script Identifier Variables

Identifier Variable	Description
ACCESS_SERVER	Returns the value "TRUE" if an access server is functional; otherwise the value is "FALSE"
AM_PM	Returns "am" if it is morning or "pm" if it is afternoon
ERROR_LEVEL	Allows you to check the error level returned by DOS or some external program (error level 0 means no errors)
FILE_SERVER	Returns the file server name
MEMBER OF	Returns the value "TRUE" if the user is a member of the "*group*" specified group; if not, the value is "FALSE"
DAY	Returns the numerical equivalent of the current day (01-31)

DAY_OF_WEEK   Returns the name of the current day of the week (Monday, Tuesday, and so on)

FULL_NAME   Returns the user's full name, as specified in SYSCON

GREETING_TIME   Returns "morning," "afternoon," or "evening" according to the current time of day

HOUR   Returns the numerical equivalent of the hour of day or night (1-12)

HOUR24   Returns the military equivalent of the hour (00-23, 00=midnight)

LOGIN_NAME   Returns the user's login name

MACHINE   Returns the six-character-long machine name for the brand of workstation the shell was written for (default is IBM_PC)

MINUTE   Returns the numerical equivalent of the current time's minutes (00-59)

MONTH   Returns the numerical equivalent of the current month (01-12)

MONTH_NAME   Returns the name of the current month (January, February, and so on)

NETWORK_ ADDRESS   Returns the network address (eight hex digits)

NDAY_OF_WEEK   Returns the numerical equivalent of the current weekday (1-7, 1=Sunday)

OS	Returns the type of operating system running on the workstation (default is MS-DOS)
OS_VERSION	Returns the version of DOS being used on the workstation (for example, v3.30 or v4.00)
P_STATION	Returns the 12-digit hexadecimal station number or node address (for example, 00001BED0A34B)
PASSWORD_EXPIRES	Use this variable in an IF...THEN statement to notify users when their passwords are about to expire
SECOND	Returns the numerical equivalent of the current time's seconds (00-59)
SHELL_TYPE	Returns the version number of the NetWare workstation shell
SHORT_YEAR	Returns the year in short format (90, 91, and so on)
SMACHINE	Returns the short machine name (default is IBM)
STATION	Returns the workstation's connection number
USER_ID	Returns the user's assigned ID number, as displayed in SYSCON
YEAR	Returns the year in full format (1990, 1991, and so on)
< >	Lets you use any DOS environment variable as a string in a login script command

How to Use the Login Script Commands

You must issue a command in order to cause a particular function to execute within the login script. By using the login script commands, you can request information from the operating system and workstation by using identifier variables. For example, to make the workstation's connection number appear upon login, use the command and identifier variable in the login script like this:

```
WRITE "Your connection number is %STATION"
```

To help you understand the login script commands, we'll review them here in more detail than in the tables. Then we'll give some examples of you how you can use them.

ATTACH

The ATTACH command is for attaching to other servers that may exist on the network. You can include this command anywhere in the login script. This command is helpful when you need to access another server for information without having to log in to the server. The command format is:

```
ATTACH [ServerName[/UserName[;password]]]
```

If you type just the ATTACH command at the network prompt, without any parameters after it, you'll be prompted to identify the file server you want to attach to and the username you're logged in under. The brackets "[ ]" represent the option parameters that are available. To attach to a file server without using a password, type:

```
ATTACH  ROCK/JOHN
```

Note: If you've synchronized your password on the server you're attaching to in the login script, you won't need to put in a password.

To attach without being prompted for your password, you can put a semicolon after the username and then type the password. For example:

```
ATTACH ROCK/JOHN;PAPER
```

For security reasons, use the password parameter sparingly.

BREAK ON or BREAK OFF

Use BREAK ON or BREAK OFF to allow (BREAK ON) or prevent (BREAK OFF) <Ctrl><Break> or <Ctrl><C> from operating during execution of the login script. The command format is:

```
BREAK ON
```

or

```
BREAK OFF
```

By default, the BREAK command is set to OFF. When you turn the BREAK command ON, it will remain valid until you turn it off.

COMSPEC

Use COMSPEC to specify the file and directory path of the DOS command interpreter, COMMAND.COM. Here are three different ways to execute the COMSPEC command:

```
COMSPEC = *n[\]filename
COMSPEC = drive:[\]filename
COMSPEC = Sn:[\]filename
```

The *n, representing the command interpreter location, is loaded from the directory to which the nth network drive is mapped. The *drive*, represents the drive letter of the directory where the command interperter is loaded. The *Sn* represents the search drive number of the directory where the command interpreter is loaded, *n* being the number. The *filename* represents the actual file name of the command interpreter. Here is a sample COMSPEC command in a login script:

```
COMSPEC=S2:COMMAND.COM
```

or

```
COMSPEC=C:\DOS\COMMAND.COM
```

We recommend that you set your COMSPEC to a command interpreter on the network rather than to one on a local workstation drive. The reason is that if you log in from another workstation, the command interpreter file may not be located on the same local drive as set in the login script.

If you don't use the COMSPEC command correctly, you'll receive a "Missing or invalid command interpreter file name" either after login or when exiting an application.

DISPLAY or FDISPLAY

Use DISPLAY or FDISPLAY to cause a message located in a text file to display while the login procedure executes. This command is useful if you want to display a message for all users or for a group of users when they log in.

Use the DISPLAY command to display regular text characters in a text file. The escape or control characters will be filtered out and not displayed.

Use the FDISPLAY command to display all characters in a text file, including escape and control characters.

The command format for DISPLAY or FDISPLAY is:

```
[F]DISPLAY [volume:directory/]filename
```

For example, if you want to display upon login a text file called SALESMES.TXT located in the SYS:PUBLIC/MESSAGES directory, type this login script command:

```
DISPLAY  SYS:PUBLIC/MESSAGES/SALESMES.TXT
```

You'll find this a useful command if you like to display the current group activities for the day. If you set it up right, you can give a secretary rights to update a text file daily. This text file can be displayed as a daily message upon login.

DOS BREAK

DOS BREAK ON allows a user to use <Ctrl><Break> to interrupt the login script execution. DOS BREAK OFF prevents the user from doing so. The command format is:

```
DOS BREAK ON
```

or

```
DOS BREAK OFF
```

DOS BREAK OFF won't let the user interrupt the login script execution with <Ctrl><Break> at any point *after* the DOS BREAK command.

DOS BREAK ON lets the user interrupt the login script execution by pressing <Ctrl><Break> at any point *after* the DOS BREAK command.

The default for the DOS BREAK command is OFF.

This command is useful when you want to make sure that certain parts of the login script get mapped while still allowing the user the option of breaking out of the login script.

DOS SET

Use DOS SET to set a DOS environment variable to a specified value in the login script. This command has the same effect as the SET command on the DOS command line. The command format is:

```
DOS SET name = "value"
```

where *name* is the name of the variable and *value* is the actual value of the variable. The command is similar to the SET command except that quotation marks are required around the value. Here's an example of how you might use this command to set a DOS environment variable for a workstation's DOS prompt:

```
DOS SET PROMPT = "$P -$G"
```

Some of your network programs may require an environment variable associated with the user's login name. You can use that type of command like this:

DOS SET *username* = "%LOGIN_NAME"

DOS VERIFY

Use DOS VERIFY to ensure that data copied from the network to a local drive with the DOS COPY command is copied correctly. The command format is:

```
DOS VERIFY ON
```

or

```
DOS VERIFY OFF
```

If you put the DOS VERIFY ON command in the login script, all data correctly copied to the local drive will be automatically verified by DOS.

If you put the DOS VERIFY OFF command in the login script, no verification of the data copied to the local drive will take place.

If you've placed DOS VERIFY OFF in the login script, you can still use a DOS command-line switch(/v) to cause the COPY command to verify correct copying. Refer to your DOS manual for more information on how to use the verification switch for the COPY command.

DRIVE

Use DRIVE to specify which drive is your default. The command format is:

```
DRIVE f:   (where f is the drive letter)
```

or

```
DRIVE *n:   (where n is the drive number)
```

Use this command in the login script when you want a certain drive to appear as the user's default drive. For example, to have the login procedure leave a user at a default database directory mapped to the M: drive, put this command in the login script:

```
DRIVE M:
```

EXIT

Use EXIT to terminate the execution of the LOGIN command. When you place this command in the login script, any other login command after the EXIT statement will be ignored. This doesn't mean that the EXIT command must necessarily appear at the end of the login script. You can use it, for example, to cause users to exit if they are part of a certain group. Upon using the EXIT command is an option to execute a .COM, .EXE, and .BAT. This useful when you want the user to go immediately into a database or a menu. The command format is:

```
EXIT
```

or

```
EXIT "filename"
```

EXTERNAL PROGRAM EXECUTION (#)

Use the EXTERNAL PROGRAM EXECUTION (#) for executing a command or program that isn't a login script command. The command format is:

 # [directory/] filename parameter line

You can also use parameters after the file name. The restrictions that apply to this command are:

- You must put a pound sign (#) before the name of the file you plan to execute.

- The file must have the extension .EXE or .COM to execute from the login script.

- The command statement must appear on the same line.

- If you're going to execute a file from one of the drives you're mapping, you'll need to map the drive before using this statement to execute the file.

You'll soon find yourself using this command frequently to execute the NetWare CAPTURE command from the login script, but you can use it for other commands as well. Here's an example of how you might use this command to CAPTURE to a printer on the network.

```
#CAPTURE S=ROCK Q=SOLID TI=10 NB NFF
```

FIRE PHASERS

The FIRE PHASERS command serves mainly to alert a user by making the workstation produce sounds like a phaser. It may sound frivolous, but this command is really useful if you're displaying something important in the login script and you want to be sure the users are paying attention. The command format is:

```
FIRE PHASERS n TIMES
```

The variable *n* represents the number of times you want the phaser sound to occur at the workstation. For example,

```
FIRE PHASERS 6 TIMES
```

would cause the phaser sounds to occur six times at the workstation.

GOTO

Use the GOTO command to execute a portion of the login script out of sequence. This command is good for creating loops. This procedure is useful if you want to repeat a sequence of commands. The command format is:

```
GOTO label
```

Label indicates where you want the script to "go to" and continue execution. For example, suppose you want to repeat a phrase such as "Happy Birthday" on the screen five times when the user logs in to the server. Type:

```
SET X = "1"
REPEAT:
SET X = <X> + "1"
WRITE "Happy Birthday!!!\n"
IF <X> IS LESS THAN VALUE "5" THEN GOTO REPEAT
```

As you can see, REPEAT is the label and the WRITE statement will be repeated five times.

IF...THEN

Use the IF...THEN command to instruct the operating system to execute commands *if* a certain condition logically exists. You can use this command in conjunction with login script commands and the login script identifier variables. Here's one example of how to use the IF...THEN command with other login script commands and identifiers.

```
IF DAY_OF_WEEK = "Wednesday" THEN WRITE "Sales meeting at 10 AM"
```

The most common use of the IF...THEN is to execute one or more specific commands if the user is a member of a specified group. For example, you might have one group on your network that needs to be mapped to one directory and another group that needs two mappings. To do this, type:

```
IF MEMBER OF "MARKETING" THEN MAP H:=ROCK/SYS:DEPT\MARKETING
```

and

```
IF MEMBER OF "SALES" THEN BEGIN
    MAP  I:=ROCK/SYS:DEPT\SALES
    MAP  J:=ROCK/SYS:DEPT\SALES\MEMOS
END
```

The IF...THEN statement can use command-line parameters to enhance the way the user logs in. For example, when a user logs in, he or she can use parameters with

410

the LOGIN command to automatically start an application. For example, for user SCOTT to have his word processor come up automatically when login is complete, he can type:

```
login SCOTT wp
```

The login script can then interpret these parameters as instructions to perform certain login script commands.

When the server interprets a login script, it knows that any percent sign (%) followed by a number in a command can correspond to a parameter used with the LOGIN command. The numbers can range from 0 to 19, %0 corresponding with the file server name, %1 standing for the username, and so forth.

For example, look at the variables in the following LOGIN command line:

```
LOGIN ROCK/JOHN WP
     %0 = ROCK
     %1 = JOHN
     %2 = WP
```

To manipulate these variables in the login script, you can use the IF...THEN statement to see if a certain condition is met. If so, a command can be executed. For example, the following script command determines which word processor a user will use as specified on the LOGIN command line (as shown above). If no word processor is specified, an IF...THEN statement is set to map the user to a default word processor.

```
IF "%2" = "WP" THEN MAP S3:=ROCK/SYS:APPLIC\DOS\WORDPERF
IF "%2" = "WORD" THEN MAP S3:=ROCK/SYS:APPLIC\WINDOWS\WORD
IF "%2" = "" THEN MAP S3:=ROCK/SYS:APPLIC\DOS\WORDPERF
```

You can use the SHIFT command, explained later in this chapter, to shift the %variable assigned to each command line parameter.

You can use relational conditions to help specify a condition when you're using the IF...THEN statement. Following is a list of these relational conditions.

Equal and Not Equal Relationships

EQUAL	NOT EQUAL
IS	IS NOT
=	!=
==	<> or #
EQUALS	DOES NOT EQUAL/ NOT EQUAL TO

Greater- and Less-Than-or-Equal-to Relationships

>	IS GREATER THAN
<	IS LESS THAN
>=	IS GREATER THAN OR EQUAL TO
<=	IS LESS THAN OR EQUAL TO

Here are some examples of relationship conditions.

```
IF DAY_OF_WEEK="02" THEN WRITE "Have a good week!!"
```

or

```
IF DAY_OF_WEEK EQUALS "02" THEN WRITE "Have a good week!!"
IF DAY_OF_WEEK=> "Thursday" THEN WRITE "We're more than halfway
there!"
```

or

```
IF DAY_OF_WEEK IS GREATER THAN OR EQUAL TO "Thursday" THEN WRITE
"We're more than halfway there!"
```

INCLUDE

Use the INCLUDE command to create login script subscripts. A subscript, which works as an extension of the login script, is nothing more than a text file with valid script commands in it (the commands described in this section). The command format is:

```
INCLUDE [volume:directory\]filename
```

For example, suppose you have a sales secretary who is required to display a schedule of each day's meetings, but you don't want to let the secretary modify the login scripts. One possible solution is to create a subscript file located in SYS:PUBLIC called SALES.INC and assign the secretary Read and Write rights. Every day the secretary can use a text editor to modify a file similar to this one:

```
WRITE " 8:30 AM - SALES BRIEFING IN CONFERENCE ROOM 1"
WRITE "10:00 AM - STAFF MEETING"
WRITE " 2:00 PM - REVIEW OF QUARTERLY GOALS"
```

In the system login script, insert the INCLUDE command directing it to the location of the SALES.INC file.

```
IF MEMBER OF "SALES" THEN BEGIN
INCLUDE SYS:PUBLIC\SALES.INC
END
```

MACHINE NAME

Use the MACHINE NAME command to set the machine name for the workstation to a specified name. This command is nessary for some programs that run under PC-DOS. The command format is:

```
MACHINE NAME = "name"
```

or

```
MACHINE = "name"
```

MAP

The MAP command has many different variations that you can use when working with network drives. Its format is:

```
MAP [option] [drive:=path]
```

MAP Command Variations

Here's a list of MAP command variations that you can use in login scripts. (Refer to the NetWare v3.11 *Installation* manual for more information about the MAP command.)

- MAP—Use this command to display the current drive mappings for the workstation.

- MAP *drive:=directory*—Use this command to map a specified drive to a certain directory.

  If you use "*1" for *drive*, the first available network drive will be mapped to the specified directory. By default, the first drive is F:, but you can modify the LASTDRIVE command in CONFIG.SYS to specify which drive is your last local drive.

  ```
  MAP  F:=SYS:USERS\PAUL
  ```

  or

  ```
  MAP  *1:=SYS:USERS\PAUL
  ```

- MAP *drive:=drive:*—Use this variation to map the first drive to the same directory as the second.

  ```
  MAP I:=F:
  ```

- MAP *drive:=directory; drive:=directory* ... —This variation allows multiple drives and multiple directories to be mapped out, eliminating the need to initiate the MAP *drive:=directory* command two or more times.

  ```
  MAP  F:=SYS:USERS\PAUL;  G:=SYS:USERS\PAUL\NOTES
  ```

- MAP INSERT *search drive:=directory*—Use the "INSERT" option to insert the new search drive into the search path, using the next available drive letter. All subsequent search drive mappings are bumped down one letter.

```
MAP INSERT S5:=SYS:APPLIC\DOS\WP51
```

- MAP ROOT—The "ROOT" option allows you to map a drive to a fake root directory. Use this command if you have applications that require reads and writes from the root directory, where most users shouldn't have rights.

- MAP DISPLAY ON—This command displays the current drive mappings when the user logs in. "ON" is the default setting.

- MAP DISPLAY OFF—This command turns off the displaying of the drive mappings when the user logs in.

- MAP ERRORS ON—This command option displays any MAP error messages that may occur while the drive mappings are being assigned. This is the default setting.

- MAP ERRORS OFF—This command option turns off the displaying of any MAP error messages that may occur while the drive mappings are being assigned.

The Shell Descriptor Area and Login Script Identifiers

Whenever the NetWare shell is loaded, the shell passes information to a descriptor area on the file server. (Shell descriptors are assigned in the SHELL.CFG file.) Unique identifiers are then assigned to each descriptor in the shell descriptor area. Here's a list of the shell identifiers.

- OS—The identifier for the DOS type descriptor.

- OS_VERSION—The identifier for the DOS version descriptor.

- MACHINE—The identifier for the long-machine-type descriptor.

- SMACHINE—The identifier for the short-machine-type descriptor.

You can use the shell descriptor identifiers in the login script for mapping drives, such as the version of DOS being used on the workstation. For example, you can use the MAP command to out the DOS version in the login script. The MAP command may look like this (where ZENITH is the long machine name set in the SHELL.CFG file):

```
MAP  S2:=SYS:PUBLIC\%MACHINE\%OS\%OS_VERSION
```

After the login script execution, the mapping will look something like this:

```
SEARCH2:=. Y:= [ROCK\SYS:PUBLIC\ZENITH\MSDOS\V4.00]
```

PASSWORD_EXPIRES

Use the PASSWORD_EXPIRES variable to let users know how many days they have before their passwords expire. You can use this variable with other login script commands, such as IF...THEN and WRITE. Here are a few examples:

```
IF PASSWORD_EXPIRES = VALUE = "1" THEN WRITE "Your password will
expire tomorrow, so be thinking of a new password!!!"
```

or

```
WRITE "Your password will expire in %password_expires days!!"
```

PAUSE

The PAUSE command is much like the PAUSE you can use in DOS batch files. You use it to pause the execution of the login script. The WAIT command will do the same thing as the PAUSE.

To use PAUSE or WAIT, put those commands in the login script at the point where you want to pause the execution of the login script. You might use this command, for example, if you've included a fairly long message in the login script that you want all users on the network to read before beginning work. The user will be prompted to strike a key when he or she is ready for the login script to continue.

PCCOMPATIBLE

Use the PCCOMPATIBLE command when including a file name with the EXIT script command on all IBM PC compatibles or less than 100-percent compatible workstations. If you've set the long machine name of your IBM PC compatible to a different name (such as ZENITH) to map out the correct DOS version (look at the MAP command) for the workstation, you'll need to use PCCOMPATIBLE (or COMPATIBLE) in the login script. For example, include the PCCOMPATIBLE command as in the script excerpt below. Remember to use the PCCOMPATIBLE command before the EXIT command.

```
PCCOMPATIBLE
EXIT "MENU"
```

REMARK

Use the REMARK command when putting explanatory text in the login script. The server ignores any text past the REMARK command when executing the login script. There are three different ways to execute this login script command:

```
REM[ARK] [text]
```

or

```
* [text]
```

or

```
; [text]
```

For example, you can use the REMARK commands like this:

```
REM This is explanatory text!!!
```

or

```
REMARK This is explanatory text!!!
```

or

```
* This is explanatory text!!!
```

or

```
; This is explanatory text!!!
```

SHIFT

Use the SHIFT command to shift the LOGIN command-line parameters to the next variable. This command allows the user to enter command-line variables in any order and still have the login interpret the variables. The command format is:

```
SHIFT [n]
```

The n represents the number of places you want shift the command line variables. You can use positive and negative numbers to move the variable in either direction. For example, a -2 would move the % variable two positions to the left. The default is 1.

When users log in, they can specify parameters with the LOGIN command. The login script then interprets these parameters as instructions to perform certain login script commands.

When the server interprets the login script, it sees any percent sign (%) followed by a number in a command as corresponding to a parameter used when the LOGIN executes. The numbers can range from 0 to 19, %0 corresponding to the servername, %1 to the username, and so forth.

For example, the following LOGIN command line would have these corresponding variables:

```
LOGIN ROCK/JOHN WP
    %0 = ROCK
    %1 = JOHN
    %2 = WP
    %3 = 123
```

To manipulate these variables in the login script, you can use an IF...THEN statement to see if a certain condition is met. A command can then be executed. For example, if specified at the LOGIN command line, the following script command could determine if the user wants to map to a word processor and/or spreadsheet:

```
IF "%2" = "WP" THEN MAP S3:=ROCK/SYS:APPLIC\DOS\WORDPERF
IF "%3" = "123" THEN MAP S4:=ROCK/SYS:APPLIC\DOS\123
```

If you use the SHIFT command, the variables will be assigned to the next parameter. In this case, 1-2-3 would be assigned %2 and WP would be assigned %1.

```
IF "%1" = "WP" THEN MAP S3:=ROCK/SYS:APPLIC\DOS\WORDPERF
IF "%2" = "123" THEN MAP S4:=ROCK/SYS:APPLIC\DOS\123
```

The end result of using the SHIFT command is that a user can include a number of different parameters in any order.

```
IF "%2" = "WP" THEN MAP S3:=ROCK/SYS:APPLIC\DOS\WORDPERF
IF "%2" = "WORD" THEN MAP S3:=ROCK/SYS:APPLIC\WINDOWS\WORD
IF "%2" = "" THEN MAP S3:=ROCK/SYS:APPLIC\DOS\WORDPERF
IF "%3" = "EXCEL" THEN MAP S4:=ROCK/SYS:APPLIC\WINDOWS\EXCEL
IF "%3" = "123" THEN MAP S4:=ROCK/SYS:APPLIC\DOS\123
IF "%3" = "" THEN MAP S4:=ROCK/SYS:APPLIC\DOS\123
```

WRITE

Use the WRITE command to display messages when executing the login script. Its format is:

```
WRITE [text string(s);... identifier(s);...]
```

Here's a list of WRITE command rules.

- Text strings must be enclosed in double quotation marks (" "). For example, the WRITE command with a text string would look like this:

```
WRITE "Hello!!!!!"
```

- The WRITE command can be executed as one command or a series of text strings or identifiers separated by semicolons (;). For example, your WRITE commands can look like this:

```
WRITE "Hello"
```

  or

```
WRITE "Hello"; LOGIN_NAME; "!!!"
```

  In this example, LOGIN_NAME is an identifier variable.

- Unless you put a semicolon at the end of a WRITE command, the next WRITE message on that line will be displayed on a new line when the login script is executed. For example, the following two text strings would appear on the same line:

```
WRITE "Hello"; LOGIN_NAME; WRITE "!!!"
```

  But these two text strings would appear on separate lines:

```
WRITE "Hello"; LOGIN_NAME; "!!!"
WRITE "Welcome to %FILE_SERVER"
```

Using Identifier Variables with WRITE

Identifier variables enhance what you can do with the WRITE command by displaying information about the server, user, and workstation parameters. Earlier in this chapter we listed the login script identifier variables that you can use. Here's an example of using some identifier variables in the login script. Notice that the identifier variables inside the quotation marks have a percent sign (%) in front of them, while the ones outside the quotation marks do not.

```
WRITE "Good %GREETING_TIME"; FULL_NAME; ", welcome to server
        SERVER_NAME!"
WRITE "Today is %DAY_OF_WEEK, %MONTH_NAME %DAY, %YEAR."
```

If you put this in the login script, when the login script executes the user will see:

```
Good Morning John Q. Public, welcome to server JUNGLE!
Today is Friday, August 2, 1991.
```

Using Super-Characters and Compound Strings

You can use *super-characters* with text strings to enhance your write commands. Enclose super- characters in double quotation marks (" ") within the text strings. Here is a list of the super-characters and their functions.

\r   Produces a carriage return
\n   Produces a new line
\"   Use for embedded quotation marks
\7   Sounds a beep

Compound strings are strings that have been combined into a single string. A string can be a quoted sequence of characters or the value of an identifier variable, including DOS environment variables. Here's a list of the operators you can use to combine strings (in order of precedence):

;   Concatenate (join together)
*   Multiply two numerical values
/   Divide two numerical values
%   Modulo (produce only the remainder of an integer division)
+   Add two numerical values

- Subtract two numerical values

\>\> Shift (truncate) to the left; for example, "2000" becomes "2"

\<\< Shift (truncate) to the right; for example, "0004" becomes "4"

Here's an example showing how you can use super-characters and the compound string operators listed above.

```
SET X = "1"
REPEAT:
SET X = <X> + "1"
WRITE "Happy Birthday!!!\n"
IF <X> IS LESS THAN VALUE "5" THEN GOTO REPEAT
```

This fancy WRITE command displays the string "Happy Birthday!!!" five times on the screen, each one starting on a new line. The DOS variable "X" serves as a counter that is incremented by one with each iteration of the loop.

Sample Login Scripts

To help you understand what a system login script looks like compared to a user login script, we've included examples of both. Both types of configurable login scripts, user and system, can use any of the login script commands and variables. Remember that the examples we're giving you here are only samples of what can be done. Use your imagination to make a login script that will fit the needs of the users on your system.

Sample System Login Script

```
******************************************************************
*     System Login Script for server COUNTER                     *
******************************************************************
*     Last modified by: Joe Supervisor                           *
*     Last date modified: August 2, 1991                         *
*                                                                *
*     Drive mapping information:                                 *
*     1. Search drive 1, 2, and 3 are specifically  used.        *
*     DO NOT MAP to those search drives                          *
*     2. Drive M: is alway used for the database                 *
*     Other login script information:                            *
******************************************************************

* System Greeting
WRITE "Good %GREETING_TIME, %FULL_NAME!"
WRITE "Welcome to server %FILE_SERVER!!!!!"
WRITE "Today is %MONTH_NAME %DAY, %YEAR."
WRITE "The time is %HOUR:%MINUTE:%SECOND."
FIRE PHASERS 5

* Set up standard mappings and environment
MAP DISPLAY OFF
MAP   *1:=ROCK/SYS:USERS\%LOGIN_NAME
MAP   S1:=ROCK/SYS:PUBLIC
MAP   S2:=ROCK/SYS:PUBLIC\%MACHINE\%OS\%OS_VERSION
  COMSPEC=S2:COMMAND.COM
DOS SET PROMPT = "$P$G"

* Set up group mappings and environment
IF MEMBER OF "WORDPERFECT" THEN BEGIN
      MAP   S3:=ROCK/SYS:APPS\WP51
END

IF MEMBER OF "SALES" THEN BEGIN
      DISPLAY  SYS:PUBLIC\MESSAGES\SALESMES.TXT
      PAUSE
      DOS  SET  USER="%LOGIN_NAME"
      MAP  M:=ROCK/SYS:DATABASE\SALEDATA
      MAP  S16:=ROCK/SYS:DATABASE\FOXPRO
      DRIVE M:
END

* Printer Groups
IF MEMBER OF "LASER1" THEN BEGIN
      #CAPTURE S=ROCK Q=LASER1 NB NFF TI=10
END

IF MEMBER OF "LASER2" THEN BEGIN
      #CAPTURE S=ROCK Q=LASER2 NB NFF TI=10
END

IF MEMBER OF "LINE_PRINT" THEN BEGIN
      #CAPTURE S=ROCK Q=LINE NB NFF TI=10
END

* Last commands for the Login Script
MAP DISPLAY ON
M A P

; End of Login Script
```

Sample User Login Script

```
MAP   G:=ROCK/SYS:USERS\JOHN\REPORTS
IF DAY_OF_WEEK="FRIDAY" THEN BEGIN
    WRITE "Remember to transfer your weekly"
    WRITE "report to Rob's report area on"
    WRITE "server HAWAII!!!"
    FIRE PHASER 5
    PAUSE
    ATTACH  HAWAII/JOHN
    MAP   H:=HAWAII\SYS:USERS\ROB\REPORTS\JOHN
END
EXIT  "JOHNMENU"
```

Troubleshooting Tips and Suggestions for Login Scripts

1. Try to keep most of the login script commands in groups. If you do, you'll find it easier to manage and you'll spend less time creating user login scripts. For example, if you have several people using an application, you may want to create a group, assign the users to that group, and then do all their mappings from the system login script as a group.

2. Include a comment area in the login script where you can note information on who modified what and any other information that may be specific to the login script. This will make your login script much cleaner and easier to troubleshoot because you can refer to what was last modified.

3. After modifying the system or user login scripts, review the modification to verify that you've used the correct syntax, then try logging in to verify that it works. If you make a mistake on a user login script, NetWare creates a backup file, called LOGIN.BAK, in the user's ID directory, located in SYS:MAIL\user_id. To return the user login script to the state it was in before the modification, simply rename LOGIN.BAK to LOGIN.

4. In some cases, you may need to include more environment space for a DOS workstation if the login script command won't add mappings or other variables to the DOS workstation environment space. (Refer to your DOS

manual for information on modifying the environment space.) For example, you may see error messages like these:

```
Could not add "USER=JOHN" to the local environment vari-
ables.
```

or

```
Could not execute external program "capture", not enough
memory.
```

or

```
There is no room to expand the PATH environment variable
with the mapping: "S16:=ROCK/SYS:PUBLIC/UTILS"
```

To increase your environment space, use a text editor to create or modify the CONFIG.SYS file with the following parameter:

```
SHELL=C:COMMAND.COM  /P  /E:512
```

The "C:" represents the disk location where the file COMMAND.COM can be found. The "/P" switch tells DOS to run AUTOEXEC. The "/E" is used to define the environmental space you want use. In this example, we use 512 bytes.

5. If you've created a system login script but not a user login script, you may get duplicate mappings (such SYS:PUBLIC and/or search mappings for DOS) or your mappings may not be as expected. You can create this problem for yourself if you map drives one way in the system login script and another way in the default login script (since no user login script exists). If so, you may want to put something in the user login script, such as a space or a REM, to ensure that the user login script will execute instead of the default login script.

6. If the machine won't execute the correct command interpreter ("Invalid COMMAND.COM"), you may want to verify that you have the same command interpreter on the workstation and file server and that your COMSPEC is correctly pointing to it. If you placed DOS under a

different machine type (such as COMPAQ or ZENITH) in the SYS:PUBLIC directory, verify that you changed LONG MACHINE TYPE in the SHELL.CFG file to the matching machine type. The machine variable should be six characters or less.

CHAPTER 17

Setting Up Menu Interfaces

Once the network and its applications are in place, you should give some thought to the things you can do to make the network easy to use and productive for its users. For most network users, the interface they see at the workstation is the network. One way that you, as a network administrator, can benefit your users is to develop a customized front-end menu that makes it easy for them to move around in the network environment.

In this chapter, we'll address several NetWare menu alternatives. The option we'll discuss in the greatest depth is NetWare's own MENU utility. Although it's not as feature-rich as some of the third- party alternatives, it's a functional and relatively easy method of creating a customized menu interface for the users on a LAN. Best of all, MENU is included with the NetWare operating system, so you can use it without incurring any additional charge.

Those of you who are experienced NetWare managers may already be familiar with MENU. But even if you haven't explored the MENU utility before, you won't find it terribly difficult to use. Following the discussion of MENU, we'll take a brief look at several third-party menu alternatives.

Examining NetWare's MENU Utility

Within NetWare, you can use COPY CON or a text editor to set up a customized menu file and then run the menu with the command-line MENU utility. You can use MENU to make it easy for users to access the applications and utilities they use all the time, or you can even set up specialized menus for different occasions and different days of the week.

NetWare's MAIN Menu

During the installation process, NetWare stores a predefined MENU file, named MAIN.MNU, in the SYS:PUBLIC directory. To see the type of menu the MENU utility creates, type **MENU MAIN <Enter>** at the command line. You'll see MENU's "Main Menu" window for NetWare.

```
╔══════════════════════════════╗
║         Main Menu            ║
╠══════════════════════════════╣
║ 1. Session Management        ║
║ 2. File Management           ║
║ 3. Volume Information        ║
║ 4. System Configuration      ║
║ 5. File Server Monitoring    ║
║ 6. Print Queue Management    ║
║ 7. Print Job Configurations  ║
║ 8. Printer Definitions       ║
║ 9. Logout                    ║
╚══════════════════════════════╝
```

As you can see, NetWare's main menu presents eight of the primary NetWare utilities and a logout alternative.

To move around in this menu, simply use the up arrow and down arrow keys to move the selection bar and press <Enter> when you reach the option you'd like to pursue. From here, the utilities operate just as they would if you had invoked them from the command line. The only difference is that when you exit a utility, you return to the main menu.

To leave the menu, you may press either <Esc> or <Alt><F10> from the lower menu levels. Then you'll see a window that says "Exit Menu?" If you select "Yes," you'll return to the command-line prompt.

Looking at the MAIN.MNU File

You can learn the basics of creating a menu script file by looking at NetWare's **MAIN.MNU** file and modify it to produce our own customized menu. To protect against accidental changes to this file, we suggest that you use the **NCOPY** command to download the **MAIN.MNU** file from the **SYS:PUBLIC** directory to your main user directory. Then you can open the file and see how it works.

If you get a message that the file can't be found, go back to SYS:PUBLIC and type RIGHTS to double-check that you have at least the RF rights (if you're not logged in as SUPERVISOR, do so now). If you have RF rights, type **NDIR MAIN.MNU <Enter>** in the SYS:PUBLIC directory to see if the file is there.

Go into a text editor or a word processor that can work with text files and open the MAIN.MNU file. You'll see the text file NetWare uses to create its main menu file. It looks like this:

```
%Main Menu,0,0,3 1. Session Management
Session 2. File Management
Filer 3. Volume Information
Volinfo 4. System Configuration
SysCon 5. File Server Monitoring
FConsole 6. Print Queue Management
PConsole 7. Print Job Configuration
PrintCon 8. Printer Definitions
PrintDef 9. Logout
!Logout
```

Using this menu text file as an example, you can determine how to build a text file of your own to create a customized menu.

How Menu and Submenu Titles Are Defined

The first line of the file—%Main Menu,0,0,3—contains a percent sign, then the title of the menu, and then a series of three numbers.

The percent sign signifies that a menu name follows (this is the title you'll see as you enter the menu screen). If you decide to create submenus, you'll need to precede these menu titles with a percent sign as well. (We'll show you how in some of the following examples.)

How a Window's Position Is Defined

The first number after the title specifies the vertical positioning of the resulting menu. Vertical placement ranges from 1, at the top of the screen, to 25, at the bottom.

The second number indicates the horizontal positioning. Horizontal placement can range from 1, the far left of the screen, to 80, the far right.

Entering zeros for either the horizontal or vertical position instructs MENU to center the menu in the middle of the screen.

As you play with the menu positioning values, you'll notice that there are often several ways to request the same position. For example, to place a menu in the center of the screen, you can state 0,0 (to signify the default setting), 12,40, or nothing.

How Menu Colors Are Defined

The third number specifies which color palette from COLORPAL you'd like to use. You can give each submenu a different color, if you wish. Here is a rundown of the predefined color settings for the numeric options 0 through 4:

Color Palette 0 (NetWare uses this for list menus and normal text):
- Background Normal is Blue
- Background Reverse is White
- Foreground Intense is Yellow
- Foreground Normal is Intense White
- Foreground Reverse is Blue

Color Palette 1 (NetWare uses this for main headers and screen background):
- Background Normal is Blue
- Background Reverse is Cyan
- Foreground Intense is Light Cyan
- Foreground Normal is Cyan
- Foreground Reverse is Blue

Color Palette 2 (NetWare uses this for help screens):
- Background Normal is Black
- Background Reverse is Green
- Foreground Intense is Light Green
- Foreground Normal is Green
- Foreground Reverse is Black

Color Palette 3 (NetWare uses this for error messages):
- Background Normal is Black
- Background Reverse is Red
- Foreground Intense is Light Red
- Foreground Normal is Red
- Foreground Reverse is Yellow

Color Palette 4 (NetWare uses this for exit and alert screens):
- Background Normal is White
- Background Reverse is Magenta
- Foreground Intense is Yellow
- Foreground Normal is Magenta
- Foreground Reverse is Intense White

If you'd like to define some color palettes of your own, you can do so with the NetWare COLORPAL utility. We'll tell how to use COLORPAL later in this chapter. In the meantime, let's look again at the format of the lines in the menu text file.

How the Menu's Options Are Defined

In NetWare's MAIN menu file, notice that the second line of the file—"1. Session Management"— begins one of the options you'll be able to select from the screen. Underneath the option, you see the command to invoke that particular option. The command is always indented at least a couple of spaces. This structure is repeated for all of the options in the menu text file.

Summary of Menu Script File Rules

When you're ready to create your own menu utility, remember the following rules:

1. Start the names of the main menu and all subsequent submenus with a percent sign (%).

2. Designate the menu's horizontal position, vertical position, and color palette, respectively, by entering the appropriate numbers for each option, separated by commas. (We'll explain how to specify what the specific numbers mean a little later on.) If you'd like to use the default positions and colors, you can enter just commas, like this:

```
%Eric's Menu,,,
```

3. Begin each menu option at the left margin; press <Enter>, then indent at least two spaces and type the command for executing each option.

4. Finally, be sure to save the file as a DOS text file. We recommend that you give the .MNU extension to the files you create. If you do, MENU will immediately recognize them as menu text files.

In our example, if you save your file as NEWMENU.MNU, anytime you need to invoke the menu you can simply type **MENU NEWMENU <Enter>**, and MENU will automatically recognize the .MNU extension. But if you name the file NEWMENU.TXT, you must include the full name of the text file, including its extension, like this: **MENU NEWMENU.TXT <Enter>**.

Creating A Custom Menu Script

To create your own customized menu, begin by planning out the programs and commands you want the menu to contain. You must decide whether all of the options should appear on a single menu, or whether you'll want to include some submenus as well. Finally, you'll need to decide what color you want the menu to be.

Let's assume you want to create a personal menu for yourself, called "Michelle's Applications." You want to make the first option "Going to DOS," which will allow you to access the command line prompt and return you to the customized menu when you're through. You also want to include options for accessing your electronic mail and word processing applications. For another option, you want to access NetWare's main utilities menu (MAIN.MNU) as a submenu of your main menu. For the final option, you want to move the Logout option out of the NetWare Menus submenu and make it an entry in your menu.

Ultimately, the "Michelle's Menu" menu will look like this:

In the course of this example, you'll learn how to run command-line utilities from MENU and how to allow users to enter command parameters.

To begin, either create the appropriate text file from scratch or take a shortcut by accessing the MAIN.MNU file you downloaded from SYS:PUBLIC. You can rename this copy something else, like NEWMENU.MNU, and use it as a template. Either way, you can define your new menu with a text editor such as WordPerfect that allows you to save your text as a DOS file.

For the sake of example, let's assume you are using the renamed MAIN.MNU file, NEWMENU.MNU. Above the %Main Menu,0,0,3 line, type the following line:

```
%Michelle's Menu,0,0
```

(For this example, you'll be using the default colors.)

Following this line, enter the main menu options you want to include:

```
%Michelle's Menu,0,0
Going to DOS
E-Mail
WordPerfect
NetWare Menus
Logout
```

If you number the options, MENU will present them numerically. If you don't, MENU will present the options in alphabetical order, regardless of the order in which they were typed in.

Now, under each of the options you've listed, enter the command you would use to invoke each program.

Under the "Going to DOS" heading, type the three lines shown here:

```
%Michelle's Menu,0,0
Going to DOS
    CLS
    prompt=Type "Exit" to return to Michelle's Menu
    COMMAND
```

The CLS command clears the screen, then DOS sets your prompt to "Type `Exit' to return to Michelle's Menu." The actual program command is COMMAND, which spawns a child COMMAND.COM process that enables you to run another application or utility. Then, when you're through with DOS, you simply type **EXIT <Enter>** to return to your menu.

Note: Once the menu is finished, you may need to increase the size of your DOS environment space for this option to work.

Accessing Network Applications in MENU

Next, enter the commands to your E-mail program and word processor under the appropriate options. Now your menu file looks like this:

```
%Michelle's Menu,0,0
Going to DOS
    CLS
    prompt=Type "Exit" to return to Michelle's Menu
    COMMAND
E-Mail
    CLS echo Loading The Coordinator II
    ATC2
    echo Exiting to Michelle's Menu
```

```
WordPerfect
    CLS
    echo Loading WordPerfect 5.1
    w p
    cls
    echo Exiting to Michelle's Menu
```

In this example, the CLS command clears the screen, and the ECHO command flashes an appropriate message on your screen. Then, the actual application you've selected appears. As you exit the application, you see the message "Exiting to Michelle's Menu." The CLS and ECHO commands are entirely optional. If you wish, you can enter just the program execution commands.

Accessing NetWare Menu Utilities in MENU

Now let's move to a trickier part. Assume that you are supervisor equivalent and that you frequently require access to NetWare's management tools. To make it easier to access the main NetWare utilities, we'll make the original MAIN.MNU file (or at least the parts of it we're interested in) a submenu of the customized menu Michelle's Menu. To do this, you'll need to indent and then type a call for the appropriate submenu underneath the "NetWare Menus" option in your file. Now the file looks like this:

```
%Michelle's Menu,0,0
Going to DOS
    CLS
    prompt=Type "Exit" to return to the Michelle's Menu
    COMMAND
E-Mail
    CLS
    echo Loading The Coordinator II
    ATC2
    echo Exiting to Michelle's Menu
WordPerfect
    CLS
    echo Loading WordPerfect 5.1
     wp
    cls
    echo Exiting to Michelle's Menu
```

```
NetWare Menus
    %NetWare Menus
 Logout
    !Logout
%NetWare Menus,0,80
1. Session Management
SESSION
2. File Management
FILER
3. System Configuration
SYSCON
4. Print Queue Management
PCONSOLE
5. Print Job Configuration
PRINTCON
```

The percent sign tells MENU to look for the NetWare Menus option as a submenu named "NetWare Menus." If you want to include submenus, you simply list the components of the submenu in exactly the same fashion that you listed the elements of the main menu, but you list the submenus at the end of the text file, after all the options of the main menu window are defined.

Notice that by moving the "Logout" option out of the NetWare Menu and up to the primary window, you save yourself from having to leave the main menu and enter a submenu every time you want to log out.

Also, notice that the submenu is positioned at 0,80, which positions it at the center on the right side of your screen. This placement allows you to have one window overlapping another.

Running Command-Line Utilities through MENU

You can also run the NetWare (or DOS) command-line utilities through MENU. Let's assume you choose to add to your personalized menu another submenu called "Command-Line Utilities."

First, add the option to your primary menu, press <Enter>, then indent and type in the appropriate submenu call, like this:

```
%Michelle's Menu,0,0
Going to DOS
     COMMAND
E-Mail
     ATC2
WordPerfect
     wp
NetWare Menus
     %NetWare  Menus
Logout
     !Logout
Command Line Utilities
     %Command Line Utilities
```

At the end of the text file, include a submenu:

```
%Command-Line Utilities, 0,1
NCOPY
     NCOPY @1"Enter Drive and Filename" @2"Enter Destination"
     dir/w @2
     pause
RIGHTS
     RIGHTS @"Enter Drive Letter"
     pause
NDIR
     NDIR @"* for files .. for Directory Path" @"Other Parameters"
     pause
MAP
     MAP @"Drive Letter or 'Enter' for All Mappings"
```

In this example, you'll notice that MENU comes with a set of command parameters that allow you to define parts of a command while you're in MENU and then finish the command with the appropriate specific information while the menu selection is displayed on your screen. Then the pause sequence allows you to watch the task you've invoked being accomplished before you return to MENU. Let's elaborate a little further.

437

To enact most DOS and NetWare utilities, you need to do more than simply type the name of the utility command. For example, to use COPY, you need to know which files, in which directories, you need to copy to where. Furthermore, you need to include this information when you run the COPY command.

MENU allows you to present these additional instructions by preceding the input with the @ (the "at") sign. (See the example below.) Any message or prompt that you want to give must apeear in quotation marks, and the quotation marks must be directly next to the @ sign.

You may also use numbers along with the @ sign to reuse a name or letter at another place. For example:

```
NCOPY
    NCOPY @1"Enter source drive/filename"@2"Enter Destination"
    DIR/W @1
    DIR/W @2
```

NCOPY @1 prompts you to specify which drive and file names you wish to copy *from*. Then the @2 prompt asks which drive you wish to copy the file *to*.

Suppose you answer the first prompt with G:*.EXE and the second prompt with F:. The DIR/W @2 command tells MENU that for whatever drive letter you entered in response to the @2 parameter (in this case, F:), MENU should display that directory using the DOS/Wide parameter (DIR/W F:). The DIR/W commands are entirely optional, of course, but if you've included them in your script, they'll allow you to watch the files being copied to the correct target drive.

Using Special Characters in Menu Files

As you can see, MENU uses the "at" sign (@), percent sign (%), and quotation marks ("") for programming purposes. Therefore, if you include these characters in your menu files, MENU will attempt to interpret them as programming signals. You may still use these characters in your menu options if you'd like, but only if you precede each special character with a backslash (\). For example, if you'd like to include the message "Copies Selling @ 50%" in the title of one of your menu options, you'll need to enter the title into your menu text file like this:

```
Copies Selling \@ 50\%
```

Entering a second backslash (\\) allows you to use a backslash as a part of your text. You can't set off internal quotation marks with a backslash, however; you'll need to use single quotation marks instead.

With these guidelines in mind, you're ready to do a little experimenting to see just what you can do with MENU. When you finish editing your script, exit your editor and save the file as a DOS text file, preferably with a .MNU extension. Then type **MENU filename <Enter>** to invoke the customized menu you've just created.

Accessing the Menu from the Login Script

When your menus are complete, you may want to make the user's work environment even easier to use by automatically invoking the user's custom menu interface from within the login script. To do this, you'll need to create a DOS file for executing the menu. For example, you may have a menu named MAIN.MNU. In this case, you could a create a batch file that looks like this:

```
MENU  MAIN
```

After creating the batch file, use the EXIT command (see Chapter 16) to execute the menu from the login script. For example, if the name of the batch file is MAINMENU.BAT, the EXIT command to execute it will look something like this:

```
EXIT "mainmenu"
```

The EXIT command puts you permanently outside the login script execution, so make sure that it appears at end of the login script or be aware that any command past the EXIT command will be ignored.

MENU and Terminate-and-Stay-Resident Programs

A word of warning: Don't try to invoke terminate-and-stay-resident (TSR) programs from MNU. Here's why: When you invoke MENU, MENU proceeds to create a working copy of COMMAND.COM and to load itself into memory. When you choose an option in your customized menu, therefore, you are also creating a "child" copy of COMMAND.COM to run the program. The copy of COMMAND.COM and the program stay in memory long enough for you to use; then the system discards them.

But if you load a TSR program, that program will sit in the memory address where it was invoked and will stay there even after you've exited and moved on. This creates an unusable memory hole. Instead of taking 12KB of memory, the TSR may be taking 40, 100, or even 172KB of memory over a period of time, and you may be unable to load your large applications into RAM.

If you want to use TSR applications, your best bet is to load them from the users' AUTOEXEC.BAT files, or include them at the end of the users' login scripts, to ensure that the programs are already loaded before users enter MENU. When you're ready to access the TSR programs, simply press the proper keys to invoke them, even if you're in MENU. Some TSRs will operate smoothly; others won't.

If your TSRs aren't cooperating, however, it may be just the order in which they're loaded that's causing them to conflict with other programs. If you're having trouble with your TSR programs—from within MENU or from without—it's a good idea to experiment with the order in which you load them before you assume any one TSR program won't work.

Using the COLORPAL Utility

NetWare's default colors for menus are blue, yellow, and white. The COLORPAL utility allows you to customize your menus' color schemes. NetWare stores the main COLORPAL table in a file called IBM$RUN.OVL in the SYS:PUBLIC directory. However, if you make changes to COLORPAL in the SYS:PUBLIC directory, these changes will affect all workstation monitors—both color and monochrome—on the LAN. For this reason, we advise extreme caution in modifying COLORPAL in the SYS:PUBLIC directory.

Your best option is to access COLORPAL from a separate directory where you have at least Read, File Scan, Write, Erase, and Modify rights. As you access COLORPAL, NetWare will automatically copy the IBM$RUN.OVL file into your working directory for you.

Changing Menu Colors for a Single Workstation

Once you've finished defining the new color scheme, map your first search drive to the directory that contains your new IBM$RUN.OVL file. NetWare starts at the first search directory when it looks for the IBM$RUN.OVL file, and if it finds the file in SYS:PUBLIC before it discovers your customized file, you'll still see the default colors on your screen.

As another alternative, of course, you can simply make it a habit to have users invoke their menus only from a directory that contains the appropriate IBM$RUN.OVL file.

Changing Menu Colors for the Entire LAN

If you'd like to change the color palettes for the entire network, run COLORPAL in the SYS:PUBLIC directory. You'll need to be logged in as SUPERVISOR to have the appropriate rights to change the IBM$RUN.OVL file.

How COLORPAL Affects Monochrome Monitors

In most cases, COLORPAL has little effect on monochrome monitors. But in experimenting with COLORPAL, you may discover that it makes some of your menu screens—particularly on monochrome Compaq and AT&T 6300 monitors—harder to read.

Here's what to do: For these types of computers, you can use an alternate overlay file called CMPQ$RUN.OVL, which is designed to provide varied shades of intensity for monochrome screens. All versions of NetWare v3.x contain the CMPQ$RUN.OVL file.

For monochrome workstations, change the short machine type specified in the boot diskette's SHELL.CFG file to CMPQ. (If you don't have a SHELL.CFG file, you'll need to create one by following the instructions in Chapter 9.)

To change the short machine type in SHELL.CFG, bring up the SHELL.CFG file with a text editor; then erase the existing short machine type (IBM) and replace it with CMPQ. If there is no short machine type is specified, insert the line

```
SHORT MACHINE TYPE = CMPQ
```

anywhere in the SHELL.CFG file.

Troubleshooting Custom Menus

It's easy to troubleshoot your menu; simply run the menu to see if it does what you expected it to do, in terms of the entries it lists, whether you've used the correct commands to invoke the applications, and so on. If the menu doesn't work, note the spot where it fails, exit the menu, and review the appropriate section of the menu text file, alongside the instructions we've given.

Other Menu Alternatives

As you can see, it's really not difficult to use MENU to create a customized front-end interface for the LAN. However, a number of third-party products are specifically designed for creating custom menu interfaces—and simplifying and foolproofing the users' access to the network—as well. In the next sections, we'll briefly cover just a few.

Saber Menu

In addition to providing the means to give users a customized interface to the network, the Saber Menu product (from Saber Software Corporation) includes such features as the ability to load and manage TSR applications (including the ability to manage the order in which the TSRs are loaded). By loading the TSRs from the Saber startup menu instead of from the user's AUTOEXEC.BAT, this scenario allows the user to choose whether or not to load a particular TSR and minimizes the temptation for the user to attempt to modify the AUTOEXEC.BAT file.

The Saber Menu also allows you to include the selection of desktop operating environments within the menu, which would assist you, for example, in managing users who may sometimes work in Windows and other times in DOS.

Saber Menu includes several menu-associated management utilities as well, such as a feature to check for a certain amount of free workstation RAM before allowing an item to be executed and controlling which items can be executed during which time periods. For example, you might want to allow users to access game programs on the network only during lunch. You can set the program to link the appropriate drives and directories automatically for specific applications, and then have them unlink when the user exits the application. Finally, the program prevents users from pressing <Ctrl><Break> during batch file execution by temporarily disabling these keyboard commands.

LANShell

Intel/LANSystems' LANShell is another popular third-party menu alternative. LANShell is specifically designed as a network administrator's tool for controlling users' access to the network. For example, the network administrator may want to present all the users in an internetwork with an identical interface and shield them from the fact that some segments of the network are using NetWare while another segment may be based on a different network operating system such as Banyan VINES.

You can set up the LANShell program to protect security by preventing users from entering the network in any other way but through the authorized menu. The LANShell program also includes a software metering function that ensures the network doesn't exceed the limits of its multiuser software license agreements.

CHAPTER 18

Resource Accounting

NetWare provides a resource accounting option in SYSCON. By activating this option, you can track file server usage and gather information necessary to charge users for various services provided by the file server. By itself, NetWare's resource accounting is not a complete system for charging and billing users. It simply accumulates usage statistics in chronological order, recording the data in an audit file on the file server. To interpret this raw data and use it to bill users, you need a third-party billing program written to NetWare's Accounting APIs.

In this chapter, we first discuss some basic concepts surrounding NetWare resource accounting. We then explain how to install resource accounting in SYSCON and assign appropriate charge rates for file server services, as well as how to remove resource accounting should you determine that you no longer need it. We'll then look at NetWare's two accounting-related utilities (PAUDIT and ATOTAL) and show how to use them to maintain the accounting audit files. Finally, we'll present some troubleshooting information for the most common problems users experience with resource accounting.

Resource Accounting Concepts

Not all LANs need resource accounting. In most business environments, the file server and peripherals are budgeted assets paid for out of capital equipment funds. Other organizations, however, must recoup at least part of the equipment costs by charging users for their use of network resources.

In this environment, NetWare's resource accounting features are indispensable. As the network supervisor, you must decide when and how to implement resource accounting. We'll begin our discussion by looking at situations in which resource accounting is useful.

Uses for Resource Accounting

The most obvious uses for resource accounting are in educational institutions and time-share services. Consider the typical university computer lab, for example. At the beginning of the term or semester, each student is assigned a temporary user account on the lab's file server and pays a set amount of money for access to the network. As a student uses the LAN, proportionate charges are subtracted from this initial account balance. If the balance runs out before the term is over, the student must pay for extra time or services.

In business settings, resource accounting can facilitate chargebacks when the same network equipment is used by more than one department. For example, suppose the Administration Department buys a disk subsystem and makes part of the storage available to the Payroll Department. The equipment purchase comes out of Administration's budget, but they want to charge Payroll for part of the expense. Administration can use NetWare's resource accounting features to track Payroll's disk storage usage and then charge Payroll's budget based on their actual use of the resource.

By the same token, you can use resource accounting to help justify future hardware upgrades or the purchase of additional LAN resources. By installing resource accounting and having it track usage without actually charging users, you can collect solid data to support your case for additional resources.

Another possible use for resource accounting is to monitor the exact usage level of various network services to charge users accordingly. If you find that some key resources are constantly in use while others sit idle most of the time, you might want to implement charges only for the heavily used resources. If certain users are taxing a particular resource, you can charge only those users for that resource.

Even if you aren't concerned about charging users for server usage, you can use resource accounting to track logins and logouts for security purposes. Regardless of whether you activate any of the charging options, resource accounting records the date and time of every login and logout attempt on the file server. This information could prove useful if you suspect that some unauthorized person is trying to break into your file server.

One word of caution: Consider the possible psychological impact of imposing usage limits on your users. As users get closer to depleting their account balance, they may become less productive, putting off certain activities to "save up" for a major task they must perform. Where LAN resources are plentiful and necessary to performing everyday work, make them available without limit to your users. Where LAN resources are not so plentiful, limited account balances might encourage users to be more careful of how they use the file server's resources.

Services You Can Charge For

With resource accounting, a file server can charge for five types of services: *disk reads* (per block), *disk writes* (per block), *connection time* (per minute), *disk storage* (per block-day), and *file service requests* (per request). You can charge for one service only or for any combination of these services.

Here's an explanation of each type of service.

Block Reads

In NetWare, a block is a unit of disk storage space on the file server. As far as resource accounting is concerned, the size of a block is 4,096 bytes (or 4KB), no matter what size was defined for the volume when it was added to the server. When you charge for block reads, you assess users for every workstation request to read a block of data from a network disk.

This type of charge is most useful when your file server provides access to a commercial database or some other information service. In most other situations, however, charging for block reads is not a good idea because it might unfairly penalize users for running large applications (such as E-mail) from the server.

Block Writes

You can also charge users for every workstation request to write a block of data to the file server's disk. This type of charge is appropriate for applications that process data mostly at the workstation and write to the file server only when users issue a save command. Most word processing programs operate in this way.

However, for database and other applications that write to disk continually, charging for block writes is inadvisable. Also, if charging users for writing data to the server discourages them from saving their work frequently, you may want to reconsider the charge.

Connect Time

In NetWare, you can charge users for each minute they remain logged in to the file server. Charging for connect time is a familiar concept to those who come from a mainframe environment or who have worked with electronic bulletin board systems. On a LAN, users might respond to a connection time charge as an implied directive to work quickly. This psychological response may not be a problem unless you want users to work more slowly and accurately.

Disk Storage

Whereas the other charges are based on a certain number of requests or minutes, you charge for disk storage in *block-days*. In other words, NetWare checks once a day to see how many blocks each user "owns" on the file server and charges the user for that number of blocks. Charging for disk space might encourage users to keep their personal directories cleaned out and store only necessary files on the server. However, users might respond by saving shared data files to floppy diskettes or to a local hard disk where other users can't access them. Make sure your users understand they will be charged only for directories and files for which they are listed as the owner.

If your intention is to limit the amount of network disk space a user can access, NetWare provides a better way to do that through the "Limit Disk Space" option in SYSCON. Using resource accounting to charge for disk storage space involves administrative details such as setting initial account balances for users, calculating the appropriate charge rate for disk usage, and so on. The SYSCON option is much easier to set up and maintain.

Going through each directory and file, checking the owner, and tabulating the total number of disk blocks for each owner takes up a good deal of the server's CPU time. Whenever possible, you should set the disk storage audit time to occur during a period of low server usage (2:00 a.m., for example). If you must audit users' disk storage during a peak period for your file server, enable the "Limit Disk Space" in SYSCON as well. With the "Limit Disk Space" feature activated, the server keeps a running total of each user's disk space and the tabulation process doesn't require nearly so much CPU time.

Service Requests

The final option is to charge users for each service request made to the file server. Since almost everything users do on the network—logging in, reading files, writing files—involves a service request, assign service request charges with care. You don't need to charge for service requests *and* for blocks written or blocks read, since they're essentially the same thing. We don't recommend charging by service requests unless the server is extremely overworked and you want to reduce the number of service requests. However, to be truly productive, LAN users must make service requests to the file server continually.

Accounting Servers

You install resource accounting and set up charge rates via the SYSCON utility. NetWare automatically makes your file server an "accounting server" when you establish accounting features on it. On an internetwork, you can define other file servers as accounting servers as well. This action authorizes these other servers to charge your users for their use of resources on the additional file servers.

If you have other types of servers (such as print servers and database servers) on your network, you can also charge your file server users for these specialized services. However, the accounting option in SYSCON only lets you authorize these servers to charge your users. You must perform the actual mechanics of setting up charge rates in a separate application written to NetWare's Accounting APIs.

The Accounting Audit File

NetWare's resource accounting option provides a way for you to keep an "audit trail" of activity on your file server. An audit trail is a detailed series of entries that documents individual transactions in the sequence in which they occurred.

Once you install accounting on a file server, NetWare creates a new file called NET$ACCT.DAT in the SYS:SYSTEM directory. In this file, NetWare records a chronological listing of all entries generated by the resource accounting feature. Every time someone logs in or out, a corresponding entry goes into the accounting audit file. If you charge for any of the services discussed above, NetWare records an entry in NET$ACCT.DAT whenever someone uses those services.

NetWare writes this raw accounting data to the NET$ACCT.DAT file in machine code that only NetWare can comprehend. The OS uses a second accounting file, called NET$REC.DAT, to translate this raw data into language humans can understand. Over time, these files become quite large as NetWare continually appends accounting data to them. Even if you don't charge users for anything, the login and logout entries alone can add up to a lot of data. To save on storage space, NetWare appends all accounting data in condensed format.

NetWare's Accounting Utilities

You use SYSCON to install resource accounting, define accounting servers, and set charge rates for the services. Once accounting is activated, you also use SYSCON to set and monitor user account balances.

NetWare also comes with two command-line utilities—ATOTAL.EXE and PAUDIT.EXE—to help you use the data stored in the accounting files to produce a printed audit trail report. Only the supervisor can run these utilities, which are located in the SYS:SYSTEM directory.

The ATOTAL (Accounting TOTAL) utility goes through NET$ACCT.DAT and totals all the transactions posted in the file. The resulting output shows daily and weekly totals for each service being charged for on the file server.

Whereas ATOTAL generates a summary of the audit file totals, the PAUDIT (Print AUDIT file) utility generates a detailed, entry-by-entry report of NET$ACCT.DAT's contents. PAUDIT uses the information contained in the NET$REC.DAT file to interpret the contents of NET$ACCT.DAT and print these contents to the screen.

Determining Appropriate Charge Rates

Perhaps the most difficult part of NetWare's resource accounting feature is determining how much to charge. First, you must define what your unit of charge will be and figure out how much of your costs you need to recover from users. From there, you'll need to do a little experimentation and research into how your people are actually using the file server.

Following the procedure outlined below will help you arrive at an appropriate charge rate for a service.

1. Define what the unit of charge will be. NetWare's resource accounting doesn't deal in dollars, pesos, or francs. Rather, it deals in *charge units*. A charge unit can represent whatever you like; for instance, you can decide that one charge unit equals one penny, one dollar, or one hundred dollars. Whatever you decide the charge unit is, it will apply consistently for all charged services.

   If you decide that a charge unit equals a dollar for disk storage, you can't redefine it as a penny for connection time.

   Generally, it's easiest to define a charge unit as the smallest monetary denomination available. In the United States, for example, you would set one charge unit equal to one penny. Whatever equivalence you choose, you have to make the appropriate conversions from charge units to real money. NetWare's resource accounting function won't do it for you.

2. Figure out how much of your costs you need to recover. Most network supervisors install resource accounting because they need to recover a certain portion of their initial equipment costs from the users. For example, suppose that in order to justify the cost of installing a LAN, your company wants to recoup $24,000 over the next two years. That means the company must collect $1,000 a month from users by charging them for file server usage. As the LAN supervisor, you might distribute this $1,000 over several types of services—perhaps half from connect time charges and half from disk storage charges. In this case, you must charge users enough to make $500 per month from each service.

3. To find out how much each service is used on your file server, set up accounting for a trial period to measure the actual file server usage. Go into SYSCON, install accounting, and set a charge rate of 1/1 for each service for which you intend to charge. (We'll show you how further on in this chapter.)

   Give your users unlimited credit before you start this trial run so they won't get locked out of the file server. Let your file server run for two or three weeks of normal LAN activity. The accounting feature will tabulate and record usage data in the NET$ACCT.DAT file.

4. At the end of the trial period, run the ATOTAL utility to total up all the accounting data. Go into the SYS:SYSTEM directory and type **ATOTAL > TRIAL.DAT <Enter>**. This command tells ATOTAL to dump its output to a text file named TRIAL.DAT in SYS:SYSTEM. (ATOTAL can take a long time to run, so don't be concerned if nothing seems to be happening for a while.)

5. When ATOTAL is finished, print out the TRIAL.DAT file, using either NPRINT or a word processor that works with DOS text files. The file will contain daily totals for each day of the trial period, as well as weekly subtotals similar to these:

```
Totals for week:
    Connect time:  8643     Server requests:   9582031
    Blocks read:  56782     Blocks written:          0
    Blocks days:      0
```

Take the average of the weekly totals to get a representative figure for how much each service is used on your file server in a week.

6. Now you need to compute the charge ratios, according to the following equation from the Novell manuals:

$$\frac{\text{Total amount you want to charge for a service}}{\text{Estimated total usage of the service}} = \frac{\text{Multiplier}}{\text{Divisor}}$$

When you divide the total amount of money you want to recoup for a given service in a week (Step 2) by the average total usage of the service in a week (Steps 3 through 5), you get a decimal result (such as 0.2) that can be represented as a fraction, or ratio (for example, 0.2 = 1/5). This ratio represents how much you should charge (in charge units) for each unit of service (each block written, or each minute of connect time).

Example of Charge Rate Calculation for Connect Time

The above procedure may seem like a lot of work, but it's really not difficult. To illustrate, here's an example of how you would calculate an appropriate charge rate for connect time.

1. Define the charge unit as one penny.

2. Assume that you want to bring in $500 a week in connect time charges. With a one-penny charge unit, that's 50,000 charge units a week.

3. After running accounting for a three-week trial period, ATOTAL shows 300,000 minutes as the total connect time for all users combined. Dividing this number by three gives you the average weekly connect time of 100,000 minutes.

4. Plugging these figures into the formula, you get:

$$\frac{50{,}000 \text{ charge units per week}}{100{,}000 \text{ minutes of connect time per week}} = \frac{1 \text{ charge unit}}{2 \text{ minutes}}$$

So, you need to charge users one charge unit (one cent) for every two minutes of file server connect time. To implement this charge rate in SYSCON, you would set the multiplier to "1" and the divisor to "2."

This textbook example works out to a nice, even ratio (1/2). However, your real-life figures probably won't. If you use a calculator to do the division, you'll most likely end up with a decimal number like 0.33165. In the charge rate "Multiplier" and "Divisor" fields, SYSCON accepts only whole numbers up to five characters long, with no decimal points. The simple solution is to round off your calculator result to the nearest whole fraction (1/3, 4/5, 17/32, or whatever). The multiplier doesn't have to be 1.

When to Remove Accounting

Tracking resource usage for the accounting feature adds an appreciable amount of overhead to the NetWare operating system. For those situations in which resource accounting is truly needed, the slight drop in performance is offset by the usefulness of the feature. If you install resource accounting on a temporary basis, you should remove it when it's no longer needed. (See the instructions under "Uninstalling Accounting," which we discuss shortly.)

Setting Up Resource Accounting

To set up the resource accounting feature on your file server, you must complete the following procedures:

- Activate the accounting option

- Set the charge rates on the services for which you will charge

- Assign user account balances

Activating Resource Accounting

Activating the resource accounting feature on your file server is simple.

1. Start the SYSCON utility and choose "Accounting" from the main menu.

2. SYSCON asks if you want to install accounting. Answer "Yes" at the prompt. The following submenu will pop up:

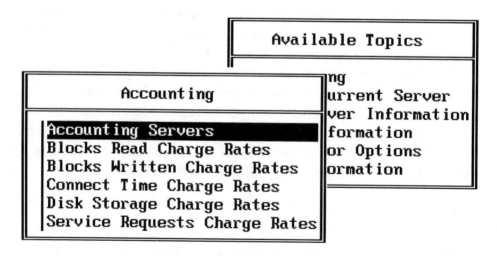

If accounting has already been installed on the file server, choosing the "Accounting" option in SYSCON takes you directly to this submenu.

SYSCON automatically sets up your file server as an accounting server authorized to charge for its services. Select the "Accounting Servers" option and you will see your file server listed. From now on, NetWare will record an entry in the NET$ACCT.DAT file every time a user logs in or out of the file server. However, no charges are levied against users for logging in and logging out.

Setting Charge Rates

The file server won't automatically charge users for anything until you set up charge rates with the other options in the "Accounting" submenu. See "Determining Appropriate Charge Rates" above for help in deciding what to charge.

Setting charge rates works the same for each option except "Disk Storage Charge Rates." Here is an example of how you would set the connection time charge rate at one charge unit for every two minutes of connect time.

1. Choose the "Accounting" option from SYSCON's main menu.

2. Select "Connect Time Charge Rates." A window will open containing a time and day grid divided into half-hour increments:

```
                                              Sun  Mon  Tue  Wed  Thu  Fri  Sat
        Connect Time Charge Rates    8:00am    1    1    1    1    1    1    1
                                     8:30am    1    1    1    1    1    1    1
                                     9:00am    1    1    1    1    1    1    1
Sunday                               9:30am    1    1    1    1    1    1    1
8:00 am To 8:29 am                  10:00am    1    1    1    1    1    1    1
                                    10:30am    1    1    1    1    1    1    1
Rate  Charge       Rate  Charge     11:00am    1    1    1    1    1    1    1
  1  No Charge      11               11:30am    1    1    1    1    1    1    1
  2                 12               12:00pm    1    1    1    1    1    1    1
  3                 13               12:30pm    1    1    1    1    1    1    1
  4                 14                1:00pm    1    1    1    1    1    1    1
  5                 15                1:30pm    1    1    1    1    1    1    1
  6                 16                2:00pm    1    1    1    1    1    1    1
  7                 17                2:30pm    1    1    1    1    1    1    1
  8                 18                3:00pm    1    1    1    1    1    1    1
  9                 19                3:30pm    1    1    1    1    1    1    1
 10                 20                4:00pm    1    1    1    1    1    1    1
       (Charge is per minute)         4:30pm    1    1    1    1    1    1    1
```

If you want, you can define different charge rates (up to 20) and vary the rates for certain time periods. For example, you might want to charge more during the day than at night. SYSCON displays the currently selected day and time period on the left side of the screen. Below that, you can see what the currently defined charge rates are. Initially, all the half-hour periods in the grid are set to Rate 1—No Charge.

3. Before you define a charge rate, you must specify the times and days for which you want the new charge rate to apply. To specify Monday 8:00 a.m. to Friday 5:00 p.m., for example, position the cursor at the 8:00am row of the Mon column and press the Mark key (F5) to mark the beginning of the period. Then move the cursor to the 5:00pm row of the Fri column (the entire block of time will be highlighted). Press <Enter> to complete the time period selection.

4. From the "Select Charge Rate" list that pops up, choose "Other Charge Rate." You will see the "New Charge Rate" window, asking you for a multiplier and a divisor:

```
                                      Sun  Mon  Tue  Wed  Thu  Fri  Sat
        Connect Time Charge Rates   8:00am  1    1    1    1    1    1    1
                                    8:30am  1    1    1    1    1    1    1
                                    9:00am  1    1    1    1    1    1    1
 Sunday                             9:30am  1    1    1    1    1    1    1
 8:00 am To 8:29 am                 10:00am 1    1    1    1    1    1    1
                                            1    1    1    1    1
 Rate ┌─────────────────────┐ge  ┌────────────────────┐1    1    1    1    1
  1  N│ Select Charge Rate  │     │ New Charge Rate    │1    1    1    1    1
  2   │ ┌───────────────────┤     │                    │1    1    1    1    1
  3   │ │ 1  No Charge       │     │Multiplier       1  │1    1    1    1    1
      │ │Other Charge Rate   │     │Divisor          1  │1    1    1    1    1
  4   └─┴───────────────────┘     └────────────────────┘1    1    1    1    1
  5              15                 1:30pm  1    1    1    1    1    1    1
  6              16                 2:00pm  1    1    1    1    1    1    1
  7              17                 2:30pm  1    1    1    1    1    1    1
  8              18                 3:00pm  1    1    1    1    1    1    1
  9              19                 3:30pm  1    1    1    1    1    1    1
 10              20                 4:00pm  1    1    1    1    1    1    1
       (Charge is per minute)       4:30pm  1    1    1    1    1    1    1
```

The multiplier and divisor determine the amount that will be charged to the user's account each minute, as indicated at the bottom left side of the screen.

5. In our example, we want to charge one cent for every two minutes of connect time. Leave the multiplier set to 1. Move the cursor to the divisor field and type "2" to set the divisor.

6. Press <Esc> twice to return to the "Connect Time Charge Rates" screen. The 2s now shown in the Mon 8:00am to Fri 5:00pm portion of the grid indicate that NetWare will use charge rate 2 (displayed as 1/2 in the rate table to the left) during that time period.

7. If necessary, repeat Steps 3 through 6 to set different charge rates for other time periods. When you're finished, press <Esc> to return to the "Accounting" submenu.

8. Follow the same process given in Steps 2 through 7 to set up charge rates for any other service for which you want to charge users. (Refer to Novell's *Concepts* manual for more examples of setting charge rates in SYSCON.) When you've set all the charge rates, press <Esc> until you return to SYSCON's main menu.

Assigning User Account Balances

Unless you specify otherwise, each user is automatically created with a default account balance of 1,000 charge units. Depending on the charge rate you set and how active your users are, 1,000 units might not last very long. Have users monitor their account balances closely, because NetWare will prevent them from using the file server when their account balance runs out (unless you give them unlimited credit). Here's how to change an existing user's account balance and credit limit.

1. Enter SYSCON and choose "User Information" from the main menu.

2. Highlight a username and press <Enter>.

3. Select "Account Balance" from the "User Information" submenu.

4. Highlight the "Account Balance" field and type in the number of charge units you want that user to have.

5. To allow a user to go "in the hole" after the account balance reaches 0, specify "Yes" in the "Allow Unlimited Credit" field.

If you type "No" here, you have the option of specifying a "Low Balance Limit." You can enter either a positive number or a negative number for the low balance limit. If positive, NetWare will start warning the user of the low balance condition before the account balance actually reaches 0; if negative, NetWare will wait until the user has gone in the hole by that amount before issuing a low balance warning.

6. Press <Esc> until you exit SYSCON. The new account balance and credit limits will take effect immediately. The user doesn't have to log out and log back in first.

If you aren't sure what to assign for an account balance, give users unlimited credit for a month or two, then figure appropriate account balances that reflect real-life system use.

The file server starts keeping track of how much each user account uses a service as soon as you define a charge rate other than "No Charge" for that service in SYSCON. However, the charges accrued are not actually subtracted from a user's account balance until that user logs out. For this reason, have your users check their account balances each time they prepare to log out. If the account balance has reached or surpassed the established credit limit, that user will not be able to log in again. Instead, the user will see the message "Attempting to login after account balance has dropped below the minimum" at the next login attempt. To rectify this situation, go into SYSCON and replenish the account balance as explained above.

Important: Warn your users that if they ever receive a message from the file server to log out because their account balance is low, they should save their files and log out immediately. If they don't, NetWare's watchdog function will automatically log them out and they will lose any data they have not saved.

If you're actually collecting money from users for their account balance, you'll have to make the necessary conversion from charge units to monetary units. With a one-cent charge unit, you would give a user 100 charge units for every dollar he or she pays. For example, if a user pays $25, assign 2,500 charge units for that user's account balance. (You can set up default account balances under "Supervisor Options" from the main menu in SYSCON to give all new users the same starting balance.)

Uninstalling Accounting

To deactivate and remove the resource accounting feature from your file server, you must first delete all authorized accounting servers (including your file server).

1. Go into SYSCON and choose "Accounting" from the main menu.

2. Choose "Accounting Servers" from the "Accounting" submenu.

3. Highlight the name of your file server in the list of authorized accounting servers and press <Del>. Answer "Yes" at the confirmation prompt. If any other servers are listed, delete them in the same manner.

4. Press <Esc>. SYSCON will ask you "Do you wish to remove accounting?" Answer "Yes," and the job is done.

Using NetWare's Accounting Utilities

The ATOTAL and PAUDIT command-line utilities help you take the network usage data stored in the two accounting files and produce usage reports and audit trail files for your records.

The ATOTAL Utility

ATOTAL, as we have seen, goes through the NET$ACCT.DAT file and totals every posted transaction. The resulting report subtotals entries by day, followed by a "Totals for week" entry. This daily/weekly subtotal format is repeated for every week contained in the current NET$ACCT.DAT file. You can draw on this summary of usage information when you need to readjust charge rates to reflect changes in file server usage patterns. Here is a sample of ATOTAL's output:

```
6/29/1991:
    Connect time: 46       Server requests:  1302
    Blocks read:   0       Blocks written:          0
    Blocks days:  78

6/30/1991:
    Connect time:  1       Server requests:         490
    Blocks read:   0       Blocks written:            0
    Blocks days:  40

Totals for week:
    Connect time: 47       Server requests:        1792
    Blocks read:   0       Blocks written:            0
    Blocks days: 118
```

ATOTAL compiles totals for only those charges you defined in SYSCON. In the sample above, the file server was set up to charge for connect time, disk storage (as indicated by "Blocks days"), and server requests.

The PAUDIT Utility

PAUDIT goes through the contents of NET$ACCT.DAT and prints an itemized usage report. This results in an audit trail record of file server activity. The PAUDIT output contains an entry for each accounting-related event on the file server—logins, logouts, and charges made to each user—arranged in chronological order.

PAUDIT itself doesn't sort the information by user or by type of charge; however, several utilities are available that do. Check with your local NetWare users group or bulletin board service.

PAUDIT normally prints its output to the screen, but you can redirect the output to a text file. Here is a sample of PAUDIT's output:

```
07/14/91 17:11:27   File Server PUBLISHER1
 NOTE: about User ED during File Server services. Logout from
 address  0000F00D:0000D800353B.
07/14/91 17:11:36   File Server PUBLISHER1
 NOTE: about User SANDY during File Server services. Logout
 from address 0000ACE2:0000000000FD.
07/14/91 18:02:49   File Server PUBLISHER1
 NOTE: about User KEN during File Server services. Logout from
 address  0000ACE2:0000000000FB.
07/15/91 7:20:20   File Server PUBLISHER1
 NOTE: about User SANDY during File Server services. Login
 from address 0000ACE2:0000000000FD.
07/15/91 7:42:59   File Server PUBLISHER1
 NOTE: about User ED during File Server services. Login from
 address  0000F00D:0000D800353B.
07/15/91 8:04:11   File Server PUBLISHER1
 NOTE: about User ED during File Server services. Logout from
 address  0000F00D:0000D800353B.
```

As you can see, each entry includes the date, time, and file server on which the event took place. The NOTE indicates which user account and which services were involved. The third line in each entry identifies the event itself (login, logout, accounting charge, and so on). PAUDIT also records an entry each time NetWare detects an intruder trying to log in to the file server and whenever the file server's system time is changed.

Even though data is stored in a compressed format in the NET$ACCT.DAT file, after a month or so the file can become unmanageably large. To create a permanent audit trail record and keep the size of the NET$ACCT.DAT audit file under control, follow the procedure outlined below on a regular basis (at least monthly).

Monthly Audit File Maintenance

Here's the recommended procedure to follow at the end of each month to clear out the NET$ACCT.DAT file and produce a printed audit trail report.

1. Total the monthly system usage with ATOTAL. Change to the SYS:SYSTEM directory and type **ATOTAL > filename**. Redirect the output into a file by including the DOS redirect symbol (>) in the command and specifying an appropriate file name for the output. If you don't, the results will be output to the screen and you will have no permanent record.

   You will see the message "Processing accounting records . . ." on the screen while ATOTAL goes through the raw data in the NET$ACCT.DAT file and compiles totals for every posted transaction. ATOTAL can take a long time to run, depending on the size of the NET$ACCT.DAT file and how many services you're charging for. You can't abort ATOTAL— once started, the utility must run to completion uninterrupted.

2. Run PAUDIT to print the audit trail. Again, redirect the output into a DOS text file so you'll have a permanent copy. For example, to save PAUDIT's output in a DOS text file named 691AUDIT.TXT, go into the SYS:SYSTEM directory and type **PAUDIT > 691AUDIT.TXT** at the command-line prompt.

   If the NET$ACCT.DAT file is large, PAUDIT can take several hours to read and transcribe the entire contents of the data file. You can stop PAUDIT at any time by pressing <Ctrl><C>.

   When PAUDIT finishes, the contents of NET$ACCT.DAT will be contained in the indicated text file. Because this file is composed entirely of

ASCII text, you can manipulate the data with almost any standard word processor or database manager. For example, you can import the contents into a database or spreadsheet.

3. Archive the NET$ACCT.DAT file to another storage medium (such as floppy diskette or tape backup). Once the data is safely printed and archived, delete NET$ACCT.DAT from the SYS:SYSTEM directory. The resource accounting feature simply starts a new NET$ACCT.DAT file if it can't find the old one.

Important: Never *delete* the NET$REC.DAT file, however. PAUDIT needs this file to run, and it won't be automatically recreated if you accidentally delete it. You'll have to restore it from a backup.

Troubleshooting Resource Accounting Problems

Most of the trouble you're likely to experience with resource accounting results from improper installation or setup. Make sure you've followed the instructions carefully and that your users have adequate account balances. Generally, the accounting-related error messages are specific and descriptive enough that you will be able to diagnose the problem easily.

The two situations described below warrant further explanation.

Problem: You're getting the error "Unable to open file NET$ACCT.DAT to add audit record" at the file server console.

Solution: NetWare's resource accounting feature is trying to append an audit entry to the NET$ACCT.DAT file, but it can't open the file. Either the accounting file has been locked erroneously or it's been corrupted. Use MONITOR to check on the lock status of the file. If it's locked, have everyone log out; then reboot the server. If the file doesn't appear to be locked, it's probably corrupt. Restore NET$ACCT.DAT from a recent backup or delete the file altogether (all previous accounting information stored in the file will be lost). Once the file is deleted, NetWare creates a new one when it needs to append information to it.

Problem: You set up your file server to charge users for disk storage, but no one's balance seems to be getting docked much except SUPERVISOR's.

Solution: NetWare only charges users for the space taken up by directories and files for which they are internally identified as the owner. When you, as user SUPERVISOR, create a directory for another user, NetWare registers SUPERVISOR as the owner of that directory. Use FILER or NDIR to check who is listed as the owner of your server's files.

Be aware also that if you use the NCOPY, FILER, or other file manager programs (including the DOS XCOPY command) to copy files, you become the files' owner because you created the new copies. As SUPERVISOR, you can use FILER to change file ownership. Also, if you use the "Move" option in FILER to move files from one directory to another, ownership does not change.

Part Four

NetWare Printing

Printing is one of the most problematic areas of dealing with computers, especially in a network environment. Yet printing is an essential function of most applications. The best network word processors or spreadsheet programs are of little value if you can't obtain a hard copy of the documents and reports they create. Like most other aspects of NetWare, setting up and maintaining printers can be difficult without a clear understanding of how the network handles print requests. But whatever effort you put into setting up network printing correctly in the first place will pay off over the long haul. Once you get all the glitches worked out, users should be able to print to network printers as easily as they can print to local printers.

This section is dedicated to helping you understand, set up, maintain, and troubleshoot NetWare printing. It also describes the many printing utilities that come with the NetWare operating system.

- **Chapter 19: Setting Up NetWare Printing** covers the basic concepts you'll need to know to successfully set up and maintain your network print servers and printers. It gives step-by-step procedures for installing print servers, configuring printers, and establishing print queues. The end of the chapter lists common problems related to printing and suggests various solutions.

- **Chapter 20: Using NetWare Printing Utilities** explains the PRINTDEF, PRINTCON, CAPTURE/ENDCAP, NPRINT, and PSC utilities in the context of day-to-day NetWare use. It describes how to run the utilities and use the various options to accomplish the kinds of tasks your users will most likely encounter every day.

CHAPTER 19

Setting Up NetWare Printing

Since the early days of LANs, users have appreciated the ability LANS offered them to share printers and other expensive peripherals. Instead of buying one printer for each user, organizations could get by with fewer printers to be shared by groups of users on the network. Though hardware prices have come down considerably in recent years, network printing is still a viable option for most purposes.

Still, setting up and troubleshooting network printing remains a tricky task. This chapter explains various ways to set up printing on your network and discusses how to diagnose problems you're likely to encounter. Before we get into the step-by-step details, however, we need to establish a conceptual background for understanding how NetWare printing works. This understanding will help you set up and maintain printing more effectively and be able to more accurately diagnose printer-related problems.

NetWare Printing Concepts

As a basis for our discussion of how printing works with NetWare, let's look at how printing works on a standalone DOS-based machine. The printer is usually connected directly to the PC through either a parallel port (such as LPT1 or LPT2) or a serial port (such as COM1 or COM2). The user then sets up each application to send printed output to whichever port the printer is connected to. When the user issues a "print" command, the application hands control over to DOS, which calls on the machine's BIOS to initialize the port and send the data one character or byte at a time to the printer. Figure 19-1 illustrates this standalone printing process.

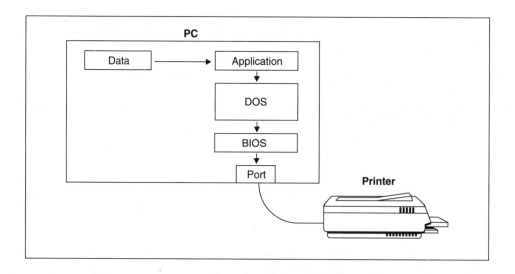

Figure 19-1: How printing works on a standalone DOS machine.

The Trouble with Network Printing

Much of the difficulty in network printing stems from the fact that most printers are not designed to be used in a network environment. Here are some of the problems that plague network printing:

- The printer interface through a computer's serial or parallel port uses protocols that are not compatible with those commonly used in networking (such as Ethernet and Token-Ring).

  This incompatibility prevents printers from being connected directly to the network cable.

- Standard printers are incapable of dealing with more than one print job at a time. If two separate print jobs were somehow to arrive at the printer together, the output would likely be a garbled mess.

- There is no standard printer "language." Each type of printer understands only a certain kind of code (such as Hewlett-Packard's Printer Control Language or Adobe's PostScript) to control the appearance of the printed output. If a job is mistakenly sent to a printer other than the one it was formatted for, the output will be unintelligible.

- Most printers are passive devices. They just sit and wait for data to arrive at their serial or parallel port, dutifully printing any data received. While many printers have status lights that indicate various operational problems (such as out of paper, low on toner, or paper jam),they lack the ability to initiate a dialog with other devices to communicate their plight. Consequently, you usually don't know that a printer is having trouble until you try to print something and can't. This annoyance becomes especially acute on a network where the printer is not within view of your workstation.

With these obstacles in the way, it's a wonder network printing works at all! But NetWare provides the pieces necessary to make it work, and if you set them up correctly you'll have an efficient mechanism for handling the bustle of multiuser print activity.

The Network Printing Model

To the user, printing on a NetWare LAN looks much the same as it does in the standalone DOS environment. But underneath are some significant differences. To start with, a printer doesn't have to be attached to every workstation on the network. You can locate printers more strategically by connecting them either to the file server or to any workstation on the LAN.

When a user issues a print command from a networked PC, the workstation shell intercepts the data to be printed and redirects it across the network to the file server. There it is placed in line, or "spooled," along with any other users' print jobs that might arrive at the server at about the same time. This storage area where jobs wait to be printed is called a print queue. Specialized print server software takes jobs from the queue on a first-in, first-out basis and passes them on to a network printer to be printed. The following figure illustrates this generic network printing model.

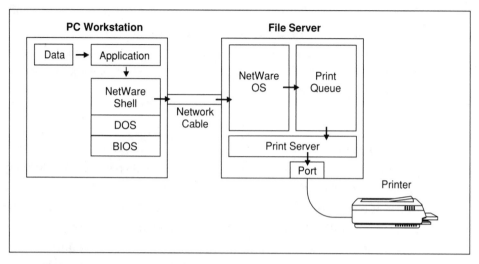

Figure 19-2: In NetWare, print jobs are redirected to queues on the file server, where they wait until the print server software sends them to the printer.

NetWare v3.11 offers four possible ways to implement the network printing software:

- Use PSERVER.NLM to provide print services as a loadable module on the file server.

- Use PSERVER.VAP to add print services as a separate, value-added process on an external router or NetWare v2.x file server.

- Use PSERVER.EXE to offload print services to a dedicated PC on the network.

- Use RPRINTER.EXE (in conjunction with PSERVER.VAP, PSERVER.NLM, or PSERVER.EXE) to print to a printer connected to a network workstation.

We'll explain more about each of these possibilities later on in this chapter.

NetWare Printing Utilities

To help you set up, control, and monitor network printing, NetWare comes with a number of printing-related utilities. You may or may not need to use these utilities, depending on your applications and how you configure printing on your LAN. Figure 19-3 lists these utilities and summarizes what each one is used for. Later in the chapter, we'll discuss how to use the print utilities in setting up and troubleshooting printing.

Utility	Purpose
PCONSOLE (Print Console)	Set up, view, and control print queues. Set up and configure print servers.
PSC (Print Server Command)	Control print servers and printers from the command line (as an alternative to PCONSOLE).
PRINTDEF (Printer Definition)	Define print devices (with their special control codes) and forms for use in PRINTCON.
PRINTCON (Print Job Configuration)	Define print job configurations for use with PCONSOLE, CAPTURE, and NPRINT.
CAPTURE	Intercept output to a local port and redirect it to a network printer (mainly used with non-network applications).
ENDCAP	End the capture of local printer ports.
NPRINT (Network Print)	Send ASCII text files or previously formatted files to network printers from the command line (similar to the DOS PRINT command).
SPOOL	Map a spooled printer number to a queue (to support applications that identify network printers by number).

Figure 19-3: NetWare printing utilities and their uses.

Network Printing Problems Solved

Through its basic architecture and its assortment of print utilities, NetWare provides a workable solution to each of the four problems mentioned above. First, the physical connection of the printer to the network takes place through ports on PCs that are connected to the LAN. NetWare's print service software uses the appropriate network protocols to transport print jobs through the cable to a networked PC. Once there, the jobs are fed to the network printer via the parallel or serial port communication protocol. Thus the networked PC acts as a kind of gateway between the network and the printer.

Second, the use of a print queue provides an orderly method for many users to send jobs to a single printer. Queuing jobs at the file server ensures that the printer has to work with only one print job at a time.

Third, most applications include a set of print drivers to interface with various types of printers. The print driver software changes a print job from whatever format it originated in to a format compatible with the target printer's printing language. The interplay between print drivers and network software is probably one of the most complex aspects of network printing. With most NetWare-aware applications, you can match up a print driver with a specific queue to ensure that output goes to the appropriate printer. For example, suppose you had both a LaserJet and a PostScript printer, and that you defined two separate print queues—one for each printer. You would then set up your application so that documents formatted with the LaserJet print driver are sent to the LaserJet queue, and those formatted with the PostScript driver are sent to the PostScript queue.

For non-network applications, NetWare provides printer definition files you can use to send printer- specific formatting instructions along with documents when you redirect them to network print queues. We'll explain more about that later when we discuss the PRINTDEF utility.

Finally, NetWare's print server software includes a rudimentary ability to discern and report printer status. Through the dedicated print server's monitor screen, various menu options in the PCONSOLE utility, or the PSC command, you can determine whether a printer is out of paper, off-line, or otherwise out of service.

Advantages of Network Printing

Besides the obvious advantages of sharing expensive printers and reducing printer idle time, network printing offers at least one other advantage over standalone printing. On a standalone system, it is not unusual for a user to sit idly by—sometimes for as long as five to ten minutes—while a long or complex graphics document prints. Unless the user has installed some kind of print buffer software, printing essentially ties up the computer for the entire time the application is formatting and sending the job to the printer.

NetWare returns control to the application as soon as the print job is fully loaded into the queue. You don't have to wait until the job has actually finished going to the printer. Because typical data transfer rates across the network are one order of magnitude faster than through a parallel or serial port (*M*bps compared to *K*bps), documents move quickly to the print queue. Once the job is fully loaded into the queue, you can move on to other tasks within your application while the job is printing.

Does the overhead associated with network printing causes a significant increase in printing time compared to standalone printing? After all, it does take a certain amount of time for the application to load a formatted document into the queue, and then for the print server to feed it to the printer. Studies of network printing undertaken by various sources don't agree on this point. For example, *Network Computing* magazine reported in the November 1990 issue that spooling (storing the job in a queue before it is sent to the printer) adds a slight delay—around 13% of the total printing time—to the printing process. In the April 1991 *Application Notes*, Novell's studies indicate that in most configurations total printing time is shorter with network printing. Either way, the advantage of getting users back to productive work sooner outweighs any small delay that might be imposed by network printing overhead.

How NetWare Print Queues Work

Because print queues are a key component in NetWare printing, you need to understand what they are and how they work. We've already explained that, conceptually, print queues are storage areas in which print jobs are temporarily held prior to being printed.

Technically, print queues are bindery objects. When you define a print queue in PCONSOLE, you give it a descriptive name. This name should identify what kind of printer the queue is associated with, where the printer is located, or what types of jobs can be sent to the queue. Examples of such queue names might be LASERJET, QMS-LIBRARY, or REPORT-Q. Print queue names can be up to 47 characters long, but cannot contain spaces. Because you might end up typing queue names quite often when using the CAPTURE and NPRINT commands, it's best to keep them short and easy to type.

The print queue name is for human users' convenience. Internally, NetWare assigns the queue an ID number, just like it does for other named objects in the bindery. Print queue IDs are eight-digit hexadecimal numbers (00050C4F, for example). You can display the ID number of a print queue in PCONSOLE. (See Novell's *Print Server* manual for the exact steps for doing this.)

For each print queue defined on a file server, NetWare creates a corresponding subdirectory in the SYS:SYSTEM directory. The subdirectory for the sample queue ID above would be named 050C4F.

When a user sends a document to a print queue, it passes through four distinct stages. You can identify these stages by the messages displayed on PCONSOLE's "Current Print Job Entries" list.

Stage	Explanation
"Adding"	The data is being formatted by the application and loaded into the queue.
"Ready"	The data is sitting in the queue waiting to be serviced by the print server. If there are no other jobs already in the queue, the "Ready" stage is very brief.
"Active"	The print server has started sending the data to the printer.
"Removed"	The data has finished being sent to the printer and is gone from the queue.

A single print queue can be serviced by up to 25 different print servers. By default, NetWare print servers poll their assigned queues every 15 seconds to see if any jobs are ready for printing. If a job becomes "Ready" right after a poll, it must wait until the next 15-second interval before its readiness is detected by the print server. This explains why a lone job in a queue sometimes goes "Active" immediately and other times stays "Ready" for a short time before going "Active."

Queue-Printer Relationships

For the sake of simplicity and manageability, you'll usually set up one print queue for each printer on your network. Then you can give the queue a name that identifies the printer it is associated with: for example, LASERJET for an HP LaserJet printer. If you have two identical printers, you can include the location in the queue name to distinguish them: for example, LASERJET_STEVE'S_DESK and LASERJET_HALL. (PCONSOLE automatically substitutes an underscore character if you try to type a space in a printer name.)

While the one-to-one approach is adequate in most circumstances, you can modify this basic setup if your needs warrant it. There are two possible alternatives: assign more than one queue to a single printer, or assign more than one printer to a single queue.

Multiple Queues to a Single Printer. NetWare allows you to associate more than one print queue with a network printer. This arrangement is useful when you have users on more than one file server sending jobs to a single printer. For example, suppose you install a wide-carriage printer to be shared by Accounting and Payroll. You then define a WIDE queue on Accounting's file server and a WIDE queue on Payroll's file server, and assign both queues to the wide-carriage printer. (Note that you can duplicate print queue names on different file servers.)

With more than one print queue per printer, you can also set the priority of the queues so that high- priority jobs get printed before all others. When you assign a queue to a printer in PCONSOLE, you are prompted for a priority level from 1 (highest priority) to 10 (lowest priority). So, for example, you can create a RUSH queue at priority 1 and designate only upper management as its queue users. Everyone else must use the regular print queue. The print server then takes jobs from the RUSH queue first (queue priority takes precedence over job sequence).

475

Another situation in which multiple queues might be helpful involves dealing with different types of paper (or *forms*, as NetWare calls them). Suppose you had preprinted forms for both checks and invoices, which you regularly print on a single dot matrix printer. To make sure checks don't get printed on the invoice forms or vice versa, you can create a CHECKS queue and an INVOICES queue. Then at check-printing time, you load the preprinted check paper into the printer and temporarily disallow the print server from servicing jobs in the INVOICES queue. (A print queue operator can do this in PCONSOLE by choosing "Print Queue Information," selecting the queue, choosing "Current Queue Status," then setting the "servers can service entries in queue" flag to "No.")

Multiple Printers to a Single Queue. One reason for choosing this configuration is to split the load on an overworked printer. When you pool two or more printers together to service the queue, the print server can send the next print job to whichever printer isn't currently busy. For this to work, the printers must be functionally identical: the same brand or type of printers using the same printer drivers.

More About Print Jobs

Once a user's data is fully loaded into the queue, it becomes known as a *print job* (sometimes also called a print queue entry or print request). Print jobs are stored as files in the print queue's subdirectory in SYS:SYSTEM. Their file names always start with "Q$" and include the last four digits of the print queue ID as the rest of the file name, plus a three-digit job number as the extension. So, for example, print job number 3 in queue LASERJET (ID number 00050C4F) would have the file name Q$0C4F.003. Each print queue can hold a maximum of 8,192 print jobs.

Because print jobs are files stored in SYS:SYSTEM, you should regularly monitor the available disk space on the SYS volume to see that there is adequate room for the print jobs likely to be in the queue at any given time. If you completely run out of space on volume SYS, printing won't be possible until you make more disk space available.

Normally, jobs print in the same order in which they arrive in the queue, as indicated by the three- digit job number. However, a print queue operator (explained below) can change the sequence of jobs in the queue.

Print Queue Operators

As supervisor, you have complete control over print jobs in the queue—not by virtue of your supervisor privileges, but because NetWare automatically assigns the user SUPERVISOR as a print queue operator of every queue. Busy supervisors can delegate these queue management tasks to other users (without having to grant them supervisor equivalence) by making them print queue operators. Here is a list of what a print queue operator can do with jobs in the queue:

- Reorder the sequence of the jobs.

- Place an operator hold on any job (so that the job remains in the queue but is not serviced until the operator cancels the hold).

- Change the number of copies, the target print server, and other parameters for any job.

- Delete any job in the queue (including the one currently printing).

- Disable the queue so that users can't submit jobs to it. o Temporarily stop all print servers from servicing jobs in the queue.

- Disallow print servers from attaching to the queue.

Print queue operators can't assign other users as operators; only the supervisor can do that.

Print Queue Users

To access a print queue, users must be explicitly defined as "queue users" for that queue by the supervisor. By default, NetWare assigns the group EVERYONE as a queue user for every print queue. If you need to, you can revoke this default assignment in PCONSOLE and restrict a certain queue to a few select users.

Users have limited control over their own print jobs. Here is what a queue user can do with his or her own job in the queue:

- Place a user hold on a job (so that the job remains in the queue but is not serviced until the user cancels the hold).

- Defer the job to be serviced at a later time.

- Change the number of copies, the target print server, and other parameters.

- Delete the job from the queue, even if it is currently being serviced.

Again, only the supervisor can make print queue user assignments.

How NetWare Print Servers Work

The other key software component of NetWare printing is the print server, which forges the link between the print queues and printers. Whether it resides in the file server or on a dedicated machine elsewhere on the network, the print server's main function is to take jobs from the queues and feed them to the destination printer.

Novell print servers can each service up to 16 network printers. Up to five printers can be attached directly to the print server. Any additional printers must be attached to workstations on the network. By installing more than one print server, you can support as many network printers as your needs dictate. Note that the print server identifies its printers by *logical* printer numbers (0 through 15), not by *physical* printer numbers (0 through 4) as in the old NetWare 286 environment. If you have older network applications that identify printers by physical printer number, check with the vendor to see if they have an updated version. If not, use the SPOOL console command to map the printer numbers to print queues.

You don't have to install a separate print server for every file server on an internetwork. A single print server can handle queues on as many as eight different file servers. You create an identical print server account on each file server, which establishes a print server object in each file server's bindery. When activated, the print server actually logs in to the file server to accomplish its work. Thus the print server takes up one "user" connection on the file server. You will even see the print server listed along with regular users in utilities such as SYSCON, FCONSOLE, and USERLIST.

Interaction with Print Queues

As we mentioned before, the print server polls its queues about every 15 seconds. When a queue contains a job marked "Ready," the next print server that polls the queue and has the proper rights to access the queue's jobs will grab the waiting job and start processing it. In doing so, the print server obtains the file handle to the file that contains the actual data.

From here, the process is slightly different for each type of print server:

- PSERVER.EXE sets up a small buffer (3KB-4KB) to contain data from the print queue. When the buffer becomes full, the print server determines if the printer is ready to receive data. If so, it sends the data to the printer.

- When you have a workstation running RPRINTER.EXE, the print server must deal with a printer not directly connected to it. In this case, the print server sends data one byte at a time from the queue to the remote printer. Through RPRINTER, the printer sends an acknowledgement back to the queue after it receives each character. (When you define the remote printer in PCONSOLE, you can specify the buffer size to accommodate printers capable of handling more data at a time.) The print server keeps track of how large the print job file is and stops sending characters when the job is finished.

Once it has finished sending the current job to the printer, the print server reverts to its 15-second queue polling mode.

Print Server Operators

NetWare automatically assigns the user SUPERVISOR as a *print server operator*, which gives you certain control privileges for the print server. As with print queues, you can offload this print server management responsibility by designating other users as print server operators.

Basically, the print server operator is charged with making sure printers are working properly and keeping them loaded with the proper paper. Here is a list of the tasks print server operators can perform, using either PCONSOLE or PSC:

- Attach the print server to other file servers.

- Determine which users should be notified if the printer needs service.

- Issue commands (such as STOP and START) to the printer.

- Change the type of paper, or forms, in the printer.

- Change the queues serviced by a printer and their priority.

- Bring the print server down.

Print Server Users

For each print server defined, NetWare automatically assigns the group EVERYONE as a *print server user*. Thus, all network users can monitor the use and status of the print server with PCONSOLE or PSC. However, users don't have to be print server users for the print server to send their jobs to a printer. As long as users are designated print queue users for a queue, the print server can service their jobs in that queue regardless of their print server user status.

Ways to Set Up NetWare Printing

With NetWare v3.11, you can connect a printer to the network in three different ways:

- to the file server directly

- to a networked PC set up as a dedicated print server

- to a DOS-based workstation on the network

480

It's possible to use various combinations of these basic configurations to connect printers wherever you need them. However, no matter which configuration(s) you choose, the general printing model discussed above holds true. All files to be printed on a network printer go first to a print queue on the file server.

The information in this section will help you decide which print server configuration will work best for your needs.

Print Server NLM (PSERVER.NLM)

In earlier versions of NetWare, the basic operating system provided both file and print services inseparably. Connecting printers to the file server was the only choice (although a few third-party vendors developed ways to use printers connected to workstations). One of the biggest problems with this setup was that it required that printers be located close to the file server. Within printer cable distance of the file server was not always the most convenient place for printers, especially when the server was locked in a separate room for security reasons. Another drawback was that the file server had to shoulder the network printing burden as well, which led to performance degradation in busy servers.

With NetWare v3.x, the print services have been pulled out of the main operating system. You no longer have the option of using "core" printing services as in NetWare v2.x; instead print services must be provided by a separate print server program running as an NLM on the file server. If locating printers close to the file server does not pose a problem for your network, you can still connect printers directly to the file server by loading the print server loadable module— PSERVER.NLM—on the file server.

The NLM-based print server boasts several advantages over the old core print services. For one, it can support up to 16 network printers. Of course, sixteen printers can't all be connected to the file server; you can use a Novell program called RPRINTER.EXE (explained later) to connect them to any workstation on the network. Also, a single NLM print server can service queues defined on up to eight file servers. These features, illustrated in Figure 19-4, give you much more flexibility in setting up your printing environment.

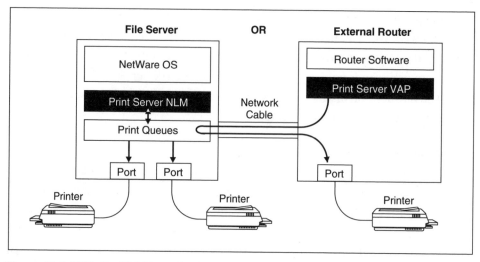

Figure 19-4: With the NLM-based print server, you have more flexibility in configuring network printing.

The print server NLM requires at least 128KB of server memory. You should also figure in about 10KB more memory per printer supported by the NLM (more if you configure multiple queues and large notify lists for your printers).

In addition to memory, NLMs also consume file server CPU time. If your file server is already under a heavy load, consider using the external print server method explained below.

Note: NetWare v3.11 also comes with PSERVER.VAP, the Value-Added Process version of the print server. While you cannot load a VAP on a NetWare v3.x file server, it can be loaded on a file server running NetWare v2.2 or v2.15c, as well as on an external router (bridge). Except for the loading and unloading procedures, PSERVER.VAP is functionally the same as PSERVER.NLM. See Novell's *Print Server* manual for more information on the print server VAP.

External Print Server (PSERVER.EXE)

NetWare v3.11 comes with the PSERVER.EXE external print server program. Moving the print server out relieves the file server from the bulk of the print service burden so it can more efficiently attend to its other duties. The file server is not entirely freed from all printing-related functions, though, because the print queues remain on the file server even when the print server software is located elsewhere.

Using Novell's external print server has the same advantages as the NLM version, with the added benefit of reducing the workload on your file server. What's more, the new version of PSERVER.EXE shipped with NetWare v3.11 provides better performance than previous versions. PSERVER.EXE supports up to 16 network printers, which can be connected to the print server itself or (with RPRINTER.EXE) to any workstation on the network. It can service queues on as many as eight file servers.

Using PSERVER.EXE requires that you dedicate a PC to function solely as the print server. A lowly 8088-based machine will do, but for performance reasons you're better off using as fast a machine as you can afford. Unless you absolutely cannot spare an extra PC on your network, the dedicated print server is the advisable configuration for most networks. Figure 19-5 shows how the NetWare external print server works.

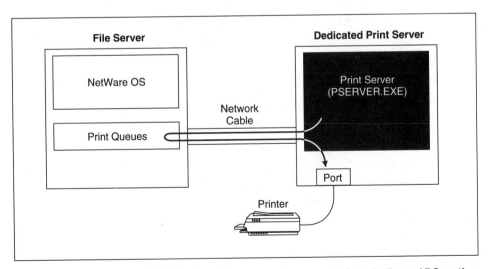

Figure 19-5: With PSERVER.EXE, the print server software runs on a dedicated PC on the network.

PSERVER.EXE requires a minimum of 256KB of memory (that includes the memory needed by DOS and the NetWare shell). You should also figure in about 10KB more for each printer the print server will support. If you configure multiple queues and large notify lists for your printers, you may need even more memory.

When you add an external print server to the network printing loop, print jobs have to travel an extra distance from the file server to the print server before they arrive at the printer. While you'd think this would significantly slow down overall printing performance, tests show that's not always the case. In a battery of tests published in Novell's April 1991 *Application Notes*, PRINTER.EXE running on a 286-based machine churned out as many (and in some cases more) graphics pages per minute than with core printing and the VAP-based print server.

Workstation-Based Printing (RPRINTER.EXE)

Whether you use the NLM-based print server or the dedicated print server, you can also use a Novell program called RPRINTER.EXE to enable the print server to send jobs to a remote printer. Novell defines a remote network printer as one that is attached to a networked PC (thus the printer is "remote" from the print server's perspective). The workstation runs a terminate-and-stay-resident (TSR) program called RPRINTER.EXE. Once run, RPRINTER stays resident in the workstation's memory until it is removed or the workstation is rebooted.

With RPRINTER loaded on a workstation, the user of that workstation can run applications and otherwise function normally on the network. However, the user cannot access the printer as a local printer in standalone fashion. Of course, the user can access it as a network printer. Like any other network printer, the remote printer must have a print queue assigned to it and be set up on the print server's list of supported printers in PCONSOLE. When run, RPRINTER configures itself based on the printer number, printer type, and other information you defined for it in PCONSOLE. Figure 19-6 shows how workstation-based printing works with RPRINTER.

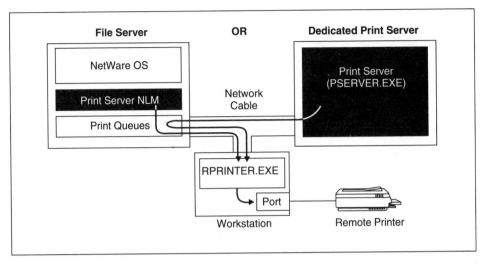

Figure 19-6: Through RPRINTER.EXE, Novell print servers can send jobs to printers physically connected to any workstation on the network.

The number of remote printers you can use depends on how many printers are attached directly to the file server or print server. You can connect up to five printers to the server, leaving a maximum of 11 remote printers. You can even have more than one remote printer connected to the same workstation by running RPRINTER once for each printer. Each instance of RPRINTER requires 8KB- 9KB of memory in the workstation (more if you set a larger buffer size in PCONSOLE).

Naturally, the type of CPU in the workstation affects remote printing performance. Printing to a remote printer connected to an 8MHz 286-based PC is slower than if it were connected to a 33MHz 386-based PC. Be aware, however, that RPRINTER can't run on some IBM PC clones. If you have trouble getting a remote printer to work, you may have to switch it to a 100 percent IBM-compatible machine.

Should the workstation user ever need to print locally to the printer, you can remove the TSR from memory by reissuing the RPRINTER command with the "-R" option. However, this option doesn't work with Novell's extended or expanded memory shell. Another alternative is to use the print server command to switch the printer to private mode.

To run RPRINTER, the NetWare workstation shell must be loaded first with a setting of "SPX connections=60" in the SHELL.CFG file. However, the user does not necessarily have to be logged in to the file server, so other users can access the remote printer even if no one is currently using the "host" workstation. In fact, RPRINTER remains in effect even when the file server goes down.

Devising a Network Printing Plan

A little advance planning will go a long way toward a trouble-free network printing setup. Take an inventory of what your users' printing needs are. Determine which users need what kind of printers (dot matrix, laser, color, plotter, and so forth). The type of printer has a profound effect on overall printing speed, so select your hardware carefully. Reliability and durability are key points to consider, since a network printer typically sees much more use than a standalone printer. Where performance is an issue, choose printers with a high pages per minute (PPM) rating (anything over 10 PPM is generally considered fast).

Next, plan the location of the printers so they will be most accessible to the individuals or groups that will use them. One of the biggest user complaints about network printing is having to hike to the printer. With the flexibility offered by Novell print servers, you can (in most cases) locate printers where you need them.

Late 1990 saw the introduction of a new class of third-party products that allow printers to be connected virtually anywhere on a Novell network. Products such as Intel's NetPort and the Hewlett-Packard LaserJet IIIsi printer attach directly to the network cable, eliminating the need for a "host" PC. If you need a network printer in a place where there is no nearby PC, these products are worth looking at.

Finally, figure how many and what types of print servers you need to handle your network printing requirements. Use the information presented above to help you determine which configuration will work best for you. As a general rule, file server-based printing can handle a workload of up to about 50 pages an hour without any noticeable drop in overall performance. If you anticipate heavier printing loads, or if your print jobs will contain a lot of graphics, it's also a good idea to write down in advance what print queues you'll create for each printer. Once you have your printing plan in place, the actual setup will go much more smoothly.

Setting Up Printing

This section gives brief, step-by-step instructions on how to set up the various print service configurations. For more detailed instructions, refer to your Novell manuals. Whichever configuration you choose, installing the printer hardware is the same. Follow the instructions under "Installing Printer Hardware" first.

Installing Printer Hardware

You must connect your network printers directly to parallel or serial ports on the file server with PSERVER.NLM, on a dedicated print server with PSERVER.EXE, or on a network workstation with RPRINTER.EXE. Most computers approved for use in NetWare networks come with at least one parallel and one serial port built in. If you need to attach more printers, you must install an add-on board with additional printer ports.

Some add-on boards require an interrupt line to signal the CPU. If so, be sure it doesn't conflict with an interrupt used by another port or add-on board in the same computer. On an AT-class machine, set the interrupt to match the port, as shown in the following chart (refer to the add-on board's documentation for exact instructions on setting interrupts).

Port	Interrupt
LPT1	7
LPT2	5
COM1	4
COM2	3
COM3	4 (shared)
COM4	3 (shared)

IBM PS/2 machines allow up to eight COM ports to be defined. In these systems, COM1 uses IRQ 4, and COM2 through COM8 share interrupt 3. Don't set a printer port to IRQ 6; most floppy disk controllers use interrupt 6. If no more interrupts are available, you can set up the printer in "poll" mode, which doesn't use interrupts. Be aware, however, that this option slows down the flow of data to the printer, and you can't use it with a remote printer.

Attach each printer to its "host" computer, using the appropriate parallel or serial interface cable. Since serial printers use the RS-232C data-transfer protocol, you must set the following parameters for them:

Baud rate   The data transfer rate—1200, 4800, and 9600 are typical values

Word size   The number of significant data bits in each character (or "word") transmitted—usually 7 or 8

Stop bits   The number of bits used to indicate the end of a character—usually 1 or 2

Parity   An error-checking method—usually odd, even, or none

Xon/Xoff   A handshaking protocol that prevents data from being transmitted faster than the printer can receive it—your printer may or may not support it

Setting Up Printing with a Print Server

Setting up printing with the Print Server NLM or PSERVER.EXE consists of six main procedures:

- Creating print queues

- Creating the print server account on a file server

- Specifying which printers the print server will support

- Specifying which queues will be serviced by each printer

- Enabling the print server to service queues on additional file servers

- Starting the print server program

Creating Print Queues

1. Log in as SUPERVISOR to the default file server of the users who will be using the printers you intend to assign to the print server.

2. Start PCONSOLE and select "Print Queue Information" from the "Available Topics" menu.

3. At the "Print Queues" list, press <Ins> to add a new queue.

4. Type a descriptive name for the print queue and press <Enter>. NetWare automatically assigns an object ID number for the queue.

5. If you want to change the default queue user (the group EVERYONE) and queue operator (the user SUPERVISOR) assignments, highlight the new queue and press <Enter>. Select "Queue Users" to add or remove queue users; select "Queue Operators" to add or remove print queue operator assignments. Press <Esc> to return to the "Print Queues" list.

6. Repeat Steps 3 through 5 for each print queue you planned to create for this file server. When you're finished, press <Esc> until you return to the "Available Topics" menu.

Creating the Print Server Account

The account you create here is the one the print server will use to log in to the file server. NetWare also builds a print server configuration file and stores it on whatever file server you are currently logged in to. Even if the print server will service more than one file server, the configuration file is created only once on the file server where you first define the print server account.

1. Select "Print Server Information" from PCONSOLE's "Available Topics" menu.

2. At the "Print Servers" list, press <Ins> to add a new print server name.

3. Type a descriptive name (such as PS-ACCTG) for the print server, then press <Enter>. NetWare automatically assigns an object ID number for the print server.

4. With the new print server name highlighted, press <Enter>. This takes you to the "Print Server Information" menu.

5. For extra security, you can assign a password that must be entered before anyone can activate the print server. Select "Change Password" and type an appropriate password in the "Enter New Password" box. Then type the exact same characters again in the "Retype New Password" entry box.

6. If you want, you can assign a longer name to the print server by selecting the "Full Name" option. A full name can help identify the print server to other users. For example, if you named the print server PS-ACCTG, the full name might be something like "Novell Print Server for the Accounting Department."

7. At this point, you can change the default print server user (the group EVERY ONE) and print server operator (the user SUPERVISOR). Select "Print Server Users" to add or remove users for the print server; select "Print Server Operators" to add or remove operator assignments.

Defining the Printers Supported by the Print Server

Now comes a tricky part where many people become confused, especially if the print server will service queues on multiple file servers. Even Novell's *Print Server* manual is unclear on this procedure. Refer to your printing plan and follow the instructions carefully to set up your printer and queue assignments correctly.

1. Select "Print Server Configuration" to access the "Print Server Configuration Menu" shown below.

```
┌─────────────────────────────────────┐
│ Print Server Configuration Menu     │
├─────────────────────────────────────┤
│ File Servers To Be Serviced         │
│ Notify List for Printer             │
│ Printer Configuration               │
│ Queues Serviced by Printer          │
└─────────────────────────────────────┘
```

2. Choose the "File Server To Be Serviced" option. You will notice that your current file server is already listed and cannot be deleted. If this is the only file server to be serviced by the print server, press <Esc> and skip to Step 3.

    If, on the other hand, the print server will service multiple file servers, you must add them to the list *now* so they will be included in the print server configuration file. Press <Ins> to get a list of available file servers. Select the ones whose queues this print server will service. (You can select up to seven other file servers, for a maximum of eight.) When you're finished, press <Esc> until you return to the "Print Server Configuration Menu." Now, to avoid getting confused, center your activity on the current file server. Don't worry about queues on any other file servers right now.

3. Select the third menu option, "Printer Configuration," to bring up a list of printers that will be handled by the print server. Initially, you will see 16 printer slots (numbered Printer 0 through Printer 15) with "Not Installed" as the description.

4. Select Printer 0 to get to the "Printer 0 Configuration" screen. This screen contains a number of fields in which you can enter information.

5. In the "Printer Name" field, type a name (up to 47 characters long) that identifies the printer and possibly its location. The name you type here will appear on the print server console screen when you bring up the print server. We suggest such names as "HP LaserJet Series II" or "Epson Printer in Accounting."

6. In the "Type" field, indicate whether the printer is physically connected to the print server or to a workstation as a remote printer. You also specify which LPT or COM port the printer is attached to. The default is "Defined Elsewhere," but

you only use this value when setting up the print server for subsequent file servers. Highlight the "Type" field and press <Enter> to bring up a list of printer types:

- For a printer that is connected directly to the print server, choose the "Local Parallel" or "Local Serial" option that specifies which LPT or COM port the printer is attached to.

- For a printer that is connected to a workstation, choose either "Remote Parallel," "Remote Serial," or "Remote Other/Unknown." If you already know what port on the workstation the remote printer is connected to, use the option that specifies that port. The "Remote Other/Unknown" option lets you reserve a slot for the remote printer now and supply the details later when you run RPRINTER.

7. The "Use Interrupts" field defaults to "Yes" and automatically selects the interrupt for whichever port you selected. LPT1 uses IRQ 7, LPT2 uses IRQ 5, COM1 uses IRQ 4, and COM2 uses IRQ 3.

   Always double-check to make sure the port in question is in fact using the specified IRQ. The documentation that came with the computer (or add-on I/O board if you're using one) should say which interrupt each port uses. If not, you might be able to use a diagnostic utility such as CheckIt from TouchStone Software or System Sleuth from Dariana Technology Group to determine which interrupt a port is using.

   If you cannot reliably determine which interrupt the printer port uses (or if the computer has no more available interrupts), specify "No" in the "Use Interrupts" field. This causes the print server to use the "polled" method of sending data to the printer. It might be slower, but you won't have to worry about interrupt conflicts.

8. In the rest of the fields, the default settings should be sufficient. You can increase the default buffer size if the printer performs sluggishly. For a serial printer, make sure the data-transfer protocol settings (baud rate, word size, and so on)

match those set on the printer itself. Press <Esc> and save the changes. Press <Esc> again to return to the "Print Server Configuration" menu.

9. If you want the print server to alert someone whenever the printer needs service, choose the "Notify List for Printer" option. Select the printer you just defined, then press <Ins>. From the resulting list of users, select the lucky one who gets to add new paper, change toner or ribbons,and perform other minor printer management tasks. This user will receive NetWare broadcast messages when the printer needs attention. You can set the number of seconds before the first message gets sent as well as how often after that the message will be repeated if the problem is not attended to. When you're finished, press <Esc> and save the changes.

10. Repeat Steps 3 through 8 for each network printer this print server will service. When you're finished, press <Esc> until you return to the "Print Server Infor mation" menu. Then move on to the next procedure.

Assigning Queues to Each Printer

Now you must match the print queues you created earlier with the appropriate printers, according to your printing plan. NetWare automatically authorizes the print server to service the queues once you map them to a printer.

1. From the "Print Server Configuration" menu, select "Queues Serviced by Printer."

2. Select a printer and press <Ins> to get a list of "Available Queues."

3. Choose the print queue you want to map to this printer. If your plan calls for only one queue per printer, leave the priority set to the default of 1. Otherwise, set the priority from 1 (highest) to 10 (lowest) according to your plan. Press <Enter> to complete the mapping.

4. If this printer will service more than one queue, press <Ins> again and map the next queue as in Step 3.

5. Repeat Steps 2 through 4 to map one or more print queues to each network printer. If your plan calls for multiple printers servicing a single queue, select that same queue for each printer (the printers must be functionally identical). When you're finished, press <Esc> until you return to PCONSOLE's "Available Options" menu.

If you're dealing with only one file server, your work in PCONSOLE is complete. Exit PCONSOLE and skip to "Starting the Print Server" for the next procedure.

If you selected other file servers in the "File Servers To Be Serviced" option, continue with the next section.

Enabling the Print Server on Additional File Servers

These instructions apply only if you configured the print server to service queues on other file servers. You must enable the print server on the additional file servers by creating an identically named print server account with the same printer definitions on each file server. To do this, you'll need supervisor privileges on each file server.

1. First use the "Change Current File Server" option in PCONSOLE to switch to one of the other file servers. If you can't attach as SUPERVISOR or as a supervisor-equivalent user, enlist the help of that file server's network supervisor.

2. Use the "Print Queue Information" option to create print queues on the new file server (if they haven't already been created). Follow the same steps as before to create the queues.

3. Use the "Print Server Configuration" option to create the print server account on the new file server. You must give it the exact same name as you did on the first file server. If you've assigned a print server password, use the same password here as well. That way you'll only be prompted for one password when you start the print server.

4. Define the same printers under "Printer Configuration" as you did on the first file server. Assign them the same printer numbers and give them the same names. However, in the "Type" field, select the "Defined Elsewhere" option. The printer types are already defined in the configuration file on the original file server, so you don't have to define them again.

5. Use the "Queues Serviced by Printer" option to map the queues on the new file server to the appropriate network printers. When you're finished, press <Esc> until you return to the "Available Options" menu.

6. Repeat Steps 1 through 5 for each additional file server you want the print server to service. When this process is completed, exit PCONSOLE.

Starting the Print Server

The print server must be fully configured as described above before you can run the software to start up the print server. Follow the instructions below for the type of print server you're using.

Starting PSERVER.NLM

Before starting the Print Server NLM, check to make sure the PSERVER.NLM file exists in the SYS:SYSTEM directory. If not, look in SYS:PUBLIC and copy it over if it's there. Otherwise, you'll have to copy the original file into SYS:SYSTEM from the NetWare PRINT-1 diskette. PSERVER.NLM requires both the CLIB.NLM and the NUT.NLM and will load them automatically if they aren't already loaded. Make sure you have the NetWare v3.11 version of all three NLMs (these should have been copied into SYS:SYSTEM during installation or upgrade).

To start the print server, type **LOAD PSERVER** *PrintServer* at the file server console. Substitute the print server name for *PrintServer*. You don't have to bring the server down and reboot it. If you want the file server to load the print server every time it comes up, include this command in the system AUTOEXEC file via "Supervisor Options" in SYSCON.

Starting PSERVER.EXE

To start the PSERVER.EXE program, it's easiest to set up an AUTOEXEC.BAT file for the workstation that will serve as the dedicated print server. The workstation must first have a SHELL.CFG that contains the line "SPX Connections=60." (The Novell *Print Server* manual states 50 SPX connections in one place and 60 in another. Actually, any setting between 50 and 60 will do.)

To start up, the print server must have access to the following files:

```
PSERVER.EXE
IBM$RUN.OVL
SYS$HELP.DAT
SYS$ERR.DAT
SYS$MSG.DAT
```

You can provide access to these files in one of two ways. The first way is to copy the files from SYS:PUBLIC to the print server's boot diskette or directory. With this method, your AUTOEXEC.BAT file should contain at least the following lines:

```
IPX
NET3
PSERVER FileServer/PrintServer
```

For *FileServer*, substitute the name of the file server on which you created the print server's configuration file. Replace *PrintServer* with the name of the print server. (Use NET4 or NET5 if the print server PC boots with DOS 4.*x* or 5.*x*.)

The second method is to create a dummy *user* account that the print server can use to log in. (Don't confuse this account with the print server account you created in PCONSOLE.) Go into SYSCON and create a user account named "PRINT." All user PRINT needs is Read and File Scan rights in SYS:PUBLIC, plus a search drive mapped to SYS:PUBLIC. NetWare grants this limited access automatically for every user created. For extra security, assign a station restriction so that PRINT can log in only from the print server PC's node address. The AUTOEXEC.BAT should look like this:

```
IPX
NET3
F:
LOGIN FileServer/PRINT
PSERVER PrintServer
```

Again, use NET4 or NET5 if the print server PC boots with DOS 4.*x* or 5.*x*, and substitute the appropriate file server and print server names.

With the PSERVER software running, the network printers attached directly to the file server, router, or dedicated print server should be available for use. (To activate remote printers, run RPRINTER as explained in the next section.) You can check your setup by going into PCONSOLE, selecting "Print Queue Information," selecting each queue one at a time, and looking at the "Currently Attached Servers" option. PCONSOLE should display the appropriate print server for each queue. If not, you've missed a step somewhere along the way. Retrace the setup procedure and make sure you have completed each step.

Starting the Remote Printer Software

You must start RPRINTER.EXE for each remote printer you defined for the print server. Run RPRINTER on the workstation to which the remote printer is physically attached. If you have more than one remote printer attached to the same workstation, run RPRINTER once for each printer.

The easiest way to run RPRINTER is through the user's AUTOEXEC.BAT file. First, however, create or edit the workstation's SHELL.CFG file to contain the line "SPX Connections=60" and delete the line "Local Printers=0" if it exists. The remote printer software doesn't have to log in to the network; it can be run as soon as the NetWare shell is loaded. This allows other users to access remote printers even when the user at that workstation isn't currently logged in. Copy the following files necessary for RPRINTER to run into the SYS:LOGIN directory of each file server:

```
RPRINTER.EXE
RPRINTER.HLP
SYS$HELP.DAT
SYS$MSG.DAT
IBM$RUN.OVL
```

Then add lines similar to the following to the AUTOEXEC.BAT file:

```
DELAY 20
IPX
NET3
F:
RPRINTER PrintServer n
PAUSE
LOGIN ...
```

Substitute the appropriate print server name for *PrintServer* and the remote printer's printer number for *n*. The "DELAY 20" line allots 20 seconds for the SPX connection with the print server to time out in the event the workstation is rebooted abruptly. Without this delay, RPRINTER will not be able reconnect to the print server immediately. You'll see the "Remote printer now installed" message if RPRINTER loads properly. The PAUSE gives the user the chance to make sure the printer is initialized. After that, the batch file can proceed to log the user into the file server as usual.

Once your remote printers are working, you might want to delete RPRINTER.EXE from the SYS:PUBLIC directory. This prevents curious but unauthorized users from running RPRINTER, which would take the slot reserved for the remote printer and render it unavailable for its intended use.

Changing the Print Server Configuration

In even the most carefully planned network, occasional adjustments to the initial setup are inevitable. However, changes to the print server configuration can be tricky. The main thing to realize is that once the print server is running, some of the changes you make to its configuration in PCONSOLE are only temporary and will be lost when you bring down the print server. Others will not take effect at all until you stop the print server and restart it.

This section is by no means an exhaustive treatment of every change you can possibly make; refer to the Novell *Print Server* manual for that. We'll just point out some common pitfalls in changing the initial printing configuration. We'll also explain how to stop and restart the print server and how to switch a remote printer from shared mode to private mode.

Changing Printers and Queue Assignments

One major cause of confusion stems from the similarity of menu choices under the "Print Server Configuration" and "Print Server Status/Control" options in PCONSOLE. These options are both found in the "Print Server Information" menu you get after choosing "Print Server Information" at the main menu and then selecting a print server from the resulting list.

In general, any changes you make under the "Print Server Configuration" option in PCONSOLE do *not* take effect until you stop and restart the print server. This is because you are essentially changing the configuration file on the file server, which the print server reads only when it initializes.

By contrast, any changes you make under the "Print Server Status/Control" option in PCONSOLE do take effect immediately, but they will be lost when you bring down the print server.

The following chart should help clarify exactly what you can do under these two PCONSOLE options.

499

Change	Print Server Configuration	Print Server Status/Control
Assign a new file server to a print server	Yes	Yes
Add or remove printers for the print server	Yes	No
Change the configuration of a printer	Yes	No
Assign new queues to a printer	Yes	Yes
Remove a queue from a printer	Yes	Yes

Any change affecting bindery objects (such as changing print queue users and operators, print server users and operators, or print server and queue names) takes effect immediately and remains in effect until changed again. If you rename or delete print queues, remember to reconfigure any network applications that were set up to recognize those print queues.

Stopping and Restarting the Print Server

The exact method for bringing down the print server and starting it back up again varies for each type of print server.

To stop a dedicated print server, go into PCONSOLE, choose "Print Server Information," and select the print server from the "Print Servers" list. Then choose

"Print Server Status/Control" and select "Server Info." In the "Print Server Info/ Status" box, press <Enter>. Choose "Down" to stop the print server immediately; choose "Going down after current jobs" if you want the server to finish what it's doing first. Restart the print server by typing the **PSERVER** *FileServer/PrintServer* command at the dedicated print server workstation.

To stop and restart the print server NLM, you don't have to bring down the file server (or router) and reboot. While you can bring down the NLM in PCONSOLE the same way as for PSERVER.EXE, going to the file server and typing "UNLOAD PSERVER" has the same effect. Restart the NLM by typing **LOAD PSERVER** *PrintServer*.

Making a Remote Printer Private

Occasionally, the user who has a remote network printer connected to his or her workstation might want to use that printer exclusively. This switch can be accomplished with NetWare's PSC (print server command). The user must know the print server name and the printer number assigned to the remote printer. The full syntax of the command is:

```
PSC PS=PrintServer P=n PRIVATE
```

You can simplify the use of the PSC by setting a DOS environment variable in the user's AUTOEXEC.BAT file. For example, if the print server is named PS-ACCTG and the remote printer is number 4, include the following line in the batch file:

```
SET PSC=PSps-acctg P4
```

The user can then type **PSC PRIVATE** at the network prompt to switch the printer to private mode. **PSC SHARED** will return the printer to shared mode.

Switching to private mode removes the printer from the print server's list of network printers. Thus the printer is temporarily unavailable to other users. Encourage users to leave the remote printers in shared mode except when it's absolutely necessary to print locally. Forgetting to return the printer to shared mode can cause problems, especially if your applications are set up to print to queues assigned to the remote printer.

Troubleshooting Printing

You can save yourself a lot of troubleshooting grief by spending the extra time necessary to properly plan and carefully set up your network printing environment. Most problems with printing are the result of incorrect or incomplete installation of the printer hardware and software. That is why we have dedicated so many pages to the setup section in this chapter.

The remainder of this chapter presents possible solutions for some of the most common problems or errors encountered when working with NetWare's print services. If you receive an error message that you don't understand, look it up in Novell's *System Messages* manual. For more help, call your Novell authorized reseller or service representative.

Problem: You are prompted for a password when you load the print server, but you didn't assign a print server password.

Solutions:

You must define and configure the print server in PCONSOLE before you run the PSERVER.EXE program. If you try to load the print server prematurely, PSERVER won't find a print server account but it will ask you for a password anyway.

If this happens after you have configured the print server, retrace the installation and configuration steps to make certain you haven't overlooked anything. Specify both the file server name and print server name when you run PSERVER.EXE. Double-check your spelling to be sure you aren't mistyping the names.

If you added a new file server to the "File Servers To Be Serviced" list under "Print Server Configuration" in PCONSOLE, be sure to create an identically named print server account on that file server. Down the print server and start it up again to put the new configuration into effect.

Problem: You are unable to attach to the specified file server when you load PSERVER.EXE.

Solutions:

First make sure you have not mistyped the file server name, print server name, or print server password (if there is one). A mistake in any one of these three entries will result in a vaguely worded message like "Access to server denied."

Type SLIST to see if the file server you need is currently up and available on the network. If the file server is down temporarily, try again after it has been rebooted. Make sure the print server has an identically named account on each file server it is supposed to service. Don't exceed the maximum of eight file servers per print server.

In most cases, you should receive a message that explains why you weren't able to attach to the file server. The possibilities are numerous:

- No more connections are available on the file server. The print server requires one user connection. Having enough connections to run the print server is mainly of concern only in the five- and ten-user versions of NetWare. About all you can do is wait until a user logs out, or upgrade to the next higher NetWare version that supports more users.

- The supervisor has disabled logins on the file server. If users can't log in, neither can the print server. Reenable the login function and load PSERVER again.

- Time, station, and other account restrictions have been imposed on the print server account.

  If you set up system-wide default account restrictions, they will apply to user and print server accounts alike. The intruder detect feature can lock the print server account as well.

  Make sure the print server account is not restricted needlessly.

- Like user passwords, the print server password is subject to expiration dates, minimum length limits, and forced periodic changes. If the message instructs you to change the print server password, do it.

- The bindery is locked. This occurs during certain maintenance procedures (such as a system backup). The bindery is usually locked only momentarily; try again in a few minutes.

- A network error is preventing the print server from attaching. Check your network boards,cabling, and other components for faulty hardware.

Problem: The workstation runs out of IPX sockets or SPX connections when you try to load PSERVER.EXE.

Solution:

The print server requires both IPX and SPX to be loaded at the workstation (SPX loads automatically with IPX). IPX allocates 20 sockets by default; you can specify more via the "ipx sockets=n" line in the SHELL.CFG file. If you get a message saying "No more IPX sockets are available," increase the current number by at least ten in the SHELL.CFG file. You also need at least 50 SPX connections to run PSERVER.EXE. If the message says you don't have enough SPX connections, add the "spx connections=50" line to the SHELL.CFG file or increase the number if the line already exists. Make sure you spell everything correctly. After changing SHELL.CFG, reboot the workstation and run PSERVER again.

Problem: The workstation runs out of memory when you try to load PSERVER.EXE.

Solution:

At a minimum, PSERVER.EXE requires 256KB of conventional memory, which includes the memory needed by DOS and the NetWare shell. However, every queue serviced, every printer defined, every print buffer, and every user on the notify list requires memory. As a general rule, figure about 10KB more memory for each printer the print server supports. To reduce the overall print server memory requirement, you can specify fewer users to be notified when the printers need service or reduce the buffer size for each printer.

If you load TSRs (besides the NetWare shell and LAN driver), try removing them or use a memory manager that can locate TSRs in expanded or extended memory.

Problem: The file server runs out of memory when you load the print server NLM.

Solutions:

The Novell manuals list two messages that indicate the file server doesn't have enough memory to run the print server: "There are no more response buffers available" and "Unable to create display portal." If you get either of these messages, add more RAM to the file server.

You can also unload any unneeded NLMs (like INSTALL) to free up server memory.

Problem: You have accounting installed on the file server, and the print server won't work because it has no account balance.

Solutions:

Installing accounting with old versions of SYSCON (prior to v3.0) can cause problems by giving the print server account a zero balance with no credit available. Check your SYSCON version with the NetWare VERSION utility. If it's below v3.0, copy the latest SYSCON.EXE file from your original NetWare diskettes or from another file server. Then remove accounting and reinstall it.

You can also just go into SYSCON and manually change the account balance.

Problem: RPRINTER.EXE doesn't initialize properly when you run it at the workstation.

Solutions:

RPRINTER needs three basic things to run successfully: (1) sufficient memory in the workstation; (2) at least 60 SPX connections; and (3) access to support files such as RPRINTER.HLP and IBM$RUN.OVL. RPRINTER needs 128KB of available conventional memory to initialize, but only 9KB to run thereafter. Remove TSR programs or use a memory manager to provide more available memory in the workstation. Check the SPX connections line in SHELL.CFG and increase the number if necessary. While you're at it, make sure SHELL.CFG does not contain the line "local printers=0." Copy the following support files for RPRINTER to the workstation's boot disk or to the SYS:LOGIN directory of each file server on your network:

RPRINTER.EXE	SYS$MSG.DAT
RPRINTER.HLP	SYS$HELP.DAT
IBM$RUN.OVL	

Make sure the print server is running and shows a slot available for the remote printer. Check the syntax of your RPRINTER command; there should be a space between the print server name and the printer number. Make sure you spell the print server name correctly and specify the printer number corresponding to the remote printer's slot. Network errors can also prevent the remote printer from initializing successfully, so check for those as well.

If the workstation crashes or needs to be rebooted, you must give the SPX connection with the print server at least 20 seconds to time out before you try to reconnect the remote printer. If you automatically load RPRINTER in the workstation's AUTOEXEC.BAT file, add a line that says "delay 20" at the beginning of the file.

RPRINTER won't run on some IBM PC clones. If you have trouble getting a remote printer to work, try moving it to a 100 percent IBM-compatible machine.

Problem: When users send documents to be printed on the network, the print jobs never even make it to the print queue.

Solutions:

First check the printer setup in your applications. Most network-aware applications let you specify a file server/print queue combination as the destination for printed output. Make sure you have spelled the file server and queue names correctly. Double-check your network printing configuration in PCONSOLE to be sure you did in fact create the print queue. Some applications will return an error indicating that the network is not accepting data. If so, cancel the print job and see if there's a network problem (network board hardware failure, shell not loaded properly, file server crash, and so on).

If you are using CAPTURE to redirect printed output for a non-network application, type "CAPTURE SH" at the workstation's DOS prompt to check the status of the ports. This command shows which port (LPT1, LPT2, or LPT3) is being redirected to a NetWare print queue. Make sure the application is set to print to that LPT port (you cannot use CAPTURE with serial ports). If not, either redo the printer setup in the application or reissue the CAPTURE command to redirect output from the right port to the right print queue.

Problem: Network print jobs make it to the queue, but don't get sent to the printer.

Solutions:

First of all, make sure the printer is turned on and that it is on-line. Paper jams, a lack of toner, and other conditions usually cause a printer to go off-line. Inspect the cable connecting the printer to the parallel or serial port. Faulty, loose, or incorrectly configured interface cables can cause a host of printing problems. If you suspect the cable, try swapping it with an identical cable that you know works. These solutions may seem obvious, but they are easily overlooked when the pressure is on.

If the printer is a new one you have just added to the network out of the box, be sure you have followed the manufacturer's setup instructions. Use the appropriate parallel or serial interface cable to connect the printer to the computer. (Use the computer's built-in ports whenever possible. Avoid using LPT ports included as part of a monitor board, as they are more prone to problems.) Run the self-test as described in the printer manual to see if the printer itself is functioning properly. Check for interrupt conflicts with other hardware in the computer. You could also try printing to the printer locally to ensure that the printer itself is functioning.

The next thing to do is check your entire network printing setup: print queues, print servers, and printers. All three of these pieces must be installed, configured, and running properly in order for jobs to get from the queue to the printer. Make sure the printer is correctly defined in PCONSOLE for the print server and that you have associated the queue with the printer. The print server should be shown as "currently attached" to the queue. Also, the print server console screen (or the PSC STAT command) should indicate that the printer is "Waiting for job."

Check the "Servers can service entries in queue" operator flag under the "Current Queue Status" option in PCONSOLE. If a print queue operator has set this flag to "No," that would prevent print servers from attaching to and servicing the queue. Another slim possibility is that the maximum of 25 print servers have already attached to the queue, preventing any further print server attachments.

If you're dealing with a remote printer connected to a workstation, make sure the SHELL.CFG file for that workstation does not contain the line "local printers=0." Also make sure the remote printer is in shared mode, not private mode. Double-check the integrity of the workstation's network connection (shell, cabling, and network board). In PCONSOLE, check the status of the print job entries in the queue. They should all say "Ready." If they say "Waiting," someone has deferred the printing until a future time.

Problem: A print job stays "Active" in the queue for an excessively long time.

Solutions:

In theory, the "Active" status indicates that the job is currently being sent to the printer by the print server. For long, graphics-intensive documents, it is not unusual for this process to take five to ten minutes or more. However, if no completed pages are coming out of the printer during this time, something is wrong. Check to see if the print server is hung. If so, reboot it and resubmit the print job. Also check for network errors.

Another possibility arises if you have queues on two file servers feeding jobs to the same printer. When both queues contain print jobs, the number one job in each queue is shown as "Active" even though only one actually is. For example, suppose a user on one file server sends a 50-page report laden with graphics. A few seconds later, a user on the other file server sends a one-page text letter. The second user's job will sit in the queue, saying it is "Active," for however long it takes the first user's job to print.

Problem: You're getting messages saying that the SYS volume is getting full. Why can't users print anymore?

Solution:

Remember that print queues are really subdirectories under the SYS:SYSTEM directory on the file server. While "in the queue," print jobs are stored as files in those subdirectories. If you run out of space on the SYS volume, there won't be room for print job files to be spooled to the print queue subdirectories. Run CHKVOL or VOLINFO to see how much space is available on the SYS volume. Archive old files and remove them from the file server to free up disk space.

Problem: The PSC ... STATUS command says a print server is not up and running, when actually it is.

Solution:

If someone who is not a designated print server user issues the PSC command to determine the status of that print server, it will erroneously report that the print server is not up and running. You get the same message if you mistype the print server name in the command. Make sure you are a print server user and that you spell the name correctly to get an accurate print server status report with PSC.

Problem: The printer is full of paper and seems to be on-line, but NetWare reports the printer status as "Out of paper" or "Not connected."

Solution:

The "Out of paper" message in NetWare can also appear when something is wrong with the physical connection of the printer to the print server or workstation. This is most likely due to a hardware problem. Turn the printer off and back on again to reinitialize it, then run the printer's self-test. If it passes, check for faulty hardware along the connection from the printer to the port.

The "Not connected" message for a remote printer indicates that the printer has been defined in PCONSOLE, but it has not yet been activated as a network printer. Run the RPRINTER program to activate the remote printer.

Problem: Print jobs are printing very slowly.

Solutions:

Check all your printer hardware connections. If you have connected a printer to an LPT port that is part of a monitor board, try switching to a built-in LPT port. The printer port's use of interrupts might be incorrectly defined in PCONSOLE. Switching from using interrupts to the "polling" method often resolves this problem.

You can speed up remote printing by moving the remote printer to a faster workstation (for example, a 20MHz 386-based machine rather than an 8MHz 286-based one).

Problem: The printer output is a jumbled stream of garbage characters.

Solutions:

The first thing to check is the printing setup in your applications. Most print jobs, with the exception of straight ASCII text files, must be formatted for a particular printer within an application. Without the special printer codes inserted by the application (in conjunction with a print driver customized for the printer), the printer doesn't know how to interpret the data being fed to it. Make sure your application is using the right print driver for the type of printer you are using.

Users might inadvertently be sending print jobs to the wrong printer (for instance, a job formatted for the HP LaserJet III going to a PostScript printer). You can help alleviate confusion by giving your queues names indicative of the type of printer that services them. Queue names like "PRINTQ_1" or "ACCTG_Q" give no clue as to what type of printer lies on the other end of the queue.

Another cause might be print jobs that leave the printer in an altered state without returning it to its defaults. For example, a spreadsheet user might switch the printer to landscape mode to print a wide spreadsheet. When the next user tries to print a business letter, the resulting output would be unusable. The solution is to use PRINTDEF and PRINTCON to create print job configurations that reset the printer after each use.

An incorrect interrupt configuration in PCONSOLE can also cause unintelligible output. Not all printer ports generate interrupts; those that don't must be set up to use the print server's "polling" method.

Problem: Whenever users print large graphics-intensive files, file server performance becomes sluggish.

Solution:

Try adding more RAM to the file server to increase the number of cache buffers. NetWare treats print jobs just like any other file sent to the file server to be stored. Thus, a print job goes first into the file server's cache memory, one block at a time, before being written to disk in a print queue subdirectory. When the job is ready to be printed, each block is read from disk and placed again into a cache buffer. Each block of the print job stays in the cache at least until the print server finishes feeding that block to the printer. Once that is done, NetWare flushes the print job from cache according to its "least recently used" algorithm so the memory can be used for other file reads/writes. Thus large print job files with lots of graphics can compete with other files being read from or written to disk for use of cache memory.

Problem: You've tried everything you can think of, but your printing problem persists.

Solution:

It rarely happens, but print queues and print server configuration files can become corrupted. When all else fails, try deleting all your print queues and print servers and starting over from scratch. Keep a written record of your entire printing configuration so you can re-create it when necessary.

CHAPTER 20

Using the NetWare Printing Utilities

If your applications are all network-aware versions designed to recognize NetWare print queues and network printers, users should be able to print without much further ado after the initial printing setup. However, some vendors do not offer network versions of their software. These types of applications are designed to send printer output only to a local printer through an LPT port. If you must use this type of non-network software on your LAN, NetWare provides a number of utilities that at least make it possible to print to network printers. These utilities include PRINTDEF, PRINTCON, CAPTURE/ENDCAP, and NPRINT.

This chapter explains how to use these utilities, not only in dealing with non-network application printing, but for everyday LAN printing needs as well. We start out with a brief look at how the NetWare printing utilities are interrelated. Then we discuss each utility in turn, examining the various options that each one offers. Finally, we describe the Print Server Control (PSC) utility, which provides command-line equivalents for many printer control functions found in PCONSOLE.

Overview of NetWare's Printing Utilities

Novell's PRINTDEF (PRINTer DEFinition) and PRINTCON (PRINT job CONfiguration) utilities are separate programs, but they are closely interrelated. Neither can offer much that is worthwhile without the other. In PRINTDEF, you define the printers, forms, and basic printing options available on the network's printers. In PRINTCON, you use the printer definitions created in PRINTDEF to set up complete configurations for specific print jobs.

Users can then include these print job configurations with the NetWare CAPTURE, NPRINT (Network PRINT), and PCONSOLE (Print CONSOLE) utilities to tell the printer how to print files from outside an application. Note that, with one exception, this is the *only* use for PRINTDEF and PRINTCON. If you never use CAPTURE, NPRINT, or PCONSOLE to print from outside network applications, you need not worry about PRINTDEF or PRINTCON. The exception is when you need to use various types of paper (forms) on the same printer. To handle this situation effectively, you must use PRINTDEF to define your forms.

Although CAPTURE, NPRINT, and PCONSOLE are separate utilities, they all recognize and use the print job configurations you establish with PRINTCON. The CAPTURE utility redirects output destined for a workstation's LPT port to the network for printing. NPRINT is a command-line utility to print a document from outside an application. By specifying various options in either CAPTURE or NPRINT, users can indicate which printer and queue they want to send files to, whether they want banners, form feeds, and timeouts, and so on. If these options are compiled into a print job configuration with PRINTCON, users can simply specify that configuration's name in the command rather than specifying each option individually. Thus, PRINTCON's print job configurations provide a time-saving way to specify these options in CAPTURE and NPRINT.

The PCONSOLE utility has its own set of defaults for printing jobs. However, if you define print job configurations with PRINTCON, you can make these configurations available for other users to select when printing a file from within PCONSOLE. (See Chapter 19 for information about using PCONSOLE to set up printing.)

While these printing utilities have been updated to work with Novell print servers, they have not changed significantly in use or in function from previous versions. If you've just upgraded to NetWare v3.11 from either NetWare v2.1x or NetWare v3.0, you'll notice some nice additions since those releases. We will point out these enhancements where applicable in our discussion of the various utilities in this chapter.

Establishing Printer Definitions with PRINTDEF

Most network applications include printer-specific drivers that handle all of a printer's functions for you. These functions often include the selection of fonts, their appearance (bold, italics, compressed), printing orientation (up-and-down or sideways), and emulation modes for standard printer types (such as Epson, IBM ProPrinter, and Hewlett-Packard PCL).

However, a new printer may have additional functionality that your application does not address. Or you may find that a printer does not reset properly after certain jobs are printed. For example, when users print sideways spreadsheets and standard business letters on the same printer, the letters might come out sideways if the printer doesn't reset to its default fonts after printing a spreadsheet. Another tricky situation arises when you must print to different types of preprinted forms (such as invoices, statements, and checks) on the same printer.

The NetWare PRINTDEF utility can help you overcome these types of problems. With PRINTDEF, you can create your own "print driver" customized for network use. Specifically, you define four aspects of a network printer:

- You first define the printer itself as a network print *device*, giving it a logical name.

- For each print device, you define a set of basic *functions*. A function is typically a sequence of escape codes that tell the printer what to do (reset, eject page, set fixed spacing, and so on).

- You then combine various functions into output *modes*. A print mode defines how you want a job to be printed (for example, draft mode, letter quality mode, and so on). One essential mode is the "reinitialize" mode to reset the printer.

- With PRINTDEF, you can also define various *forms*, or types of paper, that the printer will use. Examples of forms include letter-size bond, continuous-feed checks, wide green-bar paper, and so on.

Once defined, the printer device and its functions and modes are stored in a Printer Definition File (one with a .PDF extension). You can then import this information into a special PRINTDEF database named NET$PRN.DAT, located in the file server's SYS:PUBLIC directory.

A forewarning is appropriate here: setting up devices, functions, modes, and forms involves some effort on your part. You must be familiar with ASCII characters and control symbols, and you'll probably have to spend quite a bit of time poring over your printer's manuals. However, PRINTDEF does provide some tools for making the process as painless as possible, as we'll explain a little later.

Also, with NetWare v3.x, Novell provides predefined printer functions for a number of commonly used printers. If you happen to have one of these printers, much of the work in PRINTDEF is already done for you; you can simply import the predefined functions into the PRINTDEF database on your file server (the exact procedure is explained later in this chapter).

Here is the list of printers whose printer definition files (files with a .PDF extension) are included with NetWare v3.11. The .PDF files are automatically copied into SYS:PUBLIC during installation.

Apple Imagewriter II	HP LaserJet III/IIID
Apple Laserwriter II/Plus	HP LaserJet IIIsi-PCL
Citizen 120-D	HP LaserJet IIIsi-PostScript
Citizen 20	IBM ProPrinter 4201
Citizen 224	IBM ProPrinter II/XL
CItoh 310/315	NEC Spinwriter 2050/3050
CItoh 600	NEC Spinwriter 8810/8830
Diablo 630	NEC Pinwriter P-6
Epson FX80/FX100	Okidata Microline 192/193
Epson FX-800	Okidata 290
Epson FX86e/FX286e	Okidata 390
Epson LD-2500	Okidata Laserline 6
Epson LQ-800/LQ-1000	Panasonic 1080/1080i
Epson LX-80	Panasonic 1091/1091i

Epson LX-800
HP LaserJet I/II
HP LaserJet II/IID
HP LaserJet (PostScript)

Star NX-1000
Star Gemini 10X
Toshiba P321

Starting PRINTDEF

To start PRINTDEF, log in as SUPERVISOR or equivalent and type **PRINTDEF** **<Enter>** at the command line. The "PrintDef Options" menu appears on screen

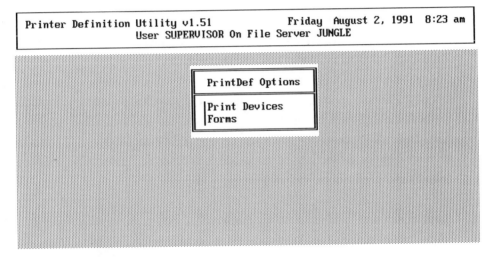

```
Printer Definition Utility v1.51          Friday  August 2, 1991  8:23 am
                    User SUPERVISOR On File Server JUNGLE
```

```
            PrintDef Options

            Print Devices
            Forms
```

Defining a Print Device

You can define print devices in any of three ways:

- Import NetWare's predefined print device definitions for one or more of the printers listed above.

- Copy print device definitions that are already set up on another file server.

- Set up your own print device definitions where they don't already exist.

Follow the instructions in the appropriate section below for the method you have chosen.

519

Importing Predefined Print Definitions

1. If necessary, start PRINTDEF by typing **PRINTDEF** <Enter> at your worksta
   tion. Then select "Print Devices" from PRINTDEF's main menu.

2. Choose "Import Print Device" from the "Print Device Options" menu.

3. In the "Source Directory" box, type **SYS:PUBLIC<Enter>**.

4. From the list of available PDFs, select the one that corresponds to your print
   device. If you select a file with the same name as an existing .PDF file in your
   server's SYS:PUBLIC directory, a "New Device Name" entry box will appear.
   Type a modified name in this box and press <Enter>.

5. Once the PDF is imported, check to see which functions and modes are included
   for the device. (To see the functions and modes already defined, select the device
   name from the list produced when you choose "Edit Print Devices." If you want
   to create additional functions or modes, do so as described under "Creating Your
   Own Printer Definitions" below.)

6. Press <Esc> until you return to the main menu. You're now ready to define
   forms, as explained under "Defining Print Forms" below.

Copying Existing Print Definitions

You can copy only one print device definition at a time from another file server's
NET$PRN.DAT file. Since the database may contain several device definitions, first
export the one you want into a .PDF file; then you can import this .PDF file into your
server's NET$PRN.DAT file.

1. Attach to the other file server as SUPERVISOR or equivalent (using the
   NetWare ATTACH command).

2. Start PRINTDEF and select "Print Devices" from the main menu.

3. Choose "Export Print Device" from the "Print Device Options" menu.

4. Select the device definition you want to copy to your file server. Then, in the "Destination Directory" box, type the directory path to your file server's SYS:PUBLIC directory (for example, JUNGLE/SYS:PUBLIC) and press <Enter>.

5. In the "Export File Name" box, type a valid name for the file you are exporting. The name must be no more than eight characters long, with no extension. It is a good idea to use a name that describes the type of printer, such as QMSPS810. Then press <Enter>.

6. Press <Esc> to return to the "Print Device Options" menu.

7. Now choose "Import Print Device" from the "Print Device Options" menu.

8. In the "Source Directory" box, type "SYS:PUBLIC" and press <Enter>. The .PDF file you just exported should now be included in the list of available printer definition files. Select it and check to see which functions and modes are included for the device. (To see the functions and modes already defined, select the device name from the list produced when you choose "Edit Print Devices." If you want to create additional functions or modes, do so as described under "Creating Your Own Printer Definitions," which follows.)

9. Press <Esc> until you're back at the main menu. You're now ready to define forms, as explained under "Defining Print Forms" below.

Creating Your Own Printer Definitions

1. Select "Print Devices" from PRINTDEF's main menu.

2. Choose "Edit Print Devices" from the "Print Device Options" menu.

3. When the list of "Defined Print Devices" appears, press <Ins> to add a new print device.

4. In the "New Device Name" box, enter a logical name for the printer. Print device names must be unique and cannot be more than 32 characters long. For example, suppose your LAN already has an IBM ProPrinter (named "IBM ProPrinter") and a Hewlett-Packard LaserJet printer (named "LaserJet1"). If you are adding a second LaserJet printer, you could assign it a name such as "LaserJet2." Press <Enter> after you type in the name.

5. Select the new printer name from the list of available printers. (You can also select an existing device from this list to add new function and mode definitions for that printer.)

Defining Device Functions

Print device functions are a series of control code sequences that the printer can interpret as commands or instructions. These control codes, or escape sequences, are usually documented in the printer's manual. With PRINTDEF, you define each function once and save those definitions for use by all current (and future) users.

Before we get into the actual steps for defining functions, we need to explain a little about PRINTDEF's delimiters. These delimiters are necessary because, unfortunately, printer manufacturers do not adhere to any common standard in establishing escape sequences for their printers. An escape sequence that means one thing to one type of printer may mean something completely different to another printer. To make matters worse, many printers require extended ASCII characters to build their escape sequence strings.

PRINTDEF handles the problem of entering extended ASCII characters by using delimiters. Delimiters allow you to group a string of characters into a single control character that both PRINTDEF and the printer will understand. The delimiters "<" and ">" say to PRINTDEF, "Any characters within these two delimiters represent one byte or ASCII character of the printer's escape sequence." For example, PRINTDEF interprets the string "<SOH>" as a single character with the ASCII value of 1. The mnemonic SOH, which stands for "Start Of Header," represents the Ctrl-B control character (see Figure 20-1).

With PRINTDEF's delimiters, then, you can enter printer control codes in whatever format you are used to. Those with previous experience in defining printers, using font editors, or creating special batch files often have their own method for representing control code sequences. Some people are accustomed to using numbers; others prefer ASCII mnemonics; still others prefer to use control characters. PRINTDEF will understand any of these methods, as long as the instructions appear within the PRINTDEF delimiters "<" and ">".

Although PRINTDEF portrays ASCII control symbols in acronym form, you may enter them in most any manner you wish. PRINTDEF also accepts two other types of delimiters to designate an ASCII character: a caret (^) followed by a character, or a backslash (\) followed by a decimal number value. For example, a Ctrl-U (^U) is the equivalent of the ASCII NAK (Negative Acknowledge) character which has a decimal value of 21. Figure 20-1 lists ASCII/control character equivalences and their delimiter acronyms.

Delim Acronym	ASCII Value	Ctrl Char	Delim Acronym	ASCII Value	Ctrl Char
<NUL>	0		<DC1>	17	^Q
<SOH>	1	^A	<DC2>	18	^R
<STX>	2	^B	<DC3>	19	^S
<ETX>	3	^C	<DC4>	20	^T
<EOT>	4	^D	<NAK>	21	^U
<ENQ>	5	^E	<SYN>	22	^V
<ACK>	6	^F	<ETB>	23	^W
<BEL>	7	^G	<CAN>	24	^X
<BS>	8	^H	<EM>	25	^Y
<HT>	9	^I	<SUB>	26	^Z
<LF>	10	^J	<ESC>	27	
<VT>	11	^K	<FS>	28	
<FF>	12	^L	<GS>	29	
<CR>	13	^M	<RS>	30	
<SO>	14	^N	<US>	31	
<SI>	15	^O	<SP>	32	
<DLE>	16	^P	<DEL>	127	

Figure 20-1: ASCII/control character equivalences and their corresponding delimiter acronyms.

If you need additional help with PRINTDEF delimiters, a full explanation is provided in the utility's help screens. Simply highlight the "Escape Sequence" field when you get to it and press <Enter>; then press the <F1> key to access the on-line help.

Here are the steps for defining new device functions for your printer.

1. Choose "Device Functions" from the "Edit Device Options" menu.

2. To define a new function, press <Ins> in the printer "Functions" window. The following form appears, containing two fields:

```
┌─────────────────────────────────────────────────────┐
│              Function Definition Form                │
├─────────────────────────────────────────────────────┤
│                                                      │
│   Name:                                              │
│                                                      │
│   Escape Sequence:                                   │
│                                                      │
└─────────────────────────────────────────────────────┘
```

3. In the "Name" field, type a name for the function. It is best to use the name given in the printer's manual. Function names must be unique for a given device, but two different devices can have functions with the same names.

4. In the "Escape Sequence" field, type the escape codes (as given in the printer's manual) that instruct the printer to perform this particular function. You have some leeway, as discussed above, in entering the escape sequences. You can insert as many escape sequences as needed in the "Escape Sequence" field.

5. When both fields contain the desired information, press <Esc> and then <Enter> to add the new entry to the list of functions.

6. Repeat Steps 2 through 5 for each function listed in the printer's manual. Note that NetWare can pass function codes to the printer only at the beginning or end

of a print job. Therefore, it is best to define only those functions that affect an entire document.

7. After inserting all necessary functions for the printer, press <Esc> to leave the "Functions" window and return to the "Edit Device Options" menu. Now you're ready to combine the print functions into print modes.

Defining Print Modes

The new list of printer functions defined above allows you to set up the modes of operation for entire print jobs. Common modes include a "reinitialize" mode that resets the printer to its default state, a "draft quality" mode for printing draft copies of long files quickly, a "letter quality" mode for printing the final output copy, and a "condensed" mode for printing spreadsheets or other reports with lots of columns. The exact modes you can define depend on the capabilities of the printer.

Here is an example of how to set up a mode for printing spreadsheet files.

1. Select "Device Modes" from the "Edit Device Options" menu.

2. Enter a name for the mode, such as "spreadsheet."

3. The resulting list of functions that you will associate with that mode appears, initially empty. Press <Ins> to display the list of all available functions.

4. Choose a function from this list. If necessary, you can choose several functions at once by highlighting each one and pressing <F5>. After marking the functions you require, press <Enter> to move those functions into the new list for the "spreadsheet" mode.

5. Note that the functions you moved appear in alphabetical order. Some modes require that the functions take place in a particular order. For instance, a printer might allow you to have the "emphasized" and the "compressed" functions in that order, so that you get text that is both emphasized and compressed. But if

you list the compressed function before the emphasized function, you will get only the compressed capability.

For these situations, you can reorder the entries as follows:

- One at a time, delete any entry that appears out of order by highlighting that entry and pressing <Del>. When you delete an entry, it reappears in the list of available functions.

- Highlight the entry that the deleted function should be in front of and press <Ins>.

- Now select the previously deleted function from the "Available Functions" list. PRINTDEF will insert it into the appropriate place in the new list, rather than appending it to the end of the list.

- Once the functions for the "spreadsheet" mode are complete and in the correct order, save the mode by pressing <Esc>. Follow these same steps to define the next mode.

The Reinitialize Mode. One important print mode for every network printer is the "reinitialize" mode. Not all applications are courteous enough to leave the printer in the same state they found it. For this reason, it's a good idea to define and use a reinitialize mode for each network printer.

For some printers, such as the HP LaserJet, the reset function is as simple as the escape sequence "<ESC>E" (note the use of the PRINTDEF delimiters). Other printers, however, don't include a reset function. In this case, you must instruct the printer to cancel any functions that may have been set by other applications or modes. Here is an example of how such a reinitialize mode would look for the IBM ProPrinter.

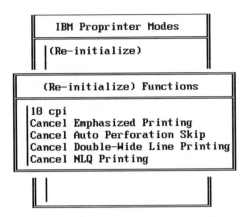

Defining Print Forms

You should define a print form for each type of paper that could possibly be loaded into your network printers. Common types of paper include letter-size bond paper, continuous-feed paper, address labels, preprinted accounting forms, and so on.

NetWare identifies forms by the name and number you assign to them. When users send a print job that requires a certain form, the print server will wait until that form is mounted on the printer before printing the job. Printing on different forms is a lot easier if you stick to only one form per printer. For instance, have one printer dedicated to printing checks and leave the preprinted check paper loaded in that printer all the time. Use another printer for printing out letters and other reports on letter size paper. That way, you or your users won't have to stop in between each print job and load the required type of paper.

Important: If you define several forms for the file server with PRINTDEF, make sure you provide your users a list of valid form names and form numbers. Depending on the queue's service mode, designating an invalid form number in a NetWare printing command can halt all printing in the specified print queue until a print server operator issues a "mount form" command. For example, suppose you define forms 0 through 2, but a user includes the "Form=5" option in a CAPTURE or NPRINT command to send a print job to queue LASERWRITER.

If the default service mode of "Change forms as needed" is ineffect, print jobs will back up in LASERWRITER, waiting for the nonexistent form 5 to be loaded. In previous versions of NetWare, you had to reboot the server to get around this problem. In NetWare v3.11, have the print server operator issue the PSC command with the "MO F=5" option, as explained under "The MOUNT FORM Option" later in this chapter.

1. To define a print form, select "Forms" from PRINTDEF's main menu.

2. Press <Ins> to bring up the "Form Definition" box. As indicated on the screen, you define each form in terms of a name, number, length (lines per page), and width (characters per line).

```
┌─────────────────────────────────────────┐
│            Form Definition               │
├─────────────────────────────────────────┤
│  Name                                    │
│                                          │
│  Number                                  │
│                                          │
│  Length                                  │
│                                          │
│  Width                                   │
│                                          │
└─────────────────────────────────────────┘
```

3. In the "Name" field, type a name for the form. The name can be up to 12 characters long. The first letter must be alphabetic, and the name cannot contain spaces.

4. Type a number in the "Number" field. The form number can be any number between 0 and 255. Assign form number 0 (the default) to the most commonly used type of paper.

5. In the "Length" field, type the length of the form. The length indicates how many lines there are per page. The number depends on how many lines per inch

the printer is set to print. For a printer set at six lines per inch, a sheet of paper 11 inches long would contain 66 lines per page. The maximum length is 255.

6.   In the "Width" field, type the width of the form. The width indicates how many characters can be printed on a full line from one edge of the paper to the other. The number depends on how many characters per inch (cpi) the printer is set to print. For a printer set at 10 cpi, a sheet of paper 8.5 inches wide could have 85 characters per line.

7.   Press <Esc> to leave the "Form Definition" box. Answer "Yes" to the "Save Changes" prompt.

Repeat the above procedure for each form. Keep a record of which form number you assign to which type of paper so you can refer to it when changing paper in the printers.

Saving the PRINTDEF Database

Once you have defined all the modes and forms you need for your network print devices, press <Esc> until you see the "Exit PrintDef" prompt. Answer "Yes" to this prompt. Then choose "Save Data Base, then EXIT" to save your new print definitions.

If you created your own printer definitions, one last step remains. That step is to import your .PDF file into the NET$PRN.DAT file on your file server. Use the steps listed under "Importing Predefined Print Definitions" above to import the definitions from your new .PDF file.

At this point, you have saved all your printer definitions and forms in the NET$PRN.DAT file. You are now ready to go into PRINTCON, where you combine the modes and forms into print job configurations that users can use with CAPTURE, NPRINT, and PCONSOLE.

Creating Print Job Configurations with PRINTCON

NetWare's CAPTURE, NPRINT, and PCONSOLE printing utilities have many possible options. When using these utilities to print files, users can specify which printer they are sending the job to, by file server and print queue name. They can also specify what form (type of paper) to use and whether the job requires a form feed after each page. All these possibilities (and more) are part of a print job's "configuration," which specifies how and where files are printed.

Frequently, users prefer a particular configuration, but they find it difficult to type all the options every time they want to print a document. They may also forget to reconfigure the printer for their job after a previous user's print job is finished.

The PRINTCON utility permits you to predefine commonly used print job configurations so users can more easily set the options available in CAPTURE, NPRINT, and PCONSOLE. You can then make the configurations defined with PRINTCON available to your users as standard choices. Users can choose the configuration that fits a particular document without wasting time specifying the individual print command options.

PRINTCON stores its data in a file called PRINTCON.DAT stored in each user's mail directory on the primary server they log in to. Users can connect to other servers, but the directory with their PRINTCON data remains on that primary server.

Since PRINTCON uses the print devices and modes defined in PRINTDEF, you should run PRINTDEF first. Also, you should already have the network printers set up with print queues on the file server (see Chapter 19).

Starting PRINTCON

To start the PRINTCON utility, type **PRINTCON <Enter>** at the command line. PRINTCON's "Available Options" menu appears:

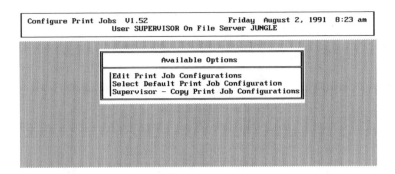

```
Configure Print Jobs  V1.52                 Friday  August 2, 1991  8:23 am
                    User SUPERVISOR On File Server JUNGLE

                           Available Options
              Edit Print Job Configurations
              Select Default Print Job Configuration
              Supervisor - Copy Print Job Configurations
```

Creating a New Print Job Configuration

Here are the steps involved in making a "Normal" print-job configuration containing all the default settings.

1. Select the "Edit Print Job Configurations" option. If this is the first time you have run PRINTCON, the resulting screen will be blank because you haven't defined any configurations yet.

2. Press <Ins> to indicate that you want to define a new printer configuration.

3. Type a name for the print job configuration in the "Enter New Name" box. Give each configuration a unique, descriptive name. Users should be able to infer from the configuration's name what its purpose is.

    As an example, let's define a general-purpose configuration that users can select for most print jobs; type the name "Normal" in the "Enter New Name" box and press <Enter>.

The "Edit Print Job Configuration" Window

At this point, an "Edit Print Job Configuration" window appears on the screen. This window is the main workspace in PRINTCON. Each field in the Edit window has a default setting already entered (see the sample screen below). These default settings are suitable for a wide variety of situations, but you can change them as you see fit.

```
╔══════════════════════════════════════════════════════════════════╗
║            Edit Print Job Configuration "Normal"                   ║
╟────────────────────────────────────────────────────────────────────╢
║ Number of copies:   1              Form name:        (None defined)  ║
║ File contents:      Byte stream    Print banner:     No              ║
║ Tab size:                          Banner name:                      ║
║ Suppress form feed: No             Banner file:                      ║
║ Notify when done:   No                                               ║
║                                                                      ║
║ Local printer:      1              Enable timeout:   No              ║
║ Auto endcap         No             Timeout count:                    ║
║                                                                      ║
║ File server:        JUNGLE                                           ║
║ Print queue:        PRINTQ_0                                         ║
║ Print server:       (None)                                          ║
║ Device:             (None)                                          ║
║ Mode:               (None)                                          ║
╚══════════════════════════════════════════════════════════════════╝
```

To move around in PRINTCON's Edit window, use the arrow keys to take you from field to field. Or you can use the Tab key to go from item to item. To see on-line help for an entry, position the cursor in a field and press <F1>.

PRINTCON's Options

Here is a brief explanation of PRINTCON's configuration options.

Number of Copies. The first entry on the screen is "Number of copies." For most print jobs (including our "Normal" example), you'll only want one copy printed. However, if you always need three copies of a certain report, you could type in the number "3" and press <Enter>. You can specify any number from 1 to 65,000.

File Contents. The "File contents" option offers two choices: "Byte Stream" or "Text." The default setting, "Byte Stream," assumes you are printing a file that was already formatted for the printer within an application such as WordPerfect or Lotus 1-2-3. This is also the setting to use when your job must download fonts on a laser printer. With this setting, NetWare simply passes along the data to the printer in a continuous stream without altering it in any way.

Change this setting to "Text" when you are sending files that consist of plain ASCII characters—with no proprietary control codes—to the printer. This is the case when you print a DOS text file. With this setting, NetWare converts tabs to spaces as it sends the data to the printer.

Tab Size. The "Tab size" option applies only if you chose "Text" as your "File contents" setting. The number you enter determines the size of tabs in the printed output. NetWare will change tabs into the specified number of spaces when the file is sent to the printer.

Suppress Form Feed. When continuous-feed paper is loaded on a printer, a "form feed" command causes the printer to advance to the top of the next page at the end of the print job. On a sheet-fed printer, where you load individual sheets of paper in a stack, a form feed causes the printer to eject a blank page. Most laser printers are sheet-fed, whereas dot matrix printers use continuous-feed paper.

The default setting of "No" for PRINTCON's "Suppress form feed" option allows the printer to advance to the next page after each job. This prevents one user's job from starting to print on the last page of the previous user's job. Set this option to "Yes" only if you find that the printer is ejecting an extra blank sheet at the end of certain jobs. This may occur with applications that automatically include a form feed at the end of a print job.

Notify When Done. The Notify feature is new in PRINTCON. Set this parameter to "Yes" if you want NetWare to send a message to the job owner when the file has finished printing. The message appears just like any other broadcast message at the bottom of the user's monitor screen. The default is "No."

Form Name. In the "Form name" field, you can specify which type of paper to use for the print job. If you didn't define any forms with the PRINTDEF utility, the field will indicate "(None defined)" and the print jobs will use whatever paper is currently loaded in the printer at the time. If you did define forms in PRINTDEF, press <Enter> in the field to bring up a list of these forms; select the form you want from this list.

Note that the form names listed depend on which file server is selected in the "File server" field. PRINTCON reads the form definitions from that server's NET$PRN.DAT file, so if you change servers, the available forms might also change.

Print Banner. By default, NetWare prints a banner page as the first page of a print job. The banner page identifies the document and the user who printed the document. NetWare has a default banner format that includes the user's login name and the name of the file being printed. (A sample banner page is shown later in this chapter.) This banner page helps users tell where one job ends and the next one begins when several jobs come out of the printer in rapid sequence.

If you don't want a banner page printed, change the "Print banner" setting to "No."

Banner Name and Banner File. When "Print banner" is set to "Yes," these two other banner options allow you to customize the banner. For example, if you are logged in as SUPERVISOR, you may want to change the name on your banner from "SUPERVISOR" to your name, thus differentiating you from other users that might log in as SUPERVISOR. If you want some other text to replace the file name on the banner, enter a different name in the "Banner file" field. Both of these entries can be up to 12 characters long.

Settings Used Only with CAPTURE

The settings thus far have been for options used by PCONSOLE, CAPTURE, and NPRINT. The parameters listed in the middle section of the "Edit Print Job Configuration" window apply only to the CAPTURE utility.

Local Printer. The "Local printer" option specifies which LPT device on the workstation (LPT1, LPT2, or LPT3) will be redirected by CAPTURE to a network printer. CAPTURE can intercept output destined for any LPT port, even if the workstation has no parallel port actually installed. The default is LPT1.

Auto Endcap. The "Auto endcap" option partly determines when the file will actually be sent to the printer. Setting this option to "Yes" causes captured data to print when you exit the current application. Setting it to "No" delays the printing of captured data until the user issues the ENDCAP command (or, if you enable timeout below, until the specified time has elapsed). "Yes" is the default setting.

Enable Timeout. The "Enable timeout" option determines when captured data will be printed in a subtly different manner from the "Auto endcap" option. Setting "Enable timeout" to "Yes" causes captured data to be printed automatically after a certain time period has elapsed, beginning with the last time printing occurred. Thus, you can print captured data without having to exit the application.

Timeout Count. If you set "Enable timeout" to "Yes," set the "Timeout count" also by entering a number from 1 to 1,000. The "Timeout count" is the number of seconds before captured data is automatically sent to the printer. With Timeout enabled, captured data will be printed when the Timeout Count is up, regardless of what you are doing in your application.

Precautions for the CAPTURE Options

The interplay between the Autoendcap and Timeout features can be tricky. If both "Autoendcap" and "Enable timeout" are set to "No," *nothing* will print until the user exits the application and runs ENDCAP. If both "Auto endcap" and "Enable timeout" are set to "Yes," data sent to the printer will be printed either when the user exits the current application, after the Timeout Count has expired, or when the user runs ENDCAP.

In some cases, you should not use timeouts to print captured data. Printing initiated by a timeout, and then interrupted by the current application, usually causes output problems. Typically, these cases occur when the current application interrupts its own printing process. For example, in WordPerfect 5.x, if you start to print a job and then go into layout mode, printing will stop for the entire time you are in layout. This problem is unavoidable in WordPerfect because the printing and layout functions share common code.

Don't use Autoendcap or Timeout when you are using CAPTURE to save screen dumps from applications to a network file that you plan to print later. If you are capturing to a file and a timeout occurs, CAPTURE closes the file and sends subsequent output to the network printer—whether you want it to or not. If you want to capture screens from several applications to a file and Autoendcap is enabled, CAPTURE closes the file and sends subsequent output to the network printer after you exit the first application.

Each case—applications that interrupt their own printing process and users who capture to a file instead of printing immediately—causes the same basic problem. At some point, the shell decides that the capture is complete and sends it to the printer. However, the capture isn't complete, and the result is unacceptable hard copy.

Specifying the Queue, Printer, and Modes

The options at the bottom of PRINTCON's edit screen allow you to specify which print queue the job goes to, which printer (device) will print the job, and which PRINTDEF mode the job will use.

File Server. The "File server" option allows you to specify which file server's print queues you want to print to. (Remember, print queues are defined on the file server, not on the print server or printer). Highlight this field and press <Enter> to view a list of current file servers. Choose the file server you want from this list.

Print Queue. Once you have chosen a file server, you must choose a queue. As explained in the previous chapter, a queue is a physical location on the server where print jobs are stored until the printer is ready for them. Highlight the "Print queue" field and press <Enter> to display a list of available queues on the selected file server. Select the appropriate one. (It helps to assign descriptive names to your print queues, such as "Dot_Matrix" or "Laser_Jet.")

Print Server. If more than one print server is attached to the queue you selected, you can choose which one you want to handle your job. Highlight the field and press <Enter> for a list of print servers to choose from. The default of "(None)" means that any available print server can handle your job.

Device. The "Device" option allows you to select a printer from those authorized to service the specified queue on the specified server. You establish print queue-printer authorization in PCONSOLE, while device names are defined in PRINTDEF. Highlight the field and press <Enter> to get a list of print devices. Choose the type of printer you want for this configuration. Leaving the field set to "(None)" will allow any printer authorized to service the print queue to print your job.

Mode. Specifying a mode in the "Mode" field can help you eliminate instances where users disrupt each other's printing. A mode is a specific kind of printing output defined in PRINTDEF—compressed mode, for example. To view the list of modes defined in the selected file server's PRINTDEF database, highlight the field and press <Enter>. If you leave this field set to "(None)," the job will be printed in whatever mode the printer happens to be in at the time.

Saving the New Configuration

Your "Normal" configuration is now complete. Press <Esc> and answer "Yes" to the prompt asking if you want to save this configuration.

Use the same procedure for creating other configurations. For example, if you use Lotus 1-2-3, you might wish to create a configuration called "Lotus" for printing spreadsheet files with CAPTURE, NPRINT, or PCONSOLE.

Designating the Default Configuration

PRINTCON designates one configuration as the default. The default configuration is simply the set of print options that NPRINT, CAPTURE, and PCONSOLE will use whenever users fail to specify another configuration. The first configuration you create is automatically designated as the default.

You can change the default configuration by choosing "Select Default Print Job Configuration" from PRINTCON's main menu. When the default print job window appears, select the configuration that you want for the default.

PRINTCON will not allow you to delete the default configuration. You can change the default and delete the old default, but there must always be one default configuration.

Copying Your Configurations for Other Users

Once you've defined print job configurations for yourself, you'll want to make them available to your users. You can do this by selecting "Supervisor -Copy Print Job Configuration" from PRINTCON's main menu. Copying print configurations in this way saves a lot of time. If you (or another user on the file server) set up PRINTCON configurations that other users want to use, PRINTCON can send any user's already defined configurations straight to any other user's mail subdirectory, where they will be accessible to that user.

Choose "Supervisor - Copy Print Job Configuration" from the main menu. You will be prompted to select a source user and a target user. For the source user, type the name of the user whose print job configurations you want to copy. The target user is the user to whom you are copying the configurations. You're essentially packaging the source user's PRINTCON file and sending it to the target user. This is more efficient than having each user create his or her own PRINTCON file.

If the target user already has something defined in PRINTCON, and you copy over to it, you wipe out what was there. Therefore, it's important for you to check with your users before you copy a PRINTCON configuration file over a particular user's own configuration file.

Specifying PRINTCON Configurations in NetWare Utilities

When users issue the NPRINT command without specifying a configuration, NPRINT reverts to the default configuration specified in PRINTCON. If they include the print job configuration option in the command (as in **NPRINT filename j=lotus**), NPRINT goes to PRINTCON and runs that specific configuration ("Lotus" in this example).

The CAPTURE command works with PRINTCON just as NPRINT does. If users type only "CAPTURE," any printing uses the default printer configuration. However, if they include the print job configuration option in the command (as in **CAPTURE j=lotus copies=5**), CAPTURE uses that particular configuration for printing. There is no need to specify things like tab settings, forms, or banners unless you want to change a parameter. In the example above, typing "copies=5" from the command line temporarily changes the "Number of copies" parameter in the "Lotus" configuration to 5.

From PCONSOLE, you can also assign different print configurations to jobs in the queue. First select "Print Queue Information" from the main menu. Then select the appropriate print queue and choose "Current Print Job Entries." Press <Ins> to add a job to this queue. Specify the directory of the file you want to print, then select that file. PCONSOLE will list your PRINTCON configurations and let you choose from them as well.

Using the CAPTURE Command

The NetWare CAPTURE command takes the place of the v2.0x SPOOL command for printing on the network. The CAPTURE command gives supervisors and users alike the ability to redirect output originally destined for a workstation's LPT ports to network printers, queues, or files. CAPTURE can redirect the output of up to three LPT ports (LPT1, LPT2, and LPT3) to various print queues or files at the same time. CAPTURE recognizes these three LPT devices as logical connections; the workstation need not have the actual LPT ports installed. By redirecting LPT ports with CAPTURE, you can print to network printers from applications that are not designed to run on a network.

CAPTURE is not usually necessary to print from applications designed to run on NetWare. With a network version of an application, the application sends print jobs directly to the network printers, rather than requiring NetWare to "intercept" jobs intended for a local printer. For example, you can set up the network version of WordPerfect so that users can select network printers as easily as if the printers were attached directly to their workstations. Network applications typically offer faster printing, increased font and formatting options, and easier printer management. Use network versions of applications whenever possible to avoid having to use CAPTURE.

There are cases, however, when you might want to use CAPTURE even with network versions of applications. CAPTURE offers a convenient way for users to print to queues on a different file server from the server they initially log in to. When you use a print server, for example, to service print jobs on more than one file server, you can use various CAPTURE commands to redirect print jobs to the appropriate printer. By using CAPTURE, users can redirect all print jobs to the server and printer most convenient for them to use. See "Using CAPTURE with Network Applications" below for other examples.

To use CAPTURE for non-network applications, you must know which LPT port the application is designed to print to. Some applications, which we'll call "dumb" applications, print only to LPT1, which is also the port to which the <Shift><PrintScrn> keyboard command prints. "Smart" applications have a SETUP or INSTALL program that allows supervisors to designate which LPT port to send print jobs to. Any application that allows you to designate a printer port can be called a smart application. The network version of Lotus 1-2-3 is an example of a smart application.

If an application does print to a port other than LPT1, make sure the CAPTURE command intercepts data at the correct port. If you change an application to print at an LPT port other than LPT1, be sure to use the correct CAPTURE options so that CAPTURE knows where to intercept that application's print requests.

CAPTURE's Options

The CAPTURE utility offers a number of options that you can add to the basic command. With these CAPTURE options, you can specify which file server, print queue, print job configuration, or printer you want to use. You can also set printing specifics, such as number of copies, tabs, banners, text names, form feeds, autoendcaps, and timeouts.

Here is a brief explanation of each of CAPTURE's options. With the exception of the "SHow" option, you can include more than one option in the same CAPTURE command. The order of the options is not important.

Specifying Where Data Will Be Printed

The following CAPTURE options allow you to specify which file server, printer, and print queue the captured data will be sent to.

Queue. Most of the time, it is sufficient to specify only the print queue you want your captured data sent to by including "Q=*QueueName*" in the CAPTURE command. NetWare assumes the queue is on your current default server. If you don't specify a queue, data will be sent to whatever queue you assigned for Spooler 0 with the SPOOL command.

Server. Include "S=*ServerName*" in the CAPTURE command if you want to send data to a print queue created on a file server other than your default file server. (Notice that this is file server, not print server. You cannot specify particular print server names in CAPTURE.)

CAPTURE no longer supports the "P=*n*" option as it did in previous versions. Train your users to send print jobs to queues rather than to printers or print servers.

Local. Include "L=*n*" in the CAPTURE command to indicate which "logical" LPT port you want to redirect data from. Replace *n* with 1, 2, or 3 (the default is 1). With CAPTURE, you can redirect data destined to LPT1, LPT2, or LPT3 even if your workstation does not have any parallel ports physically installed. CAPTURE cannot redirect data destined for a serial (COM) port.

Determining When Data Will Be Printed

The following options help determine when captured data will actually be sent to the printer. Normally, the LPT port remains captured and NetWare holds all redirected data until you issue the ENDCAP command. Only then is the data delivered to the print queue to be printed.

Autoendcap. When this option is enabled, CAPTURE will automatically end the capture without waiting for an ENDCAP command—but not until you exit an application. Every time you invoke the application's print commands, CAPTURE collects the data to be printed and holds it at the file server. When you exit the application, Autoendcap signals the file server to release all collected data and send it to the specified network print queue or printer.

Autoendcap is enabled by default. If you do not want to wait until you exit the application for files to be printed, include "NA" (for NoAutoendcap) in the CAPTURE command. To reenable Autoendcap, include the "A" option in a subsequent CAPTURE command.

Timeout. If Autoendcap is disabled, you can use the Timeout feature to tell CAPTURE how long to wait after you issue a print command within an application before the print job is closed and sent to the print queue. The default setting is "TI=0," or TImeout disabled. You can specify anywhere from 1 to 1,000 seconds for the Timeout count; for example, "TI=30" causes CAPTURE to wait 30 seconds before sending the job to the print queue.

When printing from within an application, it is generally best to set Autoendcap off and enable a timeout count appropriate for the particular application. For most applications, a short timeout of about five or 10 seconds should suffice. Desktop publishing applications like Ventura Publisher and PageMaker often need time to download fonts or format text before files are ready to be printed. To produce complicated reports, database applications might have to sort a large number of records before the report is ready to be printed. In cases like these, set a relatively long timeout count—30 seconds or more. A long timeout gives the DTP program time to format files properly and gives the database time to sort records between printing reports. If the timeout count is too short, you might get only part of your print job printed. You may need to experiment with various timeouts to find the right setting for your applications.

Keep. This option ensures that the file server will keep all redirected data even if your workstation hangs or loses power before closing the capture. You should include the "K" option whenever you plan to capture data over a long period of time (an hour or more). If your workstation does lose its file server connection before properly closing the capture, the server will wait 15 minutes, then send any partial data received to the specified print queue.

If you do not include the "K" option, the file server will discard any partially captured data 15 minutes after the workstation connection is lost.

Notify. The Notify option is a new feature of CAPTURE. Include the "NOTI" option if you want to receive a NetWare broadcast message when your job is finished printing. The message will indicate "*JobName* printed on *PrinterName*" so you know which job and printer it is referring to. With CAPTURE, the job name is usually the default "LPT1 Catch." If there is a problem with your job, NetWare will not notify you unless you were designated to receive such notifications in PCONSOLE.

If you enabled the notify option in a PRINTCON configuration and you want to override it, include the "NNOTI" option in the CAPTURE command.

Determining How Data Will Be Printed

The following options help determine how the captured data will be printed.

Job. If you have set up print job configurations in PRINTCON, you can avoid having to specify the various CAPTURE options individually by including "J=*ConfigurationName*" in the CAPTURE command. Replace *ConfigurationName* with the name of the PRINTCON print job configuration you want to use.

Copies. By including "C=*n*" in the CAPTURE command, you can specify how many copies of the job you want to print. The number of copies (*n*) can be from 1 to 256. The default is C=1.

Tabs. Most applications have a print formatter to handle margins, tabs, and other format parameters. If your application does not have a print formatter, you can include the "T=*n*" option in the CAPTURE command. The number you specify indicates how many spaces you want each tab converted to when the file prints. The number *n* can be from 0 to 18; the default is 8.

If you don't want tabs converted to spaces, include the "NT" (No Tabs) option in the CAPTURE command.

Banner Options. By default, CAPTURE inserts a banner page at the beginning of each print job. The top section of the banner page indicates the login name of the user who sent the print job, the file name and directory path, a description of the job, the date and time the job was sent, and the print queue and server that serviced the job. This information is followed by a large login name and a large banner description, as shown in this sample banner page:

```
***************************************************************************
*   User Name: KEN (3)              Queue: JUNGLE/LASERWRITER     *
*   File Name:                      Server JUN_PSERVER            *
*   Directory:                                                    *
*   Description: LPT1 Catch                                       *
*            August 2, 91 1:48pm *                                *
***************************************************************************
*                                                                *
*        K   K      EEEEE      N     N                            *
*        K   K      E          NN    N                            *
*        K  K       E          N N   N                            *
*        K K        EEEE       N  N  N                            *
*        K   K      E          N   NN                             *
*        K    K     E          N    N                             *
*        K    K     EEEEE      N    N                             *
*                                                                *
***************************************************************************
*                                                                *
*        L          SSSSS      TTTTT                             *
*        L          S            T                                *
*        L          S            T                                *
*        L          SSSSS        T                                *
*        L              S        T                                *
*        L              S        T                                *
*        LLLLL      SSSSS        T                                *
***************************************************************************
```

If you don't want a banner page printed, include "NB" in the CAPTURE command. If you do want a banner page, you can specify a different login name by including "NAME=*Name*" in the CAPTURE command. Replace Name with the user name you want to appear in large letters on the banner page. You can change the default "LST" string in the banner by including "B=*Banner*" in the CAPTURE command. Replace *Banner* with any text string up to 12 characters long. The string cannot contain spaces; use an underscore character to represent a space between words (for example, JOB_ONE).

Form Feed. By default, CAPTURE enables a form feed after each print job. Enabling form feed causes the printer to eject the final page of a print job, readying itself to begin the subsequent job at the top of the next form.

Some applications automatically eject the last page of a printed document, in which case CAPTURE's form feed will cause a blank page to be ejected after each document. To avoid wasting this extra sheet of paper, disable form feed by including "NFF" (No Form Feed) in the CAPTURE command. To re-enable form feed, include "FF" (Form Feed) in a subsequent CAPTURE command.

Form. If you have defined more than one form in the PRINTDEF utility, you can specify which form you want captured data printed on by including "F=*n*" in the CAPTURE command. Replace *n* with a valid form number. Alternatively, you can include "F=*FormName*" if you know the name assigned to the form.

Important: Train your users to specify only forms that have been defined in PRINTDEF. If they specify a nonexistent form, all printing in that print queue will halt and a print server operator will have to assist in getting the queue moving again (see "The MOUNT FORM Option" in the PSC portion of this chapter). If switching between forms becomes a lot of trouble, you can change the way the queue handles forms in PCONSOLE, as described in Chapter 19. Better yet, get another printer and use just one form per printer.

Capturing Data to a Network File

At times, you may want to save captured data to a file on the network, rather than sending the data directly to a printer. The "CR=*FileName*" option will create a file and save data to that file; replace *FileName* with a full directory path and file name, or just a file name if you want the file to be in your default directory.

The only other options you can include with "CR=*FileName*" are Autoendcap, No Autoendcap, TImeout, and Local. If you plan to save data from several applications to the same file, don't specify any Timeout and disable Autoendcap by including "NA" in the CAPTURE command. Use the ENDCAP command to signal the end of the data capturing session.

For example, to save a series of screen dumps to a file so you can include them in your customized user documentation, issue the following command before entering the application:

```
CAPTURE CR=SCREENS.CAP NA <Enter>
```

Enter the application. When the desired information appears on the screen, press <Shift><PrtScr>. CAPTURE will create the file SCREENS.CAP in your default directory (the directory you were in when you typed the CAPTURE command) and save the contents of the screen to that file. You can save as many screens as you want to the same file. When you are finished, exit the application and type **ENDCAP** **<Enter>** at the command line. The SCREENS.CAP file created is a DOS text file; you can print it out using either NPRINT or a word processor that handles DOS text files.

Viewing the Current CAPTURE Status

By including the "SHow" option, you can see the current settings used by the CAPTURE command. Typing **CAPTURE SH** will display information similar to this:

```
LPT1:  Capturing data to server JUNGLE queue LASERWRITER
       (printer 0)
       Capture Defaults:Enabled Automatic Endcap:Enabled
       Banner          :Form Feed            :Yes
       Copies          :1 Tabs               :Converted to 8
                                              spaces
       Form            :0  Timeout    Count :Disabled

LPT2:    Capturing Is Not Currently Active.

LPT3:    Capturing Is Not Currently Active.
```

You cannot include any other CAPTURE options with the "SH" option.

Using CAPTURE with Network Applications

As we mentioned earlier, CAPTURE (although designed primarily to let non-network applications print to network printers) can also be used to some advantage with network applications. Since network applications that take advantage of the NetWare environment can set up their own printing without CAPTURE, deciding when and how to use CAPTURE can be difficult. Most users just want network

example of how CAPTURE and a network application, such as WordPerfect 5.1, can work together on a network to alleviate some of the burden.

Suppose that supervisor Ryan is in charge of two file servers, ACCTG and ADMIN. User Eric belongs to a group named ADMIN that normally prints to an HP LaserJet printer through a queue named HPLASER defined on server ADMIN. From time to time, Eric logs in to server ACCTG and captures screen dumps into a file for an in-house manual he is working on.

Ryan has set up a CAPTURE command in the system login script for group ADMIN so they can print to the LaserJet printer on server ADMIN:

```
if member of "ADMIN" then begin
    #capture L=1 s=admin q=hplaser nb ti=3
end
```

The problem with this scenario is that when Eric wants to log in to ACCTG and capture his screen dumps by using <Shift><PrintScrn> (which automatically sends the contents of the screen to LPT1), he has to issue another CAPTURE command that redirects LPT1 output to a local file. Thus, he loses his LPT1 connection to the LaserJet printer on ADMIN.

There are several ways around this problem. The most obvious is to set up WordPerfect to print directly to the network printer. To do this, you enter WordPerfect's printer edit menu (press <Shift><F7>, choose "Select printer," then "Edit") and choose "Other" for the port designation. Then choose "Network printer" and specify the server and print queue names (ADMIN/HPLASER).

If you want to use CAPTURE to redirect WordPerfect's output (which defaults to LPT1) to a network printer, Eric can set up another CAPTURE command in a batch file and then switch back and forth between the default LPT1 capture to the network printer and the local file for his screen dumps. For example, a batch file named SCREENS.BAT could contain the command **CAPTURE L=1 CR=MANUAL1.SCR**. Another batch file, named RESET.BAT, would contain the same CAPTURE command as in the system login script (**CAPTURE L=1 S=ADMIN Q=HPLASER NB TI=3**). When Eric wants to do screen dumps, he attaches to server ACCTG and runs the SCREENS batch file. When he is finished, he runs RESET.BAT to return to his regular print jobs setting.

Using the ENDCAP Command

The ENDCAP command ends the effect of a CAPTURE command. Whatever printer port redirection was in effect at the workstation will be cancelled and the port will be returned to its normal status. Users might want to end CAPTURE to print to a locally attached printer for a while.

If you have set up an elaborate printing environment using CAPTURE commands in batch files or login scripts, train your users not to use ENDCAP indiscriminately. Many users will be unable to figure out why they all of a sudden can't print on the network anymore.

A new feature of ENDCAP is that you can specify which LPT port it will affect. This is useful if you have captured two or more LPT ports for different purposes.

For example, suppose you used CAPTURE to redirect LPT1 output to queue LASERWRITER and LPT2 output to a dot matrix printer through queue EPSON. To cancel the LPT1 capture while leaving LPT2 redirection in effect, type

```
ENDCAP L=1 <Enter>
```

You can also use the new "Cancel" option to end the capture of an LPT port and discard any data without it being printed. To use the above example, you would type

```
ENDCAP CL=1 <Enter>
```

To end the capture of all LPT ports, include "ALL" in place of a specific port number.

Using the NPRINT Command

NPRINT is a network printing command, similar to the DOS PRINT command. NPRINT allows you to send files to network printers without being in an application. Most of the time, you'll use NPRINT to print only DOS text files. Novell's documentation states that you can also use NPRINT to print files already formatted within an application for the printer you are sending them to. However, this does not work for very many of today's applications. Enhancements made to both printers and printing capabilities (soft fonts, PostScript fonts, and so on) over the past several years require print format codes too complex for NPRINT to handle correctly.

NPRINT's Options

NPRINT offers numerous options that you can add to the basic command. All but one of these options are the same as for CAPTURE. The duplicate options include:

Queue=*QueueName*
Server=*ServerName*
Job=*ConfigurationName*
Notify (NOTI)
No Notify (NNOTI)
Copies=*n*
Tabs=*n*
No Tabs (NT)
B=*Banner*
NAME=*UserName*
No Banner (NB)
 Form Feed (FF)
No Form Feed (NFF)
Form=*n* or *FormName*

NPRINT also offers a "Delete" option. Including "D" in the NPRINT command will automatically erase the file after it is printed.

Here's an example of how to use NPRINT to print the system login script. The system login script is stored as a DOS text file called NET$LOG.DAT in the SYS:PUBLIC directory. To send the file to queue LASERJET on the file server, type the following command at your workstation:

```
NPRINT SYS:PUBLIC\NET$LOG.DAT Q=LASERJET NB NFF <Enter>
```

The system login script will be printed with no banner (NB) and no form feed (NFF) at the end of the job.

Using the PSC Command

NetWare's PSC command gives you a quick way to check and control the status of your Novell print servers. To use all of the control options, you must be a designated print server operator for the print server. Print server users (the group EVERYONE by default) can use PSC to view the status of a network printer.

The basic command format for PSC is as follows:

```
PSC PS=PrintServer [P=n] Option
```

Replace *PrintServer* with the name of your print server, n with the number assigned to the printer in PCONSOLE, and *Option* with one of the PSC options listed below. If you leave out the printer number, PSC displays information about all printers associated with the print server.

Typing in the print server name and the printer number can get tedious, especially if you have only one print server and printer to control. To eliminate the need to include these parameters in the PSC command, type the following at the command-line prompt to set the name and number in a DOS environment variable:

```
SET PSC=PSPrintServer Pn <Enter>
```

You can also include this command in your AUTOEXEC.BAT file or in your login script to have it be automatically set when you start up your computer and log in to the network. If you put the command in your login script, remember to enclose everything after the equals sign in quotes.

You can override the default environment-variable print server and printer number by specifying a different server and number in the actual PSC command. The new server and number apply only to that command. Your defaults will still be in effect the next time you type a PSC command with no parameters.

PSC's Options

The PSC command has several options you can use to control the printer. These options are summarized below. You can abbreviate the options when you type them by including only those parts of the option names shown in capital letters.

The STAT Option

The "STATus" option causes PSC to display the current status of the network printer(s). For example, the command

```
PSC PS=ATPSERVER P=0 STAT <Enter>
```

displays information similar to the following about printer 0 on print server ATPSERVER:

```
Printer 0: LaserJet_III
Waiting for job
```

If you don't specify a printer number in the command, PSC will display information for all printers associated with the specified print server. If you specified a certain printer number as a DOS environment variable, include "P=all" in the PSC command to see all printers.

The message "Waiting for job" means the print server is active and ready to accept another print job. Other possible status messages are listed below.

Printing job	The printer is currently printing a job. Other status messages may accompany this one.
Off line	While printing a job, the printer was either turned off or someone switched it to off-line mode. (This message appears below the "Printing job" message on the screen.)
Out of paper	While printing a job, the printer ran out of paper. (This message appears below the "Printing job" message on the screen.)
Not installed	No printer has been installed for this printer number.
Not connected	A remote printer configuration exists for this printer number, but the remote printer has not been initialized with the RPRINTER command.

Paused   The printer has been temporarily stopped with the "PAUse" option.

Stopped   The printer has been stopped with the "STOp" option.

Ready to go down   The "Going down after current jobs" option was selected in PCONSOLE, and the print server is set to shut down as soon as it finishes the jobs in the queue.

Mount form n The printer is waiting for the indicated form number to be mounted.

Mark/Form feed   The printer has been stopped and is performing a "MArk" or "FormFeed" command.

In private mode   The remote printer is not available for network use because a user has issued a PSC command with the "PRIvate" option at the workstation.

Options for Stopping and Starting the Printer

From time to time, you need to halt printing on a particular printer: for example, to adjust the print position on preprinted forms, or to perform some type of maintenance on the printer. While you could run to the printer and switch it off-line, PSC provides easier ways to stop a network printer.

- The "PAUse" option simply halts the printer temporarily. If a job is currently printing at the time, it will resume right where it left off when you restart the printer.
- The "STOp" option, by contrast, halts the printer and deletes the current job (if any) from the queue.

- The "STOp Keep" option halts the printer and stops processing the current job at that point. However, the printer keeps the current job and resubmits it at the top of the queue when you restart the printer. The job will then start printing all over again from the beginning.

To restart the printer after choosing any of these options, include the "STARt" option in the PSC command. For example, the command

```
PSC PS=ATPSERVER P=0 STAR <Enter>
```

restarts printer 0 on print server ATPSERVER.

The MOUNT FORM Option

PSC provides a quick way to inform the printer that a new form has been mounted. When the printer status indicates it is waiting for a certain form number, printing will halt automatically. You (or a designated print manager) must go to the printer and load the type of paper that corresponds to the specified form number. Once this is done, you must type a PSC command with the "MOunt Form=n" option before printing will resume.

For example, suppose printer 0 indicates it needs form 1, which you defined as preprinted letterhead in PRINTDEF. Load the letterhead in the printer's feed tray, then type the following command at your workstation:

```
PSC PS=ATPSERVER P=0 MO F=1 <Enter>
```

Printing will resume until the next form change comes along.

Of course, NetWare has no way of knowing whether you have mounted the right kind of paper or not. Once you issue the PSC command saying you have mounted the requested form number, the printer will start printing again regardless of the paper in contains. This is why it is important to make a list of the form numbers and corresponding paper types for the forms you defined in PRINTDEF. Keep a copy of this list by the printer so that whoever is in charge of loading paper knows what type to use.

Other PSC Options

Often, when you mount continuous-feed forms on a printer, you have to do some adjusting to get the top of the page at the right place. PSC provides an option to help you do this. After you have loaded the forms in the printer, type the PSC command with the "MArk" option. The printer will respond by printing a line of asterisks (*) at the current position. This line of asterisks shows you where the printer will start printing the next page. If necessary, adjust the paper up or down so that the marked line is at the top of the page where it needs to be.

After you have marked up one page with asterisks, use the "FormFeed" option to move to the top of the next page before resuming printing.

In PCONSOLE, users or print queue operators can delete jobs from the queue. You can even delete the job that is currently printing. However, much of the job might already be in the printer's internal buffer, so it keeps printing for a while even after being deleted from the queue. PSC provides a quicker way to abort the current print job. The "ABort" option causes the printer to stop printing the current job, delete it from the queue, and move on to the next job in the queue.

If you want to abort the current job but then resubmit it after you change something (load different paper, for example), use the "ABort Keep" option. This aborts the current job and resubmits it in its entirety at the top of the queue.

The "PRIvate" and "SHared" options are used to switch a remote printer to private (non-network) mode and then back to regular shared (network) mode. We explained how these options work in Chapter 19.

The final option is "CancelDown." Use this option if you change your mind after selecting the "Going down after current jobs" option in PCONSOLE. It's quicker than going back into PCONSOLE to cancel the down request for the print server. You don't need to include a printer number with this option. Simply type the command as follows:

```
PSC PS=ATPSERVER CD <Enter>
```

As long as you enter the command before the end of the last print job, the print server will remain in operation. If you're too late and the print server goes down anyway, you'll have to restart it as explained in Chapter 19.

Part Five

Management and Troubleshooting

Up until now, our emphasis has been on the proper installation and setup of the network. When your foundation is secure, further management and troubleshooting is much easier. Regular daily and weekly maintenance procedures are a must if your network is to remain healthy. Of course,nothing every stays the same on a network. It's only a matter of time before you'll need to add a new hard disk, join more LAN segments, or add server memory to the server. And, with all those hardware and software components working together, a failure here and there is inevitable. This section is your guide to maintaining and troubleshooting the various aspects of your network.

- **Chapter 21: Memory Management and Performance Tuning** deals with NetWare v3.11 server memory and how it is used by volumes, file services, NLMs, and other server applications. It also explains how to optimize the use of server RAM to get the best performance.

- **Chapter 22: File System Management** explains data structures associated with the file system and how they relate to the various SET command parameters. It describes ways to tweak these parameters to tune the file system for your particular network needs.

- **Chapter 23: System Fault Tolerance** delves into NetWare's fault-tolerance features such as Hot Fix, disk mirroring and duplexing, and transaction tracking. It explains how to manage these features to give added protection to your valuable data, and gives some tips for troubleshooting related problems.

- **Chapter 24: Disk/Volume Management** contains an in-depth look at the components of NetWare's disk channel, including controllers, drivers, and the disks themselves. It explains how to add new disks and volumes, change existing ones, and oversee the health of the disk channel in MONITOR. It describes relevant SET parameters and the use of VREPAIR to fix minor disk problems, then lists common disk-related problems and possible solutions.

- **Chapter 25: LAN Driver/Communications Management** digs deeper into NetWare's LAN communication channel and explains how LAN drivers and network protocols work together. It covers the utilities for loading LAN drivers and binding network protocols to them, and guides you through the LAN I/O statistics in MONITOR. The chapter ends with common LAN driver-related problems and suggestions for resolving them.

- **Chapter 26: UPS and Power Protection** emphasizes the importance of protecting your network hardware from commercial power fluctuations, and explains how to choose the best type of UPS for your network. It covers NetWare's UPS monitoring feature and related console commands, and gives tips for troubleshooting the UPS system.

- **Chapter 27: Backup and Restore Management** explains how to implement an effective backup plan using the SBACKUP software that ships with NetWare v3.11.

- **Chapter 28: Remote Management** tells how to use Novell's RMF feature to manage scattered networks from a central management console. It briefly describes the other network management features and products available for NetWare v3.11.

CHAPTER 21

Memory Management and Performance Tuning

In Chapter 1 of this book, we discussed memory management in the context of the NetWare kernel. We stated that memory management is mostly a non-issue when it comes to NetWare troubleshooting. That statement still holds true. Memory management is, however, a performance issue in the sense that you can increase NetWare v3.11's performance considerably by fine-tuning its memory management, as explained in this chapter. This chapter also discusses some of the potential memory management problems, most of which occur when you don't have enough physical memory installed in the server machine for your particular configuration.

The key to understanding NetWare v3.11's memory management and how to tune it lies in a solid knowledge of the different types of memory the NetWare v3.11 kernel maintains, and how NetWare uses each. Once you understand the different types of memory NetWare uses, you can track each type using the MONITOR NLM. Finally, you can tune NetWare v3.11's memory management using the SET console command.

NetWare Memory Types

NetWare v3.11 has four memory types: kernel memory, which contains the NetWare v3.11 kernel (and DOS if you haven't removed it); cache memory, which is the largest single type of memory upon server initialization; permanent memory, which NetWare uses to maintain its internal data structures; and alloc memory, which NLMs can draw on for short-term memory requirements. NetWare's queue management system also uses alloc memory for queue nodes.

When NetWare v3.11 initializes, it sets up its internal data structures using small amounts of permanent memory, initializes a small pool of alloc memory, and initializes the remainder of memory as cache memory. The benefit of having more RAM installed in the server is that the server will have more cache memory, which speeds file service dramatically.

There are two types of permanent memory: permanent and semi-permanent memory. While permanent memory is used for data structures that remain throughout the duration of server operation, semi-permanent memory is used for data structures that may or may not remain in use during server operation or that are constantly changing size, such as NLM screens, transaction tracking nodes, and tracked resources.

There are three types of cache memory: file cache buffers, which are used to cache file data; cache movable memory, which is used for dynamic data structures of a long duration, such as transaction tracking tables, file allocation tables (FATs), and directory tables; and cache non-movable memory, which is used for dynamic data structures of a short duration, mostly for use by loaded NLMs. When you unload an NLM, for example, its non-movable memory goes back to the file cache buffer pool.

Upon system initialization, the permanent and alloc memory pools are small, and most of the memory within those pools is already in use. As soon as you begin loading NLMs, or when clients attach to and begin requesting server resources, the amount of memory within the permanent and alloc pools will become all used up. NetWare v3.11 will need to expand these two memory pools.

When NetWare v3.11 expands its permanent and alloc memory pools, it takes memory out of its file cache pool and assigns that memory to either the permanent or alloc memory pool. When alloc memory is released (such as when you unload an NLM), the alloc memory is recycled into the alloc memory pool. Once NetWare v3.11 has removed memory from its file cache pool into either the alloc or permanent memory pools, however, that memory never goes back to the file cache pool.

Figure 21-1 shows the MONITOR "Server Memory Statistics" screen, which displays the amount of memory in each of NetWare v3.11's memory pools.

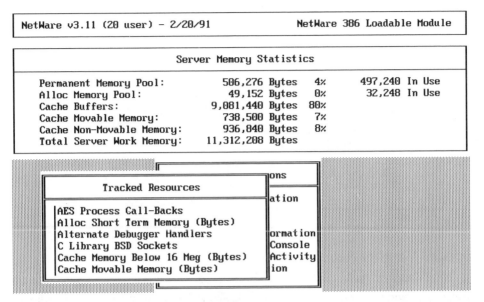

Figure 21-1: The MONITOR "Server Memory Statistics" screen displays how memory is being used in each of NetWare's memory pools.

Later in this chapter, you'll learn how to use the MONITOR "Tracked Resources" menu, shown also in Figure 21-1, to obtain information about how NetWare v3.11 is using its memory.

Volume Memory Requirements

The key to successful NetWare v3.11 memory management is ensuring there is enough file cache memory. NetWare will not mount a volume if it does not have enough memory to cache the entire FAT within its file cache memory. Even if NetWare is able to cache a volume's entire FAT, it should have lots of cache memory remaining to cache directory tables and file data. If you wish to have transaction tracking enabled, the server should have sufficient cache memory for that too.

Here's a simple way to calculate NetWare v3.11's memory requirements, given a specific volume configuration. (Note that this formula tends to overestimate memory requirements for volumes over 1.5GB in size.)

For the NetWare OS:

2MB

For each volume, add:

.023 x Volume Size (MB) / Block Size (Kilobytes)

For each name space active on the volume, add:

.009 x Volume Size (MB) / Block Size (Kilobytes)

A NetWare v3.11 server should always have a minimum of 4MB RAM.

Special Memory Requirements

While the method of estimating server memory requirements shown above is useful, you should modify it for your anticipated memory configuration. Here are some additional things to consider.

LSL Packet Receive Buffers

Each packet receive buffer requires approximately 1,600 bytes of RAM. The server will require enough memory to allocate at least one packet receive buffer for each potential user. On a 250-user server, this comes to around 400KB. If your server is running multiple protocol stacks, each protocol stack will require an additional packet receive buffer for potential users could be deleted. If your server has any EISA LAN adapters, you should allow 10 packet receive buffers for each adapter.

Indexed Files

Whenever NetWare v3.11 allocates 64 or more cache buffers for a single file, it attempts to index the file. NetWare does this by constructing a "Turbo FAT" for the file, which consumes approximately 23 bytes for each disk block associated with the file. Every large file you have on the server that is subject to frequent access by clients will probably be indexed in such a manner, with the most obvious example being database files.

Btrieve

Btrieve is a file handling engine and a set of tools for building applications, rather than an application itself. If you plan to use the NetWare server-based file handler for database applications, you should configure your server with at least 1MB of RAM specifically for Btrieve, and probably more, depending on the application. This is because Btrieve doesn't use the OS cache memory directly, but allocates memory to do its own file caching from the semi-permanent and alloc memory pools.

NLM Applications

This group includes application-specific NLMs such as NetWare SQL, Oracle, and others. You may even have developed your own NLMs. If you plan on running any NLM applications, you should research the server memory requirements of those applications before deciding on a RAM configuration for your server. These requirements can vary widely, depending on the specific application, but can easily entail several megabytes of server memory.

TCP/IP Support

Every copy of NetWare v3.11 ships with a series of NLMs to support TCP/IP. These NLMs don't provide support for the Network File System (NFS), which is a separate product, but they provide full IP routing and support for straight TCP and UDP clients. While the memory requirements of loading the TCP/IP NLMs are rather modest (less than 300KB), you must effectively double the number of packet receive buffers on the server. Plan on at least an additional 1MB of RAM.

NetWare for Macintosh, NetWare NFS, and NetWare OSI

These are the upper-layer file service modules for the respective optional protocol stacks supported by NetWare v3.11. Each one is a separately purchased Novell product. NetWare NFS and NetWare OSI both use the IP services provided by the TCP/IP NLMs, but NetWare for Macintosh requires that you load the full AppleTalk protocol stack, plus the upper-layer AppleTalk Filing Protocol (AFP) stack and the Printer Access Protocol (PAP) stack. The memory requirements for each stack depend on the number of users your server supports. Consult the documentation that ships with these products for specific memory requirements.

Our recommendation is that you always err on the side of more server RAM rather than less server RAM. NetWare v3.11 is extremely effective in using RAM to advantage. You never need to worry about having too much RAM, because NetWare uses all "extra" memory to cache its file system, which increases server performance dramatically.

Memory Use While Mounting Volumes

When NetWare v3.11 mounts a volume, it requires more memory than it does to cache the volume's FAT after mounting is complete. This is because NetWare allocates additional memory structures during the mount procedure to perform consistency checks on the volume it is mounting. For example, NetWare checks for discrepancies between the duplicate FATs that it stores on disk. NetWare also requires memory to scan a volume's TTS log file and perform transaction backouts if necessary.

Usually, this extra memory requirement isn't a problem. Most server administrators mount volumes before loading NLMs, which provides a margin for extra memory beyond the strict run-time requirements of the volume in question. However, you may experience an out-of-memory error during the volume mount process, especially if you try to mount a very large volume after NetWare has been up and running for a while.

The bottom line in this situation is that you need more memory in the server. However, you may be able to sneak by if you remove DOS from the server's memory by issuing the REMOVE DOS console command. You can also unload all unneeded NLMs. If the volume has name space support, you can use VREPAIR to remove name space support, which should reduce memory requirements for mounting the volume dramatically. However, we don't recommend this last option because it deletes extended file information that you may not be able to recover gracefully.

If you manage to get the volume mounted, you can reduce the memory required to mount it again by reducing the number of directories on the volume and consolidating files within fewer directories. However, this is not a very graceful solution either because it may disrupt applications, and will certainly disrupt users, who have probably created directories for their own reasons.

Memory Use During File Service

After NetWare v3.11 has mounted its volumes and file service is occurring, NetWare fills its file cache memory with data requested or created by client applications. For example, when a client requests data from a file, NetWare caches that data, where it remains until the client closes the file or until NetWare "steals" the cache buffer to cache more recently requested data. When a client writes over part of a cached file, NetWare flushes that cache buffer to disk.

NetWare also maintains directory cache buffers, which contain directory information. NetWare maintains directory information within its cache buffers as long as clients request data from inside a directory frequently (you can set the definition of "frequently," as you'll learn in Chapter 22).

NetWare uses all available file cache memory for these two types of caching. As long as the server has enough memory to mount a volume, file service will continue as the amount of available file cache buffers dwindles. NetWare recycles file cache buffers using a Least Recently Used (LRU) algorithm. However, as the number of file cache buffers dwindles, server performance decreases markedly. (See Chapter 22 for more explanation of the LRU algorithm.)

Memory Use by NLMs

NLMs can use permanent, semi-permanent, alloc, cache movable, and cache non-movable memory. As a rule, well-designed NLMs minimize their memory use as much as possible, thus allowing more memory to be dedicated to file system caching. (Some NLMs, such as Btrieve, allocate their own cache memory.)

Using MONITOR to View NLM Memory Usage

You can track an NLM's memory use with the MONITOR NLM. From MONITOR's "Available Options" menu, select "System Module Information" and press <Enter>. MONITOR will display a "System Modules" list, which contains an entry for each loaded module. Your server's console screen should appear similar to the one in Figure 21-2.

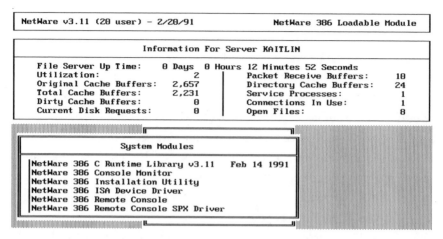

Figure 21-2: MONITOR's "System Modules" list displays the NLMs currently loaded on the server.

To track a module's memory use, highlight a module from the "System Modules" list and press <Enter>. Figure 21-3 displays the kind of information you would see for the NetWare 386 Remote Console (REMOTE.NLM)

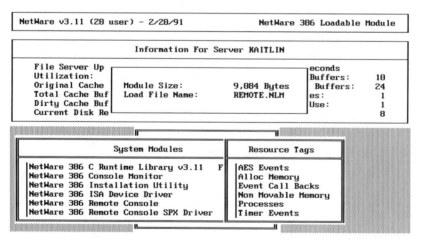

Figure 21-3: MONITOR displays the size and the resource tags being used by the selected module (in this case, REMOTE.NLM).

In Figure 21-3, you can see that the size of the REMOTE NLM is 9,084 bytes. The "Resource Tags" list shows all the types of tracked resources currently in use by REMOTE. You can tell from this list that REMOTE is using some alloc memory and some non-movable cache memory.

To see how much alloc memory is being used by REMOTE, highlight "Alloc Memory" in the "Resource Tags" list and press <Enter>. The screen will display how much alloc memory is being used by REMOTE, as shown in Figure 21-4.

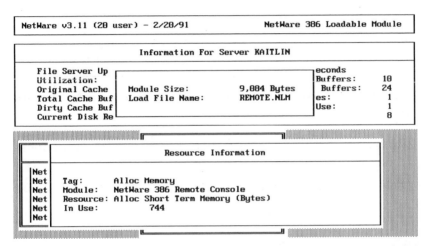

Figure 21-4: MONITOR displays how much alloc memory is in use by REMOTE.NLM.

To view how much non-movable cache memory is being used by REMOTE, press <Esc>, then highlight "Non Movable Memory" from the "Resource Tags" list and press <Enter>. Figure 21-5 shows the result.

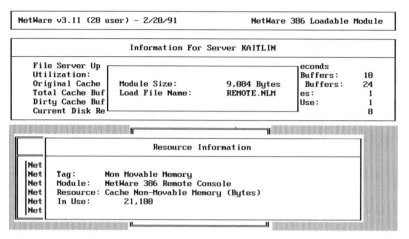

```
NetWare v3.11 (20 user) - 2/20/91          NetWare 386 Loadable Module

                    Information For Server KAITLIN

  File Server Up                                     econds
  Utilization:                                       Buffers:    10
  Original Cache   Module Size:        9,084 Bytes    Buffers:    24
  Total Cache Buf  Load File Name:     REMOTE.NLM     es:          1
  Dirty Cache Buf                                     Use:         1
  Current Disk Re                                                  8


                           Resource Information

  Net
  Net   Tag:       Non Movable Memory
  Net   Module:    NetWare 386 Remote Console
  Net   Resource:  Cache Non-Movable Memory (Bytes)
  Net   In Use:        21,100
  Net
  Net
```

Figure 21-5: MONITOR displays how much non-movable cache memory is being used by REMOTE.NLM.

You might want to experiment with MONITOR's "System Module Information" option a little bit to familiarize yourself with this excellent tool. By spending a little time doing so, you can get a pretty good idea of how NLMs use memory. You'll notice that each NLM uses memory differently.

MONITOR's "Resource Utilization" Option

As we just saw, the "System Module Information" feature of MONITOR allows you to track memory use by module. MONITOR also allows you to track memory use by type of memory. To do this, select "Resource Utilization" from the MONITOR "Available Options" menu. MONITOR will display its "Tracked Resources" list, which shows the different types of tracked resources available for investigation.

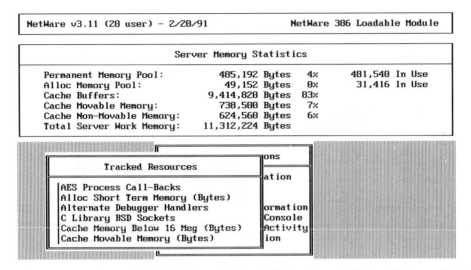

Figure 21-6: MONITOR displays a list of "Tracked Resources" that can be investigated.

To see how this option works, select "Alloc Short Term Memory (Bytes)" from the "Tracked Resources" list. MONITOR will display a "Resource Tags" list, as in Figure 21-7.

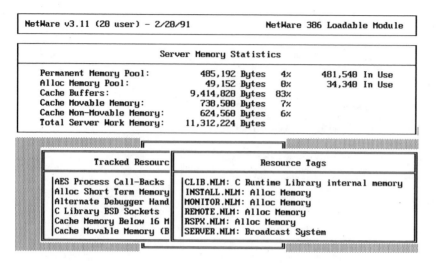

```
NetWare v3.11 (20 user) - 2/20/91          NetWare 386 Loadable Module

                        Server Memory Statistics

    Permanent Memory Pool:        485,192 Bytes    4%    481,540 In Use
    Alloc Memory Pool:             49,152 Bytes    0%     34,340 In Use
    Cache Buffers:              9,414,820 Bytes   83%
    Cache Movable Memory:         738,500 Bytes    7%
    Cache Non-Movable Memory:     624,560 Bytes    6%
    Total Server Work Memory:  11,312,224 Bytes
```

```
        Tracked Resourc            Resource Tags

    AES Process Call-Backs     CLIB.NLM: C Runtime Library internal memory
    Alloc Short Term Memory    INSTALL.NLM: Alloc Memory
    Alternate Debugger Hand    MONITOR.NLM: Alloc Memory
    C Library BSD Sockets      REMOTE.NLM: Alloc Memory
    Cache Memory Below 16 M    RSPX.NLM: Alloc Memory
    Cache Movable Memory (B    SERVER.NLM: Broadcast System
```

Figure 21-7: When you select a particular type of resource from the "Tracked Resources" list, MONITOR displays a "Resource Tags" list showing each NLM that is using that particular type of resource.

Notice the difference between the "Resource Tags" lists in Figures 21-3 and 21-7. While Figure 21-3 shows the different types of resources being used by the REMOTE.NLM module, Figure 21-7 shows all the different modules using the alloc memory resource type.

By selecting "REMOTE.NLM" from the "Resource Tags" list shown in Figure 21-7, we can verify that REMOTE is indeed using 744 bytes of alloc memory, as shown in Figure 21-8. (Notice that the data shown in Figure 21-8 is consistent with the data in Figure 21-4.)

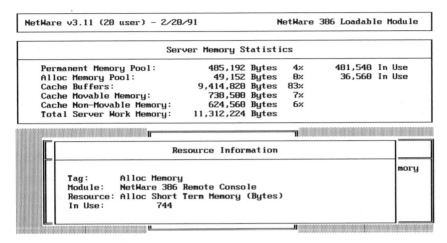

```
NetWare v3.11 (20 user) - 2/20/91          NetWare 386 Loadable Module

                     Server Memory Statistics

   Permanent Memory Pool:        485,192 Bytes   4%   481,548 In Use
   Alloc Memory Pool:             49,152 Bytes   0%    36,568 In Use
   Cache Buffers:              9,414,828 Bytes  83%
   Cache Movable Memory:         738,500 Bytes   7%
   Cache Non-Movable Memory:     624,560 Bytes   6%
   Total Server Work Memory:  11,312,224 Bytes
```

```
                   Resource Information                          mory

      Tag:      Alloc Memory
      Module:   NetWare 386 Remote Console
      Resource: Alloc Short Term Memory (Bytes)
      In Use:        744
```

Figure 21-8: MONITOR's "Resource Information" screen also shows the memory usage of a selected module.

What you've seen here is that MONITOR provides you with two easy ways to track server memory use: by module, or by type of memory.

Other MONITOR Options

You've probably noticed that you can track other resources besides memory using MONITOR, such as processes, disk activity, driver resources, receive buffers, and so on. Chapter 24 discusses the disk- related options in MONITOR, while Chapter 25 discusses the LAN driver-related options.

Here's an undocumented feature of MONITOR that can help you get a better idea of how heavily the server CPU is being used. If you add the "P" option when you load MONITOR (by typing **LOAD MONITOR P <Enter>**), the "Available Options" menu will contain an extra option called "Processor Utilization." Selecting this option displays CPU utilization percentages for the server.

MONITOR's Server Memory Statistics

Now let's change gears and look at MONITOR's "Server Memory Statistics" window. If you look at the top half of Figure 21-8, you'll see that MONITOR displays its different types of memory, how much of each type is available, and how much of the available permanent memory and alloc memory is in use. (Cache memory is always "in use.")

The MONITOR "Server Memory Statistics" display is easy to bring up on the console: simply select "Resource Utilization" from the MONITOR "Available Options" menu and press <Enter.> The top half of the console screen changes to show the memory statistics.

Permanent Memory Pool. First look at the "Permanent Memory Pool" statistic. In Figure 21-8, you can see that 485,192 bytes are available as permanent memory and that 481,540 bytes are already in use by NLMs. That means that the server has around 4KB available for permanent memory. In a situation like this, chances are good that as soon as you load an NLM, the operating system will need to "steal" memory from cache to provide enough additional permanent memory to load the NLM.

Alloc Memory Pool. You can also see that there are 49,152 bytes of alloc memory, with 36,560 of those bytes currently in use. That leaves around 12KB of alloc memory available for NLMs. Should the operating system be asked by an NLM to provide more than around 12KB of alloc memory, the operating system will have to "steal" further cache buffers and put them to use as alloc memory.

Cache Memory. It is important to monitor the percentage of total memory being used for file cache buffers. In Figure 21-8, you can see that a healthy 83% of server memory is being used as cache.

As you may have discovered by experimenting with MONITOR, the operating system itself makes use of permanent and alloc memory for directory tables, receive buffers, client drive mappings, file and record locks, and so on. As the load on the server increases, you will see the percentage of memory in use as cache decreases. File service will become marginal when cache buffers make up 20% or less of total server memory.

What to Do When Cache Buffers Are Low

There are a couple of things you can do when the server's file cache buffers diminish to a critical level.

First, remember that once the operating system "steals" cache memory in order to provide more permanent or alloc memory, it is gone for good. The gateway between cache and permanent or alloc memory is strictly one-way: out of the cache buffer pool. The only way you can reclaim memory for cache is to reboot the server. Of course, a better (and more permanent) solution is to add more memory to the server.

The "SET Maximum Alloc Short Term Memory" Command

NetWare v3.11 allows you to set the maximum ceiling for alloc memory using the SET console command. By setting the maximum amount of alloc memory the server will allocate, you can stem the flow of memory through the cache-to-permanent or cache-to-alloc gateway. The syntax for this command is:

```
SET maximum alloc short term memory: bytes
```

where *bytes* is the point at which you cut the server off from stealing more alloc memory from cache. The valid range for *bytes* is 50000 (around 48KB) to 16777216 (around 16MB). The default value is 2097152 bytes, or 2MB. If you've got between 500 and 600MB of data on your server, 2MB of cache isn't very much, especially considering that NetWare v3.11 uses this minimum 2MB pool for both directory and file caching. However, it protects you from extreme shortages of cache memory.

It's important to mention that the "SET Maximum Alloc Short Term Memory" command will not prevent the operating system from stealing further cache memory to use as permanent memory. To deny the server additional permanent memory, even when cache memory is severely depleted, can cause serious problems. Consider that the server uses permanent memory for connection tables, transaction tracking, receive buffers, process stacks, file control blocks, and other critical data structures. Denying the server permanent memory may cause data errors or a failure of the transaction tracking system, or worse. In short, permanent memory is always more important than cache memory, even when cache is depleted.

The "SET Reserved Buffers Below 16 Meg" Command

NetWare v3.11 includes a new SET command that reserves a specified number of cache buffers under the 16MB level for device drivers that can't access memory above 16MB. The syntax for this command is:

```
SET Reserved Buffers Below 16 Meg: n
```

where n is the number of cache buffers you want to reserve. The valid range is from 8 to 200; the default number is 16. This SET command can only be placed in the STARTUP.NCF file.

NetWare's Consistency Checks

All of NetWare v3.11's memory allocation and management routines perform internal consistency checks. Consistency checking is simple in concept. When NetWare initializes or allocates its different memory types, it uses a small portion of each memory object as a resource tag. A memory object's resource tag is similar to a brand, or stamp, that identifies the type of memory, why it was allocated or initialized, and which process it belongs to. Before writing data to a memory object, NetWare compares the object's resource tag with the type of data it is about to write to the object.

For example, if NetWare is going to use a memory object to record one type of transaction tracking information, it assumes the memory object is a transaction node. It therefore compares the resource tag a transaction node is supposed to have with the resource tag of the memory object. If the comparison fails, NetWare refuses to write data to the memory object and generates an error message. This is just one instance of a failed consistency check.

NetWare v3.11 performs many different types of consistency checks in many different situations. A failed consistency check is always a serious error, because it indicates some degree of memory corruption. In some cases NetWare v3.11 will shut itself down completely, but in other cases it will shut down only part of itself. Most failed consistency checks produce an error message that mentions an invalid resource tag. However, this isn't always the case.

What to Do When the Server Fails a Consistency Check

There are as many possible causes for a failed consistency check as there are lines of code loaded in the server's memory, plus a few more. However, most failed consistency checks are caused by two things: hardware faults and NLM bugs. For example, aberrant power fluctuations can corrupt server RAM. A power spike need only change a single bit of RAM to corrupt an entire data structure. This is usually the cause of failed consistency checks.

Note that the instructions for dealing with failed consistency checks, as printed in the Novell *System Messages* manual, have been replaced with newer instructions in the README.311 file. When you receive an error message for which the Novell manual refers you to the section on consistency checks, respond as follows:

- Reboot the server. If the error persists, run INSTALL to reinstall the operating system from the original diskettes.

- Check the server's system board, memory chips, power supply, and power conditioning equipment. Replace any faulty hardware.

- Remove any new hardware that you have recently installed in the server. If the error goes away, the problem is most likely with the new hardware. Check for IRQ, DMA, memory, and I/O port conflicts between the existing server hardware and the new hardware. If the hardware came with its own diagnostics, run the diagnostic tests to discover where the problem lies.

- If the error persists, make a list of all the hardware installed in the server and all actions you have taken to correct the problem. Contact your Novell service representative.

NLM bugs can cause the types of failed consistency checks that are most difficult to detect. What usually happens is that, because of a stray pointer or some other type of invalid memory reference, an NLM will write data to some area of server memory that it shouldn't be accessing. The reason this type of bug is difficult to detect is that it is difficult to reproduce. NLMs get loaded into different areas of memory each time they're executed. Operating system data structures shrink and grow dynamically. Sometimes a stray pointer does no damage to data structures; at other times, it corrupts them.

This type of error is extremely rare with the NLMs that Novell ships with NetWare. However, third- party NLMs are sometimes not as robust, especially in-house NLMs. For this reason, you should always record the server's configuration whenever NetWare v3.11 reports a failed consistency check. Perhaps you can focus the problem on a single NLM and reproduce it.

Tools for Detecting NLM Errors

Two tools that are invaluable for detecting erroneous NLM memory references are NET-CHECK and NLM-CHECK, both provided by Nu-Mega Technologies Inc. NLMCHECK.NLM is primarily a development tool, while NETCHECK.NLM is a run-time memory protection mechanism that prevents NLMs from writing to other NLM's code space.

NETCHECK uses the Intel page-based memory protection hardware to tell you exactly which NLM attempted to make an out-of-bounds memory overwrite. The best part is that NETCHECK will prevent such overwrites from reccurring. However, you can configure it to allow overwrites, and it will still inform you of them.

We recommend that you run NETCHECK on the server whenever you introduce a new NLM to the system. If the NLM runs for several weeks without any problems, you can unload NETCHECK, because you've got a rock-solid system.

SET Commands for NLM Developers

If you are developing your own in-house NLMs, there are three other SET commands you should be aware of. The first one, "SET Display Relinquish Control Alerts=On," enables the server console to display messages if your NLM fails to relinquish control of the CPU after 0.4 seconds. The second, "SET Display Old API Names=On," causes the server to display any code references to outdated APIs it encounters in an NLM. The default setting for both of these commands is "Off."

The third command enforces a kind of "pseudo-preemption" on a NetWare v3.11 server, which may be necessary with some developmental NLMs. Adjust the "SET Pseudo Preemption Time=n" only as recommended in the NLM documentation.

For more information on these SET commands, refer to the Novell *System Administration* manual.

CHAPTER 22

File System Management

The NetWare v3.11 file system is integrated tightly with the NetWare v3.11 kernel, especially when it comes to kernel memory management and process scheduling. The kernel's memory manager allocates and manages the massively-scaled NetWare v3.11 file system cache, while the kernel's process scheduler allows the file system to synchronize contending file service requests. Due to the nature of the NetWare v3.11 file system, managing and tuning it is just as much a matter of kernel tuning as it is file system tuning.

Data integrity is at least as important as file system performance, and NetWare v3.11 has significant data safeguards built into its file system. This chapter investigates NetWare file system performance and data integrity from a troubleshooting perspective. We'll look at the various data structures and caching mechanisms involved, and then look at some NetWare utilities and SET commands for managing and tuning the file system.

NetWare File System Data Structures

The NetWare v3.11 file system is highly optimized for file service performance in a networked environment. The primary means NetWare v3.11 uses to increase file service performance is caching of its data structures. Every file stored on a NetWare hard disk has its directory entry cached, and the entire File Allocation Table (FAT) of every NetWare volume is cached when NetWare mounts the volume. This makes finding a specific file (or portion of a file) within even the largest volumes quick and easy. In addition, NetWare may cache some or all of a file's data.

To know best how to troubleshoot and tune the NetWare v3.11 file system, it's important to understand its underlying data structures.

NetWare Volumes

As you read in Chapter 5, the primary data structure of the NetWare file system is the volume. We'll quickly review some of the aspects of NetWare volumes here; Chapter 24 offers a fuller explanation of volume parameters and how to work with them.

A NetWare volume corresponds to the "root" level of a DOS hard disk. You create directories, subdirectories, and files within each volume, which represents a fixed amount of disk space. Theoretically, the maximum size of a NetWare v3.11 volume is 32TB (terabytes). However, the real limit on volume size—at least with today's hardware—is server RAM. In Chapter 21, we discussed server memory management when mounting and using volumes. Recall that basic server memory requirements depend on the volume block size, the number of blocks on the volume, and volume name space support. (You may want to review Chapter 21 if you don't remember the specifics.)

You can extend a volume's size by using INSTALL.NLM to add additional segments to the volume, but you can't shrink a volume by removing segments. To shrink a volume, you must destroy the volume and re-create it, using fewer segments. These procedures are explained in Chapter 24.

The first volume you create on a server is always the SYS volume. Additional volumes—up to a maximum of 64—are optional. More than one volume may or may not be necessary, depending on which applications you plan to use with the server, which name spaces you plan to support, and other issues.

Each NetWare volume has certain data structures unique to itself. These data structures include the file allocation table and the volume directory table, both of which are cached by the server. We'll discuss both of these structures shortly.

Disk Blocks

Disk blocks are individual storage units within a volume. These disk blocks may or may not be cached, depending on specific client requests for data. By way of review, each volume has a block size, which you set when you create the volume. Possible block sizes on NetWare v3.11 volumes are 4KB, 8KB, 16KB, 32KB, and 64KB.

You can't change a volume's block size without destroying the data stored on a volume. The volume block size represents the smallest storage unit for that volume. A one-kilobyte file, although it occupies only a fraction of total block storage capacity, occupies an entire block. Files stored on NetWare v3.11 volumes exist on one or more disk blocks chained together using the volume FAT.

Disk blocks are further divided into sectors. The number of sectors per block depends on the block size, with a larger block having more sectors than a smaller block. Sectors are entirely the domain of the NetWare v3.11 file system. As a network manager, you probably won't need to be aware of them.

The File Allocation Table

Each NetWare v3.11 volume has a file allocation table (FAT) that provides the operating system with information regarding volume disk blocks and the data they contain. There is a one-to-one correspondence between entries in the volume FAT and disk blocks located on the volume. If a particular disk block is part of a file chain, that block's entry in the volume FAT contains a pointer to the next block in the file chain. Or, if the block is the last block in a file chain, it contains an end-of-file marker in place of a pointer to the next block in the chain.

Alternatively, a FAT entry may indicate that its disk block contains no file data, and is thus free for the operating system to use to extend an existing file or to create a new file.

As we discussed in the previous chapter, NetWare v3.11 attempts to cache a volme's entire FAT when mounting the volume. If NetWare can't cache the entire volume FAT, it refuses to mount the volume. By caching the volume FAT, NetWare guarantees its ability to find quickly individual blocks within a file chain. (The terms "file chain" and "file" mean the same thing in this context. Files consist of one or more disk blocks logically *chained* together.)

To find individual blocks within a file chain, the operating system must simply read data from memory to obtain the location on disk of a specific portion of a file. If the volume FAT were not cached, the operating system would first have to load a FAT entry from disk into memory, and then read the FAT entry to obtain the location on disk of a specific portion of a file.

While the volume FAT contains information that links together the individual disk blocks that make up a file, it doesn't contain the information NetWare v3.11 needs to locate the *beginning* of the file and thus to obtain a file handle for a specific file. This information is stored in another volume data structure, the volume directory table.

The Volume Directory Table

The volume directory table is a data structure that contains an entry for each file or directory located on the volume. Among other data, the volume directory table contains information the operating system can use to locate the first FAT entry for that file. Figure 22-1 is a generalized depiction of how this works.

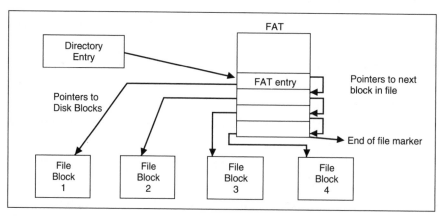

Figure 22-1: This is a generalized depiction of the relationship between a directory entry, FAT entries, and individual disk blocks that form a file chain.

Redundant Copies of the FAT and Directory Table

The volume FAT and the volume directory table are two vital data structures NetWare v3.11 uses to provide clients with access to files (and portions of files) stored on its volumes. To provide an additional measure of protection, NetWare v3.11 stores redundant copies of its volume FATs and directory tables on each volume. These so-called mirrored FATs are compared against each other when NetWare v3.11 attempts to mount a volume. If they don't match, NetWare refuses to mount the volume and requests that you run VREPAIR to fix any problems in the file system. (See Chapter 24 for more information about running VREPAIR.)

Troubleshooting FAT and Directory Table Problems

Knowing the relationship between the volume directory table, the volume FAT, and the ability of clients to gain access to specific files, you can infer what has gone wrong when clients have problems gaining access to files. For example, if there's a problem with the volume directory table, NetWare v3.11 can't know where on a volume the first block of a file is stored. The file is still intact, but since NetWare doesn't know how to locate the first block of the file, clients can't open the file (or a portion of the file) for reading or writing.

What do you think would happen if the volume directory were intact, but one of the FAT entries for a block in the file chain were corrupt? NetWare v3.11 would be able to locate the beginning of the file with no problem. However, because FAT entries contain pointers to the next block in the file chain, a corrupt FAT entry would prevent NetWare from locating the file in its entirety.

If the corrupt FAT entry represents a block near the beginning of the file chain, NetWare knows where only the first few blocks of the file are stored. If the corrupt FAT entry represents a block near the end of the file chain, NetWare can gain access to most of the file, but not to the last part. If the corrupt FAT entry represents the last block in the file chain, NetWare doesn't know where the file ends (and consequently doesn't know how big the file is, despite the fact that it can locate the entire file.)

When these types of problems occur, you should run VREPAIR on the offending volume. Virtually all file service errors on a NetWare v3.11 volume result from NetWare's inability to locate the file (or a portion of the file) on the volume, rather than from corruption of actual file data. VREPAIR is "intelligent" enough to infer this information from data stored within the physical disk blocks located on the volume and to reconstruct the volume directory table and FAT. Since, in most cases, the data stored in the various disk blocks of what used to be an intact file chain still exists, NetWare v3.11 uses the reconstructed directory table or FAT to gain access to the previously inaccessible file chain. (See Chapter 24 for more information about running VREPAIR.)

Directory Caching

Like the volume FAT, the volume directory table is cached. However, unlike the FAT, the directory table is cached as needed, rather than automatically. For example, when a client node requests a file handle, NetWare v3.11 caches that file's entry in the directory table. The directory entry remains cached as long as clients continue to request access for reading or writing to the file. When clients stop requesting access to the file, the operating system may or may not recycle the directory entry's cache buffer.

There are several reasons why NetWare v3.11 caches the volume FAT automatically, but the volume directory table only as needed. First, the directory table is used basically for one purpose—providing access to specific files—while the FAT table is used for many purposes, including fault tolerance and general file system management. Further, while an individual file may occupy many disk blocks and consequently many entries in the FAT, a single file occupies a single entry in the directory table. So caching of the FAT is more critical than caching of the directory table.

Moreover, the file system may require access to specific FAT entries for purposes other than file access operations. Also, NetWare v3.11 uses FAT entries to synchronize file cache buffers with the physical disk blocks holding the original data contained (after caching) within the file cache buffers.

Directory Hashing

To compensate for the possibility that a directory entry may not be cached, NetWare v3.11 performs *hashing* on all directory entries. Hashing is a method used by many computer applications to speed access to entries in large tables of data. When hashing is in effect, a computer can predict the location of a specific entry in a table with great accuracy. When the computer guesses wrong, it misses the entry it's looking for by only a couple of rows within the table, allowing it to find the entry by moving up or down among entries within the table.

For example, if you store two files named "PIT.TXT" and "TIP.TXT" on a NetWare v3.11 volume, the operating system processes the file names through a hashing algorithm that causes the directory entries to be placed next to each other in the volume directory table. When you later request access to "PIT.TXT," NetWare uses the same hashing algorithm to predict the location of the directory entry for

"PIT.TXT" within the directory table. It might guess wrong, placing the file pointer to the entry for "TIP.TXT." However, by moving to the next slot in the directory table, the operating system locates the entry for "PIT.TXT." Or, if that doesn't work, the operating system moves to the entry immediately above "TIP.TXT," where it will certainly find the entry for "PIT.TXT." (This example assumes there are no other files containing the same characters, such as "IPT.TXT," or "PIT.TTX," and so on.)

On the whole, hashing is a highly efficient method of speeding access to large tables, because it works perfectly most of the time. When it doesn't work perfectly, it still points to a location in the table close to the desired location. Other, more accurate methods of speeding access to large tables, such as indexing, involve overhead such as separate index files. In the case of NetWare, the additional overhead isn't worth it: NetWare would rather use its resources to provide file cache buffers.

Viewing Directory Cache Buffers in MONITOR

You can use the MONITOR NLM to track the server's use of directory cache buffers. A sample MONITOR screen is shown in Figure 22-2. The "Directory Cache Buffers" field shows the current number of directory cache buffers on the server.

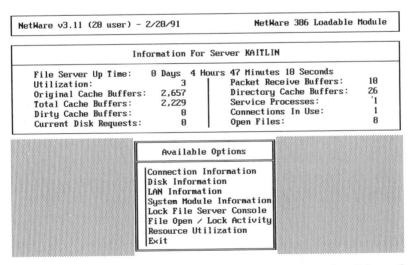

Figure 22-2: MONITOR's main screen displays, among other things, the number of Directory Cache Buffers currently in use.

If the server needs more directory cache buffers, the OS will take memory from the cache buffer pool to create more. However, this memory is not returned unless you reboot the server. Consequently, you can use the SET console command to limit the number of directory cache buffers allocated by NetWare v3.11, as we'll explain later in this chapter.

File Caching

You've just read about directory cache buffers, which NetWare uses to cache entries from the volume directory table. The most prevalent form of caching for NetWare v3.11 servers (provided they have sufficient RAM) is *file* caching. This preferential treatment reflects the importance NetWare places on its disk I/O functions. As needed, the OS can take memory from the cache buffers for other tasks or for loaded modules. But it returns this memory to the cache buffer pool when it is no longer required or the module is unloaded.

Although the cache buffer allocation mechanism is different, the principle of file caching hasn't changed form earlier versions of NetWare. Cache buffers are portions of server memory that NetWare uses to speed up reading and writing data on the server's hard disks. They act as buffers between user requests and disk drive access, capitalizing on the fact that computers can access data from memory about 100 times faster than they can from a hard disk.

Whenever a client requests access to data stored on a NetWare v3.11 volume, the operating system caches the data. Data is cached within file cache buffers on a per-block basis. That is, a client requests access to a block of data, and the operating system caches that block.

For example, imagine the file depicted in Figure 22-1, which consists of four disk blocks chained together by the volume FAT and a directory entry pointing to the first block of the file. When a client requests access to the first block of the file, NetWare v3.11 caches that block to a file cache buffer, as depicted in Figure 22-3.

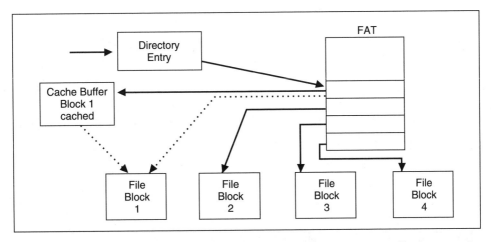

Figure 22-3: NetWare caches disk blocks to file cache buffers as soon as clients requests access to the data contained in the block.

Note the dashed line extending from the FAT to the first block in Figure 22-3. The NetWare file system preserves a link between a cached FAT entry, its cache buffer, and its disk block. This way, NetWare can synchronize cache buffers and disk blocks, and is able to report the correct error when it fails to flush a cache buffer to disk.

Cache Buffer and Disk Block Size

Remember that the default sizes of disk blocks and file cache buffers in NetWare v3.11 are both 4KB. By default, then, there is a one-to-one correspondence between a cached disk block and a cache buffer. However, as you read in Chapter 5, you can configure the operating system to allocate file cache buffers larger than 4KB (8KB and 16KB, to be specific). This is accomplished either by placing the "SET Cache Buffer Size" command in the server's STARTUP.NCF file or by adding the "-c" option to the SERVER command (as in "SERVER -c8192). This parameter cannot be changed while the server is running.

Generally, you'll get the best performance when the cache buffer size matches the disk block size specified for the volumes at installation time. If all of your volumes are using 8KB blocks, for example, you should set the cache buffer size at 8KB. If you have volumes that use different-sized blocks, set the cache buffer size to match the *smallest* disk block size.

For example, if a server has two volumes, one of which has 4KB blocks while the other has 8KB blocks, configure the server to use 4KB cache buffers. That way, when caching data from a volume with 4KB blocks, there will be a one-to-one correspondence between cache buffers and cached disk blocks. When caching data from a volume with 8KB blocks, there will be a two-to-one correspondence between cache buffers and cached disk blocks. The same relationship applies to other possible combinations of volume disk blocks and file cache buffers.

Never set the cache buffer size larger than the disk block size. Because such a mismatch would waste memory and decrease performance, NetWare won't even let you mount any volumes whose disk block size is smaller than the cache buffer size.

How Caching Works for Disk Read Requests

When a workstation sends a request to read data from a network disk, NetWare copies the entire block of data from the disk into an available cache buffer. In doing so, the OS figures that subsequent read requests from that workstation are likely to be for data in the same vicinity as the original request. When the next request comes and it *is* for data already in the cache buffer, the OS doesn't have to go to the disk. If the requested data is not already in the cache buffer, the OS has to fetch it from the disk. As before, it copies the whole block containing that data into another cache buffer in anticipation of subsequent requests in that vicinity.

Read requests can be for application or utility program files as well as for the data used with the applications. Files that multiple users access heavily are likely to remain in cache memory all the time, provided you have enough cache buffers. Users may notice that a particular application loads more quickly at times. Although other factors (such as the state of the LAN communication system) may influence how fast an application loads, the difference could very well be whether the program files are in cache memory.

The typical NetWare v3.11 server has twenty to thirty times the disk capacity as it has the capacity for caching disk blocks. All available cache buffers can become full, especially on a busy server with a limited number of cache buffers. When a new request comes along for data that is not already in cache, the OS needs a way to decide which cache buffer to overwrite. NetWare employs what is called the Least Recently

Used (LRU) algorithm in this situation. This algorithm has the OS dump the contents of whichever buffer hasn't been used for the longest time. Once that cache buffer is available, NetWare fills it with the newly requested data block from the disk.

If the OS needs another cache buffer but can't find one available, it uses the LRU algorithm again to free up another cache buffer. This recycling of the least recently used buffer continues as long as requests keep coming in for data not in cache. Obviously, the server's performance will decrease if the server keeps having to go to disk for new data. The situation can become especially aggravated if you don't have enough memory in the server and users continually load a variety of different programs.

How Caching Works for Disk Write Requests

Hard disk drives can only accept writes containing a complete sector of data. Since a disk sector is typically much smaller than the cache buffer size (512 bytes compared to 4KB, for example), NetWare has to handle write requests differently than read requests. To understand how this works, picture an empty 4KB buffer. Assuming a disk sector size of 512 bytes, this buffer could hold up to eight sectors worth of data (8 x 512 = 4,096). As data comes in needing to be written to disk, the OS starts filling up the buffer sector by sector. When a full 512 bytes are written to cache, NetWare informs the application that the write has been completed. It's "lying," of course, since the sector has not actually been written to disk yet. But this lie allows the application to move on to other things more quickly than if it had to wait for the data to make it to the disk.

At this point another algorithm, called the "aging" algorithm, comes into play. This algorithm dictates that the OS must write the data to disk either as soon as all sectors in the cache buffer have been updated, or after 3.3 seconds have passed. (This 3.3 seconds is the default delay time; you can adjust the time via the SET command, as explained later in this chapter.) This aging of write requests allows NetWare to combine multiple small writes into one larger write request, thereby cutting down on the number of times it has to access the hard drive.

When a cache buffer contains updated data that has not yet been written to disk, it is called a "dirty" cache buffer. NetWare "flushes" dirty buffers by writing their data to disk at the earliest opportunity. If the least recently used buffer happens to be dirty, NetWare will always write it to disk immediately— without waiting 3.3 seconds—before dumping its contents.

Viewing File Cache Statistics in MONITOR

The NetWare v3.11 MONITOR utility displays numerous statistics that relate to file caching on its main screen display. Type LOAD MONITOR <Enter> at the server console. If MONITOR is already loaded, press <Ctrl><Esc> and select "Monitor Screen" from the list of screens. Here is a sample of the top half of MONITOR's main screen.

```
┌──────────────────────────────────────────────────────────────────────┐
│              Information For Server KAITLIN                           │
├──────────────────────────────────────────────────────────────────────┤
│  File Server Up Time:    0 Days  4 Hours 49 Minutes 10 Seconds        │
│  Utilization:                 6  │ Packet Receive Buffers:     10     │
│  Original Cache Buffers:  2,657  │ Directory Cache Buffers:    26     │
│  Total Cache Buffers:     2,229  │ Service Processes:           1     │
│  Dirty Cache Buffers:         4  │ Connections In Use:          1     │
│  Current Disk Requests:       0  │ Open Files:                  8     │
└──────────────────────────────────────────────────────────────────────┘
```

Original Cache Buffers. When a file server boots up, it allocates all memory not used for DOS and other NetWare services to the cache buffer memory pool. The number of cache buffers the OS creates in the pool depends on the cache buffer size (4KB is the default size). If you multiply this number by the buffer size, you'll get an idea how much memory was initially allocated for cache buffers.

Total Cache Buffers. When new NLMs are loaded, or when the OS requires more memory for various tasks, the memory is taken from the cache buffer pool. Thus the original number of cache buffers decreases. "Total Cache Buffers" indicates the current number of cache buffers available in server memory. Monitor this number periodically; if your server gets low on cache buffers, you need more memory, either by unloading unneeded NLMs or by adding more RAM to the server.

By default, the absolute minimum number of cache buffers is 20. NetWare will send a warning message when it nears this low limit, and another one when the minimum number is reached. You can adjust this low buffer reporting mechanism with server SET commands, as we'll discuss shortly.

Subtracting the "Total Cache Buffers" entry from the "Original Cache Buffers" entry yields another interesting statistic. This difference between the two represents the number of file cache buffers that were depleted because the operating system needed their memory for something else, such as short-term alloc memory or for an additional receive buffer. By comparing these two items, you can see how many file cache buffers have been "allocated" by the operating system for some other use. Remember, once a file cache buffer has been allocated for some other use by the operating system, it never returns to the pool of available file cache buffers.

Dirty Cache Buffers. This number indicates how many cache buffers currently contain updated data that has not yet been written to disk. Since NetWare writes dirty cache buffers within a maximum of 3.3 seconds, this number should be very low, if not zero, most of the time. (Note that NetWare will not allow the number of dirty cache buffers to exceed 75 percent of the total cache buffers.)

The server shown above has four dirty cache buffers, meaning that four buffers contain data that is different from the data originally cached. Shortly, the operating system will flush the dirty cache buffers to disk, at which point they will become "clean." When this occurs, MONITOR updates its display to reflect the fact that there are no more dirty cache buffers.

If this number stays large for an extended time, it could mean your disk channel is too slow to handle the onslaught of disk write requests.

How Many Cache Buffers Do You eed

The number of cache buffers you need for good performance depends on how many users you have and how they access the disk. For most networks, the amount of server RAM used for cache buffers should be around 60 to 80 percent of the total. Check the percentage for your server by selecting "Server Memory Statistics" under "Available Options" in the MONITOR utility. The cache percentage should never drop below 20 percent.

However, if users start noticing significant delays in accessing the disk at 30, 40, or even 50 percent, it's time to add more memory. This is especially true if you have a lot of different programs being loaded continually, or if your users access the data on the disk randomly more than sequentially. Even though NetWare v3.*x* says it will run with a minimum of 2.5MB of server RAM, most experts recommend 8 to 12MB of memory in the server for smoother, more efficient performance.

NetWare's SALVAGE and PURGE Utilities

The NetWare v3.11 file system preserves deleted files by maintaining "invisible" entries for such files in the volume directory table. Thus, when you delete a file, it remains on disk. However, the file's directory entry remains hidden from clients, and the free space on the volume doesn't show that these deleted files exist. (As you'll read shortly, this last statement isn't entirely true, because some deleted files do count toward the volume free space statistic.)

Deleted files remain on disk until the NetWare volume runs out of free blocks, at which point it begins to use blocks occupied by deleted files. You can confirm the existence of deleted files on a NetWare v3.11 volume by executing the NetWare CHKVOL utility, which displays information like this:

```
Statistics for fixed volume KAITLIN/SYS:

Total volume space:                            280,300
K Bytes Space used by files:                    67,156
K Bytes Space in use by deleted files:          48,288
K Bytes Space available from deleted files:     48,288
K Bytes Space remaining on volume:             213,144
K Bytes Space available to MDAY:               213,144  K Bytes
```

The CHKVOL utility shows you how much space is being occupied by deleted files. Note that deleted files do not show up in DIR nor in NDIR output.

The fact that the NetWare v3.11 file system retains deleted files implies that you can recover those deleted files. In fact, you can do so, using the NetWare SALVAGE utility. Figure 22-4 shows the SALVAGE utility's main screen.

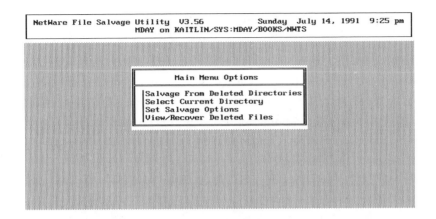

```
NetWare File Salvage Utility  V3.56          Sunday  July 14, 1991  9:25 pm
                   MDAY on KAITLIN/SYS:MDAY/BOOKS/NWTS

                          ┌──────────────────────────────┐
                          │      Main Menu Options        ║
                          ╞══════════════════════════════╡
                          │Salvage From Deleted Directories│
                          │Select Current Directory       │
                          │Set Salvage Options            │
                          │View/Recover Deleted Files     │
                          └──────────────────────────────┘
```

Figure 22-4: The NetWare v3.11 DOS SALVAGE utility allows you to recover deleted files that are preserved by the NetWare v3.11 file system.

As you can see from Figure 22-4, the SALVAGE utility affords users many options for recovering deleted files, including the ability to search for deleted files using the standard wildcard characters ("*" and "?"). Refer to Novell's *Utilities Reference* manual for instructions on how to use SALVAGE.

NetWare also maintains a special directory on each volume called DELETED.SAV. The DELETED.SAV directory contains deleted files for which the directory that used to contain the files (before they were deleted) no longer exists. As a corollary, the DELETED.SAV directory also contains entire subdirectory trees, including files, that were deleted en masse by means of the FILER utility or some equivalent method. The "Salvage From Deleted Directories" option shown in Figure 22-4 salvages files and directory trees from the DELETED.SAV directory.

Note that for security purposes, it may not be desirable to preserve certain deleted files. If you wish to PURGE a deleted file, remember that doing so renders all attempts to recover it unsuccessful. To use the PURGE utility, type the following at the workstation command line:

```
PURGE [filename | path] [/ALL] <Enter>
```

As you may have guessed from its syntax, the PURGE utility allows you to purge a specific file, or all files in a specific directory.

593

SET Commands for Tuning the NetWare File System

The NetWare v3.11 console provides a series of SET commands that allow you to tune numerous operating system parameters. These parameters control file and directory caching, file locking, workstation use of the file system, warning messages, and more. What follows is a detailed discussion of the parameters that relate to the NetWare file system, grouped according to the categories you see when you type **SET <Enter>** at the server console. (Certain SET commands that relate specifically to volumes are described in Chapter 24.)

Remember that SET commands must be issued from the server console command line, either directly to the console (or indirectly with RCONSOLE), or from the server's .NCF files. Some SET commands can only be issued from the STARTUP.NCF file when the server boots.

"File Caching" Category

Minimum File Cache Buffers

As you've read by now, NetWare v3.11 uses all available memory as file cache buffers. When another NLM or operating system process requires memory, NetWare obtains that memory by taking one or more file cache buffers and allocating them to the NLM or process requesting the memory. This depletes the total pool of file cache buffers, which, in turn, decreases file service performance.

By default, NetWare v3.11 allows depletion of file cache buffers until there are only 20 buffers remaining for file caching. At this point, NetWare refuses any further requests for memory. This refusal can limit all types of server activity, including the granting of further receive buffers and transaction tracking overhead buffers (depending on the configuration of the server in question). However, it also stops the depletion of file cache buffers.

You can change the minimum number of file cache buffers from its default of 20 to a higher number, up to 1000. To do so, use the SET command from the server console:

```
SET minimum file cache buffers=n <Enter>
```

The "SET minimum file cache buffers=*n*" command is the only one in this category that you normally need to worry about. If your server is running low on cache buffers after the OS has allocated memory from the cache buffers pool to other server processes, you can increase the minimum number of cache buffers. However, if you reserve too much memory for cache buffers, the other server processes may not have enough memory to operate effectively, and you might not be able to load additional NLMs. A better solution is to add more memory to the server.

Another reason you might want to increase the minimum number of file cache buffers is if your applications require high-performance, cached file service. Again, you don't want to set the minimum to a number so high that it restricts the operating system from expanding critical data structures such as connection tables. Nor do you want to restrict the operating system from maintaining an appropriate number of directory cache buffers, which can also decrease file service performance. You do want to prevent the loading of unneeded NLMs that will deplete file cache buffers.

Therefore, you should determine what NLMs the server will be running during normal operation and the potential memory requirements of those NLMs. Also, determine the memory requirements of the operating system during high-load points, such as the number of connections, receive buffers, and so on. Don't forget to include a liberal number of directory cache buffers in this calculation. What is left over is the amount of memory available for file cache buffers. Divide that amount by the size of file cache buffers (the default size is 4KB) and multiply that amount by 70%. The number you reach is a good minimum number. This should allow the operating system and required NLMs to obtain the memory they need, but should prevent the loading of unneeded NLMs. Thus file service performance should remain at an optimum level.

When the server reaches the minimum number of buffers specified, it displays the following message at the console: "Cache memory allocator exceeded minimum cache buffer left limit." This console alert is also written to the file server error log, which you can view from within SYSCON.

Minimum File Cache Buffer Report Threshold

The "Minimum File Cache Buffer Report Threshold" allows the OS to warn you when the number of file cache buffers nears the minimum. With the default setting of 20, NetWare will display the "Number of cache buffers is getting too low" message when the server is down to 20 cache buffers more than the minimum number specified in the previous command. You can set the minimum file cache buffer threshold report to any number between 0 and 1,000. The syntax is:

```
SET minimum file cache buffer report threshold=n <Enter>
```

It's a good idea to set the "Minimum Cache Buffer Report Threshold" to a number equal to the minimum file cache buffers. However, you don't have to do this. You may, for example, set the minimum cache buffer report threshold a small number, say 100, greater than the minimum cache buffers. By doing this, you cause NetWare v3.11 to send a warning message before the server reaches its minimum number of cache buffers.

Dirty Disk Cache Delay Time

This parameter allows you to define the maximum time a dirty cache buffer can remain dirty, after which NetWare forces the buffers to be flushed to disk by the file system. The default value for "Dirty Disk Cache Delay Time" is 3.3 seconds, which works very well for most networks. The minimum value is 0.1 seconds, and the maximum value is 10 seconds. The syntax for this parameter is:

```
SET dirty disk cache delay time=n <Enter>
```

You should ajust this parameter only if you are an experienced network manager. Under high-load conditions, the default delay time of 3.3 seconds may force the NetWare file system to flush dirty cache buffers at an inefficient time. This action can not only slow read requests, but can also drastically slow write performance by causing the file system to load the elevator in a less-than-efficient manner. In this case, you may want to raise this parameter to increase disk write performance.

Decreasing the time because you are afraid of losing data is not a good idea; it only reduces the risk by a slight margin and can drastically reduce server performance by forcing the OS to make more frequent trips to the disk. Most NCP write request packets contain between 512 bytes and 1KB of data anyway. It is better to let small write requests accumulate in the cache buffer and be written a full block at a time whenever possible. In fact, if the overwhelming majority of users' write requests are small, you might see better performance by increasing the time a little to let more requests pile up before they go to disk.

In terms of file service performance, then, decreasing the "Dirty Disk Cache Delay Time" is a relatively expensive way to gain data integrity. The NetWare v3.11 Transaction Tracking System (TTS) is actually more effective at retaining data integrity in the face of faults, and also happens to be more efficient overall. (See Chapter 23 for a discussion of the TTS.)

Maximum Concurrent Disk Cache Writes

This SET parameter determines how active the volume disk drive(s) are at flushing dirty file cache buffers to disk. It can affect the ability of the volume disk drive(s) to service read requests quickly. To improve the efficiency of disk I/O requests, NetWare uses an "elevator seeking" mechanism. When reading from or writing to a disk, the disk process places read and write requests in a queue and arranges them in order so that the read/write heads can make a smooth sweep across the disk's surface. This lets the disk drive perform more efficiently by reducing the distance the disk head needs to move across the media.

When placing read and write requests in the elevator, the NetWare file system gathers data from dirty cache buffers and read requests, and arranges the data in the elevator in the most efficient manner. If there are many dirty cache buffers, it's possible that NetWare may fill the entire elevator with write requests. This situation delays the servicing of read requests until the next elevator cycle. The maximum disk cache writes parameter allows you to specify a limit to the number of write requests NetWare can place in the elevator during a single cycle. The syntax is:

```
SET maximum concurrent disk cache writes=n <Enter>
```

By default, NetWare allows a maximum of 50 write requests to queue up before the disk head starts its sweep. The lower you set the maximum concurrent disk cache writes parameter, the more quickly NetWare will be able to fulfill read requests (on average), and the more slowly NetWare will be able to flush dirty cache buffers (the lowest you can go is 10). On average, most disk activity for a NetWare server involves reading rather than writing, so you probably won't have to change this parameter from its default value of 50 concurrent disk cache writes.

However, for servers running database applications, writing data to disk may be the most critical activity. In this case, it's important for NetWare to be able to flush dirty cache buffers as soon as possible. You can get a handle on how quickly NetWare v3.11 is flushing dirty cache buffers by viewing MONITOR's main screen. The two items to look at are "Total Cache Buffers" and "Dirty Cache Buffers." If more than three quarters of the total cache buffers are dirty at any given time, you can speed the fulfillment of disk write requests by increasing maximum concurrent disk cache writes, up to the maximum of 100 per elevator cycle.

Note that you should never use this parameter to limit the amount of time a file cache buffer can remain dirty; the "Dirty Disk Cache Delay Time" parameter is more appropriate for doing so. And the maximum concurrent disk cache writes parameter doesn't specify a given time that dirty file cache buffers remain dirty; it merely sets the relative ratio of read and write requests in an elevator cycle under high-load conditions. Moreover, this parameter has virtually no effect on the NetWare v3.11 file system under medium- and low-load conditions.

"Directory Caching" Category

Directory Cache Buffer NonReferenced Delay

You'll recall that NetWare v3.11 caches directory table entries differently than it caches file data. Cached directory entries are cached entries from the volume directory table. Directory entries always point to the first FAT entry for a file. Cached directory entries speed access to file and directory information equally.

Whenever clients request access to a file or request information about a directory or directory tree, NetWare attempts to cache the related directory information. There's an inverse relationship between directory cache buffers and file cache buffers. The more directory entries NetWare caches, the fewer file cache buffers are available for caching file data. Both types of caching increase file service performance. However, file cache buffers increase performance to a greater degree than directory cache buffers for typical applications.

The "Directory Cache Buffer Nonreferenced Delay" parameter allows you to control how quickly the NetWare v3.11 file system can recycle its pool of directory cache buffers. For example, whenever NetWare places directory table data in a cache buffer, it maintains that information in the buffer until no client uses the cached information for the time interval specified in the nonreferenced delay parameter. When the interval expires with no access to the cached directory data, NetWare recycles the directory cache buffer, making it available for caching other directory information.

On the other hand, if a client requests data from the directory table and there are no available directory cache buffers, NetWare v3.11 takes a buffer out of the file cache buffer pool and uses it as a directory cache buffer. Once a file cache buffer has been allocated as a directory cache buffer, NetWare can't return that buffer to use as a file cache buffer.

Increasing the "Directory Cache Buffer Nonreferenced Delay" parameter causes the NetWare v3.11 file system to retain directory cache buffers for a longer interval after the last access to the information they hold. This allows NetWare to use directory cache buffers more efficiently by reducing the need to recycle them. However, it has the side effect of depleting available file cache buffers.

Reducing the "Directory Cache Buffer Nonreferenced Delay" parameter causes NetWare to recycle directory cache buffers more frequently, which can slow client access to directory information. Consequently, however, it reduces the need for NetWare to remove buffers from the file cache buffer pool, thereby speeding client access to file data.

To raise or lower this parameter, use the SET command as follows:

```
SET directory cache buffer nonreferenced delay=time <Enter>
```

The default value for "Directory Cache Buffer Nonreferenced Delay" is 5.5 seconds. The valid range is from 1 second to 5 minutes. You should decrease this parameter only if the server is running low on cache buffers. You should increase this parameter only if the server has plenty of cache buffers and you determine a need to speed client access to directory information. You can view the number of directory cache buffers currently allocated by the server on the main screen of the MONITOR NLM.

Maximum and Minimum Directory Cache Buffers

Once you understand the difference between file cache buffers and directory cache buffers, it's important to note that cache memory being used to cache directory information is unavailable for caching file data. In other words, cache memory used for directory caching remains unavailable for file caching until you re-initialize the server.

Because of this memory tradeoff between directory cache buffers and file cache buffers, NetWare provides two SET parameters that establish bounds for the maximum and minimum numbers of directory cache buffers NetWare v3.11 will allocate for its file system. The syntax for these two parameters is:

```
SET maximum directory cache buffers=n <Enter>

SET minimum directory cache buffers=n <Enter>
```

The valid range for maximum directory cache buffers is from 20 to 4,000, with the default being 500; for minimum directory cache buffers, the range is from 10 to 2,000, and the default is 20.

You should use the "Maximum..." and "Minimum Directory Cache Buffers" parameters in concert with the "Minimum Directory Cache Buffer Nonreferenced Time" to set the upper and lower bounds and the rate at which NetWare will recycle directory cache buffers. If you define a wide range between the maximum and minimum parameters, it makes sense to define a relatively long nonreferenced delay time period. Conversely, if you define a narrow range between maximum and minimum directory cache buffers, it makes sense to define a short nonreferenced delay interval, which causes NetWare to recycle its directory buffers more quickly.

Dirty Directory Cache Delay Time

This parameter defines the maximum time period during which the NetWare file system will allow a directory cache buffer to remain dirty before NetWare forces the directory cache buffer to be flushed to disk.

The valid range for this parameter is from 0 to 10 seconds. However, we don't recommend that you alter this parameter from its default value of 0.5 seconds. A dirty directory cache buffer occurs when a client alters the directory structure of a NetWare v3.11 volume: for instance, whenever a client creates, renames, or deletes a directory or subdirectory. If you define this parameter as zero, it can disrupt the normal file system buffer flushing activity. The syntax for setting dirty directory cache delay time is:

```
SET dirty directory cache delay time=time <Enter>
```

Maximum Concurrent Directory Cache Writes

The "Maximum Concurrent Directory Cache Writes" parameter behaves exactly like the "Maximum Concurrent Disk Cache Writes" parameter, so we refer you to the preceding discussion for details. The valid range for the "Maximum Concurrent Directory Cache Writes" parameter is from 5 to 50 seconds, with the default being 10 seconds.

Directory Cache Allocation Wait Time

The directory cache allocation wait time parameter forces NetWare v3.11 to wait for an interval between allocation of directory cache buffers. The default value for this parameter is 2.2 seconds, meaning that NetWare can allocate, at most, one additional directory cache buffer every 2.2 seconds.

The purpose of the "Directory Cache Allocation Wait Time" parameter is to adjust how fast NetWare responds to transient load spikes. The syntax for setting the directory cache allocation wait time is:

```
SET directory cache allocation wait time=time <Enter>
```

The principle behind this parameter is somewhat arcane, however. Recall that NetWare attempts to recycle unreferenced directory cache buffers before allocating new ones. Forcing NetWare to wait for a time interval to pass before allocating an additional directory cache buffer increases the likelihood that an unreferenced buffer will become available for recycling before the minimum interval passes. This procedure tends to reduce the total number of directory cache buffers, thereby preserving more memory for use as file cache.

"File System" Category

Immediate Purge Of Deleted Files

As discussed previously in this chapter, NetWare preserves deleted files on the sever until the space they take up is needed by other files. The "Immediate Purge of Deleted Files" parameter, as you've most likely surmised, causes NetWare to purge files as soon as you delete them. Turning on this parameter, of course, prevents NetWare from preserving the deleted files.

To have your server purge all deleted files immediately, type the following command at the server console:

```
SET immediate purge of deleted files=on <Enter>
```

The default for this parameter is "off," meaning that the NetWare v3.11 file system retains deleted files.

Minimum File Delete Wait Time

The "Minimum File Delete Wait Time" parameter determines how long the NetWare v3.11 file system must guarantee that a file remains in a salvageable state after a user deletes that file. A file is in a salvageable state only as long as the NetWare file system doesn't write over one of the file's blocks. It's possible, then, for a file to be unsalvageable before the file is explicitly purged. Remember that NetWare writes over deleted (and not yet purged) files on a volume as soon as that volume runs out of unoccupied FAT entries. When NetWare does this, it's called "automatic purging."

Even if a deleted file isn't automatically purged, it's always possible that some application will use the blocks occupied by the deleted file for other data. We refer to this type of file corruptions as "random overwrite." Random overwrite can only happen to deleted files that aren't yet purged, but have been deleted for longer than the minimum file delete wait time.

Purging a deleted file, on the other hand, wipes out that file's entries in the volume FAT and obliterates the purged file's data by writing over its blocks on the volume. To set the minimum file delete wait time for a server, at the server console, type:

```
SET minimum file delete wait time=time <Enter>
```

Valid times range from 0 seconds to 7 days, while the default time is 1 minute and 5.9 seconds. Be careful when entering the time parameter, because the console will only recognize single time units, such as "1 minute," or "2 days."

If you type "SET Minimum File Delete Wait Time=1 day," for example, the NetWare v3.11 file system guarantees that you'll be able to salvage deleted files within one day (24 hours). After one day has passed, you may or may not be able to salvage the deleted file, depending on the state of the volume in question. Note that if you explicitly purge a file, the NetWare file system disregards this parameter and purges the file, just as you instructed it to do.

File Delete Wait Time

This parameter defines the minimum time a file is resistant to automatic purging. Note the difference between "File Delete Wait Time" and "Minimum File Delete Wait Time." The "Minimum File Delete Wait Time" parameter guarantees that a file won't be automatically purged or randomly overwritten for a specified time period. On the other hand, the "File Delete Wait Time" parameter guarantees only that a file won't be automatically purged for a specified time period; it doesn't protect against random overwrites.

The "File Delete Wait Time" parameter has the same valid range as the "Minimum File Delete Wait Time" parameter, but has a default value of just under five and a half minutes. The syntax for this parameter is the same as for "Minimum File Delete Wait Time."

Maximum Percent of Volume Used by Directory

Here's an interesting parameter; it defines the maximum percent of a volume that can be used for directory space. This parameter simply says that at most $n\%$ of the volume can be used to store directory entries.

If clients end up creating enough directories, it's possible for the space devoted by the file system to store directory information to exceed this parameter, thereby keeping clients from being able to create further directories. Note that this can happen with lots of free space remaining on the volume, which leads to some interesting error messages. For example, some applications, when experiencing this condition, will report that the volume is full. To set the "Maximum Percent of Volume Used by Directory" parameter, at the server console, type:

```
SET maximum percent of volume used by directory=percent <Enter>
```

The valid range for this parameter is from 5 to 50 percent of the total volume space, while the default value is 13% of volume space. You probably won't exceed the default threshold, unless you run applications that create many directories and fill those directories with small files.

Extended File Attributes

Two parameters allow you to limit the volume storage space used by Netware to store extended file attributes. Extended file attributes are pieces of information stored by files using non-DOS name spaces. Name spaces, you may recall, allow the NetWare file system to store non-DOS files, such as Macintosh and OS/2 HPFS files. These types of files have long names and other attributes beyond those of standard DOS files, and the Netware file system views these attributes as "extended attributes."

The "Extended File Attributes" parameter defines a maximum percentage of volume space to be occupied by extended file attributes. NetWare v3.11 checks this parameter when it mounts a volume. If the actual percentage of volume space occupied by extended attributes exceeds the defined maximum, NetWare won't mount the volume. Note that it's possible for a volume to mount, but then exceed this limit during file service, in which case the volume will fail to mount upon the next mount attempt.

To invoke this parameter, at the server console, type:

```
SET maximum percent of volume space allowed for extended
    attributes =percent <Enter>
```

A related parameter is "Maximum Extended Attributes per File or Path." "File or path" simply means "file or directory." To set this parameter, at the server console, type:

```
SET maximum extended attributes per file or path=number <Enter>
```

This parameter limits individual files and directories to a specific number of extended attributes. Be careful to define this parameter as a *number* rather than as a *percentage*. For example, setting this parameter equal to "15" means that each file can have at most fifteen extended attributes, not that fifteen percent of the file's storage can be occupied by extended attributes.

The valid range for "Maximum Percent of Volume Space Allowed for Extended Attributes" is from 5 to 50% of total volume space; the default value is 10%. The valid range for "Maximum Extended Attributes per File or Path" is from 4 to 512 extended attributes, and the default value is 32 attributes. Both of these default values should be sufficient. However, you may need to raise them if you have multiple non-DOS name spaces active on a volume—for example, if you support OS/2 HPFS, Macintosh, and NFS files on a single volume.

NCP File Commit

Some advanced NLM applications require direct access to the NetWare v3.11 file system. For these types of applications, the NetWare operating system provides a series of NetWare Core Protocols (NCPs). The "NCP File Commit" parameter activates a particular NCP that causes all of an application's write requests to be flushed to disk immediately. Such preemptive flushing of cache buffers can decrease overall file service performance. However, applications that use this NCP have particularly good reasons for doing so.

The default value for "NCP File Commit" is OFF. You shouldn't have to change it to ON unless the file system is having problems flushing its cache buffers. To turn this parameter on, at the server console, type:

```
SET NCP file commit=on <Enter>
```

One indication that the file system is having problems flushing its cache buffers is that the number of dirty cache buffers remains at a high level (more than 70% of total cache buffers). Note that changing this parameter is meaningless unless an application loaded on the server uses the direct file system NCPs.

Maximum Subdirectory Tree Depth

The NetWare v3.11 file system supports subdirectory tree depths of up to 100 levels. The depth of a subdirectory tree equals the number of subdirectories below the root volume. For example, "SYS:DATA\TEXT\RESEARCH" is a three-level directory structure. Some DOS applications don't work correctly with very deep subdirectory trees, and you can use this parameter to limit the depth of subdirectory trees to a level supported by specific applications. For example, to limit the depth of subdirectory trees to 15, enter the following at the server console:

```
SET maximum subdirectory tree depth=15 <Enter>
```

The default value for "Maximum Subdirectory Tree Depth" is 25 levels, and the valid range is from 10 to 100 levels. You should only change this parameter if a specific application requires greater or fewer subdirectory levels than the default of 25.

Turbo FAT Re-use Wait Time

When NetWare v3.11 clients gain access to files having 64 or more entries in the volume FAT, NetWare may choose to construct a "turbo FAT" for the file. A turbo FAT is a special cached FAT that is distinct from the volume FAT. NetWare uses turbo FATs specifically to provide clients with faster access to large files. Whenever NetWare builds a turbo FAT for a file, that file is said to be "indexed." When it constructs a turbo FAT, NetWare retains the turbo FAT in memory for a short period of time after clients close the indexed file.

NetWare retains the turbo FAT for a short interval after the indexed file is closed because overhead is involved in constructing a turbo FAT, and there's a good chance that a client will re-open the indexed file shortly. If NetWare collapses the turbo FAT prematurely, it will have to re-construct it immediately because clients still require access to the indexed file. On the other hand, if NetWare retains the turbo FAT too long, it may be tying up cache buffers that could otherwise be used to the advantage of clients that which no longer require access to the indexed file.

By changing the value of the "Turbo FAT Re-use Wait Time" parameter, you can control how long NetWare retains a turbo FAT after clients have closed the indexed file. The default value for this parameter is just under five and one-half minutes, while the valid range is from just under one second to just over an hour and five minutes. To set "Turbo FAT Re-use Wait Time," at the server console, type:

```
SET turbo fat re-use wait time=time <Enter>
```

Note that you'll encounter problems if you attempt to enter more than one time unit within a single line at the server console. For example, the line

```
SET turbo fat re-use wait time=1 hour and 1 minute <Enter>
```

won't work as you intended. The solution is to remove the "and" in between time units. For example:

```
SET turbo fat re-use wait time=1 hour 1 minute 1.2 seconds <Enter>
```

As a rule of thumb, setting a short "Turbo FAT Re-use Wait Time" causes NetWare v3.11 to use its FAT cache memory more efficiently, while setting a long "Turbo FAT Re-use Wait Time" causes NetWare v3.11 to use its FAT cache memory more effectively, albeit less efficiently. NetWare generates turbo FAT indexes using permanent memory, which it removes from available file cache memory.

So if your server has plenty of memory, you may be able to increase file service performance by increasing the "Turbo FAT Re-use Wait Time" parameter. Conversely, if your server is short of RAM, you may be able to increase file service performance by decreasing the "Turbo FAT Re-use Wait Time." In the former case, the server has all the file cache buffers it needs; in the latter case, the server is short on file cache buffers. Remember that you can determine if the server is short on file cache buffers by looking at the "Server Memory Statistics" screen of the MONITOR NLM, as shown in Figure 22-5.

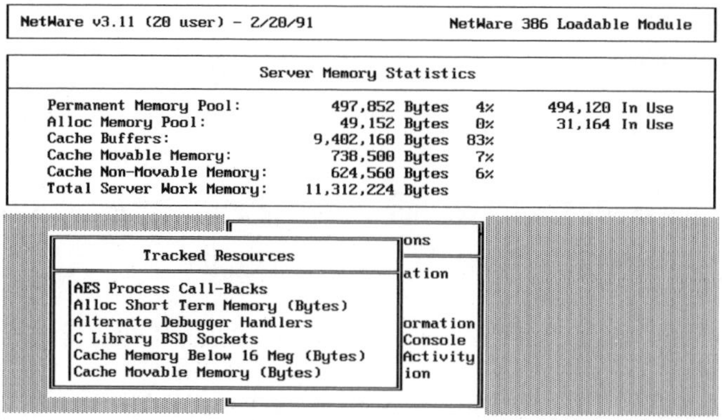

```
┌─────────────────────────────────────────────────────────────────────┐
│ NetWare v3.11 (20 user) - 2/20/91          NetWare 386 Loadable Module │
└─────────────────────────────────────────────────────────────────────┘

┌─────────────────────────────────────────────────────────────────────┐
│                    Server Memory Statistics                           │
│  Permanent Memory Pool:        497,852 Bytes   4%   494,120 In Use     │
│  Alloc Memory Pool:             49,152 Bytes   0%    31,164 In Use     │
│  Cache Buffers:              9,402,160 Bytes  83%                      │
│  Cache Movable Memory:         738,500 Bytes   7%                      │
│  Cache Non-Movable Memory:     624,560 Bytes   6%                      │
│  Total Server Work Memory:  11,312,224 Bytes                          │
└─────────────────────────────────────────────────────────────────────┘

         ┌──────────────────────────────────┐ ons
         │        Tracked Resources         │ ation
         ├──────────────────────────────────┤
         │ AES Process Call-Backs           │
         │ Alloc Short Term Memory (Bytes)  │
         │ Alternate Debugger Handlers      │ ormation
         │ C Library BSD Sockets            │ Console
         │ Cache Memory Below 16 Meg (Bytes)│ Activity
         │ Cache Movable Memory (Bytes)     │ ion
         └──────────────────────────────────┘
```

Figure 22-5: By selecting "Resource Utilization" from the MONITOR "Available Options" menu, you can view the percentage of memory available to the server for file cache buffers.

As you can see, MONITOR displays the percentage of server memory currently in use as cache buffers. The percentage displayed in Figure 22-5 is 83%. If this statistic falls below 20%, you can safely assume that the server is short of file cache buffers, in which case you may want to decrease the "Turbo FAT Re-use Wait Time" parameter.

You should also consider the behavior of your network-based data management application. (Most indexed files are part of a database application.) If your database software frequently opens and closes data files, you should attempt to synchronize the "Turbo FAT Re-use Wait Time" with the historical behavior of the database application. For example, if your database software opens a specific large file every ten minutes, performs a search on it, and then closes it, you may want to increase the "Turbo FAT Re-use Wait Time" parameter to eleven minutes. Doing so will ensure that the server doesn't have to rebuild the same turbo FAT every time the application opens a particular file.

"Locks" Category

Maximum File Locks

To control access to files, the NetWare v3.11 file system allows a client to place a lock on the file, thereby preventing other clients from writing data to the file. Obviously, this is a critical function of the file system. Each file lock consumes a small amount of server memory. You can use the "Maximum File Locks" parameter to define the maximum number of file locks NetWare will grant to clients at a given time. The syntax for this parameter, typed at the console command line, is:

```
SET maximum file locks=n <Enter>
```

The default maximum concurrent files locks is 10,000 locks, sufficient in most cases. For example, on a server with 250 active clients, each client may have an average of 40 file locks, exclusive of system-generated file locks. The valid range is from 100 locks to 100,000 locks.

Maximum Record Locks

Record locks are similar to file locks. The difference is that file locks lock the entre file, while record locks lock a portion of the file.

Record locks are used exclusively by database applications, where a file is divided into predefined logical units called "records." Usually, records within a database are all the same number of bytes. Clients require a greater number of record locks than file locks. Record locking is the mechanism that makes multiuser database applications possible, because multiple clients can be allowed to write data to the same file concurrently, provided that only a single client writes data to a specific record at a given time.

The default maximum number of record locks for a NetWare v3.11 server is 20,000, while the valid range is from 100 record locks to 200,000 record locks. Like file locks, record locks consume server memory. To set the "Maximum Record Locks" parameter, from the console command line, type:

```
SET maximum record locks=n <Enter>
```

Just as you can set the maximum number of record and file locks a server will grant, you can set a maximum number of record or file locks each client can obtain from the console command line as follows:

```
SET maximum file locks per connection=n <Enter>
SET maximum record locks per connection=n <Enter>
```

The default for maximum file locks per connection is 250 file locks, with a valid range of ten file locks to 1,000 file locks per connection. The default for maximum record locks per connection is 500 record locks, with a valid range of ten record locks to 10,000 record locks per connection.

How you set the "Maximum Record File Locks per Connection" and "Maximum File Locks per Connection" parameters depends largely on the requirements of your database application. Some database applications make use of many small files, while other database applications make use of fewer large files. Similarly, some database applications generate more record locks per client than other applications do.

Troubleshooting Application Error Messages

As you've probably realized, the NetWare v3.11 file system is a sophisticated piece of software—much more sophisticated, in fact, than the DOS file system, and more sophisticated than the Macintosh and OS/2 HPFS file systems. Applications written for non-NetWare file systems may therefore provide misleading error messages when they run with the NetWare v3.11 file system.

For example, we've seen a DOS application that, upon failing to obtain a NetWare file lock, reported that the disk had failed. In actuality, the disk hadn't failed, but instead another client held a lock on the file the DOS application attempted to open for writing. We've also seen a Macintosh application that, upon attempting to copy a directory tree to a NetWare server, reported that the disk was full. The disk wasn't actually full, but instead had exceeded the maximum extended attributes for a single directory tree.

The important thing to remember from these two examples is that most applications you'll run on your NetWare v3.11 server are not fully aware of the NetWare file system. As a result, you can't trust application error messages. To find out what's really happening, you sometimes have to ignore the application error messages and, using your knowledge of the NetWare v3.11 file system, deduce what the problem is.

In both of the examples above, what the application assumed was an error was in fact not an error, but a consequence of the design of the NetWare v3.11 file system. In such cases, you probably won't get a console error message. Your best troubleshooting strategy is to narrow the possibilities down to a group of SET parameters you can change, and then to change these parameters one at a time. For example, raise the limit on concurrent file locks and re-run the offending application.

Sometimes, however, an application error message will indicate a problem with the server. For example, a volume may actually be full or even dysfunctional. Whenever there's a problem with the server, however, you should get a host of console messages and related problems. For example, if all active clients experience problems writing data to the server at the same time, it's a safe bet that there's a problem with one or more server volumes. There are probably some error messages at the server console, too. Unlike most client applications, NetWare is very aware of itself, and usually provides informative and correct error messages.

The only way application developers can provide correct error messages for NetWare v3.11 is to build awareness of the NetWare operating system into their applications. This is a painstaking and resource-consuming effort for developers, and consequently many developers don't do it. Some do, however, and their numbers are increasing along with the popularity of NetWare. Our advice is to prefer applications that are aware of NetWare and that provide accurate error messages. By doing so, you'll place pressure on all developers to make their applications more appropriate for NetWare.

CHAPTER 23

System Fault Tolerance

In addition to file and directory caching, which increase file service performance, the NetWare v3.11 file system maintains a combination of data structures and logical mechanisms designed to increase its tolerance of faults and reduce the likelihood of data corruption. These mechanisms include maintaining redundant copies of volume FATs and directory tables (explained in Chapter 22), Hot Fix, read-after-write verification, disk mirroring/duplexing, and transaction tracking. This chapter explains the last four aspects of NetWare's fault tolerance.

Hot Fix

Hot Fix is a logical mechanism the NetWare v3.11 file system uses to protect against random media errors. ("Logical" in this context means software-based, rather than hardware-based. A "logical" mechanism is a device constructed using software, while a "physical" mechanism is a hardware device. An example of a physical mechanism to protect against random media errors is disk mirroring.)

Random media errors are a fact of life for all types of computer storage. All types of magnetic media use a coating of magnetic material that is placed on some other material, such as a platter or tape, and which the computer can manipulate to store data. Over time, small areas of a storage device's magnetic coating lose their ability to be manipulated by the computer. When this happens, the degraded area becomes "corrupt," or unsuitable for data storage. On a hard disk, "bad blocks" are areas on the disk where the magnetic coating has become degraded.

Hot Fix refers to NetWare's ability to detect bad disk blocks and redirect all read or write operations to another block within the Hot Fix redirection area of the

NetWare partition. The Hot Fix redirection area is a reserve pool of disk blocks NetWare maintains on each partition that will accept data in case other blocks on the main portion of the partition go bad. (You may recall reading about the Hot Fix redirection area in Chapter 5.) Figure 23-1 shows how Hot Fix works.

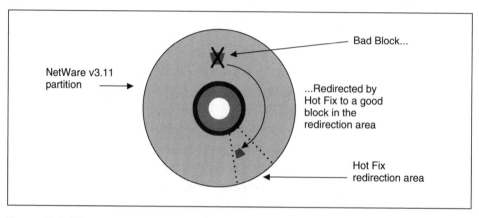

Figure 23-1: When NetWare v3.11 detects a bad block on one of its partitions, it "shuts down" the block and re-directs all input and output operations addressed to the bad block to a good block in the Hot Fix redirection area.

You determine the size of a partition's redirection area when you create the partition. By default, INSTALL installs a redirection area equal to two percent of the blocks on the partition you are creating. However, you can raise or lower the size of the redirection area (in blocks) by editing the Redirection Area field in INSTALL's "Partition Information" window, as shown in Figure 23-2.

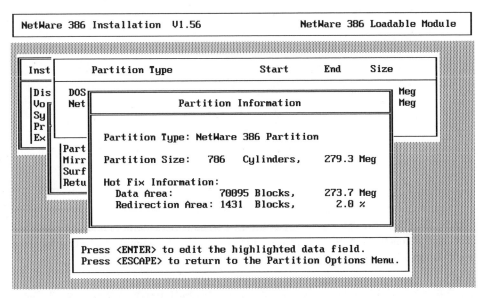

Figure 23-2: INSTALL NLM allows you to edit the size of a NetWare partition's Hot Fix redirection area in the "Partition Information" window.

Read-After-Write Verification

Hot Fix would be of little use to anyone without read-after-write verification. The concept behind read-after-write verification is simple: when NetWare v3.11 writes data to disk, it maintains a copy of the written data in memory. Immediately after writing the data to disk, it reads another copy of the written data off the disk and back into a second area of memory. It then compares the two copies of the written data.

If the two copies are equal, NetWare infers that the underlying disk block(s) are functional. (It obtained the second copy of the data by reading it from the disk blocks.) However, if the two copies are different, NetWare infers that the "disk" copy is incorrect and hence the disk blocks from which it obtained the "disk" copy are bad. Figure 23-3 shows how read-after-write verification works.

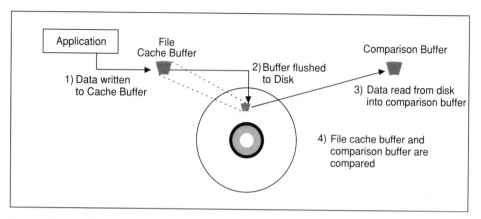

Figure 23-3: NetWare retains a copy of the written data in its memory and compares the data on the disk to the copy in memory. If the two copies don't match, the read-after-write verification fails.

One important aspect of NetWare v3.11's read-after-write verification is that it takes place "below" the file system cache. When NetWare v3.11 is writing to a cached disk block, it performs read-after-write verification when the cache buffer is flushed to disk, rather than when the data is written to cache. Figure 23-4 shows how this works.

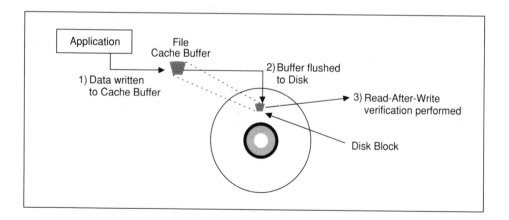

Figure 23-4: When data is cached, NetWare's read-after-write verification occurs when the cached data is flushed to disk, rather than when the data is written to cache.

616

Write Redirection

Write redirection is similar to read-after-write verification. When NetWare v3.11 writes data to disk (or flushes cached data from buffer to disk) and the write operation returns an error code, NetWare automatically redirects the data to a reserve block from the Hot Fix redirection pool. The difference between write redirection and read-after-write verification is that write redirection is triggered by an error code on a write operation, while read-after-write verification can detect data errors for write operations that return with a success code.

Read Redirection

If your server has mirrored or duplexed partitions, you can benefit from read redirection. When NetWare v3.11 attempts to read data from disk, but is unsuccessful because of a disk error, it automatically attempts to read the same data from a mirrored or duplexed partition. Whenever read redirection occurs, NetWare marks the offending disk block as "bad" and redirects all future reads or writes to a block from the Hot Fix redirection area. Even if the partition isn't mirrored or duplexed, NetWare still marks the block as "bad" and redirects all future reads and writes to a block from the redirection area. However, without mirroring or duplexing, you can't recover data using read redirection.

Read redirection is necessary to detect latent media errors. A latent media error occurs when a disk block becomes corrupt after data has been successfully written to it. Read-after-write verification can't detect latent media errors, because the media goes bad after NetWare performs read-after-write verification.

Random Media Errors vs. Bad Media

We stated earlier that random media errors are a fact of life. How, then, do you tell the difference between random media errors—a normal condition—and bad media that may be on the verge of total failure?

The answer is that random media errors occur at a constant rate, while bad media fails at an increasing rate. In other words, NetWare will detect random media errors regularly—say, one block every month. After a year or so, if NetWare begins detecting bad blocks at an increased rate (for example, one per day), you should suspect the integrity of the drive media.

Checking Hot Fix Redirection in MONITOR

The MONITOR NLM provides you with a way to track the number of bad blocks that are detected and redirected by NetWare v3.11. To view redirected blocks, follow these steps:

1. Select "Disk Information" from the MONITOR "Available Options" menu. MONITOR will display the "System Disk Drives" dialog box, which shows all the drives currently on-line.

2. Select the drive you wish to check by highlighting its entry in the "System Disk Drives" dialog box and pressing <Enter>. At this point, a window similar to the following should appear:

```
               ISA Type 028        Card  0 Controller  0 Drive 0
 ┌─────────────────────────────────────────────────────────────────────────┐
 │ Driver:              ISADISK.DSK    │  Partition Blocks:        71,526    │
 │ Disk Size:              309 Meg     │  Data Blocks:             70,095    │
 │ Partitions:                   2     │  Redirection Blocks:       1,431    │
 │ Mirror Status:      Not Mirrored    │  Redirected Blocks:            2    │
 │ Hot Fix Status:          Normal     │  Reserved Blocks:             28    │
 └─────────────────────────────────────────────────────────────────────────┘
```

In this screen, MONITOR.NLM displays data blocks, redirection blocks, and redirected blocks. You can use this information to track the rate of random media errors for a NetWare partition.

The key statistic to look is "Redirected Blocks." As we said, you should see the number of redirected blocks increase at a slow but constant rate. This is the normal behavior of a magnetic disk drive. However, if you notice that redirected blocks are increasing at a faster rate than before, you should consider yourself warned that something is wrong—or will shortly be terribly wrong—with the drive in question.

If you ever see a warning message that the server is low on redirection blocks, it means that particular network disk is about to fail. Have your users save their open files to a *local* disk if possible. Then bring down the server. Back up all data on the disk, reinitialize the drive, and restore the data. If the Hot Fix errors persist, you'll have to replace the drive.

Disk Mirroring and Duplexing

As you'll recall from Chapter 5, NetWare allows you to pair disks together to form one logical drive. Disk mirroring stores duplicate data on two hard disks connected on the same disk channel. This protects data against a failure on either disk, but not against failures in other channel components such as controllers, cables, and power supplies.

Disk duplexing is the same as mirroring, except that the two disks involved communicate with the server through separate disk channels. With disk duplexing, if any component on the disks or along the disk channel fails, data can still be written to and retrieved from the duplicate disk via the opposite channel. If a component on the channel fails, the operating system sends a message to indicate that the failure occurred.

You establish disk duplexing in the same way you establish disk mirroring, except that each of the mirrored disks speaks to the file server through its own disk channel. Once set up, you can view the mirroring status for both mirrored and duplexed disks under "Disk Options" in the INSTALL NLM. Likewise, you can use this option to establish a new mirrored disk or to temporarily unmirror and then remirror a mirrored/duplexed disk pair.

As you make changes to the status of your disks (to establish disk mirroring, or for any other reason), be sure to record the changes in your network configuration log. Keeping your logbook current will make troubleshooting and maintenance easier.

Unmirroring Disks

If you need to unmirror a disk to replace or repair it, you can do so without bringing down the file server. Here are the steps:

1. Make sure all users are logged out of the network.

2. Dismount the affected volume(s), using the DISMOUNT console command.

3. Go into the INSTALL utility and select "Disk Options" from the main menu.

4. Choose "Mirroring" from the "Available Disk Options" menu.

5. In the resulting list of mirrored partitions, highlight the one you want to unmirror and press <Del>.

NetWare will begin the unmirroring process. When it's completed, you can remount the volume if necessary to allow users to access the data while you fix the other disk. However, mirroring protection will not be available during this time.

Remirroring Disks

To remirror a disk (after one of the disks has been unmirrored, has failed and needs to be replaced or repaired, or has been shut off), you essentially follow the same procedure you followed when you established the mirrored pair.

1. If necessary, make sure no users are accessing the affected volumes and then dismount the volumes.

3. Go into the INSTALL utility and select "Disk Options" from the main menu.

4. Choose "Mirroring" from the "Available Disk Options" menu.

5. In the resulting "Partition Mirroring Status" list, highlight the partition you want to remirror.

6. Press <Ins> and select the partition to be remirrored to the one you selected in step 5.

The file server will then re-establish the mirror status and will either copy all of the data from the partner disk onto the mirrored disk (if the file server had been rebooted since the disk was unmirrored), or will copy over any changes that have been made since the disk was unmirrored (if the file server hasn't been rebooted).

Transaction Tracking

Transaction tracking is a special type of fault tolerance offered by the NetWare v3.11 file system. TTS is designed to protect database applications from possible corruption in the event of system failure during a software transaction. The TTS feature guarantees that in the event of a network failure during a transaction, one of two things will happen: The transaction will either be wholly saved or, if the transaction was only partially complete, TTS will back out the incomplete transaction and use the backout file to restore the database to its original state.

TransactionTracking is especially useful when NetWare is updating two or more records in a single file, or when updating one or more records in two or more files as a set. In both cases, TTS ensures all records are updated or none are.

Flagging a File Transactional

You apply transaction tracking to specific files by flagging them as "transactional" by means of the NetWare FLAG utility. At the workstation command line, type:

FLAG *filename* +T <Enter>

To remove a file's transactional flag, substitute a "-" for the "+" in the command above:

FLAG *filename* -T <Enter>

Once you flag a file "Transactional," it cannot be deleted or renamed unless you remove the "Transactional" attribute. Having this attribute changes the way NetWare writes data to the file. It's helpful to refer to a transactional file as the "target" file, or the target of the transaction. Whenever a client requests to write data to a target file, NetWare notes the position (offset) within the target file where the client wishes NetWare to write the data, and the length of the data the client wishes to write.

These two parameters (offset and length of the impending write) denote the data in the target file that will be written over when NetWare fulfills the client's request. NetWare then reads the existing data from the target file and writes it to a special system file used only by the NetWare OS. Thus, NetWare preserves the data that it's about to write over in fulfillment of the client's request.

With the existing file data safely preserved in the backout information file, NetWare writes the new data to the target file in the same place where the old data formerly resided. If NetWare is able to write the new data successfully (subject to read-after-write verification) to the target file, it discards the old data by deleting it from the backout information file.

However, if NetWare is unable to write the new data successfully to the target file because of some error, it returns the file to its previous state by retrieving the old data from the backout information file and writing the data back to the target file. The process of writing original data back to the target file is called "backing out" the transaction.

Transaction tracking is most appropriate for database files, which typically undergo repeated writes to the same offset. A good example is the NetWare v3.11 bindery. Whenever you change your password, NetWare writes your new password over your old password in one of the bindery files. The bindery files are always transactional files, so if NetWare experiences an error when writing your new password to the bindery, it's able to preserve your old password by backing out the transaction.

Suppose NetWare experienced an error and wrote garbled data to the offset within the bindery file that contained your password. You wouldn't be able to log in to the server, and you wouldn't be able to change your password, because you would have no idea what NetWare actually wrote in place of your password. In short, you would be out of luck. That's why bindery files are always transactional files. Transaction tracking provides NetWare with the ability to backtrack after a write error and start over.

The bindery is just one example of a good application for transaction tracking. Most database applications apply file updates in groups, such as updating all the fields of a database record. For these types of applications, NetWare provides a transaction tracking programming interface. Using this programming interface, applications can group related file updates into transactions. If NetWare can't successfully complete all updates that are part of a transaction, it backs out the transaction and allows the application to try to complete the entire transaction again from the starting point.

Transaction tracking imposes some memory and performance overhead to the NetWare v3.11 file system. First, NetWare maintains data structures in permanent memory for the purpose of tracking the state of writes to transactional files and to the transaction log file. Second, whenever an application writes data to a transactional file, it locks the area of the file that is the target of the write operation, and holds that lock until the transaction is completed by NetWare. This takes longer than the default write operation, which is a simple write to a file cache buffer. So writes to transactional file use more memory than "normal" writes, and they take a little bit longer.

On the typical NetWare v3.11 volume, most files will not be transactional files. There is no reason to flag applications as transactional. There is little benefit in flagging, say, a WordPerfect data file as transactional. WordPerfect data files are usually created and updated sequentially, and there's no repeated pattern of data in them, as there is for records in a database file. In fact, transaction tracking makes sense only for database files. And for database files, you should be willing to trade some performance for the extra data integrity transaction tracking provides.

Disabling and Enabling TTS

Transaction tracking is always on, unless you explicitly disable it from the server console. To disable transaction tracking, from the console, type:

```
DISABLE TTS <Enter>
```

After you've disabled transaction tracking, it will remain disabled, even for the server's bindery, until you reboot the server or turn it back on by typing the following command from the server console:

```
ENABLE TTS <Enter>
```

Generally, the only occasion for manually disabling TTS would be as a programming tool to test transactional applications which already include their own TTS. For most transactions, TTS takes just 40 bytes of memory. However, TTS can require as much as 400KB in applications that handle extremely large records, or facilitate multiple large tasks as a single transaction. In addition, TTS requires a minimum of 1MB disk storage space. Nevertheless, we believe that the security TTS provides for your applications is well worth the memory cost.

The Transaction Backout Procedure

In general, NetWare v3.11 doesn't back out transactions in "real time," when it suffers a fault writing the transaction to the target file. Instead, it scans the backout information file when the server mounts a volume and attempts to back out transactions as part of the volume mount procedure.

There are two exceptions to the rule that transaction backouts occur when you mount a volume. First, transaction backouts occur immediately whenever a transaction is aborted by an application. Second transaction backouts occur if a volume other than the target volume fails for one reason or another.

It may seem more appropriate to back out transactions as soon as possible after the write to the target file fails. However, this can actually decrease data integrity. Why? Well, the only reason a write to a target file can fail is the existence some kind of file system problem. Perhaps there's a hard (physical) error on the disk hosting the target file. Or maybe there's a logical error in one of the volume data structures. Either way, NetWare assumes some type of problem with the volume and refuses to back out the transaction until you've dismounted the volume and re-mounted it.

This leads to another characteristic of the NetWare v3.11 file system. It always refuses to write data to a volume that NetWare suspects may be corrupt, either logically or physically. Writing data to a corrupt volume can compound existing problems and can lead to further data loss. So NetWare forces you to dismount a volume, fix the problem, and re-mount the volume before it continues file service to the volume. The transaction backout procedure is just another manifestation of this philosophy.

If, during NetWare's scan of the backout file during a volume mount, an outstanding transaction is discovered, NetWare displays the following prompt on the server console screen:

```
Incomplete transaction(s) found. Do you wish to back them out?
```

If you answer "yes" to the prompt, NetWare backs out the transactions for you, displaying the data for each backout on the server console, including information about the transaction's target file. Depending on how some of the TTS parameters are defined, NetWare v3.11 may or may not display the transaction information on the screen as it's backing out transactions.

The TTS$LOG.ERR File

When TTS backs out a transaction, it writes a record of the backout to a transaction log file called TTS$LOG.ERR, located in the root directory of volume SYS. NetWare also records an entry in this file whenever TTS is initialized or disabled. This file is a valuable troubleshooting tool for analyzing TTS-related events on your server.

```
Backout information for transaction #82
        (original write occurred at 6/19/91 8:05:42pm)
File = SYS:SYSTEM\NET$VAL.SYS
Record offset = 0x00001CD8; Record size = 0x008E
Record data in the file before the backout =

60 A4 22 86 70 10 C0 13 27 34 3B CE C1 49 C1  D0  '".p...'4;..I..
86 AD 28 C5 CC 38 95 77 D5 18 8B 20 50 2E 09  65  ..(..8.w...P..e
21 18 8C 7E 42 37 A0 A5 22 6F AC 07 85 A7 C6  25  !.~B7.."o.....%
CF 4E 31 C2 B9 7B 64 48 91 A3 C6 3 3 10 6E 49  B5.1..{dH...3.nI.
9B 4C A9 52 09 89 2D 3A 85 82 88 2B 31 61 57  5B  ..R..:...+1aW[
CA C3 23 B9 BB 1F 4D 76 2D 84 29 B7 16 26 52  27  .#...Mv.)..&R'
13 A1 61 0E 11 1F 30 0B 39 85 CE 7D 33 05 AD  5C  .a...0.9..}3..\
B2 A5 21 B6 AD 02 5B 00 A8 D3 1D C2 81 BD 0E  58.!...[........X
88 6A A8 7B C6 7C 78 7F 69 7F CA 32    28 B7  .j.{.|x i..2(.

Original record data from the backout file (being written back to the
file) =

    00  00  00  00  00  00  00  00  00  00  00  00  00  00  00  00
    .   . . . . . . . . . . . . . .
    00  00  00  00  00  00  00  00  00  00  00  00  00  00  00  00
    .   . . . . . . . . . . . . . .
    00  00  00  00  00  00  00  00  00  00  00  00  00  00  00  00
    .   . . . . . . . . . . . . . .
    00  00  00  00  00  00  00  00  00  00  00  00  00  00  00  00
    .   . . . . . . . . . . . . . .
    00 00   00  00  00  00  00  00  00  00  00  00  00  00  00  00
    .   . . . . . . . . . . . . . .
    00   00 00 00  00  00  00  00  00  00  00  00  00  00  00  00
    .   . . . . . . . . . . . . . .
```

```
00   00 00  00   00  00   00 00  00  00   00  00   00  00  00  00
 .   ...............
00   00 00  00   00  00   00 00  00  00   00  00   00  00  00  00
 ..  ...............
00   00 00  00   00  00   00 00  00  00   00   00  00  00
 ...............

Backout information for transaction #82
        (original write occurred at 6/19/91 8:05:42pm)
File = SYS:SYSTEM\NET$PROP.SYS
Record offset = 0x00000AA0; Record size = 0x0022
Record data in the file before the backout =

06 9A B6 05 16 2C 83 C4 0E 2B C0 50 50 B8 00 00  ........,...+.PP...
50 FF 76 0C FF 76 0A FF 76 08 FF 76 06 9A B6 05  P.v..v..v..v....
16 2C  .,

Original record data from the backout file (being written back to
    the file) =

50 00 00 01 0F 53 45 43 55 52 49 54 59 5F 45 51  P....SECURITY_EQ
55 41 4C 53 01 32 20 00 00 01 FF FF FF FF FF  FFUALS.2......... FF
FF      ..
Backout information for transaction #82
        (original write occurred at 6/19/91 8:05:42pm) File =
SYS:SYSTEM\NET$VAL.SYS Original End Of File Offset = 0x00001D66;
New End Of File Offset = 0x00001CD8
```

Figure 23-5: Backout information for a garbled transaction. This transaction involved two separate writes to bindery files and a truncation of the bindery file NET$VAL.SYS.

For each part of the transaction, NetWare records the time of the write operation, the name of the file, the offset within the file, the size of the write, the data in the file before the backout, and the original data that was restored to the target file.

NetWare never deletes the TTS$LOG.ERR file or removes data from it. Over time, this log file can grow quite large. You should periodically monitor the size of the log file. When necessary, copy the file to an archive disk and delete the TTS$LOG.ERR file from the server. NetWare will automatically recreate a new log file the next time it needs to record TTS status information.

Explicit and Implicit Transactions

TTS determines the beginning and end of each transaction in one of two ways: either the application uses NetWare's TTS APIs to tell TTS when to start and stop tracking a transaction (an explicit transaction), or TTS infers the beginning and end of the transaction based on the application's use of record and file locks.

Applications that support explicit transactions include Novell's Btrieve, Verasoft's DBman, Zanthe's ZIM, and any program written in BBX (Business Basic Extended).

The majority of database applications haven't been specifically modified to support explicit TTS calls. In these programs, TTS assumes that a transaction is starting whenever the application performs a physical record lock on a file flagged "Transactional." Likewise, TTS assumes that the transaction has ended when the record lock is released.

However, some applications (such as dBASE III Plus, MicroFocus Cobol, and Revelation version G2B) don't conform to default implicit transaction assumptions. To deal with these programs, you'll have to modify the way TTS interacts with the application through the SETTTS utility.

Using SETTTS

The SETTTS utility allows you to set new transaction beginning points. Some applications require you to do this before they'll operate with TTS on a LAN.

For example, dBASE III PLUS v1.0 uses an immediate record lock within the application itself, and doesn't release the lock until you exit the program. (However, later versions of dBASE III PLUS can be run in the normal fashion.) To run dBASE III PLUS v1.0, you must use the SETTTS command from the workstation where you'll be running the application to specify the number of logical and physical record locks TTS should ignore while the application is running, like this:

```
SETTTS [LogicalLevel [PhysicalLevel]] <Enter>
```

For example, if TTS needs to ignore two logical and one physical record lock before starting a transaction, type **SETTTS 2 1 <Enter>** before you enter the application. If you need to specify only a physical lock threshold, then type **SETTTS 0 1 <Enter>.**

In most cases, the logical or physical lock threshold will be 1. If you set the threshold incorrectly, TTS may break the updates up into too many transactions or interpret all the work you do within the application as one giant transaction rather than continuously backing up each appropriate piece. Other examples of applications that require SETTTS include MicroFocus Cobol and Revelation vG2B. In general, most programs that use logical record locks require an adjustment when used with SETTTS.

If you're not sure about the program's record-locking sequence, the best thing to do is to call the software vendor. Most will be able to give you specific instructions for getting the application to cooperate with TTS.

You might also try to start the application from one workstation, then log in as Supervisor from another station and enter MONITOR. Select "Connection Information" and observe the connection at the workstation where the application is running. Next, choose "Logical Record Locks." If the program uses an initial logical record lock, you'll see which task is using the lock and the current status of the lock.

Next, escape this window and enter "Open Files/Physical Records." From the "File/Physical Records Information" menu, choose the "Physical Record Locks" option to see if there are any physical record locks on the application file in use and to check for any other open files which are listed. Add up the number of logical and physical record locks you find and enter these totals in SETTTS.

Once you establish TTS thresholds with SETTTS, the settings you specify will remain in place until you log out, issue a different SETTTS command, or reboot your workstation.

Workstation Deadlocks

As we've discussed, TTS holds workstation record locks until the end of the transaction, and doesn't release the lock until it's assured that the transaction is complete and all is correct. However, some database applications release their internal record locks before the transaction is complete. For these applications, TTS may sometimes cause the two workstations engaged in a mutual transaction to hang.

If this happens, the only thing you can do (short of disabling TTS) is to simply reboot the machines. Although it isn't ideal to reboot your workstation while you're using a database application, the good news is that TTS will have protected the database from corruption in any case.

A better approach is to ensure that your application has been tested for the ability to work correctly with implicit transactions before you buy it. If you're not sure about an application you already own, be sure to test it yourself before you release it into a full production environment.

TTS-Related SET Commands

NetWare v3.11 has a number of SET commands that control transaction tracking. Most of these are advanced parameters that should not be changed except by a knowledgeable system administrator.

Maximum Transactions

The NetWare v3.11 file system allows up to 10,000 transactions to be active at the same time. That's quite a lot of transactions, when you stop to think about it. If you have 250 users on a server, Netware will allow each user to have up to up to 40 outstanding transactions. However, the actual number of transactions your server can support depends on the amount of RAM available for file cache buffers and also for transaction overhead. Since even the most high-throughput transaction processing database applications generate transactions asynchronously, it's highly unlikely that a NetWare v3.11 server will ever obtain 10,000 concurrent transactions. As soon as a transaction is successfully written to the target file, NetWare clears the transaction, and decrements the number of outstanding transactions.

What can happen, however, is that a fault may occur on the server volume hosting the target file, while an application will continue to generate transactions. NetWare will log these transactions to the transaction log file, which is always stored on the SYS volume. (If the SYS volume goes down, NetWare stops file service.) In a situation like this, outstanding transactions can accumulate as fast as the application generates them, up to the limit of 10,000.

You can define the upper limit of outstanding transactions by using the SET console command:

```
SET maximum transactions=n <Enter>
```

For example, to set the upper limit of outstanding transactions to 1,000, at the server console command line, type:

```
SET maximum transactions=1000 <Enter>
```

While the number of outstanding transactions affects the amount of memory consumed by transaction tracking, it also affects the size of the transaction log file stored on the SYS volume. The NetWare v3.11 file system allocates blocks for the transaction log file each time a transaction is generated.

Before extending the transaction log file, Netware tries to re-use blocks allocated for old transactions that were successfully completed. Likewise, before truncating the transaction log file, NetWare checks to see if there are any new transactions that need a block from the transaction log file.

NetWare is therefore very efficient in its use of the transaction log file. However, as the number of outstanding transactions increases, so does the size of the transaction log file. So this is another resource consideration, along with the amount of memory consumed by outstanding transactions.

Auto TTS Backout Flag

As we explained above, when a crashed server that had transactional files open is rebooted, the server tells you it found incomplete transactions and asks you if you want to back them out. If you want the server to go ahead and back out transactions without this prompt, place the following command in the server's STARTUP.NCF file:

```
SET Auto TTS Backout Flag=ON
```

Starting the next time you boot the server, TTS will automatically back out any incomplete transactions. You can't issue this command at the console prompt; it must be in the STARTUP.NCF file.

TTS Abort Dump Flag

This SET command determines whether or not NetWare saves its transaction backout data to the TTS$LOG.ERR file located in the SYS volume root directory. By default, when the server fails during a data write to a file that is flagged "Transactional," the OS uses the backout data to back out the incomplete write, but does not save the data to the transaction log file.

To turn on the TTS abort dump flag, type the following at the server console command line:

```
SET TTS Abort Dump Flag=ON <Enter>
```

With this parameter set to ON, NetWare writes a copy of the original data from the transaction and a copy of the data it uses to back out transactions to the TTS$LOG.ERR file. In the event of a failure during a transaction, you can "preview" the information that is to be restored to the database by reading the TTS$LOG.ERR file. By comparing this information with what was entered at the workstation, you can determine whether the information needs to be re-entered into the database.

Note that with this paramater turned on, the TTS$LOG.ERR file will grow much more quickly than before. Be sure to monitor its size regularly and follow the log file maintenance procedures previously outlined.

TTS Unwritten Cache Wait Time

Some blocks of transactional data must wait for other transactional blocks to be written first. If the maximum time limit expires for one of these blocks, other write requests are held up while the block is written to disk. The "TTS UnWritten Cache Wait Time" parameter determines how long a block of transactional data can be held in memory before it is written to disk. The syntax is:

```
SET TTS UnWritten Cache Wait Time=time <Enter>
```

The default *time* is 1 minute 5.9 seconds. The valid range is from 11 seconds to 10 minutes 59.1 seconds.

TS Backout File Truncation Wait Time

This SET parameter determines how long allocated but unused blocks remain available for the TTS backout file. The syntax is:

```
SET TTS Backout File Truncation Wait Time=time <Enter>
```

The default *time* is 59 minutes 19.2 seconds; valid range is from 1 minute 5.9 seconds to 1 day 2 hours minutes 51.3 seconds.

Troubleshooting Fault Tolerance Problems

This section contains information that will help you deal with problems related to NetWare's system fault tolerance.

Problem: You can't flag a database file Transactional.

Solution:

The database file must be closed before you can flag it Transactional. Use MONITOR's "Connection Information" option to make sure no users have the file open, then try flagging the file again.

Problem: A database file has become contaminated.

Solutions:

A number of things can cause contaminated databases, including faulty hardware, power failures, and file locking problems.

If a faulty hard disk is the cause of your problem, first use MONITOR to check the status of the disk, repair or replace the disk, and then restore the data from a backup. (You are backing up your network data on a regular basis—right?)

In the event of a power spike or a power failure, you may need to use VREPAIR to locate and correct inconsistencies in the FATs, as explained in Chapter 24. You can use BINDFIX to correct bindery problems, as explained in Chapter 12. We also strongly recommend that you employ some type of power conditioning protection, especially on the network servers (see Chapter 26).

If your database fails due to file locking problems and you have several file servers on your network, it may be that your application is using a record- or file-locking algorithm that doesn't take the multiserver environment into account. If this is the case, you can correct the problem by ensuring that all users execute the application from the same server and from the same default drive.

Problem: The server has disabled TTS.

Solutions:

Several factors can cause the server to automatically disable TTS. First, if you run out of disk space on volume SYS (the TTS backout volume), the OS will shut down TTS. Normally, TTS requires about 1MB of free disk space in SYS to track all open transactions. If users are working with large database records, you'll need enough free space on SYS to hold the largest record.

Insufficient server memory can also cause NetWare to disable TTS. TTS needs about 40 bytes of memory per transaction. At the maximum of 10,000 transactions, TTS would need a total of 400KB of memory. If you don't have enough server memory, either unload unneeded NLMs (such as INSTALL and MONITOR), dismount rarely-used volumes, or add more RAM to the server.

Once you have freed up ample disk space or opened up some memory, re-enable transaction tracking by typing ENABLE TTS <Enter> at the server console.

Problem: The server failed while TTS was disabled.

Solution:

If the file server fails while TTS is disabled (either automatically or manually), the data in the TTS backout file is unreliable. You shouldn't attempt to back out of any transaction. The primary moral of this story is that you're better off if you don't disable TTS. If for some reason you really must disable TTS, you can at least reduce the likelihood of this type of problem by attaching a UPS to your file server and disk subsystems.

CHAPTER 24

Disk/Volume Management

Disk reads and writes are by far the two most common operations performed by a NetWare file server. The hard disk channel and its associated hardware, then, form another critical link that affects all the file server's users. In Chapter 5, we discussed how to install and configure network disk drives, controllers, and host bus adapters, along with the basics of loading a disk driver. In this chapter, we discuss NetWare disk and volume concepts in more detail. We will look at some of the utilities used to manage them and present some troubleshooting procedures for network disk problems.

When troubleshooting hard disks, it is important to distinguish between what is defined at the hard disk level and what is part of the volume definition. The "hierarchy" of definitions is illustrated in Figure 24-1.

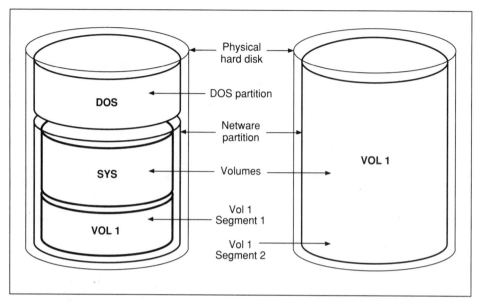

Figure 24-1: NetWare disks can be divided into partitions, volumes, and volume segments.

Disk Management Concepts

The concepts surrounding hard disks and volumes in NetWare v3.x have evolved somewhat from earlier versions of NetWare. As drive manufacturers came up with faster and larger hard disks, many new capabilities were added to NetWare to accommodate them. However, the basic building blocks remain essentially the same: disks, controllers, interface boards, and disk drivers. These components together make up what NetWare calls a disk "channel."

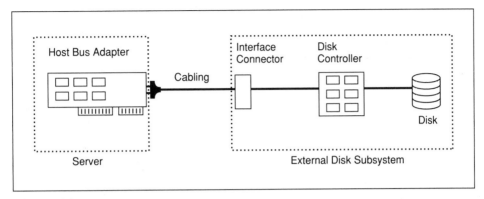

Figure 24-2: A server's disk communication channel consists of a host bus adapter, disk controller, the disk itself, and related hardware.

Disk Interfaces and Controllers

NetWare supports a wide variety of disk drives from various manufacturers. A disk's storage capacity is determined by the number of heads and cylinders the disk has and by the encoding method used to write data onto its surface. Common data encoding methods include MFM (Modified Frequency Modulation) and RLL (Run Length Limited). MFM drives typically have a maximum storage capacity of less than 80MB. Larger drives (100MB and up) use some form of RLL technology, which stores data more densely and provides faster access times.

Each disk has an associated disk controller, a circuit board that translates operating system requests into the electronic pulses that the hard disk components can understand. The disk controller is often a separate board that connects to the disk via ribbon cables. Or, some disks have built-in, or "embedded" controllers located within the drive housing itself. Disk controllers generally fall into three main categories, according to the type of interface they use:

- ST-506, one of the first standard disk interfaces for IBM PC compatibles. These controllers ypically use the MFM data encoding method, although newer ones use RLL. They can control up to two disk drives.

- ESDI (Enhanced Small Device Interface) is a more recent standard used by IBM in its PS/2 line of computers. ESDI controllers typically support up to two disk drives.

- SCSI (Small Computer Systems Interface) is a standard, hardware-independent interface used with any disk that is block-addressable. A block-addressable device looks at data storage in terms of logical "blocks" of storage area, rather than the actual physical sectors on the disk. Most hard disk and tape drives made for PCs are block-addressable. Up to seven SCSI-compatible controllers can be daisy-chained together in a "bus" configuration. Each controller can control one or two devices, for a possible total of 14 hard disk drives.

A disk controller must somehow connect into the computer's I/O expansion bus. For most internal disk drives, the controller board comes with the computer and is plugged into one of the expansion slots. Internal disk controllers often control the floppy diskette drives as well as the hard disk drives in the machine. When the disks and controllers are located outside of the computer (as they are with most SCSI drives), you need an interface board for the entire channel. Traditionally, this role was played by a Disk Coprocessor Board, or DCB. Novell originally developed a number of DCBs specifically for use in NetWare file servers, but has since licensed the technology to a number of third-party vendors. NetWare can handle up to four external disk channels (four DCBs per file server). Novell's new term for a DCB is a "Host Bus Adapter" or HBA.

Disk Drivers

A disk driver is a piece of software that serves as the interface between NetWare and a particular disk channel's controller board(s). The driver knows how the disk/controller hardware expects to receive and deliver data and what their unique capabilities are. Thus it is the code that actually talks to the disks.

In NetWare v3.x, disk drivers are NLMs with the .DSK extension. The disk drivers shipped with the OS support four main types of hard drives and controller interfaces:

- Controllers for internal disk drives, such as the Western Digital-type controller found in the IBM AT and most AT compatibles. These controllers use either the MFM or RLL encoding method and plug into the Industry Standard Architecture (ISA) bus. The disk driver is therefore called ISADISK.DSK.

- MFM-type controllers found in low-end models of the IBM PS/2 computers (such as the PS/2 Model 50). These controllers require the PS2MFM.DSK disk driver.

- ESDI controllers found in high-end models of the IBM PS/2 line (Model 60 and above). PS2ESDI.DSK is the disk driver for these controllers.

- SCSI-compatible controllers connected to the SCSI bus running off a Disk Coprocessor Board or Host Bus Adapter in the server. These use either the DCB.DSK for Novell's DCB SCSI controllers or PS2SCSI.DSK for IBM's microchannel SCSI controllers.

When you initially choose a disk driver (such as ISADISK.DSK, PS2ESDI.DSK, or a third-party driver) in INSTALL, NetWare chooses a port and interrupt for the loading driver and writes the appropriate LOAD command to the STARTUP.NCF file. NetWare can't do much of anything unless it can talk to the disk containing the SYS volume. That's why the disk driver LOAD commands must be among the first commands executed when you boot the server.

NetWare's Device Numbering Scheme

Within utilities such as MONITOR and INSTALL, and in system messages, NetWare uses three different numbering schemes to identify physical hard disks attached to the file server:

- The *physical address* of the disk channel interface board (or "card"), the disk controller, and the disk itself; for example, card 0, controller 0, drive 1. Most MFM, RLL, and ESDI controllers use the system board (identified as "Card 0") as the disk channel interface board. Systems using DCBs as the disk channel interface identify them as "Card 1" through "Card 4." SCSI disk controllers have jumpers that you set to indicate the controller address (0 through 7). The drive number will always be 0 or 1, depending on jumper settings on the disk or the order in which the disks are connected to the controller. Drives with embedded controllers are usually set to drive number 0.

- A five-digit *device code* based on the physical address, where the first two digits represent the disk type number, digit three is the card number, digit four is the controller number, and digit five is the disk number; the code for the example disk above would be 00001.

- A logical *device number* based on the order in which the disk drivers are loaded. When the first driver is loaded, the first disk (disk 0) attached to the corresponding controller 0 becomes logical device #0; the second disk (disk 1, if there is one) attached to that controller becomes logical device #1, and so on. Always load the internal controller driver first, followed by drivers for external disk channels in channel number order.

As an example, when you choose the "Disk Information" option in MONITOR, the utility lists the disks according to the following pattern:

Device #0 (21000) CDC WrenIII/Embedded SCSI

"Device #0" is the logical device number. The number in parentheses is the device code. The first two digits, 21, mean this disk is type 21; the last three digits indicate the physical address (card 0, controller 0, disk 0). The concluding character string identifies the brand or manufacturer of the disk.

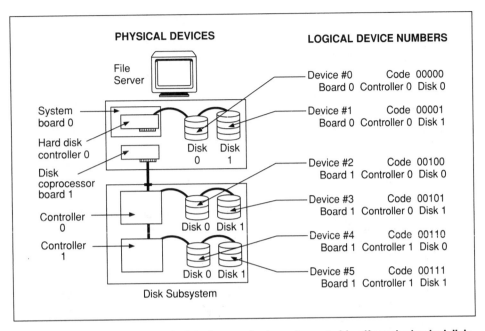

Figure 24-3: NetWare uses a logical device numbering scheme to identify each physical disk.

Note that for this logical device numbering scheme to work, you must always load the disk drivers in controller board order (load the driver for controller 0 first, then the driver for controller 1, and so on). If you don't, system messages about hard disks might identify the disks incorrectly.

Partitions

You can divide up a hard disk into *partitions* for different operating systems. NetWare recognizes DOS partitions (primary and extended) and NetWare partitions. Those for other operating systems, such as Unix, are listed as "non-NetWare" partitions. You can define only one NetWare partition per disk. The NetWare partition can be located anywhere on the disk; it doesn't have to begin at cylinder 0 as in previous versions of NetWare.

NetWare assigns physical and logical identification numbers to the various partitions created on the network disks. For example, suppose you created an 8MB DOS partition and a 32MB NetWare partition on a 40MB hard disk. NetWare refers to the DOS partition as physical partition #0, and to the NetWare partition as physical partition #1. System messages relating to Hot Fix use these physical partition numbers to report which hard disk has bad blocks that need to be redirected.

When you mirror or duplex two physical NetWare partitions together, NetWare uses logical partition numbers to refer to the paired physical partitions as one logical unit. Since you cannot mirror non- NetWare partitions, their logical partition numbers correspond one-to-one with the physical partition numbers (although the actual numbers may not be the same).

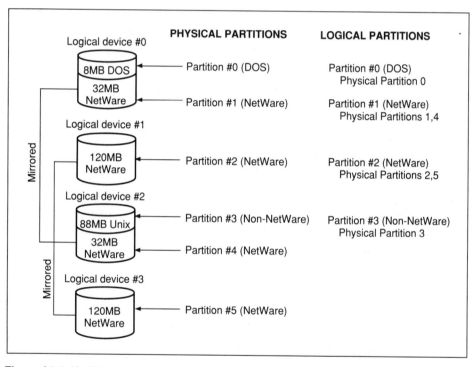

Figure 24-4: NetWare uses both physical and logical partition numbering.

Volume Management Concepts

The chart below summarizes the various maximums associated with NetWare volumes.

Maximum size of a NetWare volume	32TB (terabytes)
Maximum number of volumes per server	64
Maximum number of segments per volume	32
Maximum volume segments per hard disk	8

The main parameters you can define for a volume include the volume name, size, segments, and block size.

Volume Names

Every NetWare file server must have a volume named SYS. The SYS volume contains all of the NetWare system and public files. Beyond that, you are free to name your volumes as you please. A volume name can range from two to 15 characters long; certain characters are illegal (NetWare's INSTALL program will not let you enter invalid characters). Generally, short volume names are easier to work with than longer ones that are hard to type.

Volume names must be unique; no server can have two volumes with the same name mounted at the same time.

Volume Size

Of course, the theoretical maximum volume size of 32TB is more than current microcomputer hard disk technology and memory limitations will allow. Technically, though, the size of a volume is limited only by the size of your network disks. When you run out of space on one disk, you can extend the volume by adding another segment to it on another disk (see "Volume Segments" below). At the lower end, the minimum size for a volume is 5MB. The maximum of eight volume segments per disk implies that the most you can have is eight volumes on a single disk. You can always make a volume bigger; however, you cannot reduce the size of a volume without destroying its data.

When considering the size of a volume, keep in mind that NetWare keeps a copy of every mounted volume's directory entry tables and FATs in cache memory. A huge volume with lots of little directories and files can take up a lot of RAM. It also takes longer for NetWare to find a particular file when it has to search through thousands of entries. So don't abandon the principles of good data management. In most cases, it's better to spread the data out into two or three smaller volumes than lump everything into one gigantic volume. About the only time you'd want to define one big volume is when you have a single, large database file.

In NetWare v2.x, you had to completely fill up every NetWare partition with volumes. There was no way to leave some undefined partition space in case the volume grew faster than you anticipated. With NetWare v3.x, you can set aside some of the NetWare partition space for future growth. Generally, however, you'd want to use all the megabytes you paid for.

Volume Segments

Before NetWare v3.x, a volume could be only as big as the physical hard disk upon which it resided. As applications improved in their ability to create and maintain very large data files, Novell recognized the need to extend a volume over more than one physical disk drive. The parts of the same volume on different disks are called *segments*. NetWare numbers the first piece of a volume as segment 0 and continues up to segment 7.

Suppose, for example, that your server has one 100MB hard disk, divided into volume SYS and volume DB (both 50MB in size). Volume DB contains a single database file that is rapidly nearing the 50MB mark. To accommodate future growth of the file, you could add a second hard disk to the server and define another segment of volume DB on the new disk.

While segmenting volume over multiple disks is a lot easier than trying to rearrange all of your existing data, it has its risks. If a volume spans two disks and one of the disks fails, you lose the entire volume—unless both disks are protected with NetWare's disk mirroring feature. Novell strongly recommends that you mirror all disks that contain segments of the same volume. This implies that, in the example above, you would have to buy three new disks instead of just one: another 100MB disk to mirror the original one (which contains the first segment of volume DB), and two more disks to mirror for the second segment of volume DB. Another benefit of spanning volumes between physical disks is that NetWare can split large file writes and send part to one disk and part to the other. The split writes occur simultaneously, cutting the total write time in half.

Volume Block Size

A "block" is the smallest unit of data that NetWare reads and writes on a network disk. The default block size in NetWare v3.x is 4KB. However, when you define a new volume through the "Volume Options" in the INSTALL utility, you can increase the block size to 8KB, 16KB, 32KB, or 64KB. The block size will be the same for all segments of the same volume. However, you can set different block sizes for separate volumes on the same disk.

If the volume will store mostly small files less than 4KB in size, use the default block size. If the majority of files are more than 4KB in size, you might see increased performance by using a larger block size. Since NetWare must write at least one full block at a time, it's a waste of disk space to use large blocks with mostly small files. Even a 10-byte file, for instance, takes up 16KB on the disk if 16KB is the block size. The larger block sizes are most useful when you have mainly large database files on the volume.

Note: If you select the 32KB or 64KB block sizes, some DOS file management utilities will be unable to correctly calculate the amount of free hard disk space. Use NetWare's CHKVOL or VOLINFO utilities instead.

You can also use INSTALL to change the block size of a volume after it has been in use for a while. Make a full backup of all data before you do so. Changing block size effectively destroys the existing data in the volume. Note also that when you change disk block size, you usually need to change the cache buffer size to match (see "Cache Buffer and Disk Block Size" in Chapter 22).

Useful NetWare Commands and Utilities

This section explains some of the NetWare console commands and DOS workstation utilities that are useful in configuring and troubleshooting disk drivers, disks, and volumes. For more detailed information, refer to Novell's *System Administration* manual.

The INSTALL Utility

You can change disk-level parameters (install and remove disks, or modify partitions, Hot Fix, and mirroring) via the "Disk Options" selection of the INSTALL utility. For volume-level parameters, use the "Volume Options" selection. To access the INSTALL utility, type "LOAD INSTALL" at the server console or press <Ctrl><Esc> and choose "Install Screen" from the list of screens.

INSTALL's "Disk Options"

Under the "Disk Options" selection, you can accomplish the following tasks:

- Add new hard disks to the server and remove existing disks.

- Create and delete NetWare partitions.

- Reformat a disk and test it for bad blocks.

You can also mirror and unmirror drives, and edit Hot Fix information on a disk. These procedures are explained in Chapter 23.

Adding a New Hard Disk. When you add a new hard disk, you can either make it part of an existing volume or define a new volume on the disk. Here are the basic steps to add a new hard disk to the server:

1. If you are adding a second internal hard disk, you must bring the server down first, turn the computer off, and unplug it from the power source.

    If you are adding a new disk in an external disk subsystem, you can leave the server running. However, if you intend to add the disk to an existing channel, you must dismount all volumes contained on that channel and unload the disk driver via the UNLOAD command. Then turn off the power to the disk subsystem.

2. Install the new disk drive, following the instructions in the computer owner's manual or those provided with the disk. Then turn the computer or subsystem back on.

3. For internal drives, run the necessary setup or configuration programs so that the computer recognizes the new disk. With NetWare v3.x, you do not need to DOS format the new disk.

    For external drives, reload the disk driver and remount the volumes. If the disk is connected to a DCB or SCSI host bus adapter, run DISKSET to program the board to recognize the new drive.

4. Load INSTALL and select "Disk Options," then "Partition Tables." The new disk should be listed in the "Available Disk Drives" menu. Select the new disk and create a NetWare partition on it.

6. Either create a new volume on the disk or make the new disk part of an existing volume by following the appropriate instructions under "INSTALL's `Volume Options'" below.

Removing an Existing Disk. When a network disk starts showing signs of failure (for example, the Hot Fix Redirection area is filling up rapidly), you should remove the drive and either have it repaired or replaced. If you allow a failing disk to become unusable (to the point where Hot Fix is shut down), the disk driver can hang the server for several minutes while it attempts to communicate with the bad disk. Here are the steps to remove a network disk:

1. If possible, make a complete backup of all data residing on the disk. Proceeding with these steps will destroy any existing data, so you must have a backup in order to restore the data onto the replacement drive.

2. Dismount any volumes contained on the disk.

3. Load INSTALL and use "Volume Options" to delete the volumes that were defined on the disk. Then use "Disk Options" to delete the partitions on the disk. (If the disk partition was mirrored, you must unmirror it first.)

4. If you are *not* replacing an external disk with an identical disk, run DISKSET to remove the disk definition from the DCB or host bus adapter.

5. Unload the disk driver for the disk's channel with the UNLOAD command.

6. For an external drive, turn off the power to the subsystem. For an internal drive, bring the server down and turn it off. Then remove the disk, following the manufacturer's instructions.

7. Install and set up the replacement drive as explained under "Adding a New Hard Disk" above, only define the same volumes that were on the previous disk. Then restore the volume data from your backups.

Editing a Disk's Partition Tables. The "Partition Tables" option lets you create or delete various partitions on a network disk. The only kind of partition you can create is a NetWare partition; however, you can delete DOS, OS/2, Unix, and other non-NetWare partitions from INSTALL. This allows you to install NetWare partitions on disks previously used by other operating systems. Deleting a NetWare partition and recreating it is the only way to change the partition's size.

Note: Changing the partition table effectively destroys all data on the disk, even data in non-NetWare partitions. Make sure you have a current backup of all crucial data before you delete any partitions.

To delete a partition on an installed disk, follow these steps:

1. Load INSTALL. If the partition you want to delete is currently mirrored, unmirror it under "Disk Options." Then delete the volumes (if any) in the partition with the "Volume Options."

2. Back in "Disk Options," select "Partition Tables" and select the disk containing the partition from the list of available drives.

3. Select "Delete Partition" from the "Partition Options" menu and, if there is more than one partition on the disk, choose the partition to delete from the resulting list.

4. Answer "Yes" to the confirmation prompt. The partition is now deleted and becomes "Free Space" that can be used by NetWare.

To create a new partition, follow these steps:

1. Load INSTALL and select "Disk Options," then "Partition Tables." Choose the disk you want to create a partition on from the list of available drives. If no partition table exists on the disk, an informational message will appear. Press <Esc> to continue.

2. Choose "Create NetWare Partition" from the "Partition Options" menu. IN STALL displays a "Partition Information" window with the following default settings:

   - Partition Type: NetWare 386 Partition

   - Partition Size: All "Free Space" on the disk

   - Hot Fix Data Area: 98 percent of the partition

   - Hot Fix Redirection Area: 2 percent of the partition

   If you want to change these defaults, highlight the appropriate field and enter new numbers. You can't change the partition type, but you can reduce the partition size to leave some reserve free space for future expansion. The Hot Fix data and redirection areas automatically adjust to total 100 percent of the partition size.

3. Press <Esc> to leave the "Partition Information" window, and answer "Yes" to the confirmation prompt.

Reformatting a Disk. In certain cases, you can use INSTALL's "Format" option to salvage a failing disk. If the disk's trouble is due to shifting read/write heads or track alignment problems, reformatting can sometimes help. The basic steps are:

1. If possible, back up all data on the disk. Formatting a disk obliterates any existing data.

2. Have all users log out of the server, then dismount any volumes contained on the disk.

3. Load INSTALL. If the disk is mirrored, unmirror it under "Disk Options." Then go to "Volume Options" and delete all volumes on the disk.

4. Back in "Disk Options," choose "Format (optional)" and select the disk from the resulting list. Then choose "Format Disk Drive" from the "Format Options" menu. You will see a warning that all information on the partition will be lost. Press <Esc> to proceed.

5. Enter the interleave factor for the disk. Most MFM and SCSI-compatible disks use an interleave of 2, which is the default. ESDI drives and others using newer, faster technology use an interleave of 1. Check the disk documentation if you're not sure what interleave to select. Setting the wrong interleave can hamper the performance of the disk.

6. The formatting will begin as soon as you input the interleave. You can switch to other console utilities while the formatting is taking place (which can take hours or even days, depending on the size of the disk), but leave the INSTALL module running in the background. The formatting process will stop if you exit INSTALL before it has finished. A successful reformat is indicated by the "Completed" status; if the disk is beyond salvaging, the status will indicate "Failed."

7. Once you have successfully reformatted the disk, recreate the NetWare partition and volumes on the disk as you would for a brand new disk. Then restore the volumes' data from your backup.

Testing a Disk for New Bad Blocks. Normally, manufacturers test disks extensively at the factory and include a list of known bad blocks when they ship the drive. When Hot Fix finds bad blocks, it records their location in the bad block table as well. As necessary, you can perform a surface test of a disk to find new any bad blocks not yet listed in the table.

This surface test is no longer required at installation (as it was in previous versions of NetWare). Whereas the old COMPSURF utility performed a destructive analysis, INSTALL lets you choose between a destructive test and a nondestructive one. The destructive tests obliterates existing data, but runs faster; the nondestructive test preserves your data, but takes approximately 20 percent longer to run. Both operate in the background so you can do other things in INSTALL while the test is running. Here are the steps:

1. Have all users log out of the server. Even if you are going to run the nondestructive test, make sure you have an up-to-date backup just in case.

2. Dismount all volumes contained on the disk you want to test.

3. Load INSTALL and select "Disk Options," then "Surface Test." Select the disk you want from the list of available drives.

4. Select "Begin Surface Test" from the "Surface Test Options" menu, then choose the type of test (destructive or nondestructive).

5. The testing will run for several hours, or as long as it takes to test the total number of blocks indicated on the screen. If you need to do other tasks at the server, you can switch out of INSTALL (but leave the test running) by pressing <Alt>-<Esc>. The testing will be terminated if you actually exit the INSTALL utility.

6. When the test is completed, the screen displays the number of bad blocks found. INSTALL adds these to the existing bad block table. If you ran the destructive test, you must redefine the volume and restore its data from a backup.

7. Remount the disk's volume(s) using the MOUNT ALL command.

INSTALL's "Volume Options"

Under the "Volume Options" selection, you can accomplish the following tasks:

- Create and delete a volume

- Add a new segment to an existing volume

- Rename a volume

Creating a New Volume. Creating a volume is a slightly different procedure than adding a new segment to an existing volume. If you have no "Free Space" in any NetWare partitions, you must add a new hard disk before you can define a new volume (see "Adding a New Hard Disk" above). Here are the steps for creating a volume:

1. Load INSTALL, if necessary, and select "Volume Options." A list of existing volumes appears.

2. Press <Ins> to add a volume to the list. If there is more than one hard disk with free space, select the disk you want to create the volume on.

3. A "New Volume Information" window appears showing default settings for the block size, and the initial segment size (in blocks) and volume size (in mega bytes). Type a name for the volume in the "Volume Name" field. Change the default block size according to the guidelines given earlier in this chapter. To make the volume smaller than the entire available space, type in a smaller number of blocks. The window will show the corresponding size in megabytes in the "Volume Size" field.

4. Press <Esc> to leave the "New Volume Information" window, and answer "Yes" to the confirmation prompt.

5. You can mount the new volume either from within INSTALL or by exiting and

using the MOUNT command. To mount the volume in INSTALL, highlight the volume name in the "Volumes" list and press <Enter>. Highlight the "Status" field in the "Volume Information" window and press <Enter>, then select "Mount Volume" from the "Volume Status Options" menu.

Deleting a Volume. Obviously, you don't want to delete a volume that is currently in use. Use MONITOR to see who is accessing files on the volume, then make sure those users close their files and applications before you proceed.

1. If you want to save any data from the volume, back it up now.

2. Dismount the volume with the DISMOUNT command.

3. Load INSTALL and select "Volume Options."

4. Highlight the volume name and press <Del>. Answer "Yes" to the confirmation prompt.

Adding a New Segment to a Volume. This procedure is slightly different than creating a new volume. If you have no "Free Space" in any NetWare partitions, you must add a new hard disk before you can extend an existing volume (see "Adding a New Hard Disk" above). The volume must also be mounted on the server. Here are the steps for adding a segment to a volume:

1. Load INSTALL, if necessary, and select "Volume Options." Select the volume you want from the "Volumes" list.

2. In the resulting "Volume Information" window, highlight the "Volume Seg ments" field and press <Enter>.

3. Press <Ins> to add a new segment to the list. If there is more than one hard disk with free space, select the disk you want to create the volume segment on.

4. Type the number of blocks you want the new segment to occupy and press <Enter>. Answer "Yes" to the confirmation prompt.

Renaming a Volume. You shouldn't have to rename volumes very often. When you do, you must change any drive mappings to that volume in the system and user login scripts. If the volume name appears in any batch files or application setup screens, they will have to be changed as well. You cannot rename a volume that is currently in use. Use MONITOR to see who is accessing files on the volume, then make sure those users close their files and applications before you proceed.

1. Dismount the volume with the DISMOUNT command.

2. Load INSTALL. Then select "Volume Options" and choose the volume to rename.

3. In the "Volume Information" screen, highlight the "Volume Name" field. Type a new name over the old name and press <Enter>. Answer "Yes" to the confirmation prompt.

4. To mount the renamed volume, highlight the "Status" field and press <Enter>. Choose "Mount Volume" from the "Volume Status Options" menu.

The LOAD Command

You use the LOAD console command to load a disk driver as well as other types of NLMs. Disk drivers have their own set of possible parameters, however. These parameters are summarized below. The basic command syntax is:

```
LOAD [Path]DiskDriver [Parameters...]
```

If you don't specify a path, NetWare assumes the disk driver is in the SYS:SYSTEM directory on the file server. You can use the SEARCH console command to specify other paths for the OS to look in for NLMs.

Depending on the type of disk controller the driver is written for, you can set various hardware configuration parameters when you load the disk driver. Few controllers require all of these parameters. If you don't include any parameters, the OS will prompt you for the essential ones after you enter the LOAD command. (Generally, disk drivers for PS/2 ESDI or MFM controllers don't require these parameters because they cannot be configured.)

INT=n Tells the driver what interrupt or IRQ line the controller is set to use. Use hexadecimal notation for n (2 through 9, 10=A, 11=B, 12=C, 13=D, 14=E, 15=F).

DMA=n Tells the driver what DMA (Direct Memory Access) chan nel the controller is set to use.

PORT=nnn Tells the driver which I/O port address the controller is set to use (usually a three-digit hexadecimal address).

MEM=$nnnn$ Tells the driver which shared memory address the controller is set to use (usually a five-digit hexadecimal address).

SLOT=n In a micro channel or EISA computer, this is the only parameter you need. It indicates which slot the controller occupies. The OS reads the configuration set with the *Reference* diskette or EISA configuration program.

Of course, these parameter values must match the actual hardware settings on the board itself. Otherwise, the disk driver will probably not load.

The UNLOAD Command

The "UNLOAD *DiskDriver*" command unlinks the disk driver from the disk controller board and removes the driver from the file server's memory. Naturally, this action effectively halts any network communication with the disk(s) attached to that controller. Make sure no users are currently accessing data on the disk. It's also a good practice to dismount any volumes contained on the disks before you unload the driver. If you do not, the OS will warn you that the driver is being used by volumes and automatically dismount the indicated volumes if you proceed.

MOUNT, VOLUMES, and DISMOUNT

The MOUNT console command loads a volume on the server and makes it available to users. The disk or disks containing the volume must be properly installed with the associated disk driver loaded. The volume must have been previously defined in the INSTALL module.

The command format to load a single volume is:

```
MOUNT VolumeName <Enter>
```

To load all defined volumes at the same time, type:

```
MOUNT ALL <Enter>
```

If a volume has previously been mounted, the server will display the message "Volume *VolumeName* is already mounted."

Normally you mount all defined volumes when the server is booted by putting the appropriate MOUNT commands in the AUTOEXEC.NCF file. If, however, you have one or two volumes that are rarely used, you can leave them unmounted until they are needed. This will conserve the server memory normally taken up by the volumes if they were mounted.

To list the volumes currently mounted on the server, type **VOLUMES <Enter>** at the console prompt.

You can dismount only one volume at a time, by typing:

```
DISMOUNT VolumeName <Enter>
```

Make sure no users are currently accessing data on the volume before you dismount it. NetWare returns the memory used to cache the volume's directory table and FAT to the file cache buffer pool.

You should only use the DISMOUNT command if you know there's a problem with the volume, or if you need to perform server maintenance and you know there are no active clients using the volume. When you issue the DISMOUNT command, NetWare assumes you mean business and shuts down the volume immediately, leaving NetWare clients using the volume holding the bag, so to speak. You don't get any "Are you sure you want to do this?" types of messages; NetWare just shuts things down at once. Dismounting the SYS volume forces NetWare to close the bindery, which shuts down everything for clients.

Whenever NetWare shuts down file service to a volume, you should dismount the volume (if NetWare hasn't already done it for you) and run VREPAIR on it. (We'll discuss VREPAIR later in this chapter.) If VREPAIR can't fix the problems, you should perform a surface scan of the underlying hard disk(s) using INSTALL (see "Testing a Disk for New Bad Blocks" above).

MONITOR's Disk-Related Information

You can use the MONITOR utility to view several screens of information relating to the file server's disk drives. Type "LOAD MONITOR" at the server console. If MONITOR is already loaded, press <Ctrl><Esc> and select "Monitor Screen" from the list of screens.

Disk I/O Statistics

The MONITOR utility's main screen displays several items of information relevant to disk I/O. Here is a sample MONITOR screen.

```
NetWare 386 v3.11 (250 user) - 2/20/91         NetWare 386 Loadable Module

               Information For Server JUNGLE

  File Server Up Time:     3 Days  8 Hours 31 Minutes 38 Seconds
  Utilization:             5           Packet Receive Buffers:    100
  Original Cache Buffers:  3,613       Directory Cache Buffers:   135
  Total Cache Buffers:     1,267       Service Processes:           4
  Dirty Cache Buffers:     1           Connections In Use:          5
  Current Disk Requests:   0           Open Files:                 29
```

Current Disk Requests. This number indicates how many outstanding disk requests are queued up and ready to be serviced by the server's disk process. This is the total number of read and write requests for all disks attached to the server. A consistently large number of queued disk requests is another indication that your disk and controller are too slow.

Sluggish disk channel performance can result from two things: hardware errors somewhere along the channel, or plain old slow hardware (especially true of older MFM and ISA disk controllers). If you start seeing numerous pending disk requests along with a large number of dirty cache buffers, consider upgrading to faster ESDI or SCSI drives and controllers.

Packet Receive Buffers. These buffers are different from cache buffers, but they are involved in the disk I/O process. When an NCP disk read or write request first arrives at the server, the Link Support Layer copies the packet into a packet receive buffer. It waits there until a file service process (FSP) is available to forward the request to the server's disk I/O process. (We'll further explain the interplay between packet receive buffers and FSPs under "Service Processes" discussed shortly.)

Both the minimum and maximum number of packet receive buffers are configurable via the SET command, as is the maximum size of these buffers. At boot time, the OS allocates enough permanent memory for the minimum number of packet receive buffers specified (the default is 10). If the server runs out of packet receive buffers, it pulls memory from the cache buffer pool to create more (up to the maximum number allowable). Once allocated, this memory is not returned to the cache buffer pool. The only way to recoup the memory for cache buffers is to reboot the server.

We'll talk more about packet receive buffers in the context of LAN communication in Chapter 25.

Service Processes. Previous versions of NetWare called these file service processes, or FSPs. The concept behind service processes is the same in NetWare v3.x, although the mechanism for allocating FSPs is different. Basically, an FSP is the *only* NetWare OS process that can service incoming packets containing NetWare Core Protocol (NCP) requests for file services.

One commonly-used analogy compares an FSP to a butler in a mansion (the server). Whenever an NCP request arrives at the server, a doorman (the NetWare "polling" process) places the request in a waiting room (a packet receive buffer). From there, the request is passed to a butler (FSP). The FSP dutifully escorts the request to the disk process, waits for the request to be processed, then accompanies the results of the processing back to the door to send them on their way. The FSP then waits for additional NCP requests to arrive.

On a busy server, more than one NCP request can arrive at the same time, or additional NCP requests might arrive while an FSP is busy servicing a previous request. Rather than be caught short, NetWare v3.*x* simply allocates additional FSPs to handle the extra requests. The server boots up with zero service processes. The system typically allocates one service process to handle user logins and connections. As users begin loading applications and requesting data, the number of disk I/O requests can surpass the ability of this one service process to handle. NetWare waits a few seconds to see if the demand keeps up, then allocates another service process. Again, the necessary memory comes from the cache buffer pool and is not de-allocated until you DOWN the server and bring it back up again.

The "Disk Information" Option

The "Disk Information" option in MONITOR's "Available Options" menu leads to more specific information about each physical disk attached to the server. When you select this option, you see a list of "System Disk Drives" showing the currently attached disks identified by device number and disk driver type. Choose the disk you want and press <Enter>. The top part of the MONITOR screen changes to reflect pertinent information about that drive. The bottom part of the screen contains a "Drive Status" window.

```
┌──────────────────────────────────────────────────────────────────────────┐
│ NetWare 386 v3.11 (250 user) - 2/20/91      NetWare 386 Loadable Module    │
├──────────────────────────────────────────────────────────────────────────┤
│ ┌────────────────────────────────────────────────────────────────────┐   │
│ │         Type 320/Embedded SCSI Card  0 Controller  0 Drive 0         │   │
│ ├────────────────────────────────────────────────────────────────────┤   │
│ │ Driver:               DCB.DSK    │  Partition Blocks:     78,116     │   │
│ │ Disk Size:            305 Meg    │  Data Blocks:          77,616     │   │
│ │ Partitions:                 1    │  Redirection Blocks:      500     │   │
│ │ Mirror Status:    Not Mirrored   │  Redirected Blocks:         0     │   │
│ │ Hot Fix Status:        Normal    │  Reserved Blocks:          11     │   │
│ └────────────────────────────────────────────────────────────────────┘   │
│                                                                            │
│ ┌────────────────────────────────────────────────────────────────────┐   │
│ │                            Drive Status                              │   │
│ ├────────┬───────────────────────────────────────────────────────────┤   │
│ │ Device │ Volume Segments On Drive:       (select for list)          │   │
│ │ Device │ Read After Write Verify:        Hardware Level             │   │
│ │ Device │ Drive Light Status:             Not Supported             │   │
│ │ Device │ Drive Operating Status:         Active                     │   │
│ │ Device │ Removable Drive Mount Status:                              │   │
│ │ Device │ Removable Drive Lock Status:                               │   │
│ └────────┴───────────────────────────────────────────────────────────┘   │
└──────────────────────────────────────────────────────────────────────────┘
```

The top of the screen displays the disk type, along with the card number, controller number, and drive number. This information helps you confirm that you have selected the right disk.

Driver. This entry identifies the disk driver (such as ISADISK.DSK or PS2ESDI.DSK) chosen during installation for this disk.

Disk Size. This number indicates the total size, in megabytes, of the hard disk, including all of its partitions (not just the NetWare partition).

Partitions. This number indicates how many partitions exist on the disk. The example screen above shows two partitions. This would be the case if, for example, the disk had a DOS partition and a NetWare partition (a common setup for server booting purposes).

Mirror Status. This entry indicates the current status of the disk as it relates to NetWare's disk mirroring feature. If you are not using disk mirroring or duplexing, MONITOR displays "Not Mirrored" for each disk. If you have paired this disk with another disk via either mirroring or duplexing, the screen will indicate "Mirrored." If one disk in a mirrored pair gets out of sync (the data is no longer identical on both disks) or if it has just been replaced, you might see the "Remirroring" status. This indicates that data on one disk is currently being copied to its mirrored counterpart to restore the mirroring feature.

Hot Fix Status. As we have explained in Chapter 23, Hot Fix is NetWare's method of preventing data from being written to bad blocks on the disk. The OS reads each block of data after it is written to disk and compares it with the original data still held in memory. If the two don't match, Hot Fix rewrites that block of memory to a different part of the disk (the "Redirection" area) and records the address of the defective block in the bad block table.

The "Normal" status indicates that Hot Fix is currently operational on the disk. The "Not-hot-fixed" status indicates that NetWare has shut off the Hot Fix function on this disk. This condition occurs when a disk experiences so many write failures that the Hot Fix Redirection area is filled up with rewritten data. (The number of "Reserved Blocks" plus "Redirected Blocks" will equal the total number of "Redirection Blocks" shown in the right-hand column of the screen.) When this occurs, the disk has failed beyond NetWare's ability to use it. Remove the disk and either have it repaired or replace it with a new one.

Partition Blocks. This entry indicates the total amount of space in the NetWare partition on this disk. NetWare divides disk space into "blocks." The default block size is 4KB, although you can change it via the server SET command. Multiply the block size by the number of partition blocks to get the size of the NetWare partition in bytes.

Data Blocks. This entry tells you how much of the NetWare partition's disk space is available to hold data. The data area is what's left over after NetWare sets aside part of the partition for Hot Fix.

Redirection Blocks. This entry shows how many blocks NetWare has set aside for the Hot Fix Redirection area. By default, this is approximately 2 percent of the total blocks within the partition.

Redirected Blocks. This is the number of blocks within the Hot Fix Redirection area that currently contain redirected data. For each of these blocks, NetWare found a new bad block on the disk that wasn't listed when the disk was installed. You can gauge the health of a disk by how fast the Redirected Blocks accumulate. If the disk runs out of free Redirection Blocks (Redirected Blocks equals Redirection Blocks minus Reserved Blocks), NetWare doesn't allocate any more. Rather, it shuts off Hot Fix and reports the Hot Fix Status as "Not-hot-fixed." You'll probably get numerous other disk-related errors before this happens. Either replace the drive or have it repaired to restore Hot Fix.

Reserved Blocks. NetWare reserves a certain number of blocks within the Redirection area to hold the Hot Fix tables. The exact number depends on the size of the disk. (HL3) The "Drive Status" Window

The "Drive Status" window appears underneath the main "Disk Information" screen discussed above. This window has one informational option and five status indicators.

Volume Segments On Drive. When working on a server with multiple volumes, it's sometimes difficult to remember which volume is on which physical disk. It's even more difficult when the volumes span several physical disks. Pressing <Enter> on the "(select for list)" field brings up a "Volume Segments" window showing you all of the volume segments defined on the currently selected hard disk.

Note: If the field next to "Volume Segments On Drive" is blank, the drive is not currently active ("Inactive" is displayed in the "Drive Light Status" field). You must reactivate the hard disk before you can see the volumes. To do this, highlight "Inactive" and press <Enter>, then select "Activate Drive" from the resulting window.

For a physical disk containing only one volume, you will see a description like "110 Meg on Volume SYS segment 0." For a disk containing several volumes, the segments are displayed as follows:

```
50 Meg on Volume SYS segment 0
60 Meg on Volume VOL1 segment 1
```

This shows you the size of each volume segment on that disk, the volume names, and the segment numbers.

Read After Write Verify. This field can contain one of the following status messages: Software Level, Hardware Level, Disabled, or Not Supported. However, the last two messages do not mean that NetWare is not performing read-after-write verification on the disk. Rather, the status refers to which disk channel component—the driver, the controller, or the drive itself—is actually initiating the verification.

Some newer disk drives and controllers can perform their own internal read-

driver specification allows for a *configurable* read-after-write verification option. Most disk drivers don't support this configurability. For these drivers, the status will be either "Not supported" or "Software Level." If your driver does support configurable read-after-write verification, you will be able to highlight the field, press <Enter>, and get the "Read After Write Status" window containing three possible selections. The three possibilities are described below. (For some disk drivers, not all of these options will be available.)

• The "Software Level Verify" option means the disk driver will oversee the read-after-write verification. This is the way NetWare traditionally handles it for most disks. The driver interacts with the OS to check data written against the original data in memory. If they don't match, the driver returns a write error and Hot Fix takes over to redirect the data.

• The "Hardware Level Verify" option means the disk's controller board will verify the data as it is written to the disk, without the driver having to initiate the process. If a write error occurs, the controller signals the driver, which passes the error on to the OS. As usual, Hot Fix kicks in to have the data rewritten to the Redirection area.

• "Disable Verify" disables both the hardware and software levels of verification. Choose this option only if the hard disk provides its own internal read-after-write verification. (Check the specifications in the disk manufacturer's documentation.) As always, any write errors will be passed back up the channel to the OS. From there, Hot Fix will handle things.

Some of the disk drivers that ship with NetWare (such as the ISADISK driver) provide software-level verification as the default. Depending on the driver, you might be able to select the hardware-level or disabled verify. However, if the controller or disk is not designed to perform its own read-after-write verification, your selection won't be reflected in the status field when you return to the "Drive Status" window. Most SCSI drivers display "Not Supported" because they do not support the configurable read-after-write verify feature. Be assured, however, that as long as you use Novell-certified disk drivers, data will always be verified after it is written. This capability is part of the certification requirements.

You can turn read-after-write verification off altogether by entering the "Set enable disk read after write verify=off" command at the server console. (See "SET Commands for Disk and Volume Management" below.)

Drive Light Status. Most computers and disk subsystems have drive indicator LEDs that light up whenever a disk is being accessed. This option allows you to make the lights flash on demand, even if the disk is not being accessed at the time. This can help you identify exactly where the drive whose statistics you are looking at is located. If the driver, controller, or disk do not support the function call used to flash the lights, the status will indicate "Not Supported." Otherwise, highlight the field (which initially displays the "Normal" status) and choose "Flash Light" from the "Drive Light Status" menu. The indicator light for the currently selected disk should now flash at regular intervals.

Drive Operating Status. Use this entry with caution: it does not just control what information you see on the screen, as the description in Novell's *System Administration* manual leads you to believe. What it does is allow you to deactivate (and thereby cease all communication with) the drive for which you are currently viewing information. This is *not* something you want to do while users are actively accessing the disk. Deactivate a drive only when you want to shut it down for diagnostic purposes, or if you must replace one drive in a mirrored pair while the server is running. (The latter procedure would only work with disk duplexing. The drive would have to be located in an external disk subsystem separate from its counterpart drive, since you must shut off power to the box before you attempt to remove a drive.)

To deactivate a drive, highlight the status field (which currently displays "Active") and press <Enter>. Then select "Deactivate Drive" from the ensuing "Operating Status" menu. If the disk is still in use, you'll get a warning message that says "The selected drive is currently being used by other processes <Press ESCAPE

To Continue>." Press <Esc> but *do not* respond to the "Deactivate Drive Anyway?" prompt until you are sure nobody is accessing critical files on the disk. When you answer "Yes," any further communication with the drive over the network is impossible. All of the entries on the MONITOR screen go blank except for the driver name and the disk size at the top. The Drive Operating Status will indicate "Inactive."

If you deactivate a drive that is still in use, you'll get numerous errors both at the server and at workstations that were reading or writing data on the disk.

Removable Drive Mount Status. If you are using removable media (such as a Bernoulli box or some other removable hard disk), this entry is where you signal the OS when to mount and dismount that media. (Nothing is displayed here for non-removable disks.)

- To mount a removable drive, insert the unit and select the "Disk Information" option from the first MONITOR screen. Then choose the drive's driver/controller combination from the "System Disk Drives" list. Highlight the "Removable Drive Mount Status" field in the "Drive Status" window and press <Enter>. Then choose "Mount Drive" from the "Drive Mount Status" menu. Once mounted, the driver accepts the drive media and users can access data on the disk.

- To dismount a mounted drive, follow the same steps, except choose "Dismount Drive" from the "Drive Mount Status" menu. The OS cannot access data on a dismounted drive, so make sure no one is actively accessing data on the drive before you dismount it.

Removable Drive Lock Status. Using a similar procedure, you can lock and unlock a removable disk drive. Locking the drive prevents anyone from physically removing the media. Before you can remove it, you must unlock the disk. This gives you some security against media theft, which is a concern with removable media.

SET Commands for Disk and Volume Management

The following SET commands relate to volume capacity and disk activity. They are grouped according to the categories you see when you type "SET" at the console.

"Memory" Category

The only disk-related command in the Memory category is "Set cache buffer size=n." The default is 4,096 bytes (4KB). Other allowable values are 8,192 for 8KB buffers and 16,384 for 16KB buffers. Choose the value that matches the smallest disk block size set for your volumes. (See "Cache Buffer and Disk Block Size" above for more information.) This command must be entered in the STARTUP.NCF file, or you can specify the cache buffer size when you type the SERVER.EXE command by adding the "-c" option (for example, "SERVER -c8192").

"File System" Category

The "SET Volume Low Warn All Users" parameter defaults to ON. When the free space in a volume falls below the low warning threshold, the OS sends a "Volume...almost out of disk space" broadcast message to all users currently logged in to the server. This is a signal for users to archive and delete unneeded files from the volume. You can turn off this warning mechanism by setting the parameter to OFF. If you do, be sure to periodically monitor available volume space with CHKVOL, VOLINFO, or a similar third-party management utility.

The "SET volume low warning threshold=n" parameter determines when the OS sends the warning message described above. Before issuing the warning message, the NetWare v3.11 file system attempts to purge all deleted files eligible for purging. After attempting to purge files, if the volume free blocks are still below the warning threshold, NetWare generates the broadcast warning. The default value for n is 256 blocks; you can adjust that anywhere from 0 to 1,000,000 blocks (do not include commas if you enter a value over 999). The actual amount of storage space this parameter represents depends on the block size set for the volume. With 4KB blocks, the default of 256 translates into about 1MB of storage. NetWare includes salvageable files that have not yet been purged when it calculates the remaining free space on a volume. Thus purging files is another way to free up space on a volume.

The "Set volume low warning reset threshold=n" parameter controls when the OS will send a second volume low warning after reaching the threshold described above. As users delete files to make more space on a volume, other users might be creating new files. Also, unless deleted files are purged immediately, they take up space until the minimum file delete wait time has elapsed. As a result, the available space on an almost-full volume often fluctuates above and below the low warning threshold for a while. In this situation, you don't want users to get the volume low warning message every time the available space dips slightly below the threshold. This parameter determines how many blocks must be freed up *above* the threshold before the low warning mechanism resets. The default value is 256 blocks; allowable values range from 0 to 100,000 blocks. Again, the exact amount of disk space that represents depends on the block size. With a 4KB block size, the default of 256 means that users must delete and purge enough files to free up at least 1MB of volume space above the threshold before the OS can issue any subsequent volume low warnings.

"Disk" Category

The "Set enable disk read after write verify=off" command allows you to turn off NetWare's read- after-write verification feature ("on" is the default value). When the OS doesn't have to do any read- after-write verifying, it can perform disk writes almost twice as fast. However, try this only if you have extremely reliable disks that are all mirrored or duplexed. Without adequate data protection, the speed you gain won't be worth the potential for data loss due to write errors.

"Miscellaneous" Category

The "Display disk device alerts" parameter controls whether or not the OS displays messages about hard disks. "Off" is the default setting. If you set this parameter to "on," NetWare will display a console message whenever a disk is added, activated, deactivated, mounted, or dismounted (the latter two apply only to removable disks). These messages can be helpful when you are troubleshooting a problem with a disk driver or hard disk. Although you can set this parameter anytime by entering the command at the console, we recommend you put the command in the STARTUP.NCF file so you can see alerts as the disk drivers are loaded.

The VREPAIR Utility

NetWare's VREPAIR (Volume REPAIR) utility corrects minor hard disk problems resulting from corrupted or mismatched FAT and directory table entries. You can also use VREPAIR to remove Macintosh, OS/2, Unix, or OSI FTAM name spaces from a volume.

As explained in Chapter 22, FATs and directory tables contain critical information that the file server must have in order to locate directories and files on its hard disk volumes. VREPAIR attempts to recover data from a volume after incorrect information has been written to the volume's FAT or directory table. Bad information in these tables can result from:

- Defective or worn-out hard disks
- Unexpected power loss to the file server, or severe power fluctuations
- Shutting off the file server before bringing it down properly

Of course, the use of Hot Fix and UPS power protection, along with proper downing of the server, can help prevent these possible causes of data loss. However, disk surface defects can become so excessive that NetWare shuts off Hot Fix; other disk hardware components can also fail. Some UPS systems do not protect adequately against power fluctuations that often cause just as much damage as full-fledged outages. And if the server mysteriously hangs, you have no choice but to turn it off without issuing the DOWN command.

If files are still open when a disk fails or the server is shut off unexpectedly, file pointers used in the FAT become misaligned and no longer point to the next block of information in that file. This misalignment also affects the directory tables because they rely on the FAT tables for data retrieval. In cases like these, VREPAIR may be able to help you recover some of the data from the disk. Since NetWare keeps two copies of all FATs and directory tables, VREPAIR compares the primary tables with their duplicate copies. When it finds a discrepancy, VREPAIR uses whichever set has the most correct entry and writes that entry back into both sets of tables.

While VREPAIR can fix the directory and FAT entries, it cannot bring back data held in cache buffers that had not been written to the hard disk. VREPAIR's primary purpose is to restore the integrity of the FATs and directory tables; its secondary purpose is to recover data, if possible. VREPAIR may not be able to recover lost data at all; therefore, don't rely on VREPAIR to take the place of regular system backups.

When to Run VREPAIR

Here are some of the most common error messages that indicate the need to run VREPAIR on a volume. These messages are displayed on the server console screen, usually during the volume mounting process after you reboot a server that has gone down unexpectedly.

```
Deleted file is a Subdirectory.
Directory block is inconsistent...has several Subdirectory
    numbers.
Directory block refers to non-Subdirectory directory entry.
Directory entry contains an invalid file name.
Directory FAT chain has a hole.
Directory tree is circularly linked.
Duplicate file names in the same directory.
Error reading both copies of the directory on Server/Volume.
Error reading one copy of the directory on Server/Volume. Error
reading in volume directory.
Error re-reading in a directory entry.
ERROR: Two volume segments with same sync value have mis
    matched data.
Error writing FAT table for volume Server/Volume.
Error writing to the extended directory space.
Invalid available entry.
Invalid deleted file block.
Invalid directory number code.
Invalid Maximum Space defined in Subdirectory.
Invalid trustee directory entry.
Invalid user restriction node...too many trustees.
Invalid volume header/root directory entry.
Length differences on mirror directory chains could not be
    resolved.
Subdirectory entry and first directory block do not match.
Subdirectory entry refers to invalid directory block.
Two subdirectories reference the same first directory block.
```

Certain errors referring to name space support may also require VREPAIR. If you encounter any of the following errors when using the ADD NAME SPACE command, you might have to run VREPAIR with the "Remove All Name Space Entries" option. Then try to add the name space again.

```
AddNameSpace error reading volume header...volume is left in a
    bad state.
Error allocating new entryonNameSpaceupgrade...volume is left
    in a bad state.
Error reading directory on NameSpace upgrade...volume is left
    in a bad state.
Invalid name space value.
```

Running VREPAIR

With NetWare v3.x, VREPAIR is an NLM located on the Operating System-2 diskette. Be sure you use the version of VREPAIR that shipped with your file server's version of NetWare: the utility is not interchangeable between v3.0, v3.1, and v3.11. It is a good idea to copy VREPAIR.NLM and its name space support modules (named V_NameSpace.NLM) to the file server's boot directory: either the C: drive if you have a DOS partition, or the boot diskette if you boot from a floppy diskette. That way, you can still run VREPAIR even if the SYS volume is unavailable.

VREPAIR is a nondestructive utility; no data is written over or deleted in the volume being repaired. However, always make a full backup of your disks before running VREPAIR, just to be safe. The 3.x versions of VREPAIR do not take as long to run as previous versions; the exact time depends on the size of the volume. On a large volume (1GB or more), VREPAIR usually takes at least 30 minutes.

You can run VREPAIR on a volume while the server is up and running, but the volume must be dismounted. In most cases, a volume with even minor directory errors will fail to mount in the first place. Follow one of the two procedures below, depending on whether you want to fix directory problems or remove name space entries on the volume.

Repairing a Volume. If the volume you need to repair is mounted, make sure no users are accessing files in the volume; then use the DISMOUNT command to remove the volume from use.

1. Type "LOAD VREPAIR" at the console. If volume SYS is not mounted, specify

1. Type "LOAD VREPAIR" at the console. If volume SYS is not mounted, specify the path to where the VREPAIR.NLM file is located (for example, LOAD C:\VREPAIR).

2. Select option 2, "Set Vrepair Options," to specify how you want VREPAIR to handle writing updated FAT and Directory Entry Table information to the disk. The current settings are displayed at the top of the screen, with the alternative options in a numbered list below. The relevant options are:

Write Only Changed Directory and FAT Entries Out to Disk.. This is the default selection for the second option. By default, VREPAIR writes only updated entries to the existing tables. Use this the first time you attempt to fix a volume with VREPAIR.

Write All Directory and FAT Entries Out to Disk.. Select this alternative if the first attempt fails to correct problems on a *mirrored* volume. With this option selected, VREPAIR will write the entire updated tables to both disks. If the server had important data files open when it crashed, do *not* use this option until you have tried unmirroring the disks and salvaging the most up-to-date version of the data from one of the disks. Otherwise, you may lose part of the data.

Keep Changes in Memory for Later Update. This is the default selection for the third option. It allows VREPAIR to run faster by accumulating all changes in memory and then writing them to disk all at once when it has finished scanning the volume. Make sure you have plenty of memory available; if VREPAIR finds a lot of errors, it could run out of memory to hold them and have to abort the operation. If VREPAIR encounters more than 1,000 errors, keeping them all in memory will cause the program to run very slowly.

Write Changes Immediately to Disk. Choose this option if you have limited memory in the server, or if a lot of files were open when the volume's problem occurred. VREPAIR will run slightly slower, since it stops to write any changes

If necessary, change one of these options by typing the appropriate number at the prompt and pressing <Enter>. Then type "0 <Enter>" to return to the main menu. The remaining instructions assume you have chosen the defaults.

3. Select option 1, "Repair A Volume," from the main menu. If more than one volume is unmounted, select the one you want to repair. VREPAIR begins scanning the volume and displays the following information:

```
Total errors:
Current settings:
    Pause after each error
    Do not log errors to a file
Press F1 to change settings

Start 8:20:19 am
Checking volume SYS
```

As VREPAIR checks through the FAT and Directory Entry Tables, its progress is indicated by rows of dots across the screen.

4. When VREPAIR finds an error, the test pauses and displays both the original table entry and the proposed corrected entry in a format similar to the following:

```
Error at file entry 711
Original Entry - Deleted DOS file entry
    Name: \DELETED.SAV\REPORT.TXT
    Size: 0
    File size does not agree with allocated FAT blocks
Corrected Entry - Deleted DOS file entry
    Name: \DELETED.SAV\REPORT.TXT
    Size: 4096
<Press F1 to change settings, or any other key to continue>
```

By pressing <F1> (either after an error or any time during the test), you can set the following run-time options:

- With option 1, you can tell VREPAIR not to pause after each error it encounters. With "Do not pause" selected, the test will run faster; however, VREPAIR will no longer display the errors it finds.

- Option 2 suggests that you can log the errors into a file of your choosing. However, due to a bug in VREPAIR, anything you type at the ensuing "Error log file name:" prompt is rejected. If you need a record of which files have been damaged (so you can restore them from a backup if necessary), you'll have to manually record them as they are displayed on the screen.

- Option 3 allows you to abort the VREPAIR test. You can do this at any time during the test; however, no corrections will be made to the tables and the volume will remain in its corrupted state.

Type **0 <Enter>** to proceed with the VREPAIR test.

5. When the test finishes, VREPAIR displays the total number of FAT repairs and directory repairs,and prompts:

```
Write repairs to the disk? (Y/N): Y
```

Answer "Yes" to this prompt to have the corrected entries written to disk. Then press any key to return to the main menu.

6. Type **0 <Enter>** to exit VREPAIR.

While VREPAIR is a useful tool for fixing file and directory problems caused by power failure or downing the server improperly, it cannot always bring a volume back into an operational state. If a volume still won't mount after you have run VREPAIR on it, go into INSTALL and delete the volume. Then recreate it and restore data from the most recent backup.

If the problems persist and worsen to the point where you need to reformat the disk, consider replacing the hard drive altogether. If your site has a history of power problems, either purchase an uninterruptible power supply (UPS) or have the UPS you are using upgraded or repaired (see Chapter 26).

Removing a Name Space with VREPAIR. The procedure for using VREPAIR to remove name space entries from a volume is similar to that described above. Removing a name space destroys any extended information about files on the volume. With Macintosh files, for example, you lose long file names and Finder icons, as well as the entire resource fork of every Macintosh file entry. Only the data fork and DOS-equivalent names remain.

Follow the procedure below only if you get name space-related errors, or if you are sure you no longer need multiple name space support on the volume. (You cannot remove the default DOS name space.)

1. If necessary, remove the volume from service by typing "DISMOUNT *VolumeName*" at the console. Make sure VREPAIR's name space support modules (called V_*NameSpace*.NLM) are in the same directory as VREPAIR.NLM. Then type "LOAD VREPAIR."

2. Select option 2, "Set Vrepair Options," and specify "Remove Name Space support from thevolume" for the first option. VREPAIR lists the name spaces currently existing on the volume. Select the one you want to remove.

    Also select "Write Changes Immediately To Disk" for the third option, then type "0 <Enter>" to return to the main menu.

3. Select option 1, "Repair A Volume," from the main menu. VREPAIR begins scanning thevolume as before.

4. When the test finishes, exit VREPAIR and remount the volume.

The CHKVOL Utility

Use the CHKVOL utility to find the total space on a volume, how much space is being used by regular files and deleted files, how much space is available to all users, and how much space is available to the user who typed the CHKVOL command. The display is similar to this:

```
Statistics for fixed volume JUNGLE/SYS:

Total volume space:                       992,960 K Bytes
Space used by files:                      971,808 K Bytes
Space in use by deleted files:                 24 K Bytes
Space available from deleted files:            24 K Bytes
Space remaining on volume:                 21,152 K Bytes
Space available to KNEFF:                  21,152 K Bytes
```

This utility is helpful for quickly finding out how much volume space is still available. For example, suppose a user calls and complains that he or she can't save a file. You can ask the user to run CHKVOL to find out how much space is available on the volume, especially when the user's space must be limited.

The VOLINFO Utility

VOLINFO is similar to CHKVOL, but it displays real-time statistics at a glance for each volume on the file server. Use this utility for monitoring the directory entries as well as for monitoring usage of disk space. A sample VOLINFO screen follows.

Page 1/1	Total	Free	Total	Free	Total	Free
Volume name	SYS		VOL1			
KiloBytes	30,048	6,496	96,612	95,600		
Directories	2,432	1,390	6,528	6,525		
Volume name						
KiloBytes						
Directories						

```
Available Options

Change Servers
Update Interval
```

VOLFINO tells you the total space and the free (available) space on each volume, as well as the total number of directory entries and the number of free directory entries on each volume. The <F2> key toggles the display between kilobytes and megabytes. (VOLINFO defaults to megabyte display if the server has more than 1GB of disk space.)

Other Disk and Volume Analysis Tools

There are numerous third-party tools that can help you manage your server disks and volumes. (See Appendix D for a more complete listing.)

One tool that can help you analyze the actual use of your server's disks is the File Wizard utility from Knozall Systems. With this tool, you can determine (among other things) what percentage of usage is coming from which volumes on your disks. For example, if you run a File Wizard Volume Analysis report, and discover that your total server usage is 75%, but the usage of the server's SYS volume is running at 89%, you can see that it's time to consider either increasing the size of SYS, or moving some of the data to a volume other than SYS. If you run an Aging Analysis of volume SYS and determine that 40MB of the data stored in this volume has not been updated in the past 360 days, you can see that the volume doesn't need to be any larger—you can solve your problem much more easily by simply archiving and removing the unused files.

Another third-party tool you may want to consider is the Bindview product from The LAN Support Group. Bindview is a NetWare report generator that allows you to define any type of NetWare usage report you would like to generate. Although there are many types of uses for this type of a product, disk and volume analysis and security analysis are some of the most prevalent.

Troubleshooting Network Disk Problems

A NetWare disk channel contains numerous software and hardware components: cache buffers, disk drivers, disk channel interface boards, controllers, cabling, and the hard disks themselves. Although disk drive technology has improved remarkably over the past several years, mechanical components such as hard disks and controllers will eventually fail. The reasonable life expectancy of a hard disk in a standalone system is only three to five years. On a network, where the server's disks and controllers are in almost constant use, the life span tends toward the shorter end of the scale.

Of course, the seriousness of failures in any of these components depends on how you have implemented NetWare's fault-tolerance features such as Hot Fix, disk mirroring, and disk duplexing. Since network disks are the repositories of your critical data, we recommend that you take full advantage of these features. And, no matter how reliable you think your components are, *always* back up your data.

On the whole, hard disk-related problems are fairly easy to detect; disk failure messages are more direct and specific than most other types of network errors. However, not all disk problems generate a clear-cut error message, nor are all possible symptoms obviously disk-related. A hard disk malfunction almost always produces an error message, but a failure in the controller or other circuitry may not. Now that NetWare supports almost every conceivable type of mass storage device, from the humblest MFM disk to the flashiest optical drive, the possible combinations of disk hardware are endless. This opens the door to some insidious incompatibility problems that are very difficult to troubleshoot.

As always, you'll need your full troubleshooting arsenal to successfully diagnose and resolve disk- related problems. Keep a detailed record of all your disk channel components: manufacturer, brand name, hardware and software configurations, driver versions, and so on. Users tend to fret more when network disks go down, fearing the loss of hours or even days of tedious data entry. So be prepared for the onslaught. Whenever possible, keep spares of all critical parts in stock, and maintain a suitable service agreement for all hard-disk-channel components.

Improper installation is one of the biggest causes of disk-channel problems. Don't assume that if you've installed one disk, you've installed them all. Although the general procedure is the same, details vary from manufacturer to manufacturer. You can avoid a lot of grief by carefully following all installation instructions.

Following is a list of other common disk problems and solutions. Use this information along with the utilities previously described to help get disks and volumes back up and running. For explanations of specific error messages, see Novell's *System Messages* manual.

General Disk Troubleshooting Procedure

When troubleshooting disk problems, it's a good idea to trace along the entire disk channel, starting with the hard disk itself and working your back to the disk driver. Here is a quick list of things to check along the way:

- Make sure the hard disk and controller have been physically installed according to the manufacturer's instructions. Refer to the manufacturer's documentation to see if any jumper settings need to be made on the controller or the hard disk. If there is only one disk per controller, make sure the disk is cabled and addressed as disk 0. A second disk, if there is one, must be cabled and addressed as disk 1.

- Most SCSI disks are shipped with a jumper set to enable parity. To use the disk with NetWare, you must disable parity by removing the appropriate jumper (refer to the manufacturer's documentation for details).

- Ensure that the power supply is functioning properly, and that the cables from the power supply are seated firmly in the power sockets, both on the hard disk and on the controller.

- Check the ribbon cables between the hard disk and controller. Be sure Pin 1 of the ribbon cable (usually indicated by a colored stripe) matches up with Pin 1 of the connector.

- For SCSI drives daisy-chained to a common disk coprocessor board (or host bus adapter), make sure the last controller on the SCSI bus is properly terminated with a terminating resistor. As the first controller on the bus, the DCB should also have a terminating resistor installed. However, if the DCB is connected to internal disks, remove the terminatingresistor.

- Make sure each controller connected to the same SCSI bus has its own valid controller address (0 through 7). The controller address is usually set via jumpers on the controller board.

- Check to see that the DCB or internal disk controller board is properly installed and fully seated in the expansion slot. For a DCB, make sure the SCSI interface cable is firmly fastened to the connector on the board.

- The board's interrupt, DMA, I/O port address, and memory address settings must not conflict or overlap with those used by any other hardware in the computer. See Appendix Afor a list of commonly used hardware configurations.

- Chips or other circuitry on the controller or DCB can become faulty. If the board came with its own diagnostics, use them to identify such problems. For boards with no self-diagnostics, try swapping the board with one you know works. If the problem goes away, you probably have a bad board.

- A disk driver must be loaded with parameters that match the board's settings. Type "MODULES" to see if the disk driver you need is loaded. Disk drivers are typically loaded via LOAD commands in the STARTUP.NCF file. View the contents of that file to see the current settings of loaded disk drivers. (See "Problems When Loading Disk Drivers" below if the driver won't load.)

- Make sure the INSTALL program has been run to create a NetWare partition and one or more volumes on the disk.

- Don't overlook the possibility of hardware failure in the PC itself. To diagnose problems such as memory parity errors or bad I/O slots, see if the computer will boot with DOS only. Most PCs come with internal diagnostics programs; refer to the manufacturer's documentation for instructions.

If a hard disk is not listed when you select various "Disk Options" (to format the drive or run the surface test, for instance) in INSTALL, check all of the above plus:

- Run the DISKSET NLM to make sure the hardware configurations stored in the EEPROM chip on the DCB match the actual disk channel configuration.

- For internal hard disks, make sure you have run the SETUP (or similar) program so the computer can recognize a newly-installed disk.

Problems When Loading Disk Drivers

Disk drivers, like any other loadable modules that you link to your operating system, should be approved by Novell and certified for your version of the OS. All disk drivers available from Novell have been approved and certified for use with NetWare. Unapproved NLMs may abend the server or corrupt data. Check on NetWire or ask your Novell Authorized Reseller about the approval status of third-party disk drivers.

As with LAN drivers, you will often have fewer problems and get better performance if you upgrade your disk drivers when you upgrade the version of NetWare.

Problem: A disk driver NLM will not load.

Solutions:

First, make sure you are typing the LOAD command correctly: "LOAD *DiskDriver Parameters*" is the basic format. Check your spelling of the driver name. You don't have to specify the extension, but if you do it should be .DSK for a disk driver.

Make sure you have properly installed the right kind of controller board or DCB for the disk driver you are trying to load, and that you have a v3.x version of the disk driver. (Refer to Appendix B for a list of disk drivers and their associated hardware.) The boards must be correctly attached to powered-on disk drives for the driver to initialize properly.

Check the INT, PORT, and other disk driver parameters. These settings must match the board's actual configuration but not conflict with settings on any other hardware in the machine, including printer ports, video display adapters, and so forth. If you specify a parameter that is already in use by other hardware that NetWare knows about, NetWare will so indicate with an error message. The I/O port and shared memory addresses represent only the start of a *range* of bytes, so it is possible for them to overlap if two boards use settings too close together. Use CONFIG to see the full address ranges and the settings used by the LAN adapters in the server. If necessary, bring down the server, reconfigure the board, reboot the server, and reload the disk driver with the correct parameters.

Another common reason that a disk driver won't load is that the file server cannot find the NLM. If this is the case, you'll usually see the message "Unable to find load file *DiskDriver*." Since disk drivers must load before you can mount any volumes (including SYS), you must copy the .DSK files to the server's boot directory. In the LOAD command, specify the appropriate drive letter (A: or C:) before the driver name. If you use the REMOVE DOS or SECURE CONSOLE commands, you can no longer load NLMs from anywhere but the SYS:SYSTEM directory. You can also use the SEARCH command to tell the OS where to look for NLMs.

If none of the above solutions works, the disk hardware might be faulty. Follow the preceding checklist to isolate the problem. Repair or replace any malfunctioning disk-channel components.

Problem: When I load a disk driver, I get a message saying that the module is using old API calls. What does this mean?

Solution:

The disk driver was written for NetWare v3.0. Starting with NetWare v3.1*x*, Novell changed some of the API calls for NLMs. The old API calls will still work, but they are slower than the new v3.1x calls. Contact the disk driver vendor for a version updated for NetWare v3.1*x*.

Problems When Mounting a Volume

If a volume won't mount, check the following potential causes:

- The OS must be able to find the disk driver NLM for the disk's channel. Make sure this module is in the same directory as the other file server boot files, or use the SEARCH command to specify the path to the disk driver module. o If you store non-DOS files on the volume, the OS must be able to find the appropriate name space modules. Make sure MAC.NAM, OS2.NAM, and other name space modules are in the file server boot directory, or use the SEARCH command to specify the path to the name space modules.

- If you included the commands to load the disk driver and name space modules in the STARTUP.NCF file, check the syntax and paths to make sure they are correct.

- If the server cannot locate all the segments of a volume (if one of the disks containing the volume is down, for instance), the volume will not mount. Make sure all necessary disk drivers have been loaded. Use MONITOR to check the status of all disks containing pieces of the volume.

Problem: I get FAT or directory entry errors when I try to mount a volume.

Solutions:

Entries in the directory tables and FATs might become corrupted if the file server is shut down unexpectedly, without the DOWN command. Minor errors, such as incorrect FAT entries, will usually correct themselves the next time the OS writes to the disk. Others will be taken care of by TTS.

If errors concerning directory or FAT mismatches persist, or if they prevent a volume from mounting, run VREPAIR on the volume.

Problem: I get memory errors when I try to mount a volume.

Solutions:

The server does not have sufficient memory to mount the volume. Volumes require more memory during the mounting process than afterwards because the OS must check the consistency between both copies of the FATs and directory tables. This extra memory is taken from the cac he buffer pool, and returned to the pool after the volume mounts. Thus if the cache buffer memory pool is getting low, a volume might not be able to mount. Load MONITOR and check the percentage of available cache buffers. If it is lower than 20 percent, add more memory to the server.

Other ways to free memory for mounting volumes include unloading unneeded NLMs, downing the server and rebooting it to return memory from the permanent and alloc pools to the cache buffer pool, and reducing the number of directories on the server. It is a waste of disk space and memory to have subdirectories with only a few files in them, since each subdirectory entry takes up a minimum of one disk block whether it contains one file or twenty. A 4KB block can contain a directory entry holding information on up to 32 files. By combining directories so there are fewer directories containing more files, you can often free up some memory.

Problem: I get errors saying a volume's block allocation size, directory or FAT table blocks, number of segments, total volume size, or volume flags do not match.

Solutions:

These mismatch errors can be caused by one of two things: either two volumes on the same server have identical names, or the volume has become corrupted. Although NetWare won't let you define a new volume with the same name as an existing one, duplicate volume names can occur when you have volumes on removable media. Check all defined volume names on the server before you name a new volume. If necessary, rename one of the volumes in the INSTALL utility.

If the volume is corrupt, run VREPAIR. If that fails to fix the problem, back up the entire volume. Then run INSTALL to delete the volume and recreate it.

Other Disk-Related Problems

Problem: The server reports an error expanding a volume's directory because the directory size limit was exceeded.

Solution:

NetWare limits the number of directory blocks to 1/32 of the total volume size. Once that many blocks are used by the directory, the OS cannot allocate any more blocks for the directory table. Delete any unneeded directories or combine smaller directories into fewer, larger ones. Or add more disks to the volume.

Another limit to be aware of (although it is unlikely you will ever reach it) is that NetWare allows a maximum of 2 million files per volume.

Problem: The server reports an error expanding a volume's directory because no more disk space is available.

Solutions:

If the volume runs out of disk space, users won't be able to create any new files or directories.

Delete unused files, consolidate directories, or add more disks to the volume.

Problem: The server reports an error expanding a volume's directory because no more memory is available for the tables.

Solution:

The OS has no more memory to cache Directory Entry table. Delete unused files and directories,add more memory, unload unneeded NLMs.

Problem: The server is unable to create or write to the VOL$LOG.ERR file on a volume.

Solutions:

Either the volume has no more free disk space, or a disk error is preventing the OS from accessing the volume error log file. Check the available space with CHKVOL or VOLINFO. If space has run out, either delete all unused files or add more disks to the volume. If the error log file itself is getting too large, copy it to another storage media (floppy disk or tape backup), then delete it from the server. NetWare will start over with a new VOL$LOG.ERR file.

Run MONITOR to check for disk errors. Repair or replace any faulty disk-channel components.

CHAPTER 25

LAN Driver/ Communication Management

LAN drivers, with their associated network boards and cabling hardware, provide the physical foundation for communication in a NetWare network. The health of this LAN communication mechanism is critical to virtually all other network functions. In the Installation section, we discussed how to load a LAN driver and bind it to a protocol stack. We also covered the basics of network numbering and routing. This chapter presents a more in-depth discussion of LAN communication theory, then introduces tools you can use to manage file server LAN drivers and troubleshoot network communication problems.

LAN Communication Concepts

In a file server, LAN drivers serve as the software connection between NetWare and the physical network components. Since the LAN driver code talks directly to the network board, a given LAN driver works only with the type of board for which it was designed. However, some manufacturers build boards with look-alike interfaces so that they can be used with an existing LAN driver. (Appendix B contains a list of the server and DOS client LAN drivers shipped with NetWare v3.11 and the network hardware they work with.)

Server LAN drivers are slightly different than workstation LAN drivers. Server LAN drivers are NLMs with the .LAN extension, such as NE2000.LAN and

TRXNET.LAN; the core set is loaded into the SYS:SYSTEM directory when you install NetWare. LAN drivers for traditional DOS workstations are linked in with IPX.COM when you run WSGEN. On a DOS workstation using ODI, LAN drivers are separate .COM files (NE2000.COM, TRXNET.COM, and so on) that you configure via the NET.CFG file. For OS/2 workstations, LAN drivers are like other device drivers (NE2000.SYS, TRXNET.SYS) loaded and configured in the CONFIG.SYS file.

Whereas using ODI in a DOS workstation is optional, a NetWare v3.x file server always uses ODI to communicate with LAN drivers. In fact, the server's LAN communication mechanism is built around ODI, as shown in Figure 25-1.

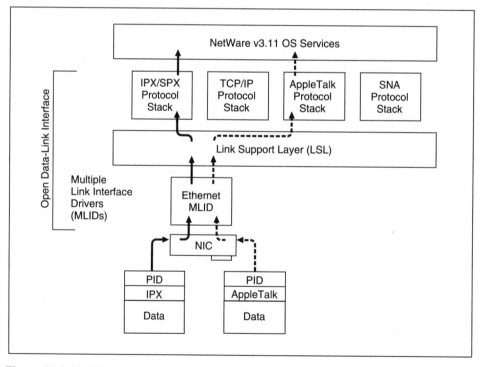

Figure 25-1: NetWare v3.x servers use an ODI-based LAN communication mechanism.

Packets, Headers, and Frame Types

Communication on a network involves breaking large pieces of data (files, usually) into small chunks called *packets*. "Packet" is the Novell term for what is called a "frame" or "datagram" in other types of networks. In addition to actual data, a packet contains control and routing information in various *headers*, plus some error checking codes.

The exact size and position of a packet's fields vary with each type of network (Ethernet, Token Ring, and Arcnet). They also vary slightly among *frame types* for the same network hardware. For example, various frame types used in the Ethernet environment are Ethernet 802.3, Ethernet II, and Ethernet 802.2. We'll talk more about frame types later in this chapter. For now, suffice it to say that network boards can communicate only with other boards of the same type transmitting packets with the same frame type over a certain kind of cabling.

To send a packet, each communication layer in turn adds its own header to the packet. Ultimately the LAN driver adds a hardware-specific header to the packet and delivers it to the network board hardware, which converts the packet into electronic signals and sends them out across the network cable.

At the other end, the signals are received by a similar network board. That board's LAN driver converts the signals back into a packet and checks the error codes to make sure the packet arrived intact. If necessary, the driver reassembles a series of packets to produce the complete message. As the packet travels up the communication layers, the headers are stripped off in reverse order and the data is delivered to its intended destination. Figure 25-2 illustrates how a request packet travels from a DOS workstation to the file server.

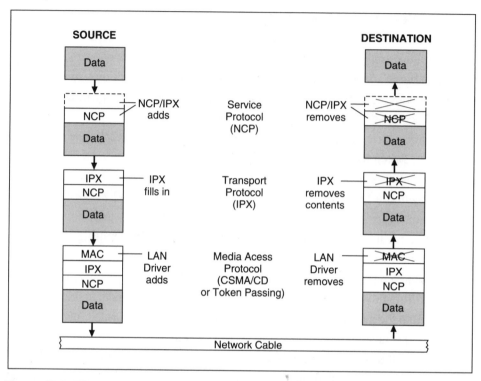

Figure 25-2: When a packet is sent, each communication layer adds its own header information, which is removed in reverse order at the destination.

In this example, the packet contains a piece of data to be written to the network disk. The workstation shell adds a NetWare Core Protocol (NCP) write request header and an IPX header to the data. IPX.COM then fills in the IPX header, which indicates the source address, the destination address, the length of the packet, the packet type, and so on. The LAN driver adds a Media Access Control (MAC) header containing source and destination addresses used for routing the packet.

At the file server, the LAN driver reads the MAC header and removes it before passing the packet up to the IPX protocol stack. From the information in the IPX header, IPX determines that this is an NCP write request. IPX removes the header's contents and passes the packet up to the NCP service protocol. NCP recognizes the packet as a write request, removes the NCP header, and passes the data to the file server's disk process to be written.

One important concept to understand for troubleshooting purposes is that packets don't always arrive intact. A number of things can cause corrupted or malformed packets: electromagnetic interference on the cable, loose or bad cable connectors, faulty network boards, and so on. The IPX/SPX protocol has a built-in mechanism for handling the occasional bad packet. When a LAN driver receives a packet that doesn't pass the error checking sequence, it discards the packet. At the sender's end, IPX waits a predetermined amount of time for a response to the packet. If none is received, the packet is re-sent and the timeout wait is increased. If there is still no response, IPX sends the packet again with an even longer timeout. This process repeats until either the packet arrives intact and a response is received, or the maximum number of retries is reached. Once IPX runs out of retries, it gives up and reports a message such as "Error sending on network" at the workstation.

The LSL and Multiple Link Interface Drivers

ODI actually consists of three basic components: the multiple protocol interface (MPI), the link support layer (LSL), and the multiple link interface (MLI). For most purposes, though, it's easier to think of these collectively as just the link support layer. We mention the subcomponents here mainly to explain the acronym MLID, which is often associated with a LAN driver. An MLID is a "multiple link interface driver," so named because it is written to Novell's MLI specifications.

Most MLIDs (LAN drivers) can be loaded more than once. Of course, you must load a LAN driver for each physical network board you install in the file server, even if two are the same type of board. Since no two boards can share the same interrupt, I/O port, or memory addresses, each LOAD command must specify different configuration parameters. There is one exception: two Token Ring boards in the same machine can share the same interrupt. Therefore the TOKEN driver can be loaded twice with the same interrupt setting.

To conserve memory space, all the LAN drivers shipped with NetWare v3.x (except the PCN2 driver) load "reentrantly." Rather than duplicating the entire driver code in memory each time they are loaded, these drivers share one copy of the driver code and certain global data. A small block of memory is then allocated for each subsequent loading to tell the OS about the different parameters used.

Another reason for loading LAN drivers more than once is to run multiple protocols over the same network board. In this case, you load the same LAN driver twice with identical configuration parameters except for the frame type. Then, instead of one physical board, the LSL sees two "virtual" boards—one for each protocol/frame type. In all, the LSL can support up to eight MLIDs and 16 protocol stacks.

With this understanding of the LSL's interaction with MLIDs, we can see how these components cooperate to get packets to the right place. When a packet arrives via a physical network board in the server, the LAN driver associated with that board checks the destination address in the IPX header. If the destination address contains the board's own network and node addresses, the LAN driver passes the packet up to the LSL. The LSL reads a protocol ID (PID) number within the packet to determine which protocol stack the packet needs to go to, then passes it to that stack through the MPI. From there, the packet is handled in the normal way by higher-level NetWare services.

If a board receives a packet destined for another network segment (either directly attached to another board in the server or accessible indirectly through the server), the packet still goes up to the LSL. The server's internal router directs the LSL to pass the packet back down to the appropriate MLID.

Transport Protocols and NetWare Streams

Previously in this book, we've talked about how NetWare Streams allows transport-independent communication in the server. In addition to IPX/SPX, NetWare v3.11's Streams supports the TCP/IP, AppleTalk, OSI TP4 (Transport Protocol Class 4), and SNA transport protocols. Applications written to take advantage of the Streams interface can access the full set of NetWare OS services regardless of which of these transport protocols the packet arrives on. One such application is the Server Backup (SBACKUP) program that ships with NetWare v3.11. With Streams installed on your file server, you can add new transport protocols or change existing ones without affecting the operation of Streams- based applications.

The following NLMs make up the NetWare Streams interface:

- STREAMS.NLM (provides application interface routines and utility routines for Streams-based server applications, a log device, and a driver for ODI

- TLI.NLM (provides the Transport Level Interface between Streams and user applications, allowing them to connect with transport level protocols)

- IPXS.NLM (lets Streams-based applications access the IPX protocol)

- SPXS.NLM (lets Streams-based applications access the SPX protocol)

Loading these NLMs adds interfaces at both the top and bottom of the protocol stacks. The "stream head" interface at the top talks to service protocols such as NCP and AFP. The interface at the bottom talks to the LSL.

Obviously, the Streams NLMs must be loaded on your server if you plan to run application NLMs that use the Streams interface. We've mentioned SBACKUP as one; check the documentation for third- party NLMs to see what their Streams requirements are. Some require only STREAMS.NLM to be loaded; others need STREAMS and TLI, but not IPXS and SPXS. Generally, if an application requires CLIB.NLM (a library of Novell C-language interface functions), you must load STREAMS.NLM before loading CLIB.NLM. If you're in doubt, go ahead and load all of the NetWare Streams NLMs in the following order: STREAMS, CLIB, TLI, IPXS, and SPXS.

Before you unload NLMs such as IPXS and SPXS that provide access to a protocol stack, remember to unload any application NLMs that might be using them.

Ethernet Frame Types

As you can see, NetWare v3.11 was designed to coexist in a multivendor, multiprotocol environment. One key concept to understand, especially in mixed networks, is how NetWare deals with the different packet formats imposed by other communication protocols.

The original Ethernet specification was developed by Xerox Corporation, then refined with the help of Digital Equipment Corporation and Intel. The refined packet specification is known as Ethernet version 2, or Ethernet II. As more and more companies embraced Ethernet technology, the IEEE 802.3 standards committee eventually stepped in to create a formal Ethernet specification.

About this same time, Novell was developing Ethernet LAN drivers based on the then-unfinished 802.3 standard. The Ethernet 802.3 packet Novell used to encapsulate IPX packets is slightly different from the Ethernet II packet, as shown in Figure 25-3. In the two-byte "Type" field, Ethernet II packets contain a protocol ID number. Novell substituted a two-byte "Length" field instead. IEEE subsequently decided to add 802.2 headers to the 802.3 specification to provide the PID and type information in the packet, thus creating a third Ethernet packet type called Ethernet 802.2.

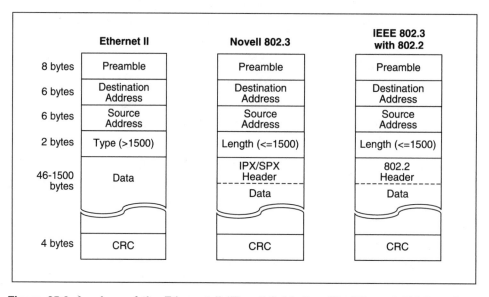

Figure 25-3: In place of the Ethernet II "Type" field, Novell's Ethernet 802.3 packet contains a "Length" field. IEEE subsequently added 802.2 headers to provide packet type information.

Because of the timing of Novell's Ethernet driver development, NetWare is the only network that uses the so-called "raw 802.3" frame type. Digital's DECnet and most of the TCP/IP community use the Ethernet II frame type, while IEEE and OSI compliant networks use Ethernet 802.2. Some in the TCP/IP community felt that Ethernet II's two-byte "Type" field was too limited, so they came up with what they call the Subnetwork Access Protocol, or SNAP, extension. Thus the fourth Ethernet frame type—Ethernet SNAP—was born.

These differing frame types are of little concern until you start interconnecting your NetWare LANs with Ethernet networks from other vendors—for example, Digital's VMS and DECnet, or TCP/IP-based networks such as the Internet. In this mixed environment, a station (be it a server, router, or workstation) must be able to recognize what frame type a packet is to know what to do with it. The key is the PID number contained either in the "Type" field, in the 802.2 header, or in the SNAP extension fields. The fact that Novell's 802.3 packets contain none of these fields causes some interesting compatibility problems.

As it happens, the two-byte PIDs in Ethernet II frames are always less than 1,500, while the "Length" field in Novell 802.3 frames always contains a value greater than 1,500. This nonduplication of values allows Novell 802.3 and Ethernet II packets to coexist on an Ethernet cabling system. However, it does not necessarily allow stations using the different Ethernet frame types to communicate with each other.

Adding 802.2-compliant devices to the network further complicates the matter. When these devices receive a Novell 802.3 packet, they try to interpret whatever follows the 802.3 header as 802.2 header information. The result is unpredictable at best. Workstations usually just discard the nonconforming packet. A router, however, might try to route the packet anyway despite the incorrect 802.2 information, causing all kinds of protocol handling errors.

To prevent these types of errors and to enable different Ethernet systems to communicate, NetWare v3.x allows you to configure file servers, routers, and workstations to recognize and properly route other Ethernet frame types. Below are some general guidelines; for specific instructions, refer to the Novell *Installation, System Administration*, and *NetWare ODI Shell for DOS* manuals.

File Server Configuration. By default, all Ethernet LAN drivers written for NetWare recognize Ethernet 802.3 packets. If you want the driver to handle an additional frame type, load the driver again with the same interrupt, I/O port, and so on, but add the "FRAME=*FrameType* NAME=*BoardName*" options to the LOAD command. For example, to enable a Novell NE2000 driver to recognize both 802.3 and Ethernet II packets, type **LOAD NE2000 [... FRAME=Ethernet_II NAME=NEII]** at the server. Giving the new instance of the driver a name makes it easier to work with this "virtual board" in subsequent commands. The new Ethernet II frame type automatically registers itself with the IPX protocol in the server. You can check this by typing "PROTOCOL" at the server console, which will display information similar to the following:

The following protocols are registered

```
Protocol: IPX    Frame type: VIRTUAL_LAN Protocol ID: 0
Protocol: IPX    Frame type: Ethernet_802.3 Protocol ID: 0
Protocol: IPX    Frame type: Ethernet_II Protocol ID: 8137
```

The next step is to bind IPX to the newly loaded driver by typing **BIND IPX TO NEII** and entering a new network address when prompted. Each frame type you load must have its own unique network address, even if it shares the same Ethernet cabling system with other frame types. Remember that you are essentially creating two "logical" network boards where there is physically only one. As far as the LSL is concerned, the 802.3 packets come from a different "board" from the Ethernet II packets. The LAN driver will now insert Novell's IPX protocol ID (8137) into the "Type" field of all Ethernet II packets so that Ethernet II stations can recognize them as IPX packets and route them accordingly.

You can also bind another communication protocol, such as TCP/IP, to the driver. Provided the TCPIP.NLM is loaded, typing **BIND IP TO NEII** and entering a unique IP network address will accomplish this task. If TCPIP.NLM is not loaded, you will get some warnings and a fatal error for the bind operation. The BIND IP command binds both IP and ARP (the Address Resolution Protocol) to the board. ARP makes the necessary translation between IP addresses and Ethernet addresses. (For more information on TCP/IP addressing and configuration, see the NetWare v3.11 *TCP/IP Transport Supervisor's Guide* that ships with the OS.)

Workstation and Router Configuration. There are two ways to configure workstations and routers to handle other Ethernet frame types. One way is to use Novell's ECONFIG utility to configure the IPX.COM shell file or the ROUTER.EXE program to use Ethernet II frame types. (This method does not work for Ethernet 802.2 or Ethernet SNAP frame types.) ECONFIG alters IPX.COM and ROUTER.EXE so that they will insert Novell's assigned protocol ID number for IPX (8137) into the Type field of each Ethernet II frame they encounter.

Here is the command format for ECONFIG:

```
ECONFIG [volume:]filename [option:parameter, [number]]
```

For *volume*, substitute the name of the NetWare volume containing the file you want to ECONFIG. *Filename* is the actual name of the file: IPX.COM or ROUTER.EXE. For *option*, use "SHELL" for IPX.COM and the LAN driver letter (A, B, C, or D) for ROUTER.EXE. For *parameter*, use "N" for IEE 802.3 frame type and "E" for Ethernet II frame type. Substitute "8137" for *number*.

The second method, which allows you to configure workstations and routers to handle IEEE 802.2 or Ethernet SNAP packets as well, is to use ODI LAN drivers. With these drivers, you specify the frame types and associated protocols you want the board to recognize in the NET.CFG file. For example, if you want a workstation's NE2000 Ethernet board to handle both Novell 802.3 packets via IPX and Ethernet II packets via TCP/IP, include the following lines in that workstation's NET.CFG file:

```
Link Driver NE2000
    Frame ETHERNET_802.3
    Frame ETHERNET_II
    Protocol IPX 0 Ethernet_802.3
    Protocol TCPIP 800 Ethernet_II
```

In the workstation's AUTOEXEC.BAT file, place the following startup commands:

```
LSL
IPXODI
NET3
TCPIP
```

The TCPIP.EXE program, included with the DOS ODI workstation software, rovides the TCP/IP protocol stack. To the LSL, it now appears that there are two boards in the workstation: one for Novell's IPX packets and one for TCP/IP's IP packets.

Other Frame Types

In the Token Ring environment, you use the default TOKEN-RING frame type for NetWare-only communications and for other protocols (such as OSI) that require 802.2 encapsulation. If you also want to connect to Unix computers over a TCP/IP-based network through the same Token Ring board, add the TOKEN-RING_SNAP frame type that supports IP services. The SNAP extension is also required for communicating through the AppleTalk protocol stack.

Likewise, IBM PC Network II adapters can use either the default frame type (IBM_PCN2_802.2) for NetWare-only and OSI communications, or the IBM_PCN2_SNAP frame type for interconnecting with AppleTalk and TCP/IP-based networks.

Arcnet boards can only use the default NOVELL_RX-NET frame type.

Useful Console Commands and Utilities

This section explains some of the console commands and utilities that are useful in configuring and troubleshooting LAN drivers and protocols. For more detailed information, refer to Novell's *System Administration* manual.

The LOAD Command

You use the LOAD console command to load a LAN driver as well as other types of NLMs. LAN drivers have their own set of possible parameters, however. These parameters are summarized below. The basic command syntax is:

```
LOAD [Path]LANDriver [Parameters...]
```

If you don't specify a path, NetWare assumes the LAN driver is in the SYS:SYSTEM directory on the file server. You can use the SEARCH console command to specify other paths for the OS to look in for NLMs.

Hardware Configuration Parameters

Depending on the type of network board, you can set various hardware configuration parameters when you load the LAN driver. Few network boards require all four parameters. If you don't include any parameters, the OS will prompt you for the essential ones after you enter the LOAD command. (Generally, LAN drivers for microchannel boards don't require these parameters in the LOAD command; the driver reads the configuration set with the *Reference* diskette.)

INT=*n*   Tells the driver what interrupt or IRQ line the board is set to use.

DMA=*n*   Tells the driver what DMA (Direct Memory Access) channel the board is set to use.

PORT=*nnn*   Tells the driver which I/O port address the board is set to use (usually a three-digit hexadecimal address).

MEM=*nnnn*   Tells the driver which shared memory address the board is set to use (usually a five-digit hexadecimal address).

Of course, these parameter values must match the actual hardware settings on the board itself. Otherwise, the LAN driver will probably not load.

Board Identification Parameters

You can add the following optional parameters to further identify the board to the OS.

NAME=*BoardName*	Assigns a unique name (up to 17 characters long) to the board. The OS associates the driver's parameters and the frame type with this board name. Most commonly used when you load the same LAN driver more than once, to distinguish between virtual boards. You can use this name to refer to the board in subsequent commands, such as BIND and UNLOAD.
NODE=*Number*	Overrides the hard-coded node address on Ethernet and Token Ring network boards. *Number* must be a valid hexadecimal address that is not being used by any other board on the same network segment.
	Don't use addresses 0 or FFFF FFFF FFFF; they are reserved for NetWare. (Not all LAN drivers support this option.)
SLOT=*n*	In microchannel and EISA machines, use this parameter to indicate which slot the board is located in. Slots are usually numbered starting with 1.

Load-Time Configurable Parameters

The following parameters can be modified only when you load the driver at the command line. Not all drivers support these parameters.

RETRIES=n Adjusts the maximum number of times the driver will try to send a packet after the first attempt fails. The default is 5 for most drivers (100 for TRXNET). Change this parameter with caution— too many retries can slow down the board's perfor mance considerably.

LS=n (Token Ring only) Defines the number of 802.5 link stations the board will open upon initializa tion. Used only when you will connect to other IBM systems (such as a mini/mainframe host or an OS/2 LAN Server) over the same Token Ring board.

SAPS=n (Token Ring only) Defines the number of 802.2 service access points the board will open upon initialization. Used only when you will connect to other IBM systems (such as a mini/mainframe host or an OS/2 LAN Server) over the same Token Ring board.

TBC=n (Token Ring only) Defines how many transmit buffers the driver will use.

TBZ=n (Token Ring only) Defines the size of the transmit buffers for the driver. The OS will allocate memory for the size and number of transmit buffers you specify.

To have the OS run the necessary LOAD commands every time you reboot the server, include the commands in the AUTOEXEC.NCF file. You can edit this file through INSTALL's "System Options" menu.

The UNLOAD Command

The UNLOAD command automatically unbinds a LAN driver from any communication protocols, unlinks it from all network boards for which it was loaded, and removes the driver from the file server's memory. Naturally, this action halts all network communication through that LAN driver, so make sure users have logged out before you unload it. If you have loaded the same LAN driver more than once for the same board, you cannot unload it for only one frame type or protocol—it's all or nothing. (If you have more than one board using the same LAN driver but with different protocols, you can use UNBIND to disable communication on one of the boards without unloading the LAN driver.)

The command syntax for unloading a LAN driver is:

```
UNLOAD LANDriver
```

Normally you unload a LAN driver to change optional parameters for the board while the server is running. For example, if you need to change the number of retries for an Arcnet board from the default of 100 to 75, type **UNLOAD TRXNET** and then **LOAD TRXNET RETRIES=75**. Be sure to specify the same hardware configuration parameters as before.

The NetWare v3.11 *System Administration* manual states that if you unload and reload the driver quickly (in less than 15 minutes), you can do it while users are logged in. Active workstations will receive the following error message if they make calls to the server while the driver is unloaded:

```
Network error on Server ServerName: Error receiving from network.
Abort, Retry?
```

According to the manual, users are to choose "Retry" once to see if there is an alternate route to the server through another network board. If they get another error, they should choose "Retry" after the driver is loaded again. Their connection will be preserved for up to 15 minutes. After that, the NetWare watchdog process automatically terminates any inactive user connections.

It is important to realize that the network error resulting from unloading a LAN driver at the server usually hangs non-ODI workstation shells. It can also cause problems for other routers on the same network segment. The safest way to change a LAN driver parameter is to have all users log out first. After you unload the driver and reload it with the new parameter, users can log back in and continue working.

You can't change hardware configuration options by unloading the driver and then loading it again. For that, you must bring the server down and actually change the settings on the board. Then reboot the server and load the LAN driver with the new settings.

If you get errors saying that the driver did not release allocated short-term memory when you unload it, contact the vendor for an updated version of the driver.

The BIND Command

A network board must have at least one communication protocol bound to its LAN driver; otherwise, no network communication can occur over that board. As discussed above, you can bind more than one protocol to the same LAN driver and network board. You can also bind the same protocol to more than one LAN driver in the server. To have the OS run the necessary BIND commands every time you reboot the server, include the commands in the AUTOEXEC.NCF file. You can edit this file through INSTALL's "System Options" menu.

Binding IPX

There are two possible command formats for binding the IPX protocol. Use the first if you assigned a name to the board when you loaded the driver:

```
BIND IPX TO BoardName NET=n
```

For example, if you named a certain board "BACKBONE," you would type the following to bind IPX to that board:

```
BIND IPX TO BACKBONE NET=BADBEEF
```

703

The only "protocol parameter" for IPX is the network number (NET=n). If you don't include it in the BIND command, the OS will prompt you for one. This number must be a valid hexadecimal network address. Use the following guidelines to determine an appropriate address:

- If the board is connected to an existing cabling system, use the network address of that system.

- If you are connecting a new cabling system to the board, choose a unique hexadecimal number between 1 and FFFFFFFE that is different from all other network addresses and IPX internal network numbers on the internetwork.

- If you loaded the driver with more than one frame type for the same board, you must enter a different address for each frame type that will exist on the cabling system.

If you did not assign a name to the board in a previous LOAD command, you must respecify the LAN driver name and parameters in the BIND command:

```
BIND IPX TO LANDriver [DriverParameters] NET=n
```

LANDriver and *DriverParameters* identify to the OS exactly which driver you want to bind IPX to. This is especially crucial if you have loaded the same LAN driver more than once in the server. Include as many parameters as necessary to distinguish the driver, and enclose them in square brackets. Make sure you use the same parameters as when you loaded the driver.

For example, if you have two NE2000 boards in the server, one using interrupt 3 and the other using interrupt 4, you would bind IPX to the second board by typing:

```
BIND IPX TO NE2000 [INT=4] NET=BADBEEF
```

If you have loaded a LAN driver more than once and you do not specify any parameters, the OS will list all instances of the driver as numbered "virtual" boards and prompt you for the one you want, then for the network number.

Binding Other Novell-Supplied Protocols

A TCP/IP transport protocol is included in NetWare v3.11. Other protocols come with optional Novell products such as NetWare for Macintosh and NetWare FTAM. These protocol stacks consist of one or more NLMs, such as the TCPIP.NLM for the TCP/IP transport protocol. You must load the appropriate protocol NLMs before binding the protocol to a LAN driver.

The basic format to bind these protocols to a LAN driver is:

```
BIND Protocol to LANDriver
[DriverParameters][ProtocolParameters]
```

Replace *Protocol* with the protocol name, such as IP or AppleTalk. If you assigned a name to the LAN driver when you loaded it, use that name in place of *LANDriver* and [*DriverParameters*]. Include any *ProtocolParameters* unique to the communication protocol, as described in the Novell documentation. IP, for example, requires that you specify an IP address.

Note: Some optional Novell products automatically insert the appropriate BIND command in the AUTOEXEC.NCF file if you install them with the "Product Options" feature of INSTALL. Check the product's documentation to see if it can be installed this way.

Binding Third-Party Protocols

Third-party vendors can also provide their own communication protocols for use on NetWare v3.*x* servers. Check on NetWire or consult your Novell Authorized Reseller for information about other available protocols. Generally, setting up the server to handle a third-party communication protocol is a four-step process:

1. Install an additional network board, if necessary, and load the appropriate LAN driver via the LOAD command.

2. Load the new protocol stack NLM(s) via the LOAD command.

3. Register the new protocol by using the PROTOCOL REGISTER command, if necessary. (See "The PROTOCOL Command" below for details.)

4. Bind the new protocol to the LAN driver by using the BIND command format for Novell- supplied protocols previously discussed.

The UNBIND Command

UNBIND removes a communication protocol from a network board and LAN driver without unloading the driver. This action halts all network communication for a particular protocol through that board, so avoid doing it when you have active users on the network. When you unbind IPX from a board, users on that board's cabling system cannot log in to the server until you rebind the protocol.

The command syntax for unbinding a protocol is:

```
UNBIND Protocol FROM LANDriver [DriverParameters]
```

If you assigned a name to the LAN driver when you loaded it, you can specify that name in place of *LANDriver* [*DriverParameters*]. Otherwise, you must identify to the OS which driver you want to unbind the protocol from. If you have loaded a LAN driver more than once in the server (either for multiple boards or for multiple frame types) and you don't specify any parameters, the OS will show you a list of numbered "virtual" boards and prompt you for the one you want.

Changing a Network Number

One reason you might want to unbind IPX is to change the network number assigned to a cabling system when a router reports an address conflict. To do this, type **UNBIND IPX FROM** *LANDriver* and select the appropriate virtual board if prompted. Then type **BIND IPX TO** *LANDriver* and enter the new network number when prompted. (You can use the DISPLAY NETWORKS command described below to see the network numbers currently in use on the internet.)

As with the UNLOAD command, the NetWare v3.11 *System Administration* manual states that if you unbind IPX and then bind it again with a new network number quickly enough (within 15 minutes), you can change the network number while users are still logged in. Active users will get the same "Network error..." message when they attempt to access the file server while IPX is unloaded.

Again, this network error usually hangs non-ODI workstation shells. It can also cause problems for other routers on the same network segment. The safest way to change a network number is to have all users log out first. After you unbind IPX and rebind it with the new network address, users can log back in and continue working.

The PROTOCOL Command

The PROTOCOL console command displays a list of all currently registered protocols and their assigned PID numbers. LAN drivers automatically register IPX with the default NetWare frame type when you load them. When you load a LAN driver with an additional frame type, the driver registers the new frame type for IPX as well. Here is a sample PROTOCOL listing:

```
The following protocols are registered

Protocol: IPX   Frame type: VIRTUAL_LAN Protocol ID: 0
Protocol: IPX   Frame type: Ethernet_802.3  Protocol ID: 0
Protocol: IPX   Frame type: Ethernet_II Protocol ID: 8137
```

When you bind a Novell-supplied protocol besides IPX to a LAN driver, the protocol automatically registers itself with the OS. For example, when you bind IP to the LAN driver using the Ethernet II frame types listed above, PROTOCOL will list the following protocols:

```
The following protocols are registered

Protocol: IPX   Frame type: VIRTUAL_LAN Protocol ID: 0
Protocol: IPX   Frame type: Ethernet_802.3  Protocol ID: 0
Protocol: IPX   Frame type: Ethernet_II Protocol ID: 8137
Protocol: IP    Frame type: Ethernet_II Protocol ID: 800
Protocol: ARP   Frame type: Ethernet_II Protocol ID: 806
```

IP needs the Address Resolution Protocol (ARP) to translate between IP addresses and Ethernet addresses, so ARP is automatically registered as well.

The PROTOCOL REGISTER Command

IPX and other Novell-supplied protocols register themselves automatically. Most third-party protocols will also. In the rare case that a protocol does not register itself, you must use the PROTOCOL REGISTER command to register the new protocol for use by a LAN driver. Make sure any protocols you use are approved by Novell.

The command format for registering a new protocol is:

```
PROTOCOL REGISTER ProtocolName FrameType PID
```

As indicated, you must specify the protocol name and the frame type that is to be bound to the communication protocol when you load the LAN driver. The PID (protocol identification number) is a unique hexadecimal number that tells NetWare how to recognize packets coming from the new communication protocol. Check the third-party documentation for the appropriate NetWare IPX protocol ID number. IBM calls this number a SAP; other vendors may refer to it as the Ethernet type, E-type, or something similar.

The CONFIG Command

The CONFIG console command is useful for determining which LAN drivers have been loaded on the server and what their configuration parameters are. Here is a sample of what CONFIG displays:

```
File server name: FS1
IPX internal network number: FADE2500

NE-2000 Lan Driver V3.10 (900308)
    Hardware setting: I/O Port 300h to 31Fh, Interrupt 3h
    Node address: 00001B082A03
    Frame type: Ethernet_802.3
    Board name: BACKBONE
    LAN protocol: IPX network BADBEEF
```

One advantage of the CONFIG display is that it shows the entire range of shared memory addresses and I/O Port addresses (300 to 31Fh in the sample above). It also displays the node address set on each physical network board, the frame type the driver is using, the name assigned to the board (if any), and the communication protocol and associated parameters (IPX and the network address in the sample above). If no protocol has been bound to a board that has a LAN driver loaded, the CONFIG display will show the message "No LAN protocols are bound to this LAN board."

The IPX internal network number shown at the top is the unique number assigned to the file server itself.

NetWare reads the network board information from the LAN driver, not from the board itself. You can thus use CONFIG to check the LAN driver settings against what is actually set on the board. You can also use CONFIG to see which interrupts and memory addresses are already spoken for before you configure and install additional network boards, add-on memory boards, or host bus adapters in the file server.

The DISPLAY NETWORKS Command

This command lists all currently recognized networks (both internal and cabling system) and their assigned network numbers. On a file server, the list includes network numbers currently used by that server and all other file servers that the internal router recognizes.

```
:display networks
    00000001  0/1  00000003  1/2  00000004  2/3
    00000051  2/3  000000BD  0/1  000000FF  3/4
There are 6 known networks
```

The two numbers after each eight-digit address indicate the number of hops (intermediate routers) that must be crossed to reach the network and the estimated time in ticks (1/18 of a second) for a packet to reach the network.

On a NetWare v3.x file server, you should see two networks that are zero hops away. One is the IPX internal network number for the server; the other is the network address of the cabling system to which the server is physically attached.

You can use this command to check communication on an internetwork. If a network exists but isn't displayed, something might be wrong with an intermediate router along the way. Either a file server or external router is down, or you have conflicting network addresses. Another possibility is a bad network board or faulty cabling system.

A similar command, DISPLAY SERVERS, displays the same type of information but lists file server names rather than network addresses.

The COMCHECK Utility

You can use the NetWare COMCHECK utility to check the communications between workstations, servers, and routers on the network. This utility helps you pinpoint possible cable problems and duplicate addresses (a frequent problem with Arcnet). COMCHECK doesn't require the server or router to be running, but the cables do have to be connected to each of the stations (workstations, servers, and routers) you want to test.

COMCHECK uses IPX to do a point-to-point test between nodes on the network. For this utility to work correctly, all the nodes you want to check must exist on the same physical cabling system. When two workstations are running COMCHECK, one will send a packet to an intended destination. If the destination workstation receives the packet, it will transmit a packet to the sender acknowledging that it still exists on the network and that it received the packet.

To use COMCHECK, first load the appropriate IPX.COM on each of the workstations you plan to check. (See Chapter 9 for more information about generating the IPX.COM file.)

If you can't load IPX.COM successfully, verify that your LAN adapter settings and IPX.COM configurations match. If they do, verify that your LAN adapter is properly seated in the bus expansion slot. If that doesn't help, check for possible conflicts between the LAN adapter and other hardware on the computer.

After you load IPX.COM, execute the COMCHECK utility (found on the WSGEN diskette) by typing **COMCHECK <Enter>** at the DOS prompt. You will be prompted to enter a unique name to identify the workstation. This can include the user's name (for example, "Scott's Workstation"). You will then see a screen containing the name you just typed, the network and node address of the workstation, and the time of the last successful communication with the workstation. The asterisk (*) next to the current date and time indicates the workstation on which you are currently running COMCHECK.

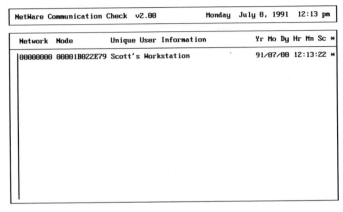

Now go to another workstation and follow the same procedure of loading IPX.COM and COMCHECK. Within 15 seconds, a screen will appear, displaying information about both workstations that are running COMCHECK.

```
 NetWare Communication Check  v2.00          Monday  July 8, 1991  12:11 pm

  Network  Node            Unique User Information       Yr Mo Dy Hr Mn Sc *

  00000000 00001B022130 Fred's Workstation               91/07/08 12:11:30 *
  00000000 00001B022E79 Scott's Workstation              91/07/08 12:11:30
```

If the second workstation doesn't appear after 15 seconds, you can suspect a cabling problem. To correct the problem, start by checking the connectors on the LAN adapter, then move out to any transceiver or hubs that may be faulty. If you have

Ethernet cabling installed, verify that the connector setting on the LAN adapter is set for the correct cable type (thick or thin).

For Arcnet communication problems, use COMCHECK to check for duplicate node addresses. A duplicate address can prevent the workstations with the same address from communicating. In fact, sometimes a duplicate address can make it impossible for any of the workstations to communicate. The node addresses are listed for each workstation on the COMCHECK screen.

There are two parameters you can adjust in COMCHECK: the *broadcast delay period* and the *dead timeout period*. The broadcast delay period represents the period of time after which an update packet will be sent out. The default is 15 seconds. Be careful setting this parameter when you run COMCHECK on a currently working network; too short a delay could flood the network with broadcast packets, causing a degradation in overall network performance.

The dead timeout period represents the period of time that COMCHECK waits, after a workstation has failed to send out update packets, before officially declaring the workstation "dead." The default timeout period is 60 seconds. When a workstation is considered dead, its name will be highlighted on the COMCHECK display screen.

MONITOR's "LAN Information" Option

The "LAN Information" option in the MONITOR.NLM utility is your doorway to a host of LAN driver information and statistics. In addition to generic statistics common to most LAN drivers, MONITOR can also display custom statistics specific to a particular board and driver. Besides alerting you to error conditions, this LAN driver information also helps you see which LAN segments are handling the most traffic.

Loading the Network Management Agent (NMAGENT.NLM) before loading a LAN driver allows the driver to register and pass network management information to other vendors' management systems (such as IBM's NetView and SNMP-based products). In NetWare v3.11, the OS automatically loads NMAGENT if you forget to.

Here's how to get to the LAN driver information in MONITOR:

1. Load MONITOR.NLM by typing **LOAD MONITOR** at the server console.

If it's already loaded, press <Ctrl>-<Esc> and select "MONITOR Screen" from the list of module screens.

2. Choose the "LAN Information" option from the "Available Options" menu.

3. Select the LAN driver whose information you want to look at. (If you have loaded the same LAN driver more than once for the same board, each instance will be listed. However, the statistics will be the same whichever one you choose.) You'll see a screen similar to the following:

```
┌──────────────────────────────────────────────────────────┐
│    NE2000    [port=300 int=3 frame=ETHERNET_802.3]         │
│                                                            │
│    Version 3.10                                            │
│    Node Address: 0000D81027A5                              │
│    Protocols:                                              │
│       IPX                                                  │
│          Network Address: 00000003                         │
│                                                            │
│    Generic Statistics:                                     │
│  ▼   Total Packets Sent:                        17,049     │
└──────────────────────────────────────────────────────────┘
```

Driver Name and Configuration. The window header shows the name of the LAN driver and the configuration parameters specified when it was loaded. These match the actual hardware settings on the board itself.

Version. The first line in the window itself identifies the version of the driver. (Generally, the LAN driver version will correspond to the NetWare OS version. In the sample screen above, driver version 3.10 means the driver was written for NetWare v3.1.)

Node Address. The next line displays the 12-digit node or station address set on the network board. Most Ethernet and Token Ring board manufacturers set this address in the board's firmware. The station address for Arcnet boards is set via jumpers or switches mounted on the board itself. Each network board in the file server will have a different node address.

Protocols. In this section, MONITOR displays the protocols currently bound to the network board. For the IPX protocol, you will also see the eight-digit network address assigned to the board. With NetWare v3.11, if you select a LAN driver bound to other protocols (such as TCP/IP or AppleTalk), you will see those protocols listed here.

Generic LAN Driver Statistics

By pressing the Down arrow key, you can scroll through the generic statistics. Most LAN drivers support these generic statistics; if not, you will see "Not Supported" on the screen. This section explains what these generic statistics mean and gives a few suggestions for using them to manage LAN driver communications. Note that all of the numbers described below represent a cumulative total since the last time the driver was loaded. Whenever you unload and reload the driver (or reboot the server), the count is reset to zero. The first two statistics are informational; the rest indicate abnormal or error conditions.

Total Packets Sent. This statistic counts the number of packets sent out through this network board to nodes connected to its cabling system. These packets come from higher-level OS routines, including NetWare's internal router. The total packet count includes all IPX, AFP, TCP/IP, and other types of packets supported by NetWare v3.11.

Total Packets Received. This statistic counts the number of packets the server has received through this network board. These can be either NCP file service requests destined for this server, packets destined to other IPX sockets on the server, or packets that must be routed to other servers through this server's internal router.

By comparing the number of packets sent and received for each network board, you can get a pretty good idea which segment is handling the most traffic. If one segment seems to be overburdened in comparison to the others, you may want to redistribute the load by moving some of the workstations to another cabling system. If all segments are equally busy and overall performance is becoming bogged down, consider adding another network board and moving some of the workstations to its new cabling system.

You can also use this information to evaluate the routing efficiency of your network. A typical internetwork setup involves a backbone cable used only for connecting file servers, with one LAN adapter (say an NE2000) providing the backbone connection in each server. A server's workstations are connected via a separate cabling system off another LAN adapter (say a Token-Ring adapter). By monitoring the Token-Ring statistics, you should be able to see how much of the traffic is generated locally. You can then monitor the NE2000 statistics to view requests routed to other servers across the internet.

If either of these totals is zero on an active network, something is preventing the board from transmitting packets. Check for hardware conflicts with other boards or components in the server. Also check for a faulty board or cabling.

No ECB Available Count. This statistic counts the number of times a request packet is sent to the file server but no ECB is available to accept it. ECB stands for Event Control Block, a structure in file server memory that NetWare uses to handle packet transmissions via IPX/SPX. Closely associated with the ECB is a packet receive buffer. (Packet receive buffers correspond to what were called "communication buffers" or "routing buffers" in previous versions of NetWare.) These buffers serve as "waiting rooms" in server RAM to store incoming requests until a service process is freed up to take care of the request. Requests in this case can be either file service requests (disk reads and writes) or packets waiting to be routed to other servers. The number of requests a server can respond to, then, depends on the number of packet receive buffers currently available in memory. This number is displayed in the "Packet Receive Buffers" field in the top half of the MONITOR screen.

Normally, the OS simply allocates more packet receive buffers when there aren't enough available. However, the OS is bound by both a lower and an upper limit. By default, the minimum number of packet receive buffers is 10 and the maximum number is 100. You can change these boundaries through a SET command that specifies new numbers for the "minimum packet receive buffers" or "maximum packet receive buffers" parameters. Novell's *System Administration* manual suggests you vary these boundaries in the following situations:

- When you want to decrease the default amount of server RAM consumed by receive buffers. At boot time, the OS automatically allocates enough memory for the *minimu n*umber of buffers. On a small network with limited file server memory, you might be able to squeeze out some additional memory for other NLMs by decreasing the minimum number of buffers (10 is the lowest you can go) in the STARTUP.NCF file. Don't get carried away, though—if the server seems to respond more slowly immediately after a reboot, change the minimum back to where it was.

- When you are using EISA or Microchannel bus mastering boards (such as the NE3200), adjust the *minimum* number of buffers so that you always have at least five buffers per board. If you start to see "No ECB Available Count" errors, increase the minimum to allow for 10 buffers per board. (You can change the minimum buffers parameter only through the STARTUP.NCF file.) You should also adjust the maximum number of buffers upward by the same number.

- When the actual number of buffers allocated reaches the upper boundary (200 by default), increase the *maximum* number by 10 until you have approximately one packet receive buffer for each workstation actively communicating with the file server. (You can issue the "set maximum packet receive buffers=*n*" command from the file server console.)

There is also a "set new packet receive buffer wait time" parameter that determines how long the OS waits before allocating another buffer. The default value of 0.1 seconds is adequate to prevent too many buffers from being created during a sudden upsurge of requests. Do *not* adjust this parameter unless it is recommended by an expert NetWare technician. It should *never* be changed if you have an EISA bus mastering board in the file server.

Another way around the problem is to increase the "maximum number of service processes" parameter via the SET command. You'll need fewer packet receive buffers if you have more service processes available to handle incoming requests. NetWare v3.1x defaults to a maximum of 20 service processes, but you can allow up to 40. The current number of service processes is displayed in the top half of the MONITOR screen.

Do *not* increase the number of service processes if your server is low on cache buffers. A small number of cache buffers limits the amount of disk data that can be held in memory, thus increasing the likelihood that service processes will have to wait for the data to be fetched from disk. Making more service processes only exacerbates the problem. Monitoring the number of service requests is also vital if you have loaded multiple name spaces on your server (such as OS/2, Macintosh, and NFS). In this environment, file service requests can tie up service processes for longer periods of time.

Finally, if your server uses either TCP/IP or OSI protocol stacks and any Novell Ethernet driver that uses a packet size greater than 1,506 bytes and frame type 802.2 or 802.2 SNAP, you must increase the default "Maximum Physical Receive Packet Size" to 1,530. Otherwise, the file server will not be able to receive the packets and the "No ECBs Available Count" will increment.

Send Packet Too Big Count. This count increments whenever the LAN driver tries (unsuccessfully) to send a packet that is too big for the board to handle.

Send Packet Too Small Count. This count increments whenever the LAN driver tries (unsuccessfully) to send a packet that is too small for the board to handle.

Network boards differ in the maximum packet size they can handle. For example, the original SMC Arcnet boards can handle only 512-byte packets, while NE1000 Ethernet boards can handle 1,024-byte packets. Some newer network boards offer improved performance by increasing the maximum packet size they can accept, but they require an updated LAN driver. Packet-too-big or too-small errors might indicate that you do not have the right LAN driver for the network board. Contact the board manufacturer for the latest driver version.

Receive Packet Overflow Count. This count increments whenever the file server receives a packet that is too big to fit in a receive buffer. You'll rarely see this happen, unless you are running an application that does not negotiate network packet size properly. Try your applications one at a time. If this counter starts incrementing with a certain one, contact the vendor for an updated version of the application software.

Receive Packet Too Big Count. This counter increments whenever the file server receives a packet that is too large.

Receive Packet Too Small Count. This counter increments whenever the file server receives a packet that is too small.

The SET command's "maximum physical receive packet size" parameter determines the size of the largest packet that can be received by any network board in the file server. The default of 1,514 (1,130 in v3.1) allows 1KB packets (data plus the packet header) to be accepted. This setting is fine for most Ethernet and Token Ring drivers and boards. If one or more of your file server's network boards can accept a larger packet size, increase the setting accordingly (4,202 for a 4KB packet is the highest you can go). You can change this parameter only by placing the SET command in the STARTUP.NCF file and rebooting the server.

Other generic statistics. Numbers in any of the remaining entries usually indicate errors due to a defective network board or a faulty cabling system.

- The "Send..." and "Receive Packet Miscellaneous Errors" entries show how many other errors have occurred when sending or receiving packets.

- The "Send Packet Retry Count" indicates how many retries occurred after the server tried to send packets but could not because of hardware errors. The OS will continue to retry an unsuccessful send operation until it either succeeds or reaches the maximum number of retries set for the LAN driver. With most LAN drivers (except TOKEN and PCN2), you can increase the maximum number of retries up to 255 by adding the "RETRIES=n" parameter when you load the driver. However, increasing the number of retries can slow down the performance of the board.

- "Checksum Errors" occur when the checksum byte at the end of a packet does not match the sum of the bytes contained in the packet. This mismatch indicates a corrupt packet.

- The "Hardware Receive Mismatch Count" tells you how many times the packet length specified in a receive packet did not match the size of the packet actually received by the board. Again, this is a sign of packet corruption.

Custom LAN Driver Statistics

The custom LAN driver statistics displayed in MONITOR vary according to the type of network board. Appendix A of the *System Administration* manual lists the exact statistics displayed by 11 of the most common LAN drivers. Not all of these custom statistics are helpful in troubleshooting; some are only informational, while others are too esoteric to be of real value. Rather than duplicate the complete lists given in the manual, we'll point out some of the main errors to watch for in each family of network boards.

Ethernet Boards

Ethernet boards include the 3C503, 3C505, 3C523, NE2, NE2-32, NE1000, NE2000, and NE3200. A solid background knowledge of the IEEE 802.3 specification will help in understanding the Ethernet custom error statistics. Figure 25-4 illustrates possible trouble spots in the Ethernet environment.

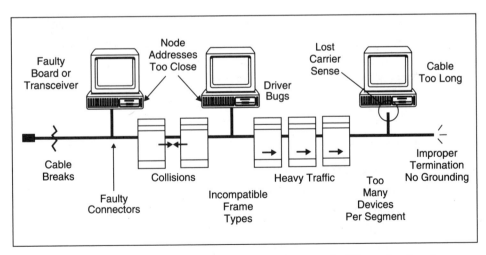

Figure 25-4: These are some of the potential trouble spots in Ethernet networks.

Collisions. A big concern in the Ethernet environment is the number of packet collisions that occur. Ethernet boards use the carrier sensing (CSMA/CD) media access method in which the driver "listens" on the cable to make sure the coast is clear before sending a packet. Once the driver gets a "clear to send," there is a slight delay before the packet is actually sent. If another board happens to send a packet during this delay, a collision can occur. Most of the time collisions are not a problem because both boards detect the collision and each resends its packet after waiting a random amount of time. The exact wait time is calculated based on the board's Ethernet address.

All of the drivers listed above (except the 3C505 and the NE3200) report some type of collision count. A "Total Collisions Count" increments every time a collision occurs. Naturally, the busier the network the more collisions you'll see. A more telling statistic is the "Excess Collisions Count," which reports how many times collisions recur after the first time. While excess collisions can indicate heavy network traffic, there are other possible causes:

- Two Ethernet boards on the same cable segment might have node addresses that are too close to each other. Since the wait time after a collision is based on the node address, the resends occur at nearly the same time and the packets collide again and again. (The boards are said to be "in sync.") Ethernet node addresses are set at the factory, but some boards allow the ODI LAN driver to override the hard-coded node address with a user-specified one in the NET.CFG file. Run USERLIST /A to make sure the address you set is unique and different enough from the existing addresses. If your hardware won't allow an address override, you'll have to swap one of the boards with another one from a different cable segment.

- The transceiver or other Ethernet hardware components might be malfunctioning. Many external transceivers have status indicator lights that show transmissions and collisions. Boards with built-in transceivers often have status LEDs on the mounting bracket. Check these lights to see if the board is functioning properly. If you suspect a faulty board, replace it. If the number of excess collisions decreases, you've found the problem.

- The cable segment might be too long or improperly terminated. This condition is usually accompanied by "Transmit Timeout Count" errors. Review the maximum cable lengths in the Novell *Installation Supplements* and make sure your segments comply. The T-connector at each end of an Ethernet trunk must be terminated, with one end properly grounded.

Heavy Traffic. Some other indicators of excessive network traffic are errors like "Enqueued Sends Count," "Back to Back Sends Count," and "Overflow Resends." These errors occur when the board is trying to send more packets than it can handle easily. If you see increasing numbers in these counters and network transmit times are slow, you need to either install an additional network board in the server to balance the load or split the network load by adding another file server.

Lost Carrier Sense. The "Carrier Sense Lost Count" increments when the transmitter on the board temporarily loses its connection with the cable. Before checking for a bad board, make sure the cable connector is firmly fastened to the board. T-connectors especially can easily jiggle loose.

Frame Types. To communicate, file servers, routers, and workstations must all be configured for the same Ethernet frame type. Ethernet 802.3 is the default frame type for NetWare-only networks. If you have loaded a LAN driver that uses another frame type (Ethernet II, Ethernet 802.2, or Ethernet 802.2 SNAP), run ECONFIG at the workstations or reconfigure the ODI drivers to match.

Faulty Board Indicators. Most of the other custom statistics for Ethernet boards—command length mismatches, DMA faults, paging errors, and overruns—indicate some type of hardware problem. Check the reset count also. If a board has to be reset often because of hardware errors, it's probably time to replace the board.

Token-Ring Boards

Although the IEEE 802.5 Token Ring specification is very complex, it does provide a sophisticated mechanism for self-monitoring and dealing with transmission errors on the ring. A technical understanding of how ring stations use the token to transmit data is essential to understanding the Token Ring custom statistics. (For a brief description of token passing, see Chapter 3 of this book.) One invaluable reference source is the *IBM Token-Ring Network Architecture Reference,* available from IBM.

Figure 25-5 shows some of the potential trouble spots in the Token Ring environment.

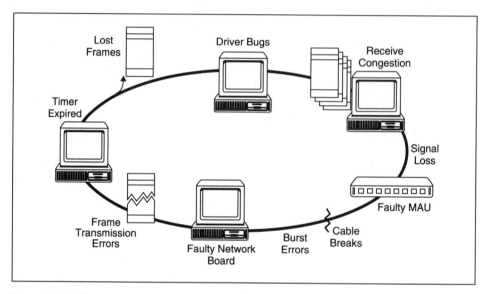

Figure 25-5: These are some of the potential trouble spots in Token Ring networks.

Hardware Problems. When a Token Ring board starts to go bad, it can experience "recoverable" hardware errors and still remain on the ring. These are reported as "Internal Errors" in the custom statistics. If the internal errors get bad enough, the board will remove itself from the ring.

Internal hardware errors can also cause a station to transmit spurious "Abort Delimiters" frames. Normally, a station transmits an abort delimiter only when it receives a data frame that is erroneously identified as the non-data token. The station changes the frame so that the Start and End Delimiters indicate an "abort" sequence.

Other hardware problems include breaks in the ring cabling and faulty multistation access units (MAUs). These can cause "Frequency Errors" (when the frequency of the incoming signal is markedly different from that of the local station's crystal oscillator) and signal loss (indicated by an error code on the "Last Ring Status" line).

"Unknown ARB Requests" usually indicate an older board that is issuing unrecognized commands to communicate with the driver via the Adapter Request Block. Newer boards use only four known commands to communicate with the driver. To prevent the board from hanging, NetWare responds to unrecognized requests and increments this counter. Although these errors are not fatal, you should upgrade the Token Ring board in the file server.

Last Ring Status. The number displayed on the "Last Ring Status" line changes whenever the status of the ring changes. Convert this decimal number to hexadecimal and look up its meaning in the chart in Appendix A of the NetWare v3.11 *System Administration* manual. The codes indicate error conditions such as an open or short circuit in the wire, signal loss on the ring, and only one station on the ring.

Receive Congestion. Since the token passing protocol allows only one station at a time to transmit data, media contention and collisions are not a concern in the Token Ring environment. The overall throughput stays fairly constant even in the face of increasing network traffic. The number of "Receive Congestion Errors," which occur when a board has no buffer space available to copy a frame addressed to it, should be low.

Frame Transmission Errors. In a Token Ring, one station serves as the "Active Monitor" and at least one other is designated the "Standby Monitor." Among other things, these stations ensure proper ring delay and data frequency, monitor the use of the token, poll the ring stations periodically, purge the ring of bad frames, and generate a new token when it is lost or corrupted. It is normal to see a small number of token errors, frame copied errors, lost frames, and burst errors in a ring. You needn't be too concerned, however, because the active and standby monitors take care of these types of errors.

Bad Correlator Count. These are critical errors because they can eventually cause the file server to crash. Numbers on the "Bad Correlator Count" line usually indicate that some software running at the server is corrupting data or code in the ECBs. Thus when the Token Ring driver requests information from these ECBs, the server is unable to respond correctly. To isolate the software that is corrupting the data, reboot the server and load the NLMs one at a time while watching this counter.

Arcnet Boards

The TRXNET driver is the main Arcnet LAN driver shipped with NetWare v3.*x*. It works with RX- Net, RX-Net II, and RX-Net/2 boards. Other Arcnet vendors provide their own LAN drivers with their boards.

One distinguishing feature of Arcnet is that the node address is set by the installer, not by the manufacturer. You set a node (station) address between 1 and 255 by manipulating switches on the board itself. No two Arcnet boards on the same segment can have the same station address. Duplicate station addresses are a common source of problems with Arcnet; they can prevent all stations on the segment from communicating with the file server.

Arcnet uses a token passing protocol in which the token is passed around in station number order. (By contrast, Token Ring passes the token in ring position order.) Since most Arcnet boards have a small (512-byte) maximum packet size, large transmissions must be broken into a sequence of smaller packets.

Figure 25-6 shows the potential trouble spots in the Arcnet environment.

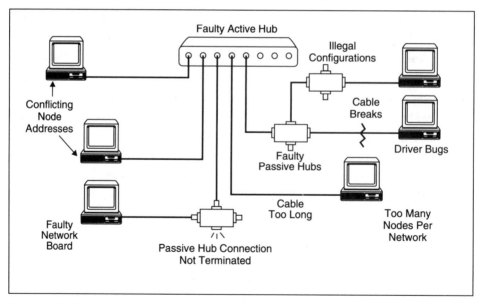

Figure 25-6: These are some of the potential trouble spots in Arcnet networks.

Retries and Timeouts. Like the other topologies, Arcnet limits the number of times a LAN driver can retry an unsuccessful send. The "Fatal Retransmissions" counter increments when this limit is reached. You can increase the maximum number of retries up to 255 for the driver by unloading it and reloading it with the "RETRIES=n" option. However, allowing more retries slows down the performance of the board.

"Timed Out Sends" occur when the server sends a packet to the driver, but the board does not respond within a certain amount of time. A small number of timeouts is not serious.

"Timed Out Receive ECBs" occur when all packets in a sequence do not arrive at their destination within a certain amount of time. Numbers here could indicate excessive network traffic.

Orphaned Packets. The "Number of Orphaned Packets" counter increments by one every time the following scenario occurs. The driver divides information in a data buffer into smaller packets and sends them out in sequence. If one of the packets arrives at the destination out of order, the sending driver cancels all the remaining packets in the sequence.

Unloaded Driver. Unloading the TRXNET driver while the driver is active can cause some curious errors. "Sends Cancelled" means the driver was unloaded when it had packets ready to send. Since the LAN driver is gone, the OS cancels the send commands. "First Halves Cancelled" means that the driver was unloaded in the middle of sending a sequence of packets, thus preventing the entire sequence from arriving at the destination intact. "Sends Ignored - Driver Shut Down" means other stations are trying to send packets to the unloaded driver.

Spurious Interrupts. A spurious interrupt occurs when the board generates another hardware interrupt while the driver is in the middle of an interrupt service routine (ISR). Normally, the driver turns off interrupts until the ISR is completed. The TRXNET driver recovers from a spurious interrupt by polling the hardware before exiting the ISR to see who issued the interrupt. If no device claims responsibility, the driver ignores the interrupt and increments the "Spurious Interrupts" counter. If you see a significant number of spurious interrupts happening, it could indicate a corrupt LAN driver or faulty board hardware. Reload the driver from the original diskette or replace the board, if necessary.

Other Communication-Related SET Commands

In addition to the SET commands described in previous sections of this chapter, NetWare v3.11 has three commands that affect the NetWare watchdog function. The watchdog's duty is to check periodically to make sure network stations are still active. If the watchdog senses no activity from a station for a period of five minutes, it starts sending watchdog packets to the station. If the station does not respond, the watchdog starts sending watchdog packets at one-minute intervals for up to 10 minutes. If the station still does not respond after 15 minutes, the watchdog assumes that the station is not active and clears the station's connection.

If you type **SET Console Display Watchdog Logouts=ON** at the server console, the server will display a console message whenever the watchdog clears a connection. The default setting is "Off." Most of the time, you won't need to display watchdog logouts; however, if stations are having connection problems, you can use this display to isolate which stations aren't successfully responding to the watchdog packets.

You can adjust the amount of time the server waits without receiving any requests from a workstation before it sends out the first watchdog packet to that workstation. To do so, enter the **SET Delay Before First Watchdog Packet=n minutes n sec** command at the server console. The default is 4 minutes 56.6 seconds (roughly five minutes). Supported values range from 15.7 seconds to 20 minutes 52.3 seconds.

Likewise, you can adjust the amount of time between watchdog packets (after the first watchdog packet is sent) via the **SET Delay Between Watchdog Packets=n** command. The default value is 10, which corresponds to 4 minutes 56.6 seconds (roughly five minutes). You can adjust the delay from one second to 10 minutes 26.2 seconds.

A new SET command in NetWare v3.11 allows you to turn off a server's ability to reply to Get Nearest Server packets from workstations. The DOS workstation shell sends these packets when trying to locate a server to attach to during the login process. If you don't want a particular server to answer, type "SET Reply To Get Nearest Server=OFF" at the server console. The default setting is "ON."

Troubleshooting LAN Communication Problems

The LAN communication system encompasses a host of software and hardware components: LAN drivers, workstation shells, protocols, network boards, cabling, connectors, hubs, wiring concentrators, bridges, routers, and so on. This multiplicity of parts makes it hard to isolate the cause of a LAN communication problem. As with other aspects of NetWare, there is no clear one-to-one correspondence between symptoms and their underlying causes. Even something as seemingly minor as a crimp in the cabling or one workstation using an old shell version can have deleterious effects on an entire internetwork. What's more, NetWare's elaborate retry and error recovery mechanisms are designed to hide minor communication problems from users. Often the only clue that something is amiss is a longer-than-normal response time.

To find and resolve LAN communication problems, you must adhere to proper troubleshooting technique. You should have already documented in your network log book all related hardware and software information, including network board and cabling types, hardware configuration settings, network and node addresses, LAN driver and shell versions, and so on. A cabling map and labels on the cables themselves will save you hours of frustration when you're trying to isolate cable failures.

No matter how intense the pressure is to get the network back up, resist the impulse to start tinkering randomly. Carefully observe the symptoms of the communication problem and try to uncover as many clues as you can. Answers to the following questions are particularly helpful:

- Does the problem affect a single workstation, a group of workstations, or everyone on the network? The scope of the problem helps determine where to start looking for its cause. If a problem is isolated to a single workstation, you can be fairly sure that the trouble is within that machine. When a problem affects a certain group of workstations but not others, look for a common link: They may all connect to the same hub or cable segment, attach to the same board in a file server/router, or use the same protocol. For network-wide problems, check your servers and routers first.

- Does the problem occur continuously, intermittently, or at regular intervals? Sporadic problems are much harder to isolate than continuous or regularly occurring ones. A general rule (to which there are numerous exceptions) is that intermittent problems are software-related, while problems that crash the network are hardware-related. Look for any relationship between the problem and some other event on the network (a workstation booting up or the server's periodic routing information broadcast, for instance).

- If the network worked before, have any components been added or modified recently?

  Every time you add a new component—be it hardware, software, driver, or cabling—or change an existing component, you run the risk of introducing a new problem on the network. Fortunately, these types of problems are easily traced to the new or changed component. Problems that occur out of the blue on a static network are much harder to isolate.

Draw upon these clues and your knowledge of how network communication protocols work to formulate a hypothetical cause of the problem. Use the "LAN Information" statistics explained above to help confirm your hypothesis. Then test one component at a time (replacing suspected bad ones with known good ones if necessary) until you find the source of the problem.

The remainder of this chapter explains common problems you might experience with NetWare's LAN communication system. For ease of reference, they are grouped according to when they are likely to occur. For explanations of specific error messages, see Novell's *System Messages* manual.

General LAN Communication Problems

Probably the two most frequently encountered error messages on a NetWare network are "A file server could not be found" and "Network error on server." The first occurs at a workstation after IPX loads and the shell tries to attach to a file server. Variations on the second message usually appear after a user has logged in successfully and has been working for a while. Both indicate that something has disrupted the communication channel between workstation and server.

Many seasoned network troubleshooters use a bottom-up approach, starting with the cabling system and working up to the network board and LAN driver. With that in mind, here's a quick list of things to check when the above errors occur.

- Anywhere from 70 to 90 percent of all LAN troubles can be traced to the cabling and associated hardware (connectors, transceivers, hubs, repeaters, and the like). That's not too surprising, since the cable is subject to so many environmental hazards: electromagnetic and radio frequency interference, cable breaks, shorts, oxidation (rust), loose or bad connectors, and so on. Improper installation of the cabling hardware is another culprit.

  Refer to Chapter 4 for specific tips on troubleshooting cabling and connection hardware.

- Check to see that the LAN adapter is properly installed and fully seated in the expansion slot. Make sure the cable is firmly fastened to the correct connector on the adapter. Many LAN adapters support more than one type of connection: BNC, DIX, and twisted pair are the most common.

- The adapter's interrupt, DMA, I/O port address, and memory address settings must not conflict or overlap with those used by any other hardware in the computer. See Appendix A for a list of commonly used hardware configurations.

- Check for duplicate node addresses. The node address is usually set on the adapter itself, but some LAN drivers allow this address to be overwritten. CONFIG will show you node addresses for file server and router boards. If the server is still up, run "USERLIST /A" at a workstation to see the node addresses for operational workstations. One telltale sign of conflicting node addresses is if one workstation can log in only when all others are logged out.

- Malfunctioning components (such as chips or transmitter circuitry) on the LAN adapter itself may be causing the problem. If the adapter came with its own diagnostics, use them to identify such problems. For adapters with no self-diagnostics, try swapping the adapter with one you know works. If the problem goes away, you probably have a bad LAN adapter.

- A LAN driver must be loaded with parameters that match the adapter's settings. In a traditional DOS workstation, go to the boot directory (the one containing files like CONFIG.SYS, AUTOEXEC.BAT, and IPX.COM) and type **IPX I** to see the current driver configuration. In a DOS ODI workstation, read the settings in the NET.CFG file. In a server or router, use the CONFIG command to display the current settings. (See "Problems When Loading LAN Drivers" below if the driver won't load.)

- In the server, at least one communication protocol must be bound to the LAN adpater for it to be able to transmit packets. CONFIG will show you which protocols are bound to each driver. (See "Problems When Binding Protocols" below if you have trouble binding a protocol to a driver.)

- In a mixed Ethernet network, make sure the file servers, routers, and workstations are configured for the same frame types. (See "Ethernet Frame Types" earlier in this chapter for more details.)

- In Token Ring networks, workstations need other programs loaded besides the shell. Load TOKREUI, DXMAID, or LANSUP.COM as instructed in the *Novell Token Ring Installation Supplement*.

- A file server cannot transmit packets on the network unless the SYS volume is mounted. Type **VOLUMES** at the console to see if SYS is mounted; if not, mount it by typing **MOUNT SYS**. If the SYS volume won't mount, check for the following potential causes:

  (1) The OS must be able to find the disk driver NLM for the disk that contains the SYS volume. Make sure this module is in the same directory as the other file server boot files, or use the SEARCH command to specify the path to the disk driver module.

  (2) If you store non-DOS files on the SYS volume, the OS must be able to find the appropriate name space modules. Make sure MAC.NAM, OS2.NAM, and other name space modules are in the file server boot directory, or use the SEARCH command to specify the path to them.

  (3) If you included the commands to load the disk driver and name space modules in the STARTUP.NCF file, check the syntax and paths to make sure they are correct.

- The server may not have enough packet receive buffers to handle traffic on a busy network. Check the current number listed in the MONITOR utility's main screen. If you don't have at least one buffer per workstation, increase the number via the "set maximum packet receive buffers=n" command at the server console.

- Don't overlook the possibility of hardware failure in the PC itself. To diagnose problems such as memory parity errors or bad I/O slots, see if the computer will boot with DOS only. Most PCs come with internal diagnostics programs; refer to the manufacturer's documentation for instructions.

Problems When Loading LAN Drivers

LAN drivers, like all loadable modules that you link to your operating system, should be approved by Novell and certified for your version of the OS. All LAN drivers available from Novell have been approved and certified for use with NetWare. Unapproved NLMs may abend the server or corrupt data. Check on NetWire or ask your Novell Authorized Reseller about the approval status of third-party LAN drivers.

Novell certification does not guarantee that a LAN driver is version-level compatible with every other network component. Avoid mixing LAN drivers and workstation shells from different versions of NetWare on the same network. When you upgrade the server OS, upgrade all LAN drivers, shells, and router software as well. A surprising number of intermittent lost connections are due to one user loading an old shell file.

Problem: A LAN driver NLM will not load.

Solutions:

First, make sure you are typing the LOAD command correctly: "LOAD *LANDriver Parameters*" is the basic format. Check your spelling of the driver name. You don't have to specify the extension, but if you do it should be .LAN for a LAN driver.

Make sure you have properly installed the right kind of network board for the LAN driver you are trying to load and that you have a v3.*x* version of the LAN driver. (Refer to Appendix B for a list of LAN drivers and their associated hardware.) Some boards must be attached to a properly terminated cabling system to load. Token Ring boards must be attached to a MAU. With most Arcnet boards, you must have at least one functioning workstation cabled to the server.

Check the INT, PORT, DMA, MEM, and other LAN driver parameters. These settings must match the board's actual configuration but not conflict with settings on any other hardware in the machine, including printer ports, video display adapters, and so forth. If you specify a parameter that is already in use by other hardware, NetWare will so indicate with an error message. The I/O port and shared memory addresses represent only the start of a *range* of bytes, so it is possible for them to overlap if two boards use settings too close together. Use CONFIG to see the full address ranges and the settings used by other network boards in the server. On Ethernet boards, make sure the connector type setting (thick Ethernet or DIX versus thin Ethernet or BNC) is set for the type of cable connection you are using. If necessary, bring down the server, reconfigure the board, reboot the server, and reload the LAN driver with the correct parameters.

Another common reason that a LAN driver won't load is that the file server cannot find the NLM. If this is the case, you'll usually see the message "Unable to find load file *LANDriver.*" Normally you load NLMs from the SYS:SYSTEM directory. By preceding the LAN driver module name with a path designation, you can load them from drive A:, drive C: (a DOS partition), or another subdirectory on the file server. You can also use the SEARCH command to tell the OS where to look for NLMs.

When loading a LAN driver from SYS:SYSTEM, you must first mount the SYS volume. If it isn't mounted, type **MOUNT SYS**. (See "General LAN Communication Problems" above for suggestions if SYS won't mount.)

The REMOVE DOS console command prevents you from loading NLMs from a local DOS drive (floppy drives A: and B: or drive C: on a DOS partition). SECURE CONSOLE prevents you from loading NLMs from anywhere except the SYS:SYSTEM directory. (See the next three problems for more details.)

If none of the above solutions work, the network board or cabling system might be faulty. Run the COMCHECK diagnostics to see if any workstations can communicate with the network board. Fix the cabling problem or replace the board as necessary.

Problem: You can't load a LAN driver NLM from a floppy diskette in drive A:.

Solutions:

First make sure the LAN driver you are trying to load is actually on the floppy diskette and that you are typing the command as "LOAD A:*LANDriver*". If you have removed DOS with the REMOVE DOS command or used the SECURE CONSOLE command, you cannot load any NLMs from drive A. Either copy the driver into SYS:SYSTEM from a workstation and try again, or down the file server and reboot it to restore DOS command capability. (If you included the REMOVE DOS command in the AUTOEXEC.NCF file, remember to delete that line first.)

Problem: You can't load a LAN driver NLM from a DOS partition on your file server.

Solutions:

First make sure you have copied the LAN driver you are trying to load to the DOS partition (usually accessed as the C: drive) and that you include the correct path in the LOAD command. If you have removed DOS with the REMOVE DOS command or used the SECURE CONSOLE command, you cannot load any NLMs from the DOS partition. Either copy the driver into SYS:SYSTEM from a workstation and try again, or down the file server and reboot it to reenable loading modules from a DOS drive. (If you included the REMOVE DOS or SECURE CONSOLE command in the AUTOEXEC.NCF file, remember to delete that line first.)

Problem: You created a SYS:SYSTEM/DRIVERS subdirectory for LAN drivers, but you can't load a LAN driver NLM from that directory.

Solution:

Make sure you have copied the LAN driver you are trying to load into that subdirectory and that you either include the correct path in the LOAD command or specify that subdirectory in the server's SEARCH command. If you have used SECURE CONSOLE, you can only load NLMs from the SYS:SYSTEM directory. Either copy the driver into SYS:SYSTEM from a workstation and try again, or down the file server and reboot it to disable the SECURE CONSOLE command. (If you included the SECURE CONSOLE command in the AUTOEXEC.NCF file, remember to delete that line first.)

Problem: When you load a LAN driver, you get a message saying that the module is using old API calls.

Solution:

The LAN driver was written for NetWare v3.0. Starting with NetWare v3.1x, Novell changed some of the API calls for NLMs. The old API calls will still work, but they are slower than the new v3.1x calls. Contact the LAN driver vendor for an updated version for NetWare v3.1x.

Problems When Binding Protocols

You should bind at least Novell's IPX protocol to each LAN driver you load. Other protocols are necessary only in mixed-vendor environments. Before you load a protocol from a third-party vendor, make sure it has been approved by Novell for use with NetWare v3.11.

Problem: IPX won't bind to a LAN driver.

Solutions:

Make sure you have loaded the LAN driver with the proper configuration settings and frame type. If you have loaded the LAN driver more than once, be sure you are correctly specifying the virtual board you want to bind IPX to. Either assign a name to the driver each time you load it, or include the distinguishing LAN driver parameters in the BIND command.

If you see router configuration errors scrolling on the console screen, the network number you assigned to the board's cabling system is conflicting with another network number. Unbind the driver and type **DISPLAY NETWORKS** to see a list of network numbers currently in use on the internetwork. Select an unused network number and try binding IPX to the LAN driver again using that number.

Problem: Other protocols won't bind to a LAN driver.

Solutions:

Novell-supplied protocols other than IPX must be loaded on the file server first. For example, before you can bind IP to a board, you must load the NetWare v3.11 TCP/IP transport NLMs by typing **LOAD TCPIP** at the server console.

Some third-party protocols have to be registered with the OS. Type "PROTOCOL" first to see which protocols and frame types are already registered. If the protocol you loaded is not listed, register the new protocol and frame type with the PROTOCOL REGISTER command.

Internetwork Routing Errrors

The most common cause of routing configuration errors on an internetwork is conflicting network addresses. Anther likely cause is improper or inefficient use of LAN communication protocols. Of course, in a NetWare network, routing is accomplished both within the file server and in external routers. Hardware failures in either of these devices will almost certainly affect internetwork routing.

One important concept to be aware of is that NetWare routers (both internal and external) use dynamic routing. Every 60 seconds, a router broadcasts information about the network segments it knows about. Other routers pick up these broadcasts and check the information against their own routing tables. As routers come up and go down, the other routers automatically adjust their tables to reflect the new internetwork configuration. You can monitor these routing information exchanges via the TRACK ON command.

Given the 60-second delay between routing information broadcasts, it is possible for a server or router to crash but still be listed for a short time thereafter in an SLIST or DISPLAY NETWORKS command. If a workstation tries to establish a connection during this time, it will receive the message "No response from given server." The RESET ROUTER command will cause a server or router to rebuild its routing tables immediately.

Router configuration errors can cause other network communication problems, so don't ignore them. The message should indicate the node address of the detecting router and which network segment address is causing the conflict. Use DISPLAY NETWORKS and CONFIG to find the network boards the offending address is assigned to. Change the address on one of them by unbinding IPX and repeating the BIND command, as explained in "Changing a Network Number" above.

Note: Once the server is up and running, you cannot change its *internal* IPX network number. You must specify a new number in the AUTOEXEC.NCF file, bring down the server, and reboot it.

Other routing-related errors may appear when IPX is unbound from a LAN driver while in use, when the LAN driver is unloaded while in use, or when the network board fails altogether. Stations communicating with other network segments through that board will no longer be able to do so. Reload and rebind the driver and protocol, or replace the faulty board, to restore routing.

CHAPTER 26

UPS and Power Protection

Any business or organization that relies on a LAN to store valuable data must protect itself against the possible loss or corruption of that data. One critical aspect of protecting data on your network disks is the use of an uninterruptible power supply (UPS). Without a UPS to provide dependable power to the file server and its peripherals, even NetWare's most sophisticated fault tolerance features cannot prevent data loss when commercial power is disrupted.

This chapter looks at the basic concepts of power protection and introduces the various types of power conditioning devices available. We explain how to set up a UPS and the file server to use NetWare's UPS monitoring feature, then discuss UPS messages and troubleshooting procedures.

The Importance of Power Protection

Power problems are a lot more common than most people think. Users often accuse software of causing hung workstations or lost data, when power disturbances are really to blame. Network technicians estimate that up to half of the service calls they receive are power-related. The following brief explanation of commercial power disturbances underscores the importance of providing ample power protection for your network.

The electrical components found in all computers, hard disks, and circuit boards are extremely sensitive to fluctuations in the power supply. In North America, commercial power companies go to great lengths to ensure that the electricity they generate is as close as possible to the standard 120-volt AC power alternating at 60 cycles per second (60Hz). (Other parts of the world have different power standards.)

Most people assume that this standard power is delivered in its pure form across the power lines. However, a number of factors can pollute electrical power before it reaches the customer. Storms, lightning, accidents, blown transformers, radio and television broadcast signals, interference from other electrical devices, large loads all coming on line at once—all of these can corrupt commercial power enough to cause problems for electronic components.

Disturbances to Commercial Power

Most of us have experienced power outages, or blackouts. This total loss of power is potentially the most devastating type of power disturbance. If the blackout occurs during a save to disk, while the file allocation table is being updated, you could lose access to some or all of the files on the disk. You also lose any data held in RAM at the time of the outage. The costs of reentering lost data far exceed the costs of merely replacing a damaged hard disk or power supply.

Though dramatic, blackouts are relatively infrequent. Other types of disturbances to commercial power can occur much more often:

- A spike is a burst of high voltage lasting only a fraction of a second. Spikes are also referred to as impulses or transients.

- Noise is the result of high-frequency, low-voltage oscillations that originate from such sources as fluorescent lights and heavy equipment motors.

- A power surge is a sudden increase in voltage that can last several seconds.

- A sag is a decrease in voltage lasting up to several seconds. Sags make up the majority of power problems.

- A brownout is a prolonged sag that usually occurs during periods of peak power usage, when the local utility company's power-producing capacity is severely drained. A typical example is a hot summer day when everyone is running his or her air conditioner at full blast.

The effects of these "less serious" power disturbances may be neither immediately obvious nor predictable. For example, they can cause glitches in the file server's internal power supply, which in turn can corrupt some of the data held in RAM. If such a disturbance occurs during a discrete operating system routine, the file server may continue to operate normally until that routine is used again. Only then will the server lock up or abend because of the corrupted data in memory.

Power surges are a common cause of hardware problems. Surges put undue stress on hardware components, particularly power supplies, and can cause them to fail prematurely. High-frequency noise or spikes can lead to read/write errors or parity errors, either of which could cause the computer to hang. Spikes can also damage hardware components. When power disturbances occur together, their potential effects are compounded. For example, slight sags in power happen frequently and may not be sufficient to adversely affect computers. If these sags occur during a brownout, though, the power level may be reduced below the acceptable power range that computer equipment needs to operate.

Types of Power Protection

For the most complete protection against data loss due to interruptions or fluctuations in commercial power, Novell recommends the use of a UPS on all NetWare file servers and attached hard disks. A UPS is a specially-designed power supply containing a battery that can provide power to the file server for short periods. If the commercial power fails, the server runs off the UPS battery until it can write all cache buffers to disk, close all files, and shut itself down gracefully.

A number of other power protection devices are currently available for computers. However, non-UPS devices do not protect your system against the full range of power problems. Some, such as surge suppressors and voltage regulators, are designed only to protect against minor power surges, spikes, and noise. They are ineffective for more serious power problems (sags and brownouts) and contain no battery backup to protect the network from blackouts. This is not to say that line conditioners, voltage regulators, surge suppressors, and the like do not have their place on a network; they are recommended for use with workstations and other less critical LAN peripherals.

Types of UPS Systems Available

Not all UPS systems are alike. Early UPS units were designed simply to provide backup power in the event of a blackout, leaving the server completely vulnerable to other types of power irregularities. Newer UPS systems are designed to protect against the full range of power problems.

The two main types of UPS systems are off-line and on-line. All UPSes contain an internal battery that produces AC power via an inverter. The inverter takes the DC charge from the battery, converts it to AC, and sends it to the computer's power supply. How and when this inverter comes into play largely determines the effectiveness of the UPS.

Off-Line UPS

In an off-line UPS, or standby power system (SPS), the inverter is normally off. Thus the file server and other attached equipment receive power directly from the commercial line as long as it is available. If the commercial power drops below a certain voltage level or fails altogether, the UPS switches from commercial power to battery power.

One drawback of this type of system is that it takes a finite amount of time for the unit's battery to kick in after it senses that the voltage has dropped. Sometimes the file server can't ride through this momentary delay and crashes anyway, especially when voltage on the power line is already low. The "switching time" of an off-line UPS is crucial. Generally, an SPS with a switching time of four milliseconds or less is safe to use with a network.

Another problem with off-line UPSes is that they typically do not perform well during sustained low-voltage conditions. Most blackouts are preceded by a brief period of low voltage. Off-line UPSes can inaccurately sense a brownout as a blackout and prematurely switch to battery. During a sustained brownout, an off-line UPS may completely discharge the battery and potentially crash the server, even though the office lights might still be on. Switching time also increases as the commercial voltage decreases. It is not uncommon for a unit with a five-millisecond transfer time at 120 VAC to exceed 20 milliseconds at 100 VAC.

The only significant advantage of an off-line UPS is its low cost. Low-end SPSes with one to three outlets, capable of supplying brief battery backup power, are available for a few hundred dollars. However, since the server remains exposed to such power disturbances as spikes, noise, surges, and brownouts, manufacturers of SPSes often recommend that a line conditioner or voltage regulator be used in addition to the SPS unit itself. This somewhat offsets the potential cost savings.

Some so-called "hybrid" UPS systems are currently being marketed. These are typically off-line SPSes with a built-in electronic or ferro-resonant line conditioner. Others feature an "enhanced" design intended to smooth out the transition from commercial power to battery power. Descriptions such as "line interactive," "no break," "load sharing," "bidirectional," and "single conversion" are often applied to these hybrids. Despite their filtering and conditioning capabilities, hybrids are fundamentally off-line UPSes. The server still runs on raw or partially filtered commercial power most of the time, giving only limited protection against potential power-line problems.

Off-line or hybrid UPSes are a poor choice for use in industrial parks, rural regions, some foreign countries, and other areas subject to low voltage or frequency instability. These systems are also unacceptable for use in facilities with on-site generators, such as hospitals, oil rigs, remote field sites, and military bases. The slightest irregularities in power can be catastrophic to sensitive process and test equipment, such as blood analyzers, positioning devices, and controlled chemical process equipment.

On-Line UPS

An on-line UPS acts like a small, solid-state generator. The inverter continuously converts commercial AC power to the DC power necessary to charge its battery. The UPS then takes DC power from the battery and uses it to create new, clean AC power in a steady 120-volt, 60Hz sine wave. The file server runs off this UPS-generated AC power at all times. Thus, an on-line UPS uses the commercial line voltage only to keep its batteries charged, never to supply power directly to the server. Since this type of UPS completely isolates the file server and its peripherals from the commercial power line (and its inherent power fluctuations) and does not rely on switching between commercial and battery power, most experts prefer on-line UPS systems for network use.

On-line UPS systems can range in price from $500 to $5,000, depending on the size of your network. When justifying UPS systems, remember to balance the costs against the value of the hardware, software, and data they protect. In most cases, proper use of power conditioning devices can actually reduce the overall maintenance costs of a network.

Intelligent Power Systems

Another new development in UPS technology is the "intelligent" power system, or IPS. These products are designed to protect the entire network (including workstations and peripherals), not just the file server. They take on-line UPS protection one step farther by providing software that interacts with NetWare itself. This interaction goes beyond a simple connection with status indicators of good power or battery charge. IPS systems use NetWare's built-in UPS monitoring functions to monitor and communicate with sophisticated power supplies, thus providing the LAN with several minutes of battery backup. During this time, the IPS transmits messages to any workstations that are still operational and orchestrates an orderly, automatic, and unattended shutdown of the network.

Implementing Power Protection on Your Network

Before you purchase and install a UPS or other power conditioning devices, double-check the commercial power available for your network. Wherever possible, network components should use dedicated power lines that provide adequate amperage for the number of systems connected. Placing computers and peripherals on the same lines as air conditioning equipment or other heavy machinery is not recommended. The surges and sags produced by such equipment can cause serious damage to network interface boards and other network components. Also make sure the power outlets are all properly grounded. Plugging a power conditioning device into a poorly grounded outlet negates any protection the device might have given your hardware.

Most authorized NetWare resellers and consultants have access to a list of Novell-approved UPS systems. The main concerns in selecting a UPS are deciding what network components (besides the file server) to protect and determining the appropriate UPS power rating for those components.

What Network Components to Protect

It won't do you much good to keep the file server running if the disk drives lose power. Therefore, Novell strongly recommends that every file server and its attached disk subsystems have UPS protection. In fact, this is a basic requirement for sites that purchase Novell's service and support package. Depending on the UPS power rating and how many receptacles it has, you can often attach the file server and its peripherals to the same UPS.

It is also a good idea to provide external routers, gateways, print servers, backup servers (with their storage devices), and communication servers (with their modems) with some kind of UPS protection. For network printers, a surge suppressor or line conditioner is usually sufficient. Many laser printers require more power than the typical UPS can provide. Also, the motors found in all printers generate voltage fluctuations that might cause problems for a UPS.

Depending on the types of applications you run on your network, you may also want to provide UPS protection for workstations. Most traditional network applications run almost entirely at the client PC, holding data in the workstation's RAM until the user issues a save command. Thus users will lose any unsaved data during a power outage, even if the file server stays up. Workstations that lose power also cannot receive UPS warning messages from the file server. For maximum protection, you might use a large UPS for the file server and its peripherals, plus a smaller UPS for each workstation. (UPS units designed to fit underneath a computer's monitor are ideal for workstations.) However, having a UPS for every workstation can be expensive. You may want to limit UPS protection to only those workstations running key applications where data loss would be critical.

UPS Power Rating

Each UPS unit should have a power rating sufficient to support all hardware that will draw power from the unit. Power ratings are normally specified in terms of volts/

amps (VA), as in 150VA or 600VA. The VA rating is obtained by multiplying a product's voltage by its amperage (since volts times amps equals watts).

To determine a sufficient power rating for a UPS, add up the individual VA or wattage requirements for each piece of equipment the UPS must supply power to. Then add about a 10 percent margin of safety to that total. Most manufacturers list the power consumption rating in watts somewhere on the equipment itself or in its accompanying documentation. If you can find only the current (given in amps), multiply that by the standard voltage (120 in North America) to get the number of watts the equipment uses.

Complex configurations require more power than simple ones. For example, a high-end engineering workstation used to run CAD/CAM programs would require a higher power rating than an IBM XT workstation used for word processing. If you aren't sure what power rating you need for a given configuration, consult with the equipment manufacturer's sales engineering staff.

Another consideration is the "inrush capacity" required for the UPS's power source to start up all connected loads at a given time. The initial power draw when computers are turned on is much higher than the normal "steady state" operating power requirement. If additional equipment attached to the UPS is powered on when the demand for UPS power is already high, a temporary overload can occur. Either the additional device will not receive power, or other equipment attached to the UPS will be shut down. Consequently, on-line UPS devices may require an inrush capacity as high as 1000 percent. An on-line UPS with insufficient inrush capacity cannot be used to power equipment up to the rated output capability of the UPS.

Finally, check the maximum duration of the UPS battery power. After a power failure, the UPS's backup power system must be able to maintain power to the server and disk subsystems long enough for the OS to write any data in memory to disk, close all open files, update all tables, and shut the file server down gracefully. You should avoid prolonged operation of the file server on UPS batteries in the absence of commercial power, except where there is a critical need. Extended battery-powered operation shortens the life of the UPS battery. Most UPS systems allow you to set a maximum time before the unit either switches back to commercial power or initiates the shutdown of the server.

NetWare's UPS Monitoring Feature

To enhance the protection offered by a UPS, NetWare v3.*x* includes a UPS monitoring feature as a NetWare loadable module. The UPS.NLM provides an interface between the UPS unit and the NetWare operating system. Through this interface, the file server can monitor the power supply and signal the OS when the power fails. NetWare then sends a broadcast message, indicating that the server is running on backup power, to any workstations that haven't been affected by the power problem. This gives users a chance to save their files quickly and log out. If power is not restored within a specified time, the server automatically logs out any remaining users and shuts itself down, making sure that all files, directories, and the FAT are internally consistent.

UPS-Monitoring Hardware

To take advantage of NetWare's UPS-monitoring NLM, your file server must have a board that contains special circuitry, cables, and a socket for connecting to the UPS unit. This UPS circuitry is included on the following boards available from Novell or its OEMs:

- The Novell Disk Coprocessor Board. Most recent versions of the DCB, the Enhanced DCB, and the combination DCB/floppy disk controller contain UPS monitoring circuitry. Older (pre-1987) versions do not.

- The Novell standalone UPS monitoring board. This is a half-size, eight-bit board whose sole function is to provide UPS-monitoring hardware.

- The Novell SS keycard. Although a serialized keycard is no longer required to run NetWare, some keycards contain the UPS-monitoring circuitry. If you have one of these keycards from a previous purchase of NetWare, you can use it to hook up the UPS.

An easy way to tell if your old keycard or DCB has UPS monitoring circuitry is to look on the metal mounting bracket on the end of the card. If it has a small, RCA-style jack that looks like you could plug a set of stereo headphones into it, that indicates UPS-monitoring capability.

Note that on an IBM PS/2 file server, you connect the UPS through the mouse port; you don't need a separate UPS board.

Setting UPS Jumpers

On the UPS-monitoring boards listed above, you must make some UPS-related jumper settings. These settings determine the board's I/O address, the battery-low input setting, and the battery on-line input setting. Different UPSes use different methods to signal when the battery is on-line and when it is low. The jumpers must be set accordingly on the UPS board in the file server for UPS monitoring to function correctly.

The jumper settings for Novell UPS-monitoring hardware are documented in the supplement shipped with the board. Make a note of the I/O address jumper setting; you'll need it when you load UPS.NLM.

Loading UPS.NLM

To activate UPS monitoring, you must load the UPS loadable module at the server. First make sure you have connected the UPS unit according to the manufacturer's instructions and installed the UPS monitoring hardware as described above. Then follow the steps below to load UPS.NLM.

1. Type **LOAD UPS** at the server console. (If the UPS.NLM file is not located in the SYS:SYSTEM directory, include the path to UPS.NLM in the command.)

2. The screen will display the following available UPS types. Type the number corresponding to the UPS monitoring hardware you have installed in the server.

```
1-DCB Disk coprocessor board (default)
2-EDCB Enhanced disk coprocessor board
3-STANDALONE Novell standalone UPS monitor board
```

```
4-KEYCARD   Novell SS keycard
5-MOUSE PS/2 mouse port
6-OTHER Third-party UPS monitoring
board
```

3. Depending on your UPS-hardware type selection, you will be prompted for an I/O port. This is the I/O port address (in hexadecimal notation) corresponding to the jumper settings or factory-preset settings on the UPS-monitoring hardware. The following chart summarizes the possible I/O addresses:

Novell disk coprocessor board	346, 34E, 326, 32E, 386, 38E
	(depends on the DCB channel number and
	version—check Novell's documentation)
Enhanced DCB	380, 388, 320, 328 (depends on channel)
Novell standalone UPS board	231 or 240 (check the jumpers)
Novell keycard	230 or 238 (check the jumpers)
PS/2 mouse port	no I/O address parameter needed

The screen will display the default value for your selected hardware. You can either accept the default or type in one of the supported I/O port values listed on the screen.

4. The "discharge time" is the estimated number of minutes the UPS battery can keep the file server operating before becoming depleted. The default is 20 minutes; the allowable range is from one to 3,976,821 minutes (over 7 1/2 years!). Obviously, no UPS can provide power for the maximum time; check your UPS documentation for an appropriate number, or go with the default for now. You will probably need to decrease the discharge time as your UPS gets older.

5. The "recharge time" is the estimated number of minutes the UPS battery needs to recharge after being totally discharged. The default is 60 minutes; allowable range is from 1 to 3,976,821minutes. Again, either use the default or check your

749

UPS documentation for an appropriate number. You will probably have to increase the recharge time as your UPS gets older. You can specify these pa rameters in the LOAD command itself by using the following format:

```
LOAD UPS TYPE=xxx PORT=nnn DISCHARGE=n RECHARGE=n
```

For TYPE, use the character string (such as DCB or MOUSE) rather than the corresponding number shown in Step 2 above. If you want UPS monitoring support to be loaded automatically when you boot the server, add this command to the AUTOEXEC.NCF file.

If your UPS hardware is not set up to match the I/O port in the LOAD UPS command, you'll see the following error messages:

```
WARNING:  UPS hardware configuration error was detected.
Check for errors in your UPS hardware configuration settings.
Module initialization failed. Module UPS.NLM NOT loaded.
```

Check the documentation for your UPS-monitoring hardware to see how the I/O address jumpers should be set for the port you are trying to enter. If necessary, down the server, remove the board, and reset the jumpers. Then try the LOAD command again.

Relevant Console Commands

Once you have loaded the UPS.NLM, you can use two UPS-related console commands to check on the status of the UPS and change the initial configuration.

The UPS STATUS Console Command

To check the status of a server's UPS, type "UPS STATUS" at the console. A screen similar to the following is displayed:

```
UPS Status for Server JUNGLE

Power being used:  Commercial
Discharge time requested:  20 min.      Remaining: 20 min.
Battery status: Recharged
Recharge time requested:   60 min.      Remaining: 0 min.
Current network power status:  normal

NOTICE: If your battery is over 6 months old, you may need to
        lower the discharge time. (Consult the UPS documenta
        tion for details.)
```

The "Power being used" line indicates whether the UPS is using commercial power or battery power.

"Discharge time requested" displays the discharge time chosen when UPS.NLM was loaded. This is the approximate amount of time the UPS can deliver battery power to the server. When the server is running on battery power, the "Remaining" time counts down to indicate how much longer the server can safely remain on UPS power.

The "Battery status" line indicates whether the battery is recharged, being charged, or low. If the battery status is low, it can no longer provide power for the full discharge time. You should either repair or replace the battery as soon as possible.

"Recharge time requested" displays the recharge time chosen when UPS.NLM was loaded. This is the amount of time the battery needs to fully recharge itself. When the server is running on battery power, the "Remaining" time counts up from zero to indicate how many minutes the UPS will need after commercial power is restored to bring the battery up to full charge.

The Current network power status line will display one of three possible messages:

- "Normal" means the server is running on commercial power.

- "Server going down in *n* minutes" means the server is running on battery power and will shut itself down in the indicated number of minutes.

- The status changes briefly to "Server down" when the remaining time has elapsed and the server commences its automatic shutdown procedure.

The UPS TIME Console Command

To change the UPS discharge or recharge time after you have loaded the UPS.NLM, type **UPS TIME** at the console. The screen will display the current settings first and allow you to change them. Use the following guidelines when adjusting these parameters.

The UPS discharge time should give users enough time to log out (if they still have power), but not unduly drain the UPS battery. The default discharge time is 20 minutes, but you can make it longer or shorter than that depending on the capacity and age of your UPS. Over time, a UPS battery can lose some of its original capacity, especially after extended periods of battery operation. As this happens, you should decrease the discharge time proportionally.

Note: If the OS receives the "battery low" signal from the UPS before the specified discharge time has elapsed, the OS will shut the server down within one minute after receiving the low-battery signal, regardless of the discharge time remaining.

The recharge time is intended to allow the UPS battery enough time to fully recharge after use. If a second blackout occurs before the recharge time is up, NetWare knows that the UPS hasn't had enough time to recharge its battery. Consequently, the full discharge time is probably not available. The OS can usually compensate by initiating the automatic shutdown sooner.

Troubleshooting the UPS System

Improper configuration and installation of the UPS hardware is one of the most common causes of problems with a network UPS system. Since every UPS is different, you must make sure the jumpers on the UPS monitoring hardware are configured to match your particular UPS. Don't just assume that the default settings will work. Consult both the UPS documentation and the documentation for the DCB (or other UPS monitoring hardware), or enlist the help of the UPS vendor if you have trouble installing a UPS on your NetWare LAN.

As mentioned earlier in this chapter, UPS.NLM will fail to load if the I/O address in the LOAD command does not match that set on the UPS monitoring hardware. Other UPS-related jumpers control how the UPS signals its on-line status, off-line status, or low battery condition. If these are set incorrectly, the UPS.NLM might load, but the monitoring function will not work properly. For example, the server might display bogus UPS battery low errors, or the UPS may indicate the server is on battery power when it is actually on commercial power.

To test the UPS monitoring function, Novell recommends that you perform the following procedure after you initially install a UPS and load UPS.NLM.

1. Have all users log out of the server. Then unload all LAN and disk drivers. (Leaving drivers loaded during the test could cause data corruption or even damage to the network boards and disk controllers if the UPS fails to function correctly.)

2. With the file server and peripherals properly attached to the UPS, unplug the UPS from the commercial power source. This simulates a power blackout.

3. Type **UPS STATUS** at the server console. Within 20 seconds, the screen should indicate that the network is on battery power and start decrementing the discharge time. If the display doesn't change, or if the server loses power altogether, the UPS is not sending the proper signals to the server. Change the jumper settings on the UPS-monitoring hardware in the server to match the signalling method used by the UPS itself.

The UPS-monitoring feature generates a number of different messages besides those displayed with the UPS STATUS command. Some are displayed on the console screen; others are broadcast to attached workstations. The following section briefly explains what the UPS messages mean and what to do when you see them.

UPS Initialization Messages

When you load UPS.NLM, the module performs an initial check of the attached UPS system to see if it is responding according to the configuration specified in the LOAD UPS command. If not, you will see one or more of the following messages.

```
WARNING: Commercial power detected off during UPS installation.
Check commercial power lines or the UPS.
```

If this message appears the first time you try to load UPS.NLM after you initially install the UPS, it indicates that the on-line jumper was set incorrectly on the UPS-monitoring hardware.

```
WARNING: UPS battery is low. Repair or replace battery.
```

During first-time installation, this message indicates the low battery jumper was set incorrectly.

```
WARNING: UPS hardware configuration error was detected.
Check for errors in your UPS hardware configuration settings.
```

This message indicates that both the on-line and the low battery settings are incorrect.

Any one of these errors causes the UPS initialization routine to fail. Double-check the jumper setting on your UPS monitoring hardware. Also make sure the UPS battery is properly connected. If necessary, use a battery tester and replace the battery if it fails the test.

Server Shutdown Messages

During a blackout, the discharge time determines how long a server can run on UPS battery power. When all but one minute of the discharge time has elapsed, the server displays the following message:

```
Battery discharge time has almost expired. The file server will
be shut down in one minuteunless commercial power is restored.
```

Ideally, all users will already have saved their files and logged out of the server by this time. If not, they will be logged out automatically in 60 seconds when the server shuts itself down. Right before this happens, the server displays:

```
UPS is shutting down server ServerName. Commercial power has
failed and the battery is too low.
```

Whenever a UPS-protected file server shuts down during a prolonged power outage, be sure to turn off all power switches to the system unit, the monitor, the disk subsystems, and any other electronic equipment on the same electrical circuit. If you leave your equipment switched on, everything tries to start back up at once when the commercial power is restored. This puts undue strain on the circuit and can cause potentially harmful voltage spikes. The same applies to workstations. Instruct your users to switch everything off if a power outage occurs. Then bring the network back up a few components at a time to lessen the drain on newly restored power.

UPS Messages Sent to Workstations

If any workstations still have an active connection to the file server while the server is on auxiliary power, the OS sends a series of broadcast messages to alert users to the emergency condition. The first message is:

```
Server ServerName on battery power. N min. remaining.
```

No matter how many minutes the message says are remaining, users should save their files as quickly as possible and log out. If they do not, the server issues one last warning:

```
Server ServerName UPS battery exhausted. Logout!
```

If users do not heed this final warning, the server sends the following message just before terminating the user's connection:

```
Server ServerName power failed. Connection terminated.
```

Any files the user had open on the server will be closed, and any data in the workstation's memory not yet saved to disk will be lost.

If by chance the commercial power comes back on before the user has a chance to log out, the server sends this message:

```
Server ServerName commercial power restored.
```

Once commercial power is restored, the UPS battery begins recharging.

Low Battery Messages

The server displays the following message when a discharged UPS battery starts to be recharged:

The UPS battery for server ServerName is recharging. The status is no longer low.

When the recharging process is complete, the server displays another message:

```
The UPS battery recharge for server ServerName is complete.
```

Over time, a UPS battery can lose much of its effectiveness, especially after periods of prolonged use. If an old UPS battery is unable to hold a charge, it sends a low battery signal to the OS, which results in the following message:

```
Server ServerName battery is low. Repair or replace battery.
```

First make sure the UPS unit is functioning properly and the battery is still connected. Check the battery with a battery tester; repair or replace the battery if it fails the test.

CHAPTER 27

Backup and Restore Management

With all of NetWare's built-in data protection features, you might be tempted to think of a backup system as an optional peripheral. This is a dangerous point of view. A backup system is an absolute necessity to the basic operation of the network. Even with reliable disks and a stable power source, you must still back up regularly to protect data against accidental deletions, hardware failure, sabotage, or disasters such as fires and earthquakes. A reliable backup and restore system is your best hedge against these threats to your data.

Whether you choose Novell's backup utilities or a third-party backup product, you need to formulate a plan for using these backup products to their fullest advantage. The conceptual information in this chapter will help you evaluate your present backup system. It also provides some guidelines for implementing an effective backup plan. The last part of this chapter explains how to use the NetWare v3.11 SBACKUP program and gives troubleshooting hints for common backup problems.

Backup Program Features

When evaluating a backup system, you should carefully consider your network requirements and the backup/restore capabilities offered by various products. The system you choose must able to completely and reliably back up and restore all files (including the bindery) on a NetWare disk, along with any rights and extended attributes associated with those files. Ideally, the system should allow you to get the network back up and running quickly, restoring everything exactly as it was before, even after a total server crash.

A wide variety of hardware is available for backing up networks. However, it is the software accompanying the hardware that marks the biggest difference between systems. Use the following criteria to evaluate the suitability of your backup system software.

NetWare File System Compatibility

NetWare has its own file system that is different from the one used by DOS. Thus, you cannot use DOS backup programs and procedures to back up NetWare disks. DOS backup programs (such as the BACKUP command) copy only the files, attributes, and directory structures that DOS recognizes. Since DOS does not recognize NetWare's bindery data, directory rights, trustee assignments, and extended file attributes, they cannot be backed up by DOS backup systems.

With the high capacity of hard disks often used in NetWare v3.x servers, large files in the multi- megabyte range are becoming more and more common. Directory structures can also grow quite large, with a single volume containing hundreds of directories and subdirectories. Some backup systems cannot handle files over a certain size or handle more than a specific number of directories.

Another important consideration for NetWare v3.11 is whether a backup program can handle the various name spaces required by NetWare for Macintosh v3.0, NetWare NFS, NetWare FTAM, and OS/2 workstations storing HPFS files on the server. If you have loaded the Macintosh name space, for example, make sure the backup program can handle both the data fork and the resource fork of Macintosh files.

Backing Up Open Files

On a typical NetWare file server, certain files are held open for long periods of time. Therefore, another important feature to look at is how the backup system handles files that are open when the backup takes place. Some programs require the file server to be down when you do the backup; in that case, all files are guaranteed to be closed, and open files are not an issue.

Programs that offer on-line backup while the server is up feature a variety of methods to deal with open files. Some systems can back up open files as long as they are flagged Shareable; if a file is open and flagged Nonshareable, the program skips over it and lists it in a log file printed after the backup. The system supervisor can then review the log file and try backing up the skipped files later when they are not open.

Other programs will stop and report that a shared file has been encountered, giving the operator the option to abort the backup, retry the file copy, or skip the file. The program maintains a list of skipped files so you can come back to them later. Usually some type of timeout feature is available to allow the system to continue if the backup is running unattended. After so many retries, the system will skip the files and continue its backup.

Backup Rate

The speed at which the backup system can copy data is another factor to consider, especially if you have a large amount of disk storage to back up. For example, backing up 200MB of data at 0.5MB per minute would take over 6 1/2 hours; at 3MB per minute, it would take slightly over one hour. Average backup speeds range from 2 to 4MB per minute, although the speed of the network hardware and the performance of the file server itself can significantly affect the backup speed.

There are other reasons to be concerned with the speed of a backup system. The longer the backup takes, the greater the chances are of a power failure during the backup. The possibility of unauthorized access to the file server is also greater—especially with unattended backup programs that log in to the server with supervisor rights. (If you are using such a backup program, check with the software vendor to see if there is a version that doesn't require the operator to be logged in as SUPERVISOR.)

Error Handling

The transfer of data to and from backup media is not an error-free process. As on a hard disk, certain areas on magnetic tape can become unable to hold data reliably. Errors caused by glitches on the physical media are called "hard errors." Errors caused by dust or micro-debris caught between the drive head and the backup media are called "soft errors" because they are not physical defects, but rather electronic misinterpretations. Backup systems vary widely in how they detect and correct these types of errors in backup and restore operations. The two main schemes are read-after-write verification and redundant copies of data on the media. Although both methods have proven reliable, both have drawbacks as well.

With read-after-write verification, the system compares each block of data written to the backup media with the data on the disk to verify that the backup copy is an exact duplicate of the original. If a discrepancy is found, the data is read again from the disk and written to a different block on the tape. The verification procedure is repeated to ensure the integrity of the backup copy. Most tape backup systems use read-after-write verification to detect errors. The drawback is that, even though data is written to the media without errors, an error can still occur when the system reads back the data during the restore process.

The redundant-copy method copies each block of data in two different locations on the media to protect against both hard errors during backup and soft errors during a restore. If soft errors occur, the system can rebuild the necessary information from the redundant copy of the data. The drawback here is that it takes longer to back up because the system has to make two copies of the data instead of just one, and you can fit only half as much data on a tape or other backup medium.

Some backup drives and controllers support a feature called Error Correction Code (ECC). With this feature activated, the hardware stores extra error correction information during each write. If a particular block is unreadable, the hardware can reconstruct it by using this extra error correction data. Check with your hardware vendor to see if your backup equipment supports ECC. If so, activate this feature for an extra layer of protection against media errors.

Backup Media Support

The type of media a backup system supports is an important consideration, especially when you're looking for new software to run with existing hardware. Here are some of the most common media used for backing up LANs.

Magnetic Tape

Magnetic tape cartridges continue to be the main medium used in most backup systems, since they are widely available at a relatively low cost. Quarter-inch cartridge (QIC) tapes come in a variety of capacities ranging from 40MB to more than 300MB. Newer systems use 8mm tape and 4mm Digital Audio Tape (DAT) cartridges capable of storing up to 2GB (gigabytes) of data.

Normally, magnetic tapes must be formatted before you can use them; buying preformatted tapes therefore saves a considerable amount of time if you need a large number of cartridges. Another important factor to consider is the interchangeability of tape cartridges. We tend to take for granted that media formatted on one machine can be ported to another machine and work just fine (as is usually the case with floppy diskettes and hard disk drives). However, some magnetic tape cartridges can only be used reliably with the tape drive on which they were formatted. Inserting the cartridge into another tape drive, even one from the same manufacturer, can result in read errors. Some manufacturers guarantee that cartridges used for backup on one tape drive can be restored from any other drive in the same hardware series; this capability ensures that, if your regular tape drive fails, you will still be able to restore data by using another tape drive.

Optical Disks

The introduction of optical disk technology several years ago saw almost immediate application in the backup products industry. Back then, the 500 to 800MB storage capacity of a single optical disk was most attractive compared to the lower capacity of QIC tapes. Early optical disks were Write Once/Read Many (WORM) media on which data could be written only once, but then read back many times. Rewritable optical disks are now available that allow you to write over data previously stored on the disk.

Removable Hard Disks

Removable hard disks can be part of the overall backup system. While removable drives, such as the Bernoulli Box from Iomega, offer limited storage capacity, they are useful for backing up critical data that must be restored quickly if lost. You can access data from a removable hard disk drive much more easily than from a tape or optical disk drive (which both write data sequentially and must perform searches sequentially).

"Convenience" Features

It is difficult to draw the line between essential backup features and those that are merely convenient. Depending on the size of your network and other factors, you may consider some of the following features a necessity.

Unattended Backup

Babysitting a backup program that requires a lot of operator intervention is, at best, drudgery. Vendors of most backup systems include in their products the ability to schedule automatic, unattended backup sessions. With this feature, you can set up these sessions to run in the middle of the night when network activity is low. If no one will be there to insert a new tape when one becomes full, make sure the hardware is capable of holding enough information that changing media is not necessary. Another solution is a jukebox system that automatically changes cartridges or optical disks when necessary. The ability to run various backup sessions through commands placed in batch files can also facilitate unattended backup.

Image and File-by-File Backups

Some backup programs make what is called an "image" backup of a disk. These programs bypass the operating system and interact directly with the disk, copying each sector in sequence. Image backups are fast because they can ignore the directory structure. You can also restore entire disks more quickly with an image backup. The drawback is that it's hard to restore a single file or directory. Also, the file server must be shut down before the image backup is performed.

The alternative is called "file-by-file" backup. This type of backup copies files separately and allows you to select exactly which files or directories you want to back up. Depending on the sophistication of the program, you can select anything from all files indiscriminately to only files with a certain extension that have been modified since the last backup. NetWare-specific programs allow you to select the bindery files only or files with a certain NetWare file attribute only. Another convenient selection feature is the ability to select only those files modified after a certain date.

File-by-file backups offer a great deal more flexibility and make it easier to locate and restore single files or directories. This type of backup can be done while the server is up and running. Most file-by- file programs allow you to restore files to a different directory than that from which they were backed up. Avoid those that do not; you'll use this feature more often than you might suspect.

About the only disadvantage to file-by-file backups is that it's easier to inadvertently overlook certain directories and files. Be sure to keep accurate backup logs and audit the system regularly to ensure that you are backing up all necessary data.

Miscellaneous Features

Other convenient backup features include media management functions that help you rotate tape cartridges and keep track of the contents of various backup media. If you have volumes larger than the maximum capacity of a single cartridge, make sure your program can span more than one cartridge in a single backup session. Where storage space is a problem, data compression can help by allowing you to cram even more data onto the backup medium. This becomes more and more important as the amount of disk storage on the file server increases. Always keep future expansion in mind when you evaluate the capacity of a backup system.

Implementing an Effective Backup Plan

No matter which backup system you select, it will do you little good if you don't use it regularly. No excuse is acceptable for missing a scheduled backup session. Problems always seem to attack your network at its most susceptible moment. If you don't have time to do the backups yourself, select a reliable assistant to be responsible for them— but oversee the backup process yourself to make sure it is properly carried out.

As with other aspects of network management, you must plan your backup strategy carefully. Here are some principles and guidelines for establishing an effective backup plan for your file server.

Recommended Backup Schedule

After you install a new backup program, you should do a full system backup. A full system backup includes all volumes, directories, and files on the file server, including the bindery files, hidden and system files, and the NetWare security associated with the directories and files. Continue to perform a full backup at least once a week. Weekly backups make it easier to restore files, because you have only a week's worth of tapes to search through.

In between the full backups, you should perform an "incremental" backup of files that have changed. Incremental backups are recommended on a daily (or, most likely, nightly) basis. Backing up only modified files conserves room on your backup media because you don't continually copy the same unchanged files over and over. Back up the trustee rights and bindery files at least once a day as well.

Depending on the applications your users are running and the sensitivity of the data stored on the server, you may need to back up modified files more often than once a day. The ultimate solution for up-to-the-minute restore capability is an on-line continuous backup system that continually copies file modifications to backup media. These types of systems allow you to restore a file as it was the instant before a problem occurred.

Once a month, go through the files on the server and archive those that are not used regularly and that haven't been changed for a long time. Regular archiving of unused files keeps the server uncluttered and makes disk space available for new files. Transfer archive files to a different type of medium, such as floppy diskettes or optical disks, or to another server. Print out a list of files archived, and store the archive medium in a safe place.

Rotating Backup Media

To reduce the risk of losing data if a tape cartridge or optical disk goes bad or gets misplaced, you should rotate your backup media. Rotation distributes backed-up data across several cartridges or disks so that the same data isn't always written to the same medium. A number of standard methods have been developed for rotating backup media. Several are outlined in the *Network Backup* report available from Novell's Systems Research Group.

To implement a media rotation schedule, you must first calculate the amount of total backup storage capacity you'll need; then buy enough media to handle two or three times that capacity. Divide the media into sets and label each cartridge or disk to identify what backup set each belongs in. Keep a written record of which volumes are backed up on which media. Also record the date of each backup, any errors encountered, and the initials of the operator who initiated the backup session.

Storing Backup Media Off-Site

While it may be convenient, keeping your backup media next to the file server is inadvisable. Should a fire or other disaster destroy the file server, your backup data will be destroyed with it. You can replace lost hardware, but it is nearly impossible to reconstruct lost data without a sound backup copy. For maximum protection of your valuable data against fires, floods, and other disasters, store the data off-site in a safe place such as a bank deposit vault or a fireproof safe.

Backup Security

Data security is a twofold concern with NetWare-compatible backup systems. The program must not only protect against unauthorized access during the backup, but also prevent nefarious users from stealing the backup cartridges and restoring the data they contain to another machine on which they have supervisory rights.

To prevent unauthorized users from accessing the server's data through the backup program, some backup systems require a password when starting up the backup or restore program. Other programs offer the ability to assign a password to each data cartridge to prevent unauthorized access to any of the data on the tape. This password is encrypted so that it cannot be read from the tape. Thus only an authorized operator who knows the password can restore data from the tape.

Another common procedure for enhancing the security of unattended backups is to create a user account named "BACKUP." This account is typically set up so that user BACKUP can log in only from a specific workstation (network and node address), with only one concurrent connection, and only during the times scheduled for regular backup sessions. A batch file is set up to log the user in at a predetermined time. The login script for user BACKUP maps the necessary drives for backing up, calls the backup program, then logs the user out as soon as the backup is finished.

The final layer of protection is to prevent anyone from interrupting the backup session to gain access to the server. Several third-party utilities are available to either disable the Ctrl-Break function or lock the workstation's keyboard with a password. (Consult your Novell reseller or NetWire for more information.)

Structuring Directories to Facilitate Backup

This last guideline does not concern your backup program, but rather how you set up the directory structure on the server. Since static files don't need to be backed up as often as files that constantly change, it's good practice to segregate static files into a volume of their own. For example, application program executable files do not change once you install them on the file server; in fact, you usually flag them Read Only to prevent anyone from altering them in any way. Data files, on the other hand, may change several times every day. If you keep all applications on the SYS volume and put data files on another volume (such as VOL1), you can back up VOL1 daily and back up SYS only monthly.

It's also a good idea to create separate volumes for Macintosh, OS/2, Unix, and FTAM files. Mixing these with DOS files in the same directories can cause problems, not only for backup programs but for day-to-day administration as well.

Backup Programs Available for NetWare v3.x

The main backup program for NetWare v3.11 is a NetWare loadable module called SBACKUP (Server Backup). Once you load the appropriate NLMs, you can run SBACKUP either at the server or from any DOS workstation via the RCONSOLE utility. SBACKUP supports all name spaces available for NetWare v3.11.

Novell shipped a backup utility called NBACKUP (Network Backup) with NetWare v3.0 and v3.1. This is essentially the same program used to back up NetWare v2.2. It is run from a DOS workstation and can handle only DOS and Macintosh files. NBACKUP is included with NetWare v3.11 for compatibility with previous versions only; it cannot back up a v3.11 server with OS/2, NFS, or FTAM name spaces loaded. We'll describe the use of SBACKUP below. Refer to your Novell documentation for instructions on running NBACKUP.

Note: The data formats of NBACKUP and SBACKUP are *not* compatible; If you back up data with NBACKUP, you cannot use SBACKUP to restore it. Always use the same utility for both backing up and restoring.

In addition, Novell has endorsed a number of third-party backup products for use with NetWare v3.x, although many good products have not yet received the official stamp of approval. Authorized NetWare resellers receive regularly updated information from Novell about compatible products. NetWire is another good source for backup product recommendations.

The SBACKUP Program

The remainder of this chapter describes how to set up, use, and troubleshoot problems with Novell's SBACKUP program.

Before we begin, however, you should be aware that Novell added a number of enhancements to SBACKUP after the *NetWare Version 3.11 Server Backup* manual was printed. Most of these additions are documented in a file called README.311 included on your NetWare diskettes. The explanations below reflect the most current software available at the time of this writing. Significant upgrades to Novell's backup programs will likely be included in future update packages. We recommend that you keep in close contact with your NetWare reseller and obtain the NetWare update kit when it becomes available.

SBACKUP Software

As we mentioned, SBACKUP is a NetWare loadable module that runs at the server. Before you can run SBACKUP, you must install a storage device (magnetic tape or optical disk drive) on the server. If you have more than one server on your network, you don't need to install a storage device on each one. A single server running SBACKUP can back up other servers over the network, as well as itself. The server to which the backup storage device is attached is called the "host" server. Other servers that will be backed up by the host server are called "target" servers.

The basic setup of both host and target servers is illustrated in Figure 27-1. Notice that the NLMs loaded in the host server are different from those loaded in the target servers.

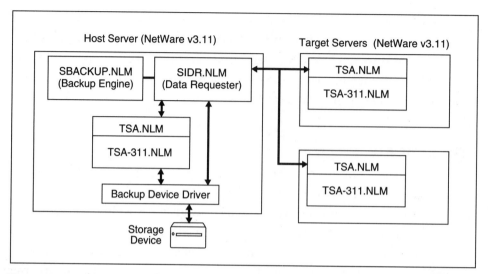

Figure 27-1: With SBACKUP, one server acts as the "host" server to back up itself and other "target" servers.

The Server Backup software is automatically installed on the file server during NetWare v3.11 installation or upgrade. However, if the installer used the "Skip" option (F7 key) to bypass the loading of files from the NetWare *Backup* diskette, you will have to copy the files manually into the SYS:SYSTEM directory.

The purpose and function of the various Server Backup NLMs are described below.

SBACKUP.NLM

This module forms the core, or "engine," of the Server Backup program. It determines what type of session is being initiated, reads and translates requests, and coordinates the activities between the other modules.

SIDR.NLM

This module is Novell's Service Independent Data Requester. It forms a data transfer "channel" through which SBACKUP can access data on other servers. The SIDR.NLM uses the Storage Management Services Protocol (SMSP) to pass data requests between the host server and the target servers.

TSA.NLM

The Target Server Agent (TSA) module sits at the other end of the channel created by the data requester (SIDR). The TSA provides a generic interface, or link, that allows the SIDR to read and write the file structures on any type of target device. A more specific module (such as TSA-311.NLM) must also be loaded on the target server to complete the link.

TSA-311.NLM

This is the specific service agent module for servers running NetWare v3.11. Because TSA-311.NLM understands the exact file structure that exists on NetWare v3.11 servers, it performs the actual data access functions. It must be loaded on a target server (along with TSA.NLM) before any actual read/write operations can take place.

Backup Device Drivers

The host server also needs a device driver loaded for whatever backup hardware has been installed. This driver controls the operation of the storage device attached to a compatible controller board in the host server.

Novell's *Server Backup* manual lists only the WANGTEK.NLM driver for Wangtek tape drives that use QIC-02 controllers. However, these are not the sole devices supported by SBACKUP. Most devices with a driver conforming to Novell's Device Independent Backup Interface II (DIBI-II) specification can be used. Several of these drivers are included with the NetWare v3.11 software. A brief list is given below; refer to the README.311 file or your Novell reseller for more detailed information.

ADAPTEC.NLM   This is a device driver for industry standard tape drives that use Adaptec 1540, 1640, and 1740 SCSI controllers. (Requires TAPEDC00.NLM.)

TAPEDC00.NLM This module provides the DIBI-II interface for the ADAPTEC.NLM device driver.

AHA1540.DSK	These are device drivers for HP Mass Storage
AHA1640.DSK	System tape drives using Adaptec SCSI controllers
AHA1740.DSK	(1540, 1640, and 1740 correspond to the controller type). These files are included on the HP driver diskette that came with the device. (Requires ASPITRAN.DSK and NOVADIBI.NLM.)
ASPITRAN.DSK	This driver provides the interface between the AHA*nnnn*.DSK device driver and the DIBI-II interface module (NOVADIBI.NLM). It is also included on the HP driver diskette.
NOVADIBI.NLM	This module provides the DIBI-II interface for the AHA*nnnn*.DSK device drivers.

Note: The ADAPTEC.NLM driver does not allow shared I/O. If you attach multiple SCSI devices to the same Adaptec controller, do not use ADAPTEC.NLM; use AHA*nnnn*.DSK with NOVADIBI.NLM instead.

For a more complete list of supported tape backup devices, refer to Appendix B.

Other Required Modules

In addition to SBACKUP and its attendant NLMs, the Server Backup program requires that the following modules be loaded on the host server:

- STREAMS.NLM
- TLI.NLM
- CLIB.NLM
- SPXS.NLM
- NUT.NLM

Make sure you have the most current versions that shipped with your NetWare v3.11 software. These files should have been copied into the server's SYS:SYSTEM directory when you installed or upgraded to NetWare v3.11.

Note that for a host server to back up its own data, you must load both TSA.NLM and TSA- 311.NLM in addition to the regular host modules.

Gearing Up for SBACKUP

To run SBACKUP, the host server must have approximately 2 to 3MB of memory above the minimum required for NetWare. You might be able to get SBACKUP to run with less than 2MB if you configure the program with fewer buffers than normal (see "Setting Server Parameters" below). But, as expected, you'll get better performance with more memory available.

Before you can load the Server Backup software and backup device drivers, you must complete the following steps:

1. Install the backup device controller in the host server. Refer to the documenta tion that came with the controller for jumper settings and installation instruc tions. Be sure to use IRQ, I/O port address, and DMA settings that do not conflict with other hardware in the server.

2. Attach the backup device(s) to the controller using the appropriate cabling.

3. Check to make sure the Server Backup software listed above has been copied into the SYS:SYSTEM directory.

4. If you are using .DSK files contained on the HP driver diskette (or on a similar driver diskette from a third-party vendor), copy the necessary files from the driver diskette to one of the following directories:

    *   SYS:SYSTEM if you want to insert the LOAD commands in the AUTOEXEC.NCF file to load the .DSK files.

    *   The boot directory (the one containing SERVER.EXE—can be on a DOS partition or on a floppy boot diskette) if you want to put the LOAD com mands in the STARTUP.NCF file to load the .DSK files.

Editing the DIBI2$DV.DAT File

Information about all supported backup device drivers and parameters is stored in a file called DIBI2$DV.DAT located in the SYS:SYSTEM/DIBI directory. You can edit this file to remove information about drivers you will not need. This is strictly optional, however. If you leave the file intact, you can select the driver you want to link when you load SBACKUP. (You can use only one backup device driver per server.)

Follow the steps below to edit the DIBI2$DV.DAT file:

1. As supervisor, change to the SYS:SYSTEM/DIBI directory and flag the file Nonshareable Read-Write by typing:

    ```
    FLAG DIBI2$DV.DAT N <Enter>
    ```

2. At the server console, load the EDIT module by typing:

    ```
    LOAD EDIT SYS:SYSTEM/DIBI/DIBI2$DV.DAT <Enter>
    ```

3. Delete all lines except those pertaining to the backup drivers you will use on the host server. Then save the file and exit the EDIT module.

4. Flag the file Shareable Read-Only by typing the following in the SYS:SYSTEM/DIBI directory:

    ```
    FLAG DIBI2$DV.DAT SRO <Enter>
    ```

Setting Server Parameters

SBACKUP will run faster if the host server has an adequate number of packet receive buffers. The minimum number the server allocates is determined by the "SET Minimum Packet Receive Buffers=n" command in the STARTUP.NCF file.

- If your host server has 4MB or less of memory, set up to 500 as the• minimum number of packet receive buffers.

- If your host server has 5MB or more memory, set up to 1,000 as the minimum number of packet receive buffers.

If you have used the **SET Maximum Subdirectory Tree Depth=*n*** command to change the maximum depth of the server's directory structure, also include a matching **SET Minimum Directory Cache Buffers=*n*** command. By setting the minimum directory cache buffers equal to or greater than the maximum subdirectory depth, you can speed up directory searches on the server (which, in turn, speeds up the operation of SBACKUP). Both of these SET commands go in the STARTUP.NCF file, so any changes will not take effect until you reboot the server.

After changing these SET parameters in the STARTUP.NCF file, reboot the server for the changes to take effect.

Loading the Backup Device Driver

After you have installed the backup hardware, you must load the driver for the backup device before you load SBACKUP. The procedure is the same as for loading other types of driver modules. Make sure the .NLM and .DSK files are either in SYS:SYSTEM or in another directory specified in a SEARCH command. You can load only one backup device driver at a time.

The command for loading a backup device driver is:

LOAD *DriverName* P=*xxx* <Enter>

For *DriverName*, substitute the appropriate driver file name (such as WANGTEK or ADAPTEC). Replace *xxx* with the I/O port address set on the controller. If you used the default I/O address when you installed the controller, you do not need to specify an address.

The driver automatically loads the other modules and files it needs to run, including the appropriate DIBI-II interface modules (TAPEDC00.NLM or NOVADIBI.NLM).

Note: To load the backup device drivers automatically when the server boots, put the LOAD command either in the STARTUP.NCF file or in the AUTOEXEC.NCF file.

If you are using the ADAPTEC.NLM driver, you can access a Tape Driver Console Screen by typing <Alt><Esc> after the module is loaded. The options available from this screen allow you to initialize the tape drive, erase data from a tape, adjust tape tension, or test for interoperability between the driver, the controller, and the tape device. See the README.311 file and the documentation accompanying your backup hardware for more information.

Loading the TSA and SBACKUP Modules

On each target file server (including the host server if it will back up itself), load the TSA modules by typing the following at the server console:

```
LOAD TSA <Enter>
```

TSA.NLM automatically loads TSA-311.NLM and the other required modules and files.

On the host server, load the Server Backup program using the following command format:

```
LOAD SBACKUP [Buffers=n Size=x]
```

The optional command parameters allow you to increase the speed of the SBACKUP program by adjusting the number and size of SBACKUP's buffers. The program defaults to four buffers 64KB in size, which should be adequate for most situations. Observe the following precautions before overriding the defaults.

- In general, increasing the number of buffers will enhance SBACKUP's performance, since the program will be able to hold more data in memory during transfers to and from the backup device. However, in adjusting the number and size of the buffers, it is possible to exceed the capabilities of your backup controller and device driver. Consult the device driver documentation for recommended settings for SBACKUP.

- You must have adequate free memory in the host server to accommodate the buffers. Multiply the number of buffers by the size to figure the total amount of memory the buffers will need. (For example, the default settings require

256KB of memory: 4 buffers x 64KB = 256KB.) SBACKUP takes the memory from the Alloc Short Term Memory pool. Use MONITOR's "Resource Utilization" option to check the amount of memory in "Alloc Memory Pool" (displayed in the "Server Memory Statistics" window).

NetWare can take memory from the cache buffer pool if it needs more Alloc Short Term Memory. Once allocated, however, this memory is not returned to the cache buffer pool even if the module that was using it is unloaded. (You can get it back for cache buffers only by rebooting the server.) The maximum amount of memory the OS can use for the Alloc Short Term Memory pool is determined by the "SET Maximum Alloc Short Term Memory=n" command. The default maximum of 2,097,152 bytes (2MB) should be plenty for your SBACKUP buffers. Increase this setting (in increments of 1MB) only if, when you run SBACKUP, the server reports that it cannot perform certain operations because it has run out of Alloc Short Term Memory.

Of course, increasing this maximum via the SET command cannot supply more memory than you have physically installed in the server. If you receive "out of memory" messages,either decrease the number of buffers down to two when you start SBACKUP or add more memory to the server.

• If you have an eight- or 16-bit backup controller, the total amount of memory used by the SBACKUP buffers *must not* exceed 16MB. If it does, the data copied to the backup device will be corrupted.

Most backup device drivers that are unable to access memory above 16MB automatically allocate enough buffers in low memory. If you get an "out of memory" message with such a driver, increase the number of reserved low-memory buffers via the "SET Reserved Buffers Below 16 Meg=n" command. The default is 16 buffers, but you can set aside up to 200. This command must be placed in the STARTUP.NCF file, so you will have to reboot theserver before it can take effect.

If you did not edit the DIBI2$DV.DAT file, SBACKUP will list the available drivers. Select the driver you need from this list. SBACKUP automatically links the chosen driver before proceeding.

When prompted, enter a username and password for the host file server. Use SUPERVISOR, unless you have created a separate BACKUP user for doing backups.

The "Main Menu" will appear. Follow the appropriate instructions below to back up or restore data.

Backing Up Data

Once you have arrived at SBACKUP's "Main Menu," the steps involved in backing up data are:

- Selecting the target server to back up o Selecting the working directory for the backup session log files

- Setting the backup options o Running the backup session

By default, SBACKUP performs a full backup of all files on all mounted volumes (including the bindery) on the target server. To do an initial full backup prior to beginning an incremental backup schedule, the only change you need to make from the defaults is to set the "Clear modify bit" option to "Yes." This clears the modified bit (archive attribute) so you can thereafter back up only files that have been created or changed since the full backup.

Selecting the Target Server

With SBACKUP, you can back up data on many target servers to the single tape drive on the host server. Only one session can be active at a time, but you can run numerous sessions without exiting the program.

1. From the "Main Menu," choose "Select Target to Backup/Restore."

2. If you have loaded other data requesters besides SIDR, SBACKUP will list them. Select the one you want to use from the list.

3. SBACKUP lists all available servers with target service agents loaded on them. Select the one you want to back up. (If you have loaded only one TSA, SBACKUP selects that server automatically.)

4. Enter a username and password for the target file server. Again, use SUPERVISOR unless you have created a separate BACKUP user account.

Selecting the Working Directory

The working directory must be on the host server. For each backup session, SBACKUP records two text files in this directory: the backup log and the error log. These files are critical to proper backup and restoration of data. The backup log contains the target server name, the backup session name, the media label, the data, and a record of which files were backed up. The error log records any errors encountered during the backup session.

Whenever possible, it's easier to use the same working directory for all backup sessions.

1. Select "Backup Menu" from SBACKUP's "Main Menu."

2. Choose "Select Working Directory." If you know the full path of the working directory, type it in and press <Enter>. Otherwise, press <Ins> to build the path one directory level at a time.

If the directory you enter does not exist, you will be asked if you want to create the path. Press <Enter> to proceed and create the new directory; press <Esc> to start over and select a different path.

Setting the Backup Options

To set the backup options, select "Backup Selected Target" from the "Backup Menu." The following "Backup Options" window appears:

```
┌──────────────────────────────────────────────────────────────┐
│                       Backup Options                         │
├──────────────────────────────────────────────────────────────┤
│                                                              │
│  What to back up:                                            │
│      File Server                                             │
│  Session Description:                                        │
│                                                              │
│  Exclude Options: See List                                   │
│  Include/Exclude Options: See List                           │
│  Clear modify bit: No                                        │
│  Append This Session: Yes                                    │
│                                                              │
└──────────────────────────────────────────────────────────────┘
```

What to back up. This field defines the largest scope of the backup session: file server, volume, directory, or bindery. To change the contents of the field, highlight it and press <Enter>. Then press <Ins> to bring up a list of other choices.

- The default setting is "File Server," which means all directories on all mounted volumes,even if you exclude specific directories under the "Include/Exclude Options" described below.

- If you select a volume, all subdirectories and files in the volume will be backed up unless you explicitly include or exclude some under the "Include/Exclude Options."

- If you specify a directory, all files in that directory will be backed up unless you explicitly include or exclude certain files under the "Include/Exclude Options."

- If you specify the bindery, the bindery files will be backed up even if they are excluded as an option.

Session Description. In this field, type a description of what you are backing up: for example, "Full COUNTER 6/30/91." The description can be up to 20 characters long and must uniquely identify the backup session. This description is recorded in the backup and error log files. It will therefore be used to identify the backup session when you need to restore data. Be descriptive enough so that you can easily tell one backup session from another.

Exclude Options. These options define what properties to exclude from the selected backup. Highlight "See List" and press <Enter> to bring up the "Exclude Options" list. This list contains two main categories of items to exclude: types of files/directories and trustee information. The default for all of these options is "No." By changing the appropriate options to "Yes," you can exclude, for example, all hidden files and directories, or files that have not been modified since the last backup.

If you don't exclude user trustee information during the backup, when you restore from this session SBACKUP will restore the trustee assignments exactly as they are now. If you have certain data areas in which trustee assignments change frequently, you may want to set SBACKUP to back up just the data without the trustee information. (Note that you can explicitly exclude *directory* trustee rights in a restore session, but not *user* trustee rights.)

Include/Exclude Options. Pressing <Enter> on this field brings up Include/Exclude lists in which you can specify certain directories and files to be included or excluded during the backup. Including and excluding is a way of narrowing down the overall scope specified in the "What to back up" option above. These options can be confusing; fortunately, you won't need to use them very often. The guidelines below might help clarify the function of these options.

- Including directories (either by name or by pattern) tells SBACKUP that, out of all the directories covered in the scope of the backup session, these are the *only* directories you want backed up. Likewise, including certain files means these are the only files you want to back up in *all* directories covered in the scope of the backup.

- Excluding works the same way, only in reverse. When you exclude s o m e - thing, SBACKUP copies everything *but* the items you have excluded. Thus, excluding a directory tells SBACKUP to back up all directories covered in the scope of the backup session *except* that one. Excluding files causes SBACKUP to skip over all files matching the specified name or pattern.

- By definition, including or excluding an item has the opposite effect on all items not specified in the list. For example, if you exclude SYS:PUBLIC during a volume backup, all other directories und er SYS are assumed to be included. If you include the file pattern "*.DOC" during a directory backup, any files in that directory with extensions other than ".DOC" will be excluded.

- Specifying a directory includes or excludes the contents of that directory *and* all subdirectories. Specifying a file includes or excludes *all* files matching the name or pattern. You can use wildcard characters (* and ?) to specify patterns. For example, to exclude all files with a .BAK extension, insert the pattern "*.BAK" in the "Files to exclude" entry. Remember, files with any other extension are assumed to be included.

  Suppose you have numerous README.TXT files in various directories. Inserting "README.TXT" in the "Files to exclude" entry will prevent all of the README.TXT files from being backed up. To designate a specific file (for example, the README.TXT file in SYS:APPS/DB), use the "Path/ file to exclude" entry.

- Exclude patterns override include patterns if they conflict. For example, if you include all files with the .TXT extension and exclude files starting with "C" (by specifying the "C*" exclude pattern), files such as CHAP1.TXT and CONFIG.TXT will be excluded.

- The "File Server Level (Exclude)" option appears only if you selected "File Server" in the "What to back up" field. This option allows you to exclude certain volumes or the bindery when doing a full server backup.

Clear modify bit. By default, the NetWare "Modified since last archived" attribute is *not* cleared during the backup session. (This attribute is the same as the DOS archive bit.) Change this option to "Yes" to do incremental backups of only those files that change between each backup session.

Append This Session. This option appears only if your backup device supports more than one session per tape. The tape drive and controller must be able to seek to the end of any existing data on the tape. The default of "Yes" allows the current backup session to start where the last one left off on the tape. If you select "No," the tape will rewind to the beginning and the current session will overwrite previous data.

Once you have specified the options you want, press <Esc> twice to save your selections and proceed with the program.

Running the Backup Session

After you set the backup options, SBACKUP displays a "Proceed with Backup?" prompt. Answer "Yes" to proceed to the "Start Backup Menu."

At this point, you need to have your backup media labeled and ready to go. On each tape cartridge, write a label such as "Backup Tape #1, 6/30/91." SBACKUP will prompt you to enter this label ID so the program can use it to identify the cartridge for a restore session.

- To start the backup session now, choose that option. Type in the media label as prompted and press <Enter>. Then insert the cartridge into the backup device and press <Enter> again to start the backup.

You can monitor the progress of the backup session by watching the information displayed in the status window. Among other things, SBACKUP displays the name of the session, the names of directories and files being backed up, and messages pertaining to the backup session. If you need to abort the session, press <Esc> any time during the backup. When the backup session is completed, press <Enter> to return to the "Backup Menu."

• To start the backup later, choose that option and specify the desired date and time at the "Start Backup Timer" prompt. Then press <Esc>. Type in the media label and press <Enter>, then insert the cartridge into the backup device and press <Enter> again. The backup session will begin at the specified date and time. You cannot set up another backup session (either immediate or deferred) until the currently specified session has run.

When a deferred backup session is completed, SBACKUP automatically exits to the "Main Menu" and logs out from the target server.

Viewing the Backup and Error Logs

To view the backup or error log for a session, choose either "View Backup Log" or "View Error Log" from the "Backup Menu." When you select the desired session, SBACKUP displays the contents of that session's log file.

It is a good idea to print both the backup and error log files for each session, so you will have a record of which files were backed up and what errors occurred. These are ASCII text files located in the working directory you specified on the host server. Backup logs are named BACK$LOG.XXX, while error logs are named BACK$ERR.*XXX*, with the *XXX* being 000, 001, 002, and so on in sequential order.

To print the log files for your first SBACKUP session (extension .000), you could use an NPRINT command similar to the following (assuming the working directory is SYS:BACKUPS):

```
NPRINT SYS:BACKUPS\*.000 Q=QueueName <Enter>
```

To exit SBACKUP, press <Esc> until you see the exit prompt, then highlight "Yes" and press <Enter>.

Restoring Data

Restoring data with SBACKUP consists of the following main steps:

- Selecting the target server to which you want to restore data

- Se lecting the working directory containing the backup log files

- Setting the restore options

- Running the restore session

Selecting the Target Server for a Restore

With SBACKUP, you can restore data only to the same type of server it was backed up from. In other words, data backed up from a NetWare v3.11 server cannot be restored to a NetWare v2.2 server. You can restore directories or even volumes to a different location from the original, provided the new destination is also on a NetWare v3.11 server.

1. From the "Main Menu," choose "Select Target to Backup/Restore."

2. If you have loaded other data requesters besides SIDR, SBACKUP will list them. Select the one you want to use from the list.

3. SBACKUP lists all available servers with target service agents loaded on them. Select the one you want to restore to. (If you have loaded only one TSA, SBACKUP selects that server automatically.)

4. Enter a username and password for the target file server. Again, use SUPERVI SOR unless you have created a separate BACKUP user account.

Selecting the Working Directory for a Restore

The working directory is the directory on the host server where the backup log files are stored. You can restore data without the backup session files, but it will take longer because SBACKUP will have to search through the backup tapes to find the session to restore. You do not need to specify the working directory if you aren't going to use the session files.

1. Select "Restore Menu" from SBACKUP's "Main Menu."

2. Choose "Select Working Directory." If you know the full path of the working directory, type it in and press <Enter>. Otherwise, press <Ins> to build the path one directory level at a time.

Setting the Restore Options

To set the restore options, select either "Restore Session" or "Restore Without Session Files," depending on whether or not you want to use the backup session files in the working directory. The following "Restore Options" window appears:

```
┌─────────────────────────────────────────────────────────────┐
│                      Restore Options                          │
├─────────────────────────────────────────────────────────────┤
│                                                               │
│  Overwrite Existing Parent: Yes                               │
│                                                               │
│  Overwrite Existing Child: Yes                                │
│                                                               │
│  Include/Exclude Options: See List                            │
│                                                               │
│  Destination Paths: None                                      │
│                                                               │
└─────────────────────────────────────────────────────────────┘
```

Overwrite Existing Parent. To SBACKUP, a "parent" is a directory. During the restore process, SBACKUP automatically creates any directory that does not already exist. By default, SBACKUP overwrites an existing directory if you restore a directory with the same name to the same location in the directory structure. The restoration includes all directory attributes and trustees as they existed at the time of the backup, unless you exclude them under the "Include/Exclude Options" below.

Change this setting to "No" if you want SBACKUP to leave existing directories as they are and restore only directories that have been deleted or that did not exist before.

Overwrite Existing Child. A "child" is a file. SBACKUP automatically creates all files that do not already exist during the restore process. Along with the data, SBACKUP restores all trustee assignments and attributes as they were when the files were backed up (unless you excluded the trustee information during the backup).

If existing files have the same name as the files being restored, the default setting of "Yes" tells SBACKUP to overwrite the existing files. Change the setting to "No" if you want to leave existing files as they are and restore only files that have been deleted or that did not exist before.

Include/Exclude Options. As with the backup options, you can explicitly designate certain directories and files to be included or excluded during a restore. Highlight this field and press <Enter> to see the list of options. These options function the same as the backup options described above.

If you use the "Destination Path" option to restore directories or files to a different location, you must specify the new path in the "include/exclude" options if you want to include or exclude portions of the restore.

Destination Paths. Use this option to restore data to a different volume or directory than it was backed up from. Highlight the field and press <Enter>.

- In the "Source Path" window, type the original path of the data as it was copied to the backup media. Use the backup log if necessary to get the path right. If you mistype the path or enter an invalid path, you may not get an error message, but the restore definitely will not work.

- In the "Destination Path" window, type the path name where you want the data restored to. If you type a path that does not exist, SBACKUP creates it automatically.

After the restore session is completed, go back into the "Restore Options" window and delete the source and destination paths. Otherwise, the next restore session will try to use the same paths.

Once you have set the restore options you want, press <Esc> to save your selections and exit the form.

Running the Restore Session

SBACKUP now asks you if you want to "Proceed with restore?" Answer "Yes," then answer "Yes" again to the "Start Restore" prompt. Insert the appropriate media as requested.

After mounting the media, SBACKUP proceeds with the restore session. You can monitor the progress of the program in the status window. Any errors that occur are displayed at the bottom of the screen.

When the restore session is completed, SBACKUP takes you back to the "Restore Menu" so you can view the error log if necessary.

To exit SBACKUP, press <Esc> until you see the exit prompt, then highlight "Yes" and press <Enter>.

Unloading the SBACKUP Modules

If your server has limited memory, it's a good idea to unload the SBACKUP modules when they are not needed. This frees up a considerable amount of memory for use by other server processes. To unload the SBACKUP modules, type the following command at the console:

```
UNLOAD SBACKUP <Enter>
```

This command also unloads the DIBI interface module (TAPEDC00.NLM or NOVADIBI.NLM) automatically.

If you want to unload the backup device driver (such as ADAPTEC.NLM or AHAnnnn.DSK), be sure to unload SBACKUP first. Otherwise, you will abend the file server.

Troubleshooting Backup and Restore Problems

Since successful backups are such a crucial aspect of data protection, you must be able to recognize and deal with problems that can occur during the backup procedure. Below are some hints that will help you troubleshoot some of the most common problems encountered while backing up and restoring network data.

Problem: What should you do about the errors listed in the error log files?

Solutions:

First of all, always print out hard copies of all log files after each backup or restore session. These files tell you not only what went wrong, but also what went right. Especially when you use the include and exclude options, you'll want to make sure the end result is what you intended. Backup logs also become an important reference when it comes time to restore. When a user requests that you restore a certain file as it existed on a certain date, you can go to the backup logs to find the precise session in which that version of the file was backed up.

After a backup session, scrutinize the section of the error log file under "The following data sets were not backed up!" Two main factors can prevent SBACKUP from backing up a file: the file is in use, or the file is flagged Execute-Only.

- *Files in use.* Since SBACKUP cannot back up files that are open, you should plan the backup sessions to occur during periods of low usage when most, if not all, users are logged out. Some system files, such as NLMs and queue files, are always open when the server is up. You normally do not need to worry about these, since you can either restore them from your original NetWare diskettes or re-create them using the NetWare utilities if they are lost. da ta files are open during a backup, you should try again to back these up as soon as possible after the backup session.

- *Execute-Only files.* You normally flag an executable file (one with a .COM or an .EXE extension) Execute-Only to prevent it from being altered or copied in any way, as an extra level of security. This attribute keeps a file from being backed up as well. Therefore, you should not flag files Execute-Only unless you have both the original and a backup copy on floppy diskettes. The only way to remove the Execute-Only flag is to delete the file and reinstall the application.

Other backup errors you are likely to see involve clearing the modified bit. If you set the "Clear modify bit" option to "Yes" but SBACKUP is somehow unable to clear the bit, the error log will say something like "The file *FileName* was not marked after backup." If you are doing incremental backups and you do not want this file backed up next time, try using the FLAG command or FILER to remove the "Modified since last backup" attribute from the file.

If you get messages saying you do not have sufficient rights to back up a directory, make sure you are logged in as SUPERVISOR or as a BACKUP user with the necessary rights to the data areas being backed up. You need at least Read, File Scan, and Modify rights to back up data.

Here are some of the most common restore errors you will encounter.

- *Incompatible NetWare versions.* You cannot use SBACKUP to restore files backed up from a v2.x, v3.0, or v3.1 server (with NBACKUP) to a v3.11 server. Novell intends to provide TSAs similar to TSA-311.NLM for these other types of servers. Until then, stick to backing up and restoring v3.11 serv ers only.

- *Directory or file already exists.* If you set the "Overwrite Existing Parent" and "Overwrite Existing Child" options to "No," SBACKUP will not restore directories or files on top of identically named ones that already exist in the destination path. SBACKUP currently does not support renaming files and directories during the restore process. If you need to restore a previous version of a directory or file that still exists, use the "Destination Paths" option to restore them to a different location.

- *Different trustee information.* When you back up directories without excluding trustee information, the trustees can change between the backup and
  the restore. The error logs report any trustee information not restored. For
  example, the message "Trustee CJONES was not restored for SYS:APPS/
  WP because trustee IDs are different!" means that user account CJONES has
  been deleted from the server and then re-created.

- *Insufficient rights.* You need at least Write, Create, Erase, File Scan, and
  Modify rights to create a directory and restore files to it. Make sure you are
  logged in as SUPERVISOR or as a BACKUP user with sufficient rights to
  do the restore.

Problem: How do you enter long names for directories and files created by
Macintosh, OS/2, or Unix users?

Solution:

Even though SBACKUP can back up and restore all NetWare v3.11 name
spaces, the program's interface recognizes directories and files by their
DOS-compatible names only. Whenever Macintosh, OS/2, NFS, or FTAM
users create a directory or save a file with a long name, NetWare automatically assigns an "eight-character plus extension" DOS equivalent name
as well.

If you have loaded multiple name spaces on a server, be careful when you
use the exclude options: you might be excluding name-space files inadvertently. The backup and error log files display the DOS-equivalent name and
the creator name space, but not the full long name of such files.

Problem: SBACKUP didn't back up all defined volumes on my server, even though I specified a full file server backup.

Solutions:

SBACKUP cannot back up or restore to a volume that is not mounted. Make sure all defined volumes are mounted before you start the backup or restore session. *Never* dismount or mount volumes while a session is in progress.

Also check the "include/exclude" options to see if you have excluded certain volumes or included only some of the volumes. Remember, if you specifically include only volume SYS, SBACKUP automatically excludes all other volumes.

Problem: The host server runs out of memory when running SBACKUP.

Solution:

SBACKUP typically requires between 2 and 3MB of memory above the minimum amount required for NetWare. If you have limited memory in the host server, reduce the number of backup buffers to two by including the "Buffers=2" parameter in the LOAD SBACKUP command. If you still get "out of memory" errors, read the other suggestions under "Loading the TSA and SBACKUP Modules."

Problem: The target server runs out of disk space when backing up or restoring files with SBACKUP.

Solutions:

During a backup session, SBACKUP creates several of temporary files named TSA$TMP.* in the SYS:SYSTEM directory of the target server. These files, which SBACKUP uses to store working information, can become quite large, especially if you have loaded non-DOS name spaces on the target server. If you do not have enough room in SYS for these temporary files,either delete unneeded files or add more disk space to the SYS volume.

Before starting a restore session, make sure you have enough free disk space in the destination to accommodate the directories and files you are restoring. If you are overwriting existing files, SBACKUP has to delete the old ones. By default, NetWare keeps deleted files on the server, which could cause SBACKUP to run out of disk space during the restore. Generally, you should have at least 20 percent more free disk space than the amount you need to restore. If free disk space is limited, use the "Set Immediate Purge of Deleted Files=On" command so NetWare will purge the files immediately upon deleting during the restore procedure. After the restore, change the setting back to "Set Immediate Purge of Deleted Files=Off."

Problem: If my host server's SYS volume is damaged, how can I restore the volume with SBACKUP?

Solution:

The main concern here is that the files needed to run SBACKUP (and usually the backup log files as well) are stored on the SYS volume of the host server. Your first line of attack is to run VREPAIR on the SYS volume. This utility can fix minor problems such as mismatched directory table and FAT entries.

In the event of a more serious SYS volume failure, you may have to reformat or replace the disk. Here is a procedure for running SBACKUP from the server's DOS boot partition to restore the SYS volume. (These instructions assume the disk is an internal hard drive capable of containing a bootable DOS partition.)

1. After reformatting or replacing the disk, boot the server under DOS. Use the DOS FDISK and FORMAT commands to create and format an active

DOS partition, just as you would during initial installation. If you booted the server from a floppy before, insert that diskette in drive A:. Other wise, copy SERVER.EXE and your LAN and disk drivers from the original NetWare diskettes to the boot partition.

2. Reboot the server and run SERVER.EXE. Load the LAN and disk drivers as usual, and configure IPX as before.

3. Load INSTALL.NLM from the *System*-1 diskette. Recreate the SYS volume as it was before, then mount the volume.

4. Load the STREAMS, CLIB, TLI, and SPXS modules, in that order.

5. From a DOS workstation, log in as SUPERVISOR and copy the following files from the NetWare Backup diskette into the indicated subdirectories of the newly created SYS:SYSTEM directory (you'll have to create the subdirectories first):

```
DR\SIDR.NLM
DIBI\WANGTEK.NLM (or other backup device driver)
DIBI\DIBI2$DV.DAT
TSA\TSA-311.NLM
```

6. Back at the server, load the backup device driver. Then load TSA and SBACKUP from the NetWare *Backup* diskette. Proceed with a full restore of the SYS volume, specifying "Restore Without Session Files."

CHAPTER 28

Remote Management

Managing a network is one of the most challenging jobs in the computer industry. Much of the challenge stems from the relative newness of microcomputer networking technology, a field that most people are still learning about and getting used to. To manage a network effectively, you need a clearly defined style of network management, a sound knowledge of your network's hardware and software components, and the ability to use network tools to troubleshoot potential problems.

This chapter gives suggestions for managing a NetWare v3.11 network, emphasizing the remote management capabilities that let you control all of your servers from a single management workstation. It also introduces some of Novell's network management tools, including NetWare v3.11's ability to work with IBM's NetView and SNMP-based network management products.

Styles of Network Management

There are two primary styles, or methods, for managing a network: centralized and distributed. In organizations that employ centralized network management, only the network administrators are allowed to control the network. By contrast, distributed network management allows the network administrator to designate workgroup leaders who have the responsibility for maintaining certain users or workgroups and certain network administration tasks. Both alternatives have advantages and disadvantages. Your own decision will depend on the size of your network and your particular network situation. The next two sections discuss both types of network management in more detail.

Centralized Network Management

Centralized network management gives the network administrator (or network administrators) complete responsibility for every aspect of the LAN. These responsibilities include adding and deleting users, modifying rights, and creating user groups. The central administrator(s) are also responsible for management tasks such as performing backups, maintaining files and directories, maintaining print services, and managing disk space, as well as providing user education and support. The central network administrator also troubleshoots any problems that arise on the LAN, such as difficulties with printing.

The primary advantage to this type of management is that it ensures that the central network administrator is aware of any problems that may be occurring and is therefore able to take corrective action. The network administrator controls every change that takes place in the network. The centralized approach also helps to eliminate potential security holes in the system resulting from a number of users having access to proprietary information.

The disadvantage of centralized network management is that the users are less aware of the network's operation and less knowledgeable about the tools they can use to solve their networking problems. If the network administrator is offsite and the network is having problems, there may be no one available to correct those problems. The centralized approach usually creates more of a workload for the central administrator, and therefore forces the network administrator to spend time on tasks that other people could accomplish with a little training.

Distributed Network Management

In a distributed network management scheme, the network administrator allows certain users to take responsibility for certain network administration tasks for their individual workgroups. These tasks could include adding and deleting users, modifying rights for certain users, and any other tasks that the network administrator chooses to delegate or distribute on a workgroup basis. (We discussed setting up user account managers and workgroup managers in Chapter 15.)

One major advantage to this type of network management is that it makes users more aware of the network and the problems that may be occurring. Network administrators tend to communicate the solutions to network problems more clearly when the management process is distributed. The distributed management scheme allows the network administrator to go offsite with less worry that the network will have problems that no one is prepared to respond to. Furthermore, this option distributes some of the more routine management tasks to others, allowing the network administrator to concentrate on the most important network issues at hand: fine-tuning and optimizing the network's performance and planning for future network growth.

One disadvantage of this alternative is that some of the distributed workgroup managers may lack the knowledge to help the users. Furthermore, the primary network administrator may not be entirely aware of the problems that exist on the network. And most importantly, a workgroup manager may risk the network's security by accidentally assigning more rights to an application or an area on the network than the users should have.

As the network administrator, you must determine which method of network management will best meet the particular needs of your LAN. If your system includes highly confidential information, you may want to choose a centralized scheme to strictly control who has access to what. If you have a large, broadly distributed network, setting up several workgroup administrators may be the better alternative.

Knowing Your Network

Few things are more frustrating than having a problem with a network component or a program that you know nothing about. Given the sheer number of products typically used on a single network, it's difficult for the network administrator to learn about everything all at once. Sometimes insufficient knowledge about products results from too little investment in time (who has time to learn about the network when there's immediate work to be done?) or too little money to invest in appropriate training.

We strongly encourage you to take the time, and invest in the training, if necessary, to gain a working knowledge of the network and the products on it. To make this process easier, you may want to delegate the responsibility for specific applications to the application gurus on your LAN or to specific workgroup managers.

As the network administrator, you should study the network, become familiar with the process of troubleshooting, and learn to continually fine-tune the performance of your LAN. Consider putting together a file of ideas and quick-and-easy fixes for the network problems most likely to occur. Store the file with your installation worksheets and make it a resource for anyone who participates in the management of your LAN.

Tools for Managing Your Network

You should become familiar with as many of the available network management tools as possible, especially those that are NetWare-specific. There are many products, both from Novell and from third-party developers, that can help you manage your network.

Management Products Available from Novell

The NetWare operating system comes with a wide-ranging selection of management utilities. We've talked about many of these, such as SYSCON, FILER, and PCONSOLE, already in this book. Two others we'll talk about in this chapter are FCONSOLE and the Remote Management Facility (RMF).

In addition to these tools, which come with the basic operating system, Novell offers numerous other tools as separate products. Here is a list and brief description of some of the NetWare management tools available from Novell.

- The NetWare Name Service (NNS) allows you to group file servers into administrative "domains" so that you can perform management activities on many servers at once. By allowing network resources to be named by domain, rather than on a server-by-server basis, NNS simplifies access to a multi-server network. The basics of installing and using NNS are described in Appendix C.

- The LANalyzer network analyzer is a useful monitoring and diagnostic tool for network managers, technical support engineers, and software developers. With the LANalyzer, you can examine activity on your network at the packet level. This capability is vital for debugging problems with protocols and application programs, troubleshooting physical-layer faults, and fine-tuning network performance.

- The LANtern network monitor gathers information from various devices on the network, noting aberrant traffic patterns and generating alerts when common problems are encountered. The LANtern monitors send data to Novell's Windows-based LANtern Services Manager, allowing you to display a graphical map of network resources and collect statistics for trend analysis.

- The Communication Services Manager is a product family that lets you connect with host- based management systems. The first communication service available is NetWare for SAA, an NLM that provides a connection to IBM SNA host systems. With this in place, the host system can receive real-time notification of faults relating to the communication services and log them for later historical analysis.

Management Products from Other Sources

A representative list of third-party NetWare management utilities and where to obtain them is given in Appendix D.

NetWare's Support for Enterprise Management Systems

An "enterprise" management system is one that is designed to manage all devices on a large heterogeneous network, regardless of vendor. In such a system, the participating devices (servers, workstations, routers, cabling hubs, and so on) contain some type of management "agent" that handles communication with a central "manager" component. Two of the most widely-used enterprise systems are the Simple Network Management Protocol (SNMP) developed for the TCP/IP community, and IBM's SNA-based NetView. NetWare v3.11 provides rudimentary support for both of these systems, thus enabling NetWare v3.11 servers to be "managed" from an SNMP or NetView management console.

The TCP/IP protocol stack built into the NetWare v3.11 OS is designed to support SNMP's Management Information Base (MIB) specification. Thus, an SNMP management console operator can request data and gather alerts from the TCP/IP stack in a NetWare v3.11 server. Novell provides a management utility called TCPCON to set up this communication between the SNMP manager and the SNMP agent in the server. The SNMP management agent, TCPCON, and related software are contained on the *SYSTEM-3* diskette that came with your NetWare v3.11 OS software. The LANtern network monitor product mentioned earlier is based on NetWare's SNMP support. The same SNMP agent can also be used with third-party SNMP managers, such as those from Sun Microsystems, Hewlett-Packard, and DEC.

IBM's NetView was originally designed to manage large SNA networks, and it is heavily slanted toward the mainframe/terminal architecture. Up until recently, managing a LAN from NetView required a rather awkward solution involving gateways and an IBM program called NetView/PC. With NetWare v3.11, Novell has included a direct entry point into NetView that eliminates the need for an external gateway and NetView/PC. Through Novell's NetView interface, a NetView host console operator can request status information and receive alerts from NetWare v3.11 servers. This NetView management agent interface, implemented via NetWare Loadable Modules, is contained on the two NetView diskettes included with the NetWare v3.11 OS software.

Setting up this management agent software on your NetWare v3.11 servers is a task that requires considerable training and expertise. If you're new to the world of enterprise management systems, we suggest you work closely with an experienced IS manager or enroll in an appropriate training program.

The FCONSOLE Utility

Those whose experience with NetWare dates back to NetWare v2.1*x* will point to FCONSOLE as one of Novell's most useful management utilities. However, with NetWare v3.*x* most of FCONSOLE's statistics reporting and management functions were moved to the MONITOR console utility. As a result, FCONSOLE is rarely used in managing a NetWare v3.*x* network. It is still a key player in managing NetWare v2.*x* networks, however.

The version of FCONSOLE shipped with NetWare v3.11 can detect what type of file server you are working with (NetWare v3.*x* or NetWare v2.*x*) and adjusts the

"Available Options" menu accordingly. For a NetWare v3.*x* server, FCONSOLE displays fewer options due to the transfer of functionality to other utilities. The remaining options allow you to send console messages, view basic information about the current server connections, down the server, change the server date and time, disable and reenable logins, disable and reenable TTS, and view the NetWare OS version information. (See your NetWare *Utilities Reference* manual for more information about running FCONSOLE.)

NetWare's Remote Management Facility

One of the most useful management tools included with NetWare v3.11 is the RMF. Starting with NetWare v3.1, Novell offered the RCONSOLE (Remote Console) utility as an optional product. A full-fledged RMF is bundled with v3.11 and includes the new ACONSOLE (Asynchronous Remote Console) utility as well as RCONSOLE.

RMF allows you to manage all of your NetWare v3.1*x* servers from one location. After setting up a workstation as the "virtual console," you can access and control all file servers that have the appropriate RMF software loaded. Specifically, RMF lets you perform the following functions:

- Execute console commands as if you were at the file server console

- Scan directories and edit text files in both DOS and NetWare partitions on the remote server

- Transfer files to (but not from) the remote server

- Install NetWare v3.1*x* on a remote server

- Upgrade a remote NetWare v3.0 server to v3.1*x*

- Reboot the file server from the remote console

Remote Management Software

NetWare's RMF consists of five main software components. REMOTE, RSPX, and RS232 are NLMs that load at the server. RCONSOLE and ACONSOLE are executable files (.EXEs) that run on a DOS workstation or standalone machine. We'll explain the purpose and function of these pieces below, in the context of the three possible RMF configurations.

Another utility included with RMF is RSETUP.EXE. RSETUP creates a file server boot disk to use when remotely installing or upgrading a NetWare v3.x server. The resulting diskette contains SERVER.EXE, disk drivers, LAN drivers, .NCF files, and the NLMs necessary to get the server up to the point where you can establish a remote connection with it. (Refer to Novell's *System Administration* manual for instructions on running RSETUP.)

Direct Connection Configuration

One way to establish a remote management session is through a direct LAN connection. This configuration is most commonly used to manage file servers on an internetwork where the servers are all connected by cabling systems. You can also successfully manage servers on a wide area network connected via a high-speed T-1 link. In either case, the IPX/SPX protocol is required.

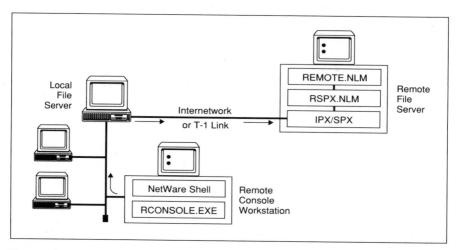

Figure 28-1: In the direct connection configuration, a workstation uses RCONSOLE to control a remote server.

In the direct configuration, the RMF software components perform the following functions:

- REMOTE.NLM, loaded at the server, handles the remote access to the server's keyboard, screen, and file system. It coordinates the flow of keyboard and monitor information to and from the RSPX.NLM driver.

- RSPX.NLM, also loaded at the server, is a communications driver that provides SPX\ support for REMOTE.NLM. It provides the data transport mechanism between the server\ and the management console client. It also uses NetWare's Service Advertising Protocol\ (SAP) to advertise that the server is available for remote access.

- RCONSOLE.EXE runs at a DOS workstation. It is a communications program that interacts with the RSPX.NLM module to provide the remote console capabilities of RMF. It uses an SPX connection to RSPX to control the transfer of screen and keystroke information to and from the remote server.

RCONSOLE can also work through communication servers such as the Novell Access Server.

Asynchronous Connection Configuration

Another way of establishing a remote session is through an asynchronous connection using modems. You typically use this type of connection to open a remote management session with a server on a distant internetwork not connected by cabling or T-1 lines. The figure below shows two possible variations on this configuration. In the first, a DOS workstation acting as remote console logs in to a local file server, then dials the remote file server's modem to establish the management session. In the second, a standalone PC establishes an asynchronous session without connecting through a file server first. Both types of remote consoles must have a modem installed.

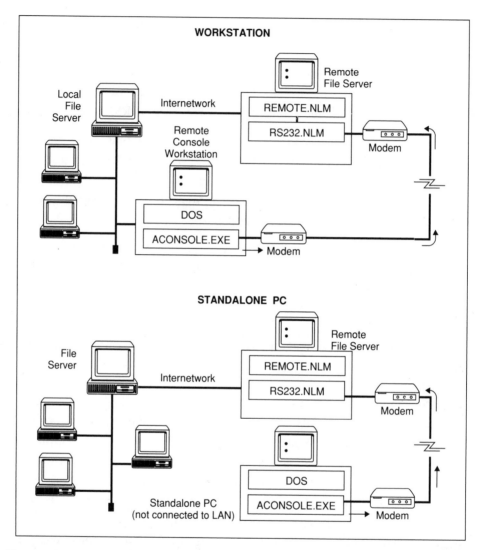

Figure 28-2: In the asynchronous connection configuration, a workstation or standalone PC runs ACONSOLE to control a remote server.

In this configuration, the RMF software components perform the following functions:

- REMOTE.NLM, as always, handles the remote access to the server's keyboard, screen, and file system. In this case, it coordinates the flow of keyboard and monitor information to and from the RS232.NLM driver.

- RS232.NLM, also loaded at the server, is an asynchronous communications driver that initializes the file server's communication port and handles the transfer of screen and keystroke information to and from REMOTE.NLM.

- ACONSOLE.EXE can be run either at a DOS workstation or on a standalone PC. It functions like many standard communications programs, allowing control of the client modem and providing a list of phone numbers that can be called. It does not use SPX, but rather interacts with the RS232.NLM module at the server to control the transfer of screen and keystroke information to and from the remote server.

The asynchronous setup is useful when some network problem prevents IPX/SPX communication with the remote server. For instance, if the server is down or a LAN driver is unloaded, you can't communicate with it using SPX. But you can open an asynchronous session with the server and reboot it, reload drivers, and remount volumes. You don't need to be logged in to any server if you have a local copy of ACONSOLE.EXE and its support files (listed under "Starting ACONSOLE at a Standalone PC" below).

Redundant Connection Configuration

The RSPX and RS232 modules can be loaded on the same server. This coexistence allows you to set up both direct and asynchronous connections, thus giving you a backup RMF mechanism should one or the other fail or become unusable for any reason.

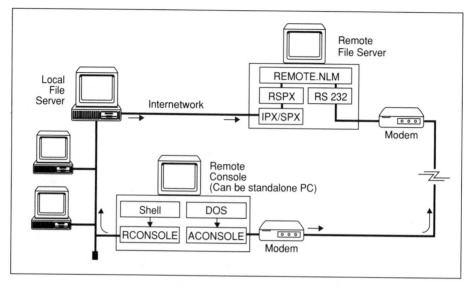

Figure 28-3: In the redundant connection configuration, you can control the remote server either directly or through an asynchronous connection.

Management and Troubleshooting Uses for RMF

Seasoned NetWare supervisors will readily see the benefits of being able to execute console commands from a workstation rather than directly at the server console. This capability makes it easier to centralize management of large corporate networks or wide area networks. By loading the RMF software on every server, network administration personnel can install, upgrade, back up, and run other server applications from a single management console.

The RMF software does not disable the regular console keyboard. It also supports up to 20 concurrent remote connections to the same file server. Thus you can have more than one person remotely controlling the same server at the same time, in addition to the regular server supervisor who has access to the console itself. While the thought of numerous people simultaneously accessing the same virtual keyboard may seem odd at first, this feature is intended to help experienced managers train novice server supervisors. For example, a training manager can open a session with a server and enter commands to show a local supervisor how to accomplish various tasks. Both users can enter keystrokes, and the same results are displayed on both the server screen and the remote console screen.

Remote access to various servers is also a powerful diagnostic and troubleshooting tool. For example, you can use it to quickly check driver configurations, network address settings, and MONITOR statistics around the internetwork.

When you're running a server application, the remote console screen need not remain dedicated until a process is completed. Once you start running a program (such as SBACKUP), you can switch to other screens or even terminate the remote console session without affecting the actual process. If you do keep the remote console session active, the remote console changes the current screen whenever the file server does. This is important when running utilities like VREPAIR that require keyboard input at various stages throughout the procedure. The OS continues to update all active screens (such as the MONITOR screen) even if they are not the current screen.

Security Precautions for RMF

Remote access to the file server console is an extremely useful and powerful feature for managing large, geographically dispersed networks. But in the hands of an unauthorized user, RMF can become a dangerous tool. If you don't carefully control access to the RMF utilities, you run the same risks as if you leave the file server console out in the open, unlocked and unattended. The following security precautions protect the server against unauthorized access via RMF.

- Only network supervisors and remote console operators should be allowed access to the RMF utilities. If it hasn't already been done, copy RCONSOLE.EXE and ACONSOLE.EXE from SYS:PUBLIC into SYS:SYSTEM. Then delete the two files from SYS:PUBLIC. This places the .EXE files in a restricted-access area so they cannot be run by just anybody.

- "Remote console operator" is not an assignable designation like file server operator or queue operator. A remote console operator can be any user to whom the supervisor has granted Read and File Scan rights in SYS:SYSTEM. The user must also know the remote console password assigned when the supervisor loads REMOTE.NLM at the server.

- The user SUPERVISOR can provide either the supervisor password or the remote password when opening a remote console session. However, if volume SYS is not mounted, the supervisor password will not work. As always, the passwords are encrypted before they are sent out over the cable.

- Once the supervisor or remote console operator gains access to a remote server, only the remote management tasks listed above can be performed on that server. Neither one can create or delete users, assign or modify trustee rights, or do anything else that isn't normally done from the server console.

- RMF does not bypass or disable the MONITOR utility's keyboard lock function. If the console keyboard has been locked with a password, both the supervisor and the remote console operator must enter that password to gain access to the remote server's keyboard.

Setting Up a File Server for RMF

To be remotely managed by RMF, a file server must have a 386 or 486 microprocessor and at least 48KB of available memory to run the remote console NLMs. The version of NetWare must be v3.10 or above, and the IPX/SPX protocols must be functioning. To support asynchronous connections, you must install a Hayes-compatible modem capable of communicating at 2400, 4800, or 9600 baud, and set to use either COM1 or COM2.

Note: You cannot load the remote management NLMs on a server running NetWare v3.0. You can, however, use RMF and the RSETUP utility to upgrade a v3.0 server to v3.11 from a remote console. See the "Remote Management" section of Novell's *System Administration* manual for instructions.

The remote management software is usually installed during initial installation. To load the remote management NLMs on a NetWare v3.1*x* server, follow these steps:

1. Make sure REMOTE.NLM, RSPX.NLM, and RS232.NLM exist in the SYS:SYSTEM directory of the server. If not, copy them in from the original NetWare diskettes.

2. At the server console, type

    ```
    LOAD REMOTE <Enter>.
    ```

    You will be prompted to enter a remote console password. This can be any unique password (not the SUPERVISOR password) up to 47 characters long. This is the password the remote console operator must type to gain access to this server.

3. To enable access to the server by a direct communication link, type

    ```
    LOAD RSPX <Enter>
    ```

    To enable access to the server by an asynchronous connection, type

    ```
    LOAD RS232 <Enter>
    ```

    For RS232, you will be prompted for the COM port number the modem uses (enter 1 for COM1, or 2 for COM2), as well as the modem speed (enter 2400, 4800, or 9600 to indicate the modem's baud rate).

Note: To load these modules automatically whenever the server is booted, place the commands in the server's AUTOEXEC.NCF file.Be sure to load REMOTE.NLM first. You can specify the remote console password and the modem parameters in the LOAD commands as follows:

```
LOAD REMOTE Password
LOAD RS232 CommPort ModemSpeed
```

Running a Remote Console Session

As mentioned before, you can run a remote console session from a DOS workstation on the LAN (via RCONSOLE), or from a standalone DOS machine with a modem (via ACONSOLE). Either way, the computer must be running DOS v2.0 or above and have at least 200KB of free memory. For asynchronous connections, the computer needs a Hayes-compatible modem capable of communicating at 2400, 4800, or 9600 baud.

Starting RCONSOLE at a Network Workstation

To run RCONSOLE, you must first log in to your local file server, then use RCONSOLE to establish a connection with the desired remote server.

1. At the workstation, log in to your local server as SUPERVISOR.

2. Map a search drive to the SYS:SYSTEM directory where the remote console files are located by typing **MAP S16:=SYS:SYSTEM <Enter>**.

3. Start up RCONSOLE by typing **RCONSOLE <Enter>**.

4. Select the server you want to establish a remote connection with from the "Available Servers" list. (The REMOTE and RSPX modules must be loaded for the server to appear on this list.)

5. In the "Password" window, type either the remote console password for the server or the SUPERVISOR password for that server. (You cannot use the SUPERVISOR password if the SYS volume is not mounted.)

6. Assuming you entered the password correctly, you will soon see whatever screen (if any) is currently being displayed on the remote server. If the "Keyboard Lock Password" box appears along with the MONITOR main screen, you must enter the keyboard password to access the server. If the remote system console screen appears, no screen is currently active on the server.

See "Remote Console's `Available Options' Menu" below for instructions on accessing the RMF menu and moving through various screens. Some of the administrative tasks you can perform remotely are described after that section.

Starting ACONSOLE at a Network Workstation

To run ACONSOLE, the workstation must have a modem installed, configured to use either the COM1 or COM2 serial port. You must first log in to your local file server, then use ACONSOLE to establish a connection with the desired remote server (which must also have a modem installed and the REMOTE and RS232 modules loaded).

1. At the workstation, log in to your local server as SUPERVISOR.

2. Map a search drive to the SYS:SYSTEM directory where the remote console files are located by typing **MAP S16:=SYS:SYSTEM <Enter>**.

3. Start up ACONSOLE by typing **ACONSOLE <Enter>**.

4. If this is your first time running ACONSOLE, select "Configure Modem" from the "Main Menu." In the "Current Modem Configuration" window, specify the COM port, baud rate, and a user connection ID of up to 40 characters. This connection ID is required before the modem will attempt to call out. Do *not* change the Reset, Initialization, Dial, or Hangup fields; these are preset to the recommended default settings. Press <Esc> when you are finished.

5. From the "Main Menu," select "Connect to Remote Location" to bring up the phone list. To add a phone number to the list, press <Ins> and type both the number and a location name for the remote server's modem. Be sure to include any outside call and long distance prefixes, as the phone number you enter will simply be appended to the dial command sent to your modem. (Refer to your modem's documentation for the exact syntax.) Press <Esc> to save the new entry.

   To modify a number already on the list, highlight it and press <F3>. Type in the new information and press <Esc> to save it. To delete a number from the list, highlight it, press <Del>, and answer "Yes" to the confirmation prompt.

6. Highlight the phone number for the desired remote server and press <Enter>. This initiates the call at the modem. As the modem attempts to make the connection, various status messages appear in the "Modem Result Codes" screen.

   Since ACONSOLE does not use SPX (which guarantees packet delivery), the program may time out when trying to send packets to or receive packets from a busy server. If you see the "Unable to Send Request to Server" or "No

Response from Server" message, press <Esc> and retry the call.

7. When ACONSOLE succeeds in establishing the modem connection, it displays the name of the server you called in the "Available Servers" list. Select it by pressing <Enter>. (The REMOTE and RS232 modules must be loaded for the server to appear on this list.)

8. In the "Password" window, type either the remote console password for the server or the SUPERVISOR password for that server. (You cannot use the SUPERVISOR password if the SYS volume is not mounted.)

9. Assuming you entered the password correctly, you will soon see whatever screen (if any) is currently being displayed on the remote server. If the "Keyboard Lock Password" box appears along with the MONITOR main screen, you must enter the keyboard password to access the server. If the remote system console screen appears, no screen is currently active on the server.

See "Remote Console's `Available Options' Menu" below for instructions on accessing the RMF menu and moving through various screens. Some of the administrative tasks you can perform remotely are described after that section.

Starting ACONSOLE at a Standalone PC

To run ACONSOLE on a standalone PC, the computer must have a modem installed, configured to use either the COM1 or COM2 serial port. The file server to which you intend to connect must also have a modem installed and have the REMOTE and RS232 modules loaded.

1. Copy the following files from the original NetWare diskettes to another diskette or to a directoryon the PC's hard disk:

    ACONSOLE.EXE
    ACONSOLE.HLP
    IBM$RUN.OVL
    $RUN.OVL

LAN$RUN.OVL
SYS$ERR.DAT
SYS$HELP.DAT
SYS$MSG.DAT

2. Insert the new diskette and go to that drive, or change to the directory containing the ACONSOLE files.

3. Start ACONSOLE by following Steps 3 through 9 under "Starting ACONSOLE at a Network\ Workstation" above.

Remote Console's "Available Options" Menu

Once you have activated the remote console, through either RCONSOLE or ACONSOLE, pressing the "*" key on the numeric keypad brings up the following menu:

```
┌────────────────────────────────────────────────┐
│               Available Options                 │
├────────────────────────────────────────────────┤
│ Select a Screen to View                         │
│ Directory Scan                                  │
│ Transfer Files to Server                        │
│ Copy System and Public Files                    │
│ End Remote Session with Server (SHIFT-ESC)      │
│ Resume Remote Session with Server (ESC)         │
└────────────────────────────────────────────────┘
```

You move around and select options in this menu just like you do in SYSCON, FILER, and other NetWare menu utilities. To select an option, highlight it and press <Enter>.

- To go directly to another active screen, choose "Select a Screen to View" and select the one you want from the resulting list of active file server screens.

- To leave the menu, press <Esc>. Once you are out of the menu, you can cycle forward or backward through the active screens by pressing the "+" or "-" key on the numeric keypad.

- As indicated, selecting "End Remote Session with Server" (or pressing <Shift><Esc> from anywhere outside the menu) ends your remote session with this server. The program redisplays the list of available servers so you can choose another server if you want. If not, press <Esc> and answer "Yes" to the confirmation prompt to exit Remote Console altogether.

Scanning Directories with RMF

Remote Console lets you scan both NetWare and DOS directories (including floppy drives) on the remote server. You can use this feature to verify that files have been correctly copied after you transfer files to the remote server.

1. Select "Directory Scan" from the "Available Options" menu.

2. In the "Enter Directory to Scan" box, type the directory path you want to scan.

   - If you want to scan a network directory, include the volume (for example, SYS:PUBLIC).

   - To scan a directory on the DOS partition, include the drive letter (for example, C:\NETWARE).

   - To scan files on a floppy diskette, type the floppy drive letter (for example, A:). Do *not* specify a local drive that does not exist on the remote server. If you do, your workstation will hang until someone presses any key on the remote file server's keyboard.

   Once you have typed the desired directory, press <Enter>.

The screen will display a list of files similar to that produced by the NDIR command, including size and last modified date/time. You can use <PgUp> and <PgDn> to scroll through long listings. Press <Esc> twice to return to the main menu.

Transferring Files to the Remote Server

Use this option to copy files from any "source" accessible to the remote console workstation to a "target" destination on the remote server. Sources and targets can be either local or network drives. The copy direction is one-way: you cannot transfer files from the remote server back to your workstation.

1. Select "Transfer Files to Server" from the "Available Options" menu.

2. Type the directory path of the source from which you want to copy files. You can use wildcard characters (* and ?) to specify only certain files.

   - To use a floppy diskette as the source, insert the diskette in drive A: or B: and include the corresponding drive letter in the path (for example, A:\ or B:*.NLM).

   - To use a local hard disk as the source, include the drive letter in the path (for example, C:\NETWARE*.*).

   - To use a network directory as the source, either type the entire path starting with the volume name or type the drive letter if you have a network drive mapping to the directory (for example, SYS:PUBLIC*.HLP or Z:*.HLP).

   Once you have entered the desired source designation, press <Enter>.

3. Type the target directory on the remote server to which you want to copy the files.

   - To specify a floppy diskette as the target, include the drive letter in the path (for example, A:\ or A:\NETWARE). Do *not* specify a drive that does not physically exist on the remote server, such as drive B: if the server has only one floppy drive. If you do, your workstation will hang until someone presses any key on the remote server's keyboard.

   - To specify a DOS partition as the target, include the drive letter in the path (for example, C:\NETWARE).

   - To specify a server directory as the target, type the entire path starting with the volume name (for example, SYS:PUBLIC).

Once you have entered the desired target designation, press <Enter>. The remote console screen will display the file names as they are transferred to the server. You can verify that the files arrived intact by using the "Directory Scan" option to check the target directory.

Copying New NetWare System Files to the Remote Server

The "Copy System and Public Files" option is mainly used when you are installing or upgrading more than one server from the remote management console. It automatically copies the necessary NetWare files to the SYSTEM, PUBLIC, and LOGIN directories on the target server.

Although the option will work in both RCONSOLE and ACONSOLE, it is *not* recommended for use over an asynchronous connection. Due to the large number and cumulative size of these files, ACONSOLE might time out during a transfer to a busy server. Phone line charges can also become prohibitive for such long transfers.

You can copy the files directly from a set of NetWare diskettes, but an easier way is to create a central "NETWARE" directory to work from. To do this, make a directory named NETWARE somewhere on your local server. (The name doesn't have to be NETWARE; any valid directory name will do.) Then create the following subdirectories under NETWARE:

SYSTEM-1
SYSTEM-2
SYSTEM-3
DOSUTIL-1
DOSUTIL-2
DOSUTIL-3
PRINT UP
GRADE
BACKUP

Use NCOPY to copy the files from each NetWare diskette to the subdirectory with the same name. For example, insert the NetWare *System-1* diskette into drive

A: and type

```
NCOPY A:*.* SYS:NETWARE\SYSTEM-1 /S <Enter>
```

This copies all files (and subdirectories, if any) from the *System-1* diskette into the SYSTEM-1 directory. Use a similar command for the other directories.

Once you have all the diskettes copied into the NETWARE subdirectories, follow these steps to copy the system files to a remote server.

1. Log in as SUPERVISOR to the server on which you created the NETWARE directory.

2. Change to the NETWARE directory. For example, if you created the NETWARE directory under SYS, type **CD \NETWARE <Enter>**.

3. Start up a remote console session as usual (see Steps 2 through 6 under "Starting RCONSOLE from a Network Workstation" above). Be sure to select the server to which you want to copy the system files.

4. Bring up the "Available Options" menu by pressing "*" on the numeric keypad, then select "Copy System and Public Files."

The remote console program looks for a file named FILEDATA.DAT in the SYSTEM-2 subdirectory of the default directory. If it finds it, the transfer begins and the file names are displayed in a window as they are copied to the target server.

If the program can't find the FILEDATA.DAT file, it prompts you to insert the diskettes one by one. You can press <F7> to cancel the operation if you didn't intend to copy the files from the original floppies. Check your NETWARE directory structure to make sure you have copied all the files into the correct subdirectories.

Specific Administrative Tasks

Using the RMF options described above, you can perform tasks involving the transfer of files, such as updating LAN or disk drivers. You can also reboot the remote server from your management console. The following sections explain how.

Updating a LAN Driver with RMF

From time to time, new or revised LAN drivers become available from Novell or from network hardware vendors. It is generally advisable to use the latest versions because they often provide bug fixes and improved performance. Here's how to use RMF and the EDIT.NLM to update a LAN driver on a remote server.

1. Start up a remote console session as usual. You can use either RCONSOLE or ACONSOLE; follow the appropriate steps as outlined above. Select the server whose LAN driver you want to update.

2. Type "*" on the numeric keypad to bring up the "Available Options" menu. Then select "Transfer Files to Server."

3. Insert the diskette containing the new LAN driver in drive A, then specify "A:" as the source directory path. Specify "SYS:SYSTEM" as the target directory path and copy the new driver to the remote server.

4. Choose "Select a Screen to View" to switch to the server console screen with the colon prompt (:). Then type **CONFIG** to display the current settings for the LAN driver. Make a note of which interrupt, I/O port, and so on the driver is using. Also note the driver's IPX network number.

5. This step is necessary only if you are running RCONSOLE. Load the EDIT module and create a file in SYS:SYSTEM called RELOAD.NCF containing the following lines (assuming the NE2000 driver is the one you want to update):

```
UNLOAD NE2000
LOAD NE2000 INT=3 PORT=320
BIND IPX TO NE2000 NET=1
```

6. In RCONSOLE, unload and reload the LAN driver by typing RELOAD at the colon prompt. You must use this .NCF file to reload the LAN driver because as soon as the LAN driver unloads, your RSPX connection will be terminated. However, the .NCF file commands will run to completion.

In ACONSOLE, just type the commands shown in step 5 at the colon prompt. Since ACONSOLE doesn't use IPX/SPX, your asynchronous connection remains intact even after you unload the LAN driver.

Updating a Disk Driver with RMF

As with LAN drivers, hard disk vendors occasionally release new or revised disk drivers for their hardware. It is generally advisable to use the latest versions because they often provide bug fixes and improved performance. Here's how to use RMF to update a disk driver on a remote server.

1. Start up a remote console session as usual. You can use either RCONSOLE or ACONSOLE; follow the appropriate steps as outlined above. Select the server whose disk driver you want to update.

2. Make sure all users are logged out of the remote server before you update the disk driver. Use MONITOR to view all current connections and send them a message to log out. Then disable further logins by typing "DISABLE LOGIN" at the colon prompt.

3. Once all users have logged out, dismount all volumes on the disks attached to the controller whose driver you are about to unload.

4. Use the UNLOAD command to unload the disk driver.

5. Type "*" on the numeric keypad to bring up the "Available Options" menu. Then select "Transfer Files to Server."

6. Insert the diskette containing the new disk driver in drive A:, then specify "A:" as the source directory path. Specify "SYS:SYSTEM" (or A: or C:\NETWARE— whatever the server boots from) as the target directory path and copy the new driver to the remote server.

7. Look at the STARTUP.NCF file with the EDIT.NLM and make a note of which interrupt, I/O port, and so on the disk driver is using.

8. Use the LOAD command to load the new disk driver, taking care to specify the same options as before.

9. Type **MOUNT ALL** to remount the volumes, then type **ENABLE LOGIN** to allow users to log back in to the server.

Rebooting a Server Remotely

Occasionally, you'll find it necessary to reboot a running server as part of your management procedures. For instance, you may have placed new or modified commands in the remote server's STARTUP.NCF file. Certain SET commands take effect only after the server is rebooted. Here's a neat trick for using RMF to reboot a server from your remote management console.

1. Using the EDIT NLM, create a REBOOT.NCF file containing the following three commands:

```
REMOVE DOS
DOWN
EXIT
```

This combination of commands yields the same result as downing the server and typing <Ctrl><Alt><Del> (a so-called warm boot). Save the file in the SYS:SYSTEM directory of the server.

2. Use MONITOR to make sure all users are logged out of the remote server. Then, at the colon prompt, type **REBOOT <Enter>**. The keyboard will be disabled while the REBOOT.NCF commands are processed. (Remember, an .NCF file runs to completion even if the remote connection is lost.)

3. When the prompt appears saying your connection is lost, press <Esc>. Then exit the remote console utility by pressing <Alt><F10> and answering "Yes" to the confirmation prompt.

4. To reestablish your remote management session with the rebooted server, open a new remote console session as usual.

APPENDIX A

Common Hardware Configurations

As you configure network boards, disk channel interface boards, and other network-related hardware, keep in mind that these add-on boards are not the only components that access the host CPU's resources. This appendix lists other hardware components typically found in IBM-compatible computers and gives the interrupt, DMA channel, I/O port addresses, and memory address ranges that they commonly use. (Some of these configurations vary from manufacturer to manufacturer; consult your hardware documentation for exact usage on non-standard PCs and components.)

The default settings for standard Novell hardware (network boards and DCBs) are also listed in this appendix. Refer to the Novell *Installation Supplements* for alternate settings.

Use these charts as a quick reference to help you avoid conflicts with internal hardware when you install network boards. Interrupts and DMA channels are given in decimal notation; I/O and RAM addresses are given in hexadecimal notation.

Standard Configurations in IBM-Compatible Hardware

Note that IRQs 0, 1, and 9 are reserved, as is DMA channel 4. These should not be used by any device. In addition, the following I/O addresses are reserved:

220-249
2F0-2F7
3E0-3E7

Device	Interrupt	DMA	I/O Port	RAM Addresses
COM1	4		3F8-3FFh	
COM2	3		2F8-2FFh	
LPT1	7		378-37Fh	
LPT2	5		278-27Fh	
If LPT3 exists:				
LPT1	7		3BC-3BEh	
LPT2	5		378-37Ah	
LPT3		-		278-27Ah
XT Hard Disk Controller	5	3	320-32Fh	
AT Hard Disk Controller	14	-	1F0-1F8h	C8000-CBFFFh
			170-177h	
Floppy Controller	6	2	1F0-1F8h	
			3F0-3F7h	
Tape Controller	5	-	280-28Fh	
Monochrome Adapter	-	-	3B0-3BFh	B0000-B3FFFh
Hercules Mono Adapter	-	-	3B4-3BFh	
CGA Board	-	-	3D0-3DFh	B8000-BBFFFh
EGA Board	2	-	3C0-3CFh	A0000-AFFFFh
VGA Board	-	-	102, 46E8h	C0000-C7FFFh
Math Coprocessor	13			
Mouse Port (Compaq)	12			
Game Port	-	-	200-209h	
Expansion Unit	-	-	210-217h	

Default Settings for ISA Network Boards

The defaults listed below are for network boards using the Industry Standard Architecture (ISA), or AT-style, bus. The settings correspond to the LAN driver's Option 0 configuration.

Settings for Microchannel boards are set automatically via the configuration option on the IBM *Reference* diskette. On Extended Industry Standard Architecture (EISA) boards, options are set automatically via the machine's SETUP or CONFIGURATION utility.

Board/Driver	Interrupt	DMA	I/O Port	RAM Addresses
NE1000	3	-	300h	
NE2000	3	-	300h	
3C503	3	-	300h	C8000h
3C505	3	5	300h	
TOKEN	-	-	A20h	D800h
TRXNET	2	-	D000h	
PCN2 (Primary)	2	-	620h	CC00h
PCN2 (Alternate)	2	-	628h	CC00h

Default Settings for Disk Coprocessor Boards

The default settings for Novell disk coprocessor boards depend on which disk channel the board is configured for. You can tell the channel from the type of PAL chips installed at position U3.11 and U4.11 on the DCB itself. The defaults are listed below. Refer to your DCB supplement or third-party manufacturer's documentation for alternate settings.

Channel	PAL U3.11	PAL U4.11	Interrupt	I/O Address
1	814-198-001	814-197-001	11	340h
2	814-198-001	814-197-002	12	348h
3	814-198-002	814-197-001	10	320h
4	814-198-002	814-197-002	15	328h

APPENDIX B

LAN, Disk, and Backup Drivers

This appendix lists the LAN, disk, and backup device drivers available for NetWare v3.11. It also shows what specific types of hardware the drivers are designed to work with.

Server LAN Drivers

The following LAN drivers ship with NetWare v3.11. They are NetWare loadable modules intended for use in the file server only.

Ethernet Drivers

NE1000.LAN	**Novell/Anthem NE1000** 8-bit ISA board (Assy 950-054401 or 810-160-001)
NE2000.LAN	**Novell/Anthem NE2000** 16-bit ISA board (Assy 810-149)
NE2.LAN	**Novell NE/2** 16-bit Microchannel board
NE232.LAN	**Novell NE/2-32** 32-bit Microchannel board
NE3200.LAN	**Novell NE3200** 32-bit EISA Bus Master board
3C503.LAN	**3Com 3C503 EtherLink II** 8-bit ISA board (Assy 2227)
3C505.LAN	**3Com 3C505 EtherLink Plus** 16-bit ISA board (Assy 2012)
3C523.LAN	**3Com 3C523 EtherLink/MC** 16-bit Microchannel board with twisted-pair wire support

Token-Ring Driver

TOKEN.LAN   **IBM Token-Ring PC Adapter II** ISA board
             IBM Token-Ring PC Adapter/A Microchannel board
             IBM Token-Ring 16/4 Adapter ISA board
             IBM Token-Ring 16/4 Adapter/A Microchannel board

Arcnet Driver

TRXNET.LAN   **Novell Turbo RX-Net** ISA board
             Novell Turbo RX-Net II ISA board
             Novell Turbo RX-Net/2 Microchannel board
             SMC Arcnet ISA and Microchannel boards

IBM PC Network Driver

PCN2.LAN   **IBM PCN Baseband** 8-bit ISA board
             IBM PCN/A Baseband Microchannel board
             IBM PCN2 Broadband ISA board
             IBM PCN2/A Broadband Microchannel board

(With v3.11, Novell has standardized on the IBM frame format; NetWare no longer supports Novell's PCN frame format.)

DOS Client LAN Drivers

The following DOS client LAN drivers ship with NetWare v3.11. They come in the form of .LAN and .OBJ files that are linked and compiled into functional IPX.COM files with the WSGEN utility. (WSGEN replaces the former SHGEN utility.) These drivers are for use in traditional DOS workstations only.

Ethernet

Novell/Anthem NE1000 8-bit ISA board (Assy 950-054401 or 810-160-001)

Novell/Anthem NE2000 16-bit ISA board (Assy 810-149)

Novell NE/2 16-bit Microchannel board

3Com 3C503 EtherLink II 8-bit ISA board (Assy 2227)

3Com 3C505 EtherLink Plus 16-bit ISA board (Assy 2012)

3Com 3C523 EtherLink/MC 16-bit Microchannel board

Token-Ring

IBM LAN Support Program

Arcnet

NetWare Turbo RX-Net boards

DOS ODI Client LAN Drivers

The following DOS ODI client LAN drivers ship with NetWare v3.11. They come in the form of .COM files that are loaded and configured via commands in the NET.CFG file. These drivers are for use in DOS workstations using the Open Data-Link Interface only.

Ethernet Drivers

NE1000.COM   **Novell/Anthem NE1000** 8-bit ISA board (Assy 950-054401 or 810-160-001)

NE2000.COM   **Novell/Anthem NE2000** 16-bit ISA board (Assy 810-149)

NE2.COM   **Novell NE/2** 16-bit Microchannel board

NE2-32.COM   **Novell NE/2-32** 32-bit Microchannel board

EXOS.COM   **Novell EXOS 205T** 8- or 16-bit ISA board

          Novell EXOS 215T 16-bit Microchannel board

3C501.COM   **3Com EtherLink** 8-bit ISA board

3C503.COM   **3Com EtherLink II** 8-bit ISA board (Assy 2227)

3C505.COM   **3Com EtherLink Plus** 16-bit ISA board (Assy 2012)

3C523.COM   **3Com EtherLink/MC** 16-bit Microchannel board with twisted-pair wire support

Token-Ring Driver

TOKEN.COM   **IBM Token-Ring PC Adapter II** ISA board

          IBM Token-Ring PC Adapter/A Microchannel board

          IBM Token-Ring 16/4 Adapter ISA board

          IBM Token-Ring 16/4 Adapter/A Microchannel board

"Turbo" Arcnet Driver

TRXNET.COM **Novell RX-Net** 8-bit ISA board

Novell RX-Net II 16-bit ISA board
Novell RX-Net/2 16-bit Microchannel board
SMC Arcnet boards

IBM PC Network Driver

PCN2L.COM   **IBM PCN Baseband** ISA board
                    IBM PCN/A Baseband Microchannel board
                    IBM PCN2 Broadband ISA board
                    IBM PCN2/A Broadband Microchannel board

(With v3.11, Novell has standardized on the IBM frame format; NetWare no longer supports Novell's PCN frame format.)

Disk Drivers

ISADISK.DSK   Built-in ISA disk controllers in IBM AT-compatibles
                    Secondary third-party ISA disk controllers
                    AT-class controllers installed in EISA computers

DCB.DSK   Novell ISA disk coprocessor boards (supporting SCSI disk channel interface)

PS2MFM.DSK   Internal MFM disk controllers in Microchannel computers

PS2ESDI.DSK   Internal ESDI disk controllers in Microchannel computers

PS2SCSI.DSK   Internal or add-on IBM SCSI adapters in Microchannel machines

Backup Device Drivers

Drivers for the following backup hardware are available for use with Novell's NBACKUP and SBACKUP programs. Contact the vendor for specific driver information.

QIC-02 Interface

Archive 2060L	60MB
Archive 2150L	150MB
Cipher 540	150MB
Emerald LAN 150-2100	150MB
Emerald LAN 150-9100	150MB
Gigatrend 103	0.3GB
Gigatrend 109	1.3GB
Wangtek 5099EQ	60MB
Wangtek 5125EQ	125MB
Wangtek 5150EQ	150MB

SCSI Interface

Archive 2060S	60MB
Archive 2150	150MB
Archive 5250	250MB
Archive Python DAT	1.3GB
Cipher ST150	150MB
Emerald Rapid Recover	150MB
Emerald VAST VAS02G-999	2.2GB
Exabyte 820	2.2GB
Gigatrend 101	1.3GB
Gigatrend 107	1.3GB
HP Mass Storage C2220A	332MB
HP Mass Storage C2221A	654MB
HP Mass Storage C2222A	1.0GB

HP Mass Storage C2224A/DAT	1.3GB
HP Mass Storage C1502A/DAT	1.3GB
Mountain 8MM	1.3GB
Maynard 2200HS	2.2GB
Sumus Gigatape 442 (Sony)	1.3GB
Tandberg TDC 3600	150MB
Tecmar THS-2200	2.2GB
Tecmar 150ES	150MB
Tecmar 525ES	525MB
Tecmar Data Vault	1.3GB
Wang DAT 1300	1.3GB
Wangtek 5099ES	60MB
Wangtek 5125ES	125MB
Wangtek 5150ES	150MB
Wangtek 5250ES	250MB
Wangtek 6130FS DAT	1.3GB

Important Note About Hardware that Uses DMA

If your server has 16MB or more of RAM, it may have problems with LAN, disk, and backup hardware that uses DMA 24-bit addressing. The main problem occurs when the board receives a 32-bit request to write to memory higher than 16MB. Since DMA uses only 24-bit addressing, the board truncates the 32-bit address and the data is therefore written to lower memory. This could overwrite portions of the OS, NLMs, cache buffers, or other vital areas in server memory.

Note that Bus Master boards or boards with programmable I/O do not experience this problem.

NetWare Name Service

To simplify the administration and use of multiple file server networks, Novell offers an add-on product called the NetWare Name Service (NNS). NNS works with both NetWare v2.*x* and NetWare v3.*x*. Without NNS, NetWare is strictly file server centric in its view of the network. In other words, user accounts are valid only on a single file server. If a user wants to access files, applications, or print queues on another file server, he or she must attach to that server under a different user account (GUEST or WP-USER, for instance). With NNS, users issue a single login command and gain access to resources on a whole group of file servers. The NNS software also makes the supervisor's job easier because you can manage a group of file servers with a single operation.

This appendix discusses the concepts behind NNS, and then outlines its basic setup on the file server and the use of the NNS utilities. It also points out some of the trouble spots you might encounter along the way.

Name Service Concepts

In small networks with just a few file servers and printers, locating a network resource is not difficult. You know exactly which server contains your database program and where the PostScript print queue is. On the other hand, in large networks with dozens of file servers and printers, the task of accessing a particular application or printer can be overwhelming. Users needing access to several servers must log in or attach to each one individually. To use a resource (an application, for instance), the user must know which server the application's files are on and specify that location in the network drive mappings.

Administering a large internetwork on a server-by-server basis becomes even more overwhelming. Even if only 25 users need to access just three file servers, you'd have 75 user accounts to create and assign appropriate rights to. Every time you physically move a resource to another file server, you have to update the mappings and login script for every user who accesses the resource.

The network industry offers several methods for simplifying the use and administration of resources on multiple servers. For example, OSI's so-called global naming specification (also referred to as X.500) outlines a system in which users can bring up a list or "directory" of network resources and choose the one they want by name. While such a system sounds good in theory, in actual practice global naming is fairly difficult to implement. The larger the network, the more complicated it becomes to maintain up-to-date information in a global database as devices are added and removed.

A Domain-Based Approach

A simpler but less global approach is a domain-based naming system such as NNS. With this system, you declare a logical group of servers to be a *domain*. You then assign names to certain resources within the domain. Once a domain is created, you can add users to it and create a *profile* for logging in to the domain. Rather than logging in to each file server one at a time, users log in once to the entire domain using the appropriate profile. According to the access rights defined in the profile, users can access resources in the domain by name without having to know exactly where the resources are located. Of course, users can still access resources outside of the domain (provided they have the necessary access rights) by explicitly declaring the location of the resource.

Although Novell's NNS allows you to define up to 400 file servers in a single domain, you would typically restrict a domain to a smaller number of servers (30 is a practical maximum). The idea is to link servers that will be administered together, so you can use NNS as a tool for managing that group of servers from a single workstation.

A file server can be in only one NNS domain at a time. Domains cannot overlap, but you can define as many domains as you need. Figure C-1 illustrates the concept of domains.

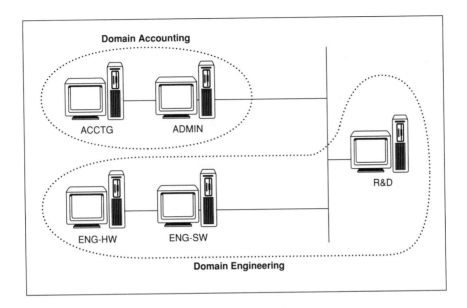

Figure C-1: With NNS, you group file servers into logical groups called domains.

In place of the system login script, NNS provides for a *domain login script* to set up the general user environment for all users in a domain. When a user logs in to a domain, this login script is executed first. Typically, it contains greetings, announcements, and DOS environment settings.

More About Profiles

An NNS profile is essentially another type of login script. The profile login script runs after the domain-wide "system" login script described above, but before the user's individual login script. Both the domain login script and the profile use standard NetWare login script commands. The profile contains drive mappings and print queue assignments to give profile users access to the servers and resources they will need within the domain. Because the NetWare shell is limited to eight server connections, a profile can include no more than eight file servers.

Users don't necessarily need to attach to every server in the domain. You can create a number of profiles for various workgroups or tasks on the network. For example, suppose the same group of writers is working on two projects. For project #1, they need access to server DOC and server TEST, while for project #2 they need access to servers DOC, EDIT, and MKTG. If you set up a separate profile for each project, the writers can specify which profile they need when they log in to the domain using their own user accounts and login names. The profile attaches each writer to the specified servers and maps drives to appropriate directories on those servers. When the needs of a project workgroup change, you can make global changes in the profile rather than in each user's login script. Note here that NNS does not provide true location-independent access to data. You still have to include the file server and volume name when you map drives in the domain profile. When the location changes, you must change the mappings in the profile accordingly.

With NNS, print queues are defined by domain rather than by individual servers. Each server in the domain has the same print queues. That way users don't have to worry about which server a print queue is defined on. If you change a print queue or add a new one, you meed only modify the profile login scripts. The NetWare Print Server (version 1.21) shipped with NetWare v2.2 and v3.11 supports NNS utilities.

The Importance of Synchronization

Within a domain, NNS creates and maintains an identical *Name Service data-base* on each file server. The database contains the same user accounts (with their passwords and login scripts), groups, print queues, and profiles. (The Name Service database supplements but does not replace the NetWare bindery for NNS users.) Whenever any of these items changes on one server, NNS automatically distributes the change to the database on every other server in the domain. Thus the servers remain synchronized with the same information.

NNS uses multiple synchronized databases rather than a single, central database to avoid having a single point of failure in the domain. If one server in the domain goes down, domain users can still access services elsewhere in the domain. However, if any changes are made in the domain while a server is down, the domain becomes unsynchronized. When the missing server is brought back up, you must make the change on that server individually to resynchronize the domain.

The following items are *not* included in the Name Service database:

- User and group object IDs

- Directories and files

- Trustee rights

- Intruder lockout and grace login information

- Disk space and volume restrictions

- NetWare resource accounting information

This information is kept in the NetWare bindery. Therefore it is not replicated and synchronized within the domain and must be administered on a server-by-server basis even if NNS is installed.

NNS Utilities

The NNS product is essentially of a set of utilities. As such, NNS can work with any existing NetWare v2.2 or v3.*x* network and requires no changes to either the operating system or the workstation shells. The main utility—NETCON—is a souped-up version of SYSCON used to create domain profiles and administer the Name Service database. The rest of the utilities are replacements for other NetWare utilities that access the bindery, modified to recognize NNS domains and names.

The NSINSTAL (Name Service installation) program copies the new Name Service utilities to the proper directories on the file server. Once the copy is successful, the program deletes the old NetWare utilities of the same name. You can run NSINSTAL from a single workstation to install the utilities throughout the internet. To avoid potential problems, you should copy the Name Service utilities to every server on the internet, even those that won't be part of a domain. The NNS utilities work the same as the regular NetWare utilities for users who aren't logged in to a domain.

One important utility to note is the NNS-aware version of SYSCON. Even though NETCON is intended to replace SYSCON, many users will habitually go into SYSCON instead. The problem is that if someone uses a non-NNS version of SYSCON to make changes on a domain server, the changes will be effective only on that server and your domain will be out of sync. To guard against this type of accidental domain corruption, copy the NNS-aware SYSCON to *every* server on the internet. The new version runs essentially the same as previous versions; however, when a user attempts a task requiring synchronization, SYSCON instructs the user to run NETCON instead.

Setting Up NetWare Name Service

This section outlines the basic procedure for installing NetWare Name Service on your internetwork. However, due to the number and complexity of the issues involved, we suggest you read the detailed instructions in Novell's *NetWare Name Service* manual.

Setting up NNS consists of the following three procedures:

- Install the Name Service-specific utilities with NSINSTAL

- Create domains with the NETCON utility

- Set up profiles with NETCON

To accomplish these tasks, you must have supervisor privileges on each file server involved. You'll probably need to enlist the help of other supervisors.

Installing the NNS Utilities

Always use the NSINSTAL program to copy the NNS utilities to a file server. NSINSTAL automatically logs in to each server, copies the necessary files, flags them with the proper file attributes, deletes the old files, and logs out. Because NSINSTAL copies the new utilities first before deleting the old ones, each file server must have at least 5MB of free disk space on the SYS volume. You'll need at least three available network drive mappings on the workstation as well.

1. From a workstation, log in to the file server you want to install NNS on first.

2. Insert the NNS "Utilities 1" diskette into drive A and type **A: <Enter>** to make this your default drive.

3. Type **NSINSTAL** **<Enter>**. The following "Available Options" menu appears:

```
┌─────────────────────────┐
│    Available Options     │
├─────────────────────────┤
│ Specify File Source      │
│ Specify Target Server    │
│ Perform Installation     │
└─────────────────────────┘
```

4. Select "Specify File Source" from this menu. A "File Source Options" menu will appear asking you to choose between "Local Floppy Drive" and "Name Service Server." Choose "Local Floppy Drive" the first time around.

    (Once you have installed NNS utilities on one file server, you can use that server as the source for subsequent copying.) After you have specified the source, press <Esc>.

5. Select "Specify Target Server" from the "Available Options" menu. A "Target Servers" list appears, initially empty.

6. Press <Ins> to add servers to the "Target Servers" list. Choose one or more servers from the "Available Servers" window that appears, and press <Esc> when your list is complete. If you haven't already logged in to all of these servers, you will be prompted to do so now.

7. Choose "Perform Installation" from the "Available Options" menu. NSINSTAL shows files being copied in the "Installation Progress" window. Insert diskettes as prompted.

8. When the "Available Options" menu reappears, press <Esc> to exit NSINSTAL.

NSINSTAL keeps a record of the installation, including any errors that occurred, in an NSINSTAL.LOG file in the SYS:SYSTEM directory of the first target server.

Setting Up NNS Domains

Once you have installed the NNS utilities, you are ready to set up your domains with the new NETCON utility. NETCON requires 640KB of memory in the workstation.

The *NetWare Name Service* manual recommends that you have all users change their passwords before you begin. This keeps NETCON from assigning random passwords to users.

1. At the DOS prompt, type **NETCON <Enter>**. The default server indicated at the top of the screen should be the main file server you want to serve as a template for the other servers in the domain. (You can switch default servers using the "Change Current Server" option.)

2. Choose "Domain Administration" from the "Available Topics" menu.

3. Select "Create Domain" from the "Domain Administration Options" menu.

4. Type a name in the "New Domain Name" entry box and press <Enter>.

5. Type the domain password and press <Enter>. Retype the domain password as prompted. Do not forget this domain password. You must enter it from now on whenever you select the "Domain Administration" option in NETCON.

6. Select "Domain Servers" from the "Domain Administration Options" menu. The "Current Domain's Servers" window appears, initially listing only the default server.

7. Press <Ins> to select other file servers to be added to the domain. Adding a server to a domain can take anywhere from a few minutes to hours, depending on how many users are defined on each server.

8. During this process, NETCON will ask you how you want to handle any user passwords that weren't changed before you started. If you have any duplicate user or group names on any of the servers in the domain, you'll see a "User/Group Name Resolution" menu that lets you choose how to resolve name conflicts. Consult the Novell *NetWare Name Service* manual if you are unsure of how to proceed.

9. Once the domain synchronization process is complete, select "Edit Domain Login Script" from the "Domain Administration Options" menu. A "Domain Login Script" box appears, initially containing the old system login script from the first server added to the domain.

10. Edit the domain login script using regular NetWare login script commands. (Remove any workgroup-oriented mappings and save them for the profile login scripts.) Press <Esc> and then press <Enter> to save your changes.

11. Press <Esc> until you return to the "Available Topics" menu.

Setting Up NNS Profiles

Your final step is to set up one or more profiles with corresponding profile login scripts for the domain.

1. Choose "Profile Information" from the "Available Topics" menu. A "Profile Names" window appears, initially empty.

2. Press <Ins> to create a new profile. Type a name (between two and 47 characters long) in the "Profile Name" entry box and press <Enter>.

3. Highlight the new profile name and press <Enter>. You'll see the following menu:

```
Profile Information

Full Name
Managers
Members
Other Information
Profile Script
Servers
```

4. Select the "Servers" option and press <Ins> to add servers to the profile. Although you can have up to eight servers in a profile, it's better to limit the

number to seven and leave a free connection for NNS to use when synchronizing changes made from a workstation. The same file server can be in more than one profile within the domain.

5. Select the "Members" option and press <Ins> to add users or groups as members of the profile. A user must be a profile member to log in using that profile.

6. Select "Profile Script" to create the profile login script. In the empty "Profile Login Script" box that appears, type the login script commands you want to apply to all members of the profile. Press <Esc> and then <Enter> to save your changes. Press <Escape> again to return to the "Available Topics" menu.

7. You should assign one of the profiles as the default to be used unless a person specifies a different profile when logging in. To do this, choose "User Information" from the "Available Topics" menu, then select the user whose default profile you want to assign. Choose "Profiles" from the "User Information" submenu, then select the default by highlighting it and pressing <Enter>. Repeat this step for each user in the profile.

8. Press <Esc> until you exit NETCON.

Using the NNS Utilities

After you've installed NNS and set up your domains, be sure to train your users on the proper use of the new utilities. They all work essentially the same as before, but many have additional domain- related options.

Users should now log in to a domain by adding the domain name (preceded by the "@" character) and the profile name to the LOGIN command. For example, user CHRIS would log in to domain "Accounting" under the AP profile by typing

```
LOGIN /PRO=AP CHRIS@ACCOUNTING <Enter>
```

You can specify the domain name in a DOS environment variable called "domain" if users routinely log in to the same domain. Set the "domain" variable in the AUTOEXEC.BAT file using the DOS SET command.

To log out of a domain, users should include the domain name preceded by @ (as in "LOGOUT @ACCOUNTING").

Other utilities have new options for domain information. A brief rundown is given below:

SLIST /D	Lists information about the current domains.
WHOAMI /D	Displays the domains you are currently in and which profile you are using in each.
VERSION /N	Displays the level of NNS awareness of a NetWare utility.
SETPASS @ACCOUNTING	Lets users change their password for the specified domain.
CAPTURE ... Q=Q2 DO=ACCOUNTING	Allows you to specify domain-wide print queues (no "S=" option is needed).
NPRINT ... Q=Q2 DO=ACCOUNTING	Allows you to specify domain-wide print queues (no "S=" option is needed).

In addition, the NNS versions of MAKEUSER and USERDEF have options for specifying a default profile in the user template.

Refer to Novell's *NetWare Name Service* manual for a complete explanation of the NNS utilities.

Troubleshooting NNS Problems

Most of the trouble you'll encounter from NNS is related to synchronization. Remember that if a server is down at the time a change is made in the domain, that server's database will not be updated. NNS will usually send an error message to that effect. Once the server is back in operation, you must go into NETCON and make the change on that server yourself using the "Synchronize Domain" option under "Domain Administration." It's a good practice to record your initial domain setup and all subsequent changes in a network log book so you can keep close tabs on your domain configuration.

While NNS is designed to make administering multiple servers easier for the supervisor, administering NNS itself can be extremely complex. Following are some hints and warnings for working with NNS. For a more complete explanation and a list of possible error messages, refer to Novell's *NetWare Name Service* documentation.

Problem: What is recorded in the SYNC$ERR.LOG file?

Solution: If problems occur during an attempt to resynchronize the domain, NETCON records an entry in a data file called SYNC$ERR.LOG in the SYS:SYSTEM directory of each domain server. You can then read this error log file and select which operations you want to retry.

Problem: You're getting errors saying that the domain can't be synchronized because the maximum attachment connections are all used up.

Solution: If you experience synchronization problems when users are attached to eight servers at once, redefine your profiles to limit the number of servers to seven. This gives NNS one free IPX/SPX connection to use for synchronization.

Problem: Can you rename a file server once it is part of a domain?

Solution: Yes, but it will work much faster if you delete the server from the domain first, rename it with the file server INSTALL program, then add it back to the domain with NETCON. Remember to change all drive mappings to that server in the domain, profile, and user login scripts.

Problem: What happens if a server is down when you delete the domain it is in?

Solution: If a server is down at the time you delete its domain in NETCON, it will appear to still be in the domain when you bring the server back up. Because a server can be in only one domain at a time, you won't be able to add the server to a new domain until you delete it from the non-existent old domain in NETCON.

Problem: Can you include Macintosh workstation users in a domain?

Solution: You can include Macintosh workstations in a domain. However, the NetWare for Macintosh utilities do not currently support NNS. Use NETCON instead of the Control Center to administer Macintosh users, groups, and print queues. (Since trustee rights are independent of NNS, you can use the Security Desk Accessory to set trustee rights for Macintosh files and folders.)

If you set up an Apple LaserWriter printer connected to an AppleTalk server with the MACSETUP program, you cannot define a domain-wide print queue for that printer. Users must send jobs to the actual print queue just as they did prior to NNS.

Problem: Can you include OS/2 workstation users in a domain?

Solution: You can also include OS/2 workstations in a domain, but you must not use the NetWare OS/2 utilities to administer the OS/2 clients. Use NETCON and the other NNS utilities instead. (You can, however, use the OS/2 utilities to set trustee rights for files and directories.)

Problem: If you upgrade to a new version of NetWare on the file server, do you have to reinstall the NNS utilities?

Solution: Generally, you do need to reinstall the NNS utilities with NSINSTAL after upgrading a file server. However, Novell says that future releases of NetWare might include enhanced versions of both Name Service and Name Service-aware utilities. Consult the upgrade documentation for any NNS-related instructions. After an upgrade (but before you rerun NSINSTAL), you can use the VERSION /N command to check the NNS status of utilities in SYS:PUBLIC, SYS:SYSTEM, and SYS:LOGIN. Make a list of any utilities identified as "Name Service" or "Name Service-aware." Then, after you run NSINSTAL, copy the new utilities you listed from the upgrade diskettes to the appropriate directories on the file server.

Problem: What precautions must you take when copying or restoring NetWare utilities from a backup?

Solution: Remember that even though the NNS utilities copied by NSINSTAL have the same names as their non-NNS counterparts, they have been modified to support domains and profile options. Copying a non-NNS utility back onto a file server can cause synchronization problems. If a user accidentally uses an old version of SYSCON to change a password, for example, it will be changed only on the server the user is currently working on. That server will then be out of sync with the other servers in the domain, and you will have to run NETCON to resynchronize the domain.

If you ever need to restore any NetWare utilities after installing NNS, be sure you restore the NNS versions of the files. If you inadvertently restore an old version, run NSINSTAL again to copy the NNS versions back to the server.

Problem: Can you still run all of your existing applications with NNS?

Solution: Once you install NNS, you must not install or use any third-party applications that directly modify the NetWare bindery. Check with the application vendor to see if the program uses the bindery or not. If so, find out if they have an NNS-compatible version of the program.

As long as they don't modify the bindery, most NetWare-aware applications will work fine even if they are not yet NNS-aware. However, some applications allow you to specify a network printer by file server name and print queue name, rather than just by parallel or serial ports. (WordPerfect 5.x is one example of such an application.) These applications do not recognize logical print queues being replicated by NNS. With these applications, users must continue to specify the actual file server and print queue as they did prior to NNS.

APPENDIX D

Sources of Additional Help

There are a number of sources for additional NetWare education and technical support. In this Appendix, we'll list some of the main sources of help you may want to consider.

Services Available From Novell

Novell provides a number of services to network administrators and users. We'll list as many of them as possible here. One helpful thing to know is that Novell recently consolidated access to all of its service programs into a single toll-free phone number: (800) NETWARE (800-638-9273). (Note that this toll-free 800 number is accessible only from the United States and Canada.)

Novell's NetWire

One of the most popular sources of NetWare support is the on-line NetWire forum, available through the CompuServe Information Service. Through the NetWire bulletin board, users can submit product questions to Novell technicians and can share technical information and ideas with other system administrators. NetWire also contains lists of NetWare-compatible products and includes Novell- provided files (such as the files for supporting Windows 3.0) that users can download.

To access CompuServe you'll need, in addition to the CompuServe subscription, a modem, a communications program, and a workstation. If you're a member of CompuServe, you can access NetWire by simply dialing in to the CompuServe number and typing **GO NOVELL** at the "!" prompt.

If you're not yet a member of CompuServe, CompuServe will give you a trial membership, with $15 of usage credit, to let you examine the NetWare service. You can get more information by calling Representative #58 at CompuServe, at (800) 848-8199 in the U.S. and Canada, or (614) 457-0802 outside the U.S.

NetWare Application Notes

Another service Novell provides is the monthly *NetWare Application Notes* publication, which provides in-depth information about designing, managing, and optimizing NetWare networks. To find out how to subscribe to the AppNotes, call the main Novell number (800) NETWARE, or call the AppNotes Hotline at (801) 429-7550.

If you're a Certified NetWare Engineer (CNE) or a Certified NetWare Instructor (CNI), Novell provides the AppNotes subscription to you free of charge.

NetWare Users International

NetWare Users International (NUI) is a Novell organization that offers users the opportunity to communicate among themselves and with Novell. NUI services include NetWare Users' Conferences in major cities, and the bimonthly *NetWare Connection magazine*.

For more information about NUI, call 1 800 NETWARE in the U.S., or FAX a request for information to (801) 429-3905.

Novell Technical Services

Novell offers users several options for direct telephone support. In addition, Novell can give you a list of certified third-party Novell Support Organizations (NSOs). For more information about Novell's technical support programs or to receive a current list of NSOs, call (800) NETWARE.

Education Programs

At this writing, 725 Novell-Authorized Education Centers (NAECs) provide technical training for NetWare network administrators and users. You can find an NAEC in your area by calling (800) NETWARE.

The CNE Program

Within Novell's education programs is the CNE program to provide resellers, independent service providers, and user technicians with advanced NetWare training.

Prospective CNEs must meet the following criteria:

- Be a NetWare user, technician, or engineer who is working for a Novell Authorized Reseller, an independent service organization, or an NSO;

- Have a working knowledge of DOS and microcomputer hardware; and

- Successfully complete the required series of CNE proficiency tests. Engineers or technicians who are already experienced with NetWare technology may be able to pass the CNE proficiency tests without completing the courses. However, every network supervisor is likely to benefit from the CNE courses Novell provides. The CNE courses are available from any NAEC.

The Certified NetWare Instructor (CNI) Program

Novell CNE courses must be conducted by a Certified NetWare Instructor (CNI). CNIs must complete an intensive training program from Novell or through an NAEC.

Publications

Here are some useful books and magazines that can provide further information about NetWare, local area networks, and related subjects.

LAN Magazine
500 Howard St.
San Francisco, CA 94105
(415) 397-1881

LAN Technology
501 Galveston Dr.
 Redwood City, CA 94063
(415) 366-3600

LAN Times
7050 Union Park Center, Ste. 240
Midvale, UT 84047
(801) 565-1060

Network Computing
600 Community Dr.
Manhasset, NY 11030
(516) 562-5071

Network World
161 Worcester Road
Framingham, MA 01701
(508) 875-6400

Bach, Maurice J., *The Design of the UNIX Operating System* (Prentice-Hall, 1986)

Case, J. et al., *A Simple Network Management Protocol*, RFC 1098 (University of Tennessee at Knoxville, 1989)

Comer, Douglas, *Internetworking with TCP/IP*, Vol. I (Prentice-Hall, 1991)

Hedrick, C., *Routing Information Protocol*, RFC 1058 (Rutgers University, 1988)

McCloghrie, K. and M. Rose, *Management Information Base for Network Management of TCP/IP-Based Internets*, RFC 1066 (The Wollongong Group, 1988)

Plummer, D. C., *Ethernet Address Resolution Protocol*, RFC 826 (Massachusetts Institute of Technology, 1982)

Postel, J. B., *User Datagram Protocol*, RFC 793 (USC/Information Sciences Institute, 1980)

Sidhu, Gursharan S., Andrews, Richard F., and Oppenheimer, Alan B., *Inside AppleTalk, Second Edition* (Addison-Wesley, 1990)

Stallings, William, *Handbook of Computer-Communications Standards* (Macmillan, 1987)

Tanenbaum, Andrew S., *Computer Networks* (Prentice-Hall, 1988)

Index

A

A file server could not be found 728
Access control rights 298, 328
Access Denied errors 366
ACCESS_SERVER 400
Account balance 457
Account limits 64
Account restrictions 307
Accounting
  API 64
  server 449
  services 63–64
ACONSOLE 801, 810, 812
ACSE protocol 92
Active hub 119
ADAPTEC.NLM 771, 775, 788
ADD command 192
ADD NAME SPACE command 669
Address Resolution Protocol (ARP) 696, 708
Addressing mistakes 113–116
AFP.NLM 209
AHA1540.DSK 772
AHA1640.DSK 772
AHA1740.DSK 772
Alerts 92
Alloc memory 35–36, 559
Alloc memory pool 572
ALLOW utility 299, 306, 312
AM_PM 400
Anti-virus software 329–330
API calls 735
AppleShare 90, 255
AppleTalk
  kernel-level support 73
  LOAD appletlk command 206
  NetWare v3.11 89
  network card 81
  physical layer 99
  protocol stacks 166, 563
  Streams 692
  suite of protocols 90
AppleTalk Filing Protocol

  (AFP) 82, 90, 563
AppleTalk Phase II 74
Application
  directories 339–340, 348
  home directories 341
  network 545–547
  NNS 849
  non-network 539
  services 26, 61–65
  subdirectories 357
Application, *continued*
  UPS protection 745
Archive attributes 305
ARCmonitor 119
Arcnet 85–87, 105, 111
  boards 698, 724–738
  cabling 114–119
  communication problems 712
  rules 117
  troubleshooting 118–120
ASN.1 protocol 92
ASPITRAN.DSK 772
Asynchronous connection 803–805
ATOTAL utility 445, 450, 459–461
ATTACH 398, 403–404
Attributes 301, 759
  delete 303
  directory 302, 311, 314
  file 303–304
  hidden 302
  purge 302
  rename 303
  security 301–305
  system 302
Audit record 64
Auto endcap option 534
Autoendcap 540
AUTOEXEC.BAT
  application effect on 359
  boot disk 327
  dedicated external router 267
  networking software 215
  ODI file 236
  RPRINTER.EXE 497
  sample 267
  TSR programs 440
  Windows SETUP program 230

workstation 93
AUTOEXEC.NCF 183, 187, 190, 196

B

Back up data 677, 778–784
Backup
    device controller 773
    device driver 10, 771–772, 775
    log 784
    media 762–763
    NetWare utilities 848
    options 780
    plan 765–768
    rate 761
Backup, *continued*
    rotating media 766
    schedule 765–766
    security 767
    server 745
    storing media 767
    system 759
    troubleshooting 788
Bad blocks 651
Banner page 533, 542
Basic components of NetWare 25
Battery status 751
Baud rate 488
Benchmark test 7
Berkeley Sockets 68, 91
BIND 178, 703–706
Bindery 62–65
    backing up 759
    BINDFIX 322
    components 305
    items not in Name Service database 839
    objects 474
    SBACKUP 778
BINDFIX utility 322–323
Binding protocols 735–736
BINDREST 323
BINDREST.EXE 291
Bindview 677
Bindview 3.0c 324
BIOS 467
Blackouts 740
Block 447
Block sizes 52, 157
BNC connectors 121

BNC terminator 121
Board name 175
Boot image file 240
Boot PROM 241
Booting from a DOS partition 133
BREAK 398
BREAK OFF 404
BREAK ON 404
Brownout 740
BTRIEVE 68
Btrieve 563, 627
BTRIEVE.NLM 186
Bus mastering boards 716
Bus topology 115
    advantages 104
    disadvantages 104
Bus type 212
Business Basic Extended (BBX) 627

C

C Library (CLIB) 58–59, 68
Cable 108
Cable, *continued*
    coaxial 212
    LAN adapter 220, 239
    patch 128
    scanners 17
    specifications 108
    tester 110
    twisted-pair 212
    Type 6 128
Cabling 729
Cabling map 727
Cache 160
    buffer 587
    buffers 52, 160, 717
    dirty buffer 589
    dirty buffers 591
    memory 559, 572
    movable memory 560
    non-movable memory 560
    original buffers 590
    system 49–51
    total buffers 590
CAPTURE utility
    applications not designed for printing 374
    domain information 845
    options 539
    print job configurations 516

print services   65, 360
PRINTCON   538
redirect printed output   508
Carrier Sense   721
CD (Change Directory)   342
Centralized network management   796
Change password   308
Charge rates   450–453, 455–457
CHKDIR utility   346, 350
CHKVOL utility   592, 666, 675
CLIB.NLM   693, 772
Client   22
Client-server model   22
CLNP protocol   92
CMPQ$RUN.OVL   441
Coaxial cable   103, 106, 212
Collisions   720
COLORPAL utility   430, 440–442
COM ports   487
COMCHECK utility   710–714, 734
   cable continuity   126, 220, 239
   workstation continuity   119, 127
Command interpreter   425
Command parameters   437
Command-line utilities   436–438
COMMAND.COM file   93, 327
Commercial power   744
Communication buffers   265
Communication protocol   77, 709, 730
Communication server   745
Communication Services Manager   799
Communications services   60
Compound strings   421
Compressed files   327
COMSPEC   398, 404–405, 425
Concurrent connections   297
CONFIG   179–181, 270, 708–709, 737
CONFIG.PST file   249
CONFIG.SYS
   application effect on   359
   boot disk   327
   conflicts with parameters   365
   conflicts with SHELL.CFG   365
   creating with DOS   236
   environmental variables   93

Configuration file   370
Consistency check   13, 205
CONSOLE command   268
Console keyboard   806
Conventional memory   222
Copy attributes   304
COPY CON   427
Copy protection   280–281
Copying new NetWare system files   816–817
CP/M   211
Create rights   298
CSMA/CD   83, 720
Current network power status   752
Custom template   387
Cylinders   151, 637

D

Daemons   97
Data
   contention   53
   directory   340
   encoding methods   637
   fork   100
   loss   668
   synchronization   51
Database servers   449
DAY   400
DAY_OF_WEEK   401
dBASE III Plus   627
DBman   627
DCB.DSK   639
Dedicated protected router   262
Dedicated real mode router   263
Default account restrictions   381
Default login script   395–396
Default Print Job Configuration   537
Delete attributes   303
Delete Inhibit attributes   304
DELETED.SAV directory   157, 335, 593
Desktop publishing   361
Device driver   57, 74
   interface   24, 57–58
   re-entrant loading   176
   support   287
Device numbering   639–641

Diagnostic services   64

DIBI2$DV.DAT file   774

Digital Intel Xerox (DIX) connector   124

DIR utility   592

Direct connection   802–803

Direct Memory Access (DMA)   173

Directory
  application   348
  attributes   302–303, 311, 314
  caching   49
  data   340
  home   341, 348
  IRM   311
  path   334
  space limit   349
  structure   768
  structure concepts   333–335
  tables   668

Dirty cache buffer   589

Dirty cache buffers   591

Dirty Disk Cache Delay Time   598

DISABLE LOGIN command   292

DISABLE TTS   623

DISABLE TTS command   57

Disable Verify option   663

Discharge time   749, 751, 752

Disk
  block   51, 52, 580–581
  channel   636, 677
  controller   637
  coprocessor boards   826
  drive   149, 637
  drives   657
  duplexing   619
  failure   677
  I/O   657
  mirroring   619
  reformatting   650

Disk Coprocessor Board
  (DCB)   134, 638, 747

Disk driver   638–639
  access server disk drive   136
  Disk Information option   660
  loading   147
  NetWare v3.x   57
  operating system driver   10
  problems with loading   681
  revised   819

Disk-space limitation   347

Diskless machines   326

Diskless workstation   240

DISKSET NLM   680

DISMOUNT   619, 656

DISPLAY   398, 405

DISPLAY NETWORKS command   73, 146, 709–710, 737

DISPLAY SERVERS command   73, 710

Distributed network management   796–798

DMA channel   823

Domain   836, 842
  login script   837
  name   844

DOS
  applications on server   339
  archive bit   783
  AUTOEXEC.BAT   327
  CD (Change Directory)   342
  COMMAND.COM   327
  CONFIG.SYS   327
  conventional memory   222
  directories   337–339
  environment   365, 434
  environment problems   225–226
  expanded memory   222
  extended memory   222
  general-purpose system   23
  IBMBIO.SYS   326
  IBMDOS.SYS   326
  MD (Make Directory) command   342
  memory location   34
  NetWare emphasis   211
  NetWare Shell   94–97
  ODI workstation   247
  ODI workstations, troubleshooting   238
  partition   135, 641, 734
  RD (Remove Directory) command   343
  server machine as workstation   134
  system files   338
  traditional workstations   688
  troubleshooting workstation   219–221
  workstation   93–95
  workstation memory   222
  workstation software   213–215
  workstation using ODI   688
  XCOPY command   463

DOS BREAK   398, 406

DOS command   268

DOS SET   398, 406–407

DOS VERIFY   399, 407

DOSGEN utility   243, 245

DOWN command   270

DRIVE 399, 407–408

Drive mappings 230, 835

Drive Operating Status 664

Drive Status window 664

Drivers 83
  disk 10
  LAN 10
  printer-specific 516

DSPACE utility 346, 346–349

Duplexing 619, 677

Duplexing partitions 153–157, 155

Duplicating node address 113

Dynamic memory allocation 32

Dynamic system 3

E

E-mail 867

Echo off statement 194

Echo on statement 194

ECONFIG utility 697

Effective rights 300–302, 320, 321, 336

8mm tape 763

802.2 frames 168

802.3 frames 167

80386 processor 282

80286 processor 282

Elevator seeking mechanism 597

Elimination 8

EMSNETx.EXE 235

ENABLE TTS 623

ENABLE TTS console command 57

ENDCAP utility 374, 547

Enhanced Small Device Interface (ESDI) 637

Enterprise management system 799–801

Erase rights 298

Error Correction Code (ECC) 762

Error log 784

Error log files 789

Error message 4, 9
  documentation 14–17
  fatal 14

ERROR_LEVEL 400

Ethernet
  adapter 126
  boards 719–721

bus topology 103
cabling 712
cabling concepts 120–127
CSMA/CD 83
frame types 220, 240, 693–698
networking hardware 84
node addresses 111
rules for thin-cable networks 122–123
star topology 105
thick cabling 123–125
thin cabling 121–123
troubleshooting tips for cabling 125–127

Ethernet II frames 167–168

EtherTalk 256

Event Control Block (ECB) 43, 715

Event Service Routine (ESR) 43, 46

EVERYONE group 281, 288

Execute Only attributes 304

Execute-only files, upgrading 278–280

EXIT 399, 408

EXPAND.EXE program 228

Expanded memory 222

Extended Industry Standard Architecture (EISA) 135, 212, 825

Extended memory 222

EXTERNAL PROGRAM EXECUTION (#) 408–409

External router 261–262, 745

F

Fatal error messages 14

Fatal errors 12

FCONSOLE operator 328

FCONSOLE utility 367, 800–801

FDISK.COM file 141

FDISPLAY 398

Fiber optic cabling 107

File 52

File Allocation Table (FAT) 82, 561, 579, 581–582, 668

File attributes 303–304, 315
  archive 305
  copy 304
  Delete Inhibit 304
  Execute Only 304
  hidden 303
  purge 305
  Read Audit 305

Read Only   303
Read Write   304
shareable   304
system   303
transactional   305
Write Audit   305
File cache   50
File cache memory   36–37
File chain   581
File Delete Wait Time   603
File lock   53, 368
File Not Found error   367
File scan rights   298
File system   24, 51–53, 81, 760
File system API   63
File Wizard utility   676
File-by-file backup   764
FILE_SERVER   400
FILEDATA.DAT   817
FILER utility   299, 306, 310–312, 343–344, 463, 593
FIRE PHASERS   399, 409
Flag   359, 362
FLAG utility   57, 279, 306, 315–316, 368, 621
FLAGDIR utility   306, 314–315
Flat memory model   31–32
Floppy drives   326
Form   544, 552
Form feed   533, 543
Form name field   533
FORMAT.COM utility   142
Formatting a disk   139
Forms   476, 517
4mm Digital Audio Tape (DAT)   763
Frame types   175, 698
difference from media types   167–172
Ethernet   721
Ethernet II   707
Ethernet network   730
packet fields   689
packet specifications   84
FTAM protocol   92, 100, 768
Full backup   778
Full system backup   765
FULL_NAME   401

Function calls   58
Functions   517

G

Gateway   745
Global naming   836
GOTO   399, 409–410
GRANT utility   299, 306, 317–318
GREETING_TIME   401
Group
administration   375, 377
bindery object   63
creating for application   363, 364
directories   329
mapping   358
security   309
WHOAMI   321
Groups option   308

H

Hard disk   646
Hard errors   761
Hardware   729
Hardware conflicts   823
Hardware Level Verify option   663
Hardware-specific modules (HSMs)   165
Hashing   584
Headers   689
Heads   637
Hidden attributes   302, 303
High Performance File System
(HPFS)   82, 88
High-impedance   114
HIMEM.SYS   222
Home directory   341–342, 344, 348
Host Bus Adapter (HBA)   638
Host server   769
Hot Fix   152–153, 613, 647, 651, 660, 677
Hot Fix Redirection area   152, 647, 661
HOUR   401
HOUR24   401
Hub concentrator   106

I

IBM PC Network II adapters 698
IBM$RUN.OVL 440
IBMBIO.SYS file 326
IBMDOS.SYS file 326
ID number 377
Identifier variables 420
IEEE 802.3 83
IEEE 802.5 84
IF...THEN 399, 410–412
Image backup 764
Implicit transactions 56
INCLUDE 399, 412–413
Incremental backup 766
Industry Standard Architecture
    (ISA) 135, 638, 825
Inherited Rights Mask 299, 312, 336
Initialization errors 12
Inrush capacity 746
INSTALL NLM 619
INSTALL utility 137, 575, 614, 646
INSTALL.NLM 148, 580
INT 25h interrupt 366
INT 26h interrupt 366
INT2F.COM file 362
Intelligent Power System (IPS) 744–745
Inter-Process Communication (IPC) 24, 44
Interleave factor 650
Internal IPX number 113, 737
Internal router 262
Internetwork Packet Exchange (IPX) 85–86
    internal network 44–49
    internal network number 709
    network number 136
    protocol 39, 703
    sockets 504
Interprocess communication mechanisms 81
Interrupt 173, 364, 365, 487, 823
Interrupt Service Routine (ISR) 725
Intruder 461
I/O
    address 174, 823
    address conflict interrupt 221
    conflict interrupt 212

port addresses 709, 823
IP 708
    network address 696
    tunneling 74
IPX.COM 213, 327, 710
IPX/SPX 166
IPXODI.COM 236
IPXS.NLM 693
IRQ 823
ISADISK.DSK 638

J

Job server 61
JUMPERS utility 214, 266

K

Kernel 25, 30–57, 34
    components 30
    memory 34
Kernel memory 559

L

LAN
    adapter 212, 220, 250, 729
    adapter address 245
    communication mechanism 688
    loading drivers 171–178
    troubleshooting communication problems 726–
        738
LAN driver 10, 39, 57, 818
    DOSODI 235
    matching LAN cards 265
    options 172–181
    parameters to match adapter 730
    software connection 687
    statistics 714–719
LANalyzer network analyzer 798
LANShell 443
LANSUP.COM 236
LANtern network monitor 799
LaserJet IIIsi 486
LaserWriter 847
Least Recently Used (LRU) 565
Library NLMs 204
Licensing rights 361

LIM specification 222
Limited grace login feature 297
Linear bus topology 103–104
Link Support Layer (LSL) 98, 166, 691
LISTDIR utility 346, 351
LOAD command 172, 654–655, 698–702, 732
LOAD MAC.NAM 291
LOAD MONITOR 571
LOAD NameSpace command 192
Loader 10, 25, 28–29, 34, 75
LocalTalk 89, 99, 255
Locking structure 373
Logging in 218, 237, 247, 253, 256
Login 446
LOGIN directory 157, 335
Login script 337, 376–377
    default 395–396
    menu, accessing 439–440
    system 396
    troubleshooting 424–426
    user 396–397
Login script commands 398–402
    # 399
    ATTACH 398
    BREAK 398
    COMSPEC 398
    DISPLAY 398
    DOS BREAK 398
    DOS SET 398
    DOS VERIFY 399
    DRIVE 399
    EXIT 399
    FDISPLAY 398
    FIRE PHASERS 399
    GOTO 399
    IF...THEN 399
    INCLUDE 399
    MACHINE NAME 399
    MAP 399
    PAUSE 399
    PCCOMPATIBLE 400
    REMARK 400
    SHIFT 400
    WRITE 400
Login script identifier variables 398–402
    < > 402
    ACCESS_SERVER 400
    AM_PM 400
    DAY 400
    DAY_OF_WEEK 401

ERROR_LEVEL 400
FILE_SERVER 400
FULL_NAME 401
GREETING_TIME 401
HOUR 401
HOUR24 401
LOGIN_NAME 401
MACHINE 401
MEMBER OF 400
MINUTE 401
MONTH 401
MONTH_NAME 401
NDAY_OF_WEEK 401
NETWORK_ADDRESS 401
OS 402
OS_VERSION 402
P_STATION 402
PASSWORD_EXPIRES 402
SECOND 402
Login script identifier variables, continued
    SHELL_TYPE 402
    SHORT_YEAR 402
    SMACHINE 402
    STATION 402
    USER_ID 402
    YEAR 402
Login security 295
LOGIN_NAME 401
Long machine type 217, 338
Long names 791
Lost data 740
Low balance limit 457
Low-impedance 114
LPT port 364, 534, 539, 540
LSL.COM 235

M

MACHINE 401
MACHINE NAME 399, 413
Machine type 64
%MACHINE variable 338
MACHINE=NAME 366
Macintosh
    Chooser 255, 258
    directories 357
    file server 339
    files 100
    installing software 255

name space   209
NDIR   352
NetWare for NLMs   258
OS   23
troubleshooting workstations   257
volumes   768
workstation   98–100
workstation users in a domain   847
MACSETUP program   847
Magnetic tape cartridges   762
MAIL directory   157, 335
Mailbox   377
MAIN.MNU file   428, 428–431
MAKEUSER keywords   384
MAKEUSER utility   62, 380, 845
Management Information Base (MIB)   799
Manual upgrade   277
MAP   399, 414–416
Map   358, 364
MAP ROOT com-
        mand   231, 362, 364, 368, 372
Mapping network drives   377
Maximum Concurrent Directory Cache
        Writes   601
Maximum Physical Receive Packet
        Size   717, 718
MD (Make Directory) command   342
Media protocols   78
Media types   167–172
Media-specific modules (MSMs)   165
MEMBER OF   400
Memory
        address   823
        alloc   559
        cache   559, 572
        cache movable   560
        cache non-movable   560
        conflicts   200–210
        kernel   559
        manager   31–38, 222, 236
        NetWare 3.x types   33–34
        permanent   559, 560
        protection   33
        semi-permanent   560
        tuning   37–40
        workstation   233

Menu script
        creating custom   432–439
        file rules   431–434
MENU utility   427
Menus, troubleshooting   442
Message Handling Service (MHS)   867
Message passing   44
Message services   65
Micro Channel   135, 212
Microchannel   825
MicroFocus Cobol   627
Microsoft Windows   96, 226
MINUTE   401
Mirroring   677
        disk   619
        feature   660
        partitions   153–157
        steps for partitioning   155
Mode field   536
Modem   329, 808
Modes   517
Modified Frequency Modulation (MFM)   637
Modified since last archived   783
Modify bit   778
Modify rights   298
MONITOR NLM   559, 565, 618
MONITOR util-
        ity   38, 71, 185, 201, 367, 585
MONTH   401
MONTH_NAME   401
MOUNT console command   656
Moveable cache memory   37
Multiple link interface driver   691
Multiple-server internetwork   112
Multiple-server network   112
Multistation Access Unit (MAU)   128, 722
Multitasking   24

N

N-series male connectors   124
Name Service database   838
Name space   75, 81–82, 668, 674, 760

Name space support   68

Named Pipes   98, 251

Named pipes interprocess communication   87–89

NBACKUP utility   768

NCOPY command   100, 428, 463, 816

NCOPY.EXE utility   277

NDAY_OF_WEEK   401

NDIR utility   330, 346, 351–356, 353, 592

NET$ACCT.DAT   449

NET$LOGIN.DAT file   288

NET$OBJ.SYS file   306

NET$PRN.DAT file   518, 520

NET$PROP.SYS file   306

NET$REC.DAT   450

NET$VAL.SYS file   306

NET-CHECK   576

NET.CFG file   93, 216, 237, 250, 720

NET3.COM   214

NET4.COM   214

NET5.COM   214

NETBIOS   251

NetBIOS   86, 98

NetBIOS emulator   215

NETBIOS.EXE file   236, 365

NETCON   839

NetFRAME   288

NetPort   486

NetView   92, 712, 799, 800

NetWare
  drive mappings   230
  expanded shell (EMSNETx.EXE)   222
  extended shell (XMSNETx.EXE)   223
  FTAM   82, 92, 705
  Macintosh   705
  Macintosh NLMs   258
  Macintosh v3.0   88, 98
  NFS   82
  OS/2 utilities   252–253
  OSI   563
  partitions   149, 641
  requester for OS/2   97, 249
  router software   264
  SAA   92, 799
  security, three types of   295
  shell   94–97, 215, 221, 227
  SQL   563
  Streams   692

test server, v3.11   289
  utilities   435

NetWare Core Protocol (NCP)   44–46, 86, 94, 690

NetWare Loadable Modules
  (NLM)   10, 29, 35, 183
  bugs   576
  environment   26, 57–61
  loading the monitor   184–186

NetWare Name Service (NNS)   798, 835
  profile   837, 843–849
  troubleshooting   846
  utilities   839–840

NetWare v3.x operating system   23

NetWare-aware applications   358–361

NetWire   227

Network
  address   41, 111
  administrator   796
  analyzer   7
  applications   545–547
  board   687
  configuration logbook   6, 15
  error logbook   15
  error on server   728
  log book   727
  management   795–797
  management tools   798
  node addresses   111–113
  number   704, 706
  print device   517
  printer   745
  traffic   721
  troubleshooting disk problems   677–686

Network Filing System (NFS)   91–93, 563

Network printing   468–469, 478
  model   469–473
  plan   486–487

NETWORK_ADDRESS   401

NETx.COM file   235, 327

NLM-CHECK   576

NMAGENT.NLM   712

Node address
  Arcnet   712, 724
  duplicate   729
  Ethernet   720
  LAN adapter   111
  MONITOR   713
  physical network board   709
  specifying station   41

Node numbers   176

Noise   740
Non-moveable cache memory   37
Non-network applications   539
Nondedicated protected mode router   263
Norton Utilities   119
Notify feature   533
Notify List for Printer   493
Notify option   542
NOVADIBI.NLM   772, 788
Novell SS keycard   747
Novell-certified hardware   290
NPRINT utility   547–548
    domain information   845
    job configurations   516
    network application printing   374
    PRINTCON   538
    printing utility   65
    TRIAL.DAT file   452
NSINSTAL   839
NSINSTAL.LOG   841
NUT.NLM   772

O

Object   306
Object supervisor   321
ODI LAN drivers   697
Off-line UPS   742, 742–743
On-line backup   760
On-line UPS   742, 743–744
Open Data-Link Interface (ODI)   80–81, 96, 165, 234
Open files   760–761
Open Systems Interconnect (OSI)   68
Optical disk   763
Oracle   563
Original cache buffers   590
OS   402
%OS variable   338
OS/2   23, 339, 352, 357
    clients   87
    device drivers   97
    NetWare requester for   87, 97
    troubleshooting workstation   254–256
    utilities   88, 252–253
    volumes   768
    workstation   248–255, 688, 848

OS_VERSION   402
OSI
    default receive packet size   717
OSI Reference Model   78
OSI TP4   692

P

P_STATION   402
Packet   39, 689, 714
    size   717
    structure of an IPX   40
Packet receive buff-
        ers   562, 658, 715, 731, 774
Parallel port   467
Parity   488
Partition   641–643, 660, 661
    DOS   135
    duplexing   153–157
    mirroring   153–157
    NetWare   149
Partition Tables option   648
Password   62, 238
    changing   308, 312
    length limitation   296
    periodic change   296
    print server   502
    security   376
    unencrypted   208
    unique   296
    user name   219, 247, 254
PASSWORD_EXPIRES   402, 416
Patch cables   128
Path space limit   349
PAUDIT utility   445, 450, 460
PAUSE   399, 416
PC Tools   119
PCCOMPATIBLE   400, 417
PCONSOLE operator   328
PCONSOLE utility   374, 516, 538
Permanent memory   35, 559, 560
Permanent memory pool   572
Physical layer tools   17
PostScript   469
Power
    disturbances   739
    outages   740
    surge   740

Preferred server   94, 218
Print
   buffer software   473
   device functions   522
   drivers   472
   forms   527–529
   job   476
   job configurations   530
   modes   525–527
   service software   472
Print queue
   component in NetWare   473
   creating   488–489
   IDs   474
   matching with printer   493
   names   474
   NNS   838
   operator   476, 477
   PRINTCON   536
   single printer   472
   special queue   70
   storage area   469
   user   477–479
Print server   61
   account   489–490
   bringing down   500
   component in NetWare   478
   configuration   495, 499
   network   449
   operator   480
   password   502
   PRINTCON   536
   software   69–71
   specialized software   469
   UPS protection   745
   user   480–481
Print Server NLM   488
Print services   65–66
PRINTCON options   532–534
PRINTCON utility   65, 387, 515
PRINTCON.DAT   530
PRINTDEF database   518
PRINTDEF delimiters   522
PRINTDEF utility   386, 515
Printer   467
   network   487
   new   509
   numbers   478
   status   472
   type   486
Printer Access Protocol (PAP)   563
Printer Control Language   469

Printer Definition File   518
Printer Name field   491
Printer-specific drivers   516
Printers   364
Printing   70
   troubleshooting   502–513
   utilities   471, 515–516
Priority   475
Profile   836
Profile name   844
Properties   306
Property data   306
Protocol   22
   decoders   17
   engine   79–81
   ID   696
   identification number (PID)   708
   stack   77
   stacks   166
PROTOCOL command   707, 736
PROTOCOL REGISTER command   708, 736
PS2MFM.DSK disk driver   639
PS2SCSI.DSK   639
PSC command   549–553
PSERVER utility   69
PSERVER.EXE   482, 496, 505
PSERVER.NLM   481, 495
PSERVER.VAP   482
PUBLIC directory   157, 335
Purge   666
Purge attributes   302, 305
PURGE utility   593

Q

Quarter-inch cartridge (QIC)   762
Queue management services   65
Queue server   61
Queue services   60–61, 70

R

RAM   24
Random media errors vs. bad media   617
RCONSOLE   594, 801, 810
RCONSOLE.EXE file   72
RD (Remove Directory) command   343

Read After Write Verify   662
Read Audit attributes   305
Read Only attributes   303
Read redirection   617
Read rights   298
Read Write attributes   304
Read-after-write verification   615, 762
Rebooting a server   820–821
Recharge time   749, 751, 752
Record lock   53
Redundant connection   805–809
Redundant copies   762
REGISTER MEMORY command   199
Reinitialize mode   526
REMARK   400, 417–418
REMOTE   801
Remote console
    operator   807
    password   807
    session   809
Remote management   802
Remote Management Facility (RMF)   72–74, 801–821
Remote network printer   484, 501
Remote program load NLM   241
Remote reset file (BOOTCONF.SYS)   246
Remote reset PROMs   326
REMOTE.NLM file   72
Removable hard disks   763
Removable media   665
REMOVE DOS command   34, 134, 205, 564, 733
REMOVE utility   306, 319–320
Rename attributes   303
RENDIR utility   346, 350–351
Requester for OS/2   249
RESET ROUTER command   73, 737
Resource fork   100
Resource Tags   567
Resource tracking   71–72
Restore
    data   785
    options   786–788
    troubleshooting   788
RETRIES parameter   177

Retry   725
Revelation version G2B   627
REVOKE utility   306, 318–319
Rewritable optical disks   763
Rights   362, 368, 759
    access control   298, 328
    create   298
    effective   300–302
    erase   298
    file scan   298
    modify   298
    read   298
    security   298–301
    supervisory   298, 300
    trustee   299
    write   298
RIGHTS utility   320
Ring topology   104–106
    advantages   105
    disadvantages   105
RMF security precautions   807–808
Root directory   372
ROUTE.COM   236
ROUTEGEN program   264
Router   30, 42, 47–49
    configuration errors   114
    dedicated protected   262
    dedicated real mode   263
    external   49, 261–262
    internal   49
    to internetwork   112
    nondedicated protected mode   263
    router   262
    troubleshooting   272–273
Router Configuration Errors   114
ROUTER.CFG file   269
ROUTER.EXE file   266
Routing   714
    errors   737–738
    table   48
Routing Information Protocol (RIP)   48
RPLODI.COM file   235, 247
RPRINTER.EXE   484–488, 497, 506
RS-232C data-transfer protocol   488
RS232   801
RSETUP.EXE   802
RSPX   801
RSPX.NLM file   72, 186
Run Length Limited (RLL)   637

Run-time errors   13
Run-time options   672

S

Saber Menu   442
Sag   740
SALVAGE utility   592
Salvageable files   666
SBACKUP utility   75, 768, 776
SBACKUP.NLM   770
Scanning directories   814
Scheduler   38–39
SEARCH console command   203
Search drive   364
Search drive mappings   367
SEARCHPATH variable   203
SECOND   402
SECURE CONSOLE command   195, 203
Security   446
   problems   320–324
   violations   323
Security equivalence   63, 300, 308, 321
SECURITY utility   323–324
Segment   653
Segmented memory model   31
Semi-permanent memory   560
SEND utility   65
Sequence of jobs   476
Sequenced Packet Exchange (SPX)   60, 86
Serial port   467
Server   22
   boot files   187
   installation steps   133–134
   internal IPX number   146–148
   machine as DOS workstation   134
   name   136, 145
   objects   62
   parameters   774–775
   preferred   218
   rebooting   820–821
   shutdown messages   755
SERVER -NA parameter   196
SERVER -NS parameter   196
SERVER -S parameter   196
Server Memory Statistics screen   560
SERVER.EXE   144

Service Advertising Protocol (SAP)   70
Service processes   658, 717
Service protocols   79
SET   232, 658, 716
   allow unencrypted passwords   208
   Auto Register Memory   199
   Auto TTS Backout Flag   630
   Cache Buffer Size   587
   cache buffer size   666
   Console Display Watchdog Logouts   726
   Delay Before First Watchdog Packet   726
   Delay Between Watchdog Packets   726
   directory cache allocation wait time   601
SET, continued
   directory cache buffer nonreferenced delay   599
   dirty directory cache delay time   601
   dirty disk cache delay time   596
   display disk device alerts   667
   Display Old API Names=On   577
   Display Relinquish Control Alerts=On   576
   enable disk read after write verify   667
   Immediate Purge of Deleted Files   793
   immediate purge of deleted files   602
   Maximum Alloc Short Term Memory   777
   maximum alloc short term memory   573
   maximum concurrent disk cache writes   597
   maximum directory cache buffers   600
   maximum extended attributes per file or
      path   605
   maximum file locks   609
   maximum file locks per connection   609
   maximum packet receive buffers   716
   maximum percent of volume space allowed   604
   maximum percent of volume used by direc-
      tory   604
   maximum record locks   609
   maximum record locks per connection   609
   Maximum Subdirectory Tree Depth   775
   maximum subdirectory tree depth   606
   maximum transactions   630
   memory management   559
   Minimum Directory Cache Buffers   775
   minimum directory cache buffers   600
   minimum file cache buffer report threshold   596
   minimum file cache buffers   202, 594
   minimum file delete wait time   603
   Minimum Packet Receive Buffers   774
   NCP file commit   605
   new packet receive buffer wait time   716
   Pseudo Preemption Time   577
   Reply To Get Nearest Server   726
   Reserved Buffers Below 16 Meg   574, 777
   TTS Abort Dump Flag   631
   TTS Backout File Truncation Wait Time   632
   TTS UnWritten Cache Wait Time   631

turbo fat re-use wait time 607
volume low warn all users 666
volume low warning reset threshold 667
volume low warning threshold 666
SETPASS utility 306, 312, 845
SETTTS utility 627
Setup Aid 128
SHARE.COM file 362
Shareable attributes 304
Shared memory 175
Shared memory addresses 709
Shell descriptor area 415–420
Shell identifiers
    MACHINE 415
    OS 415
Shell identifiers, *continued*
    OS_VERSION 415
    SMACHINE 415
SHELL.CFG file
    conflicts with CONFIG.SYS 365
    long machine type 338
    monochrome workstations 441
    remote printer 510
    RPRINTER 486
    setting commands in 93
    SPX connections 497
    Windows 229
    workstation boot disk 364
    workstation parameters 216
SHELL_TYPE 402
Shielded twisted-pair cabling 106
SHIFT 400, 418–419
SHORT MACHINE TYPE 442
Short machine type 217
SHORT_YEAR 402
SIDR.NLM 770
Simple Network Management Protocol
    (SNMP) 799
Single-user application 361
SLIST utility 145, 737, 845
SMACHINE 402
Small Computer Systems Interface
    (SCSI) 638
SNAP frames 168–172
SNMP 91, 712
Socket 41
Soft errors 761
Software Level Verify option 663

Sparse files 52
Spike 740
Spool 469
SPOOL command 478, 540
Spurious interrupt 725
SPX connections 504
SPXS.NLM 693, 772
ST-506 637
Standalone printing process 467
Star topology 105–121
    advantages 105
    disadvantages 105
STARTUP.NCF file 183, 187, 190, 594
STATION 402
Station restrictions 297, 308
Status messages 14
Stop bits 488
Storage device 769
STREAMS 59, 68, 81–83
STREAMS.NLM 693, 772
Streams/TLI 91
Striped reads and writes 52
Super-characters 421
SUPERVISOR user 281, 288, 327
Supervisory rights 298, 300
Surface test 651
Surge suppressors 741
Swapping 8
SYNC$ERR.LOG 846
Synchronization 838–839
SYS volume 157
SYS:LOGIN directory 288
SYS:MAIL directory 377
SYS:PUBLIC direc-
    tory 287, 288, 357, 428, 440
SYS:SYSTEM directory 185, 287, 288, 449
SYSCON utility
    account limits 64
    console memory alert 595
    duplicate bindery objects 288
    groups 299, 359
    home directories 344–346
    network administrator 296
    resource accounting 445
    security 306–310
    user options 280
    users 380

System Application Architecture (SAA)   91
System attributes   302, 303
SYSTEM directory   157, 335
System login script   396
System Module Information   568
System Network Architecture
    (SNA)   74, 91, 100, 692
SYSTEM-1 diskette   163
SYSTEM.INI file   230, 232

T

TAPEDC00.NLM   771, 788
Target server   769, 778, 785
TCP/IP
    default receive packet size   717
    kernel-level support   73
    linking systems   90
    LOAD tcpip command   206
    NET parameters   179
    NetWare v3.11   705
    network card   81
    NLM support   563
    protocol stack   799
    protocol stacks   166
    SNMP   799
    Streams   692
    transport NLMs   736
    Unix transport service   68
    User Data Protocol (UDP)   44
TCPCON   800
TCPIP.EXE program   698
TEMP environment variable   229
Temporary files   363, 368, 374
10Base-T   120
Test restoration   289
Third-party protocols   705–706
Time restrictions   297, 308, 382
Timeout   534, 541
TLI.NLM   693, 772
TLIST utility   312, 321
Token   83
    bus   85
    bus topology   114
    passing   83–84
    passing protocol   724
Token Ring   84, 104, 111
    board   698
    boards   721–723

Topology   103
Total cache buffers   590
TRACK OFF command   73, 270–271
TRACK ON command   48, 73, 245, 270–
    271, 737
Tracked Resources   568
Traffic   714
Transaction tracking   620
Transaction Tracking System (TTS)   50, 55–
    56, 62, 597
Transactional   57
Transactional attributes   305
Transceiver   124, 720
Transferring files   814–816
Transport Class 4 protocol   92
Transport Layer Interface (TLI)   68
Transport protocols   39, 78
Troubleshooting
    procedure   4
    tools   7, 110
Trustee assign-
    ments   309, 311, 317, 318, 336, 363
Trustee directory assignments   308
Trustee list   319, 321
Trustee rights   299, 376, 390
Trustees   62
TSA-311.NLM   771
TSA.NLM   771, 776
TSR programs   360, 440
TTS$LOG.ERR   625, 631
Turbo FAT   562, 606
Twisted-pair cabling   103, 106, 212
Type 6 cable   128

U

Unattended backup   764
UNBIND command   706–707
Unencrypted passwords   208
Unix   68, 100, 352, 641
    volumes   768
UNLOAD command   655–656, 702–703
Unshielded twisted-pair (UTP) cabling   107
UPGRADE.EXE program   277–278
UPS   741

battery power   746
initialization messages   754
jumpers   748–757
monitoring feature   747
monitoring function   753
monitoring hardware   747–748
power rating   745–747
standalone monitoring board   747
STATUS console command   751–752
TIME console command   752–754
troubleshooting the system   753–757
UPS.NLM   748–750
U.S. GOSIP 1.0 specification   92
Use Interrupts field   492
User account manager   378–379, 391
User group   389–391
User login script   396–397
USER_ID   402
USERDEF default template   386
USERDEF utility   338, 380, 386–389, 845
USERLIST/A   113, 119, 720
Username   62, 296, 375
.USR file   383

V

VAP command   263, 271–273, 280
VERSION   845, 848
Virtual memory   32
Virus   325
Virus-scanning software   327
VOLINFO utility   666, 675–676
Voltage regulators   741
Volume   51, 154, 333, 346, 643
   Block Size   159
   block size   580, 645–646
   creating   652
   directory   52
   directory table   582
   FAT table   154
   file service, primary component   157
   INSTALL, creating in   158
   level   372
   name space support   580
   names   643
   primary data structure   580
   SBACKUP   792
   segments   51, 161–162, 644–645, 662
   size   158, 643–644
   Volume Name   159
   Volume Segments   161

VOLUMES   656
VREPAIR   163, 564, 583, 633, 657, 668–674
Vrepair Options   671
VREPAIR.NLM   200, 202, 206

W

Warning messages   14
Watchdog function   458
WHOAMI utility   321–322, 845
WIN.INI file   234
Windows   339, 357
   program   96, 226
   SETUP program   96, 228, 231
Wiring concentrator   106
Word size   488
Workgroup manager   321, 328, 379–381, 392
Working directory   285, 779, 785
Workstation shell   469
Workstations   745
WRITE   400, 420–422
Write Audit attributes   305
Write Once/Read Many (WORM)   763
Write redirection   617
Write rights   298
WSGEN   93, 213

X

X.500   836
XCOPY command   463
Xerox Network Systems (XNS)   68
XMS memory manager   232
XMS standard   222
XMSNETx.EXE   235
Xon/Xoff   488

Y

YEAR   402

Z

ZIM   627

A Library of Technical References from M&T Books

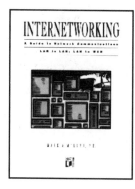

Internetworking
A Guide to Network Communications
LAN to LAN; LAN to WAN
by Mark A. Miller, P.E.

This book addresses all aspects of LAN and WAN (wide-area network) integrations, detailing the hardware, software, and communication products available. In-depth discussions describe the functions, design, and performance of repeaters, bridges, routers, and gateways. Communication facilities such as leased lines, T-1 circuits and access to packed switched public data networks (PSPDNs) are compared, helping LAN managers decide which is most viable for their internetwork. Also examined are the X.25, TCP/IP, and XNS protocols, as well as the internetworking capabilities and interoperability constraints of the most popular networks, including NetWare, LAN Server, 3+Open™, VINES®, and AppleTalk. 425 pp.

Book only   **Item #143-1**   **$34.95**

LAN Primer
An Introduction to Local Area Networks
by Greg Nunemacher

A complete introduction to local area networks (LANs), this book is a must for anyone who needs to know basic LAN principles. It includes a complete overview of LANs, clearly defining what a LAN is, the functions of a LAN, and how LANs fit into the field of telecommunications. The author discusses the specifics of building a LAN, including the required hardware and software, an overview of the types of products available, deciding what products to purchase, and assembling the pieces into a working LAN system. *LAN Primer* also includes case studies that illustrate how LAN principles work. Particular focus is given to Ethernet and Token-Ring. 221 pp.

Book only   **Item #127-X**   **$24.95**

1-800-533-4372 (in CA 1-800-356-2002)

A Library of Technical References
from M&T Books

Blueprint of a LAN
by Craig Chaiken

For programmers, valuable programming techniques are detailed. Network administrators will learn how to build and install LAN communication cables, configure and troubleshoot network hardware and more. Addressed are a very inexpensive zero-slot, star topology network, remote printer and file sharing, remote command execution, electronic mail, parallel processing support, high-level language support, and more. Also covered is the complete Intel 8086 assembly language source code that will help you build an inexpensive-to-install local area network. An optional disk containing all source code is available. 337 pp.

Book & Disk (MS-DOS)	**Item #066-4**	**$39.95**
Book only	**Item #052-4**	**$29.95**

LAN Protocol Handbook
by Mark A. Miller, P.E.

Requisite reading for all network administrators and software developers needing in-depth knowledge of the internal protocols of the most popular network software. It illustrates the techniques of protocol analysis—the step-by-step process of unraveling LAN software failures. Detailed is how Ethernet, IEEE 802.3, IEEE 802.5, and ARCNET networks transmit frames of information between workstations. Individual chapters thoroughly discuss Novell's NetWare, 3Com's 3+ and 3+Open, IBM Token-Ring related protocols, and more! 324 pp.

Book only	**Item 099-0**	**$34.95**

LAN Protocol Handbook Demonstration Disks

The set of seven demonstration disks is for those who wish to pursue the techniques of protocol analysis or consider the purchase of an analysis tool.

The analyzers will give you a clear view of your network so that you can better control and manage your LAN, as well as pinpoint trouble spots. The *LAN Protocol Handbook* demo disks are packed with detailed demonstration programs for LANalyzer® LAN Watch®, The Sniffer®, for Token-Ring and Ethernet, SpiderAnalyzer® 320-R for Token-Ring, and LANVista®. By surveying the demo programs, you will receive enough information to choose an analyzer that best suits your specific needs.

Requirements: IBM PC/XT/AT compatible with at least 640K after booting. Requires DOS version 2.0 or later. Either a color or monochrome display may be used.

Seven disks	**$39.95**

1-800-533-4372 (in CA 1-800-356-2002)

A Library of Technical References from M&T Books

LAN Troubleshooting Handbook
by Mark A. Miller, P.E.

This book is specifically for users and administrators who need to identify problems and maintain a LAN that is already installed. Topics include LAN standards, the OSI model, network documentation, LAN test equipment, cable system testing, and more. Addressed are specific issues associated with troubleshooting the four most popular LAN architectures: ARCNET, Token Ring, Ethernet, and StarLAN. Each is closely examined to pinpoint the problems unique to its design and the hardware. Handy checklists to assist in solving each architecture's unique network difficulties are also included. 309 pp.

Book & Disk (MS-DOS)	Item #056-7	$39.95
Book only	Item #054-0	$29.95

Building Local Area Networks with Novell's NetWare, 2nd Edition
by Patrick H. Corrigan and Aisling Guy

From the basic components to complete network installation, here is the practical guide that PC system integrators will need to build and implement PC LANs in this rapidly growing market. The specifics of building and maintaining PC LANs, including hardware configurations, software development, cabling, selection criteria, installation, and on-going management are described in a clear "how-to" manner with numerous illustrations and sample LAN management forms. *Building Local Area Networks* covers Novell's NetWare, Version 2.2, and 3.11 for the 386. Additional topics covered include the OS/2 LAN Manager, Tops, Banyan VINES, internetworking, host computer gateways, and multisystem networks that link PCs, Apples, and mainframes. 635 pp. approx.

Book & Disk (MS-DOS)	Item #239-X	$39.95
Book only	Item #237-3	$29.95

1-800-533-4372 (in CA 1-800-356-2002)

A Library of Technical References
from M&T Books

NetWare for Macintosh User's Guide
by Kelley J. P. Lindberg

NetWare for Macintosh User's Guide is the definitive reference to using Novell's NetWare on Macintosh computers. Whether you are a novice or an advanced user, this comprehensive text provides the information readers need to get the most from their NetWare networks. It includes an overview of network operations and detailed explanations of all NetWare for Macintosh menu and command line utilities. Detailed tutorials cover such tasks as logging in, working with directories and files, and printing over a network. Advanced users will benefit from the information on managing workstation environments and troubleshooting.
280 pp.

Book only   **Item #126-1**   **$29.95**

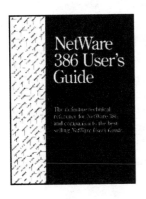

NetWare 386 User's Guide
by Christine Milligan

NetWare 386 User's Guide is a complete guide to using and understanding Novell's NetWare 386. It is an excellent reference for 386. Detailed tutorials cover tasks such as logging in, working with directories and files, and printing over a network. Complete explanations of the basic concepts underlying NetWare 386, along with a summary of the differences between NetWare 286 and 386, are included. Advanced users will benefit from the information on managing workstation environments and the troubleshooting index that fully examines NetWare 386 error messages. 450 pp.

Book only   **Item #101-6**   **$29.95**

A Library of Technical References from M&T Books

Programming in 3 Dimensions
3-D Graphics, Ray Tracing, and Animation
by Sandra Bloomberg

Programming in 3 Dimensions is a comprehensive, hands-on guide to computer graphics. It contains a detailed look at 3-D graphics plus discussions of popular ray tracing methods and computer animation. Readers will find techniques for creating 3-D graphics and breath-taking ray-traced images as, well as explanations of how animation works and ways computers help produce it more effectively. Packed with examples and C source code, this book is a must for all computer graphics enthusiasts! All source code is available on disk in MS/PC-DOS format. Includes 16 pages of full-color graphics.
500 pp. approx.

Book/Disk (MS-DOS)	Item #218-7	**$39.95**
Book only	Item #220-9	**$29.95**

Fractal Programming and Ray Tracing with C++
by Roger T. Stevens

Finally, a book for C and C++ programmers who want to create complex and intriguing graphic designs. By the author of three best-selling graphics books, this new title thoroughly explains ray tracing, discussing how rays are traced, how objects are used to create ray-traced images, and how to create ray tracing programs. A complete ray tracing program, along with all of the source code, is included. Contains 16 pages of full-color graphics. 444 pp.

Book/Disk (MS-DOS)	Item 118-0	**$39.95**
Book only	Item 134-2	**$29.95**

1-800-533-4372 (in CA 1-800-356-2002)

A Library of Technical References
from M&T Books

Advanced Fractal Programming in C
by Roger T. Stevens

Programmers who enjoyed our best-selling *Fractal Programming in C* can move on to the next level of fractal programming with this book. Included are how-to instructions for creating many different types of fractal curves, including source code. Contains 16 pages of full-color fractals. All the source code to generate the fractals is available on an optional disk in MS/PC-DOS format. 305 pp.

Book/Disk (MS-DOS)	**Item #097-4**	**$39.95**
Book only	**Item #096-6**	**$29.95**

Advanced Graphics Programming in Turbo Pascal
by Roger T. Stevens and Christopher D. Watkins

This new book is must reading for Turbo Pascal programmers who want to create impressive graphic designs on IBM PCs and compatibles. There are 32 pages of full-color graphic displays along with the source code to create these dramatic pictures. Complete explanations are provided on how to tailor the graphics to suit the programmer's needs. Covered are algorithms for creating complex 2-D shapes, including lines, circles and squares; how to create advanced 3-D shapes, wire-frame graphics, and solid images; numerous tips and techniques for varying pixel intensities to give the appearance of roundness to an object; and more. 540 pp.

Book/Disk (MS-DOS)	**Item #132-6**	**$39.95**
Book only	**Item #131-8**	**$29.95**

A Library of Technical References
from M&T Books

Advanced Graphics Programming in C and C++
by Roger T. Stevens and Christopher D. Watkins

This book is for all C and C++ programmers who want to create impressive graphic designs on their IBM PCs or compatibles. Through in-depth discussions and numerous sample programs, readers will learn how to create advanced 3-D shapes, wireframe graphics, solid images, and more. All source code is available on disk in MS/PC-DOS format. Contains 16 pages of full-color graphics. 500 pp. approx.

Book/Disk (MS-DOS)	Item #173-3	$39.95
Book only	Item #171-7	$29.95

Graphics Programming with Microsoft C 6
by Mark Mallett

Written for all C programmers, this book explores graphics programming with Microsoft C 6.0, including full coverage of Microsoft C's built-in graphics libraries. Sample programs will help readers learn the techniques needed to create spectacular graphic designs, including 3-D figures, solid images, and more. All source code in the book is available on disk in MS/PC-DOS format. Includes 16 pages of full-color graphics. 500 pp. approx.

Book/Disk (MS-DOS)	Item #167-9	$39.95
Book only	Item #165-2	$29.95

The Verbum Book of PostScript Illustration
by Michael Gosney, Linnea Dayton, and Janet Ashford

This is the premier instruction book for designers, illustrators, and desktop publishers using Postscript. Each chapter highlights the talents of top illustrators who demonstrate the electronic artmaking process. The narrative keys readers in to the artist's conceptual vision, providing valuable insight into the creative thought processes that go into a real-world PostScript illustration project. 213 pp.

Book only	Item #089-3	$29.95

1-800-533-4372 (in CA 1-800-356-2002)

A Library of Technical References
from M&T Books

The Verbum Book of Electronic Page Design
by Michael Gosney and Linnea Dayton

This particular volume introduces designers, illustrators, and desktop publishers to the electronic page layout medium and various application programs, such as PageMaker, QuarkXPress, Design Studio, and Ventura Publishing. Each chapter highlights the talents of a top designer who guides readers through the thinking as well as the "mousing" that leads to the creation of various projects. These projects range in complexity from a trifold black and white brochure to a catalog produced with QuarkXPress. More than 100 illustrations, with 32 pages in full-color, are included. 211 pp.

Book only   Item #088-5   **$29.95**

The Verbum Book of Digital Painting
by Michael Gosney, Linnea Dayton, and Paul Goethel

Contained herein are a series of entertaining projects that teach readers how to create compelling designs using the myriad of graphics tools available in commercial painting programs. Presented by professional designers, these projects range from a simple greeting card to a complex street scene. This book also includes portfolios of paintings created by the featured artists, plus an extensive gallery of works from other accomplished artists and 64 pages of full-color paintings. 211 pp.

Book only   Item #090-7   **$29.95**

1-800-533-4372 (in CA 1-800-356-2002)

A Library of Technical References
from M&T Books

Windows 3: A Developer's Guide
by Jeffrey M. Richter

This example-packed guide is for all experienced C programmers developing applications for Windows 3.0. This book describes every feature, function, and component of the Windows Application Programming Interface, teaching programmers how to take full advantage of its many capabilities. Diagrams and source code examples are used to demonstrate advanced topics, including window subclassing, dynamic memory management, and software installation techniques.
671 pp.

Book/Disk (MS-DOS)	Item #164-4	$39.95
Book only	Item #162-8	$29.95

Windows 3.0 By Example
by Michael Hearst

Here is a hands-on guide to Windows 3.0. Written for all users new to Windows, this book provides thorough, easy-to-follow explanations of every Windows 3.0 feature and function. Numerous exercises and helpful practice sessions help readers further develop their understanding of Windows 3.0 398 pp.

Book only	Item #180-6	$26.95

The Verbum Book of Digital Typography
by Michael Gosney, Linnea Dayton, and Jennifer Ball

The Verbum Book of Digital Typography combines information on good design principles with effective typography techniques, showing designers, illustrators, and desktop publishers how to create attractive printed materials that communicate effectively. Each chapter highlights the talents of a professional type designer as he or she steps readers through an interesting real-life project. Readers will learn how to develop letterforms and typefaces, modify type outlines, and create special effects. 200 pp. approx.

Book only	Item #092-3	$29.95

1-800-533-4372 (in CA 1-800-356-2002)

A Library of Technical References from M&T Books

Delivering cc:Mail
Installing, Maintaining, and Troubleshooting a cc:Mail System
by Eric Arnum

Delivering cc:Mail teaches administrators how to install, troubleshoot, and maintain cc:Mail, one of the most popular E-mail applications for the PC. In-depth discussions and practical examples show administrators how to establish and maintain the program and database files; how to create and modify the bulletin boards, mail directory, and public mailing lists; and how to diagnose and repair potential problems. Information on using the management tools included with the package plus tips and techniques for creating efficient batch files are also included. All source code is available on disk in MS/PC-DOS format. 450 pp.

Book & Disk	**Item #187-3**	**$39.95**
Book only	**Item #185-7**	**$29.95**

The Complete Memory Manager
Every PC User's Guide to Faster, More Efficient Computing
by Phillip Robinson

Readers will learn why memory is important, how and when to install more, and how to wring the most out of their memory. Clear, concise instructions teach users how to manage their computer's memory to multiply its speed and ability to run programs simultaneously. Tips and techniques also show users how to conserve memory when working with popular software programs. 437 pp.

Book	**Item #102-4**	**$24.95**

1-800-533-4372 (in CA 1-800-356-2002)

A Library of Technical References
from M&T Books

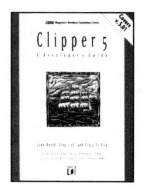

Clipper 5: A Developer's Guide
by Joseph D. Booth, Greg Lief, and Craig Yellick

An invaluable guide for all database programmers developing
applications for Clipper® 5. Provides a quick introduction to
Clipper 5 basics and discusses common programming needs
such as designing data files, user interfaces, reports, and more.
Advanced topics include networking, debugging, and pop-up
programming. Code examples are used throughout the text,
providing useful functions that can be applied immediately.
All source code is available on disk in MS/PC-DOS format.
1300 pp. approx.

Book & Disk (MS-DOS)	**Item #242-X**	**$44.95**
Book only	**Item #240-3**	**$34.95**

DOS 5 User's Guide
A Comprehensive Guide for Every PC User
by Dan Gookin

Take control of the MS-DOS® operating system with this
complete guide to using the world's most popular operating
system. *DOS 5 User's Guide* contains clear, concise explanations of every feature, function, and command of DOS 5.0.
Novice PC users will gain a quick start on using DOS, while
advanced users will learn savvy tricks and techniques to
maneuver their way quickly and easily through the system.
Practical discussions and helpful examples teach readers how to
edit text files, use directories, create batch files, and much more.
Advanced topics include using EDLIN, the DOS text editor;
configuring the system; and using the DOS shell. 771 pp.

Book only	**Item #188-1**	**$24.95**

1-800-533-4372 (in CA 1-800-356-2002)

A Library of Technical References
from M&T Books

Publishing 1-2-3
by Mary Campbell

Publishing 1-2-3 teaches users how to apply their 1-2-3 skills to create winning spreadsheets and presentations. Written for users at all levels, it outlines basic design objectives and describes important elements to consider when planning a 1-2-3 spreadsheet. In addition, this book shows readers how to enhance the features of 1-2-3 by using it with different graphics and word processing packages. Readers will learn how to use graphics packages such as Harvard Graphics and Freelance to create charts and graphs beyond the capabilities of 1-2-3 and how to import 1-2-3 spreadsheets, charts, and graphs into WordPerfect®. Covers Lotus 1-2-3 versions 2.01 through 3.1. 369 pp.

Book only   **Item #199-7**   **$24.95**

SQL and Relational Basics
by Fabian Pascal

SQL and Relational Basics was written to help PC users apply sound and general objectives to evaluating, selecting, and using database management systems. Misconceptions about relational data management and SQL are addressed and corrected. The book concentrates on the practical objectives of the relational approach as they pertain to the micro environment. Users will be able to design and correctly implement relational databases and applications, and work around product deficiencies to minimize future maintenance. 336 pp.

Book only: **Item #063-X**   **$28.95**

A Small C Compiler, Second Edition
by James Hendrix

This is a solid resource for all programmers who want to learn to program in C. It thoroughly explains Small C's structure, syntax, and features. It succinctly covers the theory of compiler operation and design, discussing Small C's compatibility with C, explaining how to modify the compiler to generate new versions of itself, and more. A fully-working Small C compiler, plus all the source code and files are provided on disk in MS/PC-DOS format. 628 pp.

Book/Disk (MS-DOS)   **Item #124-5**   **$34.95**

1-800-533-4372 (in CA 1-800-356-2002)

A Library of Technical References
from M&T Books

Using QuarkXPress 3.0
by Tim Meehan

Written in an enjoyable, easy-to-read style, this book addresses the needs of both beginning and intermediate users. It includes numerous illustrations and screen shots that guide readers through comprehensive explanations of QuarkXPress, its potential and real-world applications. *Using QuarkXPress* contains comprehensive explanations of the concepts, practices, and uses of QuarkXPress, with sample assignments of increasing complexity that give readers actual hands-on experience using the program. 340 pp.

Book/Disk	Item #129-6	$34.95
Book only	Item #128-8	$24.95

An OPEN LOOK at UNIX
A Developer's Guide to X
by John David Miller

This is the book that explores the look and feel of the OPEN LOOK graphical user interface, discussing its basic philosophy, environment, and user-interface elements. It includes a detailed summary of the X Window System, introduces readers to object-oriented programming, and shows how to develop commercial-grade X applications. Dozens of OPEN LOOK program examples are presented, along with nearly 13,000 lines of C code. All source code is available on disk in 1.2 MB UNIX cpio format. 482 pp.

Book/Disk	Item #058-3	$39.95
Book only	Item #057-5	$29.95

Turbo C++ by Example
by Alex Lane

Turbo C++ by Example includes numerous code examples that teach C programmers new to C++ how to program skillfully with Borland's powerful Turbo C++. Detailed are key features of Turbo C++ with code examples. Covers both Turbo Debugger and Tools 2.0 — a collection of tools used to design and debug Turbo C++ programs — and Turbo Profiler. All listings available on disk in MS/PC-DOS format. 423 pp.

Book/Disk (MS-DOS)	Item #141-5	$36.95
Book only	Item #123-7	$26.95

1-800-533-4372 (in CA 1-800-356-2002)

A Library of Technical References
from M&T Books

PageMaker 4 By Example
PC Version
by Tony Webster and Paul Webster

This hands-on tutorial introduces PC users to the new and enhanced features of PageMaker 4, providing them with a detailed look at this powerful and versatile desktop publishing program. It progressively covers more and more complex PageMaker operations, taking readers from basic functions to creating customized templates. Step-by-step exercises that teach readers how to apply the concepts learned to practical desktop publishing projects accompany each chapter. The supplementary disk includes tips and techniques for creating professional-looking newsletters, advertisements, press releases, and more. 617 pp.

Book/Disk (MS-DOS)	Item #151-2	$34.95
Book only	Item #149-0	$24.95

PageMaker 4 By Example
Macintosh Version
by Tony Webster and David Webster

A self-paced, hands-on guide to learning PageMaker 4.0, the premier desktop publishing program in the micro-computer market. Includes step-by-step instructions for everything from starting a new document to creating customized style sheets. Hundreds of screen shots lead readers through the concepts discussed and useful exercises reinforce each chapter's material. Readers will learn how to load files into PageMaker, edit and manipulate text, create templates, and much more. The exercise disk (Macintosh) supplements the book's exercises and teaches readers how to apply its concepts to practical desktop publishing projects. It includes tips on creating projects such as newsletters, advertisements, and press releases. 593pp.

Book/Disk	Item #121-0	$34.95
Book only	Item #105-9	$24.95

ORDER FORM

To Order: Return this form with your payment to M&T books, 501 Galveston Drive, Redwood City, CA 94063 or **call toll-free 1-800-533-4372 (in California, call 1-800-356-2002).**

ITEM #	DESCRIPTION	DISK	PRICE

Subtotal

CA residents add sales tax ____%

Add $3.75 per item for shipping and handling

TOTAL

NOTE: **FREE SHIPPING** ON ORDERS OF THREE OR MORE BOOKS.

Charge my:

❑ **Visa**

❑ **MasterCard**

❑ **AmExpress**

❑ **Check enclosed,** payable to **M&T Books.**

CARD NO. _____

SIGNATURE _____ EXP. DATE _____

NAME _____

ADDRESS _____

CITY _____

STATE _____ ZIP _____

M&T GUARANTEE: If your are not satisfied with your order for any reason, return it to us within 25 days of receipt for a full refund. Note: Refunds on disks apply only when returned with book within guarantee period. Disks damaged in transit or defective will be promptly replaced, but cannot be exchanged for a disk from a different title.

8052

1-800-533-4372 (in CA 1-800-356-2002)